Con tics

Comparative Latin American Politics

Ronald M. Schneider

Queens College, CUNY

WESTVIEW PRESS

A Member of the Perseus Books Group

Copyright © 2010 by Westview Press
Published by Westview Press,
A Member of the Perseus Books Group

All rights reserved. Printed in the United States of America. No part of this book may
be reproduced in any manner whatsoever without written permission except in the case
of brief quotations embodied in critical articles and reviews. For information, address
Westview Press, 2465 Central Avenue, Boulder, CO 80301.

Find us on the World Wide Web at www.westviewpress.com.
Every effort has been made to secure required permissions to use all images, maps, and
other art included in this volume.

Westview Press books are available at special discounts for bulk purchases in the United
States by corporations, institutions, and other organizations. For more information, please
contact the Special Markets Department at the Perseus Books Group, 2300 Chestnut
Street, Suite 200, Philadelphia, PA 19103, or call (800) 810-4145, ext. 5000, or e-mail
special.markets@perseusbooks.com.

Set in Bembo by the Perseus Books Group

A CIP catalog record for this book is available from the Library of Congress.
ISBN: 978-0-8133-4462-1

10 9 8 7 6 5 4 3 2 1

Contents

Preface

Latin America, embracing the diverse array of countries lying south of the United States in the Western Hemisphere, is both a major part of the world and its richest "laboratory" for understanding the processes of political development and their interaction with economic growth, societal modernization, and cultural influences. Its vast expanse stretches north to south for 7,000 miles from the border between Mexico's Baja California and the most populous state of the United States, California—acquired from Mexico by force over a century and a half ago—to the southernmost tip of Argentina only a short distance from Antarctica. Since much of the region is farther from the eastern United States than is most of Europe, only a relatively small portion fits the lingering stereotype of being the "backyard" of the US colossus. Moreover, from that same point south of San Diego to the easternmost bulge of Brazil, Latin America extends more than 5,500 miles from east to west.

The region's differences are so great as to raise the question of whether it has other than geographical meaning, but the term *Latin America* is firmly rooted in popular usage and embedded in the organization and operations of governments, businesses, and academic institutions. Accurately employed, the term *Latin America* includes not only the entire South American continent, but also Central America and the Caribbean as well as Mexico. The diversity among its constituent countries is striking in manifold respects: size, population, ethnic makeup, geography, resources, level of economic development, and societal dynamics as well as political development. Even with respect to language Latin America is far from homogeneous, for although it is often misleadingly referred to as Hispanic America, a third of its inhabitants speak Portuguese, Haiti is French speaking, much of the Caribbean has English as its tongue, and millions still know only the indigenous languages of their ancestors. Although Catholicism is by far the predominant religion, there are many tens of millions of Protestants and other tens of millions adhering to religions brought over from Africa or practiced in the hemisphere before the arrival of European colonizers. Not surprisingly, but sadly, lack of understanding and prevalent misconceptions characterize the fragmented and superficial image of Latin America prevailing in the United States as well as in the rest of the world.

The independence of Latin American countries came typically in the 1820s, well over a century before that of most of the Afro-Asian world. Hence a close examination of Latin America's struggles to establish viable participatory political systems provides valuable lessons concerning national consolidation and political development in new nations. Latin America's experience strongly indicates that both political institutions and their requisite congruent political culture are built over generations. Even decades prove time and time again to be far too brief and transitory spans to measure fundamental trends as opposed to mere political fads, fancies, and fashions. Moreover, because by far the greatest number of recent cases of successful democratization are found in Latin America, this region most urgently requires thoughtful comparative study. Indeed, a major aim of this book is to identify, analyze, and highlight salient lessons from Latin American experience for the current "new nations" of the Afro-Asian world. In this regard, the 1820–1930 span is more relevant in many respects than recent times, since that is when the countries analyzed here were coping with the array of postindependence problems and challenges of national consolidation that still plague over half the nations of the world. Also, at a time when the nations of eastern Europe are still attempting to install viable democratic systems, and those spun off along Russia's Asian borders are even less advanced along this treacherous road, a deeper and more systematic understanding of the analogous processes in Latin America is certainly required. Here the trials and tribulations of the late nineteenth century up through the 1920s hold more lessons than does more recent Latin American experience.

Textbooks on Latin American politics are either so massive as to be prohibitively forbidding or so streamlined as to omit any significant historical background and a coherent discussion of individual countries. Often adhering to a public policy approach, they focus on present-day governmental structures, political processes, and policy issues—sacrificing analysis of the paths by which countries, and by extension the region, arrived where they are today. This is precisely the center of my concern: to compare the political development experiences of Latin American nations.

A major challenge in understanding Latin America is its great diversity, underscored by the immense ethnic, historical, and geographic differences among its main components. The contrasts between the two nations that together contain over half the region's population at first glance overshadow any similarities, an impression only slightly reduced by closer examination and greater familiarity: Brazil is South American, Portuguese-speaking, very heavily African-influenced, and distant from the United States. Mexico is North American, Spanish-speaking, deeply Indian-influenced, and immediately proximate to the United States. Further complicating the analytical problem is the fact that the second most important pair of countries differ strikingly from each other as well as from both of the dominant dyad. Argentina is at the southern tip of South America, and Colombia borders the Caribbean. The former is largely populated by individuals of relatively recent Italian descent and enjoys close European ties; the latter's population is heavily *mestizo* (mixed Indian-European) with most of its European component descended from Spaniards who arrived during the colonial era, so it lacks Argentina's close trade and financial links to present-day Europe. The Pacific-facing South American nation of Peru is heavily Indian, whereas Venezuela and Chile are significantly more European. Together these seven countries, ranging from the region's northernmost to its southern tip and bordering both the Atlantic and the Pacific Oceans, contain four-fifths of the region's inhabitants as well as an even higher proportion of its economy. Hence, for sound reasons of parsimony and taking into account what is possible to cover within the limits of a one-semester course, they are the subject of this text.

For all its advances since rejection of the intellectually sterile historical, legalistic, institutional approach inherited from Woodrow Wilson gained headway in the 1950s, political science still lacks a single, unified, all-embracing theoretical approach. Simplistic, not necessarily simple, theories about why Latin America lags behind English-speaking North America are inadequate. "Dependency theory," which in the 1960s and 1970s was embraced by the majority of young scholars in the Latin American field, went too far in putting the blame on external factors and downplaying internal ones. Useful as a corrective to traditional institutionalism as well as deterministic versions of modernization theory, it threw the babies out with the bathwater. With the demise of the Soviet Union at the end of the 1980s, essentially economic determinist dependency approaches entered into a steep decline. The vacuum has been partially filled by a mix of "new institutionalism" and the revival of a far less mechanical and more realistic version of modernization theories tempered with concern about cultural factors. This last approach is close to my slant on analyzing and interpreting Latin American politics, and it is followed in this text as being nearest to the enduring mainstream of comparative politics.[1]

The interaction of social, economic, and cultural factors with politics is neither linear nor direct. The impact of profound socioeconomic change upon politics may at times be gradual and cumulative, but in other instances it may be delayed, pent up, and hence more explosive. Detailed treatment of all periods and administrations in every country would require a massive multivolume work with its readership inevitably limited to specialists. Nations, much like individuals, go through critical periods and transforming events as well as long stretches of routine existence. For this reason country treatment will be fuller for the more dynamic periods. Moreover, only personalities who had a catalytic influence or transforming impact upon their country will be fleshed out and analyzed in depth. The result is a treatment designed to focus on the key and the crucial rather than the routine.

Not all that transpired in Latin America in past centuries has left an operational legacy in terms of a clearly discernible imprint upon present institutions and processes. Equally clear, however, current political-governmental practices, as well as the structures through which they operate, still bear the stamp of developments buried well back in the past. The most salient aspects of this heritage, enshrined in that complex amalgam of attitudes, values, myths, and expectations usually shorthanded as "political culture," must be explored before the more relevant recent past can be discussed. For with regard to antecedent experiences and historical influences there is no rigid expiration date, much less a statute of limitations, only a rule of relevance—albeit one more stringent the more temporally remote the event. Hence, the book concentrates on the period since 1930.

No one scholar, no matter how long he or she may have labored in this field, has been able to conduct original research on all, or even most, of the countries comprising Latin America. Hence each must rely upon leading scholars on those places omitted from his or her fieldwork. As my direct experience is centered upon Brazil, with previous work on Guatemala, Cuba, and—more remotely in time—Argentina, I lean heavily for understanding of Mexico upon the outstanding scholarship of Roderic Ai Camp, Daniel Levy, Enrique Krauze, Jorge Castañeda, and George W. Grayson. On Colombia, where I have spent a little time, I rely substantially on the writings of Harvey Kline, the late John D. Martz, and Jonathan Hartlyn, and I draw heavily upon the views of Paul H. Lewis, Robert Potash, William C. Smith, Peter G. Snow, and James W. McGuire on Argentina; Peter F. Klarén, Cynthia McClintock, and Catherine M. Conaghan with respect to Peru; Daniel Hellinger and Martz on Venezuela; and Arturo Valenzuela and Paul Sigmund on Chile. On Brazil I have benefited especially from the meticulous historical work of Frank McCann, whose 2004 book does for that country what Potash's three volumes did for the understanding of Argentina. Any flaws in the interpretation of the views of these and many other talented scholars whose works I have consulted are wholly my responsibility like any other shortcomings of this book.

I wish to express my heartfelt appreciation for the constant support provided by my wife, Marva Schneider, and our children Shinelle and John. They have given me the continued zest for life and emotional stability required to persist with the tasks of research and writing a full five decades after my first book as well as providing inspiration to improve upon my previous work. At Westview Karl Yambert proved to be the book's sympathetic and efficient godfather, while Margaret Ritchie, having ably handled the task a few years ago with my previous elephantine text, again kept me on the straight and narrow with her meticulous and thoughtful copyediting. Michelle Welsh-Horst efficiently guided the transition from manuscript to finished book.

RONALD M. SCHNEIDER
Queens College, CUNY
August 2009

Notes

1. Gerardo Munck assesses approaches and conceptual contributions in his edited volume *Regimes and Democracy in Latin America: Theories and Methods* (New York: Oxford University Press, 2007), pp. 1–21, with "Touchstones for Research" on pp. 25–37.

Acronyms

AAA	Argentine Anticommunist Alliance
ABT	Alliance for the Well-Being of Everyone (Mexico)
AD	Democratic Action (Venezuela)
AD	Democratic Alliance (Brazil)
AF	Alliance for the Future (Peru)
AI-5	Fifth Institutional Act (Brazil)
AL	Liberal Alliance (Brazil)
AL	Liberal Alliance (Chile)
ANAPO	National Popular Alliance (Colombia)
ANL	National Liberating Alliance (Brazil)
AP	Popular Action (Peru)
APRA	Popular Revolutionary Alliance of the Americas (Peru)
ARENA	National Renovating Alliance (Brazil)
ASC	Social and Civic Action (Argentina)
AUC	United Self-Defence Forces of Colombia
CAEM	Center for Higher Military Studies (Peru)
CC	Civic Coalition (Argentina)
CD	Colombia Democrática
CGT	General Labor Confederation (Argentina)
CGT	General Workers Confederation (Brazil)
CIA	Central Intelligence Agency (US)
CNC	National Campesinos Confederation (Mexico)
CNOP	Confederation of Popular Organizations (Mexico)
COA	Argentine Workers' Confederation
CONADE	National Development Council (Argentina)
CONASE	National Security Council (Argentina)
COPEI	Independent Electoral Organizing Committee (Venezuela)
CR	Radical Change (Colombia)
CTM	Mexican Workers Confederation
CTV	Confederation of Venezuelan Workers
CUT	Unified Confederation of Workers (Chile)
CUT	Unified Workers Central (Brazil)
DEM	Democrats (new name of Brazil's former PFL)
DGM	General Directorate of Military Manufactures (Argentina)
EAP	economically active population
ELN	National Liberation Army (Colombia)
ESG	National War College (Argentina)
ESG	Superior War College (Brazil)
EZLN	Zapatista Army of National Liberation (Mexico)
FALN	Armed Forces of National Liberation (Venezuela)

FARC	Armed Forces of the Colombian Revolution
FCRN	Cardenist Front for National Reconstruction Party (Mexico)
FDN	National Democratic Front (Peru)
FDN	National Democratic Front (Mexico)
FDN	New Democratic Force (Colombia)
FDP	Popular Democratic Front (Venezuela)
FEB	Brazilian Expeditionary Force
FEDECAMARAS	Venezuelan Federation of Chambers and Associations of Commerce and Production (Venezuela)
FEI	Independent Electoral Front (Venezuela)
FEP	Evita Perón Foundation
FJ	Justicialist Front (Argentina)
FN	National Front (Colombia)
FLMN	Farabundo Martí Front for National Liberation (El Salvador)
FN	National Front (Colombia)
FND	National Democratic Front (Venezuela)
FRAP	Revolutionary Popular Action Front (Chile)
FREJULI	Justicialist Liberating Front (Argentina)
FRENAP	National Association of the Private Sector (Chile)
FREPASO	Fatherland Solidarity Front (Argentina)
GATT	General Agreement on Trade and Tariffs
GDP	gross domestic product
GOU	Group of United Officers (Argentina)
IBRD	International Bank for Reconstruction and Development, generally known as the World Bank
IMF	International Monetary Fund
INP	National Planning Institute (Peru)
IPC	International Petroleum Company (subsidiary of Standard Oil)
IPE	Federal Electoral Institute (Mexico)
IPES	Institute for Social Research and Studies (Brazil)
LASA	Latin American Studies Association
M–19	19th of April Movement (Colombia)
MAPU	Movement for Unitary Popular Action (Chile)
MAS	Movement Toward Socialism (Venezuela)
MDB	Brazilian Democratic Movement
MDP	Pradist Democratic Movement (Peru)
MEP	Peoples' Electoral Movement (Venezuela)
MID	Independent Left Movement (Argentina)
MIR	Leftist Revolutionary Movement (Chile)
MIR	Leftist Revolutionary Movement (Venezuela)
MIT	Massachusetts Institute of Technology
MRL	Revolutionary Liberal Movement (Colombia)
MSN	National Salvation Movement (Colombia)
MVR	Fifth Republic Movement (Venezuela)
NAFTA	North American Free Trade Agreement
OAS	Organization of American States

ORVE	Venezuelan Revolutionary Organization
PAIS	Open Politics for Social Integrity (Argentina)
PAL	Agrarian Labor Party (Chile)
PAN	National Action Party (Mexico)
PAN	National Autonomist Party (Argentina)
PARM	Authentic Party of the Mexican Revolution
PC	Civilist Party (Peru)
PC	Conservative Party (Argentina, Brazil, Chile, Colombia, Peru, or Venezuela)
PC	Constitutionalist Party (Peru)
PCB	Brazilian Communist Party
PCCh	Chilean Communist Party
PCdoB	Communist Party of Brazil
PCP	Popular Conservative Party (Argentina)
PCV	Venezuelan Communist Party
PD	Democratic Party (Argentina)
PD	Democratic Party (Chile)
PDA	Alternative Independent Democratic Pole (Colombia)
PDC	Christian Democratic Party (Argentina)
PDC	Christian Democratic Party (Brazil)
PDC	Christian Democratic Party (Chile)
PDC	Christian Democratic Party (Peru)
PDN	National Democratic Party (Venezuela)
PDR	Democratic Reform Party (Peru)
PDS	Social Democracy Party (Brazil)
PDT	Democratic Workers' Party (Brazil)
PDVSA	Venezuelan Petroleum Company
PFL	Liberal Front Party (Brazil)
PJ	Justicialist Party (Argentina)
PL	Liberal Party (Argentina, Brazil, Chile, Colombia, Mexico, Peru, or Venezuela) as well as Labor Party (Argentina)
PLM	Mexican Labor Party
PMDB	Party of the Brazilian Democratic Movement
PN	National Party (Chile)
PN	National Party (Colombia)
PNA	National Agrarian Party (Mexico)
PNP	Peruvian Nationalist Party
PNR	National Revolutionary Party (Mexico)
PP	Peronist Party (Argentina)
PP	Popular Party (Brazil)
PPB	Brazilian Popular Party
PPC	Popular Christian Party (Peru)
PPC	Popular Conservative Party (Argentina)
PPD	Party for Democracy (Chile)
PPF	Women's Peronist Party (Argentina)
PPP	purchasing power parity
PPR	Progressive Renewal Party (Brazil)

PPS	Popular Socialist Party (Mexico)
PPS	Popular Socialist Party (Brazil)
PR	Radical Party (Chile)
PR	Party of the Republic (Brazil)
PRB	Brazilian Republican Party
PRC	Conservative Republican Party (Brazil)
PRD	Party of the Democratic Revolution (Mexico)
PRF	Federal Republican Party (Brazil)
PRI	Institutional Revolutionary Party (Mexico)
PRM	Party of the Mexican Revolution
PRN	National Renovation Party (Brazil)
PRO	Republican Proposal (Argentina)
PRP	Popular Representation Party (Brazil)
PRVZL	Venezuelan Project (Venezuelan political party)
PS	Socialist Party (Argentina)
PSB	Brazilian Socialist Party
PSC	Social Conservative Party (Colombia)
PSC	Social Christian Party (Brazil)
PSCh	Chilean Socialist Party
PSD	Social Democratic Party (Brazil)
PSDB	Brazilian Social Democracy Party
PSP	Social Progressive Party (Brazil)
PSUN	Social National Unity Party
PSUV	United Socialist Party of Venezuela
PT	Workers' Party (Mexico)
PT	Workers' Party (Brazil)
PTB	Brazilian Labor Party
PTN	National Workers Party (Brazil)
PUR	Unified Party of the National Revolution (Argentina)
PV	Green Party (Brazil)
PVEM	Green Party (Mexico)
RN	National Renewal (Chile)
SENDAS	National Secretariat of Social Assistance (Colombia)
SIN	National Intelligence Service (Peru)
SINAMOS	National System of Social Mobilization (Peru)
SNI	National Intelligence Service (Brazil)
SRA	Argentine Rural Society
TEPJF	Electoral Tribunal of the Federal Judicial Power (Mexico)
UCR	Radical Civic Union (Argentina)
UCRI	Intransigent Radical Civic Union (Argentina)
UCRP	Radical Civic Union of the People (Argentina)
UD	Democratic Union (Argentina)
UDI	Independent Democratic Union (Chile)
UDN	National Democratic Union (Brazil)
UN	National Unity (Peru)
UN	United Nations
UNO	National Odrista Union (Peru)

UNIR	Revolutionary Left National Union (Colombia)
UP	Popular Union (Argentina)
UP	Popular Unity (Chile)
UPP	Union for Peru
UR	Republican Union (Colombia)
URD	Democratic Republican Union (Venezuela)
WTO	World Trade Organization

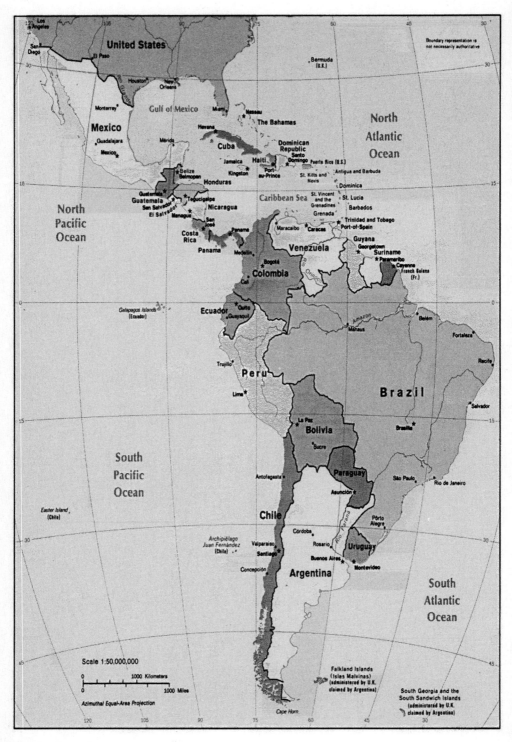

Latin America

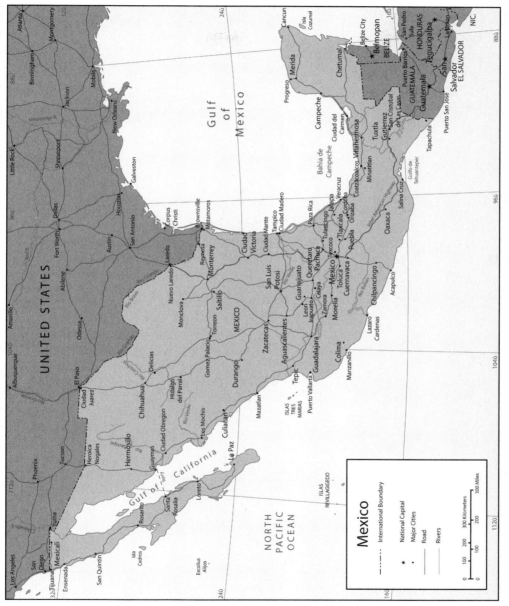

Mexico

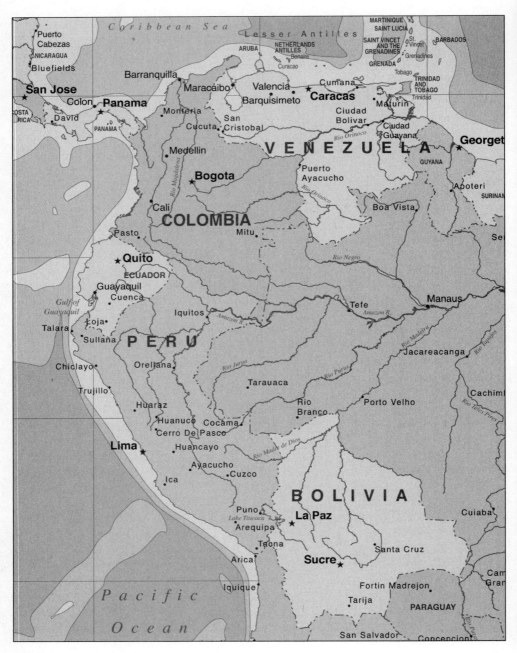

Northern South America

Brazil

Argentina and Chile

Introduction and Overview of Latin America

Latin America is a region of often perplexing contradictions stemming from the fact that rapid change in some respects interacts with intractable continuities in others. The effects of economic growth and societal modernization feed the former, whereas the latter is rooted in an authoritarian and corporatist past. To fundamentally alter institutions may take lifetimes, and alterations in the more resistant culture within which they operate take even longer—perhaps as much as three or four generations. A close-up view of Latin America underscores both its bothersome problems and its resistance to change. Yet looking back into its past brings with it a realization of how much change, some of which constitutes real and substantial political development, has taken place.

The differences from a century ago (1909) are more than dramatic, bordering upon profound. Then Brazil had been a republic for only two decades and, just fifteen years before, had traded high-handed despotic military presidents for governments dominated by oligarchic elites perpetuating themselves in power by limited and controlled elections involving very restricted participation; yet in 2002, some 120 million men and women elected an authentic man of the working class to be president. In the early twentieth century Mexico was still ruled with an iron hand by an entrenched dictator whose nearly thirty years in power would extend yet another five before its violent end ushered in a quarter century of bloody civil strife; but at the beginning of this new century it managed to transfer power peacefully from a party whose hegemony spanned over seventy years to its historical opposition. Over the same time span Argentina went from domination by an agro-producing elite to a mass-based democracy, and Colombia progressed from rule by the conservative victors of a bloody civil war to a highly competitive electoral democracy. Venezuela traveled from a traditional dictator to a modern personalist populist, Peru moved from oligarchy to mass political participation, and Chile emerged as a model of twenty-first-century democracy. This remarkable and arduous journey through political development to consolidated democracy certainly merits close examination.

The Course of Political Development

In their development toward stable participatory political processes rooted in a viable economy and functional social structures, countries do not move in a continuous or straight line. Typically there are protracted periods of stagnation or even backsliding as well as times of coasting on ebbing momentum. Fortunately most countries also experience surges of forward movement. Emphasis will be placed on these developmental spurts and the conditions and agents that caused them as well as on the conditions that led to their running out of steam. Indeed, a major aim of this book is to document the fact that political development in Latin America has rarely been a smooth, steady, and linear process. This effort also involves showing the range of variations and any possible exceptions to this rule. As a result it will be possible to relate such surges to causes in the areas of economic change, societal modernization, political leadership, altered alignments among power contenders and forces, and international factors.

Like human beings, countries do not get to select their parents or choose when and where they will be born. After widely varying prenatal experiences, generally under colonial rule, they undergo differing degrees of birth trauma before coming into being. They then start life with inherent weaknesses and vulnerabilities that may crop up at later stages of their lives as well as often with inadequate social and economic heritages. Immediately after independence the nation-state system imposes adult responsibilities upon infant political systems. Not surprisingly their performance is usually quite shaky, if not inadequate. They may eventually overcome slow and halting starts, but the very process of having to do so may further handicap them.

Every country's political past influences the present in two ways. First, there is the objective heritage in terms of governmental structures, political organizations, and policy needs addressed, or ignored, as well as the impinging socioeconomic environment. Equally important is the legacy reflected in the attitudes, values, expectations, and misgivings making up the political culture that conditions individuals' actions in the political realm. Distorted perceptions often lead to believing both that the unfeasible is possible and that what might in reality be desirable is unattainable. Hence, paths doomed to failure may be followed and those that are potentially productive may be eschewed.

To understand the present it is necessary to comprehend how it has come about. To this end a number of crucial questions concerning Latin America are best posed as backward- rather than forward-linked. What aspects of the different independence-gaining experiences are explainable in terms of the preceding colonial experience? Next, what elements of widely varying early postindependence political life had their roots in the particular manner in which independence was achieved? In turn, what differences in the second generation of national life are attributable to first-generation nuances? Hence, although this book's account of events moves forward in time, the quest for explanations is essentially retrospective. Great change has come about, but only as a result of the accumulation of lesser changes made over many generations. Our quest to understand Latin America's political development begins with an overview of the seven countries prior to 1930 (Chapters 1 through 4) before we examine them individually. There follows a synthesis of post-1930 events and trends (Chapters 5 to 9) preparatory to an examination of the several countries since 1930. The explanatory journey culminates in chapters containing analytical conclusions and observations on future challenges. Thus, the reader finishes with a solid knowledge of (1) *where* Latin America stands politically at present; (2) *how* these countries arrived at their present situation; and (3) *why* they followed their individual paths instead of going in other directions.

A good deal of progress seemed to have been made by the middle of the twentieth century (when the author began a lifetime of intense concern with the region), but some of it turned out to be illusionary, and even more was based on shifting sands. The political situation a few years after World War II was both far less participatory and markedly more unstable than it would be near the century's end. Brazil was about to embark on the last hurrah of populist strongman Getúlio Vargas, and Mexico's dominant governing party was preparing for yet another in a growing line of peaceful presidential successions, never mind that there was no real political competition. In Argentina the charismatic General Juan Domingo Perón was readying his forces for an unprecedented reelection bid with the glamorous Evita still at his side. Colombia was reeling from the murder of its most popular politician and sinking into a civil war that would claim 40,000 lives—a year! Venezuela had seen a reformist civilian regime replaced by a military junta, and in Peru an ambitious general who had recently seized power was in the process of legitimizing himself through a sham election. Chile, a bastion of constitutionality, was experiencing disillusionment with its political parties to such an extent that it would soon elect to the presidency a man who had been a military dictator in the late 1920s. For most of the region the 1960s was the disillusioning decade of the collapse of fragile and shallow-rooted populist experiments, and the 1970s witnessed a dismaying burgeoning of repressive authoritarian regimes. The sun burst from behind these gray political clouds during the 1980s, with despotism swept away by a wave of democratizing transitions—often building on the lessons of past failure. Finally, the 1990s saw consolidation of these often-imperfect democracies—with the early years of the twenty-first century raising issues of social justice and economic performance.

As essential as it is, a summation of where the countries of Latin America have arrived politically is not an answer to how they got there. The facts of what happened having been outlined in terms of events, the steps and processes of how it happened need to be examined with an eye to trends and patterns as well as paths followed, before attention can shift to causation. For although very important variations are depicted in the chapters ahead, a high-above-the-treetops wide-lens preview provides perspective on the evolution of politics for individuals down on the ground and often blindly hacking their way through decade after decade of often murky political developments. What is normal, what is backward, and what is exceptional can be assessed by students only against the backdrop of what is common. Then, looking across the region and the periods retrospectively allows judgments be made as to which countries were the ones out of step at any time or deficient or exemplary with regard to meeting specific challenges. Moreover, at any point in time Latin American political development can meaningfully be compared only to that prevailing at the time on the European continent, particularly its southern part, not to the levels achieved in the exemplary leading cases of Great Britain and the United States.

The Ethnic, Geographic, Demographic, and Economic Mosaic

Basic ethnic, demographic, geographic, and economic factors must be laid on the table before we embark on our analysis of political events, structures, and processes. The racial and ethnic complexity of Latin America is truly impressive, exceeding that of Europe. It, more than any other factor, is so dramatically varied as to call into question the validity and usefulness of one umbrella term for the region. Certainly comparison of developments in one country with those in others cannot ignore the tremendous racial variations, which exceed those of other major world regions. While some commentators go too far in saying that there are three Latin Americas—white, bronze, and black—the often underplayed racial differences are all the more crucial because the greatest variations are found in the largest and most important countries, not just in lesser exceptions to some sort of regional norm (which essentially doesn't exist).[1]

Brazil, home to over one-third of all Latin Americans (195 million of 590 million), has 98 million individuals (just over 50 percent of its population) with significant African roots, mostly mixed, but 13 million of them black. Yet its 94 million inhabitants of European extraction—roughly as many as in the rest of South America—are quite varied, with those of fairly recent Italian extraction and descendants of early Portuguese settlers the most numerous, but other Europeans common and Asian strains significant in absolute, if not relative, terms. Brazil's indigenous population has been reduced to below 0.2 percent (around 350,000 individuals). Mexicans, who at over 111 million comprise nearly a fifth of all Latin Americans, could hardly differ more from Brazilians in their origins and heritage. Persons of mixed Spanish-Indian blood predominate, while those with African roots are extremely few. But among Mexico's European population, estimated at only 9 percent, Italians are rare and Portuguese unheard of. Moreover, Indians (at 30 percent) still comprise a very sizable proportion of the country's inhabitants, and most of the majority *mestizos* are more Indian than European. Argentina, with a population of 41 million individuals, is overwhelmingly European, at some 85 percent, having all but eradicated its indigenous population during the nineteenth century, with individuals of Italian extraction easily the nation's majority, and *mestizos* less than one in seven. Colombia, whose population of 46 million is vastly different, bears a superficial similarity to Mexico in racial/ethnic makeup. Considered a *mestizo* country at nearly 60 percent, it is home to only 700,000 Indians—many with some admixture of African blood. A large proportion of Colombian *mestizos* are markedly more European, hence less Indian, than most Mexican *mestizos*. Blacks and mulattoes are nearly as numerous as Europeans in Colombia, at around a fifth of the total, but are situated at the opposite pole in socioeconomic terms and political influence, perhaps more so than their far more numerous Brazilian counterparts.

These four countries, containing two-thirds of the region's population, amply demonstrate Latin America's ethnic/racial diversity. But diversity also characterizes the middle stratum of Latin American countries. Peru's population of almost 30 million has Indians and *mestizos*—respectively, 45 and 37 percent—as the very distinct majority, with its 15 percent of European origin chiefly of Spanish extraction. It is distinguished by the fact that Asians are decidedly more numerous than persons of African ancestry. Venezuela has a racial/ethnic mosaic among its 27 million inhabitants roughly paralleling that of neighboring Colombia, although with a somewhat higher *mestizo* majority, a lower proportion of African origin, and only 2 percent Indian. Chile, population nearing 17 million, is largely fairly Europeanized *mestizos* and predominantly Spanish-origin Europeans, with only 3 percent Indians, very few Asians, and almost no one of African heritage.

Latin America is overwhelmingly Christian. It has also been essentially untouched by non-Christian immigration at a time when this has become a significant factor in making both western Europe and the United States less predominantly Christian. Cultural influences upon the region come chiefly from the United States and western European countries (especially Spain, Portugal, Italy, and France). Islamic influence is essentially nil, as are Hindu, Confucian, Buddhist, and Shinto influences. Tourist flows are similarly almost exclusively from and to the United States and western Europe.

This orientation is reflected in and reinforced by trade patterns, although not as exclusively. In addition, Latin America's continuing population expansion offsets the demographic stagnation of western Europe and the trend in this direction in the United States and increases its potential for economic growth. Hence, Latin America's importance as the third leg of the Western Christian world is not only great but also growing.

In Latin American politics, certain geographic facts cannot be ignored. Brazil, by far the largest of the region's countries (at just over 3.3 million square miles, the fifth largest country in the world), affects much more of Latin America more deeply than does second-largest Mexico. The latter is located at the northern extreme of the region and has its longest and most active boundary with the United States, its massively dominant trading partner. Within Latin America Mexico borders only Guatemala and Belize, one medium-sized by regional standards and the other tiny. In sharp contrast, Brazil, stretching 2,700 miles both north to south and east to west, occupies the heart of the South American continent and borders on the region's third- through sixth-largest countries (Argentina, Colombia, Peru, and Venezuela) as well as all other countries of the continent except Chile and Ecuador. Its Atlantic coastline of 4,600 miles equals all coasts of the United States—Atlantic, Pacific, and Gulf. Brazil is distant from the United States (which is an important, but very far from dominant, market), being closer to Africa and essentially as close to Europe as to the United States. For their part, Colombia is situated at the northern tip of South America and Argentina at its southern extreme, a position greatly limiting the number of countries with which they are in direct contact. Peru borders on four countries, while Chile has only two adjacent neighbors.

Because of these geographic factors the seven countries have had quite limited interaction. Mexico has no significant communication, much less contact, with countries in South America. Argentina and Chile lie back to back, looking out at separate oceans and with the high divide of the Andes mountains between them. Peru's very short border with Chile is in a desolate desert, and that with Brazil lies across the vast Amazon basin from that country's essentially east coast population centers. Colombia's most remote and virtually uninhabited frontier regions abut those of Brazil and Peru, and its border with Venezuela is far away from the cities of either country. This geographic isolation is even more pronounced in the case of Brazil's relationship with both of these northern "neighbors." Despite the modifications brought by instantaneous electronic communications and air transportation, it is a mistake to think that inhabitants of one of these "sister" countries have more than a rudimentary idea of what goes on in any of the others. (One exception is substantial vacation tourism by Argentines to Brazil.) The lack of interest in the other countries may be decreasing, but these countries are still very far from being brought significantly closer together.

A prevalent myth says that Latin American countries are dominated by their capital cities. Like the monoculture myth that most Latin American countries have only a single main product, it bears little resemblance to reality except in the smallest countries—where there is little room for a second metropolis, especially when the first may well not be very impressive. Starting from the top, Brazil contains two of the world's largest cities, neither of them its capital. Metropolitan São Paulo is approaching 28 million inhabitants and Rio de Janeiro has passed 13 million.[2] Impressive as these figures are, together they comprise only one-fifth of the country's population, which includes eighteen more urban regions of over a million inhabitants, totaling close to 42 million. (Belo Horizonte is over 5 million, with Porto Alegre closing in on 4 million, while Recife, Salvador, Fortaleza, Curitiba, and Brasília all fall in the over-3-million category.) Mexico City may be the world's largest urban conglomerate, inhabited as it is by at least 24 million souls, but this number constitutes just over a fifth of the country's population. Mexico's major cities in the north, led by Monterrey at more than 3 million and León, Tijuana, and Ciudad Juárez at well over a million each, are distant from the capital, and even Guadalajara (approaching 4 million) is three hundred miles from Mexico City as the crow flies, but much farther by road or rail over mountainous terrain, as is the somewhat nearer Puebla (well over 2 million). Thanks to Colombia's drug cartels, the existence of a multiplicity of large cities there is well known, no single one as populous as Bogotá, with its 7.5 million inhabitants, but together exceeding the population of the capital—led by Medellín at over 3 million inhabitants and Cali with 2.5 million. Lima, nearing 8 million, is Peru's premier city, but again owing to the Andes, there is a series of large coastal centers such as Trujillo (700,000) as well as the inland metropolis of Arequipa (800,000).

In the fourth, sixth, and seventh largest countries of the region, the capital city is more dominant and has fewer challengers. Argentina is mother to the myth of the huge head with a small body, for the city and province of Buenos Aires do contain nearly half the country's population, while Córdoba (about as far away as Brasília is from Rio de Janeiro or São Paulo) is a very distant second with 3.3 million inhabitants, followed by Santa Fé (3.2 million) and then Rosário, Tucumán, and Mendoza (around 1.5 million each). Caracas, with over 2 million inhabitants, leads other Venezuelan cities, with Maracaibo at 1.7 million and Valencia with 1.3 million, but has a relatively small share of the nation's population and is not a port, so its ability to be hegemonic is severely limited, particularly with much of the country's industry located well to the east around Ciudad Bolívar and Ciudad Guyana. Essentially Chile is the Central Valley with Concepción, Antofagasta, Viña del Mar, and Valparaiso playing third or fourth rather than second fiddles to Santiago.

The economic output of Latin America has reached an annual $6.1 trillion, raising its per capita gross domestic product (GDP) above the $10,000 level (in purchasing power parity [PPP] terms).[3] These regional averages mask extreme variations including a number of minuscule economies as well as several of world significance. Latin America includes one of the world's top economies, Brazil, at $2.0 trillion, as well as Mexico—near $1.6 trillion. Argentina, at $575 billion, is followed by Colombia (whose $400 billion does not fully reflect one of its leading industries: recreational drugs), and then Venezuela (whose $360-billion GDP fluctuates widely with the price of petroleum). Chile narrowly leads Peru $245 billion to $240 billion. Hence the seven most populous Latin American countries contribute about 88 percent of the regional GDP. Reflecting their wide variation in population, Chile has the highest per capita GDP, nearing $15,000, followed by Argentina's $14,300, Mexico's $14,200, and Venezuela's oil-skewed $13,500. Brazil weighs in at $10,100, ahead of Colombia's $8,900, which is slightly higher than Peru's $8,400. This substantial range in levels of economic development is mirrored in societal differences, including a tremendous regional gulf in Brazil between its semi-European south and laggard tropical north. In second-largest Mexico the analogous gap favors the northern part over its subtropical south. By far the smallest of these seven countries, Chile is the most homogeneous.

Leadership, Violence, and Democracy

Although it has become fashionable to deal with movements rather than personalities, leadership remains a very critical element in the Latin American political equation. Admittedly, as institutionalization advances and organizations comprising the political infrastructure acquire stability and continuity, leadership becomes less crucial as a determinant of political development. Most countries of Latin America, however, are still far from that happy juncture. This should not be surprising, as France needed a charismatic Charles de Gaulle as recently as the 1960s, while Germany required an extraordinary figure such as Willy Brandt into the mid-1970s. Even Britain sorely needed a giant the stature of Winston Churchill in the 1940s and 1950s, a leader of Margaret Thatcher's unusual talents in the 1980s, and more recently a Tony Blair. Hence dominant political figures will loom large in this study, albeit more in the account of how these countries got to where they are than since the mid-1980s. For developmental surges in Latin America usually involve a major political leader as catalyst, and such episodes have occurred at different points in time in each of the countries. Unfortunately the comparative literature on political leadership in this region is quite weak, as, for that matter, is the treatment of Latin American figures in global comparative works.[4] Hence the nature and role of leadership is a major unifying theme of this book. Indeed, a careful reading will put students in a position to critically evaluate the rankings found in Chapter 11. Leadership is sui generis, extremely resistant to analytical generalizations. Conditions and situations affect its development and emergence, but they do not determine whether an outstanding leader will come to the fore. Political recruitment processes are an important facilitating or restraining variable, with broadened participation not directly, much less immediately, resulting in wider opportunity to reach the pinnacle of power. Indeed, there is some sobering evidence that democratic electoral processes may at times reduce the chances of extraordinary individuals' coming to hold a country's top office.

People's fundamental political orientation and basic perceptions of their country are largely formed during their youth. For many, developments in their young adult years, if not before, shape the direction of their subsequent political activities. At this stage of their lives, national leaders are often seized upon as role models; for some they may even be mentors. Hence the importance of bearing in mind the context in which political figures grew up. This was the Porfirio Díaz period at the turn of the century for Mexico's great reformer Lázaro Cárdenas; Getúlio Vargas's final years in the early 1950s and the uneasy period that followed his demise, for 1995–2002 Brazilian president Fernando Henrique Cardoso; and Argentina's "false dawn" of democracy between 1914 and 1930 for Juan Domingo Perón. Hence dates of birth are provided for key political actors to establish in the reader's mind the trail back to the epoch of their socialization, particularly intense from the mid teens to late twenties. (Dates of death are included in the narrative only in the few cases where they had a direct impact upon political life, as with Evita Perón's early demise or Vargas's suicide.)

Episodes of large-scale domestic conflict mark the history of those countries that have successfully achieved economic and political development. The US Civil War, Britain's analogous strife 220 years earlier, the French Revolution, Hitler's repressive totalitarian regime and the holocaust, and the Spanish Civil War come readily to mind as examples of this inability to resolve major political issues by any means other than force of arms. Throughout the Afro-Asian world since the end of World War II, extremely bloody internal conflicts have been, and still are, dishearteningly common. Thus, by comparison Latin America's political struggles, bloody as some instances have been, are not out of line with global experience. Indeed, resort to large-scale sustained armed conflict in this region may even be a less common way of resolving intractable differences than in much of the rest of the world. Yet, despite the decreased salience of violence, it is still important, throughout the book, to look at all major episodes of violence, including those remote in time. Besides examining why major organized political violence has occurred at one time or another in almost all Latin American countries, it is important to establish whether and how such traumas have contributed to a quest for ways to avoid their recurrence. For, if learning does not take place in this field, it is unlikely to do so with respect to less calamitous events. Since there is a persistent myth that violence stems from Hispanic character traits, we will also explore the countercontention that the resort to a limited use of violence may be normal in a Latin American political system, or even necessary to its functioning. Given the many types of advantages accruing to those who control the government, emerging groups cannot count upon gaining power merely through the organization of majority support expressed through the ballot box. They may at times have to resort to violent acts, not to burn the system down, but rather to light a fire under complacent standpatters.

The broadly inclusive acceptance of competitive electoral processes as the means of arbitrating rival political ambitions and policy differences, even in tense and polarized situations, is still recent in Latin America. Thus the question is raised how deeply the roots of this democratic process may be. The wave of democratic transitions beginning in the late 1970s reflected disillusionment with authoritarian military regimes as much as, and very possibly more than, abiding faith in the long-term viability of democracy. Despite positive indications in recent years of the growing confidence of key sectors of society in the long-term workability of democratic processes, the question of what kind of democracy merits the careful consideration it receives in the chapters ahead. For as leading comparativist Howard Wiarda cautions, Latin America is "at least in part a particular Hispanic, neoscholastic, counter-reformationary, Thomistic, organicist, semifeudal, corporatist, patrimonialist, precapitalist, pre-Enlightenment, pre-Industrial Revolution, quasimedieval, pre-limited government *version* of the West."[5] The intellectual challenge is to determine how much and in what ways this cautionary diagnosis remains true and to what extent its elements are being superseded by modernizing and democratizing processes. To this end the next chapter provides both a baseline and an account of progress from colonial days until eighty years ago.

Notes

1. A perceptive and sensitive topically organized overview of the region is Ronaldo Munck, *Contemporary Latin America*, rev. ed. (New York: Palgrave Macmillan, 2008). Viewing Latin America as "part of the West, but not quite" as well as "modern, but not quite," this Argentine-born sociologist says the region can best be viewed as "more a process than a predefined entity," hence requiring hybrid and "betwixt and between" perceptions rather than rigid categorization.

2. The figures are from http://citypopulation.de.

3. See *World Development Indicators 2009* (Herndon, VA: World Bank Publications, 2009) for 2007 figures. The most recent figures are mid-2009 estimates online at the Central Intelligence Agency (CIA) World Factbook at www.cia.gov/factbook.html.

4. The literature on comparative political leadership is sparse and generally weak. Despite a lack of political science conceptualization combined with reliance solely upon English-language sources, Arnold M. Ludwig, *King of the Mountain: The Nature of Political Leadership* (Lexington: University Press of Kentucky, 2002), is the most comprehensive volume.

5. Howard J. Wiarda, *Dilemmas of Democracy in Latin America: Crises and Opportunities* (Lanham, MD: Roman & Littlefield, 2005), p. 19.

PART 1

◇   ◇   ◇

Latin America: Independence to 1930

1

Comparative Perspectives

Independence to 1930

Colonial Legacy and Achieving Independence

The protracted colonial period, from the end of the fifteenth century through the early decades of the nineteenth, witnessed the implantation of political institutions bearing the heavy imprint of medieval corporatism, in which the hierarchically organized church, military, and largely peninsular (Iberian-born) bureaucracy each enjoyed special privileges, and the Creole aristocracy (New World–born Europeans) pursued its interests through interaction with them. Royal authority was maintained through separate lines of authority and often overlapping, if not partially contradictory, instructions to the throne's three sets of representatives (church, military, and administrators). Early on, the bureaucracy became a vehicle for patronage and payoffs to reward and ensure loyalty. With time, the large landowners, particularly those who astutely allied themselves to the corporate pillars, came to be an important political factor. Late in the colonial period, intense rivalry developed between *peninsulares* and *criollos* (Spanish for "Creoles") over their conflicting commercial interests. These differences shaped their respective attitudes toward continuation of the colonial relationship.

Because of this rivalry, an "us-against-them" mentality developed and fused with the belief that politics was a zero-sum game in which any gains by one group came at the expense of others—if not in direct terms, at least in the form of foreclosed opportunities. Strong personal loyalties and intolerance of opposing views, which would later translate into intransigent partisanship, became prevalent political traits. Moreover, with power in the hands of competing hierarchical groups—the military, the church, bureaucratic authority, merchants, and large landowners—these groups became the arbiters of policy, relying on their power rather than negotiation and compromise. During the colonial era kinship ties had been very important because force and intimidation were often applied and the courts were frequently instruments of punishing enemies and rewarding friends and relatives. One could generally rely upon family, not a government that might favor your rivals and, by definition, ruthless opponents. These views and values became part of a political culture that persisted over the span of generations (for Latin America's long colonial era lasted three centuries—a far longer period than these countries' independent lives have yet spanned). In many ways these views and values would be reinforced by the strains and strife of the independence struggle.

Underlying the reservations of the economic elite concerning the one-sided nature of their relationship to the mother country, by the beginning of the nineteenth century Spain had become an inadequate industrial supplier and trading partner for its growing New World colonies. In sharp contrast, Britain was well advanced into the Industrial Revolution and experiencing rapid expansion of trade, particularly with Latin America, whose payment for British goods in silver was highly attractive within the prevailing mercantilist system. As the original conquest and settlement of the leading colonies was by now two and a half centuries in the past, the structure of society and the relations among groups had altered significantly from the early colonial era. In the view of the most influential elements, adjustments to this transformation within the bounds of empire were desirable, but if the mother country was not prepared to go halfway, then other options at least merited consideration.

Latin America's independence movements combined the selfish economic concerns and personal political ambitions of many actors with the lofty ideals and unrealistic expectations of others. Only a handful of the educated elite were imbued with ideas of liberty, republicanism, and democracy stemming from the US example and the very brief flame of the French Revolution—before it was put out by Napoleonic imperial floodwaters. For the vast majority these developments were virtually unknown or essentially irrelevant. Most Hispanic Americans were passive observers or were swept up in the course of events against their will, and politically active elements were in most instances chiefly influenced by perceptions of where advantage lay for their particular interests and where opportunity existed for their ambitions. Landowner-merchant conflict interacted with the *peninsulares-criollos* rivalries in ways that were sometimes crosscutting, but often more reinforcing.

The most basic common feature with respect to the variegated independence movements was that they were decisively catalyzed, facilitated, and in part caused by the monumental and protracted struggle, known as the Napoleonic Wars, for supremacy in Europe between globally dominant Britain and continentally hegemonic France. Had Spain not been occupied and thus temporarily incorporated into Bonaparte's domains, its Western Hemisphere possessions would not have become independent at this particular time. Instead, through entering into alliance with France in 1795, Spain had opened up a Pandora's box of unforeseen consequences that created economic and political distance between the Iberian mother countries and their American colonies. England, the dominant sea power, used its naval forces to reduce and eventually cut communications, forcing Spain to suspend its already leaky trade monopoly. The ensuing experience of trading legally with other colonies and neutral countries, especially the United States, stoked Creole desires for greater economic self-determination. The political divide widened and deepened after Charles IV granted Napoléon passage through Spain to invade Portugal, a staunch British ally. The immediate effect was the Portuguese government's 1808 move to Brazil, which transformed that disjoined array of essentially coastal colonies into the empire's administrative center based in Rio de Janeiro. The impact of the Spanish monarch's error was also felt in Hispanic America, as that same year Napoléon Bonaparte turned on his erstwhile Spanish allies, placing his brother Joseph on the throne in Madrid. Both Charles and his successor, Ferdinand, became French captives, so the "hub of all political authority" for Spain's colonies was removed.[1] Colonial elites struggled with how to maintain control without even the legitimizing and unifying symbol of a monarch at the head of the governmental hierarchy. This loss was traumatizing, as New World Spaniards, only a little over 3 million in a regional population of 17 million, feared a racial bloodbath such as the one that had recently occurred in Haiti.

This authority vacuum resulted in both the *peninsular* and *criollo* elites' setting up a variety of provisional governments, ostensibly to rule in the king's name, but in the meantime actively advancing their own interests. At that point the New World bourgeoisie were increasingly interested in equality over independence, home rule over separation, and autonomy over emancipation.[2] In Mexico City these caretaker regimes were controlled by *peninsular* loyalists, whereas in Santiago, Caracas, and Bogotá Creoles dominated the provisional juntas. The spread of *ayuntamientos* ("governing councils") to all major population centers drastically expanded political participation to less substantial businessmen and property owners. The restoration of Ferdinand to the throne in 1814 pushed Spanish America further toward independence. In Spain 12,000 liberals were jailed or exiled in a campaign to restore traditional monarchical power, and in the colonies royal use of military force, including reinforcements from the mother country, to repress independence movements hardened Creole resolve. Then, in the face of a mutiny in 1820, Ferdinand agreed to liberal reforms, a concession that while reducing tensions in Spain, divided and weakened loyalist support in the colonies by undermining confidence in the monarchy. Hence independence struggles, already under way in many parts of the region, forged ahead, proving triumphant during the 1820s. The result was instability and de facto regimes based on force, not the functioning republican regimes promised by leaders of the independence movement.

A political scientist testing explanations for revolt against the Spanish throne concludes that "by the beginning of the nineteenth century the Creole elite in each case wanted to nationalize decision-making, appropriating authority for themselves. The critical factor was the political bargaining relationship between local elites and the government of the empire and of each colony."[3] Optimistic concerning the new opportunities, the catalyzers of independence were blissfully unaware of how daunting, even perilous, the years ahead would prove to be, and how unprepared they were for the challenges ahead. The political situation prevailing in Spanish America as its component countries were looking forward to independence and finding a path to national consolidation and establishment of order was one in which

> long-term social, political, and economic change had differentiated the Spanish American empire internally and had led to the formation of consciously competing groups. When imperial legitimacy broke down, these preexisting groups turned from competition over status and wealth to competition for power. Their unrestrained conflict in the political arena led to a collapse of colonial legitimacy.[4]

As a result:

> When legitimacy was in question, many groups, both elite Spaniards and Creoles, moved simultaneously to appropriate political legitimacy. . . . Coups

and countercoups undermined the legitimacy of each of three colonial governments at the time that the legitimacy of the entire imperial system was
in question.[5]

Contrary to the expectations of the enthusiasts of independence, this turmoil
would not cease once an end to this chaotic turmoil was accomplished. Indeed, for
most of Spanish America it would increase, and in some countries it persisted for a
generation—if not even longer.

New Nations from Colonialism to Consolidation, Independence to 1870

In most countries, independence was obtained by 1830—with great variations in
the effort involved and the leadership generated. The ensuing decades witnessed
the frustration of high hopes and a substantial persistence of old patterns behind a
facade of rhetoric and cosmetic change. Often this process took place within a
context of instability mixed with dictatorial experiences (as has been the case in
the early years of almost all nations in all parts of the world). Brazil was a major exception, having in many ways experienced an exceptionally easy separation from its
mother country, involving a period in which Portugal's government was transferred
to Rio de Janeiro; once this transitional period was over, the heir to the Portuguese
throne remained as prince regent. He subsequently became monarch, and his son
would occupy the throne until 1889. Thus Brazil avoided the traumatic double
rupture of breaking at the same time both with the mother country and with the
world's established source of legitimizing political authority, that is, divine right
monarchy. At the time, the United States was the only republic in the world—still
unproven in a myriad of ways. In sharp contrast, Mexico's path to independence
was both drawn out and violent, as popular movements were bloodily repressed before an upstart adventurer proclaimed himself emperor but was soon forced out.
This train of events opened the way for a long era of *caudillo* politics, in contrast to
Brazil's stable monarchy. Antonio López de Santa Ana of Mexico and Pedro II of
Brazil were antithetical figures, each dominating the political stage for his country's
first generation of independence, the former into the 1850s, and the latter nearly
twice as long. Santa Ana would have the misfortune of presiding over the loss of
half his country to the United States, while Dom Pedro II would hold his vast
country together.

Strikingly different, Argentina's independence came early and with little bloodshed, largely because royalist forces were limited in this sparsely populated area of—at
that time—little economic value. Its liberator would then cross the Andes to help
Chile win its independence and subsequently to fight against Spanish forces in Peru.
As a result, there would be a protracted period of instability before a dictatorial
caudillo imposed order in Argentina. The ensuing authoritarian and often brutal rule
of Juan Manuel de Rosas, lasting just past midcentury, would be followed by eventually successful efforts, stretching through the 1860s, to unite the coastal metropolitan
area to the interior. (Rosas and Mexico's Santa Ana were two very distinct types of
nondemocratic political leaders, the former a product of Mexico's large area, popula-

tion, and long independence process and the latter a civilian emerging in the context of an early and easy independence in what was little more than Buenos Aires and its immediate hinterland.) By dramatic contrast, northern South America underwent a bloody armed struggle to free itself from the Spanish yoke, resulting by the late 1820s in Simón Bolívar's short-lived Gran Colombia. With Venezuela splitting off in 1830, the remainder limped along without a dominant leader until the evolution of an elitist two-party system in the 1850s and 1860s. Venezuela, an out-of-the-way traditional ranching society, spawned a durable *caudillo* pattern of politics that would continue into the twentieth century. Peru, center of Spanish rule and settlement on the continent, had resisted independence until it was imposed militarily by Bolívar's armies in the latter half of the 1820s. Hence the legitimacy vacuum had the most serious effects there, where efforts to construct a viable political system proved extremely difficult, but *caudillo* rule and its negative legacy were avoided. Chile, having won its independence early on with considerable aid from Argentina, enjoyed the best initial leadership of any Latin American country and built the foundations of a stable representative political system in the 1830s.

For these six Hispanic countries, independence did not transform the fundamentals of the inherited political-governmental system, although it did institute one very important change in removing the monarch, who had been both the legitimizer of authority and the arbiter among the rival power factors. With the disappearance of the viceroy as the king's local representative, central government institutions were greatly weakened; regions that had been victims of a lopsided center-periphery relationship often broke off. (These included Chile and Venezuela.) In all these new nations the most pressing and, as it proved, enduring problem faced in their first decades of independence was how to establish the legitimacy of their new governments. Elites were aware that Great Britain, with its parliamentary form of government, was the most advanced country in the world, but to retain monarchy would undermine the Latin Americans' justification for having separated from Spain. Thus, impelled by a deeply felt need to break with the colonial era and not follow the path being taken by their ex-rulers, they generally turned to the US republican model without seriously questioning its appropriateness, in their hurry not seriously considering whether this model had any connection to their experience and habits, much less their needs. Unconstitutional behavior and rule were almost guaranteed by the decision of the educated urban elites to adopt US-style presidentialism, separation of powers, and especially federalism. Adopted as supposed essentials of a republican system, they had no place in countries that had nothing to federalize and where legislatures and courts sorely lacked independence.

Naively, however, the region's upper classes persisted in viewing Anglo-American political institutions as responsible for the economic progress of England and the United States. Enlightenment ideas of politics were even farther from Latin American reality than from that of France, where a hopefully egalitarian revolution had spawned violent civil strife, followed by popular enchantment with imperial rule by a social upstart. (By the crucial period of the independence wars of Spanish America, the French had a restored the traditional monarchy, imposed upon them essentially by British force of arms.) Essentially realistic, those who came to occupy political offices in the new Latin American republics often ignored what high-sounding and idealistic constitutions might say:

Recognizing the need for strong leadership in these often disorganized, chaotic societies, the Latin American founding fathers entrusted the executive with strong powers, while weakening the influence of the congress and courts. The president was also given vast emergency powers frequently needed in these fractured, disorganized polities to declare a state of emergency, suspend the constitution and rule by decree. . . . The Catholic Church was often established as the official religion.[6]

Not surprisingly in the light of distinctly adverse circumstances, but dismaying to those leaders who unrealistically aspired to achieving both stability and a significant degree of democracy (at least as it was understood in those days, when Jeffersonian paternalistic elitism was being challenged only by Jacksonian ideas), effective authority in most of Spanish America reverted to audacious regional leaders, who defied the urban elites and used their private armies in a warlord manner to usurp power from those who felt entitled to it, but who generally lacked the skill, determination, and support to successfully resist the *caudillos,* ruthless mobilizers of armed support to seize power. In rare cases members of the Creole elite survived by out-caudilloing their country challengers. Chile, under the leadership of Diego Portales, was the outstanding exception; rather than copying the United States, it shaped governmental institutions to its particular conditions.

The unfortunate but fundamental fact was that, particularly in the political sphere, Latin America's lack of preparation for independence would have grave and long-lasting consequences. Given the legitimacy vacuum, the fragmentation of the old viceroyalties, and the violence involved in the struggle for independence, the initial rulers of each Hispanic country, as well as their opponents, arose from the particular processes and defining events of that country's emergence from colonial status. Over time this outcome led to a significant division between those countries that would long be plagued with a violent pattern of *caudillo* politics, those that would be able to move beyond this negative heritage, and the very few that could avoid this rudimentary level of political life, of which Brazil was the major example and Chile constituted a Spanish American exception.

Not only did the independence process heavily condition the first generation of national life, but it also significantly influenced the next one. This postindependence era of trial and error produced a number of fascinating figures and dramatic events but, generally, disappointingly little progress or positive change. Variations among countries were significant, often substantial, and in the 1850s and 1860s set the stage for greater differentiation during the final decades of the nineteenth century as some countries began to find their way while others marked time or stumbled into dead ends.[7] Not surprisingly, for most of the region, introduction to independent political life was by way of *caudillos* produced by the wars of independence. As cogently explained by Lewis:

The breakdown of civilization, the spread of chaos, the inability to conceive of a national interest, the parochial outlook, and the easy recourse to plunder that blurred the distinction between guerrilla warfare and banditry produced the local political buccaneer who acted on his own initiative without permission from his nominal commander. With no central authority to rein him in, he could consolidate his local power and enrich himself by pillaging and eliminating his immediate rivals. The wars legitimatized him, made him a prestigious local figure with an armed band at his command.[8]

Caudillism in all its variations involved use of personal appeal and leadership qualities, often bordering on the charismatic, as well as bravery and audacity, to promote allegiance to an individual in a situation where the traditional basis of monarchical authority had disappeared and no new base for institutionalizing legitimacy had yet emerged. Caudillism was particularly frequent in countries like Mexico, Argentina, and Venezuela with a deep cleavage between capital city and peripheral rural regions in which a would-be *caudillo* could build his clients, dependents, and retainers into a private army, then descend on the urban center and, conquering it, rule the country. National integration attenuated but did not eliminate caudillism, an often much misunderstood, but extremely important and persistent, feature of Latin America's political heritage. Indeed, in some instances national consolidation was brought about by one *caudillo's* dominating his rivals, then becoming a dictator, or a group of *caudillos* forming a national political machine of a warlord nature, in which they preserved local control and shared in the profits of national revenues and patronage—all this while reducing the risk of elimination by central authorities. In every instance *caudillo* rule had the effect of retarding the emergence of constitutional legitimacy, even as structured political authority did come into being. The true *caudillo* enjoyed a degree of personalist allegiance that ordinary dictators lacked, although there were both dictatorial *caudillos* and, particularly after the emergence of organized armed forces, caudillistic dictators.[9] The ideal type of postindependence caudillism could not, finally, survive the establishment of a professional military, but it could coexist symbiotically with the jerry-built nonprofessionalized armed forces that many countries had. (In some places, especially Venezuela, caudillism and militarism would eventually merge, that country's Juan Vicente Gómez being the outstanding example of a leader beginning as a *caudillo* in the first decade of the twentieth century and ending up as a militarist dictator by the 1930s.) Early in the case of Chile, a bit later in Colombia, Mexico, and Peru, and even later in Venezuela, high-status, propertied individuals in the capital used their commercial clout and dominance of foreign trade to gain control of central governments, even if in the process these elites ceded a good deal of autonomy to *caudillo* types to act as political bosses in the country's interior regions. At the same time, powerful landowners built bases of political support through patron-client relationships with their workers, retainers, and other dependents. National politics tended to become a violent struggle for political leverage, which brought with it decisive economic advantage. As development of national identity and consolidation occurred, in some countries fluid and frequently shifting alliances of urban and rural elites took form, often garbed as Conservative versus Liberal Parties—as exemplified by Colombia and, to a lesser extent, Mexico and Peru, as well as Brazil's own parliamentary monarchy version.

Fundamental economic and social change trailed independence by at least three decades, in the context of the time essentially a full generation. Creoles who had expected that freedom from colonial restraints on commerce would produce a wave of new wealth found their hopes dashed. In varying degrees the independence wars had contributed to this disappointing economic picture. Where fighting had been intense and prolonged, as in Venezuela, damage from the war was extensive. Even where the destruction of human life and economic resources had been less widespread, disruptions in systems of labor relations and financial arrangements provoked decline in important economic sectors—particularly mining, which in Mexico required half a century to regain preindependence levels of production.[10] Moreover, in much of the region, new ways had to be found to coerce labor after the tribute and labor drafts of Indians were eliminated. Overall, low economic productivity, combined with an inadequate financial infrastructure, limited both capital accumulation and inflows from abroad. Thus, in many ways the region's economies were poorer and less integrated in the first decades after independence than they had been in the late colonial period.

The negative economic conditions prevailing in the early decades of independence complicated the construction of stable constitutional governments. Political disorder was both a cause and a result of this perverse situation of economic malaise, since political instability impeded reorganization of economic systems, and stagnant economies added to political dissatisfaction. Unable to rely on the old colonial-era taxes for revenue, new governments found themselves in very tight financial straits. Their resulting weakness contributed to political instability, which in turn impeded the reorganization of economic systems disrupted by the independence struggles. Under these adverse circumstances a resurgence of development and liberalism would only occur around mid century under a new generation of leaders not directly involved in the independence struggles. To differing degrees these leaders would eliminate some of the most extreme restrictions on individual liberties and at least partially dismantle the legal framework of corporate special privileges.

Where this progress went furthest, as under Benito Juárez in Mexico, and resulted in stringent anticlerical measures—not just rhetoric—it would provoke a sometimes violent reaction. Only in Mexico, however, would reaction triumph, and there it required European armed intervention. Despite all these obstacles, national unity in combination with viable economic development had gotten under way in several of the countries during the 1860s, substantially in relatively small Chile, just barely in Argentina, and interrupted by foreign intervention and civil war in Mexico. These highly desirable developments would soon pick up momentum as the countries experienced some kind of a developmental surge, either under oligarchic formal democracies (as in Brazil, Argentina, Colombia, and Chile) or behind *caudillo*-type dictators—in pure form in Venezuela and hybrid form in Peru. Conservatives continued to rely on indirect political participation and limited regional and local self-government, and liberals advocated an enlarged and invigorated state and testing the limits of participation in representative, albeit restricted, republican politics.

Hence, although progress toward substantial political development had been halting during the first postindependence generation, by the end of the 1860s the region's countries were in many basic political ways significantly more different than they had been on the eve of independence. A greater number of differences had been accentuated by the wide variations in the process of gaining independence than had been softened or blurred, and the gaps were then widened by distinct initial experiences in their lives as separate nations. The second generation of independent existence was so heavily shaped by the experiences of the 1830s and 1840s that differentiation in some cases accelerated and in others hardened. Only in the 1850s and 1860s did countries sharing certain racial and economic features begin to follow somewhat parallel developmental paths. In the last three decades of the nineteenth century these paths began a convergence that slowly, but eventually produced common patterns.

Consolidation and Development, 1871–1899

Although major continuities remained, in important ways Latin America underwent very significant changes during the last three decades of the nineteenth century. In the first place violence, although not at the levels attained during the independence struggle, ran high as force continued to decide who would hold power in many countries. Even where there were no *caudillo*-type power struggles or foreign invaders to be expelled, as had just occurred in Mexico, large-scale bloodshed broke out. Indeed, the 1870s began with an extremely bloody war between Brazil and Paraguay, and in the 1890s Brazilian authorities ruthlessly exterminated a large community of poor rural dwellers on the implausible justification that they were subversives seeking to restore the recently abolished monarchy. In Argentina violence took the form of virtual genocide against the country's indigenous population. Supposedly civilized Colombia ended the century with an intense three-year civil war between conservatives and liberals—on both sides staunch Catholics. In the 1880s Chile and Peru fought a Second War of the Pacific, one with even more sweeping negative consequences for the loser than that of the 1830s. Just before this period began, Venezuela had its own lesser civil war, which left it under a less openly brutal *caudillo* than José Antonio Paéz had been during its first generation of independence. Even Chile experienced a brief civil war at the beginning of the 1890s, fought on the somewhat more elevated constitutional plane of reaffirming legislative prerogatives in the face of presidential encroachment. Still, although there were major negative legacies, including persistence of authoritarian mind-sets, in several important ways Latin America underwent very significant changes during the last three decades of the century. By this time several of the region's countries had fared better since independence than had others.

Brazil entered the period with its monarchy still functioning full throttle and coming off its crushing defeat of Paraguay. The shift of its economic center of gravity from the northeast and its tropical plantation products to the center-south, where coffee had become king, was well under way, bringing with it the broad stream of European, particularly Italian, immigration. The new economic elite made vigorous and persistent demands for a major voice within the parliamentary regime. But such a drastic reapportionment of representation within this federal imperial regime was totally infeasible in light of the determination of the declining elites to hold onto their governmental clout. Hence, the rising coffee-related economic elite had to wait for the establishment of a republic as a necessary, but not sufficient, condition for attaining political dominance. In fact, their progress in this direction would be severely limited during the initial presidencies of military figures with deep roots in the old order. Thus, significant political development would not occur until in the mid-1890s, when São Paulo civilians reached the presidency. Even then, the very restricted electorate had no real choice within a party system of severely limited competition based on preemptive elite agreement on an official candidate.

Mexico had just thrown off the alien monarchy imposed upon it by Louis Napoléon and returned to the interrupted liberal reforms of the Juárez era. General José de la Cruz Porfirio Díaz would rise to power in the mid-1870s, entrenching himself through a development-oriented dictatorship that would prove to be the region's longest-lived autocratic regime. For its part, Argentina had finally been unified and was being governed by leaders who were among the most intelligent and educated in the region. With peace and unity it was able to attract the torrent of Italian immigration that rapidly transformed its society. In the 1880s young and vigorous General Júlio Argentino Roca would reach the presidency, installing a centralizing and power-concentrating system that operated through a strong party that was essentially a collection of political notables who negotiated government policy while ensuring the manipulated and—if need be—fraudulent election of their candidate. Even between his presidential terms Roca remained the guarantor of this republic by and for the elites in a country awash with immigrants. Compared to these three countries, Colombia was little changed from the preceding period, entering into its coffee era without the immigration from which Brazil and Argentina were benefiting or political leadership comparable to those two countries or Mexico. The Conservative and Liberal Parties established at midcentury would compete for power in an increasingly intense manner until facing off on the battlefield as the nineteenth century came to its close.

After a conflict-ridden decade in the 1860s, Peru soon saw its first civilian president and first peaceful transition from one elected civilian to another. Subsequently the rule of its first outstanding president was interrupted by a second disastrous war with Chile. During this time Peru underwent substantial economic diversification, creating new economic elites each tied to a major export and the region from which it came. Lima grew rapidly, and amid intense intraelite rivalries, the first major impact on lagging political development was the rise to power of Augusto Leguía. Perhaps ahead of his time at this point, he would return to finish his work of transforming the "Aristocratic Republic" that had succeeded him during a 1919–1930 return to office. Venezuela entered the period just out of its bloody civil strife and had a long period of stability and economic growth and modernization under a relatively benevolent liberal *caudillo*—the first time it was catching up to its neighbors instead of falling further behind, and doing this under the least undemocratic government it would have until the late 1930s. Chile stood out as the region's most democratic country and in many ways rested on its laurels, bolstered by high nitrate exports, weathering a post–War of the Pacific conflict between congress and a president trying in vain to become a strong president as was the case in the other countries.

Authoritarian mind-sets stymied most efforts at establishing republican processes with a significant democratic component, and very little headway was made in broadening political participation. In most places executive authority dominated national legislatures, a trend most pronounced in Mexico's autocratic Díaz regime. Yet, in Chile, an attempt at presidential role expansion was stopped dead in its tracks in a violent confrontation resulting in the president's ouster and suicide. The elites in each of these countries were heavily influenced by positivism. A symbiotic fit with the goal of development, it called for controlled, evolutionary modernization. As Wiarda explains its appeal to elites and emerging middle sectors:

It advocated change and progress but not through revolutions. It was change led by the educated elites, devolving little power upon the masses. It stood for development but not genuine democratization or popular participation. It was not divisively individualistic in the U.S. sense but was centralized, organic, top-down, and corporatist in accord with long-standing Latin American traditions.[11]

Persistence and transformation of caudillism in some countries, contrasted sharply with the emergence of dominant elites, even oligarchies, in others, stand out as the most important factor differentiating these countries during the latter third of the nineteenth century. In most cases the original generation of leadership was gone by the early 1850s. A second generation, coming to power from the mid-1840s to the mid-1850s, had a different destiny in some countries than in others. The major exception was Brazil, where the monarchy provided institutional continuity, with one emperor on the throne from 1840 to 1889. Although national unity combined with economic development had begun to get under way in a few countries during the 1860s, it picked up momentum in the 1870s and 1880s. Most countries experienced some type of developmental surge, either under oligarchic formal democracies or behind *caudillo*-type dictators. Conservatives continued their preference for indirect political participation and restraints upon regional and local self-government, and liberals pushed for an enlarged and more interventionist state and expanding the limits of participation in representative republican politics.

These developments in the political sphere reflected economic and social changes, albeit often hesitantly and even belatedly. Greatly augmented demand in Europe and the United States for the region's raw materials and foodstuffs provided a favorable economic environment. Moreover, foreign capital flowed into mining, export agriculture, and the infrastructure required by a quantum leap in the movement of goods. Small local industries burgeoned along with commercial enterprises; banking and financial institutions flourished. Foreign perceptions of order and stability were essential to a continued stream of investment and access to loans, needed particularly for ports and railroads. This need for political stability to mollify foreign capitalists placed an increasing premium on control of the national government. In most countries both civilian bureaucracies and the armed forces expanded significantly as governmental control structures were strengthened and ambitious individuals were provided with employment opportunities. Since this growth of the state required increased government revenues, the extent and nature of each country's integration into the world economy were the most important differentiating factors. Political institutions responded to the development of export-import elites wishing a stronger government, not necessarily one that was more democratic or even more responsive—to others at least—and feeling that they deserved it, since burgeoning foreign trade taxes were paying the bills. In a broad contemporary sense they wanted a cross between a Bismarckian and a Bonapartist state, certainly not one with the post-1820s Anglo-American emphasis on substantially broadened participation. Elites generally considered military expenditures a necessary investment—as well as one from which they might well devise ways of deriving profit. In the cases of Brazil and Argentina, by the 1870s urban bankers and businessmen had allied with agro-producers to advocate large-scale subsidized European immigration. This drastically transformed already white Argentina and heavily black Brazil while leaving Mexico, Colombia, Peru, Venezuela, and Chile much as they had been.

Elites generally tended to endorse a congress and elections as long as these served their interests, but the several components of the elites agreed that these features could not be allowed to become vehicles for middle-class demands to attain significant leverage with respect to the allocation of public goods. "Opportunity for us and ours; regulation for you and yours" was the basic public policy rationale of sometimes allied, other times rival, elite groups. These developments interacted with leadership—forceful in many instances, but farsighted in only a few instances. The gap that widened between the modernizing urban sector of society and practices persisting in traditional interior areas was dramatic. Where the colonial period had been marked by large landholdings with an essentially captive labor force, as in Mexico and Peru, or tropical plantation agriculture had been the burden of African-origin slaves, as in Brazil, a patron-client system not only persisted but even sent down deeper roots, if not becoming the basic sociopolitical institution. Indeed, well into the supposedly modern era, landowners frequently possessed almost absolute power, at times reaching as far as life or death, in return for providing dependent clients with physical security in those situations where threats of violence existed, along with a minimum subsistence plus access to a priest. In situations where agents of the central government were far away, the area's most powerful patron took on quasi-governmental functions, in a federal system like Brazil's—where the distances from the central government were immense and communications difficult and attenuated—often legally delegated to him, in other situations on his own as the biggest shark in local waters. Moreover, at this juncture the vast majority of each country's population still dwelled in rural areas and would continue to do so for at least another long generation.

At the same time as patronal structures and practices thrived or survived in rural areas, political life became more competitive in the cities. Yet, in many ways, the emergent middle sectors there, composed of government workers, shopkeepers, professionals, and tradesmen, were also significantly dependent on patrons (hence becoming their political clients, giving rise to the frequently invoked terms *clientelism* and *clientelistic*). They did have the advantage of a significant degree of competition for their services since there often were multiple political factions seeking their support. Some of them even became middlemen in the exchange of benefits for services or made use of their ability to forge upward links to become the nucleus of a new faction. Aspiring to achieve cadet-candidate status with the elites, some posed as spokesmen and an entering wedge for the populace, many times to convince those better situated in the political order that they were worth being coopted rather than left to become increasingly troublesome. A few sincere individuals would even remain reformist.

Even in situations where the traditional system sustained substantial modification, clientelistic (political support traded for material or personal benefits) exchanges persisted, with the landowner expecting unconditional loyalty, occasionally to the feudal extreme of bearing arms and at other times blindly voting as the patron wished. For, as national politics became more complicated, patrons in a local network were often clients in a regional one, where their patron was in turn a client of some bigger fish at the national level. Even well away from labor-intensive agriculture and ranching, the patron's position rested on his links and contacts at the provincial or national level. Within the more modern milieu of the cities, this essentially patrimonial style (in the Weberian sense of accepted and expected unequal patronage-type obligations and exchanges rooted in ascribed and generally inherited status differences) survived through adapting to urban conditions. Vertical links and horizontal rivalry morphing into confrontational factional competition might come to involve different kinds of payoffs on the part of patrons—jobs or access to government agencies and social services—but come sundown, the exchange from client to patron involved whatever the latter needed to pay his upward political debts: votes in more democratic systems or times, bodies in the streets in turbulent ones. In towns and small cites the system became one of competing political factions organized around prominent families establishing patron-client relationships with elements whose support was up for grabs. Sometimes this system was incorporated into competing political parties; at other times parties vied for the support of these local political machines. By the end of the nineteenth century Brazil, Argentina, Colombia, Peru, and Chile "had developed arrangements for governing that allowed a modicum of order and material progress while continuing to limit political participation."[12] (But until well after the turn of the century there was little or no class or interest basis to these clientelistically organized building blocks of politics.)

In examining political change in the late 1800s attention must be given to the progress made by countries entering this period trailing far behind the leaders. Hence, some countries made more progress than others but remained behind them in political development. Headway was often made on one dimension while being absent in others. Voss captures the situation as one in which "the cumulative effect of the notables' response to the expanding opportunities of a market economy and of modern republican politics had reached a critical turning point by the 1870s. Their large and well-structured families enabled them steadily to broaden and deepen their involvement in the economy and public affairs."[13] The family retained its paramount role, whereas the parish and the community lost theirs as new institutions became the foundations of an industrial capitalist economy featuring greater commercialization of production and an unprecedented influx of foreign capital that "augmented the horizons of Latin America's prominent families. As a result the notables distanced themselves from those below and tightened relations with an activist national state."[14]

More often than not, the prevailing situation at the end of the century was stability that benefited the upper classes, sometimes reflected in strongman rule—varying from a sophisticated and, for the times, not undemocratic regime of channeling and balancing forces in Argentina under Roca to a harshly authoritarian regime with the most threadbare veil of republican structures and processes in Mexico under Díaz, this latter model lasting a decade into the twentieth century. In Brazil, where a republic replaced monarchy only at the end of the 1880s, elite figures started a rotation in office at the century's end, to be continued and perfected in the early twentieth century. Colombia, unfortunately, was caught up in a bloody civil war, but Peru managed to attain stable elite civilian governance during the late 1890s, while Venezuela regressed politically after the death of durable liberal *caudillo* Antonio Guzmán Blanco. What remained true for all the countries in one degree or another was that "the institutional design that was consolidated in the latter part of the nineteenth century molded state expansion, and helped explain the so-called 'oligarchic states' of the early twentieth century and their radical transformation after the 1930s." [15]

Clearly, Brazil and Mexico had followed contrasting trajectories since discovery and colonization. The hallmark of the former was that its national development was essentially evolutionary, with few sharp breaks or drastic discontinuities. This conflict-free pattern would carry into the twentieth century, as no powerful group felt dispossessed by another. Instead, those in power adjusted to sharing control with emergent elements, which did not appear suddenly but typically had been on the political scene for quite some time before causing what can best be described as changes of regime rather than of the underlying system. Even in the most important of these substitutions of one political regime for another, the old elites have never been plowed under, or even permanently swept aside. Generally old regimes have in the short run been displaced not replaced. Even such apparently "revolutionary" events in the political realm as independence (1822), the shift from monarchy to republic (1889), and the overthrow of the oligarchic republic (1930) were not in any instance accompanied by sharp social transformations or even dramatic economic innovations. Rather, they were in large part the result of substantial change in these realms of national life that had built up over time, and each landmark change of political regime was, in turn, a watershed contributing to a further round of socioeconomic developments that gradually created pressures for yet another major readjustment of the political system.

This basic pattern of political development was the opposite of Mexico's path. Settlement in the second quarter of the sixteenth century for Mexico versus significant colonization a generation later for Brazil interacted with a native civilization as the backbone of a traditional agricultural order in the former versus massive importation of African slave labor in the latter. Mexico spent three centuries as the heart of the Spanish Empire in the New World, while Brazil was the center of the Portuguese Empire. Mexico experienced a violent independence struggle involving repression of efforts to turn it in the direction of social revolution, contrasted to Brazil's remaining a monarchy under the Portuguese royal family. Violence-laced *caudillo* rule through the middle of the nineteenth century for Mexico contrasted with Brazil's peaceful stability under an emperor—as the former lost nearly half its territory to an aggressive neighbor while the latter defeated all separatist movements. In the 1860s the two largest Latin American nations continued to follow very divergent paths. Imposition in Mexico by a European power of a foreign monarch versus national consolidation under a beloved Brazilian-born monarch would be followed by the rise in Mexico of an authoritarian militarist tenaciously holding onto power for thirty-five years versus the establishment of a republic and entrenchment in its control of a civilian agro-exporting elite for Brazil.

The trajectory followed throughout the nineteenth century by Argentina was sharply different from the path taken by either Brazil or Mexico. Still, points of similarity can be found between Argentina and Mexico (a theme explored in Chapter 3). Although their colonial and independence experiences were quite literally poles apart, there is some rough coincidence between their experiences with *caudillo* rule during the 1830s to 1850s. Argentina's civil strife was to unite the metropolis with the interior, while Mexico's became submerged in the European intervention, but then, despite the primacy of immigration in the former and its almost complete absence in the latter, Díaz's Porfiriato bore a very basic functional similarity to Roca's Unicato. More important, however, the former was essentially an antipolitical development (hence ended only by revolution and protracted civil war), while the latter established the foundations for positive political change that would see Argentina become a highly regarded democracy in the first decades of the twentieth century—exactly coinciding with Mexico's protracted period of bloodshed and near chaos.

Just as there had been continuities from the first half century of Latin American independence down into and even through 1871–1899, there would also be continuities from then into the first decades of the new century. Caudillism would take a more national form, morphing into dictators bolstered by national armies. In Venezuela, Guzmán Blanco, as a financial expert, exercised a very different leadership style from that of the uneducated Paéz early in the country's history. Now Juan Vicente Gómez would use the national army he had forged against the traditional *caudillo* types, but his tactics regarding how to treat opponents still followed pages out of the playbook of Guzmán Blanco.

Great Promise to Sobering Reality, 1900–1929

The twentieth century began on an upbeat, even auspicious, note giving rise to hopes that gains made in the preceding period were a foretaste of what lay ahead. Indeed, these nations would undergo substantial changes from the end of the nineteenth century to the eve of the world's Great Depression. In an encouraging number of cases something approaching that era's less demanding standards for democracy would be approximated, but only in a few of these experiences would such gains become sufficiently rooted to survive the lack of fundamental consensus and the persistence of high-stakes, often winner-take-all, competition. Yet in a majority of countries some rough and imperfect adaptation of politics to the fundamental economic and social transformations that were taking place did occur. Even if fragile and narrowly based democratic walls subsequently could not resist the enormous strains occasioned by the Great Depression and tumbled down, foundations often survived upon which sturdier and more enduring political structures could subsequently be built. Given the distinctly different political scenarios prevailing as the period opened, this political development would occur along dramatically different paths and would leave foundations for distinct ways of getting through the difficult and polarizing decade of the 1930s.

In 1900 Brazil was still an agricultural country only a decade past monarchical rule and striving to establish viable civilian government after an authoritarian military regime and a regional civil war. It would experience a brief and rather halfhearted military reformism between 1910 and 1914 before going back to a series of undistinguished representatives of the traditional elite. This return to old-style politics would spark abortive young officer revolts in 1922 and 1924–1926, and as the structures and processes of the oligarchic republic proved outdated and inadequately representative by the end of that decade, the stage was set for revolution. Meanwhile, sustained heavy immigration was gradually turning the population more white than black and mulatto.

In Mexico the entrenched Díaz dictatorship steadfastly insisted upon maintaining the political status quo even as the economy grew and diversified because of its development policies. Hence, pressures for change built up in the first decade of the twentieth century until an essentially middle-class-led revolution tried to achieve what would soon be peacefully accomplished in Argentina, or at least to catch up with Brazil in terms of the extent of political competitiveness. In the absence of unifying leadership, this revolution led not to a reformed political system, but to the chaos of two decades of bloody civil war—the greatest wave of violence the region has ever experienced—among the elements that had quickly forced the old dictator to cut and run but then could not agree on who or what would take his place. This process consumed the lives of three presidents, a potentially great peasant leader, and millions of common citizens before, in 1928, a new strongman imposed some degree of order upon the warlord-style politics that had resulted. In the midst of the protracted violence, economic and social development had greatly suffered—even before the onset of the global depression.

In Argentina, respected President Roca returned to the presidency in 1898, providing a significant degree of stability that lasted through his death at the beginning of World War I. Following the Roca era, the country exploded into its political golden age, one in which it shone on the global scene as a stable and democratic nation when these qualities were scarce even in Europe. Sustained economic development and continuation of heavy immigration resulted in a vast increase in urbanization and growth of industry as well as emergence of politically ambitious middle-class elements. A "Tory reformer" type of moderate conservative followed up the disintegration of Roca's old party by pushing through the congress the secret ballot and nearly universal manhood suffrage. As a result, the long-oppressed radicals came peacefully to power in 1916 and remained there until 1930. Hence, effective incorporation of the middle sectors into competitive political life was complete at an early date, averting the threat of revolution and ushering in a period of democracy lasting down to an essentially counterrevolutionary outcome in 1930. During the intervening fourteen years Argentina would shine not just within Latin America, but also on the world scene, as a democratic beacon. At the same time it would become the most European of Latin American nations.

Colombia started the new century coming out of a bloody three-year civil war, to that point (and until overtaken by Mexico) the largest-scale of such fraternal strife in the Western Hemisphere outside the United States. The nation would then show a surface stability under the victorious conservatives while slowly moving toward a split in their ranks that by period's end would raise the prospect of elections in which the liberals, losers of the civil war but beneficiaries of recent socioeconomic changes, could hope to replace the victors in power. Significant economic development marked the 1920s as oil and bananas came to supplement coffee as major export crops. Hence, liberals would take advantage of the ruling party's disarray in 1930 to regain the presidency. In Peru at the turn of the century advocates of civilian and military rule were still debating the blame for their country's defeat in the Second War of the Pacific. Peru would then briefly stand out as getting on a modernizing path in 1912–1914, only to return to traditional politics before ending the period under an eleven-year reign of the same autocratic populist who had held the presidency in 1908–1912 and would resume the task of breaking the hold of the oligarchic elites.

Starting this period in a bit of a vacuum after the end of the Guzmán Blanco era, Venezuela, economically and socially the laggard of the region's larger countries, in 1908 entered the rule of its equivalent of Mexico's Díaz, a general who would remain firmly in control of the country into the 1930s, along the way getting it launched as a major oil producer. Along the way, caudillism morphed into militarism as Gómez as war minister built up an army, used it against the traditional regional caudillos, and then assumed complete control of the government for the rest of the period and into the next.

Chile began the twentieth century shrugging off the trauma of its brief 1891 civil war and with a quasi-parliamentary system in place, anchored in modern political parties dating back to the 1870s. Its "parliamentary republic," in marked contrast with Peru's "aristocratic republic" at the same time, saw refinement of its political institutions continue until the precipitous drop in earnings from nitrates in the 1920s coincided with heavy urbanization. With the Radical Party's reformist Arturo Alessandri reelected in 1925, a new more presidential constitution was of little help in stemming political decay. The military regime installed in 1927 proved mercifully short-lived—so Alessandri would be swept back into office by a 1932 electoral landslide.

Throughout these decades uneven, yet significant, socioeconomic development brought fundamental changes that heavily impinged upon politics. By the first part of the twentieth century changes readily apparent in the urban areas were greatly delayed and diluted in the interior. Indeed, moving from the capital to regional centers, to small towns, and on to the countryside, the trip was politically as much back in time as out in distance. The rural patron found himself ever more in a broker role, intermediating between his clients and influentials in government and the urban private sector who could help him produce, transport, and market his crops so as to have the wherewithal to pay off his clients. Transactions came to involve credit and subsidies, construction of roads, and, in some areas, irrigation projects. This kind of bargaining rarely took place through political parties, which were usually little more than electoral vehicles existing as urban clubs of notables during the long stretches between elections. Expanding foreign trade greatly accelerated the process of the government bureaucracy's becoming the source of clientelistic benefits and the president's becoming viewed as the superpatron. Some countries maintained or even created liberal democratic institutions to determine, or at least ratify, who would be the fortunate individual to occupy the presidency. In other cases, once in power, the nation's dominant political figure decided to stay, ignoring or eliminating inconvenient legal impediments. In most cases this *continuismo* involved support by the military to quell protests or put down attempted coups. When such military support was not forthcoming, the erstwhile strongman generally lost his hold on power, becoming just another has-been.

The early part of the twentieth century, especially the World War I era, brought an acceleration of industrialization and related "modernization" processes, including dramatic growth of urban centers, a broadening of economic opportunities, and partial reordering of society. These developments resulted in a continuing increase in the number of people making demands upon national political institutions; hence, in view of the often stringent economic limits on meeting these demands—which needed to be channeled and manipulated, if not controlled—an increase in the system's regulative, responsive, and distributive capabilities was in turn required. This broadening of functions and strengthening of implementing structures was accompanied by a broadened scope of issues with which national political institutions had to deal, such as planning, development, and social welfare—leading to increasing specialization and centralization of these institutions. These factors combined to strain governments' capabilities to extract adequate financial resources, with revenues falling behind expenditures, which, in the absence of sustained export growth or high foreign investment, required heavy borrowing.

In those countries where democratic liberal institutions blossomed, notably Argentina and Chile, the middle sectors (those varied elements of society situated between the dominant elites and the still subservient masses) sought entry into the political system often through parties, but occasionally by way of paramilitary organizations, striving in the process to weaken executive control, since their increased political participation was reflected in congress long before they could come to play a decisive role in electing presidents. Often turned back by fraud and repression, they persisted, their leaders frequently realizing that with the emergence of militant labor elements, elites currently viewing them as rivals might well come to consider them allies against a far greater threat—as many times became the case.

The period around World War I witnessed a new wave of essentially middle-class-led aspirations for democracy as narrowly understood by the empowerment-seeking middle sectors of the time. This development was frequently complicated by the efforts of urban labor in the more industrially advanced countries to be included in the broadening of participation—a trend viewed with considerable misgivings, if not downright hostility, by many middle-class elements. Hence, not only was progress in this direction very uneven, but what was accomplished almost always lacked the firm underpinnings needed to withstand a rightward swing of the political pendulum. Yet the incorporation of labor into the political process did begin in a number of countries, especially where the emergent middle class had begun to be incorporated in the preceding period. Such flourishing of liberal democracy—especially in Argentina, Chile, and Uruguay, but with fainter reflections in Peru, where it was quickly cut off by a personalist dictator, and Colombia, where its impact was attenuated by the vertical nature of its political parties—was a frustrated goal of the Mexican Revolution, where it was submerged in the protracted civil war. In Brazil, where republican government was a full generation newer than elsewhere, this trend showed only briefly before being pushed into the *tenentismo* movement of the reformist young military. Taken together, the very major exceptions of Brazil and Mexico made this democratizing trend a limited one, with the survival of a militarist *caudillo* in Venezuela through the mid-1930s further restricting it.

Overall, from the viewpoint of the late 1920s Latin America appeared to have made significant progress during the first three decades of the twentieth century. Although a considerable degree of violence had been involved, it had been largely confined to Mexico and its epic civil strife. Mexico had gained by far the biggest headlines for its revolution but was showing signs of emerging from the violent power struggle that had ensued. In bright contrast Argentina had enjoyed the greatest forward movement, coming to rank as one of the world's leading democracies. Brazil was viewed as having its early-1900s progress run out of steam, and Colombia was held up as a model of stability combined with elite democracy. Chile was recognized as going through difficult days but credited with having performed well during all but the most recent years. Peru under Leguía seemed to be lurching toward modernity, and Venezuela was praised in some quarters for stability under a dictator given a pass on his arbitrariness because of the country's rising oil exports.

Unfortunately the shallowness of the roots of development and modernization would very soon be exposed by the traumatizing impact of the Great Depression— triggered just as the relatively progressive and prosperous 1920s drew to their close. Much of what had been accomplished turned out to lack firm enough underpinnings to withstand the tsunami-force adverse impact of a sustained global economic crisis. Yet the process of incorporation of labor into the political process had begun in those countries where the middle sectors had already achieved significant entrance into politics. Following short-term interruption or even reversal of this trend, it would move forward once World War II had restored a significant degree of prosperity.[16]

Notes

1. John Lynch, ed., *Latin American Revolutions 1808–1826: Old and New World Origins* (Norman: University of Oklahoma Press, 1994), p. 88.

2. Jaime E. Rodríguez O., *The Independence of Spanish America* (Cambridge, UK: Cambridge University Press, 1998), pp. 2, 89.

3. Jorge I. Dominguez, *Insurrection and Loyalty: The Breakdown of the Spanish-American Empire* (Cambridge: Harvard University Press, 1980), p. 249.

4. Ibid., p. 253.

5. Ibid., p. 250.

6. Howard J. Wiarda, *Dilemmas of Democracy in Latin America: Crises and Opportunities* (Lanham, MD: Rowman & Littlefield, 2005), p. 110.

7. Ibid., p. 7.

8. Paul H. Lewis, *Authoritarian Regimes in Latin America: Dictators, Despots, and Tyrants* (Lanham, MD: Rowman & Littlefield, 2005), p. 14.

9. The best sources on this phenomenon are brought together in Hugh M. Hammil, ed., *Caudillos: Dictators in Spanish America* (Norman: University of Oklahoma Press, 1992).

10. On the economic situation on the eve of independence, see Richard L. Garner, *Economic Growth and Change in Bourbon Mexico* (Gainesville: University Press of Florida, 1993).

11. Lewis, *Authoritarian Regimes*, p. 75.

12. Wiarda, *Dilemmas*, p. 9.

13. Stuart F. Voss, *Latin America in the Middle Period, 1750–1929* (Wilmington, DE: Scholarly Resources, 2001), p. 163.

14. Ibid., pp. 189–190, 206–207.

15. Consult Fernando López Alves, *State Formation and Democracy in Latin America, 1810–1900* (Durham, NC: Duke University Press, 2000).

16. Paul W. Drake perceptively analyzes the region's political development in *Between Tyranny and Anarchy: A History of Democracy in Latin America, 1800–2006* (Stanford, CA: Stanford University Press, 2009). He devotes three chapters, a total of 110 pages, to the 1800–1929 period compared to only 80 for the years 1930–2006. He views the 1880s through the 1920s as the era of "partial and protected democracies."

2

Brazil

Independence to 1930

The Portuguese-colonized half of South America was fortunate in having relative autonomy in choosing its path through the first two generations of its national life. Achievement of independence without significant violence, absence of foreign interference, and stability under an enlightened ruler until almost the end of the 1880s, which included experience with an elite-dominated parliament, were advantages the other Latin American countries lacked—giving Brazil a substantial leg up on the road to political development, although not necessarily to democracy. Hence when semioligarchic republican rule proved inadequate by the end of the 1920s, new urban middle-class political forces produced by economic growth and ensuing societal changes would be prepared to move beyond the established order with a minimum of violence. By this point European immigration had reduced Afro-Brazilians to a numerically strong minority that had benefited only modestly from the late-nineteenth-century abolition of slavery.

Peaceful Separation and Preservation of Monarchy

Both in gaining independence and in filling the legitimacy vacuum that ensued, Brazil's experience differed markedly from that of all parts of Spanish America. Its remaining a monarchy for another full generation resulted in unique facets that would last throughout the nineteenth century.[1] The most important permanent result was Brazil's holding together its vast area, in contrast to the amputation of half of Mexico by the United States and the fragmentation of Spanish South America. The early nineteenth century found Portugal in another of its dynastic binds. With Queen María I on the road to outright madness, her son João ran the government, subsequently assuming the title of prince regent. In September 1807 Napoléon issued an ultimatum that Portugal must declare war against Britain, its longtime protector, or face the consequences of French occupation. Hence, in late November, the Portuguese royal family, accompanied by the civil and military bureaucracies, set sail for Rio de Janeiro under British naval escort. During a brief stopover at Salvador in January 1808, the prince regent (the future King João VI) opened Brazil's ports to trade with Britain and other countries—as much a price for British support as a sop to the colonists. Subsequently, manufacturing was permitted, institutions of higher education were founded, and naval and military academies were established. Most important in the long run, a new army composed of a mixture of Portuguese troops and local recruits was created. To coopt the local elites, in 1815 Brazil was accorded the status of a kingdom, formally coequal with Portugal—for João had declined to return to Lisbon.

By the end of the Napoleonic Wars, the colony was outgrowing its mother country, which at that time had a population just over 3 million, not intimidating to Brazilians, who by now numbered 4.5 million and were well aware of Portugal's weakness and relative poverty. Portuguese liberals convoked a Lisbon legislature in which they enjoyed a safe majority. Not surprisingly, its measures to reestablish most of Portugal's previous domination catalyzed separatist sentiment in Brazil. Thus, when João, who had become king in 1816, was summoned home in 1821, he advised his twenty-two-year-old son, Pedro, who was staying behind as prince regent, to lead the independence movement should it appear to be getting out of control. Pedro soon had cause to heed his father's advice. In the midst of clashes between Brazilian-born elements and Portuguese troops, he rejected an October 1821 order of the Portuguese parliament to return to Lisbon. Pedro's "Fico" ("I'm staying") of January 9, 1822, was followed by the appointment of a cabinet headed by native Brazilian José Bonifácio de Andrada e Silva (b. 1763). Efforts by Lisbon to tighten its hold over Brazil resulted in Pedro's dramatic cry of "Independence or death!" on September 7, 1822—commemorated as Brazil's Independence Day. Within ninety days of this challenge, he was crowned (on his twenty-fourth birthday) "Constitutional Emperor and Perpetual Defender of Brazil."[2]

Commencing national life under the rule of the man who had been governing in the name of the mother country enabled Brazil to avoid the vacuum of legitimate authority that plagued most of its neighbors, whose path to independence combined rupture with Spain and adoption of a radically different and untried political regime. Brazil's emancipation was quick, but not totally peaceful. Skirmishes and confrontations with provincial authorities and Portuguese troops loyal to João VI and the Lisbon government were handled by Brazilian troops under the command of Francisco Alves de Lima e Silva, giving a first taste of battle to the country's leading military hero—and important political stabilizer—his son, Luíz (b. 1803). While these conflicts were still continuing in the north, Brazil's first constituent assembly began to function on May 3, 1823; after six months of executive-legislative conflict, Pedro used the army to shut the assembly down (exiling Bonifácio until 1829). The emperor's version of a basic governmental charter was promulgated by decree on March 25, 1824. He appointed provincial presidents and senators (for life, from lists submitted by provincial legislatures); the lower house was indirectly elected by a very restricted suffrage.

Despite violent reaction to the establishment of a centralized regime, Brazil's territorial integrity was preserved. As if a spate of regional uprisings was not problem enough for the new nation, the emperor engaged in an expensive and unsuccessful war with today's Argentina over what would eventually become Uruguay. Indeed, by the end of the decade, the stiff-necked, impulsive, and short-tempered monarch found himself in an untenable position.[3] The ouster of French king Charles X in July 1830 had a sharp impact upon those political figures who feared that Pedro's actions were influenced by the fact that he was still heir to the Portuguese throne. In the intensifying legislative-executive conflict, the military leaned in the opposite direction from 1823, leading the emperor to abdicate in favor of his five-year-old son, Pedro. In the tripartite regency that ensued, General Lima e Silva saw his initial dominance undercut by establishment of the National Guard as a counterweight to the army. Liberal Diogo Antônio Feijó (b. 1784), who as minister of justice supervised this new armed body, came out on top. The Additional Act of August 1834, which modified the governmental system in the direction of decentralization, eliminated the Council of State and instituted a single regent—a post to which Feijó was elected in April 1835. Faced with a resurgence of conservative strength, he gave way in September 1837, being replaced in April 1838 by Pedro de Araújo Lima, the future Marques de Olinda.

Back in power, the Conservative Party curbed provincial autonomy through the Interpretive Law of 1839, leading the Liberal Party to engineer a parliamentary coup that brought Pedro II to the throne in July 1840 at the ripe age of fourteen. The man who would be the young emperor's chief adviser and military bulwark, Luíz Alves de Lima e Silva, followed up a successful 1841 campaign in Maranhão with defeat of a Feijó-led São Paulo revolt the next year (gaining each time a military promotion and a higher patent of nobility). He could then turn to the revolt in Rio Grande do Sul that had been festering since 1835, restoring order by 1845. Elevated to the dukedom of Caxias, Latin America's most accomplished military commander was named commander of the Brazilian troops sent in 1852 to help overthrow Argentine dictator Juan Manuel de Rosas, subsequently becoming war minister, a post he would hold much of the time into the 1870s—along with being president of the council of ministers (prime minister) in 1856, 1861–1862, 1866, and 1875–1878.

Meanwhile, by 1850 the elements were in place that would allow Brazil to enjoy political stability accompanied by modest economic development and limited social progress well into the 1880s. Its population had risen to near 7.5 million from just over 5.3 million in 1830, and Rio de Janeiro had grown to a city of 250,000. With British pressure bringing the slave trade to an end after 1852, more than 2.5 million slaves made up one-third of the country's inhabitants. Nevertheless, as Brazil attacked the slavery problem gradually, by 1872 over 85 percent of Brazilians were free (8.6 million out of 10.1 million). Although the main flood of immigration was still ahead, recent European arrivals were already a key component of the population in the southernmost states. Economic growth had averaged 1.6 percent annually between 1822 and midcentury, but industrialization remained in low gear. Although its great expansion was still to come, coffee already provided half the country's exports—twice the value of sugar, which it had surpassed in the 1830s. From Rio de Janeiro province, coffee was moving into the interior of São Paulo, with a consequent shift in the locus of economic power—first reflected in the emergence of the coffee nobility as a social force, but with more profound political ramifications by the 1870s. In the 1830s Brazil supplied 30 percent of the world's coffee, rising to 50 percent from the 1850s through the 1870s. As the center-south became the repository of the nation's wealth, railroad construction picked up steam, tying coffee-producing areas to booming ports, although, given Brazil's great size, not only transportation but even communication was essentially inadequate.

During the monarchy's heyday, a fairly homogeneous political class, oriented to national unity, bolstered stability. The large landowners and export producers enjoyed considerable political power, but there remained significant scope for autonomous action by middle-sector (that is, those small societal groupings neither part of the elite nor the subservient masses, but highly dependent upon the government for employment, still lacking the cohesion that by the 1920s would begin to make them a class) political-bureaucratic elements occupying the higher echelons of the centralized state administrative apparatus. The elite's ability to coopt emerging urban elements rested upon a *cartorial* state, in which appointments were exchanged for electoral support and public employment was used to provide positions in response to the clientelistic political needs of the elite. Away from the capital, decentralized but politically potent power was exercised by the provincial landed class. Given the great distances and poor communications, the Brazilian state—even at the apogee of the monarchy—had to recognize the existence of powerful local interests. These could constrain policy choices of the national government, although not force it to follow their preferred course of action.[4] The emperor remained the respected and legitimate balance wheel of the system—a stabilizing factor sorely lacking in other Latin American countries. As the fourth branch of the Brazilian constitutional system, the moderating power (*poder moderador*), the emperor could change the party in office when in his judgment such a change would reduce legislative-executive friction. Elections were indirect, with increasingly stringent income requirements moving up the ladder from local voters to provincial electors and on to those eligible to be elected. The Conservative Party, backed up by the National Guard and often manipulated by the emperor, and the Liberal Party were the linchpins in a system in which controlled elections for the national legislature were a means of legitimizing a ministry that had already been chosen by the emperor. During his long reign (1840–1889) Pedro II alternated the parties in office eleven times, always taking into account an intricate political game of intraelite interests and ambitions, which he understood as well as he did the maneuverings of notables at the provincial level to build patronage structures and establish ties with influential figures in the capital. The price for this stability was the loss of any capacity of the political parties to serve as instruments of modernization and change, which, by the way, political parties did very little of at this time in other Latin American countries.

When the Liberals returned to power in 1862, they had to turn their energies to a major international war that strained the nation's resources to the limit and allowed the Conservatives to regain control of the central government in time to garner the credit for the war's eventual success. Uruguay's independence had brought little stability to the River Plate region, and during the early 1860s Brazil intervened to aid the Colorado faction (conservatives) in its struggle with the Blancos (liberals), who turned to Paraguayan dictator Francisco Solano López for help. Small, but highly militarized, Paraguay at the end of 1864 sent forces across Argentine and Brazilian soil to reach Uruguay. With a population in excess of 9 million and the beginnings of an industrial plant, Brazil, like the North in the contemporary US Civil War, had significant material advantages over its warlike foe. At the outbreak of hostilities, Paraguay had 64,000 men under arms to only 18,000 for Brazil, which quickly mobilized its widely dispersed reserves and undertook the monumental task of transporting them and their equipment to the far-distant battlefields. When the Triple Alliance (Brazil, Argentina, and Uruguay) saw their 65,000 troops—57,000 of them Brazilian—bog down in front of Humanitá, the duke of Caxias (Luíz Alves de Lima e Silva) agreed to take command, but only if the emperor brought the Conservatives back to office. This demand met, Caxias captured Humanitá in August 1868 and occupied the Paraguayan capital at the beginning of 1869.

The war had a profound impact upon Brazil, as during the more than five years it lasted, nearly 200,000 men were mobilized, some 139,000 sent to the war zone, and at least 30,000 killed or wounded. The burdensome financial cost fed inflation and forced the Brazilian government to increase its foreign debt substantially. When the National Guard, which had provided a power base to regional political dynasties, was absorbed into the army, the political system never fully recovered from the dislocations and strains intensified by the war. Upset at having been ousted abruptly from power, the Liberals initiated a decade in opposition by issuing a manifesto in 1869 calling for electoral reform, elimination of the moderating power, and even the abolition of slavery. In 1870 alienated Liberals formed the Republican Party to work for an end to the monarchy, which nonetheless would survive another two decades. So Brazil successfully navigated the treacherous voyage from colony to nation (at a time when Germany and Italy had not yet fully achieved unification). But the road to this accomplishment contrasted sharply with the Spanish American experiences.

From Monarchy to Republic

During the 1870s and 1880s Brazil worked its way into and through a major systems change. Although the number of recent European immigrants was rising just as the ranks of slaves were thinning, the monarchy that made Brazil unique in Latin America—indeed the Western Hemisphere—was still functioning smoothly.[5] Despite three decades in power, Pedro II, just turning forty-five, was in his prime. Although the costs had been great, Brazil was enjoying the final victorious phase of the Paraguayan war, including military occupation of its troublesome neighbor. Swelling of the officer corps from roughly 1,500 to nearly 10,000 created a major demobilization problem, and the country had too many military heroes who aspired to influential governmental positions—seeing themselves as worthy successors to the country's great aging icon, the newly elevated duke of Caxias. Hence the seeds of the post-1880 decay of the monarchical system may well have been sown during the Paraguayan war, needing only sufficient irrigation during the superficially calm 1870s to ensure subsequent germination.

The war had brought with it a significant spurt of industrialization, but with a built-in lag factor before it would affect society sufficiently to have a heavy impact upon politics. Meanwhile the Liberals, smarting from their abrupt ouster from power during the war, had initiated a decade in opposition—the longest such stint in their history—calling for electoral reform, elimination of the emperor's moderating power, the disbanding of the National Guard, and even the abolition of slavery. The new generation of Conservative Party politicians was loyal to the monarchy, but unlike their distinguished predecessors, they had not experienced the "chaos, anarchy, and threatened disintegration" that had marked the 1830s, hence taking the system for granted.[6] The passage of the Rio Branco Law (the law of free birth) in September 1871 assuaged growing antislavery forces by declaring that children henceforth born to slave mothers would be free—but only when they came of age. As a result, by

1884 the number of slaves had declined to 1.24 million, and a new law then freed all over sixty years of age. By 1887 some 723,000 slaves (plus 500,000 of their children) constituted only 5 percent of Brazil's growing population—which by the early 1880s had reached 12 million (finally surpassing that of Mexico).[7] Yet this reduction in the scope of the slavery problem heartened abolitionists to press for a full end to what they viewed as a retrograde abomination. Clearly the existence and continued importance of slavery set Brazil apart from the Spanish American countries at least as fundamentally as did its monarchy. Both of these distinguishing features would soon disappear—essentially at the same time.

As in society, change in the economy was significant yet circumscribed, making its impact upon politics slow and sure rather than sudden and destabilizing. Under the forward-looking emperor the government subsidized a wide variety of economic activities, including coastal steamboats, railroad construction, modernization of the sugar industry, and European immigration. From 20 percent of central government expenditures in 1879, economic development rose to 33 percent by the monarchy's end in 1889—still well behind the cost of the military and civil bureaucracies. Foreign trade remained the major source of government revenue, and the failure of agriculture to generate sufficient income was a key restraint on industrialization. Unlike the more favorable situation of rival Argentina, Brazil's problem of a small domestic market for manufactured goods was aggravated by high internal transportation costs owing to the long distances involved. During the Paraguayan war economic growth had recovered but, after undergoing a downturn in 1876–1877, rallied strongly for the rest of the decade. Meanwhile, the land law of 1850, benefiting the coffee producers and facilitating the continuation of large plantations and *fazendas* ("latifundia"), in older areas, remained the basis of a land tenure system that would prove resistant to change down into the twenty-first century.

As Brazil moved through the 1870s and into the 1880s, the abolitionists and republicans provided the monarchy with an increasingly divisive political agenda. Yet these vociferous civilian groups by themselves were no threat to the system. The armed forces were a very different matter. A series of reform measures passed in 1873 and 1874 temporarily satisfied much of the officer corps but, as is often the wont of reforms, whetted the appetites of more radical figures. Moreover, the implementing legislation gutted this reform, reducing it to a moribund, if not completely dead, letter. Those younger officers whose wartime experience had led them to want vigorous reform of their service were discontented over indifference, if not opposition, to their proposals for modernization. The civilian elite, lulled into complacency by the absence of political adventures by the army during the long span of its dominance by the duke of Caxias (who presided over the council of ministers for the final time in 1875–1878), blindly perceived no risk in taking the military for granted (this at a time when under Díaz the military was in the driver's seat in Mexico, and when Roca was rising to dominance in Argentina on the basis of his military exploits). Thus the horizon was already clouded when economic depression was aggravated by a coffee crisis after 1880—the year in which Caxias died.

The landmark 1881 Saraiva law made parliamentary elections direct by a single class of electors, which included, for the first time, non-Catholics, freedmen, and naturalized citizens. Yet, at the same time that it took this forward step, this "reform" reduced the number of eligible voters from over 1.1 million to just above 145,000 (by eliminating the preliminary steps of the old multilevel process). The subsequent October elections dealt the first electoral reverse to the party in power in the nation's history, as the emperor maintained an unaccustomed posture of impartiality. But the establishment adapted rapidly to this modification of the rules of the political game, and clientelism at least partially replaced coercion in maintaining the essence of the old electoral politics: manageability. The Liberals' leading military figure, Marshal Manuel Luíz Osório, had passed away just before Caxias, leaving the army without prestigious old-school figures to help contain discontent. Indeed, Caxias's and Osório's heirs in the military hierarchy would ride this wave to power instead of seeking to stem it.

The growing divorce between the political elite and the military contributed to acceptance by the great majority of the officer corps of a coup engineered by a small, radicalized faction drawn chiefly from the post-Paraguayan-war generation. The government, including an aging emperor deprived of his trusted judge of the military's mood, failed to realize that military leaders could provide a very different type of opposition from that the churchmen had mounted in the 1870s on the "religious question" when the state had clashed with the upper clergy over prerogatives. When civilian governments provided members of the military with issues that united rather than divided them, they could subordinate partisan inclinations and personal rivalries to a prickly sense of corporate pride and strong institutional interests. While the Conservatives and Liberals fell over each other cultivating the generals and admirals, the small Republican Party began to work on the younger officers—particularly those who had manifested signs of dissatisfaction with the status quo. Moreover, as proved the case in many other countries, making politics a major factor in promotions and appointments proved to be a sure way to politicize the armed forces.[8]

The impact of the abolitionist cause was most strongly felt through its overlap with republicanism, as sympathy for the former led to support for the latter. Marshal Manoel Deodoro da Fonseca (b. 1827), although a confirmed monarchist, was becoming increasingly alienated from the government. Having experienced combat in the civil strife of the 1840s, he—along with his five military brothers—found an opportunity to distinguish himself in the Paraguayan war. A colonel by the conflict's end, the able, ambitious, and egoistic Deodoro was promoted to brigadier general in 1874. Advanced to field marshal, the equivalent of major general, in 1884 and named quartermaster general the next year, in 1886 he was assigned to command all military forces in Rio Grande do Sul—where the government also appointed him first vice president of that key border province. This career success fed his belief that he was the logical heir to the great influence previously exercised by Caxias. His subsequent involvement in the political dispute over the miserable state into which the army had been allowed to deteriorate was not only logical but would be far from the last time an apparently nonpolitical general with a long career marked by professionalism and adherence to authority would abruptly become highly politicized and play a key role in a regime change bordering on system transformation (as in 1955 and 1964).[9]

Deodoro aligned with the opposition Liberal Party and, aware of the emperor's advancing age and declining health, led younger officers in establishing the Clube Militar ("Military Club"), which was to play a significant role in the impending crisis as well as subsequent ones. Although cleavage on political issues had existed between the Paraguayan-war generation and the junior and mid-grade officers imbued with the positivist ideas of the leading military intellectual, Benjamin Constant Botelho de Magalhães (b. 1836), common corporate interests now crystallized in the no-holds-barred debates within the Military Club—with Deodoro as its president and Constant as vice president. Indeed, this forum for exchange of views outside the rigid hierarchy of the command structure greatly facilitated discussion moving toward action. Moreover, the War College, created in March 1889 as an extension of the Military Academy for advanced and specialized training—and commanded by Constant—had a faculty loaded with military reformers who would be part of the coming coup's leadership. Located next to cavalry and artillery barracks, the War College "infected" these line troops, rather than being contained by them. Hence, although the economic effects of abolition and their political ramifications had some impact upon the termination of the monarchy, the antislavery campaign had brought officers together with civilian advocates of a republic within the framework of a common social reform cause. Intelligently the Republican Party forged an alliance by temporarily downplaying its major goal in favor of concentrating on issues of greater immediate concern to the military—including federalism, which did not require open opposition to the constituted authorities of the empire but at the same time carried the young officers a step down the road in the direction of such a break. By early 1888 "the officers had absorbed so much republican propaganda in their studies at the military school and the Superior War College that they were ready to substitute abolitionist sentiments with republican ones as necessary to make Brazil a free Pátria."[10]

Acting as regent, on May 13, 1888, Pedro's daughter and heir ended slavery—directly affecting only 650,000 blacks (who became unemployed freedmen instead of employed slaves). The popular support gained was offset by the bitter alienation of provincial landowners, who were still important in the Conservative Party, which in June was brought back into power. Republican leaders, their party having been credited with less than one-seventh of the vote in the August 1889 elections (as blatantly manipulated as the vote that would bring down the "Old Republic" in 1930), realized their need for a prestigious military leader at the head of their movement. Heavily influenced by Constant, thirty-four-year-old Major Hermes Rodrigues da Fonseca helped convince his uncle, the malcontented Marshal Deodoro, to head the revolutionary government. When Adjutant General Floriano Peixoto (b. 1839), who, on disability leave in out-of-the-way Alagoas, had avoided involvement in the events leading up to the revolt, on November 15 added his 2,000 troops to the 600-man rebel column in Rio de Janeiro, the empire was at its end. The graying emperor was still respected, but the emerging elites could not accept the prospect of an empress dominated by an arrogant French husband—the Condé d'Eu—detested by much of the officer corps. So the royal family was sent off to Europe, where Pedro died in Paris two years into his forced retirement.

As would be the case in 1930, and even more in 1964, the coup's rapid success benefited from the government's having grossly overestimated its military strength (*dispositivo militar*), seriously misjudged the probable actions of key military figures (including the emergence of a critical "swingman"), and relied on popular support, which did not arise, to defend the regime when the crucial events were taking place in Rio do Janeiro in the first half of November. In comparative and analytic terms the decay of Brazil's imperial regime corresponded closely to Huntington's generalization concerning the fate of centralized traditional monarchies: "Such political systems ordinarily have a high degree of legitimacy and effectiveness so long as political participation is limited. Their political institutions, however, remain rigid and fragile in the face of social change. They are unable to adapt to the emergence of middle-class groups into politics."[11]

Over its sixty-seven-year life the monarchy had served its purpose. For, by the time Brazil discarded it and embarked on the republican road—which had proven so perilous and fraught with traumatic episodes for the other countries of the region—many of the most serious challenges to national integrity and identity had been overcome. Not only had the vast territory been held together, when Spanish America had fragmented, but significant gains had also been made in the process of securing borders, across which there were now eight separate Hispanic American countries. Moreover, national political institutions and processes had been consolidated, the establishment of professionalized armed forces and the alternation of parties in power being the most significant accomplishments. On the other hand, little had been lost in political development by the lateness of this adoption of a presidential republic. Mexico's republican experience had led only to the loss of half its original territory and the Díaz dictatorship. In Argentina the double break with Spain and monarchy had ushered in the dictatorship of Rosas and the political separation of Buenos Aires from the rest of the country, which was finally ended in 1861 by the military victory of the metropolis over the provinces. Even the long parliamentary experience of Chile had deteriorated by the beginning of the 1890s into a civil war between forces backing congress's supremacy and those supporting a president bent on augmenting his powers.

Now, with the monarchy's end, for the first time in Brazil's history a dictatorship was in control, legitimized only by its monopoly of force and the significant, but far from overwhelming, popular support for a republic. The crucial factor in the future course of Brazil's political development was that the Republicans had turned to the armed forces as the one institution that could put an end to the monarchy without precipitating drastic change in the distribution of power among contending social groups. For the Republican Party wanted only an alteration in the framework of government to accommodate the economic and social changes that had already occurred. With coffee's almost 5.6 million sacks in 1889 providing two-thirds of the country's exports, the coffee producers and their mercantilist associates sought greater say in national policy than the monarchy, with its ties to ossifying parties, provided. Hence this regime change did not usher in any sharp break in economic policy or new departures in the social realm. Serving in the last parliament of the empire were two Republican Party deputies, elected in 1884 from São Paulo, who soon would become the nation's first civilian presidents: Prudente José de Morais Barros (1894–1898) and Manuel Ferraz de Campos Salles (1898–1902). But first, Brazil would have to weather a stormy period of rule by a pair of autocratic militarists.

The provisional government that found itself suddenly in office on November 15, 1889, was not agreed upon what kind of a republic should be installed (much as was to be the case again after the 1930 revolution). Historical republicans, Jacobin army officers, and traditional notables seeking to salvage what they could from the sinking of the empire all vied for office and influence. Headed by a conservative militarist who had never believed in republicanism, the new government, after a short period of turmoil and strife, saw the old local and regional elites reassert their control over all but the most urban and industrializing parts of the increasingly dualistic country. As the republic's first finance minister, Ruy Barbosa (b. 1849), the epitome of the well-meaning and excessively optimistic republican civilianist cadre, implemented a moderate degree of protectionism, considering it politically crucial in consolidating the new regime. With no constitution in effect, banks emitted so much currency that the money supply almost doubled in 1890 and expanded by over 50 percent the next year. As economic interests scrambled to take advantage of the prevailing preoccupation with the nature of the emerging governmental institutions and political processes, the republican regime consumed nine finance ministers during its first seven years.

For all the government's initial uncertainty and hesitation, Brazil continued to change. Its racial composition underwent transformation as European immigrants, with Italians as the backbone, flowed in faster than African slaves had in earlier periods. From 10,000 a year in the 1850s and 1860s, they doubled to nearly 20,000 annually during the 1870s before exploding to over 450,000 in the 1880s—on their way to a record 215,000 in 1891. Indeed, of the 10 million Italians who would come to Latin America between 1870 and 1930, nearly two-fifths would settle in Brazil—and their numerous progeny would profoundly alter its society. By filling the workforce needs of the developing coffee areas, this immigration kept the former slave population at the bottom of the socioeconomic pyramid. (Over the longer run, these immigrants' impact would be felt in the political socialization they had brought from the Old World—where Italy achieved political unity only in 1868, followed by Germany in 1871.)

At this point Brazil's literacy rates, 19 percent for males and 10 percent for females, reflected the absence of educational opportunity for the vast majority of the population. As Europeanization went forward, the Afro-Brazilian proportion of the population decreased, and the indigenous population nearly disappeared. Having declined precipitously (to under 1.5 million by 1750, only 800,000 by 1819, and a mere 0.5 million by 1867), its numbers were far less than those of immigrants arriving in any two-year period. Overall, Brazil's population had risen to 14.3 million in 1889 from 11.8 million in 1880, with over two-fifths still living in the economically declining northeast region. The economic heart of the country had shifted southward into São Paulo, whose 1890 population of 1.4 million was on its way to 4.6 million by 1920, largely as a result of immigration. Still, just 11 percent lived in cities of over 10,000 inhabitants, and industry accounted for only 10 percent of the GDP.

Shadows of these changes could be discerned in the political realm. Although some planters had supported the Republican Party, from November 1889 to 1894 control of the government was largely in the hands of predominantly urban-oriented individuals, chiefly military, who took some steps inimical to the planters' interests. The nation's center of gravity had moved to the center-south, with Minas Gerais, the country's most populous state at 3.1 million in 1890, occupying a pivotal position as link between the former heartland and the soon-to-be-dominant region. Having dissolved the Chamber of Deputies and eliminated the life tenure of Senate members, Deodoro assumed the title Chief of the Provisional Government, and military men took power in a majority of states. But they would do a poor job of providing stability, much less good government.

Even before becoming war minister at the end of April 1890, Floriano Peixoto wielded great power, replacing Ruy Barbosa as first deputy chief a few months later. Four major groups had collaborated in the republican revolution and were represented in the provisional government: the historical republicans, particularly strong in São Paulo; the young civilian revolutionaries; the positivist-oriented junior officers who followed Benjamin Constant (and would be orphaned by his death in early 1891; and the senior military, who had joined or accepted the movement because of Deodoro's and Floriano's lead. At the extremes of polarization were the authoritarian-oriented Jacobin radicals and an alliance of promonarchy naval officers and São Paulo coffee-producing elites. As would be the case again in both 1930 and 1964, differences over policy as well as personal rivalries soon emerged. When the constituent assembly that was elected on September 15, 1890, met in November, the administration presented it with a draft constitution, which after some grumbling it promulgated on February 24, 1891. The following day Deodoro was chosen president over Prudente by a vote of 129 to 97, and Floriano was elected vice president by a larger majority of 153 to 57. Ominously for the future, opposition to Deodoro was engineered by Admiral José Custódio de Melo, politically ambitious president of the Military Club—with the backing of Floriano.

Unable to adapt to the restrictions of governing within the limitations of a constitution, Deodoro had difficulty in dealing with an often hostile congress. Reacting to what he viewed as unjustified obstruction, the thin-skinned president dissolved the legislature in November 1891 and imposed a state of siege. A revolt broke out in Rio Grande do Sul, and promonarchy admiral Custódio de Melo incited most of the fleet to revolt on November 23. Recognizing his position as untenable, Deodoro angrily resigned. Those who had overthrown him fared little better at governing the infant republic, narrowly avoiding institutionalizing a resort to force as means for deciding the control of political power. In the absence of channels for resolving elite differences, the military remained an uncertain arbiter. Devious where Deodoro had been direct, impassive rather than emotional, distrustful rather than open, and cautiously calculating rather than impulsive, Floriano aroused extremes of feeling. Caught between monarchical sentiment in the navy and the support of some army officers for the deposed president, and also impelled by his own authoritarian nature, Floriano was almost as far from a democratic executive as Deodoro had been.

He immediately fomented a series of local military movements (*derrubadas*) to oust all provincial presidents who had backed Deodoro in the recent crisis, thus beginning a pattern of using federal military forces to influence local power struggles that would be more the rule than the exception into the 1930s. To avoid the necessity of a direct presidential election, Floriano maintained the fiction of being "vice-president in exercise of the presidency." In February 1892 he forced dissenting flag officers into involuntary retirement. Admiral Custódio de Melo, who considered himself the author of Deodoro's ouster, interfered in government affairs beyond the normal scope of a navy minister who was also president of the Military Club. In April 1893 this ambitious officer openly broke with Floriano, and when in September federalists invaded Rio Grande do Sul from neighboring Uruguay, he led a major revolt of the fleet. After the United States thwarted his ill-conceived plan to force Floriano out of office by bombarding Rio de Janeiro, he sailed south to continue the civil war, leaving the more politically adept Admiral Saldanha da Gama and Military Club president Admiral

Eduardo Wandenkolk to lead opposition to "iron marshal" Floriano in the capital until faced in March 1894 with the arrival of a new progovernment squadron of ships hurriedly purchased in Europe. All this disorder facilitated the spread of constitutionalist sentiments for civilian rule to elements of the armed forces who lamented the negative effects on professionalism, the loss of unity, and the sacrifice of their ability to act as the moderating power (a responsibility they felt the military had assumed by eliminating the emperor).

In this trying situation, Floriano, caught up in the inexorable logic of the calculus of survival and plagued by declining health that would lead to his death within a year, had to give up any intention of staying in office in order to be able to put an end to the civil war. Agreeing to the election of a representative of the São Paulo coffee elite brought him the state troops needed to keep the rebels bottled up in the south as well as support in congress for the requisite financing. Moreover, there was an increasing tendency in many areas of the country to question the armed forces' assumption of the right to interfere in all spheres of political life and their high-handed infringement on civil liberties in the name of national security or military honor. This dissatisfaction was fueled by the government's tendency to overuse the specter of a monarchist threat (much as the communist issue would be used in the 1960s). Elections on March 1, 1894 (which Floriano had postponed from the preceding October), made Federal Republican Party (PRF) nominee Prudente de Morais Brazil's first civilian president by a margin of 277,000 votes to only 38,000 for young Afonso Augusto Moreira Pena (whose day would come a dozen years later). Beginning with this experienced politician's inauguration, representatives of the São Paulo elites occupied the presidency for twelve consecutive years. Cautious, persistent, and tenacious, new chief executive Prudente was aided by the cessation of hostilities in the south by mid-1895. Yet, to many of Floriano's supporters, found almost exclusively among the military, this taciturn representative of the São Paulo aristocracy seemed soft on reactionary interests. The relative freedom accorded to monarchist groups, contrasted to their repression under the preceding military presidents, made Prudente suspect in the eyes of exalted republicans and militant military Jacobins.

The tragic affair of Canudos, a backwater community in the interior of Bahia, soon presented these critics with an opportunity to exploit the weaknesses of Prudente's position. Only in an atmosphere of extreme political passions could the existence of a small colony of impoverished religious fanatics in the backland be seen as a monarchist plot and threat to the existence of the republic. Yet cynical manipulation of this situation created a politicomilitary crisis.[12] For Bahian officials and embarrassed military spokesmen found this conspiracy theory a convenient explanation for the inability of three successive military expeditions, each larger and better armed than the one it was sent to avenge, to defeat the small, out-of-the-way community founded by Antônio Conselheiro, a primitive mystic. National uproar exploded in March 1897 after a federal punitive expedition of 1,300 trained troops, accompanied by artillery, was all but wiped out by these poorly armed but indomitably zealous peasants. Aware that the various military factions, whose differences and rivalries had thus far allowed him to govern, might unite now that the army's reputation was on the line, Prudente sent his new war minister into the field with a well-equipped 10,000 men. On October 5 the fortified shantytown was completely demolished and its defenders were annihilated. Thus, with a total loss of some 5,000 lives on the government side and the lives of at least 15,000 humble, uneducated peasants, the traumatizing affair was ended—just in time for the choice of Prudente's successor. Paradoxically, a badly managed and perhaps unnecessary use of military force redounded to Prudente's advantage when an abortive Jacobin coup in early November left him appearing courageous, if not heroic.

Election of fifty-seven-year-old São Paulo chief executive Manuel Ferraz de Campos Salles as Brazil's second civilian president in March 1898 took place in an atmosphere of comparative calm, the winner receiving 420,000 votes to 39,000 for his outgunned opponent. The new president was a successful, moderately conservative agriculturalist.[13] Often considered the restorer of Brazil's shattered finances and credit, he inherited a chaotic financial situation rooted in a decline in coffee revenues. Under his predecessor a wide range of banks had, until 1897, been authorized to issue currency. As coffee prices continued to drop, in good part in response to an unbridled increase in production, devaluation of the exchange rate had been stepped up, causing a fall in imports and a consequent reduction in customs receipts—an important component of government revenues. This deterioration had led, by mid-1898, to the necessity of a negotiated debt moratorium. All payments on existing foreign debt were suspended for thirteen years, the creditors insisting in return upon both elimination of the budget deficit and the withdrawal from circulation of currency equal to their funding loan. In a foretaste of debt problems that would be aggravated much later by the 1988 constitution, the 1891 constitution had permitted provinces and even municipalities to contract foreign debt—a privilege they promptly abused. Much of the money borrowed was used to cover operating deficits, and by 1898 foreign debt had risen 53 percent since the establishment of the republic—requiring over half of all federal government expenditures for its service. Putting the country's finances in order required unpopular deflationary and recessive policies. The elites were chiefly interested in keeping labor plentiful and cheap through European immigration, which had the secondary effect of helping their desire to "whiten" the country's population.

Campos Salles's lasting legacy was in the political field. Reversing the policy of his predecessors, he ceased preoccupation with keeping supporters in power at the provincial level, preferring to accept whoever won the power struggle in each state as long as the state's representatives in congress lent him their support. Under the "politics of the governors," electoral fraud and coercion by state machines were tolerated, and victories by the governors' opponents were not recognized by the Chamber of Deputies. In turn, the governors extended to local elites a similar deal of patronage and services for votes. This arrangement strengthened the municipalities as a basic political unit, but in such a way as to reinforce the hold of the regional oligarchies and local clientelistic machines.

Thus, in the context of insufficient institutionalization and the persistence of the traditional sociopolitical order in the rural areas making up most of the country, the introduction of formal democracy through extension of the franchise worked not so much to make change as to bolster entrenched elites. There was a reestablishment of duality between centralized power over national matters in the hands of the federal executive and local autonomy, often bordering on license, in "lesser" matters—although these were often of life-or-death import to the bulk of the population. Under these circumstances politically active military elements disenchanted with the course of events concentrated on holding eroding positions at the provincial level, meeting with greatest success on the periphery. Undercut by the political tactics of Campos Salles, which were followed in the 1920s by a successor (Artur da Silva Bernardes) they viewed even less favorably, the military "modernizers" began thinking about how to regain control of the national government.

The political patterns of the Old Republic, as the 1889–1930 regime was called, were not what the young positivist disciples of Benjamin Constant had had in mind when they toppled the monarchy as outdated, if not retrograde. A decade into the republic, it was clear that their creation had been perverted by an unholy alliance of the new São Paulo elites and the ex-monarchical bosses in the traditional boondocks. The civilians' handiwork was, in these positivists' view, as distant from parliamentary democracy as the military interregnum had been, since in the end much of the patriarchal society was preserved. In the eyes of the dedicated advocates of a representative republic, the fact that local and regional oligarchies actually found their hand strengthened—at least on their home ground—against the new political forces that had begun to challenge their domination was an abomination crying to be corrected. The survival of what was known during the monarchy as *coronelismo* ("rule by the rural 'colonels'") was rooted in the fact that going from empire to republic at the national level did not alter basic conditions in the traditional rural areas, especially in the northeast and the north. Rural society continued to reproduce an authoritarian paternalism that provided a continuing basis for patrimonial politics. There was still a long way to go before change in political processes would catch up with the switch in governmental institutions.

The Long Process of Escaping São Paulo Domination

The twentieth century opened with São Paulo agriculturist Campos Salles, best described as moderate, opportunist, and vigilant against the excesses of the multitude, halfway through his term as Brazil's fourth president, but only the second civilian one. Generally considered the restorer of the country's shattered finances and eroded credit, he consolidated Brazil's foreign debt. His "politics of the governors," as continued by his successors, served as a means for presidents to stay above the disputes of shifting factions with little programmatic content by ceding a high degree of provincial autonomy, hence buying temporary equilibrium at the price of future crises. Electoral fraud and coercion by state political machines was tolerated as long as they played ball in national politics. By virtually eliminating any possibility of peaceful alternation in power at the state level, this concentration on the country's heartland to the neglect of other regions set up tensions that would come to a boil and burst through after 1910.

Thus, in a context of inadequate political institutionalization and the persistence of an antiquated patrimonial sociopolitical order in the rural areas that made up most of the country, formal electoral democracy with a severely limited franchise facilitated a political comeback by conservative elites entrenched at the state level—once they accepted a republic. There was a pronounced duality between centralized power over national matters in the hands of the federal executive and a wide scope for local autonomy. As McCann reconstructs the sentiment:

The Brazilian middle class saw the country controlled by rural landowners, or *coroneis*, who with their armed hangers-on constituted irregular military forces that limited the central government's ability to enforce national law. And worse, from the middle-class point of view the *coroneis*, through an elaborate alliance system, actually controlled the central government. A strong military under middle-class control might be able to impose their vision of Brazil.[14]

Grounded in the absence of real national political parties, the president's manipulative policy further weakened those feeble party structures that did exist. A chaotic scene of shifting factional alliances predominated, based on the interplay of center-state, interstate, and intrastate maneuvering in a highly federal governmental system. Under these circumstances, the military elements, which had been set back by the virtual counterrevolution implicit in the São Paulo consolidation of power, concentrated on attempts to hold their eroding positions at the provincial level. They met with greatest success on the country's periphery, where they could still use army influence over federal machinery to enhance their power in what traditionally had been local rivalries. When undercut in this enterprise by a president they viewed as more unsympathetic to their aims, military reformists would concentrate on regaining control of the central government.

In an environment of domestic peace—despite economic troubles—combined with manipulable political competition, Campos Salles chose as his successor the incumbent president of the province of São Paulo, aristocratic fifty-four-year-old Francisco de Paula Rodrigues Alves. Having served as finance minister under both Marshal Peixoto and his civilian successor, Prudente de Morais, he was admirably prepared for the presidency as shaped by his predecessor. His election in 1902 by a vote of 316,000 to 25,000 demonstrated that the system of succession via agreement among the heads of key states was working smoothly. Continuing movement toward making the federal government a condominium of conservative oligarchies, he was faced at the midpoint of his term with a revolt as proponents of a positivist military dictatorship sought to escalate into a coup the popular dissatisfaction with compulsory smallpox vaccinations. The November 1904 uprising, in which cadets from the military academy took an active role, was firmly put down. In a move that would have deep unforeseen ramifications, the academy was temporarily transferred to Porto Alegre, where the future army officers came into close contact with the Rio Grande do Sul student politicians just down the block at the law school—in some cases marrying into their families. Together, led by Getúlio Dornelles Vargas, João Neves da Fontoura, and Pedro Aurélio de Goés Monteiro, they would subsequently organize and make the 1930 Revolution.

Economically, and to an extent socially as well, Brazil had moved ahead during the dozen years of relative peace and stability under representatives of the São Paulo coffee growers and exporters. The population at the turn of the century passed 17 million, as immigration during the 1890s had risen sharply, despite civil war and economic ups and downs, to over 1.2 million, some 690,000 of whom came from Italy. The economy, which had grown only 16 percent from 1889 through 1899, expanded 4.2 percent a year from 1900 to 1909. From 1898 through 1910 coffee accounted for 53 percent of exports, and rubber, a boom-and-bust product highly subject to international demand, rose to 26 percent. Indeed, coffee production exploded from 5.6 million sacks (of 132 pounds each) in 1891 to 16.3 million in 1902—as Brazil's share of global coffee production soared to 75 percent. Highly concerned about finances, Rodrigues Alves began the economic *reerguimento* ("resurgence") characterized by tight monetary policies having recessive effects offset by amplified public works programs stressing rail and port facilities, with sewer and water systems for the capital city, which now boasted a population exceeding 800,000.

In March 1906 a new chief executive—Afonso Augusto Moreira Pena (b. 1847) of Minas Gerais—was chosen, ending the twelve-year hold of São Paulo on the presidency. But since Minas had replaced Rio de Janeiro as the second leading coffee state, this did not signify any major change in the distribution of power away from the highly influential, though not fully hegemonic, coffee elite. For Pena was an old classmate of Rodrigues Alves and had also served as his vice president. Yet a Mineiro presidency did reflect the emergence of a new balance wheel in the politics of the governors, coopting and channeling, as well as accommodating, the interests of states other than São Paulo and Minas Gerais. In August 1905 Senator José Gomes Pinheiro Machado of Rio Grande do Sul launched a brief king-making career by articulating Pena's candidacy with sufficient skill to convince São Paulo to get on board. As Minas Gerais was still number one in population, the size of the electorate, and the number of congressional seats, the elevation of its former chief executive to the presidency was logical. Essentially unopposed, Pena received over 288,000 votes to fewer than 5,000 for his token electoral sparring partner as already severely limited electoral participation slumped dramatically. Since the Federal Republican Party (PRF) was little more than a rather loose "club of oligarchs," the military, even with its internal divisions, was Brazil's closest approximation to a national political institution.

Aware of restlessness among junior and mid-grade army officers, Pena, as a wary Mineiro (a man from Minas Gerais), prudently chose as his war minister Marshal Hermes Rodrigues da Fonseca (b. 1855), articulator of the 1889 coup (as a major) and as war minister the legalist hero of the 1904 crisis. Disunity and intransigence among the civilian elites soon created a vacuum he could readily be convinced to fill, since to important elements of the armed forces he seemed to combine the best qualities of his uncle, ex-president Deodoro, with Floriano's "overlooked" virtues. Hence civilian and military founders of the republic faced off in the 1910 election. Determined to combat any resurgence of Florianism, leading sixty-one-year-old intellectual Ruy Barbosa, the epitome of civilian Brazil's finest flower, launched his antimilitarist candidacy with the backing of his home state of Bahia, São Paulo, and Rio de Janeiro, his adoptive home. Although the champion of the "civilist" (civilian) cause carried the cities of the south, the combination of state machines and military support was decisive in the interior. Official figures registered a win for Hermes by 404,000 to 223,000—both a record turnout and a record low margin of victory, as well as the first time the candidate supported by São Paulo had failed to win.

Inaugurated on November 15, 1910, the twenty-first anniversary of the republic, Hermes followed the precedent of his two military precursors rather than the live-and-let-live stance of the four intervening civilian presidents. Influenced by a new alliance of middle-class military with like-minded civilian reformers, he launched a series of "salvations," aimed at freeing oligarchic machines of local political chiefs and powerful landowning families allied with Pinheiro Machado and his embryonic

Conservative Republican Party (PRC). Influenced by Roca's policies in Argentina and aware of what Díaz had done in Mexico, Hermes felt a need to undercut the nearly complete control of political life in their states that governors maintained through clientelistic deals, nepotism, and use of patronage; electoral corruption bordering on the obscene; and violence pure and simple. Such a system of well-mounted political machines consolidated leadership of the regional chief in the states and of the *coronel* in the municipalities in such a way that the peasantry was practically feudalized. The survival of this traditional system made emergence of coherent national political parties capable of disciplining legislative politics all but impossible.[15]

But all Hermes, hamstrung by the single four-year term, which left presidents semi-lame-ducks by the end of their third year in office, could accomplish was a partial rotation of oligarchic elites and effective undermining of Pinheiro Machado's efforts to make the PRC into a real national party. Late in his administration Hermes was plagued by the Contestado insurgency, a Canudos-type situation with major political implications in a remote area disputed by the southern states of Paraná and Santa Catarina. In a period rife with corruption, unemployment, and speculation, the Contestado insurgency (named after the disputed area) survived the death of its leader in October 1912, being finally crushed by a field army of over 7,000 men in 1915 at a cost of over 300 government troops and perhaps twenty times that number of rebels killed—almost all of them humble people participating in an essentially spontaneous protest by those marginalized by the existing social order and political process.[16] In the March 1914 elections forty-six-year-old Wenceslau Bráz Pereira Gomes, vice president under Hermes, polled 92 percent of the roughly 550,000 votes, giving Minas Gerais its second president. In September 1915 Pinheiro Machado was murdered, and the PRC collapsed, once again leaving the country without a national political party. With World War I in progress, the 1918 election of São Paulo's Rodrigues Alves for a second stint as president aroused little opposition, and in keeping with the new scheme of "coffee with milk" politics (São Paulo and Minas Gerais), he had Minas Gerais chief executive Delfim Moreira da Costa Ribeiro as his running mate. As the official slate polled 99 percent of a 400,000-vote turnout, stability appeared assured. But Rodrigues Alves died in January 1919, and the vice president was too ill to take over the presidency. The compromise choice in the resulting special election was Epitácio Lindolfo da Silva Pessoa (b. 1865)—who had headed Brazil's delegation at the Versailles peace conference but would normally have been ruled out of consideration because he came from the small northeastern state of Paraíba. On April 19 he received 71 percent of the fewer than half million votes cast, as Ruy Barbosa, the William Jennings Bryan of Brazil, in his last hurrah, was credited with 119,000 votes to the victor's 341,000.

This first civilian president from outside the center-south would govern a Brazil that had changed significantly since the early 1900s. Its population had passed 22 million in 1910 on the way to 30.6 million by 1920. Rio de Janeiro was a city of nearly 1.2 million, and São Paulo, with 580,000 inhabitants, had started on the expansion that would make it the continent's premier city, but the economy, which had expanded by 77 percent from 1900 to 1913, an expansion leading to a per capita GDP rise of 35 percent, had slowed to a modest 2.4 percent annual growth rate between 1914 and 1918. Coffee still accounted for over 47 percent of the nation's exports in the 1914–1918 period; this percentage was down from its nearly 62 percent during the Hermes years. Rubber, source of 20 percent of Brazil's foreign exchange earnings during that period, now overtaken by commercial plantation production in Europe's tropical colonies, declined to 12 percent by 1922. Although immigration had fallen off during the first decade of the century, the total of 650,000 was substantial, and between 1910 and 1919 the flow rose once more, to 820,000. Although still low, literacy rates had risen by 10 percent to 29 percent for males and 20 percent for females.[17]

World War I had clearly focused the attention of both elites and government on the need to diversify industrial production so as not to be caught short in any future international crisis. Consequently, during the 1920s the government provided incentives and extended subsidies to certain priority industries. The issue of price supports for coffee became more divisive after a 27 percent fall in coffee revenues in 1920 led to further expansion of the money supply on top of the troublesome inflation of the wartime years. Political passions ran high through Pessoa's truncated tenure. The officer corps took umbrage at this cosmopolitan international jurist's appointment of civilians as service ministers and the employment of 6,000 troops in an intervention in Bahia in favor of a political ally. Although the nomination of Minas Gerais chief executive Artur da Silva Bernardes (b. 1875) for the 1922–1926 term was agreed upon by the nation's leaders in early 1921, the fact that it earmarked the presidency in 1926 for São Paulo's governor caused Rio Grande do Sul to join with Rio de Janeiro, Bahia, and Pernambuco in the "republican reaction" alliance. Hermes da Fonseca, returning from six years in Europe, threw his very considerable support to this opposition slate, which already enjoyed the backing of young military reformists and even the venerable Ruy Barbosa. The March 1922 balloting saw the government candidate win as always. But with intellectual sectors sensitized by the centennial of independence, the republican reaction refused to accept the announced results as valid, and Hermes, presiding over the Military Club, called for a "tribunal of honor" to verify the electoral results. When Bernardes was proclaimed president-elect on June 7 with the smallest margin yet (56 percent of the vote, or 467,000 to 318,000), Hermes reacted with a provocative declaration that led to his arrest. The reaction of his supporters was a revolt designed to bring the armed forces back to power. Romantic young officers organized the uprising on very short notice, and Hermes's failure to turn it into more than a gallant but futile gesture spelled the epitaph for Florianism. But out of the heroic behavior of the junior officers, who faced almost certain death, a more potent force—*tenentismo* (a reform movement of young officers)—was born as a modern movement freed from the shackles of seeking to emulate successes of an earlier era. Indeed, over a span of decades it would be unique in the annals of Latin America and in some ways of the world. McCann defines its context:

> As in the 1880s a "military question" beset Brazil's political system at a time when multifaceted frustrations gripped the army officer corps. In both periods a progressive wave had raised the level of debate about professionalism. Slow promotions discouraged junior officers who found senior officers, who had accommodated themselves to the reigning system, blocking their upward mobility.[18]

In the perspective of 1922, however, the young military rebels looked like anything but the wave of the future. Fort Copacabana under Captain Euclides Hermes da Fonseca, son of the marshal, rebelled in the early morning hours of July 5, but these gallant rebels soon found themselves in isolated resistance against the full force of the government. Under heavy fire the most militant young officers embarked upon a suicidal sally against the ground troops besieging them; only the seriously wounded Antônio de Siqueira Campos and Eduardo Gomes—twice a presidential candidate after World War II—survived to become national heroes. Bernardes was inaugurated on November 15 under the cloud of this bloodbath, and during his four years in office he enjoyed little respite from crises. Civil war broke out in Rio Grande do Sul over the outcome of the November 25 gubernatorial voting, and old scores from earlier armed struggles were settled by acts of violence crossing the line into barbarism. Long before the Rio Grande do Sul strife came to a close at the end of 1923, plans for a new revolt against the increasingly repressive Bernardes government were going forward in the nation's center under leaders with greater skill and coherence. Striking on the second anniversary of the 1922 revolt, the insurgents controlled São Paulo city before withdrawing to the interior on November 27 in the face of air attacks.

This was only the beginning of what would develop into the overture to Brazil's 1930 Revolution. Captain Luís Carlos Prestes managed to ignite the chronic powder keg of Rio Grande do Sul and, after two months of holding off government forces, marched northward to join the São Paulo rebels, a feat achieved in April 1925. With Prestes as chief of staff and Juarez do Nascimento Fernandes Távora, destined to be presidential runner-up in 1955, as commander of one of its columns, the rebel movement fought fifty battles in a fifteen-thousand-mile campaign through the country's vast interior before going into exile in Bolivia in February 1927. This saga, which outlasted the term of the target of their animosity, caught the country's imagination. Catalyzed by this dramatic insurgency, a new civilian-military coalition was emerging—one that within a short time was capable of pushing aside the decaying structures of the past four decades much as the military Jacobins, Deodoro and Floriano, and the Republican Party had done away with the empire.[19] In the lull before the storm, the presidential succession of 1926 was one of the smoothest the republic had yet experienced. The government candidate was São Paulo chief executive Washington Luís Pereira de Souza (b. 1869), with his Minas Gerais counterpart as running mate. The official results of 688,000 to 1,116 gave a grossly misleading impression of national consensus. Large coffee planters, São Paulo professionals, and the newer generation of the traditional middle class formed the Democratic Party in February 1926 to challenge the long-entrenched Paulista Republican Party. At the same time, very able and highly experienced Antônio Carlos Ribeiro da Andrada reached the presidency of Minas Gerais, from whence he contemplated his status as presumably Brazil's next president. In Rio Grande do Sul the Liberator Party (PL) was established in March 1928. Tory reformism, which had carried the day in Argentina on the eve of World War I, was finally under way, but the situation was fast slipping past the point at which its equivalent might be enough. Indeed, by 1928 the oligarchic republican regime had reached a point of deterioration similar to the decay of the empire in the mid-1880s. Those in power, however, certainly did not see the situation in such gloomy terms. Indeed, they felt that they had already weathered the worst, with smooth sailing ahead. Below the surface, however, the spread of insurrectionist sentiment among the military coincided with an increasing alienation of urban progressive groups from a political establishment unresponsive to the desire by the emergent and upwardly aspirant middle class for a significant say in policymaking and indisposed to yield to demands for any type of electoral reform. (Their Argentine counterparts had taken the high road in this respect and, as a result, had been shut out of power since 1916.) Dissension within the political elite over presidential succession combined with the impact of the world economic crisis to make the regime vulnerable and to catalyze the formation of a revolutionary coalition capable of overthrowing the established political order. This time, in contrast to the termination of the monarchy four decades earlier, nationwide mobilization and substantial fighting were required to bring about a revolution.

As the 1920s ended, Brazil's population had passed 35 million, with Rio de Janeiro a city of 1.5 million and São Paulo near 900,000. After stagnating in 1924 and 1925, economic expansion recovered to a robust 11 percent a year for 1927 and 1928—but on a fragile basis. This prosperity was highly mortgaged to coffee, responsible for 72 percent of export earnings from 1924 through 1929, a year in which GDP growth plummeted to a mere 1.2 percent—well below the population increase. For between September and December coffee prices fell by one-third, and by the second half of 1930 they were down an additional 70 percent because of a massive harvest and disastrously declining international demand. Under these conditions the president felt compelled to keep the government under the control of reliable Paulista coffee interests; reneging on the alternation understanding with Minas Gerais, he anointed São Paulo chief executive Júlio Prestes de Albuquerque as his successor. The president was soon to find that in politics, hell hath no fury like a proud and determined presidential candidate scorned.[20]

Indeed, by the late 1920s the Brazilian political system was clearly in a state of debilitating disarray, heading for outright decay—as had been the case with the monarchy a third of a century earlier. This deterioration was a function of the lack of flexibility and capacity to modernize shown by the political structures and processes, on the one hand, and of the accelerating pace of economic change and resultant societal tensions, on the other. This time bringing about a major regime change would require a serious economic crisis and the grave errors in political judgment that this crisis engendered on the part of the administration. Events over the past twenty years underscored the resilience of the oligarchic structures and demonstrated that—in contrast to circumstances in Argentina—the middle class could not hope to break through to power without the military serving as its cutting edge. For Brazil was not yet a country where the urban industrialized region could determine the course of national affairs. As Hahner aptly summarizes the situation, "Quarrels within this strong, unified elite, with its regional alliances cemented by control of a rural-based elite, never degenerated into bloody fights which might have encouraged some politicians to seek worker support for counterbalance rivals."[21]

Institutions and processes at least marginally suitable for the first years of republican government had failed over four decades to evolve beyond the amalgam with traditional practices carried over from the monarchy. The electoral process was highly fraudulent, national parties simply did not exist, and protests against the inequities of the established order were increasingly met with repression rather than compromise and evolutionary reform. In Argentina, by 1916 middle-class reformers had come to power through honest elections, and half a decade earlier Mexicans had risen up to overthrow an entrenched autocrat. But in Brazil arbitrary executive authority lacked the compensatory merits of strength and effectiveness, and the spokesmen of the often patriarchal and still essentially patrimonial regime could not point with pride to outstanding accomplishments to justify their continuing stewardship of the nation.

Notes

1. This section draws heavily upon Ronald M. Schneider, *"Order and Progress": A Political History of Brazil* (Boulder, CO: Westview Press, 1991), pp. 32–52. Excellent on the period is Roderick J. Barman, *Brazil: The Forging of a Nation, 1798–1852* (Stanford, CA: Stanford University Press, 1988), pp. 42–129.

2. Neil Macaulay, *Dom Pedro: The Struggle for Liberty in Brazil and Portugal, 1798–1834* (Durham, NC: Duke University Press, 1986), provides a nuanced treatment of this controversial figure, with these specific developments on pp. 465–487.

3. Pedro's extraordinarily long reign is ably analyzed in Roderick J. Barman, *Citizen Emperor, Pedro II and the Making of Brazil, 1825-91* (Stanford, CA: Stanford University Press, 1999).

4. See Richard Graham, *Patronage and Politics in Nineteenth-Century Brazil* (Stanford, CA: Stanford University Press, 1990).

5. This section draws substantially on Ronald M. Schneider, "Order and Progress," pp. 52–87.

6. E. Bradford Burns, *A History of Brazil*, 2nd ed. (New York: Columbia University Press, 1980), p. 156.

7. See June E. Hahner, *Poverty and Politics: The Urban Poor in Brazil, 1870–1920* (Albuquerque: University of New Mexico Press, 1986), p. 40.

8. For a meticulously reconstructed account of these developments, see Frank D. McCann, *Soldiers of the Pátria: A History of the Brazilian Army, 1889–1937* (Stanford, CA: Stanford University Press, 2004), pp. 3–10.

9. The individuals referred to here are Marshals Henrique Duffles Teixeira Lott (war minister, 1955–1960) and Humberto de Alencar Castelo Branco (president, 1964–1967). Their early careers are discussed in ibid., pp. 156, 253, 348.

10. Ibid., p. 4.

11. Samuel P. Huntington, *Political Order in Changing Societies* (New Haven, CT: Yale University Press, 1968), p. 199.

12. See McCann, *Soldiers*, pp. 31–61, as well as Robert M. Levine, *Vale of Tears: Revisiting the Canudos Massacre in Northeastern Brazil, 1893–1897* (Berkeley and Los Angeles: University of California Press, 1992).

13. This section draws heavily upon Schneider, "Order and Progress," pp. 84–114.

14. McCann, *Soldiers*, p. 88.

15. Ibid., pp. 107–157, for a full discussion of Hermes's term.

16. Todd A. Diacon, *Millenarian Vision, Capitalist Reality: Brazil's Contestado Rebellion, 1912–1916* (Durham, NC: Duke University Press, 1991).

17. Consult Hahner, *Poverty and Politics*, p. 88.

18. McCann, *Soldiers*, pp. 218–219.

19. Ibid., pp. 259–279, as well as Neil Macaulay, *The Prestes Column: Revolution in Brazil* (New York: Franklin Watts, 1974).

20. Useful for understanding politics at this juncture is Mauricio Font, *Coffee, Contention, and Change: In the Politics of Brazil* (London: Blackwell, 1990).

21. Hahner, *Poverty and Politics*, p. 291.

3

Mexico and Argentina

Independence to 1930

Situated at the two extremes of Latin America and complete contrasts ethnically, Mexico and Argentina were from colonial days different in almost all respects—the former installed in the North American continent with an immense area and large population, the second at that point quite remote, with a very much smaller population concentrated in and around Buenos Aires. Indeed, when the colonial era drew to an end for them after 1810 the two countries had very little in common, and their paths as independent nations would diverge sharply over the next century. Mexico's proximity to the United States and Argentina's freedom from contact with, much less intervention from, the hemisphere's rising power guaranteed that their developmental trajectories would continue to diverge. Moreover, both were much nearer to Europe than they were to each other and had even less in common with Brazil, which both viewed as an irrelevant oddity rather than a country from which they could learn any lessons. Mexico, with the longer and more intense colonial period and a very traumatic independence process, would reach 1930 via an extremely rocky road and without even the basic rudiments of democratic institutions and processes. Its large Indian population would still be mired at the bottom of the socioeconomic pyramid and politically marginalized. Argentina, of little preindependence consequence, would begin relatively free of a negative colonial heritage and, through being a nation of recent European immigrants and investment, construct an early-twentieth-century democratic order. Then in the face of profound economic crisis it could not sustain this progress, which would be plowed under in 1930.

Mexico to 1870:
Caudillo Dominance and Foreign Intervention

Events in New Spain, that giant-sized viceroyalty stretching from California across to Texas and down through Central America, were critically important to Spain. The source of two-thirds of Spain's colonial revenues, especially silver production, the region, governed out of Mexico City, had a population of over 6.5 million (half of all Spanish subjects in the Western Hemisphere—overwhelmingly Indians and *mestizos*), governed by only 15,000 Europeans. Having, in late 1808, routed the Creole autonomists who argued that Mexico should be a constitutional kingdom under the Spanish crown, the *peninsulares,* who were absolutists, were determined to preserve the colonial status quo.[1] They deposed the viceroy and persecuted Creoles before welcoming weaker viceroys, whom they were confident they could dominate.

Contesting the legitimacy of this Mexico City regime and other juntas set up in the wake of the French occupation of Spain, popular uprisings began in 1810, led by radical priest Miguel Hidalgo y Costilla (b. 1753), an educated *criollo* (whose family had been pushed to the brink of bankruptcy by royal tax collectors) able to inspire the Indian masses to revolt through his stirring Grito de Dolores (Cry of Pain).[2] As Indians made up 60 percent of the population, and *mestizos* another 22 percent, this unprecedented development panicked the dominant European minority—mindful of the destruction of their counterparts that had recently occurred in Haiti. By late in the year, Hidalgo's revolutionary army of 80,000 was at the doors of Mexico City, with a population of 170,000 the hemisphere's largest city. During this campaign the movement for independence began to take on the characteristics of a race and class war as the revolutionaries attacked the persons and property not only of *peninsulares,* but also of Creole elites. Repulsed near the capital by better-armed and -disciplined government forces, once back in their strongholds the popular horde executed hundreds of Europeans. By the final defeat of Hidalgo's forces in early 1811 and the execution of their leaders, some 2,000 of New Spain's 15,000 *peninsulares* had lost their lives. With Hidalgo's death, Father José María Morales y Pavón (b. 1765), of poor *mestizo* origins, assumed his mantle, mobilizing increased Creole as well as *mestizo* support. Militarily unsuccessful, this second great martyr of Mexican independence was captured and executed in late 1815.[3]

Restored to power in Spain in May 1814, King Ferdinand had annulled the liberal reforms of the Cádiz provisional Cortes (national legislature) that had so upset New World conservatives. In late 1816 a conciliatory new viceroy arrived in Mexico, but 1820 witnessed a revolt in Spain against royal absolutism. The ensuing elections of representatives to new Cortes in Madrid resulted in victory for Mexican autonomists, who viewed the prime concerns of the Spanish legislature as largely irrelevant to their needs, hence to their vision of Mexico's interests. Mexican military officers and merchants and its Catholic Church were anxious over the Spanish liberals' threat to the special privileges of the armed forces and religion. Wanting to keep these pillars of the established social order strong, and confident in their ability to keep popular forces in check, they felt a break with Spain provided their best option. Hence, in this very important part of Latin America, independence was a conservative maneuver to preserve stability and order. Against this backdrop, insurgents, led by uneducated *mestizo* Vicente Guerrero (b. 1783), were sufficiently troublesome for the viceroy to send Colonel Agustín de Iturbide (b. 1783) against them.[4] This ambitious young officer, feeling inadequately rewarded for his service to the crown, allied his men with those of his erstwhile foe behind the February 1821 Plan of Iguala. Inspired by Napoléon's example and by events in Haiti, by September this son of a Basque merchant and a Mexican mother had, on his thirty-eighth birthday, crowned himself "regent of the Mexican Empire," and by May of the following year he would be saluted as Emperor Agustín I. On his maps, his short-lived realm ran from Oregon to Panama, but he exercised effective control over only a small part of this far-flung domain.

General Guadalupe Victoria (b. 1785 as Miguel Fernández) had risen in revolt against Iturbide in October 1821 and was subsequently supported by the country's future strongman, Antonio López de Santa Ana (b. 1794), son of recent Spanish immigrants and himself a former royalist officer. After being forced to abdicate in March 1823, Iturbide attempted a comeback sixteen months later and was promptly executed. By the time a federal republic was launched in 1824 with Victoria at its helm, 600,000 deaths had occurred in the struggles begun in 1810—a tenth of the total population of slightly over 6.2 million. Thus, although Mexico was the first major part of the Spanish Empire to become independent, viable political processes would remain a distant dream as force remained the arbiter of power. In addition, damage to the economy was severe: There was not only a disturbing drop in silver production, but also the disintegration of large estates and increases in transportation costs, as 90 percent of foreign trade was funneled through the narrow Valley of Mexico to Veracruz corridor.

Establishment of the republic failed to bring a significant measure of stability, much less a taste of democracy. In the absence of political parties, politics within the restricted elites often involved the rival Masonic lodges, the York Rite and the Scottish Rite secret societies being bitterly opposed. Indeed, stability would have to wait until the 1870s, and democracy would flourish only briefly at widely separated intervals until well into the twentieth century. Even the road to consolidation proved more than bumpy; it was traumatic and nearly fatal. The blatant and brutal interference of the United States in midcentury, culminating in forceful US annexation of half of Mexico's territory, would obscure the significant leadership talents of Mexico's first dominant political figure, Santa Ana. Then the very great promise of the hemisphere's most authentic representative of the indigenous masses to reach power, Benito Juárez, would be undercut by military intervention by France, which diverted him from reform to survival.

By 1828 the York Rite faction of the Mexico City elite had won out, engineering the election of General Manuel Gómez Pedraza (b. 1789), negated through a December 1828 coup by Guerrero, Victoria, and Santa Ana. Installed as president, Guerrero abolished slavery in 1829 and forced Spanish citizens to leave the country. Santa Ana, demonstrating unusual bravery in repelling a French invasion, earned promotion to major general and became known as the Hero of Tampico, on his way to becoming Mexico's "man of destiny."[5] Overthrown at the end of 1830 by his centralist vice president, Guerrero attempted a countercoup and was promptly executed. This conflict-ridden scene set the stage for a federalist coup in 1831 that brought Santa Ana to the presidency the following year—for the first of his eleven stints in office. In 1835 this oft-absent-from-the-capital *caudillo*—since he abhorred the routine of governing and having to deal with the demands of whining politicians and clamoring businessmen—suspended the 1824 Constitution and repressed a resulting federalist revolt in the north. He turned power over to his reliable vice president, Valentín Gómez Farias, in 1833 and again in 1835—as he would in 1839, 1842, and 1843, withdrawing to his extensive holdings near Veracruz. By this time the Mexican army was made up of elements that had until recently been fighting against each other—a phenomenon that would be repeated with severely negative effects in the aftermath of the 1910 Revolution.

Captured by Sam Houston's forces when trying to quash the Texas secessionist movement in 1836 (in large part motivated by the Texans' desire to maintain slavery),

Santa Ana was coerced into recognizing that region's independence. He soon re-deemed himself by repelling a French invasion force at Veracruz in 1838, losing an arm in the process. This resilient *caudillo,* who opportunistically aligned with liberals or conservatives as the occasion dictated, returned to the presidency in 1843, only to be ousted the next year. Then in 1845 the United States annexed Texas (in clear vio-lation of its treaty obligations with Mexico) and shortly thereafter provoked a war. This crisis provided Santa Ana with an opportunity to return from exile. After fight-ing General Zachary Taylor to a draw in the north at Buena Vista in February 1847, he force-marched to Veracruz, where he was trounced by General Winfield Scott's vastly superior forces. Santa Ana's failed defense of the capital seven months later brought about his resignation and exile. Thus the shrewd politician avoided having to sign the humiliating 1848 peace treaty with the United States. As Krause captures the essence of this great *caudillo,* "In Santa Anna there was a semblance—an often grotesque mixture—of royal and popular legitimacy combined."[6] In retrospect, Santa Ana's view that it would be a century before the Mexican people would be fit for de-mocracy turned out to be not far off the mark. In his eyes, in the meantime, there was no reason despotism could not embody wisdom and virtue.

Although mid century witnessed Mexico's first fully constitutional transfer of power, a conservative-backed coup in early 1853 furnished Santa Ana a final turn in the presidency, this time supposedly as a bridge to a future European monarch. To this end he abolished the 1824 Constitution. His final, abrupt departure from power in mid-1855 was precipitated by the liberals' Revolution of Ayutla, which brought to center stage a compelling political figure starkly different in almost every dimension from the durable *caudillo.* For after November 1855 uncompromising centralist liber-als were in power in a country whose population was around 7.7 million. Benito Pablo Juárez García (b. 1806), a Zatpotec Indian descended from the region's histori-cal indigenous nobility and married to a Spanish woman, had been governor of Oax-aca and now became justice minister in the Juan N. Álvarez–Ignácio Comonfort government. Under a law with Juárez's name, the *fueros* (special legal rights) of the church and the military were abolished. Following Álvarez's resignation, the Lerdo law (named after Miguel Lerdo de Tejada) in mid-1856 drastically changed the land tenure system, and the 1857 Constitution disestablished the Catholic Church.[7]

These drastic measures led by 1858 to civil war, with the conservatives behind militarily adept General Miguel Miramón (b. 1831) controlling Mexico City, and with Acting President Juárez, ably seconded in the military field by General Santos Degollado and in the political realm by Melchior Ocampo, resisting out of Veracruz. Victorious at the beginning of 1861, the liberals indulged in violent anticlerical ac-tions and expelled the country's bishops—the result being the kidnapping and mur-der of Ocampo in May of that year. Juárez was elected president for the term ending in December 1865, at which time he was scheduled to turn the presidency over to the chief justice, General Jesús González Oretayor. But events would drastically alter that timetable.

Unable to best the liberals internally and believing that they were the only bul-wark protecting order and decency against Godless anarchy, the conservatives and the church looked for help from abroad. They found a willing partner in French emperor Louis Napoléon (Napoléon III), in power for over a decade and looking for a means to escape from the image of being just the great Bonaparte's nephew. Juárez's suspension of foreign debt payments in 1862 gave the ambitious French ruler the pretext for which he was looking, and after taking Mexico City in 1863, his invading army maintained Austrian archduke Ferdinand Maximilian von Hapsburg (b. 1832) on a Mexican throne hastily created in 1864 with the wholehearted collaboration of the conservatives and the Catholic Church.[8] Juárez's legitimate liberal government was forced to wage guerrilla warfare from the mountains. But after Prussia's defeat of Austria in the 1866 Seven Weeks' War, Napoléon III withdrew his troops in anticipation of a Prussian invasion of France, which eventually came in 1870. Thus, militarily orphaned, but erroneously believing that the masses supported him, Maximilian insisted upon carrying on what for him was a crusade, being captured and executed in mid-1867. These events brought Juárez and the liberals back to power older, if not entirely wiser, than before, with ambitious General José de la Cruz Porfirio Díaz chafing at the bit for his chance to show how the country should be run. A liberal by affiliation, Díaz in many ways had more Santa Ana than Juárez in his basic character.

Mexico to 1899: Authoritarian Modernization

Mexico, whose population had reached 9.1 million by 1872, was a model of stability and economic development in the late nineteenth century, in sharp contrast with its preceding troubles (as well as with what would soon ensue). This sharp departure from the course it had hitherto followed was of an essentially authoritarian nature under an extraordinarily effective strongman whose rule would last a decade into the twentieth century and earn itself a one-word title—the Porfiriato (after Díaz's commonly used name, Porfirio)—which became a shorthand term much like *Bonapartist* or *Bismarckian* in Europe.[9] The mid-1872 death of the liberal Juárez, only months after his reelection as president, opened the way for the rise to power of a man who would mark the transition to a kind of institutionalized autocratic rule that made a mockery of his liberal origins.

General José de la Cruz Porfirio Díaz (b. 1830) was an acutely intelligent *mestizo* from southern Mexico who abandoned education for the priesthood in favor of a military career. When Juárez became governor of Díaz's native state, the ambitious young man hitched himself to this rising star. After Juárez and many other liberal leaders went into exile when Santa Ana again seized power in 1853, the bellicose Díaz mounted guerrilla warfare. With the French intervention, this experienced military leader was promoted to brigadier general in 1862. In an audacious move he ran for the presidency against the elderly Juárez in 1871 on the slogan of "Effective Suffrage, No Reelection," which would be turned against him four decades later. Left out in the cold by a postelection Juárez–Sebastián Lerdo de Tejada alliance that gave the latter the vice presidency, Díaz essayed a failed uprising. When Lerdo (b. 1827), who succeeded to the presidency following Juárez's death, sought reelection in 1876, Díaz rebelled again, as did the head of the Mexican supreme court. Defeating Lerdo's federal forces, Díaz began his thirty-five-year domination of Mexico's political life—an era that would serve as a goal, if not a model, for subsequent Latin American strongmen.[10]

This battle-tested veteran of the struggle against the French stepped aside for an ally, General Manuel González, in 1880, resuming the presidency in 1884 with ritual reelections at the end of each term. His rule was marked by economic development and modernization from above based on a blueprint devised by a group of positivist technocrats known as Los Científicos ("the Scientific Ones"). Bearing a basic similarity to the young officers who ended the Brazilian monarchy, as well as to many Argentine intellectuals of the Sarmiento-Roca era, when push came to shove they often ended up stressing the first part of their slogan of "Order and Progress." In Camp's judgment, "Positivism became a vehicle for reintroducing conservative ideas among Mexico's liberal leadership." As aptly expressed:

> After years of political instability, violence, and civil war, these men saw peace as a critical necessity for progress. Their explanation for the disruptive preceding decades centered on the notion that too much of Mexico's political thinking had been based on irrational or "unscientific" ideas influenced by the spiritual teaching of the church and that alternative political ideas were counterproductive.[11]

In their view, this new moderate liberalism could best be inculcated in the next generation of leaders of the country through carefully supervised public education. The National Preparatory School in Mexico City was the keystone institution in their effort to create a homogeneous elite political culture. There the heirs of the upper and aspirant upper-middle classes would study under the same dedicated and highly qualified teachers. Influenced by Herbert Spencer's version of social Darwinism, they used a strategy for forging a modern Mexico that was based on the idea that for the foreseeable future an enlightened scientific elite would have to modernize the country by force.[12]

Convinced that foreign investment was the key to Mexico's future, Díaz created an environment of stability and financial responsibility conducive to such investments, concentrated on revitalizing mining and massive construction of roads and railroads. Like many other governments of the time down through South America, his was generous in making attractive concessions to maintain a steady, heavy flow of foreign investment. Between 1884 and 1910 foreign investment increased more than thirtyfold. Railroads grew from a mere 700 miles of track to over 12,000—and exports went up 600 percent during the Díaz era. Viewing Mexico's Indian masses with disdain, Díaz and his associates imported European capital and technicians instead of workers (whereas Brazil and Argentina imported workers). For although the government did try to attract immigrants, Mexico ended up with small numbers of large landowners who bought public lands at bargain prices. The privileged groups allied with them, as they diversified their investments into mining and manufacturing, shared in the country's sustained economic growth; all others benefited little. It has aptly been said by many figures that under Díaz Mexico became the "mother of foreigners and stepmother of Mexicans."

Although this attitude was politically feasible for a generation, it resulted by the end of the century in a frustrated group of upwardly mobile *mestizos* whose progress appeared blocked for lack of the right connections. Yet for decades Díaz staved off this reaction by coopting many in the emergent middle class through expansion of the federal bureaucracy—much as had been done by viceroys in the colonial era. For the Mexican state grew immensely under Díaz's Porfiriato. Successfully negotiating the consolidation of Mexico's foreign debt and starting a steel industry, Díaz presided into the new century over sustained economic development fed by foreign investment. By the end of the 1890s manufacturing employed 500,000 workers and mining another 100,000 as lead, zinc, and copper supplemented gold and silver. Precious metals dropped from 80 percent of exports to 60 percent, and other raw materials doubled from 15 to 30 percent. Urbanization helped transform the country, as Mexico City doubled its population and Monterrey and Veracruz each grew by over 450 percent. In the two-tiered society providing benefits for those of European descent and a fortunate few educated *mestizos,* while ignoring the masses, Catholic schools were permitted to serve the needs of a dependent middle stratum—as long as the church stayed clear of political affairs. For Díaz's Mexico needed obedient masses as much as it did enlightened and thinking elite sectors. Díaz placed fellow military men in many key positions, but after a quarter century in power these old comrades were increasingly replaced by young, technically better-qualified civilians. Order was maintained in the countryside not by the regular army, but through a brutal militarized police force, the Rural Guard—commonly known as the Rurales, 1,600 gunmen, many former bandits. Peons who fled the system of permanently inherited indentured servitude were ruthlessly hunted down to discourage others from attempting to escape to the growing towns and cities. Political patronage went to those who loyally served the authoritarian system and its autocratic helmsman. As Lewis describes politics under this durable despot:

> On returning to power in 1884, Díaz began tightening his grip on Mexico. He divided Mexico into eleven military zones that often were large enough to encompass two or three states. These zones were then divided into smaller military regions, and those were subdivided into even smaller subregions. Díaz personally chose the commanders of these divisions, battalions, and regiments, being careful to make sure that they were loyal. Those officers were well paid, given opportunities for graft, and frequently shifted. Thus the twenty-seven states were crisscrossed by military commands whose top leaders were capable of keeping the governors under control.[13]

By the midpoint of his rule, Díaz had put together a reliable set of governors who were reelected in noncompetitive elections as regularly as he was. It was a huge patronage machine in which scholars agree that relatives and in-laws as well as old friends and military comrades were taken care of first, in a system that was in some ways more monarchical than the Brazilian monarchy—a truly "imperial" presidency. Key regime figures included his father-in-law, Manuel Romero Rubio, as interior minister; the clever José Limantour as treasury minister; and Justo Sierra in charge of education. Crucially for the future, Díaz rejected advice to establish a political party to help institutionalize the system, preferring a style of unfettered personal leadership. Thus, when his time came to an end, there could be no question of a smooth transition. Indeed, as the century drew to a close the entrenched dictator could feel superior to the bumbling erstwhile military masters of Brazil and the São Paulo oligarch who had succeeded them in office for one puny term. Neither Díaz nor the yes-men around him had any inkling that down in Argentina a much greater degree of institution building was going on under Roca, whose heritage would live on when Díaz's work had been swept away by revolution. For as captured by Camp:

> Because Díaz held the presidency for some thirty years, a personality cult developed around his leadership. His collaborators conveyed the message that progress, as they defined it, was guaranteed by his presence. His indispensability enhanced his political maneuverability. On the other hand, Díaz put in place a political system that was underdeveloped institutionally. In concentrating on his personality, political institutions failed to acquire legitimacy. Even the stability of the political system itself was at stake because continuity was not guaranteed by the acceptability of its institutions, but by an individual person, Díaz.[14]

The very significant economic development brought about by a quarter century of Díaz's policies had led to changes in the urban sector of society that were undermining the foundations of the regime's political control. But as the century came to its close, decay of the Porfiriato was not yet in sight. Indeed, its demise was still a decade away. No one imagined that in the ensuing period the country would experience protracted civil war and stretches of near chaos. But this was the ultimate result of a repressive regime mortgaged to the strength of a single individual.

1900–1929: Dictatorship, Revolution, and Civil War

The new century opened with Mexico firmly under the control of the most powerful ruler in its history. The Porfiriato was in its prime, and Mexico City had swollen under Díaz's development-oriented policies to 345,000 souls, on its way to 470,000 by 1910—in a nation that had reached 15.2 million inhabitants. The countryside was another matter, as entire villages were having their meager holdings expropriated in order to be handed over to already large landowners or foreign land development companies. By 1910 over half of Mexico's farmland was owned by a few thousand *hacendados,* many of them foreigners, and US timber companies had forced Indians off their ancestral lands. Small farmers were being reduced to the lowly status of peons for lack of documentation of ownership and money to fight eviction through the courts. Then, in 1906, recession struck the country—all the more shocking because of the sustained growth of the Díaz era during its first thirty years. Díaz's developmental programs had given rise to significant changes in Mexican society. As vividly captured by Lewis:

> A middle class of urban professionals, government officeholders, shopkeepers, and perhaps most significantly—industrialists had emerged. These latter were mainly small entrepreneurs running family businesses: iron- and steelworks in Monterrey, textile factories in Puebla, food and beverage plants in various parts of the country. These entrepreneurs increased in number, thanks to the government's desire to promote national industry through

protective tariffs. Still, they had little access to bank credit, for their factories were labor rather than capital intensive and could compete only if they kept down wages.[15]

These new forces were acutely aware that Díaz, who was nearing eighty years of age, was not the indispensable man he had been in his prime. Moreover, the country had changed—in good part as a result of his developmentalist policies—more than he was ready to admit. As an astute student of Mexican politics encapsulated the Díaz legacy:

> As Mexico emerged from the first decade of the twentieth Century, it acquired a political model that drew on Spanish authoritarianism and paternal heritages. Like the viceroys before him, but without reporting to any other authority, Díaz exercised extraordinary power. He built up a larger state apparatus as a means of retaining power, and although he strengthened the role of the state in society, he did not legitimize its institutions. While he did succeed in building some economic infrastructure in Mexico, he failed to meet social needs and maltreated certain groups, thereby continuing and intensifying the social inequalities existing under his colonial predecessors.[16]

Juárez-style liberals had been marginalized, not destroyed, during the Porfiriato's long run, and new ideas and the germ of a spirit of revolt were emerging, fed by the writings of progressive journalists such as Ricardo Flores Magón, whose paper, *La Regeneracíon,* founded in 1900, quickly picked up an intelligent and critical readership. Although the government closed it and arrested Flores the next year, a seed had been planted, as liberal clubs had been founded throughout the country. A loosely organized circle of state governors and their supporters, mostly landowners and businessmen like themselves, were increasingly taking issue with the Científicos, looking down the pike to the old dictator's eventual retirement or death. As the yet inchoate dissatisfaction took form,

> business as usual might have continued if there had not existed widespread discontent among . . . commercial farmers, medium-size domestic businessmen and merchants, and the significantly enlarged professional and intellectual classes—as well as among more marginal elements such as shopkeepers, retail merchants, and the group generally called the petite bourgeoisie.[17]

As the time for his ritual reelection in 1910 neared, Díaz played his habitual reluctant dragon act, complaining of the sacrifices he had made for the nation and the Mexican people—complaints that had been repeatedly followed by agreement to serve one more term. This time he gave an interview to this effect to a journalist, who published it as if the dictator was serious about having competitive elections. At this point three opposition currents came together: Francisco Ignácio Madero (b. 1873), from a wealthy landowning family in the north, and his political reform movement, embodied in the Anti-Reelectionist Party; protest movements of peasants who had been pushed off the land by concentrations of ownership; and elements of the urban working class who perceived themselves as being left out of Mexico City's booming times—particularly when economic growth rates were not what they had been until 1897.

A group of educated middle-class businessmen and liberal professionals rose to the occasion behind Madero's candidacy. Arrested by Díaz, he was released after the dictator's reelection had been announced in September 1910. Fleeing to Texas, this rather bookish individual—with graduate education in Paris and at the University of California—suddenly became a popular hero and launched a revolt in November 1910 behind the slogan "Effective Suffrage, No Reelection."[18] Following Madero's February 1911 invasion from Texas, which triggered uprisings in the north led by Francisco "Pancho" Villa and in the south led by Emiliano Zapata, Díaz found that his army existed largely on paper (for commanders had long overstated their troop strength in order to pocket the surplus salaries). After three months of the defeat of his dispirited forces, Díaz decided the game was no longer worth the risk, resigned, and went into European exile in May 1911. The tyrant had been overthrown, but hopes for democracy would soon be dashed. Indeed, Mexico would enter the bloodiest and most chaotic period in its life as a nation, one that would entail by far the greatest death toll anywhere in the Western Hemisphere, with the exception of the US Civil War.

A cautious man, perhaps too mild and conciliatory for the situation in which he found himself, something of a dolphin among sharks and with a strong idealistic streak, Madero moved slowly, concentrating on electoral reforms that he believed would permit a truly representative government, which could then address the country's problems in an orderly and moderate manner. Meanwhile, as president— legitimized in November by the freest elections in Mexican history—he followed Díaz-like economic policies while leaving social policy to the governors. But labor organizers and particularly the leader of southern peasants, Emiliano Zapata (b. 1879), had a more revolutionary outcome in mind, one that stressed a serious social agenda.[19] Madero had left many individuals from the Porfiriato undisturbed in government positions and had disbanded the revolutionary army. These were fatal mistakes as they enabled General Victoriano Huerta (b. 1845), seeing himself as a more experienced and deserving replacement for Díaz, to carry out a conspiracy against him. Under Huerta's command the federal army repressed a revolt by Bernardo Reyes in mid-December 1911 and crushed a 1912 rebellion in Chihuahua headed by General Pascual Orozco—for which Madero promoted the ambitious militarist to major general. Félix Díaz, nephew of the deposed dictator, rose up at Veracruz in October 1912 but was captured and imprisoned. Then, in February 1913, a senior general freed Díaz and Reyes, a development that led the overly trusting president to place Huerta in command of the riotous capital city, where more than five hundred died in two days of fighting. The opportunistic Huerta would soon repay Madero by betraying him.

With a change of administrations looming in Washington, Republican US ambassador Henry Lane Wilson—a Díaz admirer lamenting the strongman's ouster, detesting Madero, and knowing that Democrat Woodrow Wilson would soon replace him—sped up his plotting. On February 18 Huerta arrested Madero, as Ambassador Wilson brokered a pact that gave Huerta the presidency. With this implicit blessing, Huerta had Madero cowardly murdered on February 22. This power grab by a would-be Díaz emulator ushered in the longest and most destructive civil war Latin America has seen, with a death toll well in excess of 1 million. The immediate reaction of three energetic and determined northern reformist governors was to take to the battlefield as the constitutionalists (portraying Huerta as an illegitimate usurper), with Cuahuila's Venustiano Carranza (b. 1859), Madero's war minister, as Primer Jefe ("First Chief"), backed up by the younger duo of Villa (b. 1878) of Chihuahua and Sonora's Álvaro Obregón (b. 1880). Huerta the usurper was a victim of fate in that the 1912 election in the United States had involved a split in Republican ranks between President William H. Taft and ex-President Theodore Roosevelt that let Wilson in as a minority president. Republicans of the time felt reassured to have a guarantor of stability and property rights in office in Mexico—as had been the case for nearly thirty-five years with Díaz—but a Democrat of Wilson's strong views on democracy considered Huerta a murderer. Not only did Wilson deny Huerta's de facto regime diplomatic recognition, but he also sent troops to seize the port of Veracruz to cut off supplies of weapons to Huerta's forces. Hence, defeated in June 1914 at Zacatecas by Villa's forces, and with constitutionalist armies closing in on the capital from several directions, Huerta was forced out of the presidency in July 1914. Once again, however, those who felt that the worst was over and that stability was in sight were destined for disappointment.

In October 1914 some 150 revolutionary generals met in the Convention of Aguascalientes, joined by a slew of Zapata's anarchist intellectual advisers (as the uneducated Zapata's personal skills centered on exceptional horsemanship and his image as a lover), with the constitutionalists' First Chief exercising presidential-type powers and keeping this unwanted gathering at arm's length. Convincing the United States to withdraw its troops from Veracruz in November 1914, Carranza used it as his base to wage war against the so-called conventionists. By the next August he was successful. An imposing individual at six feet four inches, with a flowing white beard, this son of a comfortably fixed *hacendado* had served as governor of Coahuila in the early stages of the revolution. A moralist reformer, he was very image-conscious, wanting to be "another Juárez, to command like Don Porfirio, and to avoid the errors of Madero."[20] "Rectification" (correction) of liberalism and the revolution was his leitmotif. To younger revolutionaries he was a somewhat antiquated carryover from a past era.

The maverick Villa continued to provide a challenge to the chief executive.[21] This son of a sharecropper who had developed a reputation as a *bandido* ("bandit") in his youth had convinced much of the populace of his northern region that, like the James brothers in the United States, he had just been reacting to oppression and injustice. His army of intensely loyal followers had reached 16,000 men by the time he defeated Huerta, giving him significant weight in what was to a high degree a warlord type of political situation. Miffed by Carranza's preference for disciplined soldier Obregón over himself—darling of the world media (with a laudatory film being made for the US public)—at the end of 1915 Villa attacked Sonora, Obregón's fiefdom. The latter would lose an arm—shades of Santa Ana—in defeating Villa, being ably seconded in this feat by Plutarco Elías Calles (eventually to eclipse Obregón politically). Villa, now a hunted guerrilla, crossed into New Mexico and sacked the small town of Columbus. The punitive expedition under General John "Black Jack" Pershing never managed to catch up with Villa in the deserts of northern Mexico, but the headlines would carry Pershing to command of the US Expeditionary Forces in World War I. (Service in the earlier war with Mexico had been a key determining factor with respect to command positions on both sides in the US Civil War.)

When Carranza's government turned a cold shoulder to their demands for "land, bread, and a roof over their heads," Zapata and his followers caused severe trouble in southern Mexico. Rebelling behind the Plan de Ayala, calling for immediate transfer of land to those who tilled it and direct election of a new government, Zapata only temporarily gained the beleaguered Villa as an ally. While liberal Carranza still had the support of the more "Jacobin" Obregón against these agrarian radicals, the elimination of Huerta had only further divided the revolutionary forces, as the sterner would-be democrat Carranza stressed the need to establish political reforms, rather than split the middle-class leadership of the revolution over the radical social measures being pushed by Zapata and Villa and their substantial armies. In 1916 Zapata was attacked by a 30,000-man federal army and pushed deep into his rural base. After putting up a good guerrilla struggle, he was lured into an ambush and shot in April 1919.

With a temporary lull in the fighting, in 1916 Carranza convoked a constitutional convention at Querétaro (north of the capital) to draft a legal framework for the revolution. In this assembly, largely comprising lawyers and intellectuals, the radicals defeated Carranza's moderate to conservative supporters on all major issues. Hence the convention produced a document whose beauty was exceeded only by, in the light of the times, its impracticality. The constitution's very idealism condemned it to remain a revered statement of aims and aspirations for several decades, not a blueprint for Mexico's governments to follow. In a country whose rich mineral deposits were largely controlled by foreign investment, this constitution declared all subsoil resources to belong to the people. With an economy still dominated by large landowners who felt entitled to act as the ultimate authority over their peons, it called for agrarian reform. In a society where factory owners were accustomed to lord it over their workers, it gave the latter the rights to organize and strike. In a highly Catholic country, it stripped the church of authority and rights that had withstood Juárez's liberal reforms a generation before. In short, it raised many hopes and expectations that, under the circumstances, could not be fulfilled—but would be of great importance farther down the road.[22] But this constitution did serve to weaken Zapata's support by projecting the image of a reform-minded government.

Gifted by the constituent assembly in May 1917 with a term as constitutional president, which he would soon find did not guarantee peace or even long life, Carranza soon faced revolt from Obregón, Calles (b. 1877), and Adolfo de la Huerta (b. 1881)—all, like him, generals by grace of their military exploits since 1911, and to varying degrees viewing the First Chief as an outdated transitional figure out of touch with their generation. Having drifted in a conservative direction and entered into an accommodative alliance with elements of the old dominant class, Carranza attempted to block Obregón—whom he correctly viewed as a potential threat to the principle of a single presidential term—from winning the 1920 elections. Behind the Plan of Agua Prieta, the Sonoran trio took up arms against him, and when the dust settled, Carranza was killed in May 1920. The way was now open for the presidency to fall into the hands of Obregón after a short rest in the interim grasp of de la

Huerta.[23] Purging Carranza supporters, the much younger Obregón soon cut the size of the army sharply from 100,000 to 50,000 men. At the same time he increased the number of officers, buying off generals and colonels by putting them on the government payroll.

Obregón, who got off on the right foot by naming progressive José Vasconcellos as education minister and lauding the great revolutionary muralists—Diego Rivera, José Clemente Orozco, and David Alfaro Siqueiros—had not hesitated to enrich himself during the civil war. Now, as his term progressed, having taken care to distribute land to former Zapata followers, he moved to the right in order to conciliate businessmen and military elements opposed to agrarian reform as well as to avoid becoming dependent on labor. Hence the Sonorans grew apart, with treasury minister de la Huerta exiting in 1923 (the year of Pancho Villa's assassination) to run for a full presidential term in the next year's balloting against Calles, who was on the ticket of the Mexican Labor Party (PLM). When, after being declared the loser, de la Huerta revolted, in what had become a habit in Mexican politics, nearly half the federal army sided with him. Obregón, who enjoyed US endorsement, crushed them as he had Villa, killing 7,000, including many of his erstwhile comrades in arms. (The contrast with Brazil at this point, when it had contained the military insurgency to the remote interior, was great; that with Argentina's apparently stable electoral democracy was total.)

Calles's victory was assured by his PLM's putting a workers' militia in the field allied to Obregón's National Agrarian Party (PNA) and its peasant army. Son of an alcoholic who had neglected his family's property holdings, Calles had been a lieutenant colonel in Obregón's Sonoran army in 1913, subsequently attacking ingrained corruption in that state as governor.[24] After working for Obregón's election, he served in the key post of interior secretary. Having traveled in Europe following his election, Calles had many ideas about what his administration needed to do. The Bank of Mexico was founded in 1925, and new petroleum and land laws were enacted—the furor they aroused in the United States being dampened by Ambassador Dwight Morrow after 1927. The National Bank of Agricultural Credit was established in 1926, and railroad rebuilding, highway construction, school building, and irrigation projects went ahead as the state's role in the economy was substantially expanded. Meanwhile, as Obregón was off crushing the Yaqui Indians and bloodily smashing Sonoran opponents, Calles guided a constitutional amendment allowing nonimmediate presidential reelection.

Calles's partiality to the PLN pushed the PNA into opposition, but this development was lost in the uproar around his decision that, unlike Obregón, he would implement the strong antichurch provisions of the 1917 Constitution. Restrictive 1926 decrees set off in rural areas a bloody revolt of Catholic peasants protesting "atheistic, socialist" excesses. In what was known as the Cristero Rebellion for its rallying cry of "Viva Cristo Rey" ("Long live Christ the King"), Catholic peasants burned schools that had been turned over to public secular education, often killing the "socialist" teachers, and blew up troop trains. For its part, the government closed down convents, and even in the capital, nuns and priests were subject to arrest for wearing clerical garb in public. Although the government could handle the National League for Defense of Religion, the devoutly Catholic peasants and their guerrilla tactics were another matter. The death toll reached at least 25,000 Cristeros—with government troop losses and those unfortunates caught in between bringing the total to 70,000.[25] At least 200,000 persons fled to the cities, and 450,000 left the country.

With many surviving revolutionary generals aspiring to the presidency, Calles saw Obregón safely through a second election in 1928, immediately benefiting from the president-elect's assassination by a fanatic Catholic in July before he could take office. This event, rather than any law or court ruling, established that the revolution's motto of "no reelection" meant never, not just immediately. Under Calles's leadership and in line with his pledge to transform Mexico from "a country of men to a country of laws," this ban was incorporated into the constitution, the presidential term was extended to six years, and the National Revolutionary Party (PNR) was created in 1928. Starting as a holding company with the surviving warlord *caudillos* and regional political bosses at its center, the PNR would take on a greater and more institutionalized role in regularizing presidential succession, in the process bringing sorely needed peace and stability. Calles was the senior survivor of the 1910 Revolution and the country's sole living ex-president as well as head of its instantly dominant political party. Thus he saw the Cristero revolt to its end and in December 1928 appointed Emílio Portes Gil (b. 1891) as provisional president, in his scheme of things a convenient figurehead. For the time being, Mexico would be run by Calles as First Chief, one in no hurry to give way to a president chosen by the people. (Although Calles looked forward to running the nation through a party under his tight personal control, his plans would soon go awry—as even the best laid plans often do.)

Argentina from Early Independence to Manipulated Elite Democracy

Having been almost as completely unlike Mexico as possible within the realm of Spanish colonization, Argentina gained its independence in a unique manner before setting out on a quest to achieve nation unification while the much larger and richer Mexico was staving off dismemberment and foreign occupation. Then, after 1870, Argentina would nearly completely remake its society through European immigration, absent from Mexico. While Mexico developed economically under the politically stifling Díaz dictatorship, Argentina would undergo a moderate form of substantial modernization led by the politically astute General Júlio Argentino Roca at the head of a unified political elite modeling themselves upon the British. Not surprisingly, the inflexibility of the Mexican political system led to its conflagration in revolution and protracted civil war, but Argentina's adaptability resulted in a rapid transition to stable democracy at the time of World War I.

Caudillo Rule and Unification

Compared to most of the rest of Spanish America and in stark contrast to Mexico's, Argentina's independence would come easily—although followed by much more turbulence than in Brazil. On the other hand, its becoming a nation would be prove more difficult, eluding the efforts of the founding fathers and being accomplished only by a subsequent generation. For the Creole merchants of Buenos Aires, finally free of colonial restraints on commerce, sought with considerable success to maintain their economic dominance over the interior, while it strove mightily to maintain the autonomy enjoyed since its original settlement by traveling down the river from what was to become Bolivia. In the area around Buenos Aires, the British strove to take advantage of the opportunities created by the Napoleonic Wars by attempting invasions in 1806 and 1807. These were repulsed by local militia under the command of French-born Santiago Linares—who, suspect because of his origins, was repaid by being overthrown in mid-1810 and promptly executed. Since this still provincial city had become the center of a viceroyalty only in 1776, before that being governed from distant Peru by extremely tenuous communications across the Andes and down through the Gran Chaco, the Spanish military presence was very weak and the Porteños, as Buenos Aires residents were known, had to shoulder the burden of re-pulsing the British largely on their own. This responsibility gave these Creoles, who had already deposed an incompetent viceroy, a sense of identity and capability.[26] As a consequence, Spanish rule was ended at the earliest date in Latin America: May 1810. This perhaps premature independence for a vast region with fewer than 600,000 in-habitants only ushered in a chaotic succession of juntas and "directors," generally with a fragile hold on the city and ephemeral control over any significant part of the interior. Although the best-remembered figure of these early years was José de San Martín (b. 1778), who had been serving as an officer in Spain, he did not govern, moving on instead with a 5,500-man army across the Andes to Chile in early 1817—never to return, dying in France in 1850.

By this point, following a rapid succession of ephemeral would-be rulers, Juan Martín de Pueyrredon had been named Supreme Director of the United Provinces of the Rio de la Plata. He moved its congress from an interior city to Buenos Aires be-fore being forced to resign in mid-1819, inaugurating a period of near anarchy. As governments came and went in a revolving door, the issue of federalism versus a uni-tary regime came to the fore with Bernardino Rivadavia (b. 1780) leading advocates of the latter, while some interior strongmen (provincial *caudillos*) allied with José Ger-vasio Artigas (b. 1764) across the La Plata estuary in Montevideo. Artigas would defeat the Spanish only to be defeated in turn by the Brazilians, who moved quickly after their independence to lay claim to the area Portugal had long coveted. By 1825 Riva-davia had forged a provisional national government, but opposition by Buenos Aires landowners opposed to his economic liberalism and modernizing policies led to its dissolution in mid-1827 in the context of war with Brazil over the area that would soon become Uruguay (and that had been in dispute between Spain and Portugal for most of the late eighteenth century). Order came, but at an extreme price, as in 1829 Juan Manuel de Rosas (b. 1793), a very wealthy and extremely well-connected landowner who had played no part in the independence struggles, was named the governor of Buenos Aires with extraordinary powers. A shrewd and ruthless *caudillo* who quickly became renowned for his courage and strength and feared for his cru-elty toward enemies, he ruled Buenos Aires with an iron hand and extended his sway over much of the interior through alliances with provincial strongmen formalized as the "Federal Pact." Cloaking himself as a federalist against Rivadavia's *unitários,* Rosas, riding the crest of successful desert and Indian campaigns, gained absolute power in Buenos Aires through an 1835 plebiscite. Reminiscent of some of Napoléon's, the announced results were an implausible 9,315 to 5.[27] The self-styled "Restorer of the Laws," known to his opponents as "Bloody Rosas," used a terrorist secret police, the Mazorca, to supplement his wily intelligence. Behind a slogan of "Death to the Vile, Filthy, Savage Unitários," he manipulated an Argentine Confederation in which his Buenos Aires government represented the other provinces in the fields of defense and foreign affairs. Between 1843 and 1851 Rosas kept his enemies penned up under siege in Montevideo. A rancher himself, he demonstrated considerable skill in maintaining alliances with provincial *caudillos* to prevent their ganging up against him until after midcentury.

Finally in 1851 *caudillo* governor Justo José de Urquiza (b. 1801) of Entre Rios province turned against Rosas and forged an uneasy alliance with the *unitários,* Brazil, and Uruguay, decisively defeating Rosas at Monte Caseros the following year. Thus Argentina had a durable *caudillo* autocrat deposed at about the same time as Santa Ana finally lost out at the other end of the region in Mexico. But instead of Juárez and the liberals aligned against European intervention as in Mexico, Argentina would see a series of elite leaders eventually bringing the metropolis and the interior—totaling close to 1.4 million inhabitants—together before heading toward a less authoritarian analogue to the Díaz regime. Argentina's constitution of 1853, with amendments to meet changing times, is still in effect today (after being temporarily replaced between 1949 and 1956). The struggle to unite the Buenos Aires region with the interior, this time under some form of democratic order, occupied the next decade and a half. Buenos Aires stayed out of the confederation formed in 1853, since the rather haughty Porteños did not want to share the revenues from their control of foreign trade, much less run the risk of being governed by people they considered inferior in both education and breeding. Under the leadership of General Bartolomé Mitre (b. 1821), they battled Urquiza. Having been exiled by Rosas in 1837, Mitre subsequently had fought in Uruguay and spent considerable time in Chile. Victory at the battle of Pavón in September 1861 ended the interior confederation and left Mitre, compared to his foes a veritable Renaissance man, in the driver's seat, so Buenos Aires gradually entered the nation with Mitre becoming Argentina's president in 1862.[28] Entrenched in power, he frequently used force against troublesome provincial *caudillos*. However, his effort to dominate the country's political life for a prolonged period failed, as the people considered Argentina's embarrassing participation as a junior partner in Brazil's war with Paraguay to be "his," not theirs, and he had to swallow the bitter pill of the 1868 election of his archrival, cosmopolitan intellectual Domingo Faustino Sarmiento (b. 1811).

Born in the northwest interior, Sarmiento, whose motto was "to govern is to educate," was an acute critic of provincial "barbarism." His book *Facundo: Life in the Argentine Republic in the Days of the Tyrants: Civilization and Barbarism*, published in 1845, was based on Facundo Quiroga, provincial *caudillo* of La Rioja province (until 1834). Sarmiento perpetuated the Porteños' sense of superiority and provided a rationale for his stress on modernization and Europeanization.[29] When he came to office, Argentina had a population of 1.8 million, of whom 500,000 lived in Buenos Aires province, with almost 180,000 in the city itself. British investment was flowing in to build railroads across the fertile pampas, and—with government encouragement—immigrants from Italy and Spain were arriving in significant numbers. (Indeed, by

1869 already three-fourths of males between age sixteen and sixty had been born elsewhere.) A golden era for Argentina was on the horizon.[30]

Unification to Roca's Elite "Democracy"

Argentina entered this period in a situation of uneasy semistability, being governed by Sarmiento, with his predecessor, Mitre, as his archrival. Successful in having Nicolás Avellaneda, his education minister, elected to succeed him in 1874, Sarmiento had to join the new chief executive in defeating a revolt led by Mitre, who fervently aspired to return to the presidency. This campaign elevated young General Júlio Argentino Roca to national prominence. Then, in 1880, Argentina, at this point a country with a population of about 1.8 to 2.4 million (the problem of estimating the number of Indians and keeping up with the influx of immigrants preventing precision), gained a new dominant figure in the person of Roca. Well aware of how Rosas had risen to power a generation before, Roca had worked his way up through the army to become a very young war minister, and in the late 1870s he had defeated both the Indians and the Buenos Aires province militia. His election inaugurated the epoch known as the Unicato, the centralization and concentration of power in terms of strengthening the federal government relative to the provinces and the president vis-à-vis the congress. Now the rapidly growing capital became a federal district, and the province was given a new capital thirty miles eastward at La Plata.

Roca's career was characterized by the kind of rapid advancement through military success that had marked the duke of Caxias in Brazil or Díaz in Mexico. (Indeed, it bore a striking parallel to Napoléon's earlier meteoric rise in France.) As a youth Roca's Unitário father had fought under José de San Martín in Chile and Peru. Júlio was born in 1843 as the middle of seven children in a relatively poor interior family. By age sixteen he was already an artillery officer under Urquiza in his unsuccessful battles against Mitre's forces. The outbreak of the War of the Triple Alliance in 1864 found him a captain and enabled the courageous young officer to rise to colonel by age twenty-eight. Helping Avellanedo defeat Mitre's rebellion in 1874 made him a general at thirty-one. Having married into a rich Córdoba family, Roca became war and navy minister in 1877 and a national hero through his desert campaign against the Indians in 1878–1879. Glorified as the Conquest of the Wilderness, this campaign allowed ranching to move south and west, leaving the rich soil of the pampas for grain, particularly wheat. Roca skillfully used this springboard to overcome Porteño opposition as the presidential candidate of the League of Governors, a loose coalition of interior caudillos seeking a president who would not be unduly beholden to their Porteño rivals. When taking office in October 1880, he was only three months past his thirty-seventh birthday. At this point a crucial bargain was made between the pampean landowners and their unruly interior counterparts, who for a share of the Buenos Aires customs revenues agreed to end their provincial *caudillo* pattern of disruptive uprisings.[31]

Roca saw the cohesive pampean elite, organized into the Argentine Rural Society (SRA) in 1866, become the backbone of the National Autonomist Party (PAN) after its formation in 1874. Controlling a productive and profitable agro-export economy, this elite—based on a concentration of landowning dating back to the Rosas era and further stimulated under Sarmiento—accumulated capital in local and foreign currency. As viewed by a modern scholar, this was "a landowning elite that was sufficiently homogeneous in economic activity and geographical concentration to allow it to constitute a national state as opposed to a set of regional fiefdoms."[32] Hence, the underlying situation was very different in Argentina from that in either Brazil or Mexico, since Brazil, given its vast area and varied regions, could not form a centralized dominant political party, whereas Mexico was under an entrenched dictator with a network of ties to regional bosses who needed no modern electoral machine. In the closing years of the nineteenth century, Argentina was run by

> a fluid, loosely organized clique of notables that chose its candidates through informal negotiation and settled disputes over credit and railway access through backroom deals called *acuerdos*. Having settled these internal conflicts, the PAN leaders doctored voting lists, bought votes, and used intimidation (taking advantage of the absence of a secret ballot) to undermine candidates running under ephemeral opposition labels.[33]

After having governed firmly and with authority during his six-year term, Roca gave way to Miguel Juárez Celman, his brother-in-law, who encountered a serious economic crisis and was faced with an attempted rebellion in the face of his institutionalization of electoral fraud before leaving office in 1890. Serving out the end of his term, Vice President Carlos Pellegrini managed to straighten out the problems of the Bank of the Argentine Nation and get the country on the road to economic recovery. Luis Saénz Peña then occupied the presidency from 1892 until 1895, when he was replaced by Vice President José E. Uriburu. By this time heavy Italian immigration—half the region's total—and substantial British infrastructure investment, the underpinnings of sustained economic growth of over 5 percent a year, were converting Argentina into Latin America's most economically developed country. Elected for a second time to the presidency in 1898, nearly two decades after his original rise to power, Roca would still be in his prime when passing the presidency to his friend Manuel Quintana in 1904. Yet pressures for political change were bubbling up through the apparently firm surface.

By 1890 urban modernizing elements led by Leandro Além (b. 1842) had founded the Radical Civic Union (UCR) to pursue reforms through the electoral process. Originating as a student movement in 1889, the UCR was joined the following year by dissident elements of the pampean elite behind Mitre, a man who had never been satisfied by any presidency other than his own back in 1862–1868. Faced with the barrier of electoral manipulation and fraud under the conservative civilian presidents, the radicals attempted coups in 1890 and 1893. Although failing at both the ballot box and the barricades for more than two decades, they would triumph in the long run. The Argentine Socialist Party (PS), founded by Juan B. Justo in 1894, but dropping the limiting words *international* and *workers* from its name the next year, encountered far less success. Competing with the anarchists for influence over the immigrant urban workers already politically socialized in Europe, the socialists would be the losers until well after the turn of the century, then face new competition from the communists. Headway for the radicals and illusions of progress for the socialists would have to wait until after Roca's death in 1914 left both the nation and the military without a strong hand at the helm.[34] In sharp contrast to Díaz, Roca had worked through parties and elections to increase the capabilities of the political system (the true measure of political development), not to function as the irreplaceable autocratic executive.

The False Dawn of Democracy

Turning the presidency over to his friend Manuel Quintana in 1904, Roca retired to the status of the country's most revered personage. Roca's 1914 demise left the nation and the military without a strong hand at the helm, but he left behind a positive heritage of economic development possessing sufficient momentum to carry on under lesser successors. Courtesy of the Roca era, by the end of the first decade of the twentieth century Argentina was the world's ninth leading nation with respect to foreign trade, but with three-fourths of its businesses owned by foreigners—overwhelmingly British. Its population of 3.9 million in 1895 had doubled by 1913, with almost half at that point immigrants or their children—predominantly from Italy—and enjoyed a level of living higher than that of the Swedes or the Swiss. A country that had had only 1.8 million inhabitants in 1869 experienced net immigration of over 2.8 million between 1880 and 1905, and the flood continued. Buenos Aires grew five times over between 1880 and 1914 to become a world-scale metropolitan center of 1.6 million. The railroad network fanning out from it across the rich soils of the pampas had burgeoned from only 2,400 miles in 1880 to 22,000 miles by the outbreak of World War I.[35]

The *estanciero* ruling class had responded positively to the opportunities provided by international markets from 1910 through World War I. Commercial agriculture adopted the latest methods and technology, diversified, and grew rapidly. By 1913 grain and meat made up 90 percent of exports, with 85 percent going to western Europe, chiefly Great Britain. In the process of this sustained economic development society became more complex, as new interests emerged to challenge the hegemonic leadership the pampean producers had consolidated over the regional bourgeoisies and society in general. These *estancieros* and their merchant and banking allies had developed a flexible network of oligarchic state institutions that afforded the means for coopting opposition elements through incorporation into the system.[36] For the political processes of the post-Roca era funneled socioeconomic conflicts into the political arena by means of carefully channeled participation and representation within the oligarchic state. Those in power consciously decided to keep politics in a struggle within a bureaucratic political class as preferable to the alternative of a pattern of revolt and repression that would leave a increasingly unreliable military, whose officer ranks were rapidly filling with descendants of recent Italian immigrants, in the position of arbiter of national destiny.

Although the radicals' 1890 revolt had failed to overturn the system, it had combined with a severe financial crisis to bring about the resignation of President Júarez Celman. The radicals' second resort to force in 1893 encountered more sympathy from junior officers, and the third UCR revolt in 1905 appeared to generate significantly broader support.[37] In this context Argentina's first democratization began in

1910 with the elevation of Roque Saénz Peña (b. 1851) to the presidency. This "Tory reformer" came to power as the result of a split within conservative ranks involving supporters of ex-presidents Roca and Carlos Pellegrini that saw the PAN disintegrate in 1909—a year marked by a bloody week of class conflict in Buenos Aires that left a dozen dead and four score injured—into a multitude of conservative provincial parties. Moderate conservatives turned reformist in fear that accelerated social mobilization could not be contained within the existing political institutions. Thus, in a strong legislative position, since the radicals had boycotted the elections, in 1912 Saénz Peña pushed through the congress a law providing for a secret ballot and expanding the electorate to include all males over eighteen, including even immigrants who had completed military service obligations. This law also guaranteed the second-place party in each province one-third of the province's congressional seats. Glancing over their shoulders at Mexico and Brazil, and looking ahead to the challenge to the socioeconomic order posed by the emerging urban working class, Saénz Peña and his followers saw the middle-class radicals as a potential ally against the masses and the emergent socialists. To some degree they may have misinterpreted indifference toward politics as a British type of respect for the elites. In any case, the 1912–1916 period saw a sudden adjustment of the political system to a half century of sustained social change. Federal supervision of the 1914 congressional elections provided a trial run for fair voting and honest ballot counting. With most UCR leaders being dissident oligarchs, moderate conservatives could contemplate a radical victory much as British conservatives had proved able to live with liberal wins in 1911. Moreover, when the dust settled after the 1916 balloting, conservatives still controlled the senate and eleven of fourteen provinces—despite the fact that the UCR had received 46 percent of the national vote and the PS 9 percent. Still, by making it much harder for conservative parties to win elections, the 1912 reforms made them less attractive vehicles for the landowners' political activities and fed the traditionally privileged political elite's aspirations for almost any kind of return to the good old days of "dependable" electoral outcomes rather than continue to witness the ascent to political office of new groups espousing policies inimical to their conservative ardor for maintaining the status quo.[38]

New president Hipólito Yrigoyen was a far different kind of leader from Roca. Born in 1853, only a few months after the battle of Caseros had toppled Rosas from power, Yrigoyen was the son of an impoverished French Basque immigrant. As a young lawyer in the early years of the Roca era, he had been a police supervisor before opting for a career as a teachers' college professor. Although several of his romances produced children, Yrigoyen never married, becoming something of a political Jesuit, devoting his very considerable talents and energies to politics—where he excelled in intrigue and behind-the-scenes wheeling and dealing. The 1896 suicide of his uncle and rival, Leandro Além, opened the way for Yrigoyen to emerge as uncontested leader of the UCR, and he carefully honed his leadership skills in the two decades before being elected president. A compulsive micromanager, he couldn't delegate authority and hesitated to give the congress any significant autonomy. This taciturn and at times enigmatic individual presented radicalism as a cause, if not a crusade, with opponents being characterized as evil and enemies of the nation. Initially Yrigoyen was more amenable to labor's demands than previous presidents, often taking an evenhanded approach to worker-employer conflicts and settling strikes with significant concessions.[39]

Although Yrigoyen used his authority to intervene in the provinces frequently and with gusto, it was only under heavy military pressure that he reluctantly agreed to repress the violent January 1919 metal workers' strike in Buenos Aires, an event stimulated, in part, by the recent Bolshevik revolution in Russia. The legacy of this "tragic week," in which at least 750 died, would hang heavy over Argentina's political life and greatly inhibit working-class support for the radicals. (In this respect, it created the opportunity for Juan Domingo Perón's rise to the political domination of Argentine labor.) Among the accomplishments of his administration were the establishment of an agency to develop the substantial oil deposits discovered in 1907, a land reform program involving nearly 20 million acres (mostly on the frontier), and a landmark university reform. Unfortunately, Yrigoyen—like his contemporaries in Brazil and Mexico—was too traditional to perceive the potential of political parties as vehicles for incorporating new elements into politics. Hence the stage was set for a situation by the 1940s in which "Argentina's least cohesive and least-organized social class became the one most fully incorporated into party politics, whereas its most cohesive and best-organized social classes were the least fully incorporated into party politics."[40]

Constitutionally limited to one term at a time, Yrigoyen gave way in 1922 to fellow radical Marcelo Torcuato de Alvear (b. 1868), a member of the Argentine Rural Society (SRA; bailiwick of the country's agricultural interests). Not wanting a pro-Yrigoyen general or a civilian to fill the critical post of war minister, he tapped Colonel Agustín Justo for the job.[41] Selection of this anti-Yrigoyen officer, the son of an ally of ex-chief executive Mitre, positioned him for a political rise reminiscent of, albeit less spectacular than, that of Roca in the 1880s. (At this juncture the *tenentes* had just staged their protest revolt in Brazil, and Mexico's professional military had been displaced by the generation of revolutionary generals that would produce the country's presidents down through World War II.) By midterm Alvear's supporters were shifting to the right, often voting in the congress with the conservatives and ending efforts to incorporate workers into party politics through the UCR. Indeed, in 1926 the powerful railroad workers' union joined municipal workers to form the Argentine Workers' Confederation (COA) as an independent political force. By this time Yrigoyen's supporters were actively hamstringing the government. During Alvear's competent but uninspiring administration (much as in 1979–1980 backers of the late Edward Kennedy would hamper president Jimmy Carter in hopes of replacing him as the Democratic nominee with their paladin), Yrigoyen deeply split the party by insisting upon returning to the presidency at age seventy-six. The aging, egoistic radical leader, austere and mysterious rather than a spellbinder, whose support now included a larger lower-middle-class component and even some moderate elements of skilled labor, was successful in this bid. On April 1 he received 839,000 votes, to 414,000 for his chief rival, selected by Alvear and tacitly backed by the conservatives.

In accomplishing this personal electoral triumph Yrigoyen created a fatal division of the party between his followers and partisans of Alvear, who wore the name "antipersonalists" as a badge of honor and would not reconcile with their rivals for over a half century (finally doing so in the 1983 elections only after decades of political turmoil and national trauma). At first, affairs progressed normally, but when the international economic crisis began to swamp the country, this representative of a fading generation had no rabbits to pull out of his top hat to salvage the situation of Argentina's hypersensitive economy. He intervened actively in interior states prior to the March 1930 congressional elections, but still his UCR would be easily overthrown on September 6, 1930. By this time the UCR leadership had become heavily middle class instead of dissident aristocrats, and as the party consolidated its electoral majority, it came to be viewed as a major threat by the country's conservative forces and their military allies. Indeed, the armed forces were so alienated that archrivals Uriburu and Justo cooperated in Yrigoyen's peaceful ouster.[42] (Clearly his nonviolent expulsion from power contrasted sharply with contemporary events in Brazil, bearing a much greater similarity to the overthrow of Pedro II in Brazil a generation earlier.)

Outstanding in many ways as a leader, but flawed in his sense of destiny, which resulted in believing himself irreplaceable, Yrigoyen was favored by having no major political figure with whom to share the Latin American spotlight. José Batlle y Ordóñez in Uruguay had far too small a stage, while many of Chilean Arturo Allesandri's best years were after 1930. Getúlio Vargas burst on the scene just as Yrigoyen exited it, and Mexico's Lázaro Cárdenas emerged from obscurity only at mid decade. Yrigoyen's bad luck was to be in his late seventies during his second term in office and to have to face the onset of the Great Depression. Still, this first, perhaps in a basic structural sense premature, democratization of Argentina was extremely significant not only for that country, but for Latin America more generally in that it demonstrated that one of the region's countries could achieve a degree of democracy arguably equal to that of the United States and ahead of or equal to that of all but the most advanced European nations.

At that time Brazil was still encapsulated in an oligarchic republic rooted in elite accommodations and electoral fraud. It would break out of this pattern only through revolution and a populist authoritarian regime headed by a personalist, albeit paternalistic, strongman. For its part, Mexico took the revolutionary road in 1910 and found itself mired in civil war through the 1920s. In Colombia the conservatives were entrenched in power, enjoying the fruits of victory in the bloody struggle at the end of the century. Chile, like Argentina, would attempt the reformist road a few years later but fall into military dictatorship by 1927, and Peru was to experience continued instability and Venezuela suffocating stability under a *caudillo* dictator. Hence Argentina's peaceful installation of a middle-class democracy at the time of World War I justifiably merited close attention, as did this noble experiment's abrupt collapse in the face of the global economic crisis in 1930.

In the context of the times, this breakdown of an extraordinarily early democracy was not an aberration, and what ensued was much more in line with the rest of the region. But the path Argentina would follow out of the Great Depression would prove much more difficult to understand, generating what for the following decade would perplex political scientists as the "Argentine Paradox." To comprehend the nature of this exceptionalism, it is first necessary to broaden our comparative scope to include other Hispanic-heritage South American nations.

Notes

1. First-rate histories of Mexico include Michael C. Meyer and William H. Beezley, eds., *The Oxford History of Mexico* (New York: Oxford University Press, 2000), and Colin M. MacLachan, *Spain's Empire in the New World* (Berkeley and Los Angeles: University of California Press, 1991).

2. Enrique Krauze, *Mexico, Biography of Power: A History of Modern Mexico, 1810–1996* (New York: HarperCollins, 1997), pp. 91–102, treats Hidalgo's preeminence.

3. Ibid., pp. 103–111, covers Moreles's revolutionary enterprise.

4. Ibid., pp. 121–129, treats this monarchical interlude.

5. Ibid., pp. 135–158, recounts the ins and outs of the Santa Ana era. Paul H. Lewis, *Authoritarian Regimes in Latin America: Dictators, Despots, and Tyrants* (Lanham, MD: Rowman & Littlefield, 2006), pp. 19–21, captures the essence of his political style.

6. Krauze, *Mexico,* p. 142.

7. Ibid., pp. 159–172, 192–204, deals with Juárez's presidencies.

8. Ibid., pp. 173–191, covers Maximilian's ill-fated rule.

9. For overviews of the Díaz period, see Michael C. Meyer, William L. Sherman, and Susan M. Deeds, *The Course of Mexican History* (New York: Oxford University Press, 2002), Chapters 26–30.

10. Krauze, *Mexico,* pp. 205–237, covers the Díaz era.

11. Roderic Ai Camp, *Politics in Mexico: The Democratic Transformation,* 4th ed. (New York: Oxford University Press, 2003), p. 35.

12. Lewis, *Authoritarian Regimes,* p. 55.

13. Ibid., p. 57.

14. Camp, *Politics,* p. 39.

15. Lewis, *Authoritarian Regimes,* p. 59.

16. Camp, *Politics,* pp. 39–40.

17. Rodney D. Anderson, *Outcasts in Their Own Land: Mexican Industrial Workers, 1906–1911* (DeKalb: Northern Illinois University Press, 1976), p. 243.

18. Krause, *Mexico,* pp. 245–273, deals with Madero and the revolution, as does Meyer et al., *Course of Mexican History,* Chapters 31, 32.

19. Robert E. Quirk, *The Mexican Revolution: 1914–1915* (New York: Norton, 1970), provides perceptive analysis. For detail see Alan Knight, *The Mexican Revolution,* 2 vols. (Lincoln: University of Nebraska Press, 1990). Also useful is Peter H. Smith, *Labyrinths of Power: Political Recruitment in Twentieth Century Mexico* (Princeton, NJ: Princeton University Press, 1979). Zapata is discussed in Krauze, *Mexico,* pp. 274–304, as well as in John Womack Jr., *Zapata and the Mexican Revolution* (New York: Knopf, 1969).

20. Krauze, *Mexico,* p. 344; the Carranza period is covered in pp. 334–373.

21. Ibid., pp. 305–333, deals with events involving Villa.

22. See Charles C. Cumberland, *The Mexican Revolution: The Constitutional Years* (Austin: University of Texas Press, 1972).

23. Krauze, *Mexico,* pp. 374–403, covers the Obregón era.

24. Ibid., pp. 404–437, deals with events during the period of Calles's domination.

25. On the religious conflict, see David C. Baily, *Viva Cristo Rey! The Cristero Revolt and the Church-State Conflict in Mexico* (Austin: University of Texas Press, 1974), and Robert E. Quirk, *The Mexican Revolution and the Catholic Church, 1910–1929* (Bloomington: Indiana University Press, 1973).

26. A standard historical survey is James Scobie, *Argentina: A City and a Nation,* 2nd ed. (New York: Oxford University Press, 1971).

27. See John Lynch, *Argentine Caudillo: Juan Manuel de Rosas* (Wilmington, DE: Scholarly Resources, 2001). Lewis, *Authoritarian Regimes*, pp. 18–19, presents a vivid sketch.

28. Ibid., pp. 88–89, provides an insightful sketch of Mitre.

29. Consult Ariel de la Fuente, *Children of Facundo: Caudillo and Gaucho Insurgency During the Argentine State-Formation Process (La Rioja, 1853–70)* (Durham, NC: Duke University Press, 2000).

30. Very useful is Fernando López Alves, *State Formation and Democracy in Latin America, 1810–1900* (Durham, NC: Duke University Press, 2002).

31. See James W. McGuire, *Peronism Without Peron: Unions, Parties, and Democracy in Argentina* (Stanford, CA: Stanford University Press, 1997), p. 30.

32. Ibid., p. 32. McGuire goes on to argue persuasively that because of this flawed foundation, Argentina went on to a series of incumbent-party hegemonies, including that of the PAN until its fragmentation in 1909, that of the Radicales from 1916 to 1930, and that of Peronism after 1946.

33. Ibid.

34. Consult David Rock, *Politics in Argentina, 1890–1930: The Rise and Fall of Radicals* (New York: Columbia University Press, 1975), and Karen L. Remmer, *Party Competition in Argentina and Chile: Political Recruitment and Public Policy, 1890–1930* (Lincoln: University of Nebraska Press, 1984).

35. See Rock, *Politics in Argentina*, as well as David Rock, *Argentina, 1516–1987: From Spanish Colonization to Alfonsín* (Berkeley: University of California Press, 1987), and Luis Alberto Romero, *A History of Argentina in the Twentieth Century* (University Station: Pennsylvania University Press, 2002).

36. Consult Paul H. Lewis, *The Crisis of Argentine Capitalism* (Chapel Hill: University of North Carolina Press, 1990), and William C. Smith, *Authoritarianism and the Crisis of the Argentine Political Economy* (Stanford, CA: Stanford University Press, 1989).

37. See Peter G. Snow, *Argentine Radicalism: The History and Doctrine of the Radical Civic Union* (Iowa City: University of Iowa Press, 1965), and Rock, *Politics in Argentina*.

38. See Douglas Madsen and Peter G. Snow, *The Charismatic Bond: Political Behavior in Time of Crisis* (Cambridge: Harvard University Press, 1991), p. 41.

39. McGuire, *Peronism Without Perón*, pp. 37–44.

40. Ibid., p. 44.

41. Consult Robert A. Potash, *The Army and Politics in Argentina*, Vol. 1, *1928–1945: Yrigoyen to Perón* (Sanford, CA: Stanford University Press, 1969), pp. 18–22.

42. Ibid., pp. 42–57.

4

Colombia, Peru, Venezuela, and Chile

Independence to 1930

The paths to national consolidation and political development for northern and western South America have been both distinct and diverse—even though their colonial experiences contained basic similarities and there were commonalities in their gaining independence. (In these respects, they come closer to the experience of Mexico than to that of either Brazil or Argentina.) Not surprisingly, each of the countries in these two regions (Colombia, Peru, Venezuela, and Chile) ended up the first century of national life in different circumstances from those of any of the others. Colombia would find its way via civil war to Conservative Party hegemony. Peru, like Mexico a major pole of Spanish colonial rule, would focus its efforts on finding an effective leader, eventually passing through a highly personalist regime that would leave the country, unlike Mexico or Argentina, stalled halfway along the road to modernity in a highly elitist "aristocratic republic." By 1930, however, it would have enjoyed a substantially modernizing regime under a unique autocratic populist. For its part, Chile, the smallest of the four countries, and formerly an appendage of Peru, demonstrated considerable skill and no little intelligence in arriving at its "parliamentary republic" by 1900, over the next three decades moving on to effective political incorporation of its middle class. At the opposite extreme, the same could not be said for Venezuela, which, having as a colony been on the fringe of important developments, failed to move beyond *caudillo* dictatorship—remaining mired at that stage even after the advent of substantial oil revenues, as the rather evil autocratic genius of Juan Vicente Gómez used them to establish militarism.

Colombia: From Bolívar's Dream to a Stable Republic

As in Mexico, reverses and frustration marked the early stages of the independence struggle in upper South America. Francisco Miranda, radicalized during a stint of army service in Spain in the 1770s, launched an 1806 invasion of Venezuela at the head of a small group of foreign volunteers. This Quixotic venture failed to find support: Although the local Creoles wanted an expansion of free trade to benefit their plantation economy, with the very recent events in Haiti very much in mind they feared the threat to their power that might result from removal of Spanish control. Hence Miranda's initial venture was easily crushed. In the vast Spanish viceroyalty of New Granada a strong loyalist faction in the capital, Bogotá, did not prevent a junta in coastal Cartagena from declaring independence in 1809. A clique of patrician Creoles who did not want full independence ousted the viceroy and proclaimed social and economic reforms in 1810. In March 1811 a "Republic of Cundinamarca" was proclaimed in Bogotá but could not withstand royalist/loyalist forces and would fall to Spanish troops by 1815.

Meanwhile, Miranda's second attempt to mount a revolution via Venezuela at the end of 1810 had resulted in his capture in mid-1812 and subsequent death in a Spanish prison. Assuming his mantle, Simón Bolívar (b. 1783)—scion of a wealthy cacao-growing family—briefly established himself in power in Venezuela in 1813 and captured Bogotá at the end of 1814. A few months later a royalist army of 10,000 men landed in Venezuela and in little over a year had retaken Bogotá.[1] The struggle heated up with Bolívar's return to Venezuela from his Jamaican exile at the end of 1816. In a little more than a year the man who went down in history as "The Liberator" had forged an alliance with José Antonio Paéz (b. 1790) and his *llanero* ("cowboy") cavalry. Aware of the need to strike Spanish royalist authority at its heart, Bolívar marched toward Bogotá, declaring the entire region independent in December 1819 at a congress he had convened at Angostura. There he was named president of Gran Colombia, embracing today's Colombia, Venezuela, Ecuador, and Panama. The trick, as had been the case of the United States after the Declaration of Independence in July 1776, was to make this assertion into a permanent fact through force of arms—but the French were no longer in a position to pull their revolutionary chestnuts out of the fire (but fortunately for these audacious patriots, Spanish military might was not as formidable as the forces George Washington and his comrades in arms had faced in 1776–1783).

Having won a major victory at Boyaca in August 1817 on the way to the capital (where the forces numbered only 3,000 a side), Bolívar consolidated his grip by triumphing again back at Carabobo in Venezuela in mid-1821. Leaving his vice president, Francisco de Paula Santander (b. 1792), in Bogotá, he moved west into Ecuador, where he had previously sent Antonio José de Sucre Alcalá (b. 1795) to support Guayaquil-based independence forces. Victory at Pichincha, near Quito, on May 24, 1822, sealed the independence of the northern portion of the Viceroyalty of Peru and paved the way for a final offensive against the remaining loyalist stronghold. Bolívar's forces triumphed at Junin in August 1824 and at Ayachucho in December. Troops under Sucre moved on to Upper Peru, which would constitute itself as Bolivia in August 1825, while in late 1826 Bolívar would leave Lima to return to Bogotá to face problems with Santander as well as with José Antonio Paéz in Venezuela (suspending many of Santander's liberal reforms).[2] In 1830 Bolívar's dream of unity for the northern tier of South America came tumbling down, burying this great historical figure in the process.[3] In addition to personal ambitions and regional rivalries, which all but doomed it from the start, Gran Colombia was plagued by very poor transportation and communications, which played into the hands of those on whom Bolívar—sitting isolated in high-altitude Bogotá—counted to do his bidding in the peripheral areas. Even in the capital, many of the local elite who remembered their former privileged access to viceroyal authorities viewed the Liberator as a Venezuelan outsider. Resigning in despair, Bolívar died on the arduous journey to the coast on his way out of the country that had proved so ungrateful. Freed from Bolívar's shadow, Santander, a lawyer from near the Venezuelan border, emerged as the dominant figure, holding the presidency of Nueva Granada, a name assumed to indicate primacy over all the former viceroyalty, as a constitution was drafted in 1832, and he was granted a new four-year term the following year. In a bloody 1837 civil war a civilian, José Ignácio de Marques, won out over Santander's choice, General José María Obando. Surviving a revolt by elements seeking greater regional autonomy, he was succeeded in 1841 by General Pedro Alcantara Herrán. Following the adoption in 1843 of a constitution strengthening the executive, Herrán gave way in 1845 to yet another Bolivarian general—in this case his own father-in-law, Tomás Cipriano de Mosquera (b. 1798), an aristocrat from Popayán. A split in conservative ranks then let the liberals slip back in as the congress chose General José Hilario Lopez in 1849, ushering in a period of reform legislation in a country nearing a population of 2.4 million—double that at the time of the independence struggle.[4]

Colombia's two-party system was solidly in place, but this did not mean that intense political rivalry was confined to the ballot box. Indeed, both liberals and conservatives were loose coalitions of factions and *caudillos*. As insightfully portrayed by Lewis:

> The party leaders were those *caudillos* with the broadest networks of relatives, friends, and clients. Minor *caudillos* attached themselves to those leaders in the expectation of sharing the rewards of victory. Defeat or disappointment might cause them to change sides, however, so the inner logic of *caudillo* politics demanded that the chief *caudillo* "must continuously find new resources of wealth which can be distributed to his following, or he must attach resources which replenish themselves."[5]

Early on in other areas as well as Colombia the chief spoils were crown possessions and the property of royalists; then came the communal lands of Indians and church holdings; and finally, *caudillos* took from rival *caudillos* (and in some cases a particularly ambitious and able *caudillo* would grab power at the national level and use the spoils "to modernize his army, overwhelm his rivals, and impose the 'blessings' of orderly despotism"[6]). Because unity was nearly impossible to achieve in mountainous Colombia, from the beginning down to the present, the distinguishing feature of Colombian politics has been two vertically organized, elite-led parties retaining a monopoly on organized political life generation after generation. For over a century and a half, the liberals and conservatives retained the support of the vast majority of politically active Colombians, dooming all efforts to create new parties—successful in almost every other Latin American country—to failure. This phenomenon has also spared the country *caudillo* rule and has limited militarism (in terms of the political involvement of professional career officers) to only one four-year outbreak (1953–1957). With General Obando (b. 1795) in office by 1853, the deeply divided liberals fell victim to an 1854 coup by General José María Melo, whose effort to change the constitution to extend his term as well as increase executive powers paved the way for the selection as president of conservative civilian Mariano Ospina Rodríguez in 1857. By mid-1861 the liberals had won out in an armed struggle, returning General Tomás Mosquera to power, enacting anticlerical measures, and adopting an extreme form of federalism that made the country essentially a confederation. Indeed, the 1863 Rionegro constitution established a system closer to that found wanting by the United States in its early days—federal in name, but confederal in substance. Sovereignty resided in the federated states, and each had its own army, with the central government handling foreign relations and having some powers in the case of foreign wars.[7]

After being reelected once again in 1866, Mosquera fell victim to a coup in May 1867. Subsequently the liberals were in power until 1880, moving against the Catholic Church—at that point by far the country's leading landowner. For the liberals held that the church was a retrograde force obstructing progress, not the glue holding the social order together as maintained by the conservatives. Civil wars and violence were rampant, with over fifty insurrections—many directed at the state administrations, which carried on most governmental activities. In 1879 dissident liberal Rafael Nuñez Moledo (b. 1825)—a positivist moving toward the right whose coup attempt had been defeated in 1877—allied with conservatives in a coalition known as the National Party (PN), promising "Regeneration." President in 1880–1882 and reelected in 1884, Nuñez ran the country, which was nearing 3 million inhabitants, until his death a decade later. His lasting contributions included shaping the 1886 unitary constitution that remained in force for over a century, establishing a strong position for the Catholic Church through a concordat with the Vatican in 1887, founding a national bank, and enacting a protective tariff. Elected to a third term in 1892, he died in office two years later. Economically the country still lacked a consistent foreign exchange earner, a vacuum increasingly filled after the barren 1870s by coffee as Colombia became a major competitor with dominant Brazil.

As time went on, power within the coalition shifted into conservative hands, and the near-hegemonic conservatives absorbed the National Party. From the mid to late 1890s Miguel Antonio Caro, author of much of the 1886 constitution, held the presidency. Elections were rigged not only to deny liberals a chance at the presidency, but also to keep them out of congress, until by 1896 General Rafael Uribe Uribe was the sole liberal in either house of congress. Under such circumstances the liberals' resort to violence was logical, so in the last years of the century the country entered one of the bloodiest civil wars in Latin American experience—a vicious struggle that would last until 1902. Undoubtedly Colombia was the period's greatest backslider, a case of political decay rather than even stagnation, much less development. Hence, no country in Latin America, perhaps none in the world, entered the new century under as unfavorable circumstances as did Colombia. The bloody civil war begun in mid-1899 and running well into 1902 left the country prostrate. Commerce was in ruins and Colombian currency almost worthless. The one positive note on the political side was that extremist factions of both the victorious conservatives and defeated liberals bore the onus for having caused the disastrous conflict. Thus the moderates of each "political religion" realized that some degree of cooperation would be necessary to rebuild the devastated economy. Before reconstruction was under way, the country received another staggering body blow: the 1903 amputation of the strategic and economically vital province of Panama by the expansionist United States.[8]

Beginning the new century in the middle of warfare, a conservative faction hoping for peace talks overthrew aged president Manuel A. Sanclemente in 1900, but, elevated from the vice presidency, José Manuel Marroquín continued all-out warfare. Four years later, with the civil war over and Panama lost, the moderate conservative leadership realized that the country required a strong leader at this juncture, and in 1904 they elected General Rafael Reyes Prieto (b. 1850) president. An upper-class man from the provinces who admired Díaz and had more than a little of Argentina's Roca in his makeup, Reyes acted decisively and with self-assurance. In the name of reconciliation he forced the conservatives to accept minority liberal representation in the cabinet as well as the national legislature. Indeed, he replaced the existing bicameral congress with a national assembly made up of three representatives of each department (as Colombia's provinces are called), indirectly chosen by department officials whom he had appointed to office.

Following a protectionist trade policy to encourage the growth of domestic industries, and building a railroad from Bogotá to the sea, Reyes realized that obtaining foreign investment and expanding trade—especially the sale of Colombia's coffee—required normalized relations with the United States. Hence he negotiated a treaty that of necessity included recognizing the independence of the breakaway Panamanian republic. Of course this treaty met heavy public resistance, since Colombians quite naturally felt that they had been victimized by a shameless land grab by a rapacious pretender to regional hegemony. Indeed, the issue of ratification of the Thompson-Urrutia Treaty invigorated the until-then quiescent opposition, and Reyes suspended the congress.[9] Thus, in June 1909, an alliance of disaffected conservatives and liberals came together in the Republican Union (UR) and won a majority in the elections for a reestablished congress. Stunned by this setback, Reyes resigned and left the country. Under the presidency of Carlos E. Restrepo from 1910 to 1914, the Republican Union held together as conservative landowners and liberal merchants found common ground in advancing the export of coffee, which had become the country's leading agricultural product. As Paul Oquist explains with regard to this country, which by 1912 contained 5.1 million inhabitants, "The state was strengthened to accommodate Colombian society to capitalist socioeconomic structures, to accelerate integration into the world capitalist system, and to compensate for the decline of traditional mechanisms of social control."[10] Conservative José Vincente Concha (president 1914–1918) initiated the trend for administrations to become more partisanly conservative, but the principle of some liberal participation survived. (When men socialized under this regime reached maturity, memories of this experience would lead them to adopt coalition government as the way out of the horrendous experience of the 1948–1956 period.)

As Marco Fidel Suárez, the illegitimate son of a peasant girl, piloted the country through the post–World War I period, a group of young emerging upper-class leaders formed a group known as Los Nuevos ("the new ones") to consider what changes were called for in light of the loss of Panama (and the opening of the canal there under US control, with no special consideration for neighboring Colombia) and the growing importance of foreign capital. Advocating a more active role for the state in guiding Colombia's development, they would furnish important political leadership from the 1930s on. The 1920s were known as the "dance of the millions" for unprecedented public spending as $173 million was borrowed abroad and $25 million was belatedly paid by the United States as an indemnity for the kidnapping of the Panama Canal project (being the amount offered Colombia in the nonratified treaty prior to Panama's secession).[11] The decade got off to a bad start politically as President Suárez resigned in 1921 in the face of substantiated charges of financial improprieties. Following an interim chief executive, Pedro Nel Ospina (b. 1858 during the presidency of his father, Mariano Ospina Rodríguez) became president in August 1922 and, as had been the case with Reyes, emphasized transportation. He was followed in 1926 by Miguel Abadía Méndez.

Change began to come in the late 1920s as oil and bananas became significant new exports and gold dropped to less than 5 percent of export earnings. Coffee, however, remained supreme—accounting for 80 percent of export earnings: Production had doubled by 1921 from 1 million sacks in 1913 and would reach 3 million sacks by 1930. A protracted and violent strike of workers and the United Fruit Company banana plantation at Santa Marta on the Caribbean coast in 1928 provoked two opposite reactions. Most conservatives approved of the repressive action taken by the Méndez government, whereas progressive liberals took the strike as a wakeup call that it was time to consider the needs and demands of the working class. Debate mounted as the next presidential elections drew near.[12] If Colombia were to become a real democracy, it was time for a fully competitive election, which the liberals would stand a fair chance of winning.

Peru: Difficult Launching, Elite Republic, Finding a Strong Leader

The area that had been the core of Spain's Spanish American empire was most deeply affected by the postindependence power vacuum. Benefiting from colonial monopolies, and fearful of the type of social violence the late-eighteenth-century indigenous revolts had threatened, many Peruvian Creoles had not been anxious to break with Spain. Having been a royalist stronghold, with most of its elites tarnished as loyalists, Peru began its life without a national hero or patriotic force—and with its population reduced to not much more than 1.2 million. After Argentine San Martín's 1821 stint as "protector" had been cut short by royalist resurgence, in 1826–1827 Bolivian-born upper-class General Andrés Santa Cruz (b. 1792) headed the government left behind in Lima by Bolívar. He was followed in power by Ecuadorian General José de la Mar from 1827 to 1829—his ascendancy arranged by the congress without resort to elections. Aristocratic aspirant General Agustín Gamarra, a former royal officer who had switched sides and become leader of Lima's north-coast-based conservatives, then held the presidency in 1829–1833 and 1839–1841; Arequipa's southern-Andes-centered liberals, who had backed de la Mar, had briefly returned to power in 1833–1834 behind Luis de Orbegoso. For much of this period no government was in full control of the country as civil strife prevailed in many areas.[13]

Santa Cruz's case was the most prominent of repeated instances in which *mestizos* who had gained distinction in the independence wars would be pushed aside by the white elites. What made it exceptional was that Santa Cruz reacted energetically and effectively. He took control of Bolivia and in 1836, through military force, Santa Cruz forged a Peruvian-Bolivian confederation under his direction, which was only broken up in 1839 as a result of defeat by Chile in the First War of the Pacific. Instability became accentuated as Peruvian president Gamarra (b. 1785) was killed in battle attempting to reannex Bolivia. His death left General Manuel Ignácio Vivanco, with a mild penchant toward education and untangling government finances, as dictator until ousted by the new king of the political hill, middle-class *mestizo* war hero General Ramón Castilla (b. 1797), in 1844. At long last Peru had a long-term strongman, as Castilla, benefiting from rising export earnings from guano, held the presidency until 1851, leading to a Peruvian state dominated by the merchant elites and their planter allies. After the ouster of his successor, José Rufino Echenique (architect of a controversial and corruption-tainted debt consolidation), by an Arequipa-based revolt, Castilla came back to power from 1854 to 1862. Castilla astutely maintained a position midway between the liberals and the conservatives. (Long sensitive to prevailing political winds, he had fought in the Spanish army against San Martín and later under the Chilean flag against the Peru-Bolivia confederation.) The emancipation of 25,500 slaves brought the number of free blacks to over 40,000.

By Castilla's time Peru had almost doubled its population from an independence day 1.2 million to near 2.3 million and had experienced a guano export boom of sufficient proportions to attract foreign investment, so Castilla could carry out limited modernization and a partial professionalization of the military. Unfortunately, his constructive work was followed by a decade of chaotic fraternal strife, leaving the country in disarray. Peru continued a complex political development replete with contradictions and partial disruptions that stopped short of clear ruptures—in part because of the lack of a single center dominating all regions. Hence the country would continue to traverse a course with almost as many ups and downs as the Andes themselves. It emerged from an unstable decade of crises in 1872 with enlightened coastal aristocrat Manuel Pardo y Lavalle (b. 1834) as its first full-term civilian president, but only after War Minister Tomás Gutiérrez ousted President José Balta. Soon both Balta and Gutiérrez were dead, the latter at the hands of an incensed Lima mob. Pardo, who survived a series of revolts fomented by Nicolás de Piérola, Balta's ambitious finance minister, was followed in 1876 by Manuel Prado—who found that, with a population reaching 2.7 million, the country was more complex than it had seemed. His assassination in 1878 opened the door for the wily and ambitious Piérola (b. 1839) to seize power. By this time the guano boom had ended, leaving the sugar-growing *hacienda* owners in the driver's seat. But railroad building, done chiefly for the mining sector, made possible livestock *haciendas*. Wool in the south became important (as oil subsequently would in the north). Intraelite conflict in the 1870s was intense.

Piérola's first stay in office was turned into a nightmare by another military defeat at the hands of Chile in the 1879–1883 Second War of the Pacific, a crushing setback that resulted in the humiliation of Chile's occupation of Lima in late 1881 and Piérola's subsequent ouster from office. The war also devastated much of commercial agriculture and seriously impaired mining output. In its aftermath Peru developed an array of export axes resulting in a more complicated structure of regional elites and masses separated into several strata. Sugar was produced in the sunnier and better-irrigated valleys of the north central coast, with cotton dominating in the less-watered valleys of the far north and the central coast. Wool in the south and rubber extraction in the east also increased in the 1890s. The large-scale sugar barons, often of immigrant origins and economically in ascension, became the backbone of the so-called oligarchy, with "plutocrats" with roots from before the Second War of the Pacific surviving on cotton as a declining element of the elite.

Resistance hero General Andrés Cáceres (b. 1833), who had carried on the struggle against Chile after the fall of Lima, had emerged by 1886 as the dominant post–Pacific War political figure, leaving the presidential office in 1890 to a friend, but retaking it in 1894. The next year the "civilianists," who had cooperated with his first administration, allied with Piérola and his newly founded Democratic Party (PD) to overthrow the personalist chief executive in a bloody civil war. Piérola was president until 1899, a fiery, but fundamentally conservative *caudillo* of a populist and provincial cast guiding the country into the inception of the twenty-five-year period known as the "aristocratic republic. This notable era saw suffrage severely restricted to literate adult males, a category that would reach nearly 15 percent of Peruvian men by the end of World War I. (Voting turnout in 1894 was a mere 4,500; a decade later it reached 147,000 of a population nearing 5 million.) With party agreements and partisan control of the electoral machinery largely predetermining the outcome of elections, as in most of the rest of the region, the cooperating elites grouped in the Civilist Party (PC) and the Democratic Party (PD) decided presidential succession in all but one instance during this quarter century.

In the first decade of the aristocratic republic and essentially down close to World War I, the basic modus vivendi among the dominant elite blocks was not seriously challenged. A liberal political economy benefited both the agro-exporters and the commercial interests of the coast, and sierra landlords retained effective local autonomy. Middle- and working-class voters were either clientelistically tied to the Civilists, a party dominated by agro-exporters, commercial interests, and the upper crust of the professions, or attracted to Piérola's Democrats. Traditional landowners could be found in either of these major parties or in the ranks of the Constitutionals and Constitutional Federalists. Both this high degree of elite consensus and the low level of central government revenue, still just half that attained during the previous period's guano boom, kept a larger role for the state at the margin of political discourse.

After 1904, during the first presidency of José Pardo y Barreda (b. 1864), son of ex-president Manuel Pardo, the alliance of the Civilists and the Constitutionalists began to lose control of the recently centralized electoral machinery. At the same time, emerging urban middle sectors started pressing for a more active government sensitive to their concerns and for a change in the system of congressional representation, which inordinately favored rural landowners. These issues were center stage in Argentina, about to become so in Mexico, and arousing concern in Brazil, but unique to Peru, a number of intellectuals were beginning to question openly the quasifeudal subjugation of the Indians. Although these pressures led to a splintering of the major parties and the emergence of new political movements, they did not cause a clear-cut realignment of the party system carried down from the preceding period.

Two governments undermined, but did not destroy, the aristocratic republic. Dissident Civilist president Augusto Leguía (b. 1863), taking power in 1908, favored urban middle-class groups and undercut his party's hegemony by decentralizing the electoral machinery. In 1912 this shrewd practitioner of the political arts threw his support to protopopulist Guillermo E. Billinghurst (b. 1851), who rode to victory on a massive mobilization of the Lima-area working class. Implementing policies favoring the urban middle and working classes, such as electoral reform and labor legislation, and using mob violence as a political resource, Billinghurst's brief and in some ways artificial equivalent of Argentina's about-to-occur middle-class democratic flourishing provoked outraged Peruvian elites to instigate a 1914 coup that cut short this laudatory but premature interlude as well as cost the idealistic president his life. Billinghurst failed to realize that Peru was far from being another Argentina—where the rise of the Radical Party to power would be the leading democratic development of the region. (Peruvian intellectuals would reluctantly try to come to grips with the essential differences between their Indian-majority country and European Argentina.)

Acting president Colonel Oscar Benevides (b. 1876) cobbled together support for the 1915 election of a unity candidate, ex-president José Pardo, who coasted through World War I on the illusionary prosperity of inflation, while mollifying the capital region's constituency, which had supported Billinghurst, by continuing there, although not in the rest of the country, progressive labor legislation. In 1919, in this partially transformed and still changing socioeconomic context, Leguía assembled a broad reformist coalition of the urban middle class, artisans, and workers to confront the diehard elements of the elite coalition that constituted the backbone of the "aristocratic republic." Refusing to be deprived of victory by electoral fraud, Leguía seized power. Acting in some ways like Yrigoyen and the radicals in Argentina, and foreshadowing to a limited extent what Getúlio Vargas would do in Brazil after 1930, during his eleven-year "encore" presidential tenure Leguía destroyed the Civilist Party. In place of this underpinning of the old order, he cultivated new political brokers in the provinces.[14]

Leguía's long return engagement as conductor of Peru's political life in the post–World War I era took place in a society significantly changed from that existing at the beginning of the century. The economic transformations were more complex than those in Brazil, Mexico, Argentina, and Colombia—if only because Peru lacked a single dominant economic focus. Coffee provided this focus for Colombia, and to a lesser extent Brazil, and for Argentina it was beef and wheat, the agro-pastoral dyad of the pampas. In Mexico's case the deciding political factor after 1910 was brute force on the battlefield, which temporarily relegated socioeconomic factors to the political sideline; besides, the economy was devastated by the near continuous warfare and the pre-1910 elites' having been displaced without yet being replaced. But contemporary political developments in Peru occurred in a context of substantial economic and social change. In the early decades of the twentieth century under the "aristocratic republic," Peru's economy was undergoing significant changes as well, leading to shifts in the power of elite sectors that would have a cumulative and, in the long run, profound impact upon national politics. Sugar, whose production had undergone rapid expansion in the mid-1890s, was overtaken by cotton as the country's leading export crop after 1910. Increased cotton production also fueled a growing textile industry in the Lima region. Copper replaced silver as the major mining export, the US-owned Cerro de Pasco Company becoming dominant by the 1920s. Wool was still significant in the south, rubber had dropped sharply, and oil was just beginning to be a factor. These economic trends were reflected in the social realm as sugar "barons," chiefly of immigrant origin, slowly became the core of the elite, bolstered by largely native-born cotton planters and commercial and financial interests tied to British investment. For sugar production was both large scale and rather highly mechanized, requiring access to foreign credit for viability. Mining as well as the plantation crops relied heavily on seasonal migrant labor, including former black slaves and Chinese coolies, as well as sierra Indians.

During this period the export of Peruvian products and the import of foreign capital and consumer goods became increasingly funneled through Lima and its adjacent port of Callao. Linked to British commercial capital, the financial and commercial sectors of the Peruvian "oligarchy," really a group of connected elites, were by early in the period concentrated in Lima, where they paid close attention to government activities. The capital was also home to the handful of Peruvian families that still owned small mines. Under protection afforded by a depreciating silver-based currency and tariffs imposed by a financially strapped government in the late 1890s, some agro-exporters, foreign firms, and immigrants began to invest in import-substitution manufacturing located in Lima. With this increase in commerce and industry, Lima began the growth that would elevate it to hegemony among Peru's urban centers, experiencing a population surge of nearly 30 percent between 1908 and 1920, from a modest 175,000 inhabitants to 225,000. After 1910 industrial growth slowed, and as inflation outpaced increases in import prices, tariff protection eroded, while the extremely successful performance of export sectors during World War I drew capital away from manufacturing. Although well-financed foreign factories survived, small immigrant entrepreneurs did not fare as well.

Not all socioeconomic developments leading to political changes were located in the capital region; others took place in the south. By the opening of the twentieth century descendants of local, English, Basque, and Catalonian wool merchants had become the core of a closely knit Arequipan elite. Extension of the southern railroad inland to Cuzco in 1907 opened new areas to the wool trade. *Haciendas* owned by interior landlords or acquired by the elite expanded at the expense of peasant communities, provoking a wave of localized rebellions. This usurpation of community land had largely stopped by the end of World War I, as the increasingly powerful urban middle class pressured the central government to be more sensitive to peasant protests. This shift in public policy gave rise to a realization that future profitability could be attained only through technological improvements like land enclosure, selective breeding, and improved pasture. This modernization was opposed by both resident *colonos,* who by tradition enjoyed the right to graze their own animals on *hacienda* land, and *comuneros,* who continued to graze surreptitiously on land they considered theirs by right. Efforts to modernize wool production bogged down by the 1920s, and for the moment alpaca exports remained more important than wool.

These changes in composition of the elite and relations among its components underlay politics for much of the period, although the emergence of a middle class enriched and complicated political life, especially as Peru moved through the 1920s. The electoral law of 1896 had replaced local caucuses with a centralized electoral system, shifting competition for control of the electoral machinery to the national level. Since suffrage was still limited to literate male citizens, the coast and the cities carried heavy weight in presidential elections. With regard to congressional elections, however, the rural regions were heavily overrepresented in both houses of the national legislature owing to quirks in the criteria for apportionment. Unlike Brazil, Mexico, Argentina, and Colombia, Peru was not a federal system, and provincial political elites were linked to competing factions at the center by a system of political brokers, rather than acting through governors.[15]

Leguía's eleven-year rule, carrying through the relatively favorable decade of the 1920s, was a lost opportunity for political development—as he was inclined to undermine and reorder traditional structures and processes, but not to replace them with new political institutions. Corruption, nepotism, and cronyism undermined the development of effective class and interest organizations, and he did not construct a new political party to replace those he had relegated to irrelevance. Hence, his personalist Democratic Reform Party (PDR) would not continue to be a significant factor once Leguía was himself off the political stage. Starting in a promising manner with an eight-hour day for factory workers, price controls on food and housing, legislation designed to protect indigenous communities, and broadening of workmen's compensation, Leguía moved toward the center-right when export prices fell in 1923.

The backbone of his constituency became the expanding government bureaucracy, the incipient industrial bourgeoisie, and the more commercially oriented landowners—with white-collar workers coopted by limited health and pension benefits not extended to the proletariat. Cognizant of the calculus of survival, Leguía split the navy from the purview of the war ministry and established a civil guard and a militarized republican guard, as well as an aviation corps under the navy minister. Peru's autocrat was a Yankee-phile who had started out as an agent for a US insurance company. Foreign experts were brought in not only as advisers, but to head new agencies requiring technical training and experience. In some ways reminiscent of Díaz in the 1890s, Leguía favored US capital over British capital, which had long ties to the Civilists, now his opponents. Seeking to resolve the lingering dispute with Standard Oil subsidiary International Petroleum Company (IPC)—which would have extremely deleterious effects in the 1960s—he granted it control of Peru's major oil field, low taxes, and exemption from royalties in return for a cash payment of $1 million and assistance in placing bonds in US capital markets. Leading to a short-term rise in oil production, this agreement was a future time bomb.[16]

The stability Leguía provided attracted foreign investment, reflected in an eruption of foreign debt from $12.4 million when he returned to power to $88.4 million by 1929—the date of his third consecutive election. In addition to expanding the government, the influx of financing allowed for the first major public works program since the guano boom. This program stimulated all industries related to construction, as well as extension of the railroad system and overdue modernization of Callao's port facilities. Five major coastal irrigation projects initiated the creation of a new group of middle-class farmers, while over 10,000 miles of roads and hundreds of bridges stimulated internal commerce. Tightened tax collection helped treble government revenues to nearly $100 million a year by the late 1920s, with expenditures pushing $80 million. The expanded role of the state under Leguía had been written into a new constitution in 1920—which borrowed heavily from that idealistic document framed by Mexico three years earlier, and as in Mexico, many of its advanced social provisions would wait another generation for implementation.

Not surprisingly, Lima grew by two-thirds under Leguía, beginning the 1930s at 375,000 including a sizable middle class. Although large factories were chiefly foreign-owned, individuals of recent immigrant origin predominated among the owners of smaller industrial establishments. Japanese Peruvians, descended from indentured servants, migrated to the cities and opened small commercial establishments or workshops, and Italians arriving in the 1920s moved into food processing and leatherworking. Leguía's policies made enemies of the agro-exporters, and his extension of governmental authority and his own political machine into the provinces alienated many traditional landlords. Concentration of urban improvement projects in the Lima area also aroused resentment in the interior. Hence, as unemployment and the consequent unrest rose in the wake of the late 1929 financial crash, an effort to overthrow the autocrat was inevitable. It would come in August 1930, but while not as severe a setback to political development as in Argentina, neither would it mark a step forward as in both Brazil and Colombia.

Venezuela: Caudillism Rampant

After declaring Venezuela's independence from Gran Colombia in 1830, José Antonio Paéz, a light-skinned *mestizo* lacking any formal education, but an able cavalry commander, launched a tradition of *caudillo* rule in this country of fewer than 800,000 inhabitants. Caudillism would persist there for over a century—longer than in almost any other place in Latin America. For seventeen years his conservatives kept their liberal rivals in check, as production of cacao, coffee, and hides recovered from the disruption occasioned by the armed struggles for independence. President from 1831 to 1835 and again from 1839 to 1843, Paéz hung like a shadow over the presidencies of José María Vargas (1835–1837) and Carlos Soublette (1837–1839 and 1843–1847). More similar to Mexico's Santa Ana than to Argentina's Rosas, albeit from far humbler beginnings, Paéz came back from his large estate in 1846 to head the army in a civil war, rebelling again in 1848.[17] By this time Antonio Leocádio Guzmán (b. 1801) had established the Liberal Party as a counterweight to the dominant landowners.

Following Paéz's next-to-last ouster, stability proved an elusive goal, and the politically dominant Monagas brothers, Generals José Tadeo (b. 1784; president 1847-1851 and 1855–1858) and José Gregorio (b. 1795; president 1851–1855), were faced with a protracted and extremely bloody armed conflict known as the Federal War between 1858 and 1863—during which 300,000 persons died in this sparsely populated country, which had managed to reach a population of 1.3 million from its preindependence 760,000. The liberals won the struggle only after they brought Paéz back from his New York City exile in 1861 and granted the old *caudillo* near-dictatorial powers, which he exercised only briefly. Of great importance for the future was the development of Guzmán's son, Antonio Guzmán Blanco (b. 1829), into a military leader of the liberal/federalist forces, resulting in a political career which would dominate the rest of the century.

Juan Cristosomo Falcón (b. 1820), a leader of the liberal/federalist side in the civil war, became president in 1863, with his vice president, wealthy financial expert Guzmán Blanco, running the country on a day-to-day basis. In 1868 José Tadeo Monagas, reincarnated as a conservative, returned via a coup for a last brief hold on the presidency before the new era dawned—as the younger Guzmán captured Caracas and seized power in mid-1870 and set out to crush the conservatives (and all other opposition). He would be the prototype for a new breed of liberal *caudillos* in the region. Coming to power by coup in mid-1870 as the country neared a population of 2 million, Guzmán Blanco was in many ways a Díaz-type developmentalist, building roads, railroads, aqueducts, port facilities, and telegraph lines. As a liberal in the mold of his father, one of the party's founders, he undercut the Catholic Church at every opportunity. Arising from the national elite, he had been a participant in the

Federal War and then served as President Falcón's successful finance minister (a post in which he amassed a personal fortune). Having been raised in Caracas, he had no regional base from which to combat local *caudillos,* but he convinced many of them to support his efforts to provide a stable environment for foreign investment in return for a share of the increased government revenues.[18]

Putting an associate in temporarily in 1877, Guzmán Blanco returned to the presidency in early 1879, a scenario he repeated in 1884–1886 with Joaquín Crespo (b. 1845) as the placeholder. During his eighteen years of dominating the country, Guzmán Blanco modernized the capital and upgraded the educational system. Infatuated to the point of near obsession with France and all things French, he spent his long 1877–1879 and 1884–1886 sabbaticals there. After two final years in power, he turned the presidency over to General Juan Pablo Rojas Paul, going into retirement when Rojas forcefully asserted his independence. Crespo seized power in 1892, gaining election two years later and serving until 1898. His handpicked successor could not withstand the onslaughts of the country's next *caudillo,* General Cipriano Castro from Táchira, who seized power in late 1899 at the cost of 3,000 lives. The forerunner of a series of dictatorial leaders from the Andean province of Táchira, Castro opted to consolidate power through development of a centrally controlled national army. Strong-arming the capital's bankers to obtain the requisite credits and raising commercial taxes, he entrusted construction of the army to his vice president, Juan Vicente Gómez (b. 1857). In a series of campaigns entailing some 12,000 deaths, Gómez crushed all would-be *caudillos.* The high-living Castro turned the government over to him in 1908 when going to Europe for medical care.

Gómez would never relinquish power, although entrusting the presidential office to close collaborators in 1915–1922 and 1929–1931, establishing a firm control that would last until his death twenty-seven years later in 1935. The political instability of the nineteenth century had prevented the emergence of an oligarchy based upon large landholdings, and Gómez maintained his power base, as had previous *caudillo* rulers, by distributing land to his cronies.[19] During the middle years of Gómez's autocratic rule, oil began to become a major factor in Venezuela's still rudimentary economy. Marginal compared to coffee or even cacao as late as 1921, by the middle of the decade oil exports earned well over three times the total of these traditional products—a ratio that would reach seventeen to one by the end of Gómez's rule. Showing a degree of foresight, Gómez limited the duration of all oil concessions to fifty years. Bringing the first significant European immigration since colonial days, the oil boom also helped shift the locus of power away from the Andean region. With everything going his way, a student uprising in 1928 was little more than a minor annoyance to the firmly entrenched strongman. Hence he permitted its leaders to go into exile rather than eliminating them—a decision that would have profound positive implications for the country, as they would become the backbone of the forces working effectively to build a democratic Venezuela after Gómez's demise. (Indeed, their most prominent leader, Rafael Caldera, would twice occupy the presidency, the last time in the 1990s.)

With Gómez still in his prime, Venezuela was the only one of the South American countries for which 1930 would not mark a significant political watershed; that would be delayed five years until his death. In the northern part of Latin America, Mexico's analogous break with the past came with Cardenas's election in 1934, as for very different reasons it, too, was insulated from the full political impact of the stress generated by the world economic crisis.

Chile: They Did It Their Way

In dramatic contrast to laggard Venezuela, Chile had the greatest success in achieving political development of a democratic nature during its first century of national life. Although its compactness and homogeneity were certainly advantages in this respect, its decision to innovate, adapting rather than blindly adopting the US model, was a major contributing factor. As a benefit of remoteness, it was used to a higher degree of self-government than the other countries, especially Peru and Mexico. The independence of this southernmost Andean country was inextricably tied up with the leadership of Bernardo O'Higgins. He was born well south of the Central Valley in 1778 as the illegitimate son of Ambrosio O'Higgins, an Irish colonel serving in the Spanish army, and his birth coincided with Chile's becoming a captaincy general, with the ensuing increased autonomy from Peru. Nine years later, his father became head of Chile's colonial administration, and in 1796, he was promoted to viceroy of Peru, dying there in 1801. Raised by friends of his distant father, in 1794 Bernardo was sent to Spain to further his education, but he quickly moved on to England, where he came in contact with Francisco Miranda and his revolutionary ideas concerning Latin American independence.[20]

With Chilean elites divided over who should govern in Ferdinand's name during the French occupation of Spain, O'Higgins became a lieutenant colonel of cavalry and was elected to the Chilean congress at the beginning of 1811. Defeated by Spanish forces at Rancaugua in late 1814, he fled to Argentina, returning with San Martín two years later. In early 1817, they won the decisive battle of Chacabuco. A few months later O'Higgins triumphed at Maipó and began a six-year stint as newly independent Chile's "supreme director." After resigning in 1823 in the face of mounting landowner and church opposition to his reform measures, he assumed a field command under Bolívar for the final stages of the war in Peru, dying in Lima in 1842.

Following O'Higgins's departure from office in 1823, liberal general Ramón Freire, champion of the *pipolos* ("novices"), was in and out of power until the *pelucones* ("bigwigs") won the 1829–1832 civil war and inaugurated three decades of conservative rule. By this time this country of 1 million inhabitants had produced a leader strikingly different from the era's typical *caudillo* ruler. After April 1830, Diego Portales Palazuelos (b. 1793), a brilliant and energetic businessman from Valparaíso serving as minister of war, navy, interior, foreign affairs, and finance (in essence almost everything of real importance)—first under President Francisco Ruiz Tagle and then, after engineering his ouster, behind General Joaquín Prieto—dominated government policy. Viewing the Catholic Church and the landowning aristocracy of the Central Valley as bulwarks of order, he created a civil guard to maintain order and act as a political counterweight to the army. During the short time before his tragic early death this exceptionally able statesman engineered a settlement between the conservative-centralist and liberal-federalist factions that brought political peace. His views on a centralized presidency were in large part incorporated into Chile's long-lived 1833

Constitution, under which an indirectly elected president, eligible for a second five-year term, appointed the intendants who headed the provincial governments and were held in line by his extensive emergency powers.[21] A bicameral congress was chosen indirectly by an electorate restricted by literacy and property qualifications. Although presidents often fixed elections, this system was advanced for the times. (Britain began to expand its very limited electorate only in 1832, and the United States was still adapting to Jacksonian democracy.)

In addition to creating conditions for economic progress, Portales placed heavy emphasis on education. He worked assiduously for Chilean victory in the war against the Peruvian-Bolivian confederation, instituting conscription and acting as de facto quartermaster general. This work was abruptly ended when he was bayoneted to death in 1837 by rebellious troops being sent to the First War of the Pacific, and he became an iconic heroic model. Prieto, who had been reelected in 1836, presided over the final military victory at the battle of Yungay in early 1839. Hence, in 1841, General Manuel Bulnes, nephew of Prieto and popular hero of Indian and antibandit campaigns even before earning battlefield laurels, was elected president and presided over a postwar economic boom. Facilitated by his close relationship to the outgoing chief executive and his engagement to the daughter of the 1827–1829 president, Bulnes's accession provided for a peaceful transition of power. (His favorable reputation would carry his son Anibal to the presidency in 1876, a John Adams–John Quincy Adams–like father-son phenomenon that would be repeated on several occasions, as late as the 1990s.) Liberal Manuel Montt Torres (b. 1809), Bulnes's interior minister, became president in 1851 after his predecessor defeated conservatives rebelling against the loss of their preferred position. Chilean elections were still heavily manipulated by the executive, albeit no more so than elsewhere in the region.

Chile continued on its remarkably stable constitutional road in 1861, after Montt's second term, in which he stressed communications, transportation, and education. Although the outgoing chief executive strongly preferred Antonio Varas, his former interior minister, the victor was conciliation candidate José Joaquín Pérez Masayano (b. 1801), who included all significant factions in his cabinet and permitted a modestly larger role for the congress—a shrewd and statesmanlike measure that continued the unique Chilean trend toward lowering the stakes of political competition by not making it the winner-take-all proposition it was in most of the other Latin American countries. (Brazil, owing to the moderating influence of the monarchy, was the other exception.) Hence, in 1866, Pérez was unopposed for a second term. Tensions were greatly eased by the emergence of Chile as the world's leading copper exporter, so the outlook for the ensuing period was bright—in sharp contrast with the outlook for its Andean neighbors.

In this essentially democratic country, the region's most politically advanced, new alignments emerged by the end of the 1860s, and the Catholic Church was reemerging as a powerful political factor. The Liberal-Conservative Fusion Party and the National (Monttvarista) Party, which had been effective vehicles for coopting newly wealthy elements, would soon be faced with a challenge from the more urban and middle-class Radical Party (PR). The changing of the guard was reflected in the fact that the chamber elected in 1870 contained no less than five future presidents. A ban on reelection enacted in 1870 put an end to the almost automatic decade-long two-term presidencies. Subsequent Chilean presidents, some of them sons of pre-1850s chief executives, served single five-year terms. Fusionist liberal Federico Errázuriz Zanartu (b. 1825) held office in 1871–1876 before his power base fell apart over anticlerical legislation, and a liberal-radical coalition subsequently enacted a series of reforms, including restrictions on the use of emergency powers, the reduction of senate terms from nine to six years, and the dropping of property requirements for voting. As the political parties became better structured in a country whose population had reached 2 million by 1880, restrictions on freedom of speech and assembly weakened.

The smashing 1879–1883 military victory over Peru and Bolivia in the Second War of the Pacific was enough to make most Chileans all but forget the demoralizing bank collapse of 1877–1878, and the acquisition of nitrate-rich regions in the peace settlement would pay dividends down through the 1920s. In 1881, following the capture of Lima, Conservatives attempted to regain power behind the candidacy of war hero General Manuel Baquedano, but he was defeated in a violent and bribery-ridden election by Domingo Santa María, a member of the incumbent cabinet. Santa María fought a rearguard action against demands of congressional leaders for a greater say in cabinet appointments and free elections and sought to reduce the influence of the Catholic Church. José Manuel Balmaceda Fernández (b. 1840), Santa María's loyal interior minister, was elected in 1886, subsequently denouncing "congressional dictatorship" resulting in what he decried as a "bastardized parliamentary system" and advocating a more active state and greater regulation of the foreign-owned nitrate companies. Concerned that Balmaceda was determined to establish strong executive supremacy (as Roca was doing in Argentina and Deodoro and Floriano were seeking to impose in Brazil—not to mention the centralized autocracy of Díaz in Mexico) in January 1891 a strong majority of national legislators voted to depose the potential tyrant. This confrontation unleashed a civil war that was won, after eight months of fighting, by procongress forces only when troops commanded by German general Emil Körner Henze switched sides. Balmaceda reacted to the collapse of his dream of dominance by committing suicide.[22]

Hence late 1891 witnessed the election of Admiral Jorge Montt Álvarez (b. 1845) as president within a system of a very strong congress and active political party competition—a far cry from Brazil's dominance by military presidents, Díaz's stranglehold on Mexico, Roca's centralization and concentration of authority in Argentina, or Colombia's resort to a bloody civil war to establish one-party hegemony. Elected in 1896, Federico Errázuriz Echaurren (b. 1850) would die in mid-1901, but the pattern of the "parliamentary republic," in which presidents were less important than in other Latin American countries, would last to 1924. Indeed, as the century came to its end, Chilean democracy was rooted in the economic prosperity resulting from the country's favored position as a nitrate producer just as this mineral was in demand not only for fertilizer, but even more for explosives in the age of European arms races featuring battleships utilizing ever larger cannon, hence needing increased amounts of explosive. What would prove extremely destructive for Europe was a boon to Chile.

The early years of the new century brought no sharp change to Chile, as the parliamentary republic with its emphasis on parties and legislative politics (along with encouraging British investment in nitrate production) continued, under a series of highly respectable, if undistinguished, presidents, beginning with Germán Riesco Errazuriz in 1901, followed by yet another Montt, this time Pedro (b. 1846), in 1906, and ending with José Luis Sanfuentes in 1915–1920. With nitrates, source of half the country's foreign exchange earnings from 1900 to 1930, in high demand, stability ruled through World War I—although five men occupied the presidency in the decade following Montt's mid-1910 resignation brought on by ill health. By 1920 this socioeconomic normality had changed drastically with the precipitous fall in demand for this essential component of explosives, and copper had not yet come to fill the gap. Politics was taking on an increasingly urban cast as Santiago reached 500,000 inhabitants by 1920 on its way to 713,000 by 1930. The landowning Central Valley elite managed to maintain the entrenched clientelistic system by absorbing commercial and incipient industrial elements. Yet dissident regional oligarchies in the north and south allied with new urban middle-sector elements and dissident middle-class groups to press for the political and social reforms their radical counterparts were achieving in Argentina.[23]

The intransigence of the Conservative and Liberal Parties, in sharp contrast to the flexibility shown by their Argentine equivalents, led in 1920 to the centrist wing of the latter joining the Radicals and Democrats in the Liberal Alliance (AL) behind Arturo Alessandri Palma (b. 1869), who had been first elected to the Chamber of Deputies in 1897 and to the Senate in 1915. Lacking a majority in the congress, Alessandri—soon to be revered as the "Lion of Tarapaca" (a reference to his home province)—resigned in September 1924 when right-wing obstruction led to military interference in governmental affairs. Having high-mindedly stressed that his democratic principles prevented him from countenancing political interventions by the armed even to his benefit, by the next March Alessandri was back in office under a new, more presidential constitution providing for direct election of the president for a six-year term, separation of church and state, elimination of congressional votes of censure of ministers, and a requirement that the legislature act promptly on proposals deemed urgent by the executive. Proportional representation applied to twenty-nine Chamber constituencies and ten for the Senate. Finding himself in the uncomfortable position of governing by decree at the sufferance of War Minister Colonel Carlos Ibáñez del Campo (b. 1877), in October Alessandri resigned for a second time—almost at the end of his term. Running in a context of economic recovery, Ibáñez gained election as president in March 1927. Like so many other Latin American chief executives, he fell afoul of the economic crash. With prices in a freefall, vital foreign exchange earnings from nitrates began a fall in 1930 that would reach 70 percent by 1933. Not surprisingly, Ibáñez's dictatorial regime ended in chaotic 1931.[24]

Notes

1. Consult Anthony McFarland, *Colombia Before Independence* (Cambridge, UK: Cambridge University Press, 1993), pp. 332–346, and David Bushnell, *The Making of Modern Colombia: A Nation in Spite of Itself* (Berkeley and Los Angeles: University of California Press, 1993), pp. 32–41. Specifics on the independence struggle are covered in Jaime Rodríguez O., *The Independence of Spanish America* (Cambridge, UK: Cambridge University Press, 1998), pp, 150–157.

2. See Bushnell, *Making of Modern Colombia,* pp. 55–60, as well as Frank Safford and Marco Palacios, *Colombia: Fragmented Land, Divided Society* (New York: Oxford University Press, 2002).

3. Bushnell, *Making of Modern Colombia,* pp. 67–73, evaluates 1826 to 1830.

4. Ibid., pp. 83–99, deals with 1832–1848.

5. Paul H. Lewis, *Authoritarian Regimes in Latin America: Dictators, Despots, and Tyrants* (Lanham, MD: Rowman & Littlefield, 2006), p. 29.

6. Ibid., p. 27.

7. Bushnell, *Making of Modern Colombia*, pp. 130–146.

8. Ibid., pp. 148–154.

9. Ibid., pp. 155–160.

10. Paul Oquist, *Violence, Conflict, and Politics in Colombia* (New York: Academic Press, 1980), p. 154.

11. Vernon Lee Fluharty, *Dance of the Millions* (Pittsburgh: University of Pittsburgh Press, 1957), is the classic work on this period.

12. Bushnell, *Making of Modern Colombia,* pp. 164–180, covers the post-Reyes years.

13. See Lewis, *Authoritarian Regimes,* pp. 25–26. Peter F. Klarén, *Peru: Society and Nationhood in the Andes* (New York: Oxford University Press, 2000), provides a sound historical treatment.

14. An unpublished manuscript by John Gitlitz was very helpful on the interaction of economics, social change, and politics in Peru's development.

15. Consult Peter F. Klarén, *Modernization, Dislocation, and Aprismo* (Austin: University of Texas Press, 1973).

16. See *El Convenio Greene-De la Flor y Pago a la IPC* (Lima. Peru: El Populista, 1979).

17. Lewis, *Authoritarian Regimes,* p. 23. On the legacy of this type of beginning see Daniel C. Hellinger, *Venezuela: Tarnished Democracy* (Boulder, CO: Westview Press, 1991). Also useful is Robert L. Gilmore, *Caudillism and Militarism in Venezuela, 1810–1910* (Athens: Ohio University Press, 1964).

18. See George S. Wise, *Caudillo: A Portrait of Antonio Guzmán Blanco* (New York: Columbia University Press, 1951). Also of use is Gilmore, *Caudillism and Militarism.*

19. See Lewis, *Authoritarian Regimes,* p. 64. The atmosphere of the period is caught in Thomas Rourke (pseudonym of J. D. Clinton), *Gómez, Tyrant of the Andes* (New York: William Morrow, 1936).

20. A useful source is Simon Collier and William E. Slater, *A History of Chile, 1808–1994* (Cambridge, UK: Cambridge University Press, 1996), which provides details on O'Higgins.

21. Consult Lewis, *Authoritarian Regimes,* pp. 38–42. There is some dispute among Chilean political scientists on the contribution of this governmental framework to the country's relative stability. For a measured view on this issue see Federico G. Gil, *The Political System of Chile* (Boston: Houghton Mifflin, 1966).

22. For perspective consult Brian Loveman, *Chile: The Legacy of Hispanic Capitalism* (New York: Oxford University Press, 1979).

23. See Karen L. Remmer, *Party Competition in Argentina and Chile: Political Recruitment and Public Policy, 1890–1930* (Lincoln: University of Nebraska Press, 1984).

24. For details on the latter part of the period, see Frederick M. Nunn, *Chilean Politics, 1920–1931: The Honorable Mission of the Armed Forces* (Albuquerque: University of New Mexico Press, 1970).

PART 2

◇ ◇ ◇

Latin America Since 1930

5

Comparative Perspectives

Latin America Since 1930

The partial dawning of liberal democracy that took place in Latin America in the early twentieth century, best exemplified by Argentina and Chile, but with more elitist shadows in Brazil, Peru, and Colombia, was short-lived, while it was stillborn in Mexico and aborted in Venezuela. It was caught between populist pressures for enhanced participation and an abrupt end to the economic growth of the 1920s—which caused conservative groups to turn to regimes that would protect their particular interests in the face of decreased resources. Indeed, many of these elements, especially the landowners, had, at best, ambivalent feelings about recent democratic trends and were ready to sacrifice them in order to preserve their own well-being. The notable, and very major, exception was Brazil, where the 1930 Revolution and the ensuing Getúlio Vargas regime allowed that country to catch up in a number of ways, whereas the former leaders in political development backslid as in Argentina, rallied modestly in the case of Colombia, or at best marked time. Indeed, the Brazilian case—and that of Mexico once it climbed out of the anguish and destruction of civil war in the 1930s under Lázaro Cárdenas—was in the forefront of a phase in which urban groups, including the new industrialists and labor sectors, bypassed or misused parliamentary and electoral processes in efforts to attack executive power. These actions were mediated and at times diverted by political entrepreneurs who, by adapting to changing conditions, became leaders of the emerging populist groups.

Rather than a revolutionary rising of the masses, the maneuvering of political brokers—displaying varying degrees of personalism—along the border between the establishment and the emergent populist groups was a hallmark of the period. Politically astute individuals, their varying degrees of skill leading to wide variations in results, sought to use the emerging urban masses to play a quite complex and often sophisticated game of facilitating their rise to power as well as the often more difficult task of holding onto it. Here Vargas (president of Brazil 1930–1945 and 1951–1954) overlapped with Juan Domingo Perón (president of Argentina 1945–1955 and 1973–1974), starting earlier in a less-developed society. Both of these charismatic leaders, as well as Cárdenas (president of Mexico 1934–1940), exercised control through essentially corporatist regimes stressing a strong state, an ordered and integrated society, and cooperation between business, labor unions, and their governments. Although their often narrow and spottily implemented welfare programs and officially sponsored unionism were often lacking in scope, substance, and depth, they significantly enhanced the regime's cooptative capabilities and affected the nature and operation of political institutions. New political interests were built into the system through bureaucratic means involving channeled, if not controlled, consultation with networks of councils and committees that linked government agencies with the burgeoning agents of sectoral groups. The legislative role expansion, until recently viewed as desirable by modernizing factions, gradually lost favor to the degree that it was perceived as decreasing governmental effectiveness by facilitating special interests and fostering stalemates and impasses.

As time went on and the region moved into post–World War II prosperity, the belief that the growth of the middle classes of Latin American society, rooted in economic development and societal modernization, would lead to greater stability and democracy proved illusory. By the 1960s, if not earlier, it had become clear to scholars, if not always to practicing politicians, that political development could not precede social structures and processes, which in turn must occur in response—often substantially delayed—to economic achievements. Varying experiences also demonstrated that progress in the political sphere might not follow as a matter of course but instead might often lag well behind these socioeconomic factors. When this discontinuity occurred, the potential for a catch-up spurt of political development increased, but whether it occurred or not depended heavily upon the presence of adequate political leadership, which could catalyze and constructively channel the mounting dissatisfaction and effectively spread a realization of the need for significant readjustments in the political-governmental sphere. From the 1920s into the 1950s such leadership had often emerged, but in the crucial 1960s it was in short supply.

A difficult new challenge was emerging with respect to broadening the base of participation to include at least a few favored rural groups, an incorporation that had already happened in Mexico under Cárdenas. Tried and true mass-based political parties of a populist character often proved ineffective, and government social service agencies of a quasi-corporatist nature fell behind the demand. Hence patron-client relationships persisted, sometimes less directly, with new political brokers skilled in getting out votes, delivering warm bodies for demonstrations, and distributing low-level favors including local patronage as a service to high-status patrons—who now were often elected officials or upper-echelon bureaucrats. Competition for benefits became intense, and the early 1960s witnessed an alarming surge in the military playing an increasingly active arbiter role, especially in countries where the long-dominant leader was gone or had exhausted his political magic (as had happened in both Brazil and Argentina by the mid-1950s). Soon the overwhelming majority of the region's countries were headed into military rule, as in the wake of Fidel Castro's rise to power in Cuba. Their armed forces grew impatient with faltering civilian rule, often mistaking uproar for looming revolution and confusing the inevitable messiness and theatrical confrontation of political bargaining with dangerous conflict, to the extent of perceiving a system and society in crisis. Time and time again, the military was ready, usually eager, to "save" the nation from the peril of greatly exaggerated, even imaginary, pro-Soviet subversion.

The military generally proved ill qualified to govern, but extremely loath to admit this deficiency—much less relinquish power. To their credit, the region's countries eventually forced their armed forces back to the barracks. Usually, however, when military regimes gave way to civilian government, it was to groups the military had earlier pushed aside in its rush to seize the reins of power. The return was essentially to what had existed before, not to anything that had developed during the military suspension of "politics as usual." In no case was power turned over to political forces of the left; in most cases it was given to center and center-right establishment political groupings. Hence there was no sudden emergence of pluralist political systems; the restored governing elites generally practiced politics essentially as they had learned to in the 1940s and 1950s. The 1980s were years of transition to civilian competitive politics, and the 1990s were a decade of consolidating electoral democracy. Deepening it and improving its quality remained for the opening decade of a new century and a new millennium.

The individual paths followed by these countries within this general pattern merit close examination. To begin with, 1930 was a watershed, not merely a landmark, for Latin America. The profound economic crisis that put an abrupt end to the era of prosperity and optimism had its most devastating effects in the political realm in Argentina, where it not only destroyed that country's recent democratic experiment but also actually swept away much of the political development and social progress achieved during the 1880–1914 Roca era. Indeed, Argentina would not enjoy a full return to democracy until after 1983—a hiatus of more than a half century. Rather than being such a great leap backward, Brazil's 1930 Revolution swept aside the outdated and inherently fraudulent "old republic," in its wake accomplishing much of the political development achieved in Argentina almost a generation earlier. However, Brazil accomplished this development in a very different manner, relying upon Vargas's astute management of the crisis period and eschewing political parties in favor of cooptative manipulation and construction of an efficient state machinery within a semicorporatist framework. Although the profound democratic elements of 1916–1929 Argentine political life would be absent—for after 1930 they were finished and gone there—they would make their belated appearance in Brazil between 1946 and 1964. Pushed to the back burner during two decades of military rule, they would reemerge stronger than before in the mid-1980s.

In dramatic contrast to Argentina and distinctly differing from Brazil, for Colombia 1930 afforded the beleaguered liberals the opportunity to achieve electoral victory for the first time in the twentieth century and provided the country with a dozen years of democracy before hostile forces spun out of control. Only after two bouts of dictatorial rule—the first under a fascistic civilian, the second under an ambitious military man—would reason prevail and democracy be restored in 1957, this time managing to last. In Peru, the one essentially Indian country of these seven, the heritage of 1930 was less positive than in Brazil or Colombia, but less negatively retrograde than in Argentina. It ended the eleven-year constitutional, albeit not fully democratic, government of autocratic populist Augusto Leguía (the closest to an outstanding political leader the country had yet produced) without ushering in any real improvement, much less meaningful political development. Intense animosity between the country's one modern political movement, the Popular Revolutionary Alliance of the Americas (APRA), and the country's armed forces precluded progress and pushed political development far into the future—with violence, political instability, and gross electoral manipulation extending into the late 1960s, to be replaced by a rather modern military regime until a transition to a shaky democracy in the mid-1970s.

For much smaller Chile, where a historically stable democracy had recently succumbed to the permanent collapse of the world nitrate market, 1930 heralded the imminent end of Ibáñez's brief military interlude, with restoration of the pre-1927 democratically elected government coming after two years of frenetic maneuvering. This blissful state would endure until 1970 and the election of a Marxist-minority president in the midst of a polarized Cold War environment. Salvador Allende's ouster and death three years later pulled Chile back to the then-prevailing Latin American mean, with the resulting Augusto Pinochet dictatorship lasting until 1989. Then Chileans would insist on a return to their country's historical norm: full democracy. Since then Chile has freely elected the longest series of highly capable presidents in the history of any Western Hemisphere country (the United States not excluded), a winning streak at four and still counting.

Mexico appeared to take 1930 in stride, but in light of the special circumstances prevailing, this appearance was somewhat misleading as 1930 did mark the onset of very crucial changes that would become increasingly apparent after 1934. The country's economy and society had been so devastated by decades of rampant civil war that there was little damage a world economic crisis could add to the toll. Politically matters were finally on the upswing as an inclusive political party designed to channel presidential succession into the electoral arena had been launched in 1929 and placed under the direction of Cárdenas, who in 1934 would be the first Mexican chief executive in six decades democratically elected and free from actual or threatened armed revolt by disappointed aspirants. Indeed, he was the first Mexican president chosen by a mass electorate and would turn out to be the greatest political leader in Mexico's history. Hence the 1930–1933 period turned out to be one of setting the stage for the near-immediate coming of perhaps the most important of the region's contemporary political watersheds: the long-delayed implementation of the goals of Mexico's 1910 Revolution. Subsequent political development, although far less dramatic, was continuous within a framework of institutional stability until reaching full democracy at the dawn of the new century.

Thus, Venezuela is the only country for which 1930 was not at least a major landmark. The delay came by way of the most deeply entrenched dictator in the region's experience. Tucked away in his quite isolated country, impervious to external economic shocks (as oil was far less subject to a sharp drop in demand than Argentina's beef and wheat or the coffee of Brazil and Colombia), seventy-eight-year-old Juan Vicente Gómez took his own good time to die, passing away with his boots on at the end of 1935. Only then would the winds of change finally make themselves felt, slowly and softly at first before picking up to gale force at the end of World War II. Then a brief preview of democracy would be followed by a decade-long relapse to militarism before the 1958 restoration of a social democratic polity that would flourish for a quarter century before failing to retain the loyalty of a new generation extremely frustrated by not receiving the same benefits from a system rooted in parties and leaders seemingly unable to extend the full incorporation achieved by the middle class and skilled urban workers to the less fortunate masses. Out of this political malaise emerged in the 1990s the charismatic, colorful, and controversial Lieutenant Colonel Hugo Chávez Frías.

By this time the region had lived through the Great Depression of the 1930s, World War II, the Cold War, and into the era of global terrorism, with the specter of another global economic crisis hanging as a dark cloud over the future. Neither being responsible for any of these developments nor having significantly affected the course of world affairs, these Latin American countries reached 2010 determined to reduce their vulnerability to the international factors impacting upon them with such crippling negative impact. In their minds the new global economic crisis unleashed in 2008 must not be allowed to have the devastating political impact of its predecessor eighty years before.

From Great Depression to Cold War, 1930–1955

The abrupt end of the essentially prosperous post–World War I decade, followed by its antithesis, the Great Depression, had a profound effect throughout the Western world. Not only did this catastrophe reinvigorate interest in Marxism-Leninism, which had ebbed during the good times of the 1920s, but it fueled a rise in the fascist regimes that would dominate most of western Europe even before, in late 1939, the Axis powers resorted to war to seek domination. Fascism came to power in Italy under Benito Mussolini in the mid-1920s, with Adolf Hitler and his Nazis gaining control of Germany in 1933. Holding sway over much of Spain after its civil war broke out in the mid-1930s, Generalissimo Francisco Franco's Falange organization, a crossbreed of Spain's traditional authoritarian Catholic corporatism with modern fascism's rejection of individualism and many aspects of modernization, was in full control of that country by the 1940s (and would prevail until the mid-1970s). A similar regime was already entrenched in Portugal under Antonio de Oliveira Salazar.

　　Given the close historical links and blood ties between most Latin Americans and Spain, Italy, and Portugal, interest in the competing ideologies of communism and fascism rose sharply during the first half of this period. The former, a hard sell in deeply Catholic societies, created a great deal of concern while failing to develop into a mass political movement. In Brazil, Vargas would play these two forces off against each other, not only neutralizing them, but also essentially neutering them by 1938. In postrevolution Mexico, with no significant Italian population, fascism never got beyond the curiosity stage, and Cárdenas defanged communism. In Argentina, where the potential was much greater, the Peróns coopted communism's labor base and absorbed fascism within their populist version of authoritarian corporatism. Staunchly Catholic Colombia, which did not receive a significant influx of European immigration in the decades before or during this period, was barren land for both these modern ideologies. In different ways this would be the case in the medium-sized countries as well. Peru would see a staunchly conservative military determinedly stymie the spread of a indigenous Marxism to its predominantly Indian society. In Venezuela Gómez's *caudillo* dictatorship would give way to a pair of far lesser military successors before a national brand of social democracy flourished ever so briefly until it was repressed by a new military dictator. In the sharpest of contrasts Chile continued highly attuned to European political currents, with socialism, communism, and fascism all vying for influence among its comparatively highly educated electorate.

　　In this international context for Latin America, the years from 1930 through 1955 were a maelstrom in which countervailing and contradictory trends were at work as each country strove to cope with its particular form of the often-traumatic impact of the global economic crisis, World War II, and the US-Soviet confrontation escalating into the Cold War—giving this period the character of a three-act play with no comedy, some tragedy, and a great deal of drama. Through it all, the pace of socioeconomic change varied greatly across the region, accompanied by major differences in its political effects. Still, as in the preceding period, violence and destruction were minor compared to that in Europe or Asia, hosts to the two world wars.

Although the timing and the directions might be nearly unique to each country, few of the region's countries avoided dramatic swings of the political pendulum. To add a good deal of excitement to events, in keeping with a world trend that produced Winston Churchill, Franklin D. Roosevelt, Adolf Hitler, Joseph Stalin, Benito Mussolini, Francisco Franco, and Mao Tse-tung, a number of truly remarkable political leaders came to the forefront across Latin America. Indeed, these exceptional individuals outnumbered the region's total of such salient figures up to that time and have not come close to being matched in subsequent periods. Their heritages are still strongly felt today. In large part because of these great leaders, for three of the four major countries this was the most significant and transforming period in their national life. It spanned the entire Vargas era in Brazil; included the developments preparing the way for Perón's rise in Argentina, as well as his stay in power; and covered the establishment, institutionalization, and flourishing of the hegemonic governing-party system in Mexico.

All these considerations and the accompanying drama were highly apparent in Brazil, where Vargas came to power in 1930, survived a civil war and both communist and fascist armed revolts during the 1930s, was ousted in 1945, and, after triumphantly returning to the presidency through popular election, died by his own hand in 1954. His political legacy, especially as applied to industrialization and the incorporation of the urban working class, would stretch on as a determining factor well beyond the end of this period, so that understanding this legacy is imperative for comprehending the political development path Brazil has since followed.

In Mexico Cárdenas, a dedicated and effective populist reformer, as close to a reincarnation of Benito Juárez as might ever be seen, threw off the tutelage of his erstwhile patron, Plutarco Elías Calles, and transformed politics and society more in six short years, from 1934 through 1940, than they had been changed in the quarter century since the 1910 Revolution—or would be over the next six decades. Largely on the momentum he built up, the dominant party would cruise through not only the rest of this period but also the following one, and on into the 1980s.

Argentina went through a failed effort to return to the oligarchic past, followed by an attempt to limit the damage and get back on a democratic track. With World War II breaking out, this was impossible: In light of the tensions between a British-controlled economy and an essentially Italian population, this balancing act gave way in the mid-1940s to the rise of populist-nationalist-authoritarian Peronism under Juan Domingo and Evita Perón—clearly both among the region's all-time most charismatic leaders. By the end of this period Evita was dead, and Juan was on his way into exile. But Peronism would remain a potent factor in Argentine life, not just through the ensuing decades but also into the next century.

At the same time, Colombia was the most tragic victim of the inability to participate in the forging of great and essentially positive legacies à la Brazil, Mexico, and Argentina. After starting out well, in the late 1940s Colombia descended into the depths of barbarous civil war and repressive dictatorship after its candidate for transformational leadership was brutally murdered on the eve of attaining power. However, by the end of the period democratic forces were rallying for a successful comeback.

Peru's tortuous political trajectory began with the vacuum left by Leguía's overthrow and ended with the eight-year rule of a military strongman. Its constant theme was the emergence of APRA as the country's most deeply rooted popular movement, and the intransient refusal of the armed forces to allow this nemesis access to power. This impasse would persist through the entire next period (and on down to 1985). For Venezuela, this quarter century opened with one dictator and closed with another, but in between, momentous developments took place that soon after would usher in an era of stable democracy. Gómez's finally passing away in 1935 initiated a transition that eventuated in reformist civilian rule in 1945–1948. Although a military authoritarian then emerged, civilian democratic forces dramatically reasserted themselves by 1958. Chile saw the fall of its erstwhile military strongman in 1931, leading to the election of a string of responsible civilian governments including even the return of General Ibáñez, this time as elected constitutional president for the 1952–1958 term.

Thus by midcentury the four-fifths of Latin Americans living in these seven countries on balance enjoyed political development along with substantial economic growth—the fruits of which were still heavily skewed toward the elites and the more favored elements of the middle class. Organized elements of the working class were recipients of social welfare benefits, although more in Argentina and Chile than in Mexico, with Brazil and Colombia still lagging in this field—but closing the gap. Peru and Venezuela still trailed farther behind but were no longer condemned to seeing this gap widen. Mexico's gains were the most institutionalized and so would survive the next period. A reversal was under way in Argentina but would be delayed nearly a decade before occurring in Brazil. Only Mexico, where the military were no longer a major political factor, would escape the wave of authoritarian military regimes that marked the next period—while Colombia and Venezuela ended this period on the verge of democratic transitions.

Into the Inferno and the Hard Road Back, 1956–1979

In contrast with the preceding quarter century, by the mid-1950s Latin American politics had become essentially nonideological. The dominance of the Institutional Revolutionary Party (PRI) over Mexico had reached the point where it had in effect become much more *Institutional* than *Revolutionary*, in fact a vast patronage-dispensing machine that might well have caused Cárdenas to roll over (and over and over) in his grave. In Brazil a doctrine of "developmentalism" was taking hold under the guidance of the new president, Juscelino Kubitschek. At just that point the Argentine armed forces ousted Perón from power but found little resonance for their negative message of antipopulist anticommunism. Relieved by a decrease in the horrendous violence of 1948–1953, Colombia was torn between the reactionary brand of authoritarian corporatism preached by Laureano Gómez, clearly in decline, and the business-oriented liberalism gaining favor among sectors of the entrepreneurial stratum. *Aprismo* (the ideology of APRA) was losing meaning if not necessarily supporters in Peru, having become just another political party more than a movement, much less an ideology. But among the armed forces, catalyzed by the 1959 Cuban Revolution, a national security doctrine developed and took on an ideological nature. It would be used not only to justify the sweeping wave of military coups that characterized the 1960s, but also to rationalize the armed forces' actions once in power. In some cases, most traumatically following the 1973 overthrow of the Salvador Allende government in Chile and the "dirty war" in Argentina a few years later, these authoritarian military regimes would carry ruthless repression to the extreme of institutionalized terrorism. In other countries, such as Brazil and Peru, insurgencies would be mercilessly crushed without a societywide reign of terror.

Thus the quarter century from the middle of the 1950s to the end of the 1970s saw most Latin American countries falter in their efforts to make representative systems work. They fell instead, many for protracted periods, under the ironfisted control of authoritarian military regimes. Indeed, competitive, constitutional, democratic governments and political processes were so eclipsed as to appear to be a scattered few exceptions to the rule of the collapse of populism and rise of a new militarism—often institutionalized in the "national security state." By the mid-1970s such repressive regimes were overwhelmingly predominant in the region, much more than elected civilian governments had been at the beginning of the 1960s. Just as these promising civilian governments had been inundated by the flood tide of rampant militarism beginning in 1962, the late 1970s witnessed a resurgence of effective demands for political liberalization and democratization, unleashing forces that would blossom within a few years into a tidal wave of transitions to democracy.

In retrospect, leadership was not as lacking in the downhill first half of this period as is often perceived by observers and students of the area. Indeed, a strong case can be made that presidents in a quite wide range of countries grappled responsibly and tenaciously with problems that were beyond resolution, given the unfavorable conditions prevailing at the time. Juscelino Kubitschek in Brazil and Rómulo Betancourt in Venezuela were the outstanding success stories, although at the time overshadowed by the dramatic appeal of Fidel Castro in Cuba, but Colombia's Alberto Lleras Camargo, Arturo Frondizi of Argentina, Peru's Fernando Belaúnde Terry, and Eduardo Frei Montalva in Chile represented effective democratic leadership under very trying circumstances.

In something of a paradox, outstanding political leadership would generally not be a major factor in the climb out of the depths of the political inferno that got under way in important parts of the region during the late 1970s, although its absence among the military did contribute to erosion of support for the authoritarian option. Failure of authoritarian regimes to deliver on promises of greatly improved economic performance and the waning of fears of possible leftist revolutions that had led elites and a panic-stricken middle to turn to the military in the 1960s played much more important roles in this democratic recovery. The striking exception was in Brazil, where Tancredo Neves was highly instrumental in turning gradual political opening into full and rapid democratization—but this would take place in the early 1980s.

Brazil entered this period on the upswing from the jolting crisis that had brought about Vargas's demise. Kubitschek, elected in late 1955 and taking office early the next year, would prove to be one of the most effective chief executives in the history of the republic—ranking very high even in the wider regional experience. After broadening and deepening the foundations for sustained development that Vargas had begun, he presided over an election in 1960 that brought a more-than-somewhat-quixotic populist to power—only to crash under the weight of his own grand schemes and bizarre manipulations less than a year later. Very ordinary João Belchior Marques Goulart, the vice president who succeeded Jânio da Silva Quadros, was no match for a polarizing situation, being ousted at the end of the first quarter of 1964 by a conservative military movement enjoying wide support from both civilian elites and the middle class. By the end of the 1970s a series of military presidents would have led the country down into a repressive, although economically successful, authoritarian regime and then turned the corner to put it on a path of liberalization morphing into political opening. By striking contrast, Mexico would leave the period as firmly under the control of its long-hegemonic party as at the beginning, although with pressure for change mounting. In compensation for this lack of real choice as its presidential successions became so institutionalized as to be highly predictable, it would be the only country to avoid military intervention and the ensuing agonies of rule by the armed forces. On balance, Mexicans clearly came away the winners in this bargain.

These twenty-five years would be both turbulent and violent for Argentina. Beginning with military rule in the aftermath of Perón's ouster, the country underwent a protracted period in which neither military nor civilian governments could provide long-term stability. Perón returned to power triumphantly in 1973, the key factor in averting a slide into undeclared civil war, only to die the next year. Back in power by 1976, the military would still be searching in vain for a blueprint for political viability when the 1970s came to an inglorious close. Colombia would emerge early from an essentially hideous ten years to find not only political viability but also democracy under a series of coalition governments operating within the innovative framework of the National Front (FN). By period's end, however, it would be plagued by insurgency and massive illegal drug-trafficking enterprises threatening to become a state within a state. Peru went through a roller-coaster period, beginning on a positive note with the election of a civilian to replace General Manuel Odría in the presidency. The continuing virulent hostility of the armed forces toward the country's most significant political party caused a brief interruption of progress toward democracy in 1962–1963 and the establishment of a sui generis nationalist-reformist military regime in 1968, with a transition back to civilian rule barely under way at the end of the 1970s. For Venezuela this period marked a high point in the establishment of a stable, highly participatory political system on the rubble of a ten-year military dictatorship. After getting through the first eighteen years reasonably well, in 1973 Chile experienced by far the most serious political crisis in its history, leading to a repressive authoritarian regime beyond Chileans' worst nightmares that would make the name Pinochet globally infamous.

Semiauthoritarian Mexico was the exception to the spread of military regimes in this period, and Colombia and Venezuela escaped from military rule near its beginning, while Peru appeared to have done so only to see the military come back to power briefly in 1962–1963 and for a longer stay in 1968–1974. Hence Brazil and Argentina best fit the wider Latin American pattern (one followed by most of the mid-sized and small Hispanic-heritage countries) for the 1960s and 1970s and were nearing the end of prolonged military domination as the period ended. Moreover, having entered the period in significantly different situations, they followed distinct paths through it, Brazil having a much less repressive political regime and a better-managed economy, leading to its military being in a position to shape the upcoming transition, while manifest incompetence would cost the Argentine counterparts all control over the course of events.

Twilight of the Generals
and Dawn of Democracy, 1980–1999

As was clear by the end of the 1970s, political development in Latin America, although often painfully slow and extremely uneven, had also been significant and widespread, a fact dramatically brought home during the last two decades of the twentieth century. Movement toward developing viable participant-representative political systems both surged ahead and demonstrated great resilience and staying power during the 1980s and 1990s. As late as the mid to late 1970s authoritarian political regimes, some of a truly despotic nature, were still entrenched in Brazil, Argentina, Peru, and Chile. Indeed, in South America only Colombia and Venezuela were clearly democratic, while the PRI-dominated regime in Mexico showed strong authoritarian tendencies. Yet by 1989 the final belated return to democracy was under way in Chile, and by the end of the 1990s, never had so many of the region's countries and such a high proportion of its population lived under governments of their own choosing that were fundamentally adhering to constitutional principles. At long last, viable representative political systems with substantial democratic processes predominated in this diverse and far-flung expanse.

Contrary to the belief in the United States that proximity to the "beacon of democracy" would be a powerfully positive factor, the heartland of Latin American democratic consolidation was in the distant southern portion of South America. There, where Brasília, Buenos Aires, Santiago, and Lima are at least as far from New York and Washington as are the countries of central Europe, consolidation of stable democracies took root (with Colombia already there, but Venezuela beginning to slip). Moreover, although Argentina and Chile are essentially European-populated, often considered an important contributory factor to democratization, the greatest rate of progress in such positive political development was to be found in Brazil—where 98 million persons of primarily African ancestry coexist with 94 million of European extraction. And the more advanced southern part of this nation of subcontinental proportions lies farther from the capital of the United States than does Moscow. (The distance from São Paulo and Rio de Janeiro to Lisbon and Madrid is roughly the same as to New York.) Equally disturbing to conventional wisdom concerning the presumptive positive political influence of the US example was the fact that a disproportionate share of Latin American laggards on the road to democratic political development were among those countries geographically closest to the United States. Thus Mexico was late to board the democratization bandwagon—getting there only after 2000.

Elections either increase or decrease the probability of certain policy outcomes; they do not determine that something will happen, although they can virtually eliminate certain options. In these respects the Brazilian balloting of 1994 and 1998 and the Mexican voting from 1994 through 2000 were of critical importance. In the first of these cases the elections made possible economic stability and fiscal modernization that could establish a viable base for social reforms in half of South America. The Mexican experience opened the door to determining whether Latin America's second most populous country could make an essentially peaceful transition to the kind of political democracy that Brazil had achieved between 1984 and 1994. Elsewhere in the region, especially in Argentina, Colombia, Chile, and even Peru, elections proved a vital part of political development.

The 1980s burgeoning of democracy saw Brazil embark upon and consolidate the longest period of stable democratic government in its history, one involving a massive expansion of participation to a still growing electorate reaching 110 million by the end of the century. Not only did military rule come to an end after 1984, but both governmental structures and political processes also became significantly stronger and much more broadly based than during the 1946–1964 period of democracy laced with recurrent crises.

Approaching democratization in a radically different context, Mexico underwent a wrenching process of dismantling a system of single-party hegemony and overcoming hurdles and setbacks to arrive by 1999 on the verge of fully competitive national elections, which would result in the opposition's capturing the presidency, a feat never accomplished in the twentieth century and almost unheard of in the nation's long history. Argentina returned to democratic civilian rule in 1983, amid the trauma of a dismally unsuccessful military adventure and, with serious hiccups along the road, put together the longest-sustained democratic experience in its history, one involving far wider participation than in either its 1916–1930 halcyon years or the Perón era.

Below the radar, in spite of very serious strains, rooted in an intractable drug and insurgency problem, in Colombia a string of popularly elected presidents serving out their full terms and turning power over to constitutionally chosen successors reached eleven by the end of the period. Along the way, the crutch initially provided by the National Front was discarded in favor of full competition.

Peru began the period with a return to democratic civilian rule under the same man the military had ousted in 1968. Subsequently, at long last, it elected an Aprista (a member of APRA) to the presidency, only to have him perform disastrously, leading the country to turn to a political outsider for a two-term administration marked by highs and lows, ending unfortunately on the latter.

With its once vaunted democratic system floundering, Venezuela resorted to reaching into the past for its presidents in a vain attempt to stave off lower-class voter disenchantment with the parties that had served the country well from the 1940s into the beginning of the 1990s.

Chile had to wait until almost the midpoint of the period to rid itself of an oppressive military regime but made up for lost time when it did return to democracy.

Entering the New Century, 2000–2010

For Latin America the 1900s had been a decade characterized by generally middle-of-the-road neocapitalist governments relying heavily upon participating in globalization by opening up their economies and privatizing investment-starved state enterprises in keeping with the so-called Washington Consensus among most of the region's leaders (which assumed that free-market economies and freer trade were congruent with increased democracy). The results of this strategy were often disappointing to downright disillusioning for the majority of the population—especially the underprivileged lower classes. As a consequence, the twenty-first century began with a wave of efforts to find ways of combining newly established democratic politics with populist, if not necessarily clearly progressive, social policies. In the ongoing tension between badly needed economic growth and fear of reawakening the dreadful dragon of inflation, 1990s progress in taming the latter subsequently tempted policymakers to embrace the former as public opinion increasingly shifted, sometimes very vocally, in favor of priority for development over price stability. This attitude provided a very serious challenge to several Latin American countries, because the less fortunate sectors of society, although sometimes expressing a theoretical preference for democracy, were more concerned about development and security. They, unlike their better-off compatriots, often preferred strong, even authoritarian, government—if it delivered in the economic realm—to democracies that failed to do so and did not firmly maintain order.[1]

Hence a very important question for Latin America as a whole is whether or not the democratic governments of the first decade of the twenty-first century will prove increasingly responsive to social sectors that heretofore have either received empty promises or merely token benefits. These broad elements at the bottom of the social pyramid fall into two major groupings: the urban underprivileged and the neglected rural masses—each in absolute, if not relative, terms more numerous in Brazil than in any other country, followed by Mexico. Authoritarian regimes of the 1960s and 1970s throughout Latin America had very little motivation to concern themselves with either segment; the initial wave of democratic administrations first gave priority to economic reconstruction before turning to the concerns of the urban middle classes and organized skilled workers. Even administrations four or five times removed from their country's initial democratic transformation found that a priority for economic stability severely circumscribed the growth required for more distributive policies.

In Brazil not only did Fernando Henrique Cardoso leave social justice and income redistribution on the back burner, but Luis Inácio Lula da Silva, his historically much more leftist successor, continued this strategy. The conservative victory behind Vicente Fox in 2000, combined with his party's 2006 win, guaranteed there would be no shift toward distributive policies in Mexico until at least after the 2012 elections. Colombia opted for a middle-of-the-road chief executive in Álvaro Uribe in 2002; with his 2006 reelection, any priority for social issues was pushed up past 2010. Argentina's turn-of-the-decade economic and social collapse condemned the administration of Néstor Kirchner to a situation where, in 2003–2005, economic recovery of necessity dominated the policy agenda, and the global recession crimped plans of his wife and successor to shift toward more progressive social policies. Hence, for the nearly 400 million of the region's 590 million inhabitants dwelling in the four largest countries, social justice continued to be limited chiefly to the levels of political rhetoric and campaign debate, not of current policy—leaving only Chile and Venezuela doing much about social issues, since Peru continued to have severe budget constraints, combined with important social groups' becoming increasingly restless.

Given significant structural differences in the economies of the several Latin American countries, there was a sharpened awareness among politically relevant groups that what was needed, or what might be politically feasible, in one country was not the same as in another—even if they might be neighbors geographically. Hence a growing division emerged between those nations in which democracy and development appeared to go hand in hand and those where formally democratic governments fell short in the sphere of economic performance, particularly where this shortcoming was compounded by dramatic rises in crime and public disorder. Management of the economy became the number-one priority for governments, especially in the more urban and developed countries, but with less favored sectors of society expecting to see positive results reflected in their levels of living, not just in macroeconomic indicators. Electorates in each country had little interest in overall Latin American economic figures, even positive ones, if their nation lagged behind and their sector of society was still being shortchanged. Indeed, only the more privileged strata had any concept of Latin America, much less a sense of Latin American identity. Hence at the end of the first decade of the twenty-first century challenges remained daunting and tensions showed few signs of easing.

Yet the early 2000s witnessed several important landmarks in Latin America: the election of an authentic representative of the working class to the presidency of Brazil, its largest country; victory of the opposition in Mexico for the first time in the life of even its most senior citizens; the remarkable recovery of Argentina from a crisis that had brought it to the brink of chaos, with a revolving-door presidency leading to the holding of new elections in early 2003; the elevation to power in Colombia, through its 2002 elections, of a hard-hitting law-and-order politician committed to reversing the tolerance shown to the guerrillas by his predecessor; and the full consolidation of restored democracy in Chile. Even Peru has climbed out of virtual ungovernability, while Venezuela is hailed either as a shining experiment with Bolivarian socialism or a tragedy of authoritarian populism.

Since 2010–2012 will see critical elections in almost all these countries, their recent electoral developments require close examination, especially in Brazil, with its great expanse, massive electorate, extremely fluid multiparty system, and dysfunctional electoral system—all defying predictions. Everywhere, voter concerns, issues, and responses from contenders take on increasing relevance as attention turns to electoral campaigns. The overall regional processes and distinguishing features of national experiences having been delineated, the distinct paths followed by each country require close examination before meaningful conclusions as to causation and implications for the future can be drawn. As Brazil and Mexico tower above the other countries in terms of population, size, and economic weight, the journey begins with them.

Notes

1. In addition to the *Journal of Democracy*'s coverage of elections, Web sites of the Americas program of the Center for Strategic and International Studies and the Latin American Programs of the Woodrow Wilson International Center for Scholars are useful for keeping abreast of events and trends in the fields covered by this book.

6

Brazil Since 1930

From 1930 to 2010 Brazil would make very substantial progress in the realm of both political development and the establishment of democracy. The early decades saw both, but substantially more of the former than the latter. Then post–World War II headway with respect to democratization would be swept away, not just eroded, during twenty years of military rule (1964–1984). After 1985 the two processes would progress hand in hand within the context of a much more economically developed and socially modern nation than that existing in 1930. The country would find the center-left party in power from 1995 through 2002, squaring off against the progressive party that had succeeded it in a seventh consecutive electoral contest for the presidency. The nation had well over 190 million inhabitants with an economy having reached $2 trillion and growing international recognition as a major actor on the world scene. The road had not been easy, and severe setbacks had interrupted progress along the way, but what had been a fraud-ridden elite-dominated republic in decay in 1930 had become a highly participant, consolidated democracy by 2010. Women had made great strides, and Afro-Brazilians were less disadvantaged than ever before.

The Vargas Era

For Brazil 1930–1955 was a momentous period, dominated from beginning to end by Getúlio Dornelles Vargas (b. 1883).[1] Taking place in an atmosphere of economic crisis, the 1930 elections were the traditional system's last chance to show whether it could adapt to the country's changing circumstances, and the governing elites of the "old republic" (1889–1930) failed the test. Never in the four-decade life of the republic had the government's candidate lost, and these arrogant movers and shakers saw no reason to change what seemed to them to be natural, if not ordained by God. Hence, many people inherently averse to revolution ended up throwing themselves into one behind Vargas, a moderate leader who personally sought compromise and conciliation until the last moment—indeed, a man who would have been pleased to become president in partnership with the established elites, if they had only let him attain office through the electoral process.[2]

The core of the revolutionary movement that triumphed in October 1930 was the *tenentes,* who had gained conspiratorial experience and popular renown during their armed struggle against the Artur da Silva Bernardes government. The revolutionary movement's success, however, required alliance with a broad coalition of political forces with power bases in a number of key states, a feat for which an experienced leader would have to be found outside the *tenentes'* ranks—a role tailored to Vargas's multifaceted talents. Born in the late years of the monarchy on a ranch in the interior of Rio Grande do Sul (Brazil's rebellious southern state), and raised the son of a leader of state militia forces involved in that frontier area's bloody civil strife of the 1890s, he joined the army at sixteen but resigned from the military preparatory school as result of a disciplinary incident, an action that left him a hero to his classmates and greatly facilitated his dealings with his generation of military leaders. Returned to the ranks as a sergeant, this feisty cowboy type (*gaucho*) saw brief combat service during a 1902 border dispute with Bolivia. Entering state politics in 1908, after graduation from law school in Porto Alegre, where he established a reputation in student politics, Vargas was quickly recognized as possessing unusual leadership talents. Elected to the state legislature in 1909, he soon rose to the position of majority leader. In 1922 Vargas was elected to the congress, where he functioned as leader of his state's delegation. In 1926 he achieved the rare distinction of being appointed Brazil's finance minister despite not coming from the São Paulo–Minas Gerais coffee elite. In November 1927 he was elected governor of his home state, where he cemented a close relationship with rising young officers who had attended the military academy in Porto Alegre while he and his closest associates were studying down the street at the law school.

The revolutionary movement was a heterogeneous amalgam of groups desiring sweeping political changes, if not a new social order, with elements violently opposed to the incumbent administration's control of presidential succession but devoid of any wish for more than moderate political and administrative reforms. Its civilian and military components were both essentially bourgeois. Presidential succession served as the issue around which fragmented opposition forces joined in a movement cohesive at least insofar as its immediate objective—attainment of power—was concerned. If government leaders thought that the 1930 election might defuse the growing crisis, they were sorely mistaken. Although Minas Gerais and Rio Grande do Sul jointly gave Vargas nearly 600,000 votes, he was credited with only 200,000 in all the rest of the country, whereas the official candidate, Júlio Prestes de Albuquerque, was given a national total of 1.1 million. Credibility was the issue in a country with a long tradition of creative vote counting, as Vargas's backers believed fervently that reluctantly crediting their leader with 44 percent of the vote was tantamount to admitting that he had been the real winner. This certainty of fraud grew as the Liberal Alliance (AL) totaled up their estimates of actual voting in the rest of the country— beginning with Rio de Janeiro, where the electoral books did not come close to balancing. Catalyzing the decision to raise the banner of revolt was the assassination of Vargas's running mate on July 26. Forty-year-old Lieutenant Colonel Pedro Aurélio de Góes Monteiro, a native of the northeastern state of Alagoas, although his military education as well as his in-laws were based in Rio Grande do Sul, rapidly emerged as the movement's effective chief of staff. Yet, despite more than a year of contingency planning, the civilians and military who would soon mobilize the most extensive revolutionary movement in Latin America's history were seeking a peaceful compromise until the last moment.

Launched on October 3 in Rio Grande do Sul, the revolt immediately drew into its wake the powerful 14,000-man federal force there, as well as the state militia. Marching northward and picking up reinforcements in Santa Catarina and Paraná, by week's end the rebel column was preparing for battle with legalist forces loyal to the government massed in southern São Paulo. Meanwhile rebel units had scored a series of successes in the distant northeast, and by October 23 rebel forces from Minas Gerais were on the verge of invading Rio de Janeiro. Aided by the intervention of the archbishop, senior generals convinced the president to resign on October 24, taking power temporarily as a "pacifying junta." Ten days later Vargas assumed office, promising a program of "national reconstruction," an amalgam of the Liberal Alliance program and a laundry list of demands of the diverse groups that had supported the revolt. The army was left deeply divided since, as shown by McCann, it had been split into six groupings: the *tenentes;* Góes Monteiro's moderates; opportunistic adherents; resisters; pacifiers; and fence-sitters.[3] Through moves more heavy-handed than those adopted in 1889 by Deodoro da Fonseca after overthrowing the monarchy, the provisional government established itself as a dictatorship with vast discretionary powers. Representative bodies were dissolved, and interventors, trusted political figures appointed by Vargas to replace the elected governors and carry out his wishes, had nearly total powers in the states. Large numbers of politicians associated with the ousted government were arrested. Senior military officers who had viewed Vargas only as a lesser evil than an extensive civil war were alarmed by the influence of the *tenentes,* whom they viewed as undisciplined, politically ambitious upstarts. Historical revolutionaries (those who had supported the 1920s rebellion) distrusted senior officers and midgrade legalists (officers who had remained loyal to the elected government) as opportunists lacking loyalty to revolutionary goals. Moreover, the *tenentes* and the dissident oligarchs had become belated allies only as events moved from the electoral arena to armed revolt. Key to the situation as 1930 ended was that

> 1930 was a reformist movement rather than a truly revolutionary one. It did not intend to eliminate poverty or even redistribute national wealth or income; it did not propose to cut up the huge *fazendas* that dominated agriculture and restructure landholding more equitably; it did not set out to eliminate illiteracy. The revolutionaries wanted an honest government that would promote modernization that included industrialization and economic development but with little re-stitching of the social fabric.[4]

The urban middle classes—including the military—took a leading part in the 1930 Revolution but lacked the independence to formulate a political program or establish autonomy from dissident elements of the oligarchy, who also participated in the revolution or quickly aligned themselves with the new regime once it was established. These eventually conservative groups realized that electoral democracy under the existing socioeconomic system would result in a return to power of the class of landowners and export merchants, whose political dependents and hangers-on greatly outnumbered the urban voters. Thus, finding in Vargas a leader in whom they could place their trust, the emerging middle-class groups submerged their reformist ideas and accepted a paternalistic regime without parties or elections, but one in which they could play a major role in a rapidly expanding bureaucracy. As in 1889, the army was the vehicle for dissident elites and the middle class to overturn old governmental institutions. When the military returned to the barracks, the civilian middle class could not hold onto political power in a still essentially patrimonial society, yet they could reap individual benefits from the clientelistic *cartorial* system by again agreeing to be coopted.

Hence, instead of a pluralist democracy, a populist authoritarian regime emerged under Vargas and built up the urban working class as a potential power factor in a corporative institutional structure (one based upon societal groupings, not individual pluralism). The middle class gained control of the *cartorial* state apparatus but did not come to control the political system as a whole. Government continued to serve the interests of the class that controlled the economy, as it looked out for the immediate needs of a middle class that asked for little more than guaranteed employment by the government or as a direct result of its development projects and social programs. As the industrial bourgeoisie developed as a potentially significant political factor (basically sympathetic to modernization), the astute Vargas began to move toward also using the industrial, essentially urban, working class as a political base for his increasingly developmentalist and nationalist policies.

During the Vargas period the state employed, with substantial success, the powerful instrument of patronage to coopt effectively much of organized labor into a "system of State tutelage and control" that would persist beyond the 1960s.[5] Most critical to the failure of the 1930 Revolution to develop into a sharp rupture with the past was the fact that the *tenentes* ("lieutenants"), rebellious young officers who constituted the cutting edge of the movement for political reform, had no one view of an appropriate role for the working class. Indeed, the civilian middle class, for all their espousal of political democracy, were not strongly inclined toward social reforms. This being the case, the armed forces became the key factor in events of the Vargas period, exercising "the function of arbiter that the body politic destined for them."[6]

Even without rupture, Brazil was transformed under Vargas: During the fifteen years of his initial stint at the nation's helm, the hegemony of the traditional agricultural elites was broken, new industrial elements came to exert significant influence on national policy, and the middle class developed political muscle and savvy. Under stop-and-go government sponsorship, determined by Vargas's reading of the political winds, the working class gradually assumed a position on the political stage, although no more central than upstage left. Vargas's long stay in power accelerated economic development; created a structured, if coopted, labor movement; strengthened the central government immensely; and greatly expanded the scope of the government's activities—in the process, raising and broadening aspirations for participation. In some ways the transformation exceeded that achieved after 1945 by Juan Perón in Argentina, since Vargas needed to cover ground already traversed by Argentina under the radicals in 1916–1930.

Far from homogeneous in their political orientation, the *tenentes* shared several attitudes setting them apart from the civilian liberal constitutionalists, who were preoccupied with democratic forms whereas the *tenentes* were concerned about the substance of vaguely articulated social and economic reforms. They also manifested an elitist approach to "national regeneration" from the top, frequently shading into authoritarian nationalism (a tendency also found among rising Argentine officers of the same generation). Although the communists and other radical movements were quite weak, their noisiness led both the old elites and the emerging middle class to a near obsession with the proletarian threat. Many failed to grasp the wisdom of Vargas's creation of a labor ministry so as to better control the workers, as well as his subtle use of manipulative paternalism. The elements considering themselves owners of the revolution were so varied as to defy orchestration. Hence Vargas's ability to work with them all and keep them from each other's throats was more phenomenal than merely exceptional. Its roots went back into his youth, when he had undertaken a military education that, even if not completed, gave him deep insight into the thought process of the contemporary military generation as well as close personal ties with many of them. Well aware that the Liberal Alliance's common denominator was opposition to the Washington Luís government rather than hostility toward the established order, Vargas also understood all the feuding civilian components of the movement that had brought him to power just as well as he understood the military. Moderately conservative to liberal, the dissident elites of advanced states such as Minas Gerais and São Paulo wanted a system of formal representative democracy in which the power of the rural oligarchic machines was curbed by the elimination of their ability to manipulate electoral results. This degree of political development had been accomplished in Argentina at the time of World War I, so the Brazilians thought it could be done in their country in fairly short order. Groups opposed to the old government in the smaller states were even less interested in reform. They just wanted to receive from the new government what their rivals had got from the old. Progressive elements saw electoral reforms as an opening to empowerment of the middle class to enact an agenda of economic and social reforms.

Before Vargas could do more than allot power at the state level to trustworthy elements and establish a minimally effective federal executive, he was faced with a counterrevolutionary threat. The São Paulo uprising, threatening disaggregation of the revolutionary forces, erupted in part because Vargas's hand-picked interventor was an outsider, a fact underscoring how much the former holders of power had lost; instead of governing the country, they were not even allowed to govern their own state. Essentially the revolt occurred because São Paulo had not been militarily defeated during the revolution: Its congressional representatives had given up in the face of the federal army's withdrawal of support for the government at the same time as people back home in São Paulo were preparing for a battle they were confident they could win. Hence, Vargas's conciliatory convocation of May 1933 elections for a constituent assembly had no effect, and the proud Paulistas' resort to force to reverse a course of affairs desired by most Brazilians cost them dearly in the long run by confirming suspicions that the São Paulo Democratic Party believed in democracy only as long as it served the party's hegemonic designs.

Rio Grande do Sul remained loyal to Vargas, and Minas Gerais sent militia, dooming the May 1932 revolt to failure—as 80,000 federal troops took five months to crush the valiant struggle by 70,000 Paulistas hoodwinked by their leaders into believing that help would come from other states. These oligarchs failed to enlist the support of the state's growing working class, for whom they harbored disdain and distrust. Following a policy of conciliation with the people of São Paulo, if not with the revolt's instigators, Vargas held elections on May 3, 1933, for a National Constituent Assembly. These elections were marked by a confusingly large number of new parties, often existing only at the state level as fronts for established interests and old leaders The 214 winners were joined by 40 handpicked representatives of social groupings. With senior officers replaced by individuals who had proved their loyalty and ability on the battlefield, and with the prospect of a united Paulista opposition eliminated through the appointment of a favorite son to govern there, Vargas was in a strengthened position. Moreover, *tenentismo* was nearly eliminated as a political force, and the army "came closer than at any previous time to enjoying a monopoly of force within Brazil."[7]

Chosen president in July 1933 for the 1934–1938 term by the National Constituent Assembly by a vote of 175 to 59 over a civilian rival, Vargas would govern under a constitution reflecting the divisions within Brazil's body politic. The core of the 1891 charter and its classic presidential institutions were preserved, with the addition of political reforms dear to the liberal constitutionalists and socioeconomic guarantees demanded by the *tenentes* and their reformist civilian counterparts. The transition from dictator to constitutional chief executive led Vargas to pay more attention to the claims of organized political groups. Ineligible to succeed himself, he had to deal with others' presidential ambitions and their impact on the 1934 congressional elections and the subsequent indirect selection of governors. With his skillful support, forces supporting Vargas's appointed interventors came out on top in all major states, in many cases confirming the interventor as elected governor. Yet political polarization soon disrupted the atmosphere of harmony accompanying Brazil's successful recovery from the Great Depression, which had played a major role in the 1930 Revolution. For strong ideological movements of the left and right took center stage away from the intramural squabbles of the government's supporters. By 1935 Luís Carlos Prestes for the Communist Party and Plínio Salgado for the incipient fascistic movement calling itself the Integralists were attracting the attention of the urban populace. In March 1935 the National Liberating Alliance (ANL) was launched as a united front for the illegal Brazilian Communist Party (PCB) and other radical leftist forces, including some alienated *tenentes*. Poorly planned, the November 1935 communist-led revolt was a total fiasco that left an anticommunist legacy in the military that was still operative a generation later. Allying the Catholic Church and propertied interests with the military to combat most progressive forces, the communist blunder enabled Vargas to lay the groundwork for his own coup and establishment of a long-term dictatorship.

The year 1937 was the most momentous for Brazil since 1930. While the public's attention was focused on the contest for Vargas's successor, scheduled for election in January 1938, crucial developments were taking place behind the scenes, where the president skillfully undermined political rivals and created a favorable situation among the military. At the end of 1936 he installed General Eurico Gaspar Dutra (b. 1883) as war minister, and soon after, his amicable rival Góes Monteiro (b. 1889) became armed-forces chief of staff. By mid-1937 both the presidential campaign and Vargas's conspiracy to derail it were in high gear. One candidate—Armando de Salles Oliveira—was depicted as a Paulista oligarch dedicated to restoring that state's hegemony; the other—José Américo de Almeida—was pictured as naive and dangerously demagogic. Both portrayals were quite close to the truth. Hence much of the political elite and a growing number of the middle class were susceptible to the idea that the elections should be postponed if a suitable unity candidate could not be found. Astutely riding on a controlled escalation of the crisis, Vargas fostered polarization by, on the one hand, encouraging the Integralists to act openly and aggressively and, on the other, reactivating the specter of communist subversion through the hoax of a sensational communist plan that created an atmosphere of near hysteria. Yet the most important element in establishing an authoritarian regime was the army, and its support for Vargas's initiatives required agreement on a mutually beneficial plan for the years ahead.[8]

With full military support and a sigh of relief from many sectors of society, on November 10, 1937, the congress elected in 1934 was closed, and a new constitution was declared to be in effect. The eight-year run of the Estado Novo (the "New State," named after Salazar's corporatist regime in Portugal) had begun. Vargas was able to assume the stance of a unifying symbol in a situation where polarization provided salience to both communism and fascism, while the majority rejecting both extremes was divided between the traditional socially sterile constitutionalism of one presidential candidate and the fundamental, often incoherent populism of the other. As the 1937 Constitution's articles concerning representation and legislation never went into effect, Vargas continued to enjoy the power to legislate by presidential decrees. The communists having eliminated themselves from contention through their 1935 fiasco, the only challenge to Vargas's new order came in May 1938, when the Integralists joined with some liberal constitutionalist conspirators in a poorly executed coup attempt. Suspicious that political parties might prove a vehicle for the rise of rivals, Vargas also viewed them as electoral trappings irrelevant to his needs and objectives. His basic pattern of manipulative paternalism, shifting gradually toward personalistic populism, required no intermediary structures. In this area Vargas was not innovative, preferring to turn existing forces to his use and to destroy those he could not utilize. He also preferred to exploit personal rivalries among leading figures, often turning yesterday's opponents into today's allies rather than having to deal with institutionalized power contenders.

Vargas did not drastically change his political style or the institutional structure of the Estado Novo during the eight years of its existence, but he did adapt pragmatically to altered conditions as the processes of industrialization and urbanization gradually modified the societal foundations of the polity. National integration continued to progress, and the federal executive developed capabilities far beyond those of the pre-Vargas era. An array of administrative agencies was established to deal with matters previously outside the scope of public policy, but now of concern to the centralized, increasingly interventionist state. Moreover, a wide variety of government corporations and mixed capital enterprises came into being to play ever more important roles in development—along with a network of organizations designed to tie urban workers to the government through both a dependent union movement and a rudimentary social welfare system. Thus, there were multiple interests seeking to influence public policy, but after 1937 there was no legislative arena and no opportunity to mobilize electoral support and bring it to bear upon the executive. Vargas was an exceptionally astute political balancer, conciliator, and manipulator, but he was overextended, requiring development of structures for linking state and society. With parties ruled out, the answer was an informal, but effective, network tying together the Vargas-appointed interventors, the growing array of governmental agencies, and sectoral organizations fostered by the basically corporatist design of the regime. Masterfully orchestrated by Vargas, this arrangement provided a means for accommodating emerging interests while easing the decline of traditional elites by continuing to provide opportunity to influence the decisions most vital to their economic interests. The resulting system of cooptative clientelism (selectively using patronage and benefits to gain and hold political support) enhanced the viability of the Vargas-designed system by channeling the concerns of politically relevant elements into narrow struggles over policy in particular areas—hence away from questions of the regime's basic orientation and underlying priorities. On balance this system worked better than the system uneasily in place in Argentina, that being forged in Mexico, or even the electoral democracy in Colombia.

The Brazil of the 1940s had evolved considerably since the 1930 Revolution. Population had grown to over 41 million (on its way to 52 million by 1950), with the state of São Paulo surpassing Minas Gerais. By 1940 urbanization had lifted Rio de Janeiro to 1.9 million inhabitants, followed by São Paulo with 1.3 million. A sustained surge of import-substitution industrialization was narrowing the gap between agriculture and industry as proportions of GDP, although the former still provided two-thirds of the national employment. Internal economic activity was overtaking external demand as the principal determinant of the accumulation of capital. The hegemony of the traditional coffee bourgeoisie had ended because coffee had fallen as a proportion of agricultural production from nearly 50 percent in the 1920s to 30 percent by the mid-1930s, and only 16 percent after 1939. Urban, modernizing sectors of society were increasingly penetrated by the governmental capabilities of the executive, and as the central government came to affect the lives of a larger proportion of the population directly, more frequently, and in a wider variety of ways, the regime built a multiclass base, even if it was not yet reflected in the sphere of political organization. The foundation for significant political mobilization had been laid.

World War II had a profound impact upon the Brazilian armed forces, especially officers of the *tenente* generation. Initially Vargas used the war to his advantage, channeling military energies into the war effort while rallying popular support in the name of national defense. Politically active officers were sent to the United States for training, then on to Italy to fight, and in general the armed forces were pleased with the new equipment they received and the favorable position relative to Argentina that Brazil came to enjoy. Both Dutra and Góes Monteiro—whose rival ambitions Vargas played against each other as skillfully as Napoléon had done with Charles Maurice de Talleyrand and Joseph Fouché—underwent a shift from sympathy for Hitler's Germany to support of the Allies. But this transformation carried the generals on to becoming champions of liberal democracy, and they would eventually join the movement to oust the dictator from power—if only to avoid the danger of being dragged down with him in the face of growing sentiment for a return to representative government. The Brazilian Expeditionary Force (FEB) returned from Italy covered with glory just in time to take part in the intense political maneuvering that characterized the second half of 1945 in Brazil.[9]

Aware that the Estado Novo could not carry over into the postwar era without major modifications, in 1943 Vargas had begun preparations for an eventual return to competitive politics by forging a political organization capable of mobilizing public support for a contest at the polls. Building upon the foundation of amplified social programs for urban workers and the government's close control over their unions, he began to organize a machine that could rapidly be transformed into a party. Industrialization became the touchstone of a program designed to appeal not only to workers, but to urban commercial and entrepreneurial interests, government employees, and the military as well. The sage politician realized that he was faced with a challenge far different from those of 1932 and 1937, as presidential aspirant Dutra could not be expected to support his continuation in power, and the opposition's Brigadier Eduardo Gomes (b. 1896) was the leading paladin of the *tenentes* by now pushing into senior office ranks. Determined that if he could not hold onto power directly, it must pass to his allies and supporters rather than to his critics, Vargas played out what seemed to be a losing hand in such a way as to maximize the possibilities of a future comeback.

On April 7, 1945, representatives of all political currents opposed to Vargas founded the National Democratic Union (UDN); Vargas immediately countered with the Social Democratic Party (PSD), essentially a holding company of state political establishments. Elections were convoked for December 2, and on July 17 Dutra was nominated by the PSD, being succeeded as war minister by army chief of staff Góes Monteiro. Vargas shifted his attention to launching the Brazilian Labor Party (PTB), a vehicle for channeling electoral support from the government-controlled labor unions. By yielding to the irresistible, Vargas was able to depart from office with honor and dignity and, more important, without having opened an irreparable breach with the armed forces. As Vargas was suspect in the eyes of the United States, burned by Perón's successful maneuvering in Argentina at this time, Dutra's military supporters allied with those of the UDN's Gomes to thwart any continuist designs the president might harbor, and the head of the Brazilian supreme court temporarily assumed the presidency on October 30. The Estado Novo was over, but Vargas was still politically potent, and the institutional structure he had devised remained untouched. Elected to the senate from both São Paulo and Rio Grande do Sul, this short, middle-aged man would continue to cast a long shadow over Brazilian politics. His ouster was largely a reaction by the old landowning and mercantile elite, in alliance with much of the middle class, against the processes of change that threatened to undermine the continued conservative dominance of politics and to use the state to further the interests of the dominant groups rather than those of an emerging urban working class. In this the elite and the middle class were rowing against the current, much as their Argentine counterparts had done in the 1930s, and the ambivalences of the middle class would in the longer run lead them back to Vargas. For at this juncture the Brazilian middle class was undergoing a transformation catalyzed by the entrance of a new generation of technical and administratively oriented personnel and a "new intelligentsia" concerned about development problems. In the immediate postwar period these still insecure elements feared losing their recent gains through the rise of the working class and the extension of expensive social benefits to them.

The growing middle class, more concerned about its patronage positions than about radical changes in the system, permitted consolidation of democratic forms without correlative social policies. In a framework of contact between the state and the urban masses through the intermediary of populist leaders, personalities took precedence over programs and, even more, over ideologies. In sharp contrast with Mexico or even Peronist Argentina, Brazil's political parties, suffering from a lack of coherence and organization, as well as from their essentially conservative orientation, were inadequate vehicles for the socialization of the new urban masses entering the electorate. Thus, as would be repeated in the 1980s, whereas vociferous nationalists proclaimed the advent of the era of ideological politics and were followed by the relatively highly politicized leadership of unions and "popular" organizations, the masses turned instead to a direct link between their votes and a political leader with a significant degree of charisma. Clientelism continued to hold the middle class to the established political leadership and the existing parties in terms of an exchange of votes for employment or a specific favor. But this arrangement could not work for the urban masses when the electorate expanded far beyond the patronage potential even of the *cartorial* state. From a million in 1908 and 2.7 million in 1934, the electorate had grown to over 7.4 million by 1945 (and rose another 1,100 percent by 1989).

Even Dutra's December 2, 1945, election depended far more upon the durability of the forces solidly in control of a majority of the states plus the urban masses' response to Vargas's populist appeals than on the lackluster candidate. For its part, Gomes's campaign had difficulty avoiding the essentially negative image of being against everything Vargas stood for. With almost 6.2 million individuals voting, the vast majority for the first time, Dutra defeated the opposition's Gomes by a margin of better than 3 to 2 (3.25 million to 2.04 million); the Communist Party standard bearer trailed with nearly 570,000. Well over 60 percent of the victor's margin came from São Paulo and Rio Grande do Sul, with much of the rest run up in Minas Gerais—as the Vargas-founded PSD and PTB delivered massive pluralities. The Dutra government turned out to be a temporary interruption of Vargas's work, not its derailment, much less its end. This sixty-year-old career army officer who took office on January 31, 1946, was experienced only in the intraregime politics of the Vargas era. Owing to his cautious nature, Brazil failed to receive strong or imaginative presidential leadership during this crucial period of transition from a relatively closed discretionary regime to an open, competitive, and representative system. Without guidance from Dutra, the new congress produced in September 1946 a constitution designed to curb executive power and guarantee federalism. State elections in January 1947 resulted in Adhemar de Barros's creating the Social Progressive Party (PSP) and becoming São Paulo governor. This creation of a party dominant in the leading state would have the effect of preventing the development of true national parties, as the PSD, UDN, and PTB would be relegated to secondary importance in the country's most populous and important state. The most negative heritage of the ballyhooed "restoration of democracy" was failure to lay a foundation for a functional party system, a detrimental shortcoming that handicaps Brazilian political development down to the present. Vargas's continuation as the potentially dominant figure for two of the three major parties, combined with the fact that opposition to him was the unifying factor and guiding principle of the third, drastically inhibited the development of parties along modern programmatic lines or into institutionalized vehicles for political mobilization.

The PSD, the party of the political "ins," supplied the majority in the 1946–1950 congress, occupied most executive positions under Dutra, and controlled the greater proportion of state administrations. Essentially nonideological, it combined dominant rural machines of the post-1930 period with businessmen and industrialists who had benefited from Vargas's increasing orientation toward economic development. It had the support of a high proportion of the new bureaucratic stratum, and its ranks were swelled by patronage-seeking opportunists (an element adhering to all subsequent governing parties). In its early years the UDN was an alliance of political "outs," and the PSD was a coalition of holders of power, which originally brought together the political chiefs of rural cliques not favored by the interventors or the governors who replaced them, including some of the most reactionary landowners, with urban commercial-industrial interests containing a high proportion of bankers, administrators of large companies, and offspring of prestigious families, as well as independent professionals and white-collar employees from the private sector. Despite a classically liberal tendency in the larger cities, because of malapportionment of congressional seats, the UDN came increasingly under the sway of its conservative rural wing. Its antithesis, the PTB, was still important only in the major industrial centers.

Governing with little opposition from the UDN, Dutra aimed at long-term stability, but his antilabor and anticommunist orientation made his term one of drift and the accommodation of retrograde forces. Vices of the Estado Novo were eliminated, but most of its virtues were also lost, and some of the least desirable features of the pre-Vargas system reemerged. A return to elections and a functioning congress enabled the old agricultural interests, through their controlled voters, to regain much of the power they had held before 1937, if not 1930. Large agriculturalists and associated mercantile interests strove to preserve an economic order based on agro-exports and unhindered access to imported manufactured goods. This resurgence of rural interests conflicted with the demands of business, banking, and an emerging industrial sector for fiscal policies promoting industrialization and tariff protection for their products. Despite unimaginative governmental policies, annual real GDP growth under Dutra averaged 6 percent, fully double the rate of population increase.

By 1950 there was a generalized nostalgia for the dynamic Vargas years. On April 19 Vargas accepted the PTB nomination, having already reached an agreement with Adhemar de Barros for PSP support—critical in São Paulo. He used his still-heavy influence within the PSD to ensure the selection of a weak candidate with appeal limited to the same sectors as that of the UDN standard bearer. Vargas also made deals with PSD gubernatorial and legislative candidates who wanted PTB votes in return for supporting him in the presidential balloting. Thus, although PSD candidates were victorious in most of the country, Vargas carried seventeen states plus the federal district (the city of Rio de Janeiro) with 3.9 million votes (nearly 49 percent) to 2.3 million (almost 30 percent) for the UDN's Gomes and fewer than 1.7 million (better than 21 percent) for the demoralized PSD nominee. The marriage of the predominantly rural-based traditionalist PSD and the largely urban, development-oriented PTB that Vargas forged in 1950 would survive, although with mutual infidelity and bickering, until 1964. Vargas's blend of clientelistic and populist policies shaped the PTB, deeply affected the PSD, and thwarted repeated efforts to infuse programmatic or ideological content into these parties. The proportions of the mix were to vary, as the PTB grew in strength relative to the PSD, and developmentalists and reformers increased within their ranks.[10]

Accustomed to governing free of restraints, Vargas was uncomfortable operating within an institutional structure designed to minimize his freedom of action. Moreover, Dutra's narrow interpretation of presidential powers and hands-off attitude with respect to party politics created a situation in which each move by Vargas to provide strong presidential leadership was attacked as an indication of dictatorial proclivities. In turn, Vargas was impatient with shortsighted obstruction of policies designed to modernize the nation and attacks upon his evolutionary approach to social welfare for the urban working class—whom he wished, in a neo-Bismarckian manner, to bring into politics within the system under the auspices of a government-linked party, as Cárdenas had done in Mexico and Perón was doing in Argentina. Vargas wanted to function as before as manipulator of existing political interests as well as mediator between these and the interests of emergent groups, being at his best as the resourceful conciliator of policy alternatives put forth by contending political forces. Beginning in a favorable economic context resulting from the demand for Brazilian products spurred by the Korean War, Vargas strove to make industrialization and diversification common denominators for a policy involving an active role for the state and a significant degree of government planning.

As long as the US administration of Harry S. Truman was willing to provide assistance for basic planning studies, Vargas turned a deaf ear to radical nationalists while maintaining his populist stance by advocating measures of economic nationalism. Near the end of 1951 he submitted to the congress a bill creating a mixed-capital corporation to explore and exploit Brazil's oil resources—which US experts had declared were extremely limited. Conservative military elements not reconciled to Vargas's victory over *tenente* hero Gomes lent a ready ear to Washington's laments over Vargas's unwillingness to join in the Korean War, embracing the perverse logic that participation in World War II created a moral obligation to align with the United States in subsequent conflicts. Hence radicalization of political life took place during the latter half of 1953, a period in which the end of the Korean conflict eroded demand for Brazilian exports, and a hostile Republican government replaced a sympathetic Democratic administration in the United States. With Vargas's term having reached midpoint, elements of the armed forces not only once again suspected Vargas of harboring designs to continue in office, but this time felt he had backing from Argentine strongman Perón. As would be the case again in the early 1960s, inflation served as the catalyst of social tensions and raised dilemmas of financial policy that the administration had sought to avoid. Wage restraints and credit restrictions, essential for economic purposes (as a former finance minister, Vargas was unique among Brazilian presidents—and most other Latin American chief executives—in recognizing the importance of sound fiscal and financial policies), undercut his efforts to build up support among labor and the new industrialists. The cost of living had risen 21 percent in 1952, twice the rise in the preceding year, and inflationary pressures were growing. The US administration of Dwight D. Eisenhower, with its policy largely shaped by Secretary of State John Foster Dulles, refused to consider any moral obligation to continue Truman's commitment to developmental assistance. Instead, Brazil was told that it should make conditions more attractive for US private investment. As a gesture of good faith, Vargas should withdraw support for Petrobrás, the state petroleum company recently approved by the congress.

The backbone of the anti-Vargas movement polarizing politics and pushing confrontation in place of conciliation was an alliance of the UDN with the strongly anticommunist wing of the armed forces. Defeated at the ballot box in 1945 and 1950, they had a commitment to democratic processes that had worn thin. An abortive attack on the life of strident Vargas critic Carlos Lacerda on August 5, 1954, gave the bitterly frustrated outs an opportunity to destabilize the president. As a military-run investigation uncovered involvement of Vargas cronies in unsavory dealings, and as leading generals refused his offer to take a leave of absence, the seventy-one-year-old Vargas shot himself on August 24. His eloquent suicide note swung public opinion against his enemies, whom he depicted as greedy reactionaries and unpatriotic instruments of rapacious foreign interests.

With Vargas abruptly gone from the stage he had dominated for so long, tension between pro- and anti-Vargas forces dominated the political scene. In the midst of advanced stages of campaigning for the October 3, 1954, legislative and gubernatorial elections, with presidential balloting only a little over a year away, Vice President João Café Filho (b. 1899) assumed a caretaker role, supported by a mixture of non-Vargist political forces, including the pro-Dutra wing of the PSD. The outcome of elections held only forty days after Vargas's death was surprisingly normal, resulting in a standoff between Vargas's heirs and his foes. As usual, the chief concern of politicians was to win, so national issues took a backseat to local questions and alliances of convenience. When the dust settled, the PSD had held onto its leading position with 114 Chamber of Deputies (lower house) seats, the PTB had edged up to 56, and the UDN had slipped to 74. Thus Café Filho and his successors would have to govern all the way to February 1959 with a congress little changed from that elected with Vargas in 1950.

With a president to be chosen, Brazil had no respite from campaigning, as the PTB and PSD allied behind Minas Gerais governor Juscelino Kubitschek de Oliveira (b. 1902) with Vargas protégé João Belquior Marques Goulart (b. 1918) for vice president. Ranking *tenente* Juarez do Nascimento Fernandes Távora (b. 1898) ran for the UDN-PDC coalition, with Adhemar de Barros (b. 1901) making a determined São Paulo–based bid. Largely on the strength of a home state margin of 430,000 votes, Kubitschek, with nearly 3.1 million votes, beat Juarez Távora by a 470,000-vote margin while receiving only 34 percent of the record 9.1 million ballots cast. Anti-Vargas forces tried to block the personable Kubitschek's inauguration, installing the presiding officer of the Chamber of Deputies as acting president, but the PSD-PTB coalition thwarted this ploy by substituting the senate's president, who, backed by the war minister, held office until Kubitschek took over in early 1956.

Although Vargas was gone, this rotund grandfatherly figure would continue to cast a long shadow, and the political patterns he had fostered would persist. Although his legacy was not embodied in a party as Cárdenas's was in Mexico or Perón's was in Argentina, it would be as lasting. Up through the military takeover in 1964, Brazilian governments would be based on a loose coalition of industrialists, commercial sectors linked to the internal market, technical elements of the middle class, and the organized component of the working class. But when the process of development threatened to bring significant socioeconomic changes, the military, with the support of conservative interests and the traditional sector of the middle class, would intervene.

Progressive forces failed to create a new party, resting instead on the inadequate basis of an eroding alliance between the PSD, strong in the congress, and the PTB, with popular support in urban areas. Vargas's heirs would run up against a hard wall of obstruction thrown up by those closely linked to the old agrarian interests and entrenched in the government machinery.

The Road into and back from Military Takeover, 1956–1979

Even after the substantial modernization of government and politics during the long Vargas era, personalities continued to take precedence over programs. Alongside still relatively effective clientelistic politics, new types of populist leaders emerged, some owing more and some less to Vargas's example. The basically conservative orientation of major parties and the heavy, if not predominant, rural influence in their leadership prevented close identification of urban voters with them. The masses turned instead to a direct link between their votes and political leaders with some degree of charisma. Clientelism continued to be the basis for holding the middle class to established political leadership and existing parties through exchange of votes for employment or favors. But it could not work for the urban masses, as the electorate grew beyond the patronage potential of the *cartorial* state. From 1 million in 1908 and 2.7 million in 1934 balloting, the electorate had passed 7.4 million by 1945, subsequently growing exponentially. As Vargas left no true heir, the peculiar Brazilian form of populism he had embodied, combining features of urban machine politics with personalism, emotional appeals, and effective performance in the material realm, assumed several distinct forms as aspiring leaders adapted it to the peculiar characteristics of the constituents they were wooing in their state. João Goulart on the left, rooted in Rio Grande do Sul, attempted rather ineptly to carry on the labor-oriented nationalism of Vargas, only to be outdone by his own brother-in-law, Leonel Brizola (b. 1922), who modernized the appeal to workers with a more stridently ideological brand of nationalism. Like his nemesis, Carlos Lacerda (b. 1914), he effectively exploited the new medium of television to transcend the limitations of public appearances to communicate with the masses. For on the right in Rio de Janeiro it was the crusading anticommunist zeal of Lacerda and his mystique of intransigent opposition, in a system where opportunism and accommodation predominated, that gained a fanatic following. Centered in São Paulo was the conservative brand of Adhemar de Barros, blending massive public works expenditures with demagogic campaigning and skillful exploitation of graft and patronage to electoral ends. The antithesis to this patronage approach was the moralistic messianism of Jânio da Silva Quadros (b. 1917), the ascetic giant killer capitalizing on the popular desires for an end to the corruption and controversy of Adhemarism and Goulart's perversion of Vargism. These strains of populism shared an appeal to the swelling mass urban population, which had been poorly assimilated and was plagued by the insecurities of city life as have-nots. Restless, but largely nonradical, the middle class also gave substantial support to populist politicians.

First up was the transitional Kubitschek, the quintessential Brazilian "cordial" man, impossible to dislike and folksy in a natural-seeming manner. Elected with a plurality in November 1955 in a close three-way race, this grandson of a Czech immigrant earned a unique place in the annals of Brazilian politics by being more popular at the end of his term than at its beginning. Indeed, he is often considered Brazil's best single-term president. Born in Minas Gerais in 1902, after being orphaned he worked his way through medical school, graduating in 1927 and doing surgical internships in Paris, Vienna, and Berlin. Serving in the congress during Vargas's first democratic period (1934–1937), he returned there in 1946 after having been mayor of Belo Horizonte, Brazil's third largest city. Elected governor of Minas Gerais at the time of Vargas's triumphal 1950 return, this leader of the moderate and modern wing of the PSD earned a reputation as a builder and an effective developmentalist that propelled him to the presidency.[11] Kubitschek brought to office all the legendary facility for political maneuvering and compromise of an experienced Mineiro (a man born in Minas Gerais) politician. His Programa de Metas ("Program of Goals") promised "fifty years' progress in five" and emphasized transportation, energy, steel, manufacturing, and construction of a new capital in the sparsely populated interior. Offering something to nearly every relevant group, his program's long-run effect was consolidation of Brazil's industrialization by building up the requisite infrastructure while implanting heavy industry—especially automotive—and fostering a capital goods sector. A dynamic and pragmatic centrist, "JK" gave economic development marked priority over social welfare measures, which he postponed to an expected second term in 1961–1965. He carefully avoided the kind of confrontation that had cost Vargas his office and life, leaving the economic and political interests of the powerful landowning forces in his party untouched in exchange for their support in promoting industry and some steps toward the modernization of urban society—in a rapidly urbanizing country. The significant and painless economic growth during his term, over 8 percent a year, could not be duplicated by his immediate successors owing to the limits of import-substitution industrialization and the high level of inflation that was the legacy of his single-minded determination to attain goals his critics had scorned as impossibly ambitious.

As war minister, Marshal Henrique Duffles Teixeira Lott (b. 1894) was both a strong bulwark against plotting and conspiracies and a restraint upon the president's freedom of action. Kubitschek's amiability and moderate nationalism dispelled lingering suspicions among the officer corps concerning his Vargist origins, and his infectious enthusiasm for Brazil's future disarmed all but the most hardened of his opponents, moving the country closer to a national consensus on many basic issues than had existed since before the 1920s. Thus, his term was the apex of reasonably functioning representative politics, and the October 1958 congressional and partial gubernatorial elections were largely free of polarization. The 326-member Chamber of Deputies chosen to serve for the last two years of Kubitschek's term and the first years of his successor's was little changed from that elected four years earlier. Since Kubitschek could not stand for immediate reelection, the outcome of governorship races had important implications for the future, particularly Brizola's win in Rio Grande do Sul and the defeat of Adhemar de Barros by Quadros's candidate in São Paulo.

A stiffening of attitudes by the US government and international financial institutions, frustrated in their efforts to force the determined Kubitschek to cut sharply back on his development program in order to curb inflation, had unfortunate effects. The structuralist-monetarist controversy, previewed under Vargas, but sidestepped by the Café Filho government in 1954–1955, was joined full force as Kubitschek would not risk the stagnation that austerity programs had brought, and were bringing, to other countries in the region. In mid-1959 this chilling of relations was aggravated by a negative US response to a Kubitschek proposal for a joint crusade against underdevelopment in the hemisphere. (This Operation Pan-American provided the inspiration for the John F. Kennedy administration's 1961 Alliance for Progress.) Kubitschek's failure to give in to US wishes infuriated top US policymakers, especially Secretary of State Dulles. Inside Brazil the consensus on developmental nationalism that Kubitschek had skillfully forged began to disintegrate in the face of polemical exchanges between economic liberals' advocacy of orthodox fiscal measures and radical nationalists' attacks on foreign capital and external influences. Viewed by many Brazilians as a fearless patriot standing up to the forces that had laid Vargas low, Kubitschek preserved his prestige and personal popularity by staying above the partisan squabbling engendered by the proximity of presidential succession. Brazil's population was up to 70 million, with over 31 million classified as urban dwellers. Life expectancy was nearing fifty-three, compared to under forty-three in 1940, and infant mortality was dropping dramatically. The doubling of industrial production during Kubitschek's term was reflected in the presence of 2.9 million employees of industry in the labor force of 22.7 million—a significant rise from 1.6 million in 1940. Indeed, by 1960, industry accounted for 25 percent of GDP compared to 23 percent for agriculture. Exceeding most of his goals, Kubitschek had built an automotive industry from scratch to 321,000 vehicles in 1960. He had laid the foundation for Brazil's post-1967 economic takeoff, but the first three years of his successor's poor management in the midst of renewed political instability led to the overturning of the political system Kubitschek's adroitness and economic successes had bolstered.

By 1960 the balance in the PSD–PTB alliance had shifted to a point where the latter could demand a greater say in picking the presidential candidate, with nationalist credentials of key importance. Kubitschek acquiesced in the choice of Marshal Lott, despite his lack of popular appeal, since an opposition victory served his longer-run objective of not facing a formidable candidate in a 1965 comeback bid. Hence the electorate's hopes came to rest upon Quadros, a new and exciting type of populist politician promising to reform or dismantle the system rather than manipulate it. Viewed by many as a political messiah, as well as São Paulo's first real chance to regain the presidency it had lost in 1930, Quadros pledged to sweep out the accumulated corruption and inefficiency of three decades of the Vargas succession while setting Brazil's administrative house in order, maintaining the momentum of development, and remembering the common people, whose interests had been largely neglected by Kubitschek's emphasis upon infrastructure growth over social development.[12] Quadros appeared to much of the electorate to be the best bet for a sound administration, if not the nation's savior. To the UDN, having lost three times in a row with distinguished *tenentes* as candidates, he was the sole hope of finally attaining power. For in contrast to Kubitschek's step-by-step rise through the PSD machine, "Jânio," as he was popularly known, relied upon a charismatic appeal and highly unorthodox campaign techniques, in which he frequently changed party label in order to build an image and a following that transcended the lines of Brazil's fragmented political organizations. But in a bid for national office he needed the electoral machinery of a major party, so he accepted UDN endorsement. Having been catapulted to national prominence by his dramatic 1954 defeat of Adhemar de Barros for the São Paulo governorship, he was elected to the congress in 1958 and on October 3, 1960, sailed into the presidency with nearly 5.6 million votes to Lott's fewer than 3.8 million and de Barros's distant 2.2 million. In amassing a record plurality, he carried all of Brazil's major states, something not even Vargas had accomplished. The PTB's Goulart's narrowly achieving reelection as vice president seemed to be of secondary import at the time.

Quadros began the lamentable process of dissipating the positive heritage left by Kubitschek, a development that would pave the way for the most dismal decade in Brazil's life as a nation, 1963–1973. Betrayal of the people's hopes through erratic Bonapartist behavior (updated via Charles de Gaulle and Fidel Castro) left a pall of disillusionment when the providential man irresponsibly fled after eight short months, contributing to a perilous radicalization as some sought in doctrinaire programs or radical ideology to remake institutions and practices that the demagogic populist leader had so completely failed to deliver. Lending depth to the crises of 1962–1964 was a growing tension between modernizing sectors of Brazilian society and those opposed to fundamental change in the patrimonial order—rooted in clientelism, cooptation, and the *cartorial* state—that had successfully withstood the 1930 Revolution and the postwar "reestablishment of democracy." As the progressives were concentrated in the center-south and traditional forces were still dominant in the northeast and north, efforts to bridge this cleavage through accommodation and conciliation fell flat. Direct popular election of the president combined with gross underweighting of the modernized regions and excessive overrepresentation of the most backward states guaranteed a congress far more conservative than the executive.

By the early 1960s economic development had so transformed urban Brazilian society that the old rules of the patrimonial political game no longer applied. But these changes had not yet reached the hinterlands, still the locus of power between presidential elections because of the grotesque legislative underrepresentation of the most populous states. This duality would prove a debilitating dilemma for civilian governments and would even be a thorny problem for the military ones that took over after 1964. The classic urban-rural gap had its most negative impact in sprawling, federal Brazil. At the local and state levels of the northeast, north, and center-west, essentially archaic patron-client political structures proved highly resistant to the limited reflections of the ongoing economic and social transformation of the area below the eighteenth parallel. From this tenacity of traditional politics in the interior stemmed repeated electoral victories at the state level that enabled these rural-based conservative elites to exert heavy influence, if not always control, within the decentralized national structures of the UDN and the PSD. Through this pernicious phenomenon, patronage politics and clientelism persisted at the national level even in the face of sustained economic growth and strong modernizing influences. In a system in which sectoral organizations, not parties, were the vehicles for urban interest groups, the inadequately organized middle classes would, under perceived threat to their level of living, come to view the army as the defender of their basic interests, a shift in viewpoint that led to a breakdown in the developmentalist coalition that had been shaped

by Vargas and had functioned effectively during the brief Kubitschek era. (It is tantalizing to think how differently events might have played out if presidential reelection
had been permitted in 1960, rather than not being adopted until the 1990s.)

Quadros, saddled with the congress elected in 1958, before the modernizing impact of Kubitschek's policies had been felt, realized that in dealing with grave financial
problems and the woeful state of administrative machinery, he would encounter strong
opposition from entrenched interests and alienate much of his UDN backing. Unable
to communicate his face-to-face persuasiveness to the nation as a whole from the isolation of the still-raw, new capital Brasília, far distant from major population centers,
Quadros opted for risky measures to impact an inherently slow-moving congress. In
August 1961 a rash plan to mobilize popular pressure on the congress to grant him
extraordinary powers backfired, and the all-out gamble of a resignation ploy ended
his presidency. While Goulart meandered home from a state visit to China that had
focused attention upon his leftist inclinations, congressional leaders and the military
ministers, anxious to avoid a clear rupture of constitutionality but unwilling to trust
Goulart with full presidential powers, worked on a compromise solution. On September 2 the congress approved a parliamentary form of government, and five days
later Goulart became president with a Council of Ministers headed by Tancredo de
Almeida Neves (b. 1910), an experienced Minas Gerais politician who had held the
justice portfolio at the end of Vargas's last term. The disaster of civil war had been
avoided, but it was a stay of execution, not a permanent reprieve. During the two
and a half years of Goulart's presidency, crucial events occurred that carried Brazil
down the slippery road to a crisis of the system as political issues, particularly those
with deep social and economic roots, went quickly from highly divisive to positively
indigestible.

Traditional agrarian interests at first continued to find allies in the congress to
thwart executive initiatives. Then, when the 1962 elections resulted in a weakening of
conservative numbers and resolve, the agrarians responded by allying with urban
elites, who were being dislodged from the levers of political power, to do away with
electoral and legislative processes that no longer served their purposes. To accomplish
this, they exploited the government's mistakes to convince centrist elements of the
dire threat posed by "demagogic" radicalism. Even more important, their allies inside
the armed forces did the same vis-à-vis moderates within that ultimately decisive institution. For there was a well-defined military nucleus frustrated by the fact that
each time the military had pushed Vargas and his heirs out of power (1945, 1954, and
1960), the "misguided" electorate quickly opened the door for their return (in 1950
by again electing Vargas, in 1955 by choosing Kubitschek, and in 1961 through
Quadros's resignation). A tragic case of political mobilization for structural reforms
leading instead to a preemptive counterrevolution gave the right its chance to take
power by force. (There are strong parallels in this respect between 1961–1964 in
Brazil and what had taken place in Venezuela in the years immediately preceding
1948, as well as what would occur in Chile just before 1973. In addition, it happened
at the same time as the military was ousting the civilian president in Argentina.)

The polarization leading to the breakdown of Brazilian democracy was fed by
both shortsighted opposition to change by intransigent conservative elements and
detachment from reality on the part of the extreme left, whose wishful thinking ran
wild during 1963 and early 1964, eventually turning into suicidal self-delusion remi-

niscent of that of the National Liberating Alliance militants in 1935. Goulart's short-comings aggravated the crisis and hastened its unfortunate denouement, but the difficult dilemmas in the early 1960s would have severely tested the mettle of Kubitschek or even Vargas. Goulart, spooked by the prospect of being outflanked on the left by brother-in-law Brizola and convinced of the need to recover full presidential powers, responded to the congressional election campaign by shifting to a stridently radical nationalist stance. On October 7, some 15 million Brazilians, of the 18.5 million eligible, chose a congress scheduled to hold power until February 1967, as well as governors in half the states. Money poured into conservative campaigns by the United States served to neutralize patronage favors and massive expenditures for left-wing candidates made by the Goulart administration—and also served to further inflame passions. Brizola launched himself onto the national scene by receiving a record vote for congress from Rio de Janeiro even though his entire political career had been in Rio Grande do Sul.[13]

The resulting lower house saw the PSD, PTB, and UDN at relatively equal strength with 119, 104, and 97 seats, respectively, leaving just 89 seats to the ten minor parties. Only if Goulart would walk a tightrope between insistent demands for basic reforms coming from the majority component of his PTB and the conservative rural-based core of the PSD could the Vargas-designed alliance be maintained and the administration retain a viable congressional base. Unfortunately the event marking the high point of Goulart's abbreviated term also distorted his political perspective. On January 6, 1963, a plebiscite favored a return to presidentialism by 9.5 million to only 2 million opposed. By interpreting this five-to-one preference for a presidential system rather than the existing hybrid regime as a vote of confidence and a personal mandate, Goulart grievously miscalculated his position. Pushing for policies injurious to the interests of the established power structure, he catalyzed a backlash mobilization capable of swamping the left's noisy campaigns and demonstrations when push really came to shove. Wage increases spurred inflation to over 80 percent for the year as per capita GDP growth turned negative. Since even in politically troubled 1961 the economy had grown by 7.9 percent, Goulart was vulnerable to charges of economic mismanagement. As presidential succession was scheduled for 1965, the semi-lame-duck president had to cope with rival political ambitions within as well as between parties. The situation was greatly complicated by the fact that marriage to a sister of Goulart's wife made the highly ambitious Brizola ineligible for the presidency, driving him toward increasingly extreme positions involving, at the minimum, militant demands for constitutional change and, at the maximum, threats of political pyromania. Goulart's brand of patronage-oriented, paternalistic populism, largely devoid of ideological content, proved inadequate in the rapidly polarizing political situation, and he became increasingly open to rash and ill-considered advice that aggravated the perilous political polarization.

The broad-based conspiracy that soon brought down Goulart was already well advanced. Retired general Golbery do Couto e Silva (b. 1911), later to be the chief idea man of the moderate wing of the military rulers, used the Institute for Social Research and Studies (IPES) as a nexus for antiregime planning, taking an active role in the search for a prestigious senior general in the Rio de Janeiro area to assume a leadership position. General Humberto de Alencar Castelo Branco (b. 1897) filled the bill admirably. A hero of the Italian campaign who enjoyed a reputation for scrupulously

avoiding involvement in civilian political affairs, he had developed a following among
those who were by now middle-grade officers during a long tenure with the Command and General Staff School and, among more senior officers, through his service
as commandant of the Superior War College (ESG). By late 1963 he had condition-
ally agreed to assume military leadership of the movement, as long as plans to move
against Goulart rested upon his violation of accepted rules of the political game.[14] At
the end of February 1964 Goulart took a number of measures bordering on demagoguery that indicated that he had stopped listening to Kubitschek and was falling
more under the influence of Brizola. Deciding to go all out for the mobilization of
mass pressures for basic structural reforms, he imposed agrarian reform by executive
decree on March 13, also nationalizing private oil refineries. As the Easter holidays
neared, governors of five of the country's six most important states undertook close
cooperation with each other and distanced themselves from the federal executive.
When 2,000 discontented servicemen gathered at a communist-controlled union on
the night of March 25, Goulart stepped over the line by agreeing to demands including the appointment of a new navy minister. Within a few days, essentially conservative Minas Gerais was in open revolt. As troops descended on Rio de Janeiro on the
night of March 31, Goulart fled to his home state, leaving the incendiary Brizola the
impossible task of mounting armed resistance.

The forces that overthrew the Goulart government with surprising ease were
united chiefly by agreement that the radicalization and lack of discipline of the preceding weeks were intolerable. Beyond a shared determination to end "subversion,"
the various components of the March 31 movement possessed no consensus as to
what should come next. As had been the case in 1930, the wide scope of participation brought with it a high degree of heterogeneity. Historical conspirators within
the military who advocated a prolonged period of purges stood alongside conservative UDN elements who wanted the lengthy period of political dominance they had
expected to have after the 1960 election. These two groups coexisted uneasily with
moderates, to whom Goulart had been acceptable as long as they could expect a return of Kubitschek to power by 1966. Relations were equally shaky with the legalists, who had reluctantly acted only when they were convinced of Goulart-Brizola
efforts to subvert military discipline and "illegitimately" change the constitution.

Concerned over having gone farther than ever before in exercising the moderating power, the armed forces decided to establish a semiconstitutional regime to replace the provisional Revolutionary Supreme Command that had been instituted by
General Arthur da Costa e Silva (b. 1899). Castelo Branco was the near-consensus
pick of the military conspirators to serve out at least the remainder of Goulart's term,
and the congress duly ratified this choice on April 11. By this time the Revolutionary
Supreme Command had issued an "institutional act" barring from political life for
ten years the "corrupt" and "subversive" elements linked to the overthrown regime,
including elected officeholders.[15] Against the wishes of the hard-liners (*linha dura*),
the president let his major discretionary powers under the first Institutional Act ex-
pire, bolstering the reservations of these younger officers of a radical rightist position
that the Castelo government was overly concerned about moderation and rationality.
Indeed, there was a general feeling among the military that power could not be allowed to fall back into the hands of the Vargas lineage as in 1951, 1956, and 1961.
How long the military should itself hold power was another matter. Forces advocat-

ing the traditional arbiter function with a quick turnover of power to reliable civilians carried the day in April 1964 and remained in control of the situation until October 1965. Only with the 1967 presidential succession did it become apparent that a long authoritarian night under elements determined to be the nation's ruler was inevitable. Castelo and his close advisers, including Generals Golbery and Ernesto Geisel, believed that basic flaws in the country's political structures needed to be remedied and that the punitive phase of the revolution had to be put behind them so that the government could come to grips with underlying structural problems. Meanwhile, economic recovery was essential, so Planning Minister Roberto de Oliveira Campos was free from the considerations of political feasibility and electoral repercussions that had constrained previous stabilization efforts. GDP growth of 3.4 percent in 1964, 2.4 percent in 1965, 6.7 percent in 1966, and 4.2 percent the following year was remarkable for a period of adjustment and austerity, leaving cosmopolitan diplomat Campos with an enviable international reputation.

Despite deep reservations by those opposed to rapidly reopening political competition, Castelo insisted on going ahead with direct election of governors in October 1965 in the states where they had been chosen in 1960. This test of public reaction to his brand of tutelary democracy saw candidates associated with the revolution carry most states, but the public perception was one of repudiation of the administration in major population centers. In the resulting behind-the-scenes military crisis, a sweeping Second Institutional Act was issued, and Costa e Silva consolidated his position as the leading contender to succeed Castelo, with existing political parties dissolved and the choice of the new president resting with the congress. Soon a two-party system was imposed, consisting of the government-sponsored National Renovating Alliance (ARENA) and nominally opposition elements banded together in the Brazilian Democratic Movement (MDB). Although the latter had only 21 senators and 150 deputies, they came from such a wide range of interests and ideological positions that the party would never achieve a significant degree of unity or even coherence.

In February 1966 the Third Institutional Act decreed indirect selection of governors, convoked congressional elections for November 15, and made mayors of state capitals appointive. In these conditions the MDB decided not to contest the presidential race, so on October 3 Costa e Silva became president-elect under circumstances closely paralleling those of Floriano's selection to succeed Deodoro nearly three-quarters of a century before. (This move to a more authoritarian regime occurred at almost the same time as Argentina was taking steps in the same direction.) While the regime shaped a new constitution, congressional balloting strengthened the government's hand, with ARENA winning over two-thirds of the seats in the Chamber of Deputies and electing eighteen of twenty-two senators on well over 8.7 million votes to 4.9 million for the MDB. Yet in a harbinger of things to come, the opposition won by large margins in Rio de Janeiro and Rio Grande do Sul and came close to winning in São Paulo.[16]

The inauguration of the amiable, rather ordinary Costa e Silva to succeed austere military intellectual Castelo ushered in a protracted period during which the presidency was occupied by someone committed to the idea of the armed forces as the country's proper and semipermanent ruler. Well intentioned in a number of ways, but also ill prepared in many areas of public policy, Costa e Silva found himself facing a "broad front" of opposition linked to ex- and would-be presidents

(Kubitschek, Quadros, Goulart, and Lacerda). More troublesome was criticism from the Catholic Church and student organizations. Caught up in Cold War conceptions, the conservative military were dismayed by the church's lack of appreciation of their self-perceived saving of Catholic values from destruction by Marxist-Leninist forces—confusing sincere concern about democracy with subversive sympathies. Lack of presidential leadership by the later part of 1968 combined with an insubordinate mood in the congress and terrorist acts by both political extremes to create a crisis. When on December 12 the Chamber of Deputies refused to strip an aggressively hostile congressman of his parliamentary immunity, the government reacted with unexpected vigor. The truly draconian Fifth Institutional Act (AI-5) granted broad discretionary powers to the president and began a new round of cancellations of legislative mandates and suspensions of political rights. Brazil moved to the brink of unrestricted military dictatorship. At least 1,400 individuals were punished under AI-5, and all elections scheduled before November 1970 were canceled. Then, as August 1969 ended, the nation awoke to the news that Costa e Silva, who had been considering moves to ease political restrictions, had suffered an incapacitating cardiovascular problem. The service ministers vetoed assumption of the presidency by the civilian vice president, forming a junta instead. For the fourth time since 1964, progress toward political normality was bulldozed into oblivion by military imposition of a more arbitrary regime than had previously existed. A military equivalent of the College of Cardinals both chose General Emílio Garrastazú Médici (b. 1905) as president and decreed an extensive set of constitutional amendments further increasing centralization of power in the hands of the federal government and augmenting the already heavy concentration of authority in the executive. After ten months of forced recess, and minus the large number of its most independent members who had fallen afoul of the Institutional Act, a chastened congress was summoned back to ratify the military's decision.

"Project Brazil: Great Power" was the leitmotif of Médici's administration, one in which high rates of economic growth coexisted with ruthlessly effective repression. Energized by the death of the most prominent guerrilla leader, Médici made it clear that in his "revolutionary state" the president retained emergency powers as leader of the revolutionary movement as well as chief executive. Economic growth had held at 9.5 percent in 1969, after an astounding jump to 9.8 percent in 1968, and was accelerating. As Brazil won its third soccer World Cup championship in the past four tries in mid-1970, making up for 1966's failure, the regime had relative ease in diverting public attention from politics. After state legislatures confirmed presidential choices for governors, on November 15 congressional elections afforded the registered electorate of 29 million (in a population approaching 95 million) a chance to choose between ARENA loyalists and surviving MDB candidates. Not surprisingly the government party garnered 220 of 310 lower-house seats and victories in 40 of 46 senate races, on the strength of 10.9 million valid votes to the MDB's 4.8 million. Yet the opposition retained a solid base of support in the most advanced regions of the country. The Médici government combined improved intelligence, systematic use of torture, and more sophisticated counterinsurgency tactics to destroy the violent left. Brutally efficient, and focused, repression was not nearly on the same scale or with as great a disregard for human life as in Argentina.

Much of the public remained mesmerized by economic growth, which, fueled by heavy industrial investment, steamed ahead at 10.4 percent in 1970, 11.3 percent in 1971, 12.1 percent in 1972, and 14.0 percent in 1973. Hailed as the "economic miracle," this growth involved low rates of inflation (under 20 percent a year), a tenfold increase in foreign exchange reserves, and sharply rising exports at $4 billion in 1972 and $6.2 billion the following year. The flies in the ointment were extremely inequitable income distribution, failure of growth to improve levels of living for the underprivileged masses, and neglect of pressing social problems. Still the government scored resounding victories in the November 1972 municipal elections. Moreover, Médici did not lose control of the succession process.

Highly respected army minister General Orlando Geisel, to whom Médici delegated authority in the matter of the succession, decided that his younger and more intellectual brother, Ernesto (b. 1908), was best qualified for the presidency. Announced as the government candidate in June 1973, Ernesto Geisel was named to the presidency on January 15, 1974, by an electoral college composed almost exclusively of the incumbent congress. This choice of a close disciple of late ex-president Castelo Branco had momentous implications for Brazil, as it restored control to moderates rather than right-wing ruler types. The next five years would be a reversal of the past half decade, as champions of the military as arbiter outwitted and outfought the entrenched hard-line advocates of indefinite military rule. The new president and his team of Castelo heirs—in the face of heavy resistance within the armed forces and only limited understanding and sporadic cooperation from a distrustful civilian opposition—steered the country through a phase of decompression of the repressive authoritarian regime and set it firmly on the path to political "opening" (*abertura*) before selecting a successor to carry this process on to democratization. To this final end, Geisel installed General João Baptista de Oliveira Figueiredo (b. 1918) as head of the National Intelligence Service (SNI).

Although coming to power in the midst of a continuing economic boom, the austere German Lutheran Geisel was clearly not going to outperform his predecessor in the growth realm. The global energy crisis had already begun during the last quarter of 1973, so the boom was due to lose steam, although not end. To repeat the economic rationality of the Castelo period, Geisel appointed João Paulo dos Reis Velloso (b. 1931) as planning minister, with brilliant young economist Mário Henrique Simonsen (b. 1935) as finance minister. Closely advised by Golbery, Geisel operated with a flexible timetable for dismantling the repressive apparatus that had burgeoned under Médici and for subsequently turning the country out of the cul-de-sac of authoritarianism. His first task was to become the effective leader of the military institution as well as head of government. At the center of Geisel's decision to begin decompression (*distensão*), as blueprinted by Golbery largely on the basis of the ideas of preeminent political scientist Samuel P. Huntington, was his perception that under Médici the security apparatus had gained a dangerous degree of autonomy.[17] Being held responsible by the public for human rights violations had widened the gap between the military and the centrist-to-moderately-reformist elements of Brazilian civil society. With the guerrilla threat eliminated, repression was dysfunctional, and its practitioners needed to be reined in. If Geisel had to act autocratically at times to remove obstacles to *distensão*, or if he even had to resort to authoritarian measures to

avoid losing essential military support, so be it, as he was concerned about the end result, not popularity along the way.

The first step was handpicking governors, all duly confirmed by state legislatures
in October 1974. Then he insisted on holding essentially free congressional elections
on November 15. With an electorate of 35.8 million in a population nearing 105
million, the turnout of 29 million matched 1970's total of voter registration. The balloting resulted in a strong MDB comeback, scoring a 16 to 6 victory in senate races
and electing 45 percent of the lower house. The government was sobered more than
shaken by the poor showing of its party's senatorial candidates, since ARENA retained a decisive 204 to 160 edge in the lower house—compared to its previous 220
to 90 advantage—and an even more comfortable margin in the upper house, where
holdovers gave it 46 seats to the MDB's 20. Indeed, in the view of its strategists, opposition gains were healthy in that they reflected the return to normal channels of
electoral politics by alienated elements that had abstained or nullified their ballots in
1970. Then, in the local elections of November 1976, some 18 million votes were
cast for ARENA's candidates compared to 13 million for the MDB's. Yet the opposition elected mayors or a majority of councilmen in 63 percent of cities of over
250,000. Still, the most important result was confirmation of the government's belief
that it could retain sufficient control of the system at the national and state levels in
1978 with ARENA as its vehicle, although this feat might require some judicious
tinkering with electoral rules.

By this time a balance had been reached between the early and unrealistic desire
of the military holders of national executive power to prioritize highly rational technocratic planning over political considerations and the requisites of maintaining electoral support, which early on had been scorned as distorting the quest for
development by interjecting clientelism, regionalism, personal gain, parochialism, and
vested interests. Having failed in the electoral realm, especially in congress, to replace
politicians with roots in pre-1964 political life with a new technocratic stratum,
regime strategists settled for these carryover elements' adapting, at the national level
at least, to the realities of dealing with the more technocratic mind-set of the higher
appointed bureaucrats. This adaptation required politicians to accept a lesser role in
policymaking and concentrate instead upon affecting implementation. In return, administrators learned the necessity of acquiring skills in dealing with political interests
and taking into account electoral politics as a relevant consideration. In the resulting
synthesis, military and civilian technocrats generally headed such ministries as planning, finance, education, health, communications, and foreign relations as well as often interior, industry and commerce, and mines and energy. Since the number of
ministries proliferated from fifteen in 1967 to twenty-seven by 1984, this division of
labor left a substantial number of cabinet positions, along with many important agencies, to be filled by politicians.[18]

As had been the case with Vargas in the 1930s, the military governments were able
to introduce a high proportion of more technocratic individuals as indirectly elected
governors and appointed capital city mayors. Still, two-thirds of the governors chosen
in 1974 and 1978 (before a return to direct election in 1982) were continuing political careers begun under the pre-1964 multiparty system. Of the senators elected up
through 1978, 86 percent had held elective office prior to the military regime. Even

in the lower house of congress three-fifths of the members elected after the military took power had begun their political careers before 1964. Moreover, the traditional recruitment channel of coming up through local and state elective office persisted. Indeed, as had been the case with President Hermes da Fonseca's *salvações* in 1911–1913 and Vargas's initial use of *tenentes* as appointed state chief executives, military governments came to realize that, as much as they might have wished to undermine if not replace personalist and clientelist politicians with individuals closer to the profile of those they appointed to federal executive positions, pursuing this aim would have led to an unacceptable risk of opposition electoral victories. The technocratic option, at its peak under Médici, had resulted in the regime's 1974 electoral setback, causing Geisel to very rationally pull back and mend political fences. This acceptance of politics as necessary would prove to be an essential step along the road back to democracy.

Relaunching *distensão* was complicated by mediocre economic performance. The ambitious Second National Development Plan for 1975–1979 had been undermined by the soaring price of crude oil and the heavy investments required by consequent efforts to reduce dependence upon petroleum imports. During 1974 problems were most evident in trade, as doubling imports resulted in a $4.7-billion deficit. Foreign exchange reserves dropped, and foreign debt rose. GDP growth, largely a carryover from the Médici years, was 9 percent, but inflation edged up to 35 percent. This economic downturn was more evident in 1975 as GDP growth declined to 6.1 percent and inflation leveled off. Although in 1976 the expansion of the GDP improved to 10.1 percent, inflation jumped to 46 percent. But the last years of the Geisel government took place in a deteriorating economic environment as growth fell to 5.4 percent in 1977 and 4.8 percent in 1978. With a rapid rise in foreign debt, balanced trade in 1977 and 1978 wasn't enough, since surging debt service required a large sustained inflow of capital. Structurally, the Brazilian economy of the late 1970s had been substantially changed since the military's seizure of power. By 1978 agriculture was down to 14 percent of GDP and industry up to 33 percent. Steel production exceeded 9 million tons by 1979, triple that of 1964, with the auto industry producing nearly a million vehicles. Electrical generating capacity had doubled between 1964 and 1971 and again by 1978. This transformation was reflected in the workforce, where, by 1978, 20 percent of the economically active population (EAP) was employed in industry and 40 percent in the service sector, with agriculture down to 36 percent—compared to 14, 26, and 60 percent, respectively, in 1950. Indeed, during the 1970s industrial employment grew by well over 500,000 a year, and jobs in the service area by nearly 900,000 annually.

In 1977 Geisel and his advisers were faced with finding a way to guarantee an ARENA victory in the next year's national elections while heading off hard-line war minister Sylvio Frota's unwanted presidential candidacy. They skillfully won the behind-the-scenes battle that had been brewing since 1975. Placing the congress in temporary recess, Geisel decreed changes in the rules of the electoral game, including extending his successor's term to six years. With one senator from each state chosen indirectly, the government was assured of retaining control of the upper house and thus reinforcing its majority in the electoral college. By reaffirming Geisel's determination to keep decompression within limits and control its pace, these decisive moves contributed to the military support necessary for dealing with the succession question. Frota was astutely maneuvered into overplaying his hand and was dismissed in October, opening the way for Figueiredo's nomination by ARENA in April 1978, preceded by elimination of the sweeping powers of AI-5. So on October 15 the electoral college ratified Figueiredo, and the selection of governors went smoothly with the exception of São Paulo, where upstart Paulo Salim Maluf (b. 1931) defeated Geisel's choice at the ARENA convention. Then, with Brazil's electorate up to 46 million in a population of 114 million, nearly 38 million of whom went to the polls on November 15, the government party elected 231 federal deputies to 189 for the opposition. Even more than had been the case in 1974, the gross underrepresentation of populous urban states was crucial to ARENA's comfortable margin of seats; in terms of popular vote, the difference was only 250,000 votes—at a bit over 15 million to 14.8 million. The government also won fifteen of the twenty-three senate seats at stake (even though the popular vote was 57 to 43 percent in favor of the MDB).[19] State electoral colleges chose twenty-two other senators, with ARENA gaining all but one. These mixed results were advantageous for the process of political decompression and its transformation into *abertura,* since the electoral vitality of the MDB convinced wavering elements associated with the regime of the need for continuing political reforms, and ARENA's firm control of congress and the state legislatures forestalled any reaction by hard-line elements in the armed forces. A moral victory for the opposition drew it further into the game of liberalization through elections—the slow and conflict-free road. Indeed, the extreme left, especially its violence-oriented component, was essentially irrelevant from this point on, and its irrelevance helped the new government to contain attempts by the radical right to derail *abertura.*

Following Geisel's end-of-year revocation of banishment orders against a number of exiles, Figueiredo was inaugurated as constitutional chief executive on March 15, 1979. For the first time since 1926, one Brazilian administration was followed by another committed to continuing its policies. Not only did Golbery continue as presidential chief of staff, but Simonsen also stayed on, shifting over to the planning ministry. Thus this was a government reflecting all major currents within both the military establishment and the technocratic stratum. The economic legacy was mixed, as GDP growth reached 7.9 percent in 1979, but inflation doubled to 77 percent. Defeated on the question of making adjustments to the harsher economic realities imposed by the global energy crisis, Simonsen gave way in September to Costa e Silva–Médici–era economic czar Antônio Delfim Netto (b. 1928) and his idea of a quick fix by way of a 30 percent currency devaluation.

Attention was focused on that month's sweeping amnesty law and the November reformulation of the party system. The Social Democracy Party (PDS) replaced ARENA as the government's electoral and legislative bulwark, and the MDB became the Party of the Brazilian Democratic Movement (PMDB); the Popular Party (PP), the Brazilian Labor Party (PTB), and the Democratic Workers' Party (PDT) were also legally recognized. As all had roots from before the military took power, the only really new factor on the party scene was the Workers' Party (PT), headed by São Paulo metalworkers' leader Luis Inácio Lula da Silva (b. 1946). Far from having the immediate impact many observers predicted for a socialist party, or being a transitory phenomenon, it would gain the presidency—but not until early in the next century.

Transition to and Consolidation of Democracy, 1980–1999

Political development surged ahead in the region's largest country during the 1980s and 1990s, in a near straight line and at an almost breakneck pace. Beginning with a return to the direct election of governors in 1982, the transition process progressed through the selection of a civilian president by an electoral college in 1984, on past balloting for a congress with constituent powers in 1986 and its drafting of a new constitution in 1987–1988, and finally to the direct election of a younger-generation president at the end of 1989.[20] The consolidation of democracy then overcame the trying challenge of mass disillusionment and unscheduled presidential succession, for when a cloud of corruption engulfed the successor Fernando Collor de Mello administration in 1992, Brazil proved its political maturity through a fully constitutional process of impeachment untainted by military interference. In 1994 Brazil's rapidly expanding electorate decisively chose a very highly qualified chief executive and granted him an unprecedented second term in 1998. But this democratic transformation did not come easily; indeed, it was carefully crafted.

As 1980 opened, Figueiredo had settled in as president with the daunting mission of conducting Brazil's transition to an elected civilian government. The economic legacy he inherited from ex-president Geisel was mixed, with GDP growth in 1979 having reached a robust 7.2 percent but inflation doubling to 77 percent. Terrorist bombings, largely the work of the extreme right although blamed on the left, escalated in May. The Figueiredo government reaped the debt whirlwind as it encountered the full impact of the second oil shock of 1979, with interest rates zooming to the stratosphere. As interest payments erupted from $2.7 billion in 1978 to $7.5 billion in 1980, debt service exploded from $8 billion to $11.3 billion. Rapid export growth was eaten up by resurgent oil prices that pushed imports from $13.7 billion in 1978 to $23.0 billion in 1980. Although economic growth in 1980 was a high 9.2 percent, inflation had climbed to 110 percent—a warning of problems ahead. The full brunt of recession was quick in arriving, with GDP in 1981 shrinking by 4.5 percent—6.6 percent in per capita terms—with minimal impact on inflation, which hovered at 95 percent as exploding debt service payments of $15.4 billion and $18.3 billion the following year depleted foreign exchange reserves. Instead of responding to the oil shock and zooming interest rates through an adjustment program that would entail economic slowdown and consequent political unpopularity, Figueiredo pushed ahead along the lines that had brought public support during the early years of his presidency, before suffering a temporarily incapacitating heart attack in September 1981. In sharp contrast with the 1969 presidential incapacitation, the regime's inner circle decided to allow the civilian vice president to assume office on an interim basis, and an atmosphere of political normality was maintained.

In this context, the November 15, 1982, direct elections for the congress, the state legislatures, and the governors were a triumph of moderation and political modernization. The mixed results encouraged all major political actors to pursue their objectives through normal legal channels.[21] The progovernment PDS won in a majority of states, guaranteeing control of the senate, a near majority in the lower house, and a majority in the electoral college, which would choose the new president two years later. Yet return to direct elections created a situation in which the federal government would at times need to compromise. Such opposition victories as occurred were accepted by the armed forces with resignation, not the indignation that similar results had triggered in 1965. Turnout was a high 48.5 million of the registered electorate of 58.6 million. The moderate-opposition PMDB won in the ten states with three-fifths of the country's population and nearly 75 percent of its GDP. For the first time the government party failed to get a majority of the valid votes for the lower house yet held onto its plurality, as the strongly oppositionist PDT received only 2.4 million votes—mostly in Rio de Janeiro and Rio Grande do Sul, Leonel Brizola's two strongholds—while the less strident PTB garnered 1.8 million votes, and the PT, led by eventual president Lula da Silva, trailed with 1.4 million ballots, more than three-fourths of them in São Paulo.

With the elections over, the government admitted that the country was on the verge of insolvency. Not only had 1982 been a bad year economically, but 1983 was even worse in almost every way. Inflation more than doubled, from 100 percent to 211 percent; GDP growth went from a minuscule 0.5 percent to a miserably negative 3.5 percent; and the current accounts deficit rose from $11.7 billion to $16.3 billion. After mid-1982, Mexico's virtual bankruptcy and foreign debt moratorium raised prospects of default and brought home to the international banking community its dangerous overexposure in Latin America. Only a hastily assembled emergency package of financing prevented Brazil's defaulting on interest payments, with amortization having been quietly suspended at midyear. By dint of a 23 percent devaluation of Brazil's currency, exports were made competitive, as Brazil embarked full steam ahead on a strategy of obtaining increased trade surpluses to offset the drying up of loans and credits so as to keep up interest payments as an inducement to banks to roll over the principal. Still, for 1982–1988, the drain caused by debt service's exceeding new loans reached a staggering $39 billion, as the principal totaled a monumental $140 billion. Brazil's success in damage control by drastically curbing oil imports while increasing exports was substantial, with 1983's trade surplus of $6.5 billion, eight times that of the preceding year, doubling in 1984 before slipping slightly in 1985, as, with interest rates moderating, debt service payments remained flat and exchange reserves rose from their dangerously low level. Registered foreign debt rose sharply, nearing the $100 billion level, and inflation leveled off at 224 and 235 percent, with GDP growth a satisfactory 5.3 percent in 1984 and a robust 7.9 percent the next year.

Unwilling to accept a long-term recession as the price of international solvency, Figueiredo failed to implement the anti-inflation measures agreed upon with the International Monetary Fund (IMF). As had been the case in 1982, the proximity of elections critical for the country's return to fully competitive political life made this a sound decision. Although the tiring government, limping into its sixth year, was losing control over *abertura,* it still appeared that Figueiredo's successor would come from within the governing party, if not the administration. Yet the controlled political opening quickly became a transition to democracy, as initiative escaped from the president's hands in the short span of June through August. Figueiredo's failure to indicate a preferred successor led to the sudden disaggregation of the PDS as Maluf continued his relentless drive to gain the support of convention delegates and electoral college members. This intelligent, but unscrupulous, clientelistic demagogue's success in winning the PDS nomination through lavish expenditures and promises of future favors and benefits catalyzed a backlash coalition of moderate regime elements and centrist opposition groups.

Following the failure of a massive campaign in favor of the direct election of the president to amend the constitution, Minas Gerais governor Tancredo Neves emerged as the anti-Maluf contender. In the behind-the-scenes maneuvering that has historically proven to be the key to Brazilian politics, this shrewd veteran with roots back in the Vargas era had no peer. The pragmatic moderate wing of the PMDB was joined by "Liberal Front" PDS dissidents behind vice president Aureliano Chaves de Mendonça in a Democratic Alliance (AD) that rapidly went from bandwagon to steamroller. Its mass rallies served as a constant reminder to the 686 electors, almost all of whom would be facing the electorate in 1986, of the political peril in going against the surging tide of public opinion—and appearing to have sold out to the blandishments of the country's consummate corrupter. Hence, on January 15, 1985, the electoral college opted for the confidence-inspiring Neves by an overwhelming margin of 480 to 180.

As had been the case in 1822, 1889, 1930, and 1946, many elements of Brazilian society expected that regime change would lead almost automatically to a substantially transformed political system. But this was a transition without rupture, one in which heavy participation by experienced politicians and powerful interests associated with the prior order would guarantee that although the bottle might be new, the contents would taste much like the old: clientelism laced with patronage and a dash of demagoguery. The transition to a viable system of competitive civilian politics after twenty-one years of military rule was by itself an arduous task, even without a transformation of long-established practices and ingrained behavior. The first task on the new government's agenda was establishing a workable relationship between the executive and legislative branches of government while infusing responsiveness into the ponderous state machinery built up since 1964. Then came the laborious process of shaping a new constitutional framework for a complex society with enormous inequalities and developmental needs. There would be early elections for the mayors of state capitals and strategic cities, appointed under the military regime, followed in 1986 by balloting for all governors, two senators per state, and a full array of federal and state legislators. Two years later came elections in over 4,000 municipalities as a prelude to 1989's first direct presidential elections in almost three decades—which required restructuring of the party system. If this political agenda were not formidable enough, there was also the task of husbanding a still fragile economic recovery and dealing with the forbidding social deficit accumulated during over nearly twenty-one years of military rule.

Brazilians had faith that Neves would find a way to pilot the country to the promised land of democracy and prosperity. Yet he would die of natural causes without even being inaugurated, leaving the task to the vice president, José Sarney, an accommodationist politician from a second-line state in the northeast. Liberal elements looked askance at his close ties to the military and his essential conservatism. This mistrust left Sarney with no option but to follow the course that was most natural for him: govern in collaboration with the center and center-right. São Paulo congressman Ulysses Guimarães (b. 1916) assumed leadership of the center-left PMDB orphans, now junior partners in a government in which they had expected to rule the roost. Yet much was accomplished in the early years of this accidental president's extremely challenging term. Legislation in May 1985 removed restrictions on the organization of political parties, made presidential elections direct, and extended the vote to illiterates. But most of the congress had been elected in 1982 on the ticket of the military regime's governing party and were deeply suspicious of anything advocated by the PMDB's progressive wing. In the economic sphere the new government inherited an improved, and in most ways still improving, situation. Initially dependent on export expansion, economic recovery broadened into domestic commerce and agriculture. Internal consumption became the engine of economic growth as real salaries rose as part of a dramatic GDP expansion of 7.6 percent in 1986 (on the heels of 1985's 7.9 percent). The warning signs of falling exports and rising debt service in 1986 were overlooked in the euphoria of a spectacular drop in inflation from 235 percent in 1985 to only 65 percent in 1986.

This positive performance resulted from the Cruzado Plan, which combined a new currency with price and rent and mortgage freezes and a new wage system. The plan's rousing success in the short run led the government to continue it unchanged through the late-year elections. With monthly inflation rates cut to 2 percent, savings were funneled into productive investment rather than the merry-go-round of financial speculations that had become rampant. But economics, like politics, depends on collective human behavior, and an unbridled consumption boom resulted. With elections in November 1986 that would determine the nature of the governmental system and the tenure of the incumbent government, neither the president nor the PMDB could resist continuing a program that had produced massive public support for the regime. Hence an artificial atmosphere of prosperity guaranteed a massive electoral victory for the PMDB, with the Liberal Front Party (PFL) picking up the leftovers. Thus, on November 15, a high proportion of the more than 69 million eligible citizens elected a congress that would also function as a constituent assembly to write a new constitution. As it would be the country's national legislature through 1990, with senators serving until early 1995, this body would play a crucial role in the consolidation of Brazil's still fledgling democratic regime. With governors and state legislatures also being chosen, the Democratic Alliance came away with all state governors, three-fourths of the federal Chamber of Deputies, and four-fifths of the federal senate. The existing opposition parties barely survived, and two dozen new parties failed to find voter responsiveness. Electing 261 federal deputies, the PMDB held a majority in the 487-member lower house, and its 45 senate seats gave it an even larger senate majority. Twenty-two of twenty-three governorships went to PMDBers, although some were in coalition with the PFL, whose 119 deputies were down by only 10 from its founding, and whose 16 senators were more than it had had going into the elections. The PDS paid dearly for its alignment with Maluf, as it fell from the 165 deputies and 31 senators it had had in 1985 to only 33 and 5, respectively. On the left, the PDT found little solace in 23 deputies—virtually unchanged—and the PT made much over having doubled its congressional representation, although this number was only 15 deputies on 5 percent of the vote (up from 3.3 percent in 1982).

Public disillusionment came quickly as inflation climbed toward record heights and Sarney decreed a moratorium on foreign debt interest payments rather than take steps to reduce consumption—at that point the engine of Brazil's inflation. The inevitable result was a drop in foreign investment combined with a rise in the remission of profits and dividends and rising capital flight. In recognition that incumbent Dilson Funaro, despite his earlier contributions, was now a liability, Sarney continued the dizzying pace of a new finance minister each year, considering them expendable lighting rods. As the changes quickly made were already overdue, inflation exploded from an unacceptable 416 percent in 1987 to a disconcerting 1,040 percent in 1988, whereas economic growth was a depressing negative 0.1 percent despite a surge in exports to nearly $34 billion, producing a record $19.2 billion trade surplus, which was badly needed in light of the $26.1 billion expended on debt service.

On October 5, 1988, a new and in ways contradictory constitution was promulgated, giving states and municipalities fiscal resources for which they been accustomed to bargain with the central government. This enormously detailed document also enshrined, in many cases in an anticipatory and philosophical manner, the social and political incorporation of rural workers and others who had been left out of previous reforms. Then late-1988 elections for over 4,300 mayors and 43,600 municipal councilmen, while mobilizing 75.8 million voters, did little to clarify the confused presidential succession picture. The two largest cities were captured by the PT and the PDT, but neither of these parties of the left demonstrated significant strength on more than a regional level. The numerically dominant, but internally divided, PMDB fell far short of its Cruzado Plan–inflated 1986 election triumph, yet it remained Brazil's largest party, electing over 1,800 mayors on 25 percent of the national vote compared to more than 1,400 for the PFL on just over 15 percent of the total. The party system's continuing fragmentation was reflected in the fact that the PT made only incremental progress toward becoming more than just a São Paulo party, coming away with only 38 mayors. For its part, the PDS was a poor third nationally with close to 450 mayors, and the PDT garnered fewer than 200 mayors. The PSDB (Brazilian Social Democracy Party) proved to be still a party of many chiefs and few Indians, trailing far behind the PTB, which elected almost 400 mayors. (Few dreamed that in the next two decades no progress would be made in reforming the increasingly dysfunctional party system.)

As 1989 opened the dreaded dragon of stagflation was a reality, but by February everything else took a backseat to the direct election of a president for the first time since 1960. As with Quadro's 1960 election, the results would lead to extreme frustration. With the stand-alone election coming near year's end, inflation near 1,800 percent, GDP growth only 3.3 percent, and foreign debt service exploding to $43.6 billion, Sarney's approval rating not unexpectedly plunged, since throughout the developed world management of the economy is always near the top of voters' concerns. Only a small minority of Brazil's voters identified with the two score political parties competing, if rarely competitive. Finding little appeal in ideologies and relatively uninterested in specific policies, voters were looking for a candidate, not a party, and were ready to vote for a perceived savior. With many of the major party nominees in the senior citizen category, like seventy-three-year-old Guimarães of the PMDB, a fresh new face captured the voter's fancy. Fernando Collor de Mello

(b. 1948), the handsome and athletic son of an old-line northeastern politician, was the near-perfect media candidate.

Economically conservative, but socially centrist, Collor gained the nomination of a minor party, then set out with enormous energy and determination to woo the voters of the major parties. Substituting talk about modernization and blistering attacks upon corruption and abusive bureaucratic privileges for any profound criticism of the existing order, he made moralization and scathing denunciation of politicians the heart of his appeal. Leaving the left to Lula da Silva and Leonel Brizola and the right to Maluf, Collor went after the center, the center-right, and the center-left, but chiefly the great number of voters looking for someone deserving their trust. At just over 82 million the electorate was swollen by the inclusion of sixteen- and seventeen-year-olds. Nearly half the prospective voters were under thirty, and fewer than 15 percent above age fifty, so almost none had ever voted in a presidential election. Hence on November 15 the vast majority voted not even for the man, but for his image. When the dust settled, only Collor and Lula were left standing for the final round—a battle for the support of the majority of the electorate orphaned by the elimination of the also-rans upon whom they had pinned their hopes.[22] On December 17, after a final televised debate in which media professional Collor outdid the proletarian Lula, 35.1 million voters chose Collor, and 31.1 million backed Lula. Lula had picked up 19.5 million votes since the first round as opposed to 14.5 million for Collor, but Collor's 9-million-vote lead in the first round had been too much to overcome, at least with the impact of television factored in.

Collor's initial economic program was reasonably successful. The economy's excessive liquidity was reduced, and other measures, including privatization, fiscal reforms, and improved tax collection, were aimed at keeping inflation down by transforming the huge prospective public-sector operating deficit into a small surplus. Price increases for 1990 were just under 1500 percent, falling to 480 percent in 1991. GDP shrank by 4.4 percent in 1990, and a minuscule 0.9 percent growth the next year was canceled out by the same slight shrinkage in 1992. Trade surpluses did remain substantial (at $10.9 billion, $10.6 billion, and $15.2 billion for 1990, 1991, and 1992, and foreign debt service was cut from 1989's nearly $44 billion to a three-year average of only $17 billion. With the initial euphoria dissipating, 84 million registered voters went to the polls on October 3, 1990, to fill the 1,700 posts of governor, vice governor, senator, alternate senator, federal deputy, and state legislator. Again the elections underscored the weakness of Brazil's political parties, and with local and regional issues playing an important role there was a strong center-right tilt in both the new congress and the lineup of governors. The gross underrepresentation of São Paulo, combined with the grotesque overrepresentation of the smaller agrarian states, made progressives' efforts to increase their weight in the congress an uphill battle. The PMDB, weakened by the schism that had given birth to the PSDB, suffered further erosion of its erstwhile dominant position, as its former partner PFL moved up to near parity in the congress and to the lead in governorships. The PSDB showed it had a long way to go, coming in sixth with only 37 deputies to the PMDB's 109 and the PFL's 86. The PDT took consolation in Brizola's recapturing the Rio de Janeiro governorship, and in holding even with 47 deputies, edging out the PDS at 43, for third place. Collor's National Renovation Party (PRN) finished fifth with 40 deputies. The PTB's 36 seats in the lower house pinned the PT back in eighth place with 35 (to go with a single senator and no governor), an outcome demonstrating that the PT was far from being a national party.

By July 1992, congressional investigations had uncovered major campaign finance irregularities and highly organized influence peddling conducted by the president's closest collaborator. Hence Collor, who turned out to be as complete a charlatan as Quadros had been three decades earlier, saw his presidency end just after its scheduled midpoint as the impeachment process ran its course with a decisive lower-house vote on September 29 to remove him pending his trial in the senate. Yet this crisis was a positive landmark, for the armed forces played no discernible role—in stark contrast to the unscheduled ends to presidential tenures in 1969, 1964, 1961, 1954–1955, 1945, and 1930. Vice President Itamar Augusto Cauteiro Franco (b. 1930) assumed the vacated office, becoming the sixth citizen of Minas Gerais to attain Brazil's presidency (partially compensating for Tancredo Neves's demise in 1985). An undistinguished politician, who after occupying the presidency would serve as his state's governor, Franco picked some able individuals to help his government escape from mediocrity, the most distinguished being his foreign minister, Fernando Henrique Cardoso, a renowned sociologist and PMDB senator from São Paulo. The October 3 municipal elections, on the second day of Franco's tenure, were remarkably unaffected by the national political crisis, with no party dramatically improving its position over the very mixed results of 1988. For the first time, runoffs were held in municipalities of over 200,000 registered voters, so the dust did not settle until after November 15. The top prize, São Paulo, fell to Maluf, who thus put an end to a streak of setbacks dating to his presidential defeat in 1984. He then merged the PDS and the Christian Democratic Party (PDC)—which had elected 211 mayors—into the Progressive Renewal Party (PPR). Nationally the PMDB elected 33.7 percent of the 4,762 mayors, followed by the PFL with 20.3 percent, the PDT with 7.9 percent, and the PDS with 7.6 percent. The PSDB won 6.7 percent of the mayoral races and the PTB 6.4 percent. The PT continued its slow drive toward becoming a national party by emerging on top in fifty-four cities. December 29 witnessed the senate's overwhelming vote to complete the impeachment process by removing Collor permanently.

Economic performance in 1993 was mixed. Inflation shot up to a record 2,670 percent, but the stagflation of recent years was broken by a 4.2 percent GDP growth, which was back where it had been before the 1990 disaster. Exports were a high $39 billion, producing a healthy $13-billion trade surplus and bringing foreign exchange reserves up to $32 billion. The inflow of investment exceeded $7 billion, pushing stock market prices up 100 percent in real terms, and new foreign loans reached $10 billion. With a weather eye on the success of Argentina's anti-inflation program, Cardoso reluctantly assumed the finance ministry in May 1993, never imagining the full benefits of this move. Announced early in 1994, the Real Plan's main features went into effect at midyear, most dramatically a partial and indirect shift to a dollar–linked new currency, the real, but also including the elimination of governmental deficit financing. The plan's instant success and credibility quickly transformed Cardoso into the government's stop-Lula presidential candidate and then, by August, into the leader on his way to becoming a prohibitive favorite.

The October 1994 elections dwarfed even those of 1989–1990, as almost 12,000 candidates sought the favor of nearly 95 million voters to fill over 1,700 positions. Although Lula's presidential campaign built up early momentum, since he had never really stopped running, Cardoso, who had stepped down as finance minister in March, had the advantage of much stronger coalitions and candidates at the state level as he ran on an alliance of the PSDB, the PFL, and the PTB. His decisive card was the success of the Real Plan, as dramatically falling inflation rates, combined with euphoria over the July World Cup soccer triumph, left voters in an optimistic mood. Brazilian voters, having been stung the last time around, went for performance and credibility. Cardoso's being author of the Real Plan was enough, added to an image for personal integrity and responsibility, as well as a more presidential demeanor than that shown by Franco, and an international reputation as a progressive scholar of development problems. Cardoso won over a large proportion of voters whose favorite party had backed its own lesser candidate. On October 3 some 78 million voters gave Cardoso 34.4 million votes, twice Lula's 17.1 million. Cardoso carried all states except Rio Grande do Sul and the Federal District as not only was Lula swamped in his wake, but the array of also-rans suffered single-digit electoral humiliation. Candidates associated with Cardoso won all key statehouses, with ex-president Sarney engineering the election of his daughter as governor of their home state, to solidify his position as a power in the PMDB. The lineup in the lower house was the PMDB 107, PFL 89, PSDB 62, PPR 53, Lula's PT 49, PP 36, Brizola's PDT 33, PTB 31, Brazilian Socialist Party (PSB) 15, Liberal Party (PL) 13, and the Communist Party of Brazil (PCdoB) 10. Hence Cardoso embarked on what was expected to be a single term as president with his core coalition having more than enough legislators to push his working majority near the three-fifths level needed for constitutional amendments—although party discipline was notoriously weak, requiring judicious use of patronage and pork. Accustomed to playing a leading role in the congress, Cardoso started auspiciously. The new currency demonstrated great strength relative to the US dollar, and foreign exchange reserves piled up to near $40 billion, while Brazil continued to run large trade surpluses despite increased imports. Inflation for 1994 was 930 percent, but for the six months that the Real Plan was in effect, it was only 22 percent—well under half the monthly rate before it went into effect—and GDP growth was a lusty 5.9 percent.

Born in 1931 in Rio de Janeiro to a family with a long tradition of army generals, Cardoso made his academic career in São Paulo. Fourteen at the time of Vargas's 1945 ouster and twenty-three when Vargas took his own life, Cardoso followed a long and gradual path from left toward center, particularly from the 1970s on. Owing to close associations with individuals and movements of the far left, he found it prudent to go into exile in Chile after the military takeover in 1964. There he played a leading role in developing dependency theory (the popular political science approach of the 1960s and 1970s) before accepting a professorship at the working-class suburban branch of the University of Paris, where the spring 1968 uprisings involved many of his students and colleagues. Following his return to Brazil later that year, Cardoso began to moderate and modify his views, and running for the senate in 1978, he polled one-sixth the vote of the winner, but as first alternate he moved up when André Franco Montoro (b. 1916) was elected São Paulo governor in 1982. Following a narrow loss to ex-president Jânio Quadros in the 1985 race for São Paulo mayor, a valuable learning experience in political campaigning, Cardoso was comfortably returned to the senate in 1986, continuing to function as the Sarney government's leader in the congress. In 1988 Cardoso took a major part in forming the PSDB as a split of progressive elements from the nonideological PMDB. Throughout the events of the early 1990s, Cardoso maintained credibility as a pragmatic social democrat—staying out of Collor's cabinet because of pressure from his party before becoming foreign minister under Itamar Franco. During the 1994 campaign, assuming the appealing political persona of "FHC," he demonstrated greatly improved campaign skills, accepting advice from such electoral whizzes as Antônio Carlos Magalhães and ex-president Sarney when operating outside Brazil's developed urban center. At the same time he projected a carefully honed image of competence and reliability through the electronic media.

As president, Cardoso had ex-president Sarney and PFL leader Antônio Carlos Magalhães as major allies as they rotated in the senate presidency. In contrast to the revolving-door that had prevailed since 1985, Pedro Sampaio Malan (b. 1943) was a fixture as finance minister. Since the Real Plan had carried Cardoso to the presidency, he was determined to maintain its integrity against demands from political forces for "flexibility," a euphemism for electorally popular loosening of the purse strings. Indeed, the touchstone of Cardoso's first term was the continued success of his economic program.[23] In 1995 the cost of living increase dropped dramatically to 22 percent, followed by 9 percent in 1996, and less than half that in 1997. Although economic growth fell off to a still healthy 4.2 percent in 1995 and slipped to 2.7 percent in 1996, some 40 million new consumers had been brought into the money economy as a result of inflation's demise. In this highly favorable environment Cardoso's backers held firm in the October 1996 municipal elections.

The PSDB began its rise toward national leadership by edging out the PMDB with more than 13 million votes to just over 12.7 million, but the PMDB bested the PSDB in the election of mayors 1,295 to 921. Actually, the PFL, with almost 10.1 million votes, was second in terms of city halls won with 934, and the PPR came in fourth both in votes (at 9.8 million) and in mayors elected (with 625). Still struggling to become a truly national party, the PT was fifth in electoral support with 7.9 million votes but, owing to its concentration in the large cities, came away with only 110 mayors, whereas the PDT's just under 7 million votes resulted in its control of 436 local executives. The favorable results for the progovernment parties bolstered Cardoso's prospects of reelection, and the fact that the four major parties received only 46.6 million votes demonstrated the highly fragmented nature of the increasingly dysfunctional party system. (At the same time, a single party continued its dominance of Mexico, while Argentina and Colombia had essentially two-party systems, with Chile featuring competition between two stable and programmatic coalitions.) In what would be the beginning of a prolonged trend, rural areas were left out of the progress so visible in cities and towns. The predictable result was a continuing rise in violent struggles over land as the government's modest agrarian reform program whetted the appetites of militant landless groups far faster than it could satisfy their desires. For social democratic initiatives were beginning to reach much of the urban low-income population as amplified public health, education, and social security programs were supplemented by new cash-income transfer programs as payments for children to stay in school and grants for basic food needs. Overall, social spending rose from only $1.3 billion the year Cardoso took office to $12.3 billion by the time he left office eight years later.

Cardoso's popularity in largely urban Brazil led to the passage in 1997 of a constitutional amendment permitting presidential reelection (extended also to governors and mayors). This measure, paralleling actions recently taken in Argentina and Peru, greatly strengthened Cardoso's hand and removed the specter of approaching lame-duck status, as most politicians worked with the probability that he would be at the country's helm through 2002. Cracks in the global economy—specifically the Asian currency crisis—led to a program of fiscal constraints in late 1997 as $10 billion in foreign exchange reserves were expended to fight off a concerted attack upon the overvalued real. (In keeping with the position it had taken in Mexico in 1994, but in sharp contrast with the Bush administration's attitude toward Argentina a few years later, the Clinton government helped out by brokering an IMF package that helped bolster the real until Brazil rebuilt its foreign exchange reserves.)

Backed by an alliance of his own PSDB, the PFL, the PMDB, the PPR, and several smaller parties, and with economic growth rallying to 3.3 percent, Cardoso was able to enact major fiscal and administrative reforms in 1998 while accelerating the process of privatizing state enterprises begun under Collor and continued at a slow pace by Franco. Hence not even the negative impact of the Asian and Russian market collapses could derail Cardoso's reelection steamroller—as Brazil won its fifth soccer World Cup. In October he received 35.9 million votes to 21.5 million for Lula. Moreover, with an electorate greatly expanded to embrace two-thirds of the country's population—compared to one-sixth in 1946—the array of parties backing Cardoso rode the wave of popular support for his management of the economy to retain their decisive congressional majorities.[24] Continued political stability thus assured, an IMF-led $42-billion financial support program was put in place in November 1998, and significant parts of the requisite fiscal, pension, and administrative reforms were duly enacted during 1999. Highly symbolic was the creation at the beginning of Cardoso's second term of a ministry of defense headed by a civilian (replacing the separate service ministries headed by military chiefs). This move was followed by devaluation of the real, which had been under attack by international speculators and now was allowed to find its market value relative to foreign currencies. By the end of 1999 international confidence in Brazil's future was again on the upswing—based on the government's demonstrated competence—although concern over social problems, particularly urban violence, rural land seizures, and ineffective police work, was on the rise.

From Cardoso to Lula and Beyond

The 2000s opened with Brazil entering year two of Cardoso's second administration. The country's thousand top politicians, along with hordes of lesser politicos, soon turned their attention to positioning themselves, engaging in slate making, arranging finances, and beginning to campaign for the October 2000 nationwide municipal elections—which in turn marked the onset of maneuvering for the late 2002 elections not only for the presidency, but for governorships and national and state legislative positions (as had occurred in 1998).[25] This time, however, with the incumbent ineligible to run for another term, the municipal elections might significantly impact the presidential succession. Trends observable in the late 1990s were confirmed by the nationwide balloting in all 5,559 municipalities at the beginning of October 2000 following intense campaigning varying from very modern techniques in the great urban centers to tried-and-true patronal and rural machine methods in the vast hinterlands. With a record 84.5 million turnout, up sharply from 1996's 74.1 million, change was incremental, not dramatic, hence providing only limited clues to what might be expected two years later in the presidential sweepstakes. The PT's increase to 14.1 percent of electoral support (over 11.9 million votes), although far below its leaders' optimistic predictions, finally established it as one of Brazil's big four, although still the least of them. On the other side of the political spectrum, the conservative PFL essentially held its ground with 15.4 percent (13.0 million votes). The PSDB, Cardoso's own party, retained the lead in the electoral derby by a nose over the more clientelistic and opportunistic—hence less cohesive—PMDB at 16.0 to 15.7 percent (over 13.5 million to nearly 13.3 million voters). A number of the medium-sized parties demonstrated electoral viability, but not to a degree that would justify dreams of going it alone on a national scale in 2002.[26] In terms of offices won, the PMDB led with 1,257 mayors and 11,373 city council members, compared to 1,028 and 9,649 for the PFL, and 990 and 8,515 for the PSDB (totaling 3,275 and 29,537, respectively, some three-fifths of the total). These results demonstrated that, although these three parties were national parties enjoying support from large numbers of elected officials and the many times larger number of functionaries these dignitaries employed, they were far from dominant. The proportion of women winning mayoral posts remained static at 5.7 percent. Although the requirement for the share of women on party slates rose from 20 to 30 percent, the number elected to city councils rose only marginally to 11.6 percent.

In the aftermath of the elections Cardoso sought in vain to enact priority legislation during 2001 before national and state electoral considerations came to the fore once more. One of his problems, fatal if he wished to manage the succession process, was his inability to bring about sustained economic growth sufficient to generate an increase in per capita income. His reelection had been greatly facilitated by GDP growth of 2.7 percent in 1996, rising to 3.2 percent in 1997 before stagnating the next year. Then, in 1999, economic growth was an anemic 1.4 percent, and memories of recovery to 4.1 percent in 2000 could not make up for a pronounced slump in 2001. In sharp contrast with Argentina's unprecedented contemporary woes, the Brazilian economy performed at least marginally well in Cardoso's eighth and final year in office. The ratio of public debt to GDP in 2002 was a worrisome 58 percent, but the federal government's primary fiscal surplus was over 3 percent of GDP, and the trade surplus was a robust $13 billion—breaking the old 1994 record of $10.5 billion only three years after enduring a $6-billion trade deficit in 1999 (on the heels of an $8.6-billion imbalance in 1998). Moreover, Brazil began to carry the day within the mechanisms of the World Trade Organization (WTO) in its challenging of unfair subsidies and restrictions on the part of the industrialized powers.

Lula's presidential campaign had been going on nearly continuously since his first bid in 1989—embracing his unsuccessful runs in 1994 and 1998. Now this mature campaigner knew after three losses in a row that to win he needed to build a broad coalition of parties, including some that were part of Cardoso's legislative base. In this enterprise Lula had three things going for him. First, his electoral allies knew that he would have to keep his promises to them, for there was no way that he could come close to building a working majority in the congress without having them as partners. Lula's second, and reinforcing, asset was the fact that these parties had a long record of adhering to whatever government was in power, being accustomed to the patronage and perks of being part of the government and unsuited to, as well as unfamiliar with, the role of opposition. His third advantage was the appreciation on the part of important PFL, PMDB, PTB, and some PPB leaders of his popularity with the masses—a part of which they would like to have rub off on their anointed candidates during what promised to be very difficult races at the state level. Once the PSDB insisted that the administration's standard bearer had to come from its ranks, only elements of the factionalized PMDB and the divided PFL could join behind Lula. He demonstrated his availability for alliances by selecting seventy-one-year-old José Alencar of the small centrist Liberal Party (PL), a successful Minas Gerais businessman, to serve as his running mate. Along with Lula, Governors Roseana Sarney of Maranhão and Anthony Garotinho in Rio de Janeiro emerged as early front-runners, but their candidacies wilted under attacks by the government's candidate, health minister José Serra. Ms. Sarney was knocked out by the exploitation of financial scandals involving her husband and ran for the senate instead; Garotinho was weakened by division of the Evangelical movement upon which his hopes rested.

In the first round on October 6, 2002, Lula garnered 39.2 million votes (46.4 percent) to Serra's 19.6 million (23.2 percent). Garotinho made a respectable showing with 15.1 million votes (17.9 percent), and Ceará statesman Ciro Gomes slipped from his 1998 third-place performance with 10.1 million ballots cast in his favor (12.0 percent). An impressive 94.3 million, some 82 percent of a registered electorate of 115.3 million, went to the polls. The October 27 runoff was anticlimactic as Lula trounced Serra 52.8 million to 33.4 million—57.6 percent to 36.4 percent (62.5 percent to 37.5 percent in terms of valid votes—null and void are also tabulated as being part of the total turnout). On the congressional side, the PT elected 91 to the 513-member lower house compared to 84 for the PFL, the PMDB's 74, and 71 for the PSDB. Fifth place went to the PPB at 49, followed at a distance by the PTB and the PL with 26 each and the PSB and PDT at 22 and 21 seats, respectively. Counting holdovers, the PFL and the PMDB led in the senate with nineteen each, trailed by the PT with fourteen and the PSDB with eleven. The PDT held five seats, and the PTB, PSB, and PL each held four of the eighty-one seats.

Because the PT had under 18 percent of the chamber and slightly less in the senate, Lula was left with a major challenge in mounting a congressional majority, reflecting his party's continued fragility in many parts of the country—worrisome in light of his determination to seek reelection in 2006. (The simple math was that his own party could take him only a third of the way to a working majority in either house, with smaller parties of the left woefully unable to fill the gap.) This weakness of the PT compared to the popularity of its candidate was confirmed in the governorship elections, where the PT won only three of twenty-seven races, no improvement over 1998. The PSDB, despite its presidential candidate's defeat, led with seven states (containing 52 million voters); the PMDB had five (embracing an electorate of 24 million), and the PFL and the PSB with four each also outperformed Lula's party. The PT was victorious in only three unimportant states, whereas the PSDB carried off the major prizes, São Paulo and Minas Gerais, and the PMDB swept the south—Rio Grande do Sul, Paraná, and Santa Catarina—as well as winning control of the

Federal District and retaining the governorship of Pernambuco. Bahia and Maranhão were the PFL's major electoral spoils.

The beginning of a process of undermining hegemonic political machines in states hitherto noncompetitive was almost lost in the drama of Lula's election. With the 1985 return to democracy, governors had reemerged as powerful political brokers, and persistence of a deep historical legacy of party system under development still prevented the subordination of regional interests to national parties and their concerns. Up to the end of Cardoso's second term, at least seven states, several of them among the country's larger electorates, remained bastions of oligarchical clientelism. Collectively these machine-dominated states had only seen 13.6 percent of state assembly seats go to parties of the left as recently as 1998. In 2002 this proportion rose to 21 percent, on the way to 26 percent in 2006. Change in the governorship contests was even more dramatic, trebling from 10.8 percent in 1998 to 34.4 percent four years later (although slumping to 25.1 percent in 2006). Although these figures were well below those in the six most politically competitive states, they heralded a change that was likely to be heavily felt the next time around.[27] The process initiated was one of the Lula government's strongly undercutting the old accommodation between center-right forces dominant at both the state and national levels by establishing vertical competition between a center-left federal government and markedly more conservative state political machines and alliances.

There would be municipal elections again in 2004, general elections in 2006, and municipal balloting once more in 2008—before yet another general election in 2010. Hence Brazilian voters would go to the polls a dizzying six times between 2000 and 2010—within the context of a party system as fragmented as that of the legendarily dysfunctional French Third Republic between 1874 and 1940. By contrast, Mexico would have only two presidential and two midterm elections over the same span, all structured by an essentially three-party system, roughly the same calendar as Argentina, which would see a single party dominant.

A crucial consideration for the future was the fact that Lula's election had resulted in large degree from support by dissident leaders of the Cardoso-era governing coalition, eager to even scores and strengthen their position within their own parties. Ex-president Sarney blamed Serra for derailing his daughter's presidential campaign, whereas Magalhães resented having been forced to resign the senate presidency as well as his senate seat over a technical violation of rules. With a Serra victory, the rivals of these two lords of Brazilian politics would consolidate control over the PMDB and the PFL, respectively; by helping elect Lula this pair of hardy political perennials could look forward to being crucial power brokers in the fragmented 2003–2006 congress and to influencing the presidential succession. Neither of these grizzled veteran wizards of Brazilian politics had any reason to remain allied with the new president except in terms of a satisfactory arrangement with respect to cabinet posts and patronage in politically strategic agencies. Both sage veterans of political wars kept a wary weather eye out for opportunities to increase their influence—a development more likely the greater the difficulties encountered by the administration's PT nucleus. Hence, while stockpiling financial resources for future campaigns, of necessity Lula focused on the task at hand: how to obtain a working majority in the congress. (This burden was different from that borne by other Latin American presidents at the time, who, with the exception of Alejandro Toledo Manrique in Peru, either had a legislative majority stemming from their election or could form one via alliance with a single party.)

Lula handled organizing his government with skill and a solid perception of political realities. He and his close associates knew that translating his landslide electoral victory into effective support for his administration would be as difficult as it was essential. Starting with under one-fifth of the seats in each house of the congress for his own party, the president-elect needed to turn his electoral allies into reliable coalition partners. Lula also demonstrated considerable skill in establishing reasonable working relationships with the governors of the most important states and, where this was not possible, with the mayors of major metropolitan centers—particularly when, as in the case of São Paulo, they came from the PT's ranks. For behind the rhetoric of electoral politics all major political actors shared a realization that Brazil had essentially found the road toward economic viability during the Cardoso years and had no desire to jeopardize the foundations that were finally in place. Government funds and employment were somewhat less available for patronage purposes, and expenditures at the state and local level were now disciplined by the 2001 Law of Fiscal Responsibility.

The central figures in Lula's administration were longtime close associate, PT head, and campaign manager José Dirceu Oliveira da Silva (b. 1946), originally from Minas Gerais, as chief presidential assistant, and Antonio Palocci (b. 1960), as finance minister (both soon to become the center of campaign-financing scandals that would involve them in legal proceedings through 2009). A two-term mayor of the sizable city of Ribeirão Preto, Palocci had played a major role in 2002 campaign fundraising. Important supporting roles were filled by economics professor Guido Mantega (b. 1949) with the planning portfolio; personal intimate José Genoino (b. 1946), yet another Paulista, who had been the PT's losing candidate for governor of São Paulo, installed as the PT's president; and Luiz Dulci (b. 1956), labor activist and PT general secretary from Minas Gerais, as secretary general of the presidency. Contrary to the expectations of those remembering Lula's historical militant socialism and the PT's ideology, but in keeping with his newly found belief that without sustained development distributionist policies would lack viability, there was a striking continuity with the policies of the outgoing administration. This continuity was also highly conditioned by the new chief executive's need to rely heavily on the same parties as had his predecessor within a presidential system with many semiparliamentary features, and with ex-president Sarney presiding over the senate (as he had done for portions of Cardoso's administration). Priority was given to enactment of the very social security, pension, and tax reforms that Lula and the PT had vehemently opposed when they were the backbone of the opposition to Cardoso's government—and which had been well advanced in the legislative process until sidelined by electoral politics in 2002.[28] In addition there were the imperatives of an IMF requirement of a primary budget surplus of 3.75 percent of GDP in 2003 and the need for $14 to $16 billion in new foreign investments and financing to supplement the hoped-for record trade surplus in order to keep Brazil's balance of payments in order. For widespread, even if unfounded, fear on the part of investors that Lula would reject market discipline and even repudiate Brazil's foreign debt had caused the real to lose half its value in 2002 while GDP shrank nearly 6 percent and the costs of borrowing soared. Lula had tried to defuse these concerns (and lock up PMDB and other center-conservative votes) by swearing during his campaign to fulfill the inherited IMF agreement.

Party switching is commonplace in Brazil, and the government managed to expand and consolidate its legislative base by attracting congress members seeking the ample advantages of executive favor. This feat came with a heavy delayed price as the government would be shaken to its foundations starting in mid-May 2005 over damning evidence that the PT had used illegal funds to pay many of these party jumpers to switch parties. The president's major success was in adding parties to his coalition through a combination of patronage and policy moderation. First, the PMDB came aboard in mid-2003, followed soon after by the PPB, recast as the Popular Party (PP). Looking ahead, the administration hoped for a groundswell of support to propel the PT along the road to becoming a truly national party. Campaigning for the most important local elections not only in Brazil's experience but, by a large margin, in that of the entire Latin American region, took place in a mixed political environment. On the negative side, by April 2004 Lula found himself mired in a corruption scandal that caused his approval rating to sink below 50 percent for the first time. Presidential chief of staff José Dirceu came under heavy attack for allegedly covering up a series of incidents of party-related corruption, a development that led the government to increased dependence on Sarney to keep the congress from open rebellion.

As the economy grew in 2003 by a meager 0.5 percent, the revelation that during his first year in office the left-leaning president had invested in development projects only a tenth of the amount Cardoso had in his final year in office further undercut the administration and, by putting it on the defensive, discombobulated its original electoral strategy of turning the local balloting into a referendum on the national administration. Economic recovery after midyear was a badly needed boon for the government. Economic growth reached 5.2 percent, and burgeoning exports—at $94 billion, up sharply from $73 billion in the preceding year, which in turn constituted a 21 percent rise over 2002—provided a trade surplus of a record $33.6 billion (compared to the old mark of $24.8 billion in 2003). Thus per capita GDP was again on the rise. For after reaching 5.7 percent in the decade beginning in 1971, this crucial index of economic health had been marginally negative for the next ten years (down 0.37 percent), before rising a very modest 1.1. percent from 1991 through 2000—all on the strength of that year's 4.3 percent economic expansion, nearly 3 percent over population growth. Belief that a resumption of economic growth was sustainable helped alleviate the problem of public sector debt, which had risen above half of GDP. Industrial production began to rise in August 2003, and a year later output was running nearly 10 percent over the corresponding month of the previous year and up nearly 8 percent since the beginning of 2004.

The big question was whether economic recovery would balance out the bad news on the sociopolitical front sufficiently to permit the PT to expand its electoral base beyond the large cities, thus improving Lula's chances of reelection, or whether a rival party would emerge as a heavyweight foe capable of mounting a formidable challenge. Two things were certain from the election results: First, this municipal balloting accurately reflected what the total national electorate of 121.4 million individuals—twice the number in Latin America's next largest country, Mexico—wanted from local authorities and politicians; second, given the nature of Brazil's fragmented multiparty system as well as its particular brand of federalism, the very mixed character of the results kept them from casting much light on presidential succession. The most dramatic immediate impact was the runoff defeat of PT São Paulo mayor Marta Suplicy by the runner-up from the 2002 presidential sweepstakes. José Serra's election in this city of nearly 7.8 million voters both resurrected his presidential hopes and, to the extent coattails were perceived to be involved, transformed the PSDB's able, young, and personable two-term governor of that electorally huge state, Geraldo Alckmin, into an alternative presidential candidate for his party. "Marta's" defeat, along with the PT's loss of important interior cities such as Campinas and Ribeirão Preto, cost the party many thousands of patronage positions, which in most cases fell into PSDB hands.

Nationally the relative shares of voter support and offices won reflected a moderate acceleration of trends visible over the past dozen years rather than any sharp shift. The PSDB, while closely trailing the PT in total national first-round votes 15.7 million to 16.3 million (16.5 percent to 17.1 percent), came away with a marked advantage in terms of offices, with 874 mayors to 411 (sixth place) as well as a healthy lead in population governed. While slipping to third place with 14.2 million votes (15.0 percent), the PMDB garnered almost a million more than it had the previous time around and still retained the lead with 1,056 mayors (a drop from 1,257). The PFL sagged from 13.0 million votes to 11.3 million (15.4 percent to 11.8 percent) and came in third with 794 mayors, increasing the likelihood that it would join a coalition in 2006. But although the PSDB and the PT—the parties of the leading presidential contenders—forged to the fore, two-thirds of Brazilian voters continued to prefer other parties (the PMDB, the PFL, and the PP together almost equaling the two leaders' votes, leaving another third for the lesser parties).[29]

If the 2004 elections had brought a major disappointment for a PT that imagined being in power nationally would yield a quantum increase in votes, 2005 was a nightmare for Lula and his party. By May, reform legislation was stalled, and although congressional allies remained as part of the government bloc, their support became less reliable as the question of presidential succession loomed. Then politics was thrown into confusion and the government into disarray in midyear by a series of financial scandals dwarfing those of a year earlier, but involving some of the same pivotal figures. Revelations concerning substantial bribes for lucrative contracts in the post office, where the PTB was ensconced as a reward for congressional support, merged with the disclosure of a scheme of payments to congress members for switching to parties allied with the PT. Under the relentless glare of the press and the start of new congressional investigations, all roads eventually led to the powerful and arrogant José Dirceu. Soon the administration's strongman was forced to resign and was expelled from the congress. Other presidential intimates, including the PT's secretary general and treasurer, were deeply implicated in a scheme with its roots back in the murky dealings of campaign financing for Lula's 2002 presidential run. Indeed, these illegal activities were clearly larger and more systematic than those resulting in Collor's 1992 impeachment. Concerned about maintaining foreign confidence in the economy— Brazil's strongest trump with 3.5 percent growth, exports up 25 percent for a record $40-billion trade surplus, and foreign debt down to 50 percent of GDP from 65 percent in 2000—the opposition at first refrained from attacking the president, while maximizing the damage done to his party, its allies, and Lula's reelection prospects. The PSDB was determined to run a candidate, believing that a greatly weakened president, one perhaps having to answer impeachment charges, was a favorable scenario.

Surprising outside observers, these misdeeds as well as a series of subsequent scandals had very little impact upon Lula's popularity (falling more on the shoulders of congress) and detracted relatively little from the generally favorable public evaluations of his government. Acceptance of corruption as long as it was accompanied by positive performance, especially in the economic realm, remained part of Brazilian political culture, greater in less-developed regions and among individuals of a conservative and/or authoritarian outlook. Much as authoritarianism had been forgiven during the 1969–1973 "economic miracle," corruption was tolerated in light of the administration's highly satisfactory management of the economy. A very capable foreign scholar of this phenomenon concludes that

> the apparent failure of repeated high level scandals to influence significantly the national electoral process of Brazil suggests a parting of worlds, from an earlier phase of elite-dominated electoral process, a la [Joseph] Schumpeter, to a vibrant new grassroots democracy, one that could care less about political elites and their internecine struggles for self-aggrandizement.[30]

Another bothersome problem for Lula arose over the control of his party. In 2001 its moderates had received 51 percent of convention votes against 36 percent for the radicals and 13 percent for a less extreme group. Now many PT militants were criticizing the government's economic policies and insisting that Lula should follow party ideology, not heed the wishes of his allies.[31] In September the government managed to install ex-labor minister Ricardo Berzoino as PT president with great difficulty and only after important elements, including a number of congressmen, ex-education minister Christovam Buarque, and other party founders, had jumped ship for a new, ideologically pure leftist party. Thus efforts toward reelection in 2006 had to center upon retaining support from parties well to the right of the PT.

On October 1, 2006, an electorate swollen to 126 million set the stage for a showdown between the two front-runners. Lula counted upon positive economic performance to pull him through to a second term, while the PMDB's fifty-three-year-old São Paulo governor Geraldo Alckmin Filho, also supported by the PFL, strove to overcome lack of voter recognition and the incumbent's popularity with lower-income groups. A strong late surge by the challenger made inroads on Lula's formidable lead, resulting in a 48.6 to 41.6 percent outcome that brought on an intense runoff campaign addressed to the 10 percent of voters whose candidates had been eliminated. A complicating factor was the absence from the second ballot of those governors and senators elected on October 3 allied to one or the other of the presidential contenders.

In São Paulo, with 28 million voters, the 58 to 32 percent governorship win by Serra helped Alckmin to the 54.2 to 36.8 percent victory over Lula that essentially carried him into the runoff—where his reduced 11.7 million to 10.7 million edge all but sealed his defeat. In Minas Gerais, with an electorate of 13.7 million, the massive reelection landslide by the PSDB's Aécio Neves (a grandson of Tancredo positioning himself as a prospective future president) did not translate into a win for Alckmin, who polled only 40.6 percent (compared to Neves's 77 percent), as Lula won the presidential race with 50.8 percent. With Neves no longer on the ballot, Lula raised his percentage of the runoff vote to almost 65, in effect dooming Alckmin to defeat. In Rio de Janeiro, where both the PSDB and the PT lacked significant support, the PMDB's Senator Sérgio Cabral was elected governor with 41.4 percent of the vote—aided by an alliance with the PP and the PTB, as ticket-splitting voters in the runoff lifted Lula by 20 percent and Alckmin failed to improve significantly on his first-round support. When two-thirds of Bahia's 9.1 million voters supported Lula in the first round before giving the incumbent a towering 78 percent in the runoff, it no longer mattered that his opponent carried Rio Grande do Sul with 56 percent, Santa Catarina with 57 percent, and Paraná with 53 percent (falling off somewhat in the runoff). When the dust settled on October 29, Lula had triumphed with 58.3 million votes to 37.5 million for his challenger, a resounding margin of 60.8 to 39.2 percent. The PSDB could take little consolation from the fact that it had won in states totaling 51 percent of the country's GDP. Despite his personal electoral triumph, Lula was faced with a slightly weakened position in the congress as the PMDB, which again did not run a presidential candidate, replaced the PT as the ranking party in the lower house with 89 seats, as the president's party fell to 83 (compared to the 91 elected in 2002), and the PSDB elected 66 and the PFL 65. Reflecting Brazil's highly fragmented party system, lesser parties won 210 of the 513 chamber seats. (By contrast, a few months earlier 90 percent of the congressional seats in Mexico had gone to just three parties.)

The undercutting of dominant patronage machines continued apace as the existence of vertical competition involving a left-leaning, change-oriented federal government destabilized established state-leader-dominated electoral machines. In Brazil's extremely fragmented party system the forging and sustenance of a winning coalition at the state level was both complex and often costly—as well as requiring unusual political skills. Accomplishing this feat was made even more difficult by an electoral system that fostered intraparty fragmentation and set supposed party colleagues against one another in a fierce fraternal rivalry for votes that might spread across the entire state or be funneled into intense competition for the votes of the same municipalities—since there are no formal electoral constituencies within the states. Party leaders are essentially powerless to impose order, much less discipline, as there is also no form of a party list or ordering. In this very fluid context local bosses, most often mayors, frequently tend to be fickle if not duplicitous in giving their support, always on the lookout for a better offer and switching their choice from one patron to another they think more likely to win and hence be in a position to honor his patronage promises.

This uncertain situation comes into play even more heavily when the opposition candidate at the state level enjoys backing from a federal government that has many ways of directing resources to the municipalities without going through the state administration, a situation particularly prevalent in the vital fields of health and education. Under these circumstances maintenance of a dominant electoral coalition became even more laborious than its original construction. Bosses, especially in once noncompetitive states, increasingly had to deal with many more potentially undermining factors than did their counterparts in other Latin American countries, especially Argentina, but including Mexico, Chile, Colombia, and even Venezuela, with their much more structured and disciplined party systems

By 2006 the keystone Bolsa Familia ("Family Grant") program, within the context of centralizing other antipoverty measures in a ministry of social development, came to exert very significant influence on electoral politics, directly affecting over 40 million of the country's poorest inhabitants in 11.5 million households. This governmental largesse was fundamental to Lula's landslide victories in the poverty-plagued northeast and north, enabling him to handily neutralize his losses in the more developed, urban and industrialized states of the south and center-south. Moreover, with concurrent state and national elections since 1994 and presidential reelection permitted since 1998, the interdependence of elections at both the state and federal levels had increased significantly, especially in years like 1998 and 2006, when the incumbent president was standing for reelection.

The election over, 2007 was comparatively uneventful. Voters who had gone to the polls every even-numbered year since 1994 could turn their attention to other matters. Still dependent upon its more conservative allies, the administration followed a tightrope strategy that "required tradeoffs between responding to investors and satisfying the hopes of domestic constituencies that had voted for change."[32] In the latter respect Lula's most effective tool was still the Family Grant program, which was extended further during his second term. Administration hopes were that this extremely popular grant program, combined with continued economic growth, would be sufficient to propel the PT to the lead among Brazil's parties in the 2008 municipal elections, thus enhancing prospects for electing a PT stalwart as president in 2010—when there would be a real question of how much of his great personal popularity Lula might be able to transfer to a lesser and relatively unknown PT candidate who would have greater difficulty in constructing electoral alliances than Lula, with his uniquely long and broad coattails, had experienced. Once again the ingrained realities of Brazil's peculiar party and electoral system would turn what might be reasonable elsewhere into a pipe dream.

Hence the late 2008 elections in Brazil's 5,563 municipalities took on added significance because the fortunes of the major 2010 presidential contenders were at stake. São Paulo governor Serra, a strong favorite for the PSDB nomination and pronounced leader in early polls regarding the presidency, was committed to the candidacy of Alckmin (his predecessor in the state house), whereas to be a possible successor to Lula, the PT's Marta Suplicy needed to regain the São Paulo city hall from which Serra had ousted her in 2004. After a hotly contested first round of balloting, "Marta" and her six-party "New Attitude for São Paulo" coalition proved to have extensive support, garnering 33 percent of the total. Unfortunately for her comeback hopes and the PT's 2010 presidential aspirations, Democrat party (DEM) incumbent Gilberto Kassab ran up a 34 percent share. With Alckmin's elimination, Serra moved behind Kassab, who had been his vice mayor before he moved to the governorship, also backed by the PMDB in a runoff in which the third- and fourth-place finishers, the disappointed Alckmin and seventy-six-year-old hardy perennial Paulo Maluf of the PP, would have a decisive voice. The October 29 second round went to Kassab by a landslide margin of 60.7 to 39.3 percent—a major blow to the PT since at a whopping 1,338,000 votes the margin exceeded their defeat the previous time around. Thus the PT would have to pin its hopes outside the premier municipality.

Although São Paulo proper, the center of the sprawling metropolitan region, and its 8.2 million voters were the major prize, in this immense urban conglomerate the two concentric rings of industrial suburbs that surround the capital were equally populous: Guarulhos, with its population of 1.3 million, and São Bernardo do Campo, with just over 800,000 inhabitants, both favored the PT over the PSDB—the first by a large margin and the second by only 10 percent; Osasco's population of 715,000 gave the PT a bare majority (with the PSDB its chief challenger). Along with the mixed results in five other cities, each of around 400,000 inhabitants, this outcome in the São Paulo suburbs narrowed the PT deficit but still left it trailing the PSDB. Results were even more mixed in the other major centers dispersed through the interior of São Paulo state (whose population is more than equal to California's and on a par with Argentina's), including Campinas, with a population of well over a million, where 725,000 voters cast two-thirds of their ballots for the PDT candidate; greater Santos, whose million-plus showed a strong preference for anti-PT parties; São José dos Campos (population 610,000), which opted for the PSDB; Ribeirão Preto (at 570,000 inhabitants), where a DEM-PMDB alliance defeated the PSDB and the PT trailed far behind; and Sorocaba, whose population of 580,000 endorsed the PSDB by over 79 percent to under 13 percent for the PT. Together with a dozen slightly smaller other cities, these urban centers furnish over 5 million voters to São Paulo's nearly 30 million total; added to the votes of the metropolis's suburbs this number more than equals the electorate of the state capital. So although far from dismal for Lula, the outcome in Brazil's premier state was clearly much more encouraging to the PSDB than to his government's hopes for continuity.

If the São Paulo results eliminated the PT's leading presidential contender and left Serra in a strong position to become the PSDB nominee, Minas Gerais was also of great significance. There, Belo Horizonte, with nearly 1.8 million voters in the central city, was crucial to the hopes of Minas Gerais governor Aécio Neves— grandson of Tancredo Neves—to establish himself as a major presidential contender. To this end he put together a slate of the PSB's Márcio Lacerda, his secretary of economic development, and Roberto Carvalho of the PT, a proxy for incumbent mayor Fernando Pimentel. On the popularity of the governor and mayor, they were swept into office on a tidal wave of runoff votes—polling 767,332 votes (nearly 60 percent of the total), leaving the PMDB well back in the electoral dust. This hard-earned result was a severe setback to the radical wing of the state PT, which, led by former governor Patrus Ananias, a member of Lula's cabinet, and secretary general of the presidency Luiz Dulci, had striven to channel PT votes in the first round to the PCdoB candidate as a sign of repudiation of the Neves-Pimentel alliance. In addition to the favorable outcome in the state capital, slates led by the PSDB or with Neves's party as a major coalition member proved victorious in a large proportion of the state's other 852 municipalities, including such population centers as Juiz da Fora, where the PSDB won in a runoff, and Uberlândia, where a PP candidate won in the first round. PT elements friendly to Neves and Pimentel won in the industrial suburbs of Betim and Contagem. Overall in Minas Gerais, the PSDB led with 160 mayors to 120 for the PMDB, 109 for the PT, and 99 for the DEM. Still the wide assortment of lesser parties came away with 42 percent of the state's mayors— enough to keep them in the alliance game looking ahead to 2010 and posing a challenge to Neves to catalyze the solid support of the over 16 million Mineiro voters essential to his presidential hopes.

In Rio de Janeiro, neither the PT nor the PSDB was a major factor, as PMDB governor Sérgio Cabral managed to get young Eduardo Paes elected as mayor in a very close runoff over former guerrilla-turned-environmentalist Fernando Gabeira. Ex-presidential third-place finisher Garotinho and his also ex-governor wife demonstrated that, no match for Cabral within the capital's PMDB convention, they still had some political clout as they did well in the interior of the state, winning in Campos (population 440,000) with a highly dramatic 79 percent tidal wave. The major Rio de Janeiro suburb of São Gonçalo, with a population of nearly 1 million, provided the PDT with a significant victory, echoed even more emphatically by the 490,000 residents of neighboring Niterói. The PT scored resounding victories in Nova Iguaçu, with 860,000 inhabitants, as well as in Belfort Roxa (population 500,000), both of which gave the PT nearly two-thirds of their votes. The PSDB's one major victory was in Duque de Caixas (865,000 inhabitants). Hence the country's third-largest electorate remained up for grabs in 2010 (and would be the focus of competing efforts at coalition building).

With Bahia having Brazil's fourth-largest electorate at 9.2 million, the intense mayoral contest in Salvador (population 2.9 million) held national significance, but since Bahia was the transitional state between the politically lagging northeast and the progressing center-south, the intensification of the 2006 shift away from PFL hegemony throughout the state was at least equally important, particularly since political life there was in a state of flux, with old alliances sorely taxed and historical animosities persisting. To a very significant degree the future of the DEM as a major national party was at stake, since its dominance in Bahia had long maintained that party as the smallest of the big four, keeping it from sliding down into the second echelon of Brazil's parties. With the mourning period barely over for Antônio Carlos Magalhães, the renowned "bulldozer" of Brazilian politics, forger of the potent political machine known locally as Carlism, and the leading figure within the DEM nationally, the party's fate was in the hands of his grandson, the young federal deputy Antônio Carlos Magalhães Neto, in the contest for mayor of Salvador against both incumbent João Henrique Carneiro of the PMDB and PT standard bearer Walter Pinheiro. The latter pair advanced to the runoff with 31 and 30 percent to Magalhães's respectable 26.7 percent, with a greatly relieved incumbent winning out by a margin of 753,000 votes to 535,000 (in percentage terms 58.5 to 41.5) with heavy support from Magalhães and his DEM. With victories in 43 municipalities including the major interior urban center of Feira de Santana (population 585,000), Magalhães's DEM remained a significant factor although just a shadow of the invincible juggernaut it had been prior to 2002. Statewide the PMDB led the PT with 116 mayors to 69 as smaller parties, led by the PSDB at 27, came away with 201 city halls, usually on broad multiparty coalitions. These results consolidated the 2006 trends, when after the governorship and presidential balloting 105 mayors, many elected in 2004 as PFL, switched to the PMDB—which had had only 15—while the PT had added only 7 party shifters.

Rio Grande do Sul, whose nearly 8 million voters often pay scant attention to national trends, featured the race for mayor in Porto Alegre, with its population of over 1.4 million, where the PMDB successfully reelected José Fogaça. Elsewhere in the state the PT carried the nearby industrial centers, but the PMDB did well in the state's interior. Despite controlling the governorship, the PSDB finished back with the middle-weight parties. Moreover, by late 2009, amid the presidential succession maneuvering the governor would be struggling to stave off impeachment.

The rest of the country reflected few dramatic changes from the balance of forces evident in 2004 and 2006. The only thing abundantly clear was that a great deal of creative alliance building would take place during 2009, as PT chances of retaining the presidency without Lula on the ballot would require an even broader coalition than had reelected him. Moreover, although polls showed Serra well in the lead, they also indicated that Neves would stand a good chance of defeating prospective PT candidates, strengthening his determination to challenge the PSDB's senior figure in a party primary. What was certain was that in this highly dysfunctional party system (linked to an even more dysfunctional electoral system), political life would be complicated by the fact that the largest single party, the PMDB, remained plagued with the frustrating dilemma of being nationally broad-based with an array of electorally strong regional leaders, but no one dominating national figure. Indeed, its most influential leader was ex-president Sarney, once again ensconced as senate president (but beleaguered by a host of patronage scandals), clearly a kingmaker, not a prospective candidate, and highly motivated to further the career of his daughter, for a third time back in as governor of Maranhão. He and other party leaders might well fall back on the common denominator strategy of the past two presidential elections: refraining from running or formally allying with a presidential candidate in order to allow the party's state organizations to make the most advantageous alliances, aimed at electing a maximum number of governors and senators. This unique situation lent itself to highly creative alliance building, potentially able to accommodate up to six parties—with the governorship and two Senate seats going to the three strongest and the positions of vice governor and alternate senators rewarding less electorally potent political forces. Thus, given the country's extremely wide array of parties, the bargaining and political courting involved would be at times not only very inventive and highly flexible, but downright kaleidoscopic.

In the field of electoral politics Brazil is as different from other Latin American countries as it was governmentally under the nineteenth-century monarchy. Lacking any strong, disciplined, programmatic parties of truly national scope, it has parties that are essentially loose federations of state organizations, most of which are controlled by a few highly influential politicians. Indeed, in 2007 an experienced politician who had been selected by Tancredo Neves to be his political coordinator and served as José Sarney's first justice minister aptly summed up the situation as one in which "Brazil has never had, doesn't have, and will never have real political parties."[33]

In particular, senators, with their eight-year endlessly renewable terms, vary widely in political importance—the key variable being their electoral clout back home rather than the size of their state. In a few cases (like those of Sarney and the late Antônio Carlos Magalhães), they are their state's dominant figure, the governor or the capital city mayor—or even both—being a product of their electoral engineering, often along with one or both of the other senators. In other cases the reins of political power are in the hands of the governor, to whom senators often owe their election and frequently aspire to succeed in the statehouse. Anyone aspiring to become president must know precisely what are the shifting sands of often delicate, even fragile, relationships between the political notables of the country's relatively small number of states—whose ranks also include big-city mayors and heads of regional electoral machines.

This rich assortment of savvy individuals spread across the vast expanse of this highly federative nation often act behind the scenes and in the shadows, subject to public scrutiny only when push comes to shove in the arena of electoral politics. What they have done in past presidential successions and state politics is the best—although still imperfect—guide to their prospective roles and actions in the crucial 2010 presidential campaign, one still in the preliminary stage. Close-to-the-vest consideration of potential future benefits and ongoing calculation of candidates' odds of winning further complicate their electoral maneuvering. (As is often the case with respect to free-agent negotiations in professional sports, bargaining is generally going on with several parties simultaneously in a game bearing as many of the characteristics of an auction as of a courtship.)

Very little internal party democracy exists, as these leaders rely primarily upon alliances with local leaders dominant in various parts of their state. This rather antiquated and highly personalistic political structure thrives in large part from the lack of any formal electoral constituencies for either national or state legislators (or even at the local level for municipal councillors). Moreover, the extremely low and lax requirements for status as a legal party lead to excessive fragmentation. In sum, Brazil's is a system in which, at all stages, strength attracts strength, as candidates for governor strive to be allied with presidential contenders who can broaden their electoral appeal, at the same time that the presidential contenders seek alliances with the strongest gubernatorial aspirants in the hope that their support will carry over into the contest for the country's top executive office. Hence, getting one's party's nomination is the first, and often the simplest, step on the road to the elusive goal of the presidency. For this reason, in this huge federal system, where every vote counts in what is a straight popular-vote race (since there is no form of an electoral college), uncertainty generally rules until a very late point in the campaign, and observers hoping to have any real understanding of what is going on have to keep tabs on a confusingly large number of actors, not just those at center stage. (As is demonstrated in the following chapters, this is a dramatically different type of electoral politics from that in other Latin American countries.)

Hence who will be Brazil's next president is a major uncertainty for the region. Early polls had the PSDB's Serra with a substantial lead, but he faced a determined primary challenge from Aécio Neves, who in turn was being wooed by important PMDB leaders. Lula worked hard to transfer his popularity to Dilma Rousseff, who had no electoral experience and needed to overcome voter reservations concerning her continuing battle with lymphatic cancer as well as possible fallout from a senate investigation into financial scandals at PT-controlled Petrobrás. Meanwhile, some diehard PT stalwarts clung to hopes that there might be (as in Venezuela and Colombia) a referendum on removing term limits that would open the way for Lula's reelection. Senator Marina Silva, who considered herself better qualified than Rousseff, left the PT in August 2009 to become presidential candidate for the Green Party (PV), with other PT figures also seeking greener pastures. What was clear in this clouded picture was that 2010 shaped up as the most wide-open and competitive presidential election in the country's history, with party alignments and voter loyalties even more fluid than usual.

Certainly Brazil will be much more apparent on the world scene during its next presidential term as the soccer World Cup, by far the most global of all sports events, returns there in mid-2014 just as Brazil's election campaign shifts into high gear. Past experience indicates that if at that time Brazil were to add yet another championship to its already leading total, the chances of the incumbent's electoral fortunes would rise significantly. However, the past casts no light on how much a victory in the 2010 World Cup would bolster Lula's ability to transfer this favorable bump to another candidate.[34] As always, the real world is the only laboratory political scientists have, so it is necessary to closely observe relevant developments as they occur.

Notes

1. The place to begin is J.W.F. Dulles, *Vargas of Brazil* (Austin: University of Texas Press, 1967). See also Robert M. Levine, *Father of the Poor: Vargas and His Era* (New York: Cambridge University Press, 1998), as well as Levine's *The Vargas Regime: The Critical Years, 1934–1938* (New York: Columbia University Press, 1970).

2. This treatment draws heavily on Ronald M. Schneider, *"Order and Progress": A Political History of Brazil* (Boulder, CO: Westview Press, 1991), pp. 106–186.

3. Frank D. McCann, *Soldiers of the Patria: A History of the Brazilian Army, 1889–1937* (Stanford, CA: Stanford University Press, 2004), p. 299.

4. Ibid., p. 308.

5. June E. Hahner, *Poverty and Politics: The Urban Poor in Brazil, 1870–1920* (Albuquerque: University of New Mexico Press, 1986), p. 292.

6. McCann, *Soldiers*, pp. 259ff., delineates with care divisions within the army.

7. Ibid., p. 331.

8. Roots of the Estado Novo are ably analyzed in ibid., pp. 406–439.

9. See Frank D. McCann, *Brazilian-American Alliance, 1937–1945* (Princeton, NJ: Princeton University Press, 1973).

10. Detail on this period can be found in Dulles, *Vargas*, as well as J.F.W. Dulles, *Unrest in Brazil: Political Military Crises, 1955–1964* (Austin: University of Texas Press, 1970).

11. Unfortunately there is no adequate biography of Kubitschek in English, although he did publish a detailed autobiography and several volumes of memoirs in Portuguese.

12. The enigmatic Quadros died in 1992 after a political comeback that led him once more to the São Paulo mayor's chair.

13. The Chamber of Deputies had been enlarged from 326 to 409. Turnout at 14.7 million was nearly two and a half times that of 1945. The author spent most of the year closely observing the campaign throughout the country.

14. See J.F.W. Dulles, *Castello Branco: The Making of a Brazilian President* (College Station: Texas A&M University Press, 1978), and J.F.W. Dulles, *President Castello Branco: Brazilian Reformer* (College Station: Texas A&M University Press, 1980).

15. More than 2,100 individuals were punished with loss of political rights; some 4,500 (1,700 civilian and 2,800 military personnel) were forced to retire from government service. Consult Maria Helena Moreira Alves, *State and Opposition in Military Brazil* (Austin: University of Texas Press, 1985).

16. See the detailed treatment of these elections in Ronald M. Schneider, *The Political System of Brazil: Emergence of a "Modernizing" Authoritarian Regime, 1964–1970* (New York: Columbia University Press, 1971), pp. 178–195.

17. On the views of Geisel and Golbery, see Alfred Stepan, *Rethinking Military Politics: Brazil and the Southern Cone* (Princeton, NJ: Princeton University Press, 1988), pp. 33–44.

18. This key aspect is ably explored by Alessandra Carvalho, "As Relações Entre a Lógica Technocrática e a Dinâmica Eleitoral do Regime Military Brasileiro," presented at the Latin American Studies Association's congress in Rio de Janeiro, June 11–14, 2009 (available on the LASA Web site).

19. The author conducted an exhausting, if not exhaustive, program of interviews and campaign observations in all major Brazilian cities from June until after election day, with results incorporated into Schneider, *"Order and Progress,"* pp. 282–283

20. Ibid., pp. 286–385, covers developments up to 1990, and Ronald M. Schneider, *Brazil: Culture and Politics in a New Industrial Powerhouse* (Boulder, CO: Westview Press, 1996), pp. 100–136, 161–168, carries the story into early 1995.

21. The author's detailed observations of the 1982 campaign and analyses of the results can be found in a series of twelve reports beginning in June 1982. See in particular Ronald M. Schneider, *Brazil Elections Series, Final Report: Results and Ramifications* (Washington, DC: Center for Strategic and International Studies, December 1982).

22. See the author's series of six reports, done with the collaboration of William Perry, *The 1989 Brazilian Elections*, especially No. 5 "The Final Tally" (Washington, DC: Center for Strategic and International Studies, January 1990). Most of PSDB standard-bearer Mário Covas's 7.8 million supporters went over to Collor, along with the lion's share of Maluf's 6 million votes and at least half of the 3.2 million electors favoring the PMDB's Ulysses Guimarães.

23. The plan, with careful monitoring and fine-tuning by Cardoso and his economic team, remains one of the world's most successful examples of a rational and politically viable economic policy, in its essential features still being continued by his opposition—who originally condemned it as an electoral fraud—fifteen years later.

24. The approval for reelection is covered in Maurício A. Font, *Transforming Brazil* (Lanham, MD: Roman & Littlefield, 2003), pp. 58–61. The electorate was just under 110 million, an increase of 15 million since 1994.

25. See Maurício Font and Anthony P. Spanakos, eds., *Reforming Brazil* (Lanham, MD: Lexington Books, 2004).

26. Changes from 1996 were very limited for the three largest parties as well as the PPB and many of the midsized parties. The PT demonstrated the greatest growth, a gain from 10.6 percent of the vote to 14.1 percent, hardly spectacular and coming essentially at the expense of the PDT, reflecting the declining appeal of its aging leader, Brizola, contrasted with Lula's moderating and maturing stature. (The PDT fell from 13.4 percent to 6.6 percent as its loss of nearly 4.4 million votes corresponded closely to the PT's gain of almost 4.1 million.) Very useful work on this and other elections has been done by Professor David Fleischer of the Universidade Federal de Brasília.

27. See André Borges, "The Decline of Political Bosses: Unstable Clientelism, Vertical Competition and Electoral Change in the Brazilian States," paper presented at the Latin American Studies Association congress in Rio de Janeiro, June 11–14, 2009 (available on the LASA Web site).

28. For perspective see Eliana Cardoso, "Monetary and Fiscal Reform," and Sonia Diaibe, "Social Policy Reform," in Maurício A. Font and Anthony P. Spanakos, eds., *Reforming Brazil* (Lanham, MD: Lexington Books, 2004), pp. 29–51, 71–91.

29. Strictly applying the criteria for the number of municipal legislators, the courts reduced the total from 60,276 to 51,748. In late 2009 the affected municipalities obtained legislation raising the numbers by over 7,000. However, legal obstacles remained to their retroactive application to the 2008 balloting.

30. Daniel Zirker, "The Corruption Conundrum in Contemporary Brazil," paper presented at the Latin American Studies Association's congress in Rio de Janeiro, June 11–14, 2009 (available on the LASA Web site). For a convincing analysis of corruption's roots in the

country's political culture, see also José Álvaro Moisés, "Corrupção Política e Democracia no Brasil Contemporâneo," presented at the same LASA panel.

31. Emir Sader, "Taking Lula's Measure," *New Left Review*, 33 (May-June 2005), pp. 58–80, is an articulate leftist critique of the PT government by a disaffected party founder. More balanced is Wendy Hunter and Timothy J. Power, "Lula's Brazil at Midterm," *Journal of Democracy*, 16:3 (July 2005), pp. 127–139.

32. Lourdes Sola, "Politics, Markets, and Society in Brazil," *Journal of Democracy*, 19:2 (April 2008), pp. 31–45, republished in Larry Diamond, Marc F. Plattner, and Diego Abente Brun, eds., *Latin America's Struggle for Democracy* (Baltimore: Johns Hopkins University Press, 2008), pp. 124–138. See also Wendy Hunter and Timothy J. Power, "Rewarding Lula: Executive Power, Social Policy, and the Brazilian Elections of 2006," *Latin American Politics and Society*, 49 (Spring 2007), pp. 1–30, as well as Joseph L. Love and Werner Baer, eds., *Brazil Under Lula: Economy, Politics and Society Under the Workers' President* (New York: Palgrave Macmillan, 2008).

33. Fernando Lyra, *Daquilo Que Eu Sei: Tancredo e a Transição Democrática* (São Paulo: Editora Iluminuras, 2009), p. 231.

34. As with all propositions in political analysis, this one needs to be reassessed and finetuned in light of what impact the 2010 World Cup has on the ongoing presidential campaign, especially as Brazilian hopes were running high and its hordes of avid fans hungered for the elation brought on by the 1994 and 1998 triumphs. The 2014 tournament to be held in Brazil (for the first time since 1950) will be the most geographically dispersed in history, with games to be held not only in São Paulo, Rio de Janeiro, and Brasília, but also in Salvador, Recife, Fortaleza, and Natal in the northeast; Porto Alegre and Curitiba in the south; and Belo Horizonte, Cuiaba, and Manaus in the interior. Its impact upon that year's presidential election may well be heavier, given the intense and "up close" immediate drama of its taking place across the country, with Rio de Janeiro hosting the championship game (a dress rehearsal for the 2016 Olympic Games).

7

Mexico Since 1930

Mexico would use the eighty years from 1930 to 2010 to catch up with the rest of Latin America in political development and to make a strong start in becoming a democracy. Without a great transforming leader such as Lázaro Cárdenas del Rio (b. 1895) at the beginning of this difficult journey, it is doubtful that it would have been accomplished. The vehicle through which this construction of a viable political system was undertaken was not only the complete antithesis of Brazil's path, but also distinct from the path of any other Latin American nation: a disciplined and hegemonic political party. In many ways Mexico's large indigenous population remained at least as disadvantaged as African-heritage Brazilians if better off than Peru's Indians.

Institutionalizing the Revolution, 1930–1955

Within the National Revolutionary Party (PNR), the holding company of regional political bosses and near warlords created by recent ex-president Plutarco Elías Calles in 1929, this godfather-like inveterate political schemer and manipulator was the kingmaker and the power behind the throne in a system called the Maximato in honor of his title as Jefe Máximo ("Maximum Chief") of the revolution.[1] Pascual Ortiz Rubio (b. 1877) of Michoacán was the candidate chosen to win by the boss-of-bosses in November 1929's less-than-honest presidential election. Intellectual José Vasconcellos's campaign against the official candidate faced an impossible uphill battle, including intimidation, and in March Calles's paramilitary "Gold Shirts" fired on a mass rally in Mexico City. The usual postelection uprising by supporters of a loser was repressed at the cost of a thousand dead and twice as many wounded—which, in a country inured since 1910 to counting fatalities in the tens of thousands, was taken as good news and a favorable portent.

The decisive factor in Mexican elections at this point was not the votes cast but their creative counting, in which the PNR excelled as much as Argentina's conservatives—or as the Brazilian oligarchic regime would for the last time in 1930. When Ortiz Rubio exited the presidency in September 1932, having found out to his great chagrin that being president did not provide the freedom of initiative and action it had before the straitjacket of a Calles-run government party, Calles replaced him with Abelardo Rodríguez (b. 1889), who had become wealthy as a rumrunner during the

US prohibition era and who was happy to have the job under any restraints. During the Maximato, Lázaro Cárdenas, a *mestizo* who was the former governor of Michoacán, led an ascending reform faction within the party seeking to revive the Sonorans' strategy of an alliance with worker and *campesino* sectors. Seen by Calles as the most solid of the competing revolutionary generals, Cárdenas had been a captain during the bloodletting between revolutionary rivals in 1913–1914 and had become a colonel before the end of 1915, then a brigadier general in 1920. While excelling as a staff officer, he had fought against Zapata, Villa, the Yaqui Indians, Venustiano Carranza, and Adolfo de la Huerta—before becoming a major general in 1928 at age thirty-two. November 1930 had found this rising politician presiding over the PNR, a post he held—and used to good advantage—until August 1931. Moving over to govern Michoacán, with radical Francisco Mugica as a mentor, he embarked on a dramatic acceleration of land reform.

At the 1933 party convention Cárdenas secured the presidential nomination, saw his campaign program adopted as the PNR's "six-year plan," and changed the basis for membership in the party to individual instead of affiliation of entire organizations, the better to use the party as a mobilization vehicle. At the center of his political strategy was state building, particularly the need to strengthen still fragile political institutions. In this respect Calles's PNR, within which Cárdenas rose to power, was not the kind of party Cárdenas felt Mexico needed. This great reformer would give it one good renovation and then guide his successor toward another thorough overhaul. The end result would be a party that could get the job done for another fifty-five years even with ordinary drivers at the wheel. Easily elected after a vigorous campaign in which he sought as much to get to know the Mexican people as to become a friendly paternalistic personality to them, exuding simplicity and sincerity, the thirty-nine-year-old Cárdenas reinvigorated agrarian reform, distributing vast amounts of land to individual *campesinos* (loosely translated as "peasants") and even more to Indian villages in the traditional communal landholding form of the *ejido*. By the end of six years he had distributed 18 million hectares (over 43 million acres) to 800,000 peasants and rural laborers. Cárdenas also implemented the provision of the 1917 Constitution for seventh-day pay, giving workers the equivalent of a 16 percent pay raise, and he greatly increased investment in education, particularly at the primary level and in small towns and rural areas long overlooked by the federal government. A proponent of a mixed economy, Cárdenas worked to make the state sector stronger and more autonomous. In June 1935 Cárdenas made his coalition with labor both stronger and more open.

This action brought to a head the conflict with Calles, who had long chafed at Cárdenas's independent ways, resulting in an intense power struggle that the highly determined and fearless Cárdenas won, ending Calles's ability to be more than a pebble in his shoe by shipping him off to California in April 1936. The remaining members of Calles's faction might prove an annoyance in the 1938 congressional elections, but most of the grief came from elements on the right longing for some of the coziness they had enjoyed with governments during the Maximato. Establishing civilian control over the military was a Cárdenas priority in pursuit of his overarching goal of strengthening and fortifying a viable political system that could be entrusted to civilian rule without military interference. This was no small task, as the army had come to play an important, indeed, highly favored, role under Díaz, was a crucial factor in the 1911–1919 outright civil war, and was featured in the sporadic resort to force during the 1920s. Although the government built up worker and peasant militias as a stopgap, the longer-run institutional solution was to establish an academy to educate lower-class young men to become professionalized, apolitical officers. In the years before these young men could have a cumulative effect on the ethos of the Mexican military, largely composed of self-made officers who had earned commissions and promotion on the battlefield and become retainers of the regional warlord class that had emerged from the decades of conflict, other steps would have to be taken. Cárdenas's war minister put into effect, with Cárdenas's firm backing and prestige as a revolutionary general, such fundamental measures as transferring officers without reassigning their men and directly paying soldiers instead of having this done by "their" officers. A decree limiting military service to a maximum of thirty years meant that all who had begun their careers with the revolution would be out at the beginning of Cárdenas's successor's term.[2]

The government's close ties to both labor and the peasantry were institutionalized in 1936 through the Mexican Workers Confederation (CTM), an umbrella union organization, and the National Campesinos Confederation (CNC), a massive outreach to peasants and rural workers in 1938. Then in March 1938 Cárdenas reorganized the PNR as the Party of the Mexican Revolution (PRM), composed of four functional sectors: the workers, organized in the CTM; the peasants, embodied in the CNC; the military; and the "popular sector" embracing the middle class, particularly organized public employees along with some liberal professionals. The last two years of Cárdenas's presidency featured boldly nationalizing the country's petroleum resources and turning them over to development and production by a state entity, Pemex (Petróleos Mexicanos). With war clouds darkening over Europe, Cárdenas took advantage of a fortuitous window of opportunity. Using a provision of the 1917 Constitution reaffirming the Spanish royal principal that all subsoil resources belong to the nation, he took physical possession of the oil fields, agreeing to subsequent payment to their chiefly foreign owners within strict limits. Given the perilous situation they found themselves in, Britain and the Netherlands had more urgent matters on their plate than jumping to the defense of Royal Dutch Shell, which Cárdenas would then put forward as a model for the resolution of the compensation issue with US companies.

With many US investors already up in arms over the land expropriations, media uproar and congressional lobbying were raucous—full of accusations of communism and demands for military intervention. The extremely tense situation was defused by the fact that the Democrat Franklin D. Roosevelt, rather than a Republican, was in the White House and that, with war on the horizon, he did not want a disgruntled neighbor on a long, exposed land border. Hence he sent Josephus Daniels as a special envoy. As he was a respected southern gentleman newspaper publisher from South Carolina (and FDR's boss as Secretary of the Navy in World War I), his endorsement of Cárdenas as a nationalist reformer, not a communist, averted an official crisis. As Cárdenas and his advisers must have expected, adverse economic fallout from the oil expropriation was heavy and damaging, leaving the economic situation in 1939 and 1940 alarmingly bleak.[3]

Cárdenas pulled back from populism near the end of his administration with a sharp reduction in land distribution and the choice of his long-term associate, the moderate Manuel Ávila Camacho (b. 1897), as his successor.[4] Most likely Cárdenas decided, quite wisely, that after the hubbub and turmoil of his term and the major long-term programs he had launched, a period of consolidation was in order. Aware of the mounting opposition that his sharp turn to the left had aroused, he could best preserve political order by agreeing to a more centrist successor and wrapping the publicly little-known candidate in his legitimizing cloak. Besides, Ávila Camacho had enough of a revolutionary background not to be a red flag to military elements, who still had most of their teeth and claws and were being recruited by an opposition candidate. In making his decision on such sound political considerations, Cárdenas taught an important lesson to future Institutional Revolutionary Party (PRI) presidents about taking the needs of the next six years into account as much as continuity of policies or personal preferences in making a wise choice of successor. In any case, the great man's decision not to try to keep a hand on the tiller or a foot on the accelerator once he had passed the sash on to his successor was a salutary example— particularly in light of Calles's penchant and precedent in the opposite direction. (Indeed, this astute consideration was appropriate for other countries as well, although unfortunately rarely followed as incumbents elsewhere most frequently strove to impose successors whom they could influence, if not control.)

In the 1940 election, Ávila Camacho, a rancher who had served as Cárdenas's chief of staff in 1919 and as his defense minister in 1940, found an old revolutionary general, Juan Andreu Almazán, running against him with the support of the large industrialists centered in Monterrey, aggrieved foreign investors, diehard praetorian (politically interventionist) elements of the military, and middle-class sectors feeling threatened by the rise of labor. In the face of electoral defeat, merited or fraudulent, Almazán rebelled, but the uprising found less support than similar reactions had in the past, and it would be the last serious effort to contest Mexico's presidency by force of arms. If Cárdenas's had been a transformational government, Ávila Camacho's presidency was in many ways a transitional one. It began a shift away from social reform toward industrial modernization that quickly coopted much of Almazán's support, converting some into enthusiasts (since many political participants as well as observers had assumed that Cárdenas, still in his prime of life, would attempt to control his successor à la Calles). As the war in Europe and the subsequent direct involvement of the United States lifted Mexico out of the economic slump of 1939–1940, the new administration's investments in infrastructure and public works rose sharply. A treaty concerning migrant farm workers (*braceros*) with the United States eased unemployment.

Accepting counsel from ex-caretaker president Abelardo Rodríguez rather than the rival Calles or Cárdenas factions in the party, and spurning its far-left fringe, Ávila Camacho forced Soviet sympathizer Vicente Lombardo Toledano out of the leadership of the CTM, bringing in Fidel Velásquez, who would serve to keep labor in line with the party and government through the 1980s. There was no sharp break in the government-labor domestic relationship; it just ceased to be monogamous—that is, being faithful to a single partner—on the government's side as business and property-owning elements gained influence. This shift was gradual and sweetened by the establishment of a social security system in 1941 and its gradual implementation over the next few years. Ávila Camacho also consolidated civilian control over the military.[5] His aim of increasingly subordinating the party to the government required a preliminary move and new legislation before a drastic restructuring of the party at the end of his term. In the 1943 congressional elections active involvement in the nominating process resulted in a significant increase in the political weight of the party's popular sector, reorganized into the national Confederation of Popular Organizations (CNOP) and including middle-class groups, which came away with 75 of the PRM's 144 seats in the lower house, to 46 for the *campesino* sector and only 23 for labor. The 1946 election law strengthened the electoral machinery while centralizing its control in the federal government's hands, done of course in the name of reducing fraud at the local level. This law also eliminated regional and ad hoc parties by requiring a membership of at least 30,000 with a minimum of 1,000 members in each of two-thirds of Mexico's states. Ideological parties were restricted by a ban on those of the extreme left or right, acceptable in a context of the war against fascism just ending and the threat of international communism just rising, as well as proscription of religious parties—a preemptive strike against the conservative Catholic National Action Party (PAN), founded in 1939 by Manuel Gómez Marín, which was seeking to recast itself as a Christian democratic party, as was happening in Italy and Germany. The PAN had been allowed in 1943 to participate in the congressional balloting, and thus the political camel was given a chance to stick its nose into the electoral tent. Indeed, beginning with 4 of its 110 Chamber of Deputies (lower-house) candidates recognized as winners in 1946, this little acorn would by the end of the century have grown into a sturdy tree.

After declaring in December 1945 that he was a "believer" (the code word for Catholic), thus reducing tensions carrying over since the 1920s, Ávila Camacho—who had appointed José Vasconcellos, the 1929 victim of electoral fraud, to head a splendid new national library (Biblioteca México)—continued his pursuit of national unity by amending the constitution to remove its most onerous anti-Catholic restrictions in the field of education. Then, at a national convention in January 1946, he unveiled ideological and structural changes packaged as being in keeping with the brave new postwar world of which Mexico was an increasingly important part. With "Democracy and Social Justice" as the new slogan (replacing "For a Workers' Democracy"), and the Institutional Revolutionary Party as the government party's new name (replacing Party of the Mexican Revolution, or PRM), membership in the official party was henceforth individual and direct, not collective and intermediated by its functional sectors. In recognition of the progress made in the professionalization of the armed forces, the military lost its status as a separate sector, being folded into the popular sector, which was made more accessible to private-sector white-collar workers, professionals, and small businessmen. The net result was a more centralized and hierarchical party in which sharply reduced debate within the no-longer-autonomous sectors (especially labor and *campesinos*) would soon be reflected in lessened debate in the congress and a decisive strengthening of the government's position vis-à-vis the PRI. Calles had built a party, Cárdenas had made it his kind of party, and Ávila Camacho transformed it into "the" party, at least for the next half century—requiring only periodic tune-ups.

The presidency of Miguel Alemán Valdés (b. 1902), Ávila Camacho's interior minister, marked a turning point in Mexican politics in several ways. With his 1946 election the torch was passed to a new generation of civilian politicians not only without personal participation in the revolution, but having had little involvement in the ensuing period of civil war.[6] As Alemán was the son of a revolutionary officer, the age of the generals was over, and the military accustomed itself to a low profile within an increasingly civilian-dominated PRI. Alemán's term represented consolidation in the power of a PRI faction far more probusiness and hence dramatically less nationalistic and reform-minded than the waning Cárdenas wing. This trend would reach the point where pursuit of political stability through economic growth would become the basic premise of the political system, seen as an operational imperative by subsequent administrations. Increasingly the quest to sustain economic growth would lead first to opening the doors wider to foreign investment, then to massive international borrowing and a burgeoning foreign debt. This quest would, unfortunately, also mark the emergence of large-scale corruption as a distinguishing characteristic of Mexican politics.

In order to promote growth without generating high inflation, a priority in a country that by 1950 had reached a population of 27.8 million, Alemán's government acted through PRI-affiliated unions to suppress labor's wage demands. A new strategy of stable development was instituted, based on the promotion of industrialization through subsidizing domestic industries and a massive infrastructure-improvement program featuring expansion of the generation and transmission of cheap hydroelectric energy. A balance-of-payments problem and rising inflation led to an unpopular devaluation of the peso in 1948, followed by another in 1952. The lessons seemed to have been learned, and there would not again be an economic crisis until 1976. But at the end of his term Alemán, later to live and die as one of Mexico's richest businessmen, faced opposition not only to his policies, but also to his divisive, rather than consensual, style. Running roughshod over party factions and refusing to enter into the traditional negotiating over the selection of governors, he was determined to impose a conservative candidate to succeed him, upon party leaders who felt it was time for the pendulum to swing in the other direction before reformist elements might begin to feel the party had deserted them.

Further undermining the autocratically inclined president, the government's heavy involvement in the economy provided ample opportunities for large-scale corruption, and its tolerance by the administration eventually sparked public outcry and even protests from within the PRI. As captured by a close student of Mexican politics, the Alemán administration became noted for "the corruption accompanying all of these grandiose economic projects, and for the very profitable economic strangleholds reputedly held" by some of the administration insiders and their favorites.[7] Indeed, corruption became an integral part of the Mexican political system—a problem that would only worsen by the 1980s, when billions of dollars from drug trafficking would lead to rampant graft and fraud not related to productive economic growth.

Hoping to restore faith in the ruling party, Alemán compromised on Adolfo Ruiz Cortines (b. 1890), his interior minister and a former governor of Veracruz, who enjoyed a reputation for probity.[8] General Miguel Henríquez Guzmán insisted on running as a dissident in the 1952 election, getting 16 percent of the vote. This would prove to be the last time in three and a half decades the PRI would come up against an unwanted electoral challenge as it completed its transformation into a hegemonic, near-monopolistic official party allowing only marginal and essentially symbolic opposition. Waving the banner of "consolidation and moral reform," Ruiz Cortines moderated his predecessor's policies without abandoning their basic thrust. The

economy continued to grow, and as the construction boom ebbed, money was channeled into public health programs and improvement of benefits to those workers already eligible rather than meeting reformers' demands for the extension of coverage
to other groups. The concentration of new jobs in urban areas in and around Mexico
City gave rise to the proliferation of shantytowns and a growing urban underclass.

The continuation of Alemán's sharp cutback in land distribution to the rural populace nourished a reappearance of the Cárdenas faction of the party as champions of
the agrarian and labor constituencies, which were as heavily emphasized in the
party's formal facade as they were marginalized in its policymaking functions. This
progressive sector was opposed by a hard-right Alemanist faction, allowing the president to assume the role of evenhanded mediator and spokesman for the party's center. "The very existence of contradictory interpretations of the Revolution made it
both necessary and possible for President Ruiz Cortines to exercise judgment independent of both and fully responsible to neither. He took a moderate stand in the
center of the broad political spectrum embraced by the PRI."[9] In exercising this
leadership style, Ruiz Cortines relied on the power of his office and the machinery of
government, not personally being or seeking to seem a particularly strong or dominating leader. In an important sense this stance simplified the succession dilemma, to
which Ruiz Cortines turned his attention after the 1955 midterm congressional
elections, in which women could vote for the first time, a right they had acquired in
the first year of his term. (At this juncture, Brazil was still staggering from Vargas's suicide and Argentina had just put an end to the Perón era. Colombia was seeking a way
out from under its only military dictator, and Venezuela was still under the latest in a
succession of military *caudillos*. In Peru a military president was in the process of
peacefully leaving power, but in Chile a former military strongman from the 1920s
was governing as a duly elected constitutional president.)

Institutionalized Stability and Economic Viability, 1956–1979

This quarter century, in comparison to the preceding one and the one to follow,
would be remarkably unremarkable and, in contrast to the rest of the region, free of
crises. The hegemony of the PRI continued essentially unchallenged under a series of
competent, but noninnovative, chief executives, with only Adolfo López Mateos
(president 1958–1964) doing much to instill some traces of new life into the graying
party still coasting on the conquests and accomplishments of Cárdenas in the late
1930s. Weathering a few significant ripples of discontent stemming in part from the
example of the Cuban Revolution, the well-institutionalized system demonstrated
residual momentum combined with occasional dashes of resilience.

The period found Ruiz Cortines well past the midpoint of his uneventful administration, and with the economy on the upturn. The 1958 elections brought his
choice, ex-labor minister López Mateos (b. 1910), to the presidency with just over
90 percent of the votes cast.[10] The conservative National Action Party (PAN) put
up a sacrificial opposition candidate, Luis H. Álvarez, a textile manufacturer from
Chihuahua, and the two other legal parties, existing primarily to give an appearance of democracy and legitimacy to the process, entered congressional candidates

but voted for López Mateos. The Popular Socialist Party (PPS) had been founded by the aging Vicente Lombardo Toledano after his Marxism had found no welcome in the PRI. The Authentic Party of the Mexican Revolution (PARM) was a club of retired army generals serving as window dressing on the right of the PRI as the PPS did on its left. For an improved public image of the regime, the PAN was credited with six chamber seats—one more than in 1952 and the same as in the 1955 midterm balloting.

In a term that overlapped the Cuban Revolution, for which many Mexicans felt a visceral sympathy, López Mateos made a swing back to the center from his predecessor's more probusiness policies—packaging this change as a move to the left and a return to Cárdenas-like policies. Benefiting from substantial prosperity, López Mateos cultivated an image of being "widely loved and a great compromiser."[11]

Yet his power base was rooted firmly in the party, and he carefully avoided offending any significant faction. Hence, in a booming economy, López Mateos kept unions relatively satisfied and moderately extended social services. Progress in these respects in the urban sector, as well as public works, particularly low-cost public housing, partially masked the continuing poverty of the rural masses, which the president sought to appease by stepping up the distribution of land. At the end of his term López Mateos boasted that he had turned over more land to the *campesinos* than even Cárdenas had. He failed to note, however, that, compared to the prime lands given out by Cárdenas, much of this land was semiarid and unproductive, located in some degree of proximity to hydroelectric complexes, but often lacking developed irrigation systems. But he demonstrated some concern about distribution of the wealth built up under his predecessors.

The 1964 election of Gustavo Díaz Ordaz (b. 1911), López Mateos's minister of *gobernación* (like Britain's Home Secretary, with control over public safety and justice), went smoothly: The PRI candidate received 89 percent of the ballots cast. Congressional and gubernatorial elections confirmed the PRI's political stranglehold. Díaz Ordaz's *sexénio*, as Mexico's nonrenewable six-year presidential term is known, did not go as smoothly as that of his predecessor (yet fared better than elected governments in Brazil, Argentina, or Peru—which would all be replaced by military regimes during Díaz Ordaz's term). Provisions had been made in 1963 for a small number of congressional seats to go to parties obtaining at least 2.5 percent of the vote, even if they failed to carry any of the 178 districts. (This proviso was used in a flexible manner by the government as a form of cooptative charity to keep docile splinter parties around and in the process to project an external image of being essentially democratic rather than, as critics charged, a veiled form of authoritarianism.) This reform resulted in a lower house in which the PRI had 175 seats for its 86.3 percent of the vote, compared to 20 seats for the PAN on 11.5 percent of the vote, balanced by 10 seats for the tame PPS and 5 for the even tamer PARM, even though their slivers of the electoral pie had been only 1.4 percent and 0.7 percent, respectively.[12] Taking office near the end of 1964, Díaz Ordaz came to exemplify the strength and power of the presidential office independent of the incumbent's leadership shortcomings. Unlike López Mateos, he lacked the will and ability to conciliate rather than alienate important interests within the broadly inclusive type of hegemonic party the PRI had become. Power contenders around him were frustrated by his failure even to communicate the idea that compromise was viable. (In this sense he was a throwback to Alemán.) Luck was not totally on Díaz Ordaz's side. He would have to cope with the severe political unrest of 1968 on the occasion of Mexico's hosting the Olympic Games—only two years before it was scheduled do the same in an election year for the soccer World Cup on the sixtieth anniversary of the 1910 Revolution. On October 2 thousands of students took to the streets to protest the lack of political liberty, the economic decline, and the government's failure to meet the social needs of a rapidly expanding population. The students were fired upon by the police and the army; 325 were killed and many more wounded, with large numbers roughly rounded up and jailed.

The 1970 succession was heavily influenced by this violent student unrest of the second half of 1968. Government figures preferring negotiation to repression were discredited in the president's eyes, as were professors in general. The elimination from consideration of the presidential chief of staff and Mexico City's mayor, both betting favorites in the early stages of the race, opened the way to the presidency for the hard-line interior minister, Luis Echeverría Álvarez (b. 1922). Indeed, a number of well-placed insiders have claimed that the rather Machiavellian Echeverría stoked, if not lit, the fires that consumed the presidential ambitions of his two main rivals, who, after the bloody massacre of student demonstrators, saw their prospects in steady decline. Echeverría's chances were aided in early 1969 by Díaz Ordaz's serious eye operation, his wife's nearing insanity, and his son's drug problems. By June 1969 Echeverría knew that he was the president's choice, and in late October, he was formally endorsed by the party.

Although Echeverría's election was not quite as easy as that of 1964 (he was credited with "only" 86 percent of the votes), neither was it a real contest in the sense of any possibility that he might lose. On the congressional side, the PRI came away with all 178 district seats (on 80.1 percent of the vote), and the PAN received 20 seats in a national bonus for its 13.9 percent of electoral preferences (with the PPS and PARM holding the same small share of the vote they had in 1964). Echeverría had the distinct benefit of presiding over an oil-exporting country during the good years of high crude prices, so he could maintain the image of a populist without having to upset those economic fat cats with whom the PRI had developed a close, at times incestuous, relationship. His policy of "shared development" called for the workers and peasants to receive a more equitable share of a growing economic pie, but without that share's coming at the expense of the middle class or the entrepreneurial stratum. His goals of doubling the production of petroleum, electricity, and steel required heavy foreign borrowing, and this would lead to an economic crisis toward the end of his term analogous to that in the final stage of Alemán's stewardship. (Yet, by comparative standards, particularly within Latin America, a quarter-century spread between economic crises was a noteworthy accomplishment—credit for which belonged to Ruiz Cortines, López Mateos, and even Díaz Ordaz, not the man under whom the streak came to its end.)

Díaz Ordaz had demonstrated, by Mexican standards, inept, sometimes hesitant, and sometimes arbitrary leadership; Echeverría went to the other extreme, showing "a style of rule that was neither institutionalized nor bureaucratized. It was extremely, urgently and intensely personal."[13] In the eyes of a perceptive student of Mexican politics, he "exemplified the degree to which the authoritarianism inherent in his office could be used to fit the personal style of the incumbent, in this case the style of an insatiable power seeker."[14] Damaging to the party was his war with the business community, at least those large-scale elements aligned with the PAN. Showing how far Echeverría had come from the Alemanist model, he massively increased public intervention in the economy, requiring an alarming degree, in the eyes of many, of deficit financing. As depicted by Camp:

> During the early 1970s the government bought or gained control of hundreds of businesses and industries, placing more economic and human resources in the hands of government managers than at any time before. At the end of his administration, Echeverría further alienated the private sector by attempting to expropriate valuable lands in the northwest.[15]

Increasing petroleum exports led to large international loans for development projects.

By the end of Echeverría's term, the country faced an economic crisis requiring a measure that PRI governments had avoided since 1954: a substantial devaluation of the peso. This would, of course, be left until the 1976 election had been safely won, not difficult since the PAN was too internally divided to field a candidate, so the election was a walkover. A three-year stabilization agreement was signed early with the International Monetary Fund (IMF), with the requisite austerity measures in terms of limits on the deficit, cuts in expenditures, more careful husbanding of revenues, and wage restraints left on his successor's doorstep as an unwanted housewarming present. Yet, in Mexico, and certainly most other countries around the world, as long as one's predecessor bequeaths the presidency to one, and not to a bitter rival, complaining about the legacy would be in bad political taste.

Echeverría initially gave the impression that his interior minister was close to being heir apparent. But this young contender, still in his thirties, became a stalking horse, if not a decoy, as the president shifted his support to an individual of much more limited political assets, one who was thus more likely to realize that he owed his rise to El Presidente.[16] Echeverría realized all too well that in choosing him, Díaz Ordaz had not found a successor who had any strong sense of loyalty. Indeed, by the end of his first year as president, the split between Echeverría and his predecessor was complete. The transition had taken place in a context of economic growth, but this favorable economic context would deteriorate, and with it the political fortunes of the heir apparent, Mário Moya Palencia. At thirty-seven the youngest interior minister in Mexico's history, he fell victim to the tradition of each age cohort's getting two bites at the presidency. Echeverría turned increasingly to the more mature José López Portillo.

Brash and overconfident, Moya built too much of an independent political following, a no-no in a system in which presidents sought to have a successor who would feel indebted to them for such a great honor and opportunity. Brought into the government in late 1971, López Portillo (b. 1920) was appointed finance minister in 1973. Although foreign debt quadrupled from $5 billion to $20 billion between 1970 and 1976, López Portillo received high grades in management of the economy from a president harboring some quite particular ideas concerning finance and fiscal policy. In selecting López Portillo to be his successor, Echeverría was seeking to minimize the chance that he would be reduced to a limping duck as political interest in general and interests as actors turned their attention to the man who would be the country's boss for the next six years. In an attempt to salvage his place in history, Echeverría lowered the voting age to eighteen and embarked on a last-minute campaign of distributing land to peasants.

Elected easily at the end of 1976, with 94 percent of the vote, López Portillo enjoyed the support of an enlarged Chamber of Deputies, in which the PRI had all 195 district seats on 80.1 percent of voter preferences, and the PAN was allowed to retain its 20 allotted national pool seats despite a drop in its share of the vote to 8.5 percent. The PPS saw its portion of these cooptative "good behavior" seats rise to 12 and the PARM's to 9—as they raised their vote to 3.0 percent and 2.5 percent, respectively.[17] The new president had considerable success in reducing the harm and alarm his predecessor had left behind, working assiduously to heal the rift between the government and the private sector. Like Ruiz Cortines and López Mateos, he radiated confidence and political stability, adopting an economic discourse stressing an "alliance for profits" soothing to business sectors offended by Echeverría's populist stance. A combination of the Arab oil embargo and the growing Mexican petroleum reserves allowed for a trebling of production and a twelvefold increase in earnings by 1980—making Mexico, or at least its government, wealthy. On the down side, López Portillo invested billions in a highly touted rural development effort with highly disappointing results, and corruption and graft reached new highs.[18] López Portillo played as fast and loose with prudent financial policies as he had facilitated Echeverría in doing. After chafing under the restraints of the IMF agreement, interpreted by him more as guidelines than as rigid limits, by the end of his term he had turned developmentalist. Unrealistically expecting continuing high crude prices to produce growing revenues, López Portillo followed unwise policies similar to those of John V. Lindsay as mayor of New York City in the early 1970s—spending next year's projected higher revenues this year. Foreign debt continued to soar in the face of profligate spending—on the way to $60 billion by the end of López Portillo's term in 1982, a tripling in only six years. Although the rest of this decade would see more of the same, the 1990s would witness a democratic transformation of Mexican politics. (At this point Brazil's political opening had reached the stage of holding direct elections for governors, while Argentina's military rulers had just seen their master stroke of taking the Falkland Islands back from the British [and hence being able to restore the name of Islas Malvinas] blow up in their faces. Usually democratic Chile was at the midpoint of the repressive Pinochet dictatorship, while Peru had recently reinstalled the civilian president ousted by the armed forces back in 1968.) Constitutional governments in Colombia faced the dual plagues of stubborn insurgency and increasingly powerful drug cartels, and democratic administrations in Venezuela were declining in terms of both effectiveness and public support.

From Hegemonic System
to a Full Democracy, 1980–1999

Compared to that of Brazil or Argentina, for most of the 1980s and into the 1990s Mexico's political development seemed limited and, in the eyes of many observers, inadequate. Yet in retrospect it appears that this once-monolithic single-party system did a better job of a controlled transition to full competitiveness than communist analogues were able to do in the former Soviet Union and Eastern Europe. Taking into account the extreme difficulty and perils of opening up a semiauthoritarian system without exposing its political processes to dangerous breakdown, Mexico handled the problem quite well. Certainly leadership passed into the hands of a younger, technically well-qualified generation, and the 1994 election was not marred by fraud as had been that of 1988, or even the amount of fraud customary before that excess. The winner undertook to make the next elections free and democratic even at the risk of the PRI's loss of the power it had held since the 1920s.[19] Although corruption continued to be a major problem, Mexican's traditional high tolerance of graft and fraud was substantially diminished during the last part of this period, and the increased degree of political competitiveness ushered in the beginning of higher standards and more effective controls. Comparative examination of the near-universal phenomenon of politically related corruption strongly indicates that a wave of major scandals is usually more related to an erosion of the tradition of impunity and the resulting public outcry and even outrage replacing the former sense of resignation, than it is a reflection of increased corruption. Essentially, what was long taken for granted becomes no longer acceptable, a significant step forward.

The great progress Mexico made toward putting an entrenched semiauthoritarian system behind and transforming it into a functioning democracy was not apparent until the end of the 1990s, when an opposition candidate won the presidential elections—unheard of since the Liberal Party's victory way back in the mid-1850s. This was a momentous event for Mexico and for Latin America, extending the benefits of competitive electoral democracy to over 100 million individuals in one fell swoop. It caught many observers by surprise, since at the beginning of this period the system of single-party hegemony established at the end of the 1920s had appeared to be firmly in place, a judgment that could still be accurately made in the mid-1980s, and many experts believed into the late 1990s that the PRI would do anything to hold onto power, not open the system up to full competition. When the period began, as had been the case for decades, it was a foregone conclusion that the next president would be whoever was the PRI standard bearer, with the incumbent president, within very loose constraints, deciding his successor's identity. Hence, by early in his presidency, López Portillo knew that shaping the succession process was his top priority, along with making sure, or at least being assured, that the economy would not go completely off the tracks. Given his role as chief architect of economic policy in the preceding Echeverría administration, López Portillo was confident that he knew what had to be done. As had been the case a dozen years earlier, he, like Díaz Ordaz, would handle the succession through a process of elimination rather than starting with an heir apparent.[20] Hence the all-important choice would eventually fall upon someone who had earned it as the *sexénio* progressed, not on any of the early favorites. Indeed. the original pair of front-runners, ensconced in the ministries of finance and planning and budget, had carried on a monumental and ill-concealed struggle over the 1978 budget that exasperated the president and resulted in both of those presidential wannabes' leaving the cabinet and being effectively exiled from the center of governmental and political affairs.

As the central economic policy issue shifted in early 1980 to Mexico's entry into the General Agreement on Trade and Tariffs (GATT), one potential candidate after another fell by the wayside. On June 1, 1981, Jorge Díaz Serrano, the powerful and prestigious director general of Pemex and a longtime close associate of the president, suddenly cut crude oil prices in order to cope with an abrupt destabilization of the international market caused by Saudi Arabian policy changes. He was immediately and opportunistically attacked by the secretary of patrimony and industrial promotion. Forced to resign by a concerted attack campaign, he, too, bit the dust. (In the brutal game of politics it mattered nothing that events proved him to have been right, as attempting to row against the tide Mexico lost $1 billion in crude sales in July alone.[21])

With economic problems mounting as 1981 wore on, López Portillo turned increasingly to the optimistic bearer of good economic tidings, planning and budget minister Miguel de la Madrid Hurtado (b. 1934). During the crucial third quarter of 1981, de la Madrid found a useful new ally in the person of young Carlos Salinas de Gortari (b. 1948), whose deficit projections were closer to de la Madrid's uncritically optimistic ones than to the politically ambitious finance minister's realistically pessimistic, indeed alarming, estimates. Only after de la Madrid won the battle of dueling estimates and was safely launched as the PRI candidate in late September 1981 were his and Salinas's deficit projections revised upward. In the real world, as distinguished from the insulated presidential palace, 1981 was a nearly disastrous year economically for Mexico. Overproduction of oil turned into a glut resulting in sharply dropping prices for crude. This fall in oil prices, combined with stagnant exports, devalued currency, and high foreign debt, frightened investors, who pulled their money out of Mexico—which was turned overnight from belle of the ball to wallflower. As described by a close student of Mexican affairs:

> Instead of putting the brakes on the state's economic expansion, López Portillo actually stepped on the accelerator. In his last year in office, without warning or consultation, he announced nationalization of the domestic banking system. With a single decree, the president increased state control over the economy. . . . The move exacerbated the business community's lack of trust in the government and strongly encouraged the flight of capital from Mexico, primarily to the United States.[22]

López Portillo reacted by instituting exchange controls to protect the peso, but by 1982 inflation had soared to 100 percent, the peso had lost 40 percent of its value, and the economy was shrinking. The disillusioned president's option for finance specialist de la Madrid over PRI head Javier García Paniagua was too far along for him to reverse course when he finally came to realize that de la Madrid seemed determined to chart his own course even before the election, rather than waiting until after his inauguration. In this decision, the future president may have had little choice, since his erstwhile sponsor's legacy was no longer a positive one. In the eyes of a leading Mexican statesman-scholar:

> The political crisis he [de la Madrid] inherited from López Portillo in the wake of the bank nationalization and the virtual expropriation of dollar-denominated savings not only severed the fragile strands of trust between the system and the middle classes who had thrived on the former's success

but also destroyed complicity and convergence of years past between the business elite and the political establishment. Nevertheless the political crisis of 1982 pales next to the country's economic collapse. De la Madrid inherited a government devoid of hard currency, without reserves, and with public finances in a shambles and the country's foreign credit practically exhausted.[23]

The 1982 election, conducted under significant reforms introduced in 1977 (the Federal Law of Political Organizations and Electoral Processes), went reasonably smoothly, with de la Madrid receiving nearly 72 percent of the vote to just over 16 percent for the sacrificial lamb candidate of the opposition PAN. Three-quarters of registered voters turned out on election day. This record total of 22.5 million actual voters—in a country with 73.1 million inhabitants—was three times that of 1958 and up by 5.6 million over 1976, partially disguising the fact that the PRI's winning percentage was well below the huge margins rolled up in the preceding four presidential sweepstakes. The requirements for minimum membership to qualify as a legally recognized political party (common to other Latin American nations since they differ from the US concept of parties as essentially private, rather than public, entities) had been lowered, and the lower house's size had been increased to 400, with 100 seats reserved for minority parties on the basis of proportional representation— compared to the 30–40 seats these parties had been getting since 1964. By encouraging three new splinter parties to participate through the certainty of getting at least a handful of seats, the 1977 law had had the effect of raising the non-PRI representation from 17.4 percent in 1976 to 21 percent in 1979—as the PAN actually won 4 of the 300 single-member district seats. (These are, as in the United States or the United Kingdom, geographical constituencies from which just one member is elected— unlike the more widely used method of proportional representation that uses large constituencies electing a multiplicity of legislators.) Now the breakdown of the new chamber was 299 for the PRI to 51 for the PAN, with four minor parties awarded 17, 12, 11, and 10 seats from the proportional pool—very little change from the midterm results of 1979. Indeed, the PRI's reduced 69.3 percent share of the vote yielded 3 more PRI seats, and the PAN demonstrated significant, but nonspectacular, progress, going from 10.8 percent of the vote to 17.5 percent.[24] Little did the president-elect imagine that this would be the last controlled succession, more because of divisions taking place within the mammoth PRI than because of the growth and diversification of the opposition.

With over half the government's revenues going to debt service, prices soaring, and labor becoming unruly, de la Madrid shifted to full alignment with IMF policies, including curbing inflation, privatizing many government holdings, and lowering tariffs. To distract attention from the country's economic woes, he initiated a crusade against corruption under the banner of "moral renovation." He also began to open Mexico's closed, nearly monopolistic, political system by acknowledging PAN victories in a number of municipalities. In 1985 two major earthquakes in central Mexico created a heavy burden of disaster relief and reconstruction. Budgetary restraint required the reduction of subsidies and cutbacks in government investments, along with a hiring freeze. Then, near the end of his term, a drastic devaluation of the peso triggered a staggering surge of inflation. Wage and price controls were instituted, and a $3.5-billion loan from the United States partially eased the revenue shortfall from the continuing drop in oil prices. The midterm congressional elections provided a misleading picture of normality, as the PRI's 289 seats in the lower house were 10 fewer than before, but the PAN also dropped 10 seats—a much more significant proportional loss from 51 to 41. The former's share of the vote slipped 4.3 percent to 65.0 percent, and the latter's 15.5 percent marked a decline of 2 percent.[25]

As the long era of PRI dominance moved toward its eventual end, Mexico's unique presidential succession process underwent significant change. López Portillo had chosen de la Madrid through a process that had begun with the elimination of candidates with whom he had had longer and closer personal ties. From the beginning of his term, de la Madrid seriously considered only two possibilities. The first, respected finance minister Jesús Silva Herzog, born the same year as the president, was a peer of de la Madrid in almost every significant respect. However, the eventual winner was Carlos Salinas, the much younger budget and planning minister, who positioned himself as a generational change who would still ensure continuity of de la Madrid's priorities. Salinas rooted his bid in a close association as a trusted collaborator of de la Madrid going back to 1979, when de la Madrid had occupied this ministerial post and Salinas was his closest aide—moving up to the cabinet post in 1982 when de la Madrid became president. Although his personal relation with the president did not extend back as far in time as that of Silva Herzog, de la Madrid and Salinas had in common that both had earned graduate degrees at Harvard.[26] Moreover, although not yet forty, Salinas was the son of an old-line PRI politico and thus not a party outsider.

Starting from behind, Salinas worked harder and with greater determination than his rival. He quietly built support within the party-government machine, while Silva Herzog, an academic rather than a political insider, was busy courting the international community, the media, and business (none of which had an impact on Mexico's peculiar succession process). Wisely, Salinas's closest alliance was forged with the presidential chief of staff, Emilio Gamboa Patrón. Battle was openly joined over the 1984 budget and reopened the next year. As revenues fell during what was known as "The Crisis," Salinas refused to cut expenses, earning the gratitude of government agencies and governors. Silva Herzog fought against raising taxes to cover these expenditures, and his public acclaim began to irritate the proud de la Madrid. When crude oil prices dropped to a devastating $8 a barrel in early 1986—costing Mexico some $6 billion in anticipated revenue—Silva Herzog increasingly appeared to the president as too concerned about his image and seeming presidential rather than about furthering the interests and objectives of the incumbent chief executive. In the escalating intramural warfare between the two economic ministries, the president sided with Salinas against further deep budget cuts, ensuring Salinas's ascension and leading to Silva Herzog's resignation. Salinas added to his prestige when the United States, the IMF, and the World Bank approved a massive $9-billion assistance program for Mexico without requiring either the spending cuts or the tax increases that Salinas's critics had insisted the international agencies would demand. All that remained was for the president to protect his chosen one by concealing his preference, publicly posing Alfredo del Mazo and Manuel Bartlett alongside Salinas as presidential possibilities so that the hard-fighting and determined Bartlett would not concentrate his fire solely on Salinas.

In March 1987 Cuauhtémoc Cárdenas Solórzano (b. 1934), son of the revered 1934–1940 president, and Porfirio Muñoz Ledo, leaders of the "democratic current" within the party, both of them feeling that they richly deserved a chance to be the official candidate, publicly split with the PRI. The interior minister's reaction seemed too conciliatory in the eyes of a president hostile to PRI dissidents, costing that hopeful any slim chance he might still have had for the coveted presidential backing. Hence, in early October 1987, the PRI ratified the president's choice of Salinas and bestowed the party's nomination on him. (This adherence to an established succession process contrasted drastically with the nearly contemporary chaotic contest in Brazil that brought Collor to power as well as with the adoption of a party primary in Argentina that would shortly facilitate the rise of a comparative outsider.)

The campaign saw each of the candidates put forth a very different view of the causes of the economic situation, one in which, in fact, per capita GDP was down 12.4 percent; workers had lost 40 percent of their purchasing power since de la Madrid's election; 1987 inflation stood at 160 percent; and the country's foreign debt had passed $100 billion. Although defending de la Madrid's free-market policies, of which he had been a major architect, as having brought prosperity for most of the term, Salinas prudently withheld endorsement of NAFTA (the North American Free Trade Agreement), in light of widespread fear that it would create a very unbalanced partnership. Cárdenas took a nationalistic line, denouncing excessive foreign influence and defending state enterprises, while calling the de la Madrid government dictatorial and depicting Salinas as representing the status quo. PAN standard bearer Manuel Clouthier, an energetic and outspoken northern businessman, advocated removing existing barriers to private investment and questioned Cárdenas's commitment to spreading democracy into all sectors of national life, depicting him as an unbridled leftist.[27]

The July 6, 1988, elections took place under changes enacted in 1986, and the momentous official results—in which participation dropped sharply to only half the registered electorate—were 50.7 percent for PRI candidate Salinas; 32.5 percent for Cárdenas, running on the ticket of the National Democratic Front (FDN) and 16.8 percent for PAN nominee Clouthier. This bare majority for the PRI candidate was crucial, as less than 50 percent would have required ratification by the lower house of the congress. Although both passions and accusations of fraud ran high, one credible analysis indicated that manipulation of ballot counting was used to get Salinas's vote above 50 percent, but that the manipulation was not sufficient to have robbed Cárdenas of victory. Other observers were less sanguine, Cárdenas's backers arguing that he actually received more votes than Salinas.[28] After some hesitation by the government and belligerent bluster from the opposition, Salinas was certified as having been duly elected, and public outcry died away much as it would in the United States in the aftermath of George W. Bush's disputed 2000 presidential win over Al Gore.

Cárdenas carried his home state of Michoacán by a landslide and also took Baja California del Norte, Morelos, and Mexico State, possibly also Guerrero and maybe Oaxaca. Belying its tranquil public face, the PRI was severely shaken, although not yet trembling. Its 50.4 percent of the chamber vote was sharply down from its 1985 percentage, but the party still came away with 260 seats (233 from districts and 27 from the proportional pool), in a body enlarged to 500, compared to the PAN's jump up to 101 seats (on a modest increase in electoral share to 17.1 percent); the Cardenista Front for National Reconstruction Party (FCRN) won 51 seats (with 10.5 percent of the vote), and the Party of the Democratic Revolution (PRD) 26 seats (putting it close on the heels of the Authentic Party of the Mexican Revolution, PARM, at 28). Thus the divided opposition took 48 percent of the chamber seats, a quantum leap over any past performance. Cárdenas, after touring the country leading protest rallies, assumed a major role in organizing the PRD as a prospective national political force.

The scandals and criminal charges that surrounded Salinas after leaving office, many stemming from illicit activities by his brother and cronies, should not obscure the fact that his management of the economy was in many ways superior to that of most other Mexican presidents and a large proportion of his Latin American contemporaries. Facing an inherited mountain of foreign debt, he carried through a massive privatization of state enterprises, blocked from going further by the "untouchable" status accorded by Mexicans to Pemex. Within five years Mexico's economy went from critical to essentially sound, with GDP growth high enough, despite population growth, to chalk up sustained per capita gains. Foreign investment by the end of Salinas's term had risen from $13.5 billion to $60.6 billion (compared to an $8-billion increase under de la Madrid), and inflation had dropped from 52 percent when he took office to 8 percent in 1993. Salinas's biggest gamble, one he considered unavoidable, was negotiating, signing, and ratifying NAFTA before the end of his term. Previously, his heavy emphasis on privatization had augmented government revenues but had also provided opportunities for the enrichment of friends and family. Some of the new revenues did go into Salinas's trademark project, the National Solidarity Program, designed to encourage grassroots organization and leadership, but also clearly useful in providing electoral support and enhancing the president's popularity.[29]

With the PRI's dominant electoral support a thing of the past, Salinas, unlike any of his predecessors, was well aware that whomever he chose as his successor would face a stiff challenge at the polls. Thus he had to choose a candidate who could win, perhaps even more than one who would continue Salinas's policies and keep on some of his key associates. Salinas also realized that he would have to take into account the increased sensibilities of individuals and factions because the party was still in a state of shock over its narrow escape from disaster. As an experienced political insider, Castañeda portrays Salinas's mind-set as centering on

> the need to take excruciating pains to keep the ruling party united, not promoting pasarelas (street demonstrations and rallies) or publicly parading the candidates, to avoid encouraging feelings of defeat or open manipulation among disappointed hopefuls or their followers by refusing to place losing prospects in delicate positions, and to ensure that the real sources of power in Mexico got to know the possible candidates and would be willing to applaud whichever of them he chose.[30]

Salinas was, however, unaware that he would have to make the choice of a successor twice, the second time under dire circumstances and severe time constraints. Moreover, he realized that he could not afford to provoke another division of the party. As Castañeda aptly puts it, "The job description required a PRI politician with technical training and ideological, regional, personal, and age-group affinity with Salinas."[31]

Salinas attempted to manage the succession much along the lines followed by Echeverría in 1976. Early favorites quickly blotted their copybooks: In the president's view, Mexico City mayor Manuel Camacho was too preoccupied with keeping active in national government matters (rather than devoting himself to his present office), and finance minister Pedro Aspe, with an economics doctorate from the Massachusetts Institute of Technology (MIT), repeated Silva Herzog's mistake of becoming the focus of too much public credit as architect of the administration's reforms and innovations. As Castañeda points out, "The idea of handing over his legacy, his place in history, and his own and his family's integrity to an individual endowed with a personality and international recognition of his own has never been a seductive one to any Mexican president."[32] The new factor was the need for a candidate able to win against stiff competition from both Cárdenas and the PAN—a stronger candidate from a political point of view than Salinas had been. Salinas and de la Madrid were both intellectual, highly educated, technocratic types; their successor had to be someone who could go out on the campaign trail and mix it up with his challengers in a verbal slugfest if necessary, or in a personality pageant if that was what it took. The PRI had never lost. To keep this tradition going, it could not afford to back a loser, but the mood of the electorate was difficult to judge. In the 1991 midterm congressional voting—with turnout up to 61 percent—the PRI had won a heartening 321 of 500 chamber seats, receiving 61.4 percent of the vote to the 17.7 percent that gave the PAN 90 seats (the PRD settled for 40, since many who had voted for Cárdenas did not carry their enthusiasm over to little-known congressional aspirants), thus regaining the three-fifths majority lost in the midst of the torrid presidential race of 1988.[33]

In contrast to rivals Camacho and Aspe, Luis Donaldo Colosio (b. 1950) was an expert on campaigns and elections. He had served as Salinas's campaign manager beginning in 1987. After starting the new administration as national party head, and having a short experience in the senate, Colosio was named minister of social development in late 1991—an assignment that made him familiar with the country and the country with him, largely through the Solidarity Program of bringing services and benefits to the community level. The strong impingement of international factors severely constrained the window for announcing the succession decision. The announcement had to be made after the November 1 Mexican state-of-the-union address and the US ratification of NAFTA—a date beyond Mexican influence, much less control—and before the mid-December onset of end-of-the-year festivities. Hence late November 1993 saw the PRI formally nominate Colosio, who compromised with Salinas on Ernesto Zedillo Ponce de León (b. 1951) as his campaign manager. (At this time Fernando Henrique Cardoso was beginning his rise to the presidency in Brazil, Carlos Menem was well into his very successful first term as Argentina's chief executive, Alberto Fujimori was riding high in Peru, Chile was moving toward into its second presidency since the reestablishment of democracy, and in Colombia Ernesto Samper was locked in a close race with a conservative rival, who would be his successor. Venezuela was in the last government of its established parties, with Hugo Chávez impatiently waiting in the wings.)

By the beginning of 1994 tension between the president and the candidate had become palpable. The trigger was the peasant rebellion in Chiapas, where rebels of Mayan extraction seized several towns and, calling themselves the Zapatista Army of National Liberation (EZLN), issued a list of demands for reforms and democracy; almost 200 deaths resulted from clashes with the army.[34] This development provided Colosio's critics an opportunity to rally around the shocked president, who gave Camacho, whom Colosio had bested in the presidential succession process, the highly visible role of mediating this globally watched insurrection as the head of a team including members of the PRD and PAN. Camacho's departure from the cabinet made him legally eligible for the presidency, a fact that stirred up in Colosio nightmares of a Salinas reversal. Salinas put this fear to rest only on the eve of Colosio's March 23, 1994, assassination while campaigning in Tijuana. This tragic event created a need to decide upon a new candidate in a matter of days. Once the idea of a constitutional amendment was discarded as impractical, no viable alternative to Zedillo emerged. He alone combined prospects for continuation of the president's economic policies and members of his team.

Having won the battle for the PRI's nomination, Zedillo faced real competition for election. If Salinas had been overconfident in 1988, Zedillo could not afford to be, for all eyes were peeled for electoral fraud, and he strongly desired to enjoy a greater aura of legitimacy than had the administration from which he was emerging.[35] His party was deeply split between an open-up-to-meaningful-competition wing and a hold-the-line, clamp-down faction insisting on the need to carry PRI control into the twenty-first century at any cost. The left opposition, banded together in the PRD, running Cárdenas for a second time, exuded a good deal of optimism. Indeed, the PRD's leadership felt that, if not the real winner in 1988, Cárdenas had come at least as tantalizingly close to victory as François Mitterand had in France in 1974 before his 1981 election as president. Cárdenas, as PRI governor of his father's state of Michoacán from 1980 to 1986, had actively sought the governing party's 1988 presidential nomination and regarded Salinas as having been too young and politically inexperienced to have earned the nomination fairly. However, in his second presidential campaign, Cárdenas had little new to say, and the collapse of the Soviet Union made his basic stump speech seem oddly dated, almost a rerun of 1988. The right-wing opposition PAN came up with an effective candidate in Diego Fernández de Cevallos, its floor leader in the lower house, thus dividing the anti-PRI voters.

Cárdenas focused his campaign on the unfairness of existing economic, social, and political practices, promising protection of workers' rights and the environment, and calling for "true" democracy. Bluntly labeling Salinas's administration repressive and dictatorial, he cautioned that the government needed to be much more selective about foreign investment, rejecting what might infringe on national sovereignty. Fernández, having by far the best slogan in "For a Mexico without lies," pictured himself as the only true democrat in light of Cárdenas's deep roots in the PRI and association with past governments. Fernández was by far the most skilled debater among the presidential hopefuls, and he homed in on the issue of poverty, asking Zedillo how he could praise Salinas and trumpet his administration's accomplishments when 40 million Mexicans were living in poverty. Fernández appeared to be more populist than the 1988 PAN standard bearer, and his populism helped soften the party's conservative reputation. Attacked from both left and right, Zedillo had no choice but to remind voters that the PRI was the best hope to meet their needs, since Salinas had been the engineer of the country's economic recovery.

When the dust settled after the midyear balloting, Cárdenas had slipped badly to 16.6 percent of the vote, compared to nearly 26 percent for Fernández. The winner, with 48.8 percent, was Zedillo—as turnout had recovered sharply to nearly four-fifths of those eligible. With the law having been reformed to prevent the plurality party from allocating itself seats from the proportional pool to guarantee a majority, the new Chamber of Deputies had 300 from the PRI, 119 from PAN, 71 from the PRD, and 10 from the minor Workers' Party (PT). In the senate, doubled in size from 64 to 128, the breakdown was 96 seats for the PRI, 24 for the PAN, and only 8 for the PRD. Yet the PRI's sharp drop to 50.3 percent of the congressional vote, coupled with the PAN's rise to 25.8 percent and the PRD's 16.1 percent, constituted a clear wakeup call to the lifetime ruling party.[36] The key question was one that deeply divided the party: Should they accept the challenge or dig in to hold onto power in any way possible?

In the normal course of events, Zedillo, at forty-five, would have been a contender for the 2000 elections, rather than for those of 1994, but he advanced early to the presidency (just as César Gaviria had been forced to step up ahead of time in 1990 in Colombia after the murder of Luis Carlos Galán). Graduating from the National Polytechnic Institute in 1972, between 1974 and 1978 Zedillo earned both a master's degree and a doctorate in economics at Yale, with a dissertation on the management of public debt. Hence, if not equaling the incomparable intellectual credentials of Brazil's Cardoso, he clearly exceeded those of Argentine contemporary Carlos Saul Menem, and more than measured up academically to the chief executives of Colombia, Peru, Venezuela, and Chile. After almost a decade of steady career progress within the Central Bank, Zedillo moved to the number two post in the budget and planning ministry in 1987 and went on to become its head in 1988, before becoming secretary of education in 1992.[37] Upon Zedillo's assuming the presidency on December 1, 1994—in a country whose population had swollen to 94 million—friction between him and Salinas was immediate, fostered by both the ex-president's brother and the finance minister, Pedro Aspe, who had been instrumental in withdrawing support from the highly overvalued peso, the results being a tailspin exchange rate and the concomitant sharp economic contraction—with GDP shrinking by 7 percent in 1995 and bank bailouts amounting to $80 billion. As Camp sees it:

> The result of the crises caused by the devaluation of the peso is that Mexico faced negative economic growth in 1995, a loss of somewhere between 250,000 and 1 million jobs before the end of the year, a reversal of foreign investment and capital flight, a dramatic rise in inflation exceeding 50 percent yearly, an extraordinary rise in private-bank interest for mortgages and loans far above the inflation rate, and numerous business closures and bankruptcies, including the threat of important state governments declaring financial insolvency.[38]

Zedillo's administration placed the blame for the crisis, which was far more serious than that of the mid-1980s, at the door of the Salinas administration for having let the peso become excessively overvalued, whereas Salinas viewed Zedillo as having been the biggest beneficiary of his prudent avoidance of upsetting the economic picture on the eve of the elections. Salinas's brother's arrest on a multitude of corruption charges in February 1995 and revelations that he might have misappropriated over $100 million poured gasoline on the fire. As the ex-president's own legal problems multiplied, Zedillo was freed of his legacy and able to embark on his own project for democratization. His most important decision was not, as had been the case for so long, whom to chose as his successor, but how competitive to make elections as part of the larger question of how far to go in making Mexico truly democratic—in which case the future selection of the PRI nominee for the presidency would lose its decisive significance. Unable to count upon economic growth to bolster his administration, Zedillo had little choice but to focus upon weeding out institutionalized corruption and initiating political reforms. To this end he took the unprecedented step of selecting an attorney general from an opposition party, the PAN. Arresting the ex-president's brother on murder charges gave Zedillo's flagging popularity a boost. By 1996 the economy was demonstrating signs of recovery, which Zedillo underscored by paying back two-thirds of the US emergency loan. Two years of extreme austerity paid off in GDP growth of 7.5 percent and inflation of only 15.7 percent in 1997. Yet the severely negative impact in the social sphere was reflected in a sharp rise in the proportion of those living in extreme poverty (most of who had already been below the poverty line) from 16 percent in 1992 to 28 percent by 1999.

The July 1997 congressional elections—involving balloting for the Federal District governor for the first time since 1924—provided an indication of how political winds were blowing. Cárdenas kept his presidential hopes alive by winning in the capital with a respectable 48 percent of the votes. Nationwide, the PRI came in first in the midterm congressional balloting with 39.1 percent of the votes, followed by the PAN with 26.6 percent and the PRD at 25.7 percent. The slippage from 1994, when congressional elections had coincided with presidential balloting, was significant, with the PRI falling to 239 seats (from 300), the PRD exploding from 71 to 125, and the PAN climbing very modestly to 121 (from 119). But although the PAN and the PRD voted together to freeze the PRI out of top congressional offices, the PAN frequently sided with the PRI on economic and budget issues. Although the PRI lost 19 senate seats in 1997, it retained a majority in the upper house of 77 out of 128. Importantly, the clean and fair elections, such a dramatic break with the past, significantly bolstered Zedillo's public approval.[39]

As 1999 saw attention focus on the 2000 elections—including an open battle for the PRI presidential nomination—Cárdenas began to fade because there had been highly unrealistic expectations of what he could do as mayor about Mexico City's manifold problems when in fact he had to depend on the PRI-controlled federal government for financial resources. But the PAN's Vicente Fox Quesada (b. 1942), former governor of Guanajuato, towering over the other candidates at six feet six inches in his trademark cowboy boots, forged ahead of the PRI's lackluster Francisco Labastida Ochoa—winner of a hotly contested November 1999 primary. Fox's *Y* for "Ya," understood as "We've had enough; now's the time," was a catchy slogan, and as he was the candidate of the businessman's party, his campaign did not lack for funds. (At this point, while Cardoso was into a second term in Brazil, Menem had just failed to gain a constitutionally very questionable third term in Argentina, and Colombia was limping along unable to resolve the drug-trafficking and guerrilla problems threatening to turn it into a failed state. Chávez had attained power in Venezuela, and Chile was celebrating a decade of reestablished democracy, whereas Peru was heading into a major crisis as Fujimori was determined to hold onto power at any cost, even that of destroying his hitherto generally positive legacy.)

Democracy Established, Progress Stalemated, 2000–2010

The significance of developments in Mexico during the first years of the new century cannot be underestimated, for they constitute the greatest step in the country's political development since the halcyon days of the Cárdenas administration in the late 1930s and are clearly more significant than contemporary developments in Brazil as well as much more positive than those in Argentina. With the opposition victory in the July 2000 presidential elections, federalism and the separation of powers, long vitiated by the hegemonic position of the PRI, finally had an opportunity to emerge as vital aspects of a broadly participant, highly competitive political system. The greater responsiveness to "outsider" elements of society provided by this transformation greatly reduced the prospect of widespread, protracted political unrest. Camp eloquently captures the watershed nature of this development:

> The victory of a party other than PRI essentially stood the Mexican political model on its head, destroying permanently the incestuous, monopolistic relationship between state and party. Such a relationship no longer exists. The future of the Mexican electoral process from 2000 forward relies heavily on the behavior and organizational strength of the three leading political parties, the PAN, PRI, and PRD, and on citizen perceptions of their candidates. It also relies on citizen views of the performance of the parties' candidates in office, particularly in executive posts.[40]

The once stodgy and Catholic Church–linked PAN had been reinvigorated during the 1980s as ranchers and industrialists alienated from the governing PRI by the 1982 bank nationalizations entered its right-of-center opposition. PAN's respectable showing in 1994 coupled with the country's financial competitiveness crisis of that year and the next led to its continued growth, further stimulated by indications of PRI vulnerability as well as increasing signs of government intentions to conduct free elections in 2000.[41] Hence the tall, quasi-charismatic Fox's dynamic campaign resulted in a plurality of 42.5 percent of the national vote, to 36.1 percent for the PRI's unexciting Francisco Labastida Ochoa and only 16.6 percent for the PRD's Cárdenas. The PAN along with its small ally, the Green Party (PVEM), came away with 38.2 percent of the chamber vote and 208 seats, whereas the PRI retained 209 seats on 36.9 percent of the vote. The PRD ran a poor third, winning only 51 seats on 18.7 percent of the vote. The PRI lost control of the senate, with only 60 seats (including holdovers), but the PAN still trailed at 51 senators, three times the PRD's 17 seats.[42] As in Argentina in 1916, the opposition had finally captured the presidency, but without control of congress—where hard bargaining would be required.

In contrast to the alliances crucial to Lula's 2002 election in Brazil, the outcome of Mexico's presidential succession was the product of long-term trends of levels of economic and social development, regionalism, and urbanization. For some time the opposition had been strong in the relatively high-income Federal District and Baja California; now they fared even better. (This situation paralleled developments in Brazil with respect to São Paulo and Rio de Janeiro beginning in 1978.) As with the government party in Brazil in the final stages of the authoritarian regime the PRI's base of electoral support increasingly narrowed to the less-developed and less-urban areas of the country—which were also the educational laggards. As Camp points out, Fox was backed by 60 percent of university-educated voters and 53 percent of those who had made it through high school, whereas for Labastida these figures were 22 percent and 28 percent—insufficient to compensate for the fact that he racked up votes among those whose formal education was limited to six years or less, since in Mexico these numbered only two-fifths of the voters.[43] Mexico, perhaps even more than Brazil, has become an urban country, and Fox obtained the lion's share of urban votes, whereas the rural bastion of the PRI contained only a fifth of the electorate. (This voter behavior confirms an observation the author made many years ago that in most cases little can be done to change the political behavior of rural populations unless they cease to be rural via the mechanism of internal migration to towns and cities.) Like Lula in Brazil, Fox was viewed as the candidate of change. He transcended the limits of his party's popularity through a personal organization known as the Friends of Fox.[44]

The first opposition president in the memory of any Mexican came to office with only minority support in the congress and amid unreasonably high expectations, since it was such an unprecedented event. Fox soon found that, no matter how arduous campaigning might have been, governing was much more frustrating and stressful. The euphoria of breaking the PRI's seven decades of hegemonic rule dissipated quickly in the face of a public expecting rapid changes and immediate results. Fox's task of organizing his government was much easier than that Lula was to encounter in Brazil two years later, since he drew only on his party and respected independents, but in the end these would not result in a reliable congressional base of support. He would have to negotiate with the PRI and PRD on a case-by-case basis as his predecessor had learned to do, particularly after 1997. In contrast to Lula, he did not have to abandon his historical ideological positions, nor did he have to worry about dissipating the suspicions and overcoming the reservations of foreign investors—as did both Lula when he came to office in 2003 and Argentina's Néstor Kirchner later that year. On the negative side, Fox faced opposition from two highly organized parties, one with a broader national base than his PAN and positioned to occupy the center of the political spectrum, while the other was firmly entrenched on the left.

Fox organized his administration, criticized for lack of cabinet coherence, and operated the resulting government showing little regard for the PAN machinery still controlled by 1994 standard bearer Fernández de Cevallos and party traditionalists. He had to deal early with the conflict between foreign minister Jorge Castañeda, an expert on presidential succession with roots well left of the party, and interior minister Santiago Creel, who strongly desired to be the 2006 nominee. Castañeda, whose presidential aspirations were increasingly apparent, was subsequently eased out of the government. To further complicate Fox's task, the ingrained inefficiency

of huge petroleum entity Pemex was a burdensome carryover from the statist traditions of the long PRI era. In 2002 major oil producer Mexico ran up a trade deficit
just under $8 billion while spending $10 billion on petrochemical imports. Even
Venezuela's oil company produced 195 barrels a day of crude per worker, more than
double Pemex's meager 87 barrels (with a private giant like Royal Dutch Shell
reaching 300 barrels per employee). To aggravate matters, Mexico's foreign debt had
ballooned to $76 billion, as foreign direct investment fell sharply from $16 billion in
2000 to $11 billion in 2002.

Many of the benefits of NAFTA predated Fox's assumption of power, and after
September 11, 2001, his vaunted rancher-to-rancher "Amigo" relationship with US
president George W. Bush was buried in the debris of the World Trade Center, with
any special relationship between the two countries forgotten amid the hubbub of the
war on terrorism. Fox counted upon making progress on bothersome bilateral issues
to distract Mexican attention from limited movement on domestic issues, and his ace
in the hole was the prospect of special treatment for the millions of Mexican migrants concentrated in those parts of the United States that had been forcibly taken
from Mexico in the mid-nineteenth century. Economically, the more than 5 million
Mexicans illegally in the United States were a vital part of the Mexican economy
through at least $14 billion a year in remittances (a third higher by some estimates).
Adding to Fox's woes, the midterm congressional balloting of July 2003 did not
bring the relief for which he was hoping. Instead, the PRI rebounded to 224 chamber seats on 35 percent of the vote (plus 17 seats for their Green Party allies), whereas
with the support of just 30.5 percent of voters the PAN dropped to 155 seats—only
30 percent of the total. The PRD recovered from its poor 2000 showing by electing
96 to the lower house compared to the 53 it had held. With a low 42 percent
turnout, the balloting was no real indication of what 2006 might bring. In the eyes of
a seasoned observer, Mexico had "a constitutionally mandated majority presidential
system operating like a parliamentary system."[45]

To divert attention from a legislative stalemate, a special prosecutor appointed by
Fox sought in mid-2004 to indict aging ex-president Echeverría for the killings of
student protesters back in 1971. This was another step in a flawed strategy of launching investigations "aggressive enough to undermine the chance of legislative cooperation, but not decisive enough to satisfy the appetite for vengeance."[46] At the end of
August, on the eve of his state of the nation address, and facing protest marches by
dissatisfied workers and farmers, Fox threatened to establish a truth commission to
investigate abuses committed by the PRI during its long dominance if the supreme
court refused to hear the case against Echeverría. But despite such public muscle flex-
ing, he was reaching the point where he would have to struggle against continued
erosion of his authority as he entered the stage of his term analogous to that of Cardoso in Brazil following the 2000 municipal elections—a semilame duck. Like Fernando Belaúnde Terry in Peru in the early 1980s as well as Cardoso in 2002, this
freewheeling personalist appeared to have no viable successor at hand—and little
time to come up with one. Fox remained personally popular, but this popularity did
not extend to his party or government.

Hence, following the few, if strategic, gubernatorial elections of 2004, Mexico's
electoral outlook was as uncertain as that of Brazil, with the mid-2006 election perhaps as likely to bring the PRI back to power as to continue the PAN's fingertip hold

on the presidency, and the PRD's fortunes on the rise in urban centers. The PRI, winner of four of six recent governorship elections, underwent reorganization at the hands of party president Roberto Madrazo Pintado (b. 1952), who became the party's nominee in November 2005. This old-line politico paid lip service to modernization but resorted to all the old win-at-any-cost tactics of the pre-Zedillo PRI.[47] The PRD's hopes were pinned on Mexico City's progressive mayor Andrés Manuel López Obrador (b. 1954), a very popular figure whom the government was trying to en-snare in a web of essentially trumped-up corruption charges, as the PAN and PRI joined in congress in April 2005 to strip him of the legal immunity attached to his office. Conservative ex-energy minister Felipe Calderón Hinojosa (b. 1962) exploited serious miscues by Creel to wrest the PAN nomination from the erstwhile favorite in a hotly contested primary. The next president would be one of these three, but which one would depend upon the course of the most competitive, as well as the most par-ticipatory election campaign in the country's history.

The only Latin American election at all comparable to that of Brazil in scope, the 2006 Mexican election differed sharply both in not having an incumbent running and in having a three-way plurality vote, without provision for a second round. Moreover, the party systems of these two giant countries were near polar opposites, with the three largest parties concentrating over 90 percent of the Mexican votes compared to under 50 percent in Brazil. Colombia's 2006 presidential election was more similar to that of Brazil in featuring a popular incumbent but differed sharply with respect to the party system. For its part, the 2007 presidential balloting in Ar-gentina would lack an incumbent as in Mexico, but as in Colombia but certainly not in Brazil, it would feature one party much stronger than all of its rivals.

On July 2, 2006, the Mexican presidential sweepstakes, involving the future of nearly one-fifth of Latin America's population, took place with well-merited sus-pense. López Obrador had been hotly pursued by the fast-closing Calderón, as Madrazo of the once-hegemonic PRI faded in the stretch, particularly after his party suffered a serious reverse in the March 12 balloting in populous Mexico State. López Obrador, an aggressive and demagogic speaker, focused his campaign on the issues of poverty and continued state control of the energy sector, whereas Calderón, well fi-nanced and with a noncharismatic but modestly appealing personality, stressed the generally sound economic situation and the need to attract foreign investment to keep development on track. This polarization left the PRI to stake out an intermedi-ate position and seek to arouse nostalgia for the Zedillo years—a strategy hampered by its candidate's lack of personal appeal. Although López Obrador took great care during the campaign to disassociate himself from Venezuela's Chávez, attack ads by the PAN had a telling effect, and López Obrador's intemperate personal diatribes against President Fox, who still enjoyed a high degree of respect, if not great popular-ity, backfired as did his failure to participate in televised debates. Moreover, Calderón hammered away incessantly on the themes of López Obrador's alleged fiscal irre-sponsibility and authoritarian personality.

As a result the extremely close balloting yielded a razor-thin 233,000-vote margin in favor of Calderón—at 35.85 to 35.33 just over 0.5 percent of the more than 41 million votes cast in a 58 percent turnout—with Madrazo finishing a poor third (at 22.2 percent of the vote).[48] As unlike a majority of Latin American countries, Mex-ico has neither an electoral college nor provision for a runoff, a highly emotional

López Obrador immediately claimed fraud and demanded a recount, mobilizing a protracted series of determined mass demonstrations in Mexico City, his electoral stronghold. Although he failed to obtain the nationwide recount he demanded, the Federal Electoral Institute (IPE) did order a five-day partial recount (from August 9 to 14) restricted to about 9 percent of precincts, which altered the tallies only marginally.[49] In the congressional balloting the PAN fared well with 206 of the 500 chamber seats—on one-third of the vote—to 160 for the PRD and its two minor allies (Convergéncia and the Workers' Party PT) and 121 for the PRI (on 29 and 28 percent of the vote, respectively). This result accompanied a solid plurality for Calderón's party in the senate, where it ended up with 52 of 128 seats to 33 for the PRI (as the PRD came away with 26 and its allies another 10). Thus the PAN improved sharply in the lower house and the PRD less so, both at the expense of the PRI. As a result, the PAN replaced the PRI as the leading party, with the PRD moving up to be the ranking opposition. The former moved quickly to name former presidential hopeful Santiago Creel as its leader in the chamber, while the PRI fell back on Emilio Gamboa Patrón, presidential chief of staff under de la Madrid in the 1980s.

A final decision came on September 5 with the definitive ruling by the Electoral Tribunal of the Federal Judicial Power (TEPJF) upholding Calderón's election (coming four days after the PRD's congressional delegation had blocked the president from delivering his state-of-the-union address in person). Even as his followers became divided over the tactic of obstruction and disruption of public order, on October 20 López Obrador had himself proclaimed the country's alternative president, while Calderón was announcing his cabinet prior to his December 1 inauguration. Eventually, the capital city's population tired of the traffic-disrupting PRD demonstrations, and in the end about two-thirds of adult Mexicans expressed confidence that the electoral officials had done all that could be reasonably expected to produce a clean vote count. As 2007 progressed, political life in Mexico City returned to normality, with the PAN generally bargaining fairly successfully with the PRI and accommodationist elements of the PRD to enact necessary legislation.

Calderón certainly had a very tough row to hoe during the first half of his term, concentrating on crime, corruption, and management of the economy, bringing the army in to bolster failing efforts on the drug front. His ability to make more headway on the closely interrelated drug-trafficking, corruption, and violent-crime front would depend heavily upon the outcome of the mid-July 2009 congressional and municipal elections, a type of off-year balloting that had not treated his predecessor kindly. The stakes were even higher in light of the fact that any prospective large-scale cooperation from the United States would depend heavily upon the Barack Obama administration's perception that Calderón had sufficient backing from the Mexican people—in short, that he could be considered something of a Mexican Álvaro Uribe (Colombia's highly successful contemporary chief executive).

Alas, that was not to be the case. Instead, the PRI staged a dramatic comeback while the PRD fell back to well below where it had been in 2000. Much like the PT in Brazil, it flourished only when benefiting from the coattails of a popular presidential candidate. With the electorate having grown to over 78 million, the PRI received 36.7 percent of the national vote for the lower house compared to 28 percent for the PAN and a mere 12.2 percent for the PRD. This outcome resulted in the PRI's jumping ahead of the PAN 241 seats to 147, giving the dominant party of the twentieth century a narrow working majority in the 500-member Chamber of Deputies, as the allied Green Party (PVEM) won 17 seats. The PAN's drop from the plurality of 206 it had previously enjoyed left the president's party needing to cultivate PRI support for all legislation, because the PRD's slide to only 72 seats eliminated it as a viable ally. The PRI also demonstrated the residual strength of its party machinery in the partial governorship elections. Hence the only silver lining for Calderón was the fact that the PRI was much more pragmatic than the PRD and motivated to avoid appearing obstructionist as it looked forward to the 2012 succession with effective party president Beatríz Paredes taking over its leadership in congress and Mexico state governor Enrique Peña emerging as a prospective presidential contender buttressed by PRI control of 95 of that populous state's 125 cities.[50]

Notes

1. Enrique Krauze, *Mexico, Biography of Power: A History of Modern Mexico, 1810–1996* (New York: HarperCollins, 1997), pp. 438–480, treats the Cárdenas era.

2. See Joe C. Ashby, *Organized Labor and the Mexican Revolution Under Lázaro Cárdenas* (Chapel Hill: University of North Carolina Press, 1967), and Roderic Ai Camp, *Generals in the Palacio, the Military in Modern Mexico* (New York: Oxford University Press, 1992).

3. See Edmund D. Cronon, *Josephus Daniels in Mexico* (Madison: University of Wisconsin Press, 1960). Veteran historian Charles D. Ameringer perceptively points out that the economic difficulties resulting from the partial shutdown of oil production owing to a shortage of skilled personnel following the nationalization was a major consideration in Cárdenas's decision to "put the revolution on hold" and opt for a "unifying" successor rather than the "logical" progression to the more leftist Francisco Mugica. See his *The Socialist Impulse: Latin America in the Twentieth Century* (Gainesville, FL: University Press of Florida, 2009), p. 79.

4. Krauze, *Mexico,* pp. 491–525, deals with Ávila Camacho's term. Still useful on this generation is Howard F. Cline, *Mexico: Revolution to Evolution, 1940–1960* (New York: Oxford University Press, 1963).

5. See Krauze, *Mexico,* pp. 508–510. Ávila Camacho's appointment by Cárdenas as war minister in 1940 had given him control over the army in the run-up to the election.

6. Ibid., pp. 526–600, analyzes the Alemán government.

7. Robert C. Scott, *Mexican Government in Transition* (Urbana: University of Illinois Press, 1964), p. 250.

8. Krauze, *Mexico,* pp. 601–624, surveys the Ruiz Cortines administration.

9. Scott, *Mexican Government,* p. 207.

10. Krauze, *Mexico,* pp. 625–644, covers the López Mateos years. From this point on, the most useful single book for understanding Mexican developments in a broad context is Daniel Levy and Kathleen Bruhn, with Emilio Zebadua, *Mexico, The Struggle for Democratic Development* (Berkeley: University of California Press, 2001).

11. Kenneth F. Johnson, *Mexican Democracy: A Critical Review* (New York: Praeger, 1978), p. 42.

12. López Mateos's handling of the succession process is discussed in Jorge G. Castañeda, *Perpetuating Power: How Mexican Presidents Were Chosen* (New York: New Press, 2000), pp. 423, 133–143. Election results are tabulated in Roderic Ai Camp, *Politics in Mexico: The Democratic Transformation,* 4th ed. (New York: Oxford University Press, 2003), pp. 190, 193.

13. Peter H. Smith, *Labyrinths of Power: Political Recruitment in Twentieth-Century Mexico* (Princeton, NJ: Princeton University Press, 1979), p. 280.

14. Johnson, *Mexican Democracy,* p. 52.

15. Camp, *Politics,* pp. 245–246.

16. Echeverría's management of the succession process is analyzed in Castañeda, *Perpetuating Power,* pp. 25–43, 144–153.

17. See the treatment of the 1976 election in Daniel Levy and Gabriel Szekely, *Mexico: Paradoxes of Stability and Change* (Boulder, CO: Westview Press, 1981).

18. This mismanagement is detailed in Luis Rubio and Robert Newell, *Mexico's Dilemma: The Political Origins of Economic Crisis* (Boulder, CO: Westview Press, 1984).

19. The rich literature on this period includes Levy and Bruhn, *Mexico;* Kevin Middlebrook, ed., *Dilemmas of Change in Mexican Politics* (La Jolla: Center for U.S.-Mexican Studies, University of California San Diego, 2002), and George W. Grayson, *Mexico, From Corporatism to Pluralism?* (Ft. Worth, TX: Harcourt Brace, 1998).

20. Castañeda, *Perpetuating Power,* pp. 45–61, 155–175, covers López Portillo's management of succession.

21. See Francisco Flores-Macías, "What Is the Value of National Oil Companies? Exploring How Petróleos Mexicanos Internacional Became a Profit Maximizer (1976–1989)," presented at the Latin American Studies Association's congress, Rio de Janeiro June 11–14 (available on the LASA Web site).

22. Camp, *Politics in Mexico,* p. 246.

23. Castañeda, *Perpetuating Power,* p. 63.

24. Camp, *Politics,* pp. 190, 193, has the results of these elections.

25. Ibid., pp. 187–190, 193, has useful discussion of this election.

26. Castañeda, *Perpetruating Power,* pp. 63–88, 177–203, 205–211, deals with de la Madrid's term with a focus on the succession process.

27. Useful are Victoria E. Rodríguez and Peter M. Ward, eds., *Opposition Government in Mexico* (Albuquerque: University of New Mexico Press, 1995), and Kathleen Bruhn, *Taking on Goliath: The Emergence of a New Left Party and the Struggle for Democracy in Mexico* (University Station: Pennsylvania State University Press, 1997).

28. Consult Camp, *Politics in Mexico,* pp. 191–193, and Castañeda, *Perpetuating Power,* pp. 230–239.

29. Information on Salinas is found in Castañeda, *Perpetuating Power,* especially pp. 205–206.

30. Castañeda, *Perpetuating Power,* p. 90, with pp. 89–129, and 212–230, treating the process by which Colosio and Zedillo were selected. On political changes preceding this crisis, see Jorge I. Dominguez and James A. McCann, *Democratizing Mexico: Public Opinion and Electoral Choices* (Baltimore: Johns Hopkins University Press, 1996).

31. Castañeda, *Perpetuating Power,* p. 94.

32. Ibid., p. 93.

33. See Camp, *Politics,* pp. 193–194.

34. The Chiapas uprising and its ramifications are discussed in Castañeda, *Perpetuating Power,* pp. 105–109, 199–201, 222–225, 229–230. Also consult Neil Harvey, *The Chiapas Rebellion: The Struggle for Land and Democracy* (Durham, NC: Duke University Press, 1998).

35. Zedillo as candidate is discussed in Castañeda, *Perpetuating Power,* pp. 124–129; his performance is assessed in Camp, *Politics in Mexico,* pp. 34, 256–258.

36. Camp, *Politics,* pp. 194–196, deals with the 1994 elections.

37. Zedillo was perhaps even more of a highly educated technocrat than Salinas or de la Madrid, although by way of Yale rather than Harvard. Roderic Ai Camp provides a wealth of material on this stratum of the Mexican governmental elite in *Mexico's Mandarins: Crafting a Power Elite for the Twenty-First Century* (Berkeley: University of California Press, 2002), and *Political Recruitment Across Two Centuries, 1884–1993* (Austin: University of Texas Press, 1995).

38. See Camp, *Politics,* p. 250.

39. Ibid., pp. 196–197, treats this election, as does David A. Shirk, *Mexico's New Politics: The PAN and Democratic Change* (Boulder, CO: Lynne Rienner, 2004).

40. Camp, *Politics*, p. 197. See also Roderic Ai Camp, *Mexico's Military on the Democratic Stage* (Northport, CT: Praeger, 2005).

41. The election is discussed in Camp, *Politics,* pp. 174–176, 199–205, and in greater detail in Chappell Lawson and Jorge Dominguez, eds., *Mexico's 2000 Elections* (Cambridge, UK: Cambridge University Press, 2000).

42. See Camp, *Politics,* pp. 190–193.

43. Ibid., p. 202.

44. Ibid., p. 204.

45. M. Delal Baer, "Mexico at an Impasse," *Foreign Affairs*, 83:1 (January-February 2004), p. 106. See also Chapell H. Lawson, "Fox's Mexico at Mid-Term," *Journal of Democracy*, 15:1 (January 2004), pp. 139–152.

46. Baer, "Mexico," p. 102.

47. See Denise Dresser, "Fox's Mexico: Democracy Paralyzed," *Current History*, No. 679 (February 2005), pp. 64–68, where she calls Madrazo "the old system at its worst," as well as Joseph L. Klesner, "Electoral Competition and the New Party Hope in Mexico," *Latin American Politics and Society*, 47:2 (Summer 2005), pp. 103–142.

48. See Luis Estrada and Alejandro Poire, "Mexico's Contentious Election." *Journal of Democracy*, 18:1 (January 2007), pp. 73–87, reprinted in Larry Diamond, Marc F. Plattner, and Diego Abente Brun, eds., *Latin America's Struggle for Democracy* (Baltimore: Johns Hopkins University Press, 2008), pp. 217–231.

49. Consult Andreas Schedler, "The Mobilization of Distrust in Mexico," *Journal of Democracy,* 18:1 (January 2007), pp. 88–102; and Jorge G. Castañeda and Marco A. Morales, "Looking to Mexico's Future," *Journal of Democracy*, 18:1 (January 2007), pp. 103–112, reprinted in Diamond, Plattner, and Abente Brun, *Struggle,* pp. 232–246, 247–256.

50. See Andrew Selee and Katie Putnam, "Mexico's 2009 Midterm Election: Winners and Losers" (Washington, DC: Mexican Institute of the Woodrow Wilson International Center for Scholars, July 2009).

8

Argentina Since 1930

From the onset of the Great Depression to the end of the first decade of the twenti-eth century Brazil made the long and challenging journey from an oligarchic repub-lic to its present status as a major world economic power and the third most populous democracy on earth. Over the same span Mexico climbed out of the hole resulting from two decades of highly destructive armed civil strife to finally achieve democ-racy, only to find itself mired in a new wave of violence rooted in its location as the main route for drug trafficking to the lucrative US market. During these eighty years Argentina experienced a roller-coaster ride from the destruction of its carefully mounted formal democracy, through a period of civil-military twilight, to the enor-mous promised and substantial accomplishments of the Perón era, and back into an extremely cruel form of authoritarian military rule before managing to restore de-mocracy in the 1980s and undertake the daunting task of its consolidation and preservation. Its trials and tribulations, experiments and disappointments, and ulti-mate success in this zigzag road toward political development provide a host of les-sons and contribute greatly to forming an accurate picture of present-day Latin American politics.[1]

Democracy's End Through the Perón Regime

Argentina's 1930 Revolution had very little in common with the simultaneous events in Brazil, much less with what had taken place in Mexico in 1910. Except for a deceptively similar name for this event, it was in reality a great leap backward, as conservative forces in alliance with the right-wing military sought to reestablish an updated approximation of Argentina's pre-1912 political system. The military's vio-lent overthrow of the democratically elected government was, however, the first rup-ture of established institutional order since the beginning of Argentina's centralized era in 1862, and it both ushered in a protracted period of political instability and led to over a half century of a "civil-military twilight" in which full democracy was never restored. The fascistic "integral nationalists" led by General José Félix Uriburu moved quickly to fill the vacuum left by Hipólito Yrigoyen's quite peaceful ouster on September 6, 1930. Heavily influenced by a German military adviser when serv-ing as army inspector general during the 1922–1928 Marcelo Alvear government, this ambitious officer was close to a secret "lodge" of disaffected officers and had re-tired early in Yrigoyen's 1928–1930 encore administration. Uriburu was far more extreme politically than the mainstream of the officer corps, and his provisional gov-ernment included mid-grade officers who, when occupying higher posts in the 1940s and 1950s, would be inveterate plotters. Thwarting Uriburu's ambitions as well as those of the fascistic Argentine Civic Legion (LCA) General Agustín P. Justo (b. 1878), the leader of the constitutionalist wing of the army, assumed the presidency through elections in November 1931. When Alvear's candidacy was vetoed by the government, the antipersonalist radicals decided to boycott the election.[2] Because Yrigoyen and his followers contested the revolution's legitimacy, maintaining that Yrigoyen was still the legal president and would be into 1934, they were banned from taking part in the election. (Hence Justo's presidency coincided with the initial stages of Vargas's rule in Brazil as well as Cárdenas's coming to power in Mexico and the first four years of his government.)

Justo, an Alvear-era war minister who had led the opposition to Yrigoyen's return to power, represented the Concordáncia, an alliance of conservatives and antiperson-alist radicals. His six-year administration (beginning in February 1932), although not the second coming of Roca, compared favorably with the regimes of most of his contemporaries, although not equaling those of Vargas or Cárdenas.

In 1933 Justo's government signed the much-criticized Roca-Runciman Pact, which granted the British preferential economic treatment in return for Britain's pledging to keep its beef purchases at the 1931 level. Given Argentina's extremely heavy dependence on meat exports, chiefly to Britain, this arrangement was as es-sential for Argentina as Vargas's moves to prevent a collapse of coffee sales were to Brazil. Mexico's agriculture was still recovering from the devastation of two decades of internal warfare, so foreign markets were not a major concern for Cárdenas. Sur-viving the impact of the world depression better than its less developed neighbors, but with its foreign exchange reserves drained, Argentina left the gold standard in 1933 (the year that also saw Yrigoyen's death). Import substitution industrialization provided for Argentina's gradual recovery from the depression. In the process pam-pean landowners learned to compromise with industrial entrepreneurs and foreign financial interests.[3]

This so-called infamous decade of the 1930s, in which both the November 1935 gubernatorial elections and the March 1936 congressional balloting were rigged, wit-nessed a changing of the guard when antipersonalist radical Roberto M. Ortíz (b. 1886) became president in a late 1937 election, the second in succession in which extensive fraud was used to frustrate the Radical Civic Union (UCR), which be-lieved that Alvear was the true winner despite the 57 percent of the vote officially credited to Ortíz. This well-intentioned centrist, who had been Alvear's public works minister and Justo's finance minister, upon taking office in February 1938 enjoyed the full backing of Justo, still the respected role model for much of the officer corps. Indeed, Justo and other constitutionalist officers blocked a coup attempt that had Or-tíz on the ropes in August 1938. Subsequently the president stepped up efforts to cul-tivate support among the officer corps. The economic policies of the Ortíz government were essentially inward-looking, with growing state involvement, but the political atmosphere was increasingly marked by cynicism, corruption, disillu-sionment, and a sense of dispiriting resignation. The traditional agricultural elites were determined to regain control of the presidency in order to use the government to defend their interests in the face of the lingering depression. (This situation contrasted both with that in Brazil, where analogous groups were already in control of the government and other interests were trying to break their hold, and—even more sharply—with the militantly progressive Cárdenas government in Mexico.)

With the antipersonalist radicals controlling the lower house but the conservatives holding a majority in the senate, Ortíz followed a reasonably moderate course until blindness resulting from diabetes forced him to hand over power in mid-1940 to sixty-seven-year-old conservative vice president Ramón S. Castillo. (Thus fate doomed Ortíz, unlike his Brazilian and Mexican contemporaries, to have only a brief and ultimately transitory watch at his country's helm.) Real wages had doubled during the 1920s, so workers were far from happy when they held level through the 1930s.

With war already raging in Europe, its impact on Argentine politics was heavy. In World War I, when both Britain and Italy were on the same side, Argentine sympathy had been solidly with the Allies. Now business sectors were again on the side of Britain and the Allies, but much of the military, given their overwhelming Italian origins, sided with the Axis. Working to block Justo's interest in returning to the presidency à la Roca four decades earlier, Castillo had been able to name his own cabinet after Ortíz's formal resignation in August 1940. As the 1943 elections came nearer, Castillo threw his support to the extremely right-wing presiding officer of the senate, Robustiano Patrón Costas. A wealthy sugar planter from the interior, this political boss of Salta had a bad reputation with respect to the treatment of his workers and was viewed as imperious and inflexible. (Castillo's short, if ultimately eventful, stay in power coincided with the apogee of Vargas's Estado Novo in Brazil as well as the first half of Ávila Camacho's post-Cárdenas administration in Mexico.)

Higher field-grade army officers, majors to colonels, despite division into semi-secret groupings known as *logias*, increasingly agreed on one thing: The elections could not take place under Castillo's direction, since under his government's concept of "patriotic fraud," in the counting of ballots, if not in their casting, Patrón Costas would be the certain winner. Wide as their ideological differences were on a traditional left-right continuum, these rising officers shared a nationalist orientation with an inclination toward national power and independence that led them to support industrialization. None of these views were compatible with those of the British-capital-linked agro-export producers hoping to see Patrón Costas lead the country into the post–World War II era. Moreover, the senior officers were very upset over the heavy US military aid to archrival Brazil after it joined the Allies in August 1942. But with the war shifting against the Axis powers, a particularly acute shift with respect to Italy, Castillo was wedded to the Patrón Costas option in the presidential balloting scheduled for September 1943. Many officers were increasingly reluctant to be associated with yet another fraudulent election.[4]

One of the most important of the activist officers by 1943 was Colonel Juan Domingo Perón. Perón was decidedly the most important individual in twentieth-century Argentina, very probably the outstanding leader in the country's history, and a strong contender for that distinction with regard to all Latin America. A far more complex figure than the rather cardboard caricature in the musical *Evita,* he was in many ways a typical Argentine, although on a larger-than-life scale. This exceptional man came from family roots similar to those of much of Argentina's population. His paternal great-grandfather, a Perrone, had migrated from Sardinia in 1827, married an English girl, and become a moderately successful merchant specializing in imported footwear. Hence Juan Domingo's grandfather could become a doctor and a man of letters of considerable material worth and substantial social standing. He further broadened the family's gene pool by marrying a Uruguayan of southern French ancestry. This distinguished Buenos Aires man-about-town's early death at age fifty had a decidedly adverse impact upon the Perón family fortunes.

Juan Domingo's father had been born in 1867, and his mother was a Spanish-Indian woman not formally married to Don Mário Thomás Perón. The future Argentine strongman came into the world on October 8, 1895, in a small town on the pampas, moving as a little boy to a Patagonian sheep ranch that his downwardly mobile father managed. Sent to the capital for schooling in 1904, the embryonic charismatic *caudillo*, lacking money for the private schools required for pursuing a medical career, entered the National Military School in 1911. Thus his socialization spanned the late Roca era and overlapped the ferment that preceded the rise of the radicals to power. Making his mark more in sports than in the classroom, having early in life become an expert horseman and excelling at boxing and fencing, Perón, the youngest in his class, graduated 43rd of 110 in December 1913. After several routine interior assignments, the twenty-four-year-old first lieutenant began teaching at the Non-commissioned Officers' School in the capital, a post he would hold until March 1926. By then a captain, he undertook studies at the Superior War College (ESG), graduating near the top of his class in January 1929 and marrying at that point. Having demonstrated intellectual capacity, as well as leadership potential, he continued to teach military history while assigned to the general staff. Playing a cautious and discrete role in the 1930 Revolution, Perón became a supporter of General Justo and was promoted to major at the end of 1931. During Justo's presidency Perón wrote intensively, manifesting an affinity for the ideas of Oswald Spengler and admiration for the conventional quartet of Alexander the Great, Julius Caesar, Frederick the Great, and Napoléon Bonaparte, as well as expressing strong views on the state's need to avoid internal conflict by regulating all aspects of national life. After two years as a military attaché in democratic Chile, Lieutenant Colonel Perón returned to his beloved Buenos Aires in 1938. In the aftermath of his twenty-nine-year-old wife's tragic death from uterine cancer, he was sent in February 1939 to observe Benito Mussolini's crack Alpine troops. While in northern Italy he assiduously read the basic documents of the fascist regime, took advantage of his proximity to Milan to take some courses in organizational theory, and toured wartime Europe, visiting Nazi Germany and returning by way of Franco's Spain.[5] Once home in early 1941, Perón, a tall, handsome individual with widely recognized leadership abilities, rapidly emerged as a key figure within the not-so-secret military "lodge" founded in March 1943 known as the GOU (Group of United Officers) with its slogan of "Government, Order, and Unity" and General Edelmiro J. Farrell as its patron. With Justo's early-1943 death (following those of Alvear and Ortíz the preceding year) having removed a constitutionalist restraining influence over the still largely apolitical mass of the army, a broad-based conspiracy ousted Castillo on June 4, 1943, eliminating the prospect of elections through which the Concordáncia would remain in power. As 10,000 troops marched on the presidential palace and fatalities were held to 70, few observers had any idea that this would be the end of civilian rule until 1958.[6]

The initial president of the de facto regime, pro-Ally Arturo Rawson (twelfth in seniority among Argentina's active-duty generals), who considered breaking diplomatic relations with the Axis powers, was swept aside in two days and replaced by the war minister, General Pedro P. Ramírez, the chief organizer of Castillo's ouster (and sixth in seniority), whose views were closer to those of the GOU, with General Farrell becoming war minister. (At this point Juan Carlos Onganía, who would govern Argentina in 1966–1971, was just a junior first lieutenant.) Now a colonel, Perón became Farrell's undersecretary, maneuvering skillfully through the politically dangerous shoals. In what was by late 1943 a "Francoist" regime (one bearing basic similarities to Spain under Francisco Franco), Perón became head of the national labor department in October and was upgraded two months later to a cabinet post as secretary of labor and social security. When the vain and somewhat lazy Farrell replaced Ramírez as president in late February 1944, a month after his sudden severing of relations with Germany and Japan, fast-rising Perón became minister of war in June and vice president in July before adding the title of president of the National Council for the Post-War Era the next month. While heading the war ministry, he astutely built support within the military by greatly expanding the upper levels of the officer corps. The number of the army's general officers was increased from twenty-five to thirty-seven, with full colonels upped by 25 percent and lieutenant colonels increased from 233 to 420. Needless to say, Perón had a great deal of say in the ensuing orgy of promotions and an even louder voice in the reshuffling of assignments.[7]

The strategy Perón had evolved for ensuring his country's advancement without undue disorder amid a conflictual world called for a systematic effort by the Argentine state to organize workers and channel social conflict in order to prevent revolution. This effort would require someone with an enlightened mind coupled with unwavering determination to be at the helm, probably for a lengthy period of time. Such an individual needed to combine the strong points of Franco and Mussolini with an updated version of Roca's political sagacity and an understanding of the Argentine people. Looking around, but not long for far, Perón found no one fitting the bill for Argentina's providential man nearly as well as he did. (History has amply confirmed his judgment as it has the certainty of Churchill, Charles de Gaulle, and Franklin D. Roosevelt that they were what their country needed in its particular time of crisis.)

With his eye on the need for a power base outside the armed forces, Perón worked assiduously to gain influence and followers within the labor movement. In 1943 a minimum wage was instituted, a system of labor courts was set up to adjudicate employee-employer disputes, and an end-of-year "thirteenth month" bonus was required. In 1944 Perón reached out to the rural underclass with a "Statute of the Peons," extending to them some of the rights and benefits previously accorded to urban labor. Between 1943 and 1946 the number of people covered by social security trebled. Meanwhile, Perón forged a single national labor central, the General Labor Confederation (CGT), and issued a corporatist labor code similar to that proclaimed by Vargas in Brazil. Hence, in October 1945, on the eve of his fiftieth birthday, Perón was in a position to bid openly for the presidency.[8]

Possessed of astute political acumen and adroit skill at manipulation coupled with a magnetic personality and a flair for showmanship, Perón polished the latter with enthusiastic and extremely close coaching from twenty-six-year-old Eva María

Duarte. A kindred spirit, Evita, also born without the church's formal blessing, had made it in from the boondocks and up from the street the hard—or easy—way, depending upon one's perspective, and was an extremely ambitious and strikingly attractive actress cum radio personality who knew a winner when she saw one. Soon she moved in with the tall, handsome widower Perón, launching a symbiotic partnership that would end only with her greatly premature death in mid-1952.[9] Conservative forces were panicked by the possibility of Perón's rising even higher and in mid-September 1945 organized a mass march—perhaps nearing 250,000 persons—for "the constitution and liberty," but a coup attempt by disaffected army units a few days later in Córdoba fizzled out. Yet, encouraged by this demonstration of anti-Perón sentiment, Perón's enemies and rivals within the regime, jealous of his popularity and wary of being eclipsed by his meteoric rise, convinced insecure president Farrell to dismiss him on October 9, 1945, for having used his government position to further his electoral ambitions. Trying to put the best face possible on this potentially crippling setback, Perón claimed to have voluntarily resigned in order to pursue his presidential candidacy without conflict of interest. He asked for, and received, a chance to bid the Argentine people farewell, using it to announce a major wage increase that he "hoped" the government would honor. Alarmed by his audacity and the favorable public response it elicited, on October 12 his enemies arrested Perón and had him confined on an island in the La Plata estuary (where he would be sent again by military opponents in September 1955).[10]

Throwing caution to the wind, Evita infused backbone into hesitant labor leaders and effectively stirred up Buenos Aires's urban masses—the *descamisados* ("shirtless ones," in the sense of not wearing shirts with collars). A fervent and highly vocal demonstration in the city's center on October 17, involving a march sponsored by the CGT, the largest demonstration Buenos Aires had ever seen, involving 300,000 persons, convinced the vacillating Farrell to reverse course. Moreover, Perón's intramural foes were unwilling to shed blood over the issue, with General Eduardo J. Ávalos—remembering the "tragic week" a quarter century earlier—opening the gates by refusing to repress the demonstrating masses. Thus Perón returned in triumph, making a devastatingly dramatic appearance in front of a hysterical mass of Porteños from the balcony of the presidential palace at the centrally located Plaza del Mayo.[11] He then resumed his whirlwind campaign, which led to a decisive victory in Argentina's first fully free and competitive election since 1928, announcing formation of the Partido Laborista (Labor Party, or PL). In December the cowed government, reconciled to his election, issued a wage and bonus decree clearly bearing Perón's stamp—and well calculated to bolster his vote.

In recognition of her crucial role when Perón's fate hung in the balance and her immense popularity with the lower classes, Evita became the second Señora Perón at a private ceremony on October 23 and would soon be Argentina's youngest and most glamorous first lady, indeed very likely the hemisphere and even global leader in these respects. Still, many senior army officers considered her unfit for that lofty position, and further elevation would be a bone of contention between Perón and the other generals. The campaign was an intense and spirited one, with the radicals allying with socialists and communists behind a unity slate composed of somewhat antiquated José Tamborini for president and Ricardo Balbín, leader of the UCR, for vice president. To counter, Perón selected J. Hortensio Quijano, a dissident radical, as his running mate. The US government, viewing the opposition Democratic Union (UD) with favor, was bitterly opposed to Perón and less than two weeks before election day released a "Blue Book" denouncing his supposed fascist ties.

This blatant attempt to influence the election had a boomerang effect, giving credence to Perón's attacks upon the opposition slate as an unholy "capitalist/communist alliance." On February 24, 1946, Perón received 52.4 percent of the record vote, 10 percentage points ahead of the UD coalition standard bearer. His 2.84 million votes were far and away the most any president had ever received, coming from an electorate of males eighteen and over, some 700,000 larger than in 1937—of whom all those under twenty-six had never before voted for a president. Perón had 304 of 376 votes in the electoral college, a two-thirds majority of seats in the lower house of the national legislature, twenty-eight of the thirty senate seats being contested, and all provincial governors.[12] With his gala inauguration on June 4, the Perón era, Argentina's most defining period, was fully under way. As a sign of his authoritarian side, all supreme court judges were summarily replaced. (Perón had paid very close attention to Vargas's modus operandi, ironically achieving power just after his senior Brazilian semi-soul-mate had been forced out of power. Vargas would, however, be back in office during all but the critical last year of Perón's second term. His overthrow and suicide would precede Perón's ouster by just over a year, and it is hard to imagine that the success of the Brazilian military conspirators did not serve as an encouragement to the Argentine officers plotting Perón's ouster.)

The country over which General Perón (promoted on the eve of his taking office) would govern for nearly a decade was far more complicated than it had been at the time of his political socialization. Fed by immigration, mostly from Italy, its population had passed 15 million, with almost 3 million in the capital and another 1.5 million in its suburbs. While industry had surpassed agriculture as a proportion of GDP, most of it was small and low-tech. The country's industrial plant and infrastructure were rundown after a long lack of renovation stemming from the depression and wartime. Although the country had been neutral during the war and had faced only an imagined threat from Brazil, the armed forces absorbed 43 percent of federal government outlays and 6 percent of GDP, with most of it going to the 138,000-man army. The General Directorate of Military Manufactures (DGM), established in 1941, was expanding into a wide variety of ancillary activities. Because all but two of the army's forty-four generals were senior to Perón, they had some difficulty in accepting the sudden role reversal—subordination to their former subordinate. Unlike the president, two-fifths of them had been born in Buenos Aires and half were sons of immigrants.[13]

For Perón, becoming president was more like a return to power than a transition. His determination to do things his way was exemplified by his choice of an inexperienced thirty-three-year-old as finance minister, so that until 1949 the real economic czar would be Miguel Miranda operating out of the Central Bank presidency. It was clear that import substitution industrialization was bottlenecked, requiring either a broadening of the internal market or an expansion of exports, optimally both. October saw the proclamation of a five-year plan featuring an ambitious program of industrialization, the implementation of which was marred by a good deal of inexperience, substantial mismanagement, and more than a hint of corruption. Yet between 1943 and 1948 GDP rose over 25 percent, hitting 8.3 percent in 1946 and a very impressive 13.8 percent in 1947. In January 1947 the government used some 150 million British pounds ($750 million) from the blocked (nonconvertible) sterling accounts run up by Britain during the war to purchase the country's railroads—a step that was psychologically satisfying, but creating a drain on the already strained government financing of badly needed repairs and reequipment as well as operating costs. Similar expenditures to buy out British-owned public utilities imposed the double burden of a high purchase price and the need to make heavy investments in maintenance and expansion. At that juncture, a young radical politician, Arturo Frondizi (destined to be elected Argentina's president in 1958) denounced a proposed oil exploration deal in Patagonia by Standard Oil of New Jersey as a betrayal of nationalist principles. It would be a long time before Perón could again be criticized for insufficient nationalist zeal, but when it did happen during his second term, it would inflict a serious political wound. (Alejandro Lanusse, who would be the military president who found himself compelled to hand the presidency back to Perón in 1973, was a cavalry first lieutenant.)

Heavily conditioned by political considerations, Perón's development policies contained fundamental contradictions. His encouragement of light industry required increasing capital goods imports, but with investment in agriculture down, failure to generate sufficient export earnings created a severe bottleneck. Perón's nationalism discouraged foreign investment, and his prolabor and anticapitalist rhetoric put off domestic entrepreneurs—especially with regard to long-term investments. Yet there is no question that the first years of Perón's government were better for Argentina's workers than even the preceding Farrell-Perón regime had been. Between 1946 and 1949 real wages went up 60 percent, and even more for unskilled workers than for skilled ones. Consumption was stimulated and pressure put on prices as purchasing power rose. To come up with the vast increase in revenues required by his social programs, Perón elevated protective tariffs and heavily taxed rural exporting elites. In 1946 he established the state-controlled Argentine Institute for Trade Promotion, deeply infringing on a sphere that had been the private sector's.[14]

Perón made no secret of his distaste for political parties, considering them anachronistic and stressing that Peronism was a movement, not just a party. As soon as the Labor Party (PL) had served its electoral purpose, he dissolved it, forming in June 1946 the Unified Party of the National Revolution (PUR) in its stead. By 1949 this party would become the Peronist Party (PP), but he wanted it to remain an electoral vehicle and not gain autonomy from his personal control or play a major role in government. To this end he kept the Women's Peronist Party (PPF) under Evita's leadership separate and used the Evita Perón Foundation (FEP), along with the CGT, to dispense patronage. Indeed, throughout his career Perón would take pains to see that potential rivals would not find an organizational base in a structured, hierarchical party.[15] As part of his preference for direct links to the populace, Perón gave Evita wide leeway to expand the activities of her foundation. Already in charge of the labor secretariat, she gathered funds for the FEP from unions and "voluntary" contributions from businesses. The vast sums collected were used to build apartment complexes, orphanages, homes for the elderly, clinics, and even schools. They also funded programs for distributing food, clothing, and medicine to the needy. This wide array of social welfare functions blurred the line between Peronism and the government, leaving grateful beneficiaries feeling indebted to the Peróns.

In the March 1948 congressional elections the Peronists received 60 percent of the vote and a two-thirds majority in the lower house (the senate being chosen indirectly by the provinces). Needing to amend the constitution to permit reelection, Perón held elections in December for a constituent assembly to revise the 1853 Constitution, winning 66 percent of the vote and two thirds of the assembly's seats. After only two months' work the assembly produced a new constitution, which was promulgated on March 11, 1949—strengthening presidential powers, permitting reelection, and confirming Perón's 1947 extension of the vote to women. But a major economic crisis in 1949 was kicked off by a January stock market crash triggered by Perón's dismissal of economic czar Miranda, who had held his position since the administration's inception. The dropping of the economic pilot was a response to a precipitous drop in economic growth—from 1947's almost 14 percent to a scant 1.2 percent in 1948 on the way to a negative 4.6 percent for 1949. Moreover, inflation rose from 13.1 percent in 1948 to 31.1 percent for 1949. The exhaustion of the game plan, if not the basic model, resulted in large part from the fact that the drive for industrialization had created a great jump in imports just as export earnings declined in response to sagging prices and a loss in world market share.

Perón's reelection was not a civic festival, as his initial elevation to power had been. The campaign was marked by the harassment of opposition candidates and the use of government machinery on behalf of the Peronists. A long-simmering feud between Perón and Alberto Gainza Paz, internationally renowned publisher of the country's most prestigious newspaper, *La Prensa,* came to a head in January 1951 with the closing of the newspaper, aggravated by its expropriation in April. Perón's intention to make Evita even more of a coleader by elevating her to the vice presidency stirred up opposition from those elite sectors still considering her that immature, upstart *puta* ("whore"), a reference to her bed-hopping rise from obscurity.[16] Significant military elements felt that Perón had to be stopped before achieving a second term. By early 1951 Major General Eduardo Lonardi (who would be Perón's bête noire in 1955) was the center of one group of plotters, while retired Brigadier General Benjamín Menéndez was the hub of a rival conspiracy. With the elections moved up three months to November 11, time was running short. An abortive coup by Menéndez on September 28 weakened the anti-Perón movement's base by triggering a wave of purges and forced retirements, but these left deep scars that would come back to haunt the nation's strongman. A State of Internal Warfare was decreed, remaining in effect for the rest of Perón's presidency. An honorable man, Lonardi requested retirement so that he could continue plotting in good conscience.

The conspirators had been undercut by Evita's announcement at the end of August that she was resigning the vice presidential nomination that had been bestowed upon her. By this time it was a very poorly kept secret that she had been suffering from uterine cancer for some time, refusing to undergo a hysterectomy until November 5. The balloting six days later saw an enthusiastic turnout of 7.6 million, including women for the first time in a presidential election. Perón finished well ahead with 61 percent of men's votes and 64 percent of women's, whereas 32 percent of the voters, some 2.4 million, cast their ballots for the radicals' Ricardo Balbín (who would try again for the presidency in 1958). Peronism came away with all governors and 135 of the 149 lower house seats.[17] Vice President Quijano died just before the April 1952 reinauguration, which was also marred by the beloved (by many) and hated (by few)

Evita's excruciating illness. Her tragically premature death on July 26, 1952, led to a massive outpouring of grief and sympathy, with 2 million mourners at her state funeral, but down the road it would create serious problems for the charismatic, but already overextended, leader of the Argentine nation.

In February 1952, facing high inflation (36.7 percent in 1951 and 2 percent higher in 1952, along with the prospect of a foreign exchange crisis, the government announced the most ambitious economic stabilization program in Argentine history. It included a two-year wage freeze and, perhaps even more jolting to Argentines, deep cuts in domestic beef consumption to allow increased exports. Economic growth, which had recovered to 4 percent in 1951, plummeted to an unprecedented negative 6.3 percent for 1952. To emphasize that these sacrifices were temporary, Perón unveiled a second five-year plan at year's end. The situation was not helped by persistent rumors propagated by the opposition that as much as $700 million had been diverted through the Evita Perón Foundation into overseas bank accounts. Then, too, central government payrolls had soared as the number of federal public employees rose from a little over 200,000 in 1945 to nearly 400,000 by 1955.[18]

Perón was never one to stay on the defensive for long. In an act of major symbolic import, the Jockey Club, shrine of the country's traditional propertied elites, was burned to the ground on April 15, a fate shared by the headquarters of the Socialist Party (PS). Then, in July 1953, in a surprise turnaround, Dr. Milton Eisenhower, educator brother of the incumbent US president, arrived on a special mission. This highly publicized rapprochement with the United States was followed by a new and much relaxed investment law, which made possible foreign investments in the exploration and development of Argentine oil fields and signaled a new era in Perón's hitherto quasi-neutralist foreign policy. Economic growth recovered sharply to 7 percent in 1953, remaining at a satisfactory 3.8 percent in 1954. Under these at least temporarily favorable conditions, Perón called elections for the congress and a new vice president for late April 1954, with Peronists getting 69 percent of the vote and filling the vacant vice presidency with Admiral Alberto Tessaire. Perón also moved ahead to complete the organization of a broad Peronist movement having the Peronist Party (PP), the Women's Peronist Party (PPF), and the CGT as its three pillars.

Hence, in late 1954, Perón appeared solidly in power. But the crisis that would topple him by September 1955 had already begun to take form. Worn down from riding the two horses of keeping the military in line and at least partially filling the void, left by Evita's death, in dealing with labor and the masses, the fifty-eight-year-old president filled the vacuum in his personal life with fourteen-year-old Nelly Rivas. But this lapse in morality would be more a pretext for the church's turning against him than its cause. In point of fact, the church had long felt deeply threatened by the state's moving into the social welfare field, which it considered its private preserve, through Evita and her foundation's multifarious activities, even if such activities were essentially competitive rather than fully preemptive. A divorce law passed in December 1954 was a further serious provocation of the church and anathema to fervent Catholics.[19] Having the pretext for a break with Perón, the church needed opportunity. Negative popular and military reaction to his April 1955 contract with Standard Oil of California (SOCAL, a rival of ESSO despite their common roots) to explore for oil in Patagonia left Perón looking vulnerable. Thus, when the next month the government removed religious instruction from public schools, replacing it with what the church considered political indoctrination under the guise of citizenship lessons, the church, almost certainly in consultation with the Vatican through the papal nuncio, girded for war. Unwisely as it proved, Perón was ready, even eager, to meet this remaining institutional bastion of independence on the political battlefield. Congress immediately passed a law calling for elections to a convention to revise the constitution on all aspects relating to the church. With backing from disgruntled sectors of the armed forces, the church defied Perón by organizing a 100,000-person Corpus Christi procession in the center of Buenos Aires in early June. When Perón retaliated by expelling two non-Argentinean members of the Catholic hierarchy, within his legal rights, but a radical rupture with custom, he was publicly excommunicated on June 16. Legalities aside, war between church and state had been declared by both sides. The church rallied support by publishing an "Episcopal Declaration Denouncing Religious Persecution in Argentina." It continued to defy Perón by going ahead with the organization of a Christian Democratic Party (PDC) along the lines of the dominant political force in Italy, in whose formation the Vatican had played a key role in the immediate postwar years. It was no coincidence that on the same day Marine Corps Rear Admiral Samuel Toranzo Calderón led a revolt, which was bloodily repressed. The church, now further upset by the regime's organization of youth branches and rescinding of long-established subsidies to Catholic schools, added its active encouragement of military conspiracies to that already furnished by the restive conservative elites, now out of power for a dozen long years.

The original leader of the second coup was Major General Pedro Eugenio Aramburu, recently appointed to head the Superior War College (ESG). When he backed off, retired General Eduardo Lonardi took over, launching the revolt in Córdoba on September 16, three months after its ill-fated precursor. Rear Admiral Isaac Rojas threw his weight behind Lonardi in a self-styled "revolutionary council" and its pretentious claim to be the "liberating revolution." Perón sought to ride out the storm, but hundreds of civilians were killed when navy pilots strafed the Plaza de Mayo in front of the presidential palace (Casa Rosada) in an effort to kill Perón. Although his most fanatical followers retaliated by attacking priests and burning churches, Perón threw in the towel in the face of air force threats to destroy valuable oil refineries and demolish port facilities. Two days following Perón's resignation on the night of September 19, the interim military junta gave up negotiating, and on September 23 Lonardi was duly sworn in.[20] Military purges occurred rapidly, with all admirals, except Rojas, as well as 45 captains forced into retirement from the navy, a fate in store for 63 of 86 army generals and about 1,000 officers of less elevated rank.

Lonardi's most serious mistake may have been an act of omission: failure to name Aramburu war minister. This well-connected active-duty general pushed him out on November 13, though not quite as quickly as Ramírez had forced Rawson out back in 1943. Aramburu found himself originally hemmed in by a "revolutionary military council," soon downgraded and more prosaically renamed the Military Advisory Board. So the momentous period that had opened in 1930 with Yrigoyen still living in a fool's paradise ended with Perón on his way to exile and Aramburu believing that the tasks facing him were manageable and would mark an end to Peronism—indulging in a pipe dream, for Perón would return to power in the mid-1970s, and eventually Peronists would be governing the country not only throughout the 1990s, but in the early years of the next century. Perón's ouster came only a year after Vargas's demise in Brazil and just before Colombia rid itself of the only military dictator in its history—one who had sought to pose as a neo-Peronist (soon also the fate of a copy-cat in Venezuela). A more authentic disciple was entrenched as constitutional president of Chile, while a slightly more traditional military strongman was preparing to leave power in 1956 in Peru.

Peronism Versus Military Rule, 1956–1979

The complexity of Argentine politics during 1956–1979 all but defies explanation. Starting and ending with authoritarian military figures in power, in between it saw presidencies by each wing of the radicals as well as a dramatic return to power by Perón. During this time a variety of economic game plans would be introduced, then generally abandoned in midstream as a new chief executive abruptly took power. Several grandiose political strategies were devised by heads of government and their brain trusts, failing because of either faulty premises or excessive rationality detached from any deep understanding of persisting, albeit perverse, political realities. In many important ways Argentina's turmoil was nearly the polar opposite of Mexico's extreme stability under a hegemonic party during the same period. Although Brazil would also spend much of the period under military rule there would be important differences: (1) Brazil would begin the period under civilian government and enjoy perhaps the most democratic and progressive administration in its history in 1956–1960 before the military seized power in 1964; (2) once in, the military remained continuously instead of coming in and out; and (3) the careful and gradual Brazilian transition was well under way by the end of this period, whereas in Argentina the authoritarian right would still be in place, in some ways at its most repressive, at the end of the period.

Although out of power and in exile far away in Spain, Perón would still cast a long shadow over Argentina not only until his death in 1974, at a time when he was back in the presidency, but through the rest of the century and into the next. No matter what strategy the forces that ousted him might adopt, they could not break Perón's hold on the hearts and minds of a very sizable segment of the Argentine people or even prevent this support from extending into a new generation. Direct military rule, government by one of the rival radical parties, then by the other, and renewed military rule would be tried, but in 1973 Perón triumphantly returned to power. With his death, the third Señora Perón would inherit the presidency and then be overthrown by the military in 1976. This coup resulted in a highly authoritarian regime and a prolonged state of virtual civil war, with the situation improving only in 1983.

The first eighteen years of this post-Perón period witnessed a great chasm between what the forces that had opposed and finally overthrown Perón had hoped to accomplish in the political realm and the vastly different outcome of their efforts. At the core of this at times grotesque gap between the military's perception of reality, largely shared by the radicals, and the objective reality of Argentina was the unprecedented continued loyalty of millions of Argentines to Perón the man, to the Peronist movement, and eventually to Peronist myths. Government after government operated on the erroneous assumption that societal elements "misled" by Peronist demagoguery could be converted. This wildly overoptimistic thinking was closely linked to a belief that as his place of exile moved farther and farther from Argentina (Paraguay to Venezuela, then on to the Dominican Republic and finally to Spain) and the aging process inexorably continued, Perón would cease to exercise his, to them, irrational sway over the Argentine masses. Clearly they failed to realize that charisma, like beauty, is in the eye and heart of the beholder.

The groups that so unsuccessfully strove to build a sanitized post-Perón political order failed completely to foresee the vast appeal the aging *caudillo* would have to a younger generation—which to a large extent turned him into what they wanted him to be. Hence the military and their allies acted on the faulty premise that time was definitely and distinctly on their side. Perón and Peronism were in their eyes—blinded, as is so often the case in politics, by the distorting lens of wishful thinking, compounded by misreading their enemy—transitory phenomena. In their thinking, by way of contrast to that of the armed forces, the radical parties and the economic elites were permanent institutions that could and would outlast what they saw as a pernicious plague.[21] How very wrong they were is clear from the fact that since the late 1980s, Peronism has been the strongest political force in Argentina, coming, under Carlos Saul Menem, to enjoy an even broader and better structured popular base than that built by Perón, with help from Evita, during the immediate post–World War II decade. It would seem, as students of Argentine political life have asserted, that after 1955 Argentina had two different and distinct political subcultures, one of which viewed the pre-Perón years as the country's golden age and 1943–1955 an abomination, and the other viewing Perón's years in power as Argentina's finest epoch, unfortunately sandwiched between two despicable eras. No wonder compromise was nearly impossible to achieve.

The "National Liberating Revolution," as the anti-Peronist forces pompously called themselves, was divided from the start. Provisional president Lonardi (b. 1894) was out of step with the majority current in the armed forces. He and his backers believed that it was necessary to try to work with the labor leaders, who demonstrated an inclination toward some degree of cooperation with their new regime, even if they were Peronists. The liberal faction of the army strongly disagreed with any leniency toward Peronists and ousted Lonardi on November 13, 1955. General Aramburu (b. 1903), their leader, ensconced as provisional president, cracked down hard on all aspects of Peronism, intervening in the CGT as well as many of its member unions. Nullifying the 1949 Constitution in April 1956 and replacing it with the constitution of 1853 had the effect of wiping out the rights workers had gained under Perón. The Peronist Party was outlawed, and its party and union activists were barred from political positions. All visible Peronist symbols—pictures, plaques, statues, and buildings—were razed. Following Lonardi's death in March, Aramburu draconianly repressed an attempted Peronist countercoup in June 1956, breaking an unwritten rule of Argentine politics by having its leader, a retired general, and twenty-seven other rebel officers executed.

As Aramburu consolidated his hold, most prominent nationalist generals were forced out in November, with the vice president Rojas shown the gate at year's end.[22] (At this point Alejandro Lanusse, to be the last military president before Perón's return to power in 1973, was a lieutenant colonel in the grenadiers regiment.) As officers purged under Perón returned to active duty, much as in Brazil in the early 1930s, over 1,000 army officers and a large number of noncommissioned officers, as well as over 100 naval officers, were forced out, and the anti-Peronist purges extended to the labor unions. Moderate civilian allies, alienated by Aramburu's extreme measures, broke with the government and, under the leadership of future president Arturo Frondizi (b. 1908), founded the dissident Intransigent Radical Civic Union (UCRI). Constituent assembly elections in late July 1957 saw the two radical parties at almost even strength as Balbín's Radical Civic Union of the People (UCRP) edged Frondizi's UCRI by 2.11 million to 1.85 million votes (24.2 percent to 21.1 percent). Blank votes, a great many cast by Peronists, reached 2.12 million—some 24.3 percent.[23]

The February 23, 1958, presidential elections gave the UCRI's Frondizi a decisive 4 million to 2.4 million win over the UCRP's Balbín—on whom the military were counting to win. Frondizi's 45 percent of the vote, more than double the UCRI's proportion seven months earlier, removed any doubt that he was the beneficiary of the Peronists' support. Unhappy that a deal between Frondizi and Perón had decided the electoral outcome, the Aramburu regime acquiesced in Frondizi's inauguration with obvious reluctance.[24] He entered office on May 1—ending thirty-two months of military rule—with the support of all governors and all of the senate, as well as holding 133 out of 187 seats in the lower house. But he was soon weakened by defections over his July decision to allow foreign companies to invest in the petroleum industry. Further narrowing of his political base resulted from the resignation of vice president Alejandro Gómez, implicated in a conspiracy centering on an army commander-in-chief who resisted being replaced—a development that made the senate's presiding officer, José María Guido, next in line for the presidency. Frondizi's response was to declare a state of siege. Moreover, the military insisted on the resignation of his chief adviser, Rogelio Frigerio, and despite the relegalization of the CGT, Perón broke openly with Frondizi, seriously embarrassing him by publicizing the text of their supposed secret preelection agreement.

At this point, the Argentine military were deeply divided between the so-called Azules ("blues"), believing that the military should be subordinated to constitutional authority, and the Colorados ("reds"), who held that the military should exercise power until the task of eradicating Peronism had been accomplished, "cost what it may cost." (Onganía, who would reach the presidency in 1966, had just been promoted to brigadier general and was for a time at least closer to the Azules than to the Colorados.) After another failed military coup in June 1959, accompanying a wave of strikes and social unrest, one of many such buffetings he would have to survive, Frondizi invited his erstwhile rival and critic Álvaro Alsogaray, a champion of private enterprise and brother of a highly placed and extremely political general, to become economics minister. The ensuing austerity program ended Frondizi's honeymoon with labor. Economic growth, 5.1 percent in 1957 and a robust 6.1 percent for 1958, had tumbled precipitously to a negative 6.4 percent, accompanied by 113 percent inflation, a situation calling for this new economic doctor with a new magic elixir in his bag.[25]

As the ailing economy seemed to respond quickly with GDP growth of 7.8 percent and inflation of 27 percent in 1960 and 7.1 percent economic expansion for 1961, Frondizi's fortunes appeared to be on the rise, but they would crash with a dismal economic performance in 1962—a shocking negative 1.2 percent, on its way down to a negative 2.4 percent in 1963. (At this time similar poor economic performance in Brazil was greasing the slides for Goulart's ouster and the onset of military rule.) But by then Frondizi would have been relieved of his office and was hence free from responsibility for a recalcitrant economy. Long before that point he had abandoned his populist grand strategy of winning the Peronist masses over to his UCRI through the benefits and lure of rapid industrialization and settled for the calculus of survival. The first step in his disillusionment in this respect was the 1960 congressional elections, which showed that Peronist voters were still loyal to their leader; Frondizi's hopes that this loyalty might change by 1962 proved vain.[26] The ultimate failure of the Frondizi administration, despite its often quite able and generally courageous leadership, demonstrated that intransigence and unwillingness to compromise on fundamental questions still characterized Argentina's major political actors.

During his forty-seven months in office, Frondizi faced thirty-eight conspiracies and confrontations with military elements, usually being forced to back down on some action or policy he wished to pursue in order to move the country ahead. Showing such extreme political weakness, Frondizi could not give Alsogaray the firm support required to effectively implement his policies in a difficult economic context. Moreover, electoral imperatives led to large increases in government spending prior to the 1960 midterm elections, a loosening of the purse strings that Frondizi anticipated repeating in 1962. Seeking a lightning rod, if not a sacrificial lamb, for the lack of sustained economic progress, Frondizi dismissed Alsogaray in March 1961—a move certain to enrage Alsogaray's brother Júlio, a seasoned conspirator. Overall, Frondizi could not satisfy either leg of his restless Peronist-labor or impatient center-right-military constituencies. By late 1961 foreign policy came to be an aggravating, not just complicating, factor in his survival equation. Heading toward the second midterm elections in his scheduled tenure, Frondizi found his 1958 understanding with the Peronists that he would allow their participation in the next presidential election a two-edged sword. The military had swallowed their sworn enemy's 1960 legislative gains because these were only partial elections, but a similarly strong performance in 1962 might give them control of the lower house, if not the senate. (Up to this point Frondizi had a weather eye cocked toward Quadros's inventive, but ultimately self-destructive, maneuvering in Brazil.)

A gesture to mollify the Peronists, the September 1961 award of a medal to expatriate Ernesto "Che" Guevara, now an official of Fidel Castro's Cuban regime, raised military hackles.[27] At the January 1962 meeting across the river at Punta del Este, Uruguay, of hemispheric foreign ministers, a two-thirds majority vote was required to suspend Cuba's membership in the Organization of American States (OAS), and the United States was hard-pressed to cobble together this majority. The Argentine military demanded a vote against the Castro regime; Peronists, entrenched in control of the labor movement, were equally adamant that Argentina cast the vote necessary to "save" Cuba from the "imperialists'" underhanded blow. In a futile attempt to avoid either horn of this politically explosive dilemma, Frondizi had his representative abstain. This abstention infuriated both sides because it forced the United States to make an unsavory deal with Haitian tyrant François Duvalier in order to prevail, but it did not prevent the two-thirds vote for Cuba's ouster. The Argentine military and the Peronists agreed on only one thing, that Argentina's abstention was a cowardly act on Frondizi's part, not one of statesmanship. (In Argentine political culture, the word *intransigent* bore the positive connotation of standing firmly for one's principles;

compromise carried with it the negative connotation of lacking the courage of one's convictions.)

Retribution by the military would follow swiftly, with a full-blown crisis erupting on February 2. Frondizi had justified letting the Peronists run in the March 18 elections as providing an opportunity to destroy the myth of their invulnerability, but their Popular Union (UP) front party won the Buenos Aires gubernatorial race with 37 percent of the vote to 23 percent for the UCRI. Nationally the two Peronist groupings, the UP and the Justicialist Front (FJ), elected ten of fourteen governors and won thirty-two congressional seats to the UCRI's twenty-five places in the lower house and the UCRP's twenty. Soon, however, a coup would deprive the Peronists of the fruits of electoral victory. While frantically searching for a solution to the volcanic backlash unleashed by the Peronists' "sensational" showing, Frondizi encountered a UCRP preferring a military coup to entering a national union coalition with their estranged former UCR brothers. Indeed, the situation with respect to the radicals was, and would continue to be, reminiscent of the Protestant Reformation and the Counter-Reformation. So, unable to form a coalition, at dawn on March 29, 1962, Frondizi was unceremoniously thrown out of office as Yrigoyen had been in 1930. As in that case, leaders or the rival political factions of the military agreed on the need to remove the president, although disagreeing on what should ensue.

Whereas the interventionist Colorado or *gorila* faction of the armed forces, with General Júlio Alsogaray (b. 1918) in the van, desired a return to military rule à la 1955–1957, influential "swingman" (pivotal figure) General Onganía (b. 1914 and three years' senior in service) was a relative legalist, as was another president-to-be, Colonel Alejandro Augustín Lanusse (b. 1918). With a wave of induced retirements in April, Onganía shot up twenty-six spots in seniority, becoming army commander-in-chief. Júlio Alsogaray became army undersecretary, with his brother Álvaro as economics minister, a post to which he would return much later in Argentina's tragic political saga. Thus entrenched, Onganía managed to avoid the creation of a military junta.[28] In consultation with ex-president Aramburu and other key officers, he and his backers came up with a quasi-constitutional way out. Since the vice president had resigned back in November 1958, the next in succession was the presiding officer of the upper house of the congress, José María Guido. In this confrontation of ruler versus arbiter military groupings the latter won out on the basis of greater unity of purpose and esprit de corps. By the night of September 22 the danger of a hard-line coup was over and Guido was in the hands of the legalist faction. During his less than a year and a half in office the mild-mannered Guido was satisfied with his interim status, acting as little more than a figurehead behind whom the armed forces called the shots. The legalist elements of the army, led by Onganía and following a tradition going back to general/president Justo in the 1930s, insisted on holding presidential elections in July 1963, confident that the UCRP would win in balloting in which neither the UCRI nor the Peronists would be in a position to mount a serious contest. The Colorados, behind aged warhorse General Benjamín Menéndez, General Federico Toranzo Montero, and always troublesome retired admiral and one-time vice president Rojas, saw their coup plans flop in early April 1963.[29]

The UCRP fell back on Arturo Umberto Illia (b. 1900), a provincial leader from the interior with minimal qualifications to govern the country, particularly under difficult circumstances. Yet, overlooking the fact that the UCRP had competed with the

UCRI for Peronist support in 1958, the military viewed him with favor. On July 7, 1963—with 9.7 million, some 86 percent of the registered electorate, casting their ballots—this above-middle-age country doctor received a bit over 25 percent of the vote and 169 of 476 electoral votes, which in light of 19 percent blank ballots gave him an adequate edge over the UCRI's Oscar Alende (with 16.4 percent of the votes) and ex-chief executive General Aramburu, who retained the support of 13.8 percent of voters.[30] As the smaller parties cast their electoral votes to Illia, he took office in October, with Guido apparently relieved to be off the hot seat. As his party held only 72 of 192 seats in the lower house, the new president's alliance-building skills would be severely tested. Wisely he retained Onganía and the rest of the military high command and adopted a "hands-off" policy toward the military.

The neo-Peronist Popular Union (UP) had been legalized for these elections, joining the UCRI in a national and popular front. Engaged in a power struggle with dissident Peronist Augusto Vandor, entrenched in control of the "62 Organizations," the strongest component of the labor movement, Perón insisted on Vicente Solano Lima of the small Popular Conservative Party (PCP) as the front's candidate. Two weeks before the elections he was removed from the ballot as being a mere stalking horse for Perón. This proscription led Perón, from exile, to order his followers to cast blank ballots. But in the partial midterm elections of March 1965 the predominantly Peronist UP won 31 percent of the vote to the governing UCRP's 30 percent, with other neo-Peronist parties receiving 7 percent. (The Justicialist Party PJ had been legalized in January, but this ruling was overturned on February 26, and it was forced back into the cover of a multiparty front.) This development left the government with sixty-eight seats in the lower house, as the Peronists rose dramatically from eight to fifty-two deputies. Moreover, they had carried the country's two largest cities: Buenos Aires and Córdoba.

Illia's problems began to mount with his decision to support the April 1965 US intervention in the Dominican Republic, resulting in bloody riots by students and workers. His inept handling of the crisis alienated both Onganía and General Lanusse, the general staff's assistant chief for operations. The former resigned over the appointment of a new army secretary and began planning Illia's ouster. In this plan the key plotter was General Alsogaray, ensconced in the strategic post of commander of the army corps in the greater Buenos Aires region.[31] Meanwhile, leaning more toward the structuralist (need for fundamental economic reforms) than the monetarist (priority for fiscal policies) side, Illia had opted for a nationalist stance and reversed Frondizi's oil concessions while initially giving favorable wage increases. Although his government's early economic results were satisfactory, with robust GDP growth of 10.3 percent in 1964 and 9.1 percent in 1965, 1966 witnessed a sharp economic slump featuring a near stagnation 0.6 percent rise in GDP (a decrease in per capita terms) and inflation back up to 32 percent. Foreign capital failed to meet the country's investment needs, even though it bought up many Argentine firms, but it served to undermine the none-to-strong entrepreneurial spirit of local capitalists. Foreign debt, slightly under $380 million in 1961, rose to $526 million by 1965.[32]

As Vandor afforded an option of neo-Peronism without Perón (like Fernando Belaúnde Terry and his Popular Action Party did in Peru vis-à-vis the military's veto of APRA), the 1966–1967 round of governorship elections took on great strategic importance. In a showdown in Mendoza in April 1966, Perón's candidate defeated

Vandor's by 102,000 to 62,000—giving victory to the Democratic Party (PD), an irreparable setback to the idea nourished in some military circles of negotiating "acceptable" Peronists for the major provincial executive elections in 1967 as a prelude to a tacit alliance with Peronists independent of the old man. These members of the military had hoped that the gubernatorial elections would show that Perón's personal appeal and electoral influence had waned, but this was clearly not the case—so a very different approach would have to be found. As Illia's shortcomings became patent, inviting invidious comparison with Frondizi, the military removed him faster than they had Frondizi. By this point many of them had soured on civilian politicians in general and the parties in particular, holding that the Peronists, UCRI, and UCRP had all proved incompetent at governing. Moreover, by 1966 the armed forces had taken over many of Argentina's South American neighbors and were poised to do so in others. Mixing ideas of both military factions, General Onganía had garnered the support of officers who, in principle, favored civilian rule—although with the military close by as arbiter—but disillusioned with its prospects under present circumstances and hence willing to assume a ruler role.

Finally a coup on June 28, 1966, brought the reluctant dragon turned eager beaver to power. Onganía gained the public's attention for his "Argentine revolution" when he promised that he would stay in power until all its goals were achieved no matter how long it might take. To clear the way for rebuilding the country politically, all parties and legislative bodies were dissolved and the supreme court was dismissed. Strengthening the presidential staff while reducing the number of ministries and secretariats, Onganía shifted a significant share of decision making into the hands of the National Security Council (CONASE) and National Development Council (CONADE). In the view of a perceptive scholar, the Argentine government had proven to be big, but not strong or intelligent.[33] Álvaro Alsogaray became secretary general of the presidency, from whence he could supervise the impressive sounding System for National Planning and Action for Development and Security.

Scalded by his earlier experiences, particularly that under Frondizi, Alsogaray had no problems with Onganía's strengthening of the government's repressive capabilities if this repression would further insulate economic planning from disruptive conflicts within the entrepreneurial class—much as was the case with Roberto Campos in Brazil at the time. This tendency had the backing of Alsogaray's brother Júlio, installed as the army's commanding general. The resulting policy mix was "an intertwining of liberal orthodoxy, mercantilism, and technocratic interventionism" that reflected the debate raging in the academic and business communities.[34] This debate brought with it a continuing tension and rivalry between economic liberals and nationalists (a rivalry resolved in Brazil by that point in favor of the former).

As his confidence increased with experience as president, Onganía increasingly sided with the monetarists against structuralists and their insistence on basic reforms, installing Adalberto Krieger Vasena as a type of economic czar in December 1966. A liberal representative of industry and agro-business with close ties to transnational interests, Krieger Vasena strove to deepen Argentina's industrialization with an eye to exportation. Convinced of the need for free trade and less governmental paternalism and interference, he was neither an orthodox monetarist nor a structuralist, believing that Argentina's inflation had shifted from demand-generated to cost-pushed. In his view the answer was to hold wage increases behind the previous year's inflation through an "incomes policy" of administered wage and price controls, while providing credit to the private sector slightly ahead of past inflation, but keeping expansion of the money supply behind it. This formula worked primarily to the advantage of urban industrialists and foreign investors. In 1965 GDP growth had been a very robust 9.1 percent, plummeting to 0.6 percent in 1966 before rallying to 2.6 percent for 1967 and 4.4 percent in 1968. Concentration, centralization, and denationalization went forward, and after 1968 there was an addition to the policy mix of an increased public sector role in maintaining aggregate demand along with an active fiscal policy. In point of fact, the Onganía government's management of the economy was one of its strong points, as the period from March 1967 to May 1969 witnessed the most successful economic turnaround since that under Perón in 1952. (This boom coincided with the beginning of Brazil's "economic miracle," which would last to 1974.) Even with 1969 expansion of GDP at 8.5 percent, however, not everyone was satisfied. Many entrepreneurs favored greater emphasis on privatization and dismantling of the state sector, and there was a conflict brewing in the agricultural arena between the large cattle and grain-export-oriented producers and smaller farmers producing for the domestic market—a cleavage found in many countries of the region.

Criticism of schemes from within the administration's brain trust to create corporatist legitimacy and a "communitarian" (social cooperation) ideology also mounted. Onganía's government included a "patriarchal and traditional" group of loyalists, "authoritarian liberals" with deep reservations concerning the nationalist and corporatist leanings of the "authoritarian nationalists" and the technocratically inclined "professionals."[35] Both elements who could be described as developmental nationalists and the nationalist populists had divergent ideas of what should be the aims of Onganía's heralded transformation of the nation. The former feared continued denationalization of the economy, and the latter thought that negative effects of the present economic program could raise sociopolitical unrest to dangerous levels. The national populists went beyond opposition to orthodox economic policies, also entertaining serious misgivings about Onganía's long-range sociopolitical project.

By late May 1968 Generals Alsogaray, an avowed opponent of the nationalists, and Lanusse were questioning the corporatist project and raising in the backrooms of the regime the issue of whether Onganía was the proper interpreter of the military's "revolution" or essentially a delegate of his fellow officers, as he was president of the military junta—which had installed him—as well as of the Argentine nation.[36]

The response of this imperious, even imperial, president, who manifested pronounced Gaullist inclinations (as this dominant leader of France had triumphed over his opponents in mid-1968) was to move against both Alsogaray brothers. In August 1968 the more trustworthy Lanusse became the new army commander-in-chief, and Onganía began to favor the paternalists, advocates of a more active state role in the economy. With ex-president Aramburu and Alsogaray almost openly conspiring by mid-1969, the last thing Onganía needed was a social explosion. But the traumatizing Cordobazo broke out on June 28, with 13,000 workers and students rioting through the country's second city, Córdoba (from which the episode got its name). Their ranks swollen by striking workers of foreign-owned auto plants, the next day they controlled 150 square blocks of the city's center. For several days intense media coverage treated the rest of the country to the spectacle of destructive mobs running wild. Rigorously repressed by the army, although not without difficulty and significant bloodshed, this shocking event punctured the government's carefully cultivated image of invulnerability.[37] (At this time Emílio Garrastazú Médici in Brazil was in firm control of a stable and prosperous country.) To Onganía's dismay, within six months a number of guerrilla movements were active, with the growing sense of malaise fed by the leftist Peronist self-named Montenero terrorists kidnapping and executing ex-president Aramburu for his alleged crimes against Peronism and the Argentine people.

Hoping to use Krieger Vasena as a scapegoat for economic discontent, Onganía dropped his erstwhile economic pilot but gained very little from the move (as, once intense military plotting is under way, currying favor with well-placed economic groups is generally too little, too late). He alienated Lanusse by naming a retired general and Buenos Aires province governor as interior minister without consulting the army commander-in-chief. As they were the protectors of the regime, the officer corps wanted a larger say in its policies, whereas Onganía acted increasingly as if he alone possessed the revealed truth handed down to him from on high. By this point Onganía's base of support was perilously thin, and opposition to him had significantly broadened and deepened. In this deteriorating environment Lanusse was able to forge a consensus in early 1970 for putting an end to Onganía's corporatist designs and starting a slow transition to civilian rule. A face-to-face meeting between Onganía and Lanusse at the end of April failed to clear the air. In late May Onganía told senior commanders that his project of the "three periods" (in which the economy had to be set in order before he began a restructuring of society, which needed to be completed before he turned to construction of a new political system) might require ten to twenty years. Lanusse responded by calling for a "Great National Accord" involving closer consultation with reliable civilian forces, a proposal whose logic called for a new hand at the country's helm.[38]

Problems with labor, chronic for all Argentine military regimes, peaked in the Onganía years. Perón had left behind the best-organized and most politically sophisticated and conscious labor movement in Latin America, and subsequent governments' efforts to depoliticize it had met with very limited success; indeed, taken collectively these efforts had added up to abject failure—beginning with Aramburu's interventions and purges of the CGT and its member unions. Labor leader Vandor had made a try at Peronism without Perón, a project in which he met determined opposition from José Alonso, toward whom the Onganía government had tilted. A December 1966 general strike had ended a relative honeymoon between Onganía and the trade union movement, at the same time making Vandor and his associates overconfident. After Vandor's loss at political arm wrestling with Perón back in 1966, the government had struck back hard during the second quarter of 1967 to put him on the defensive. Within a year a dissident body, a radical populist CGT de los Argentinos, led by Marxist Raimundo Ongaro, had made serious inroads among the newer service sectors, particularly public sector employees and those in state enterprises. Both of the rival CGTs (paralleling the UCRI-versus-UCRP contest to be viewed as the legitimate heir to the old UCR) laid claim to about 500,000 affiliated workers. Not to be outflanked, Vandor moved to the left and sought to mend his fences with Perón. By the beginning of 1969 a substantially weakened Ongaro-led insurgent CGT de los Argentinos had become strong chiefly around Córdoba, where it was associated with the violent events of the Cordobazo. Vandor's murder, probably at the hands of Montenero guerrillas in the middle of 1969, had left a major vacuum in the labor field and a smaller one in the political arena. Even more serious political fallout had resulted from the murder of Aramburu, viewed by many key figures as the man who might be used to govern the country during a transition back to civilian rule. His death required reassessment of the options.

Seeing the handwriting on the wall, in early June 1970 Onganía sought to remove Lanusse from command of the army but, after several rounds, ended up being the odd man out. In ousting Onganía from office, the armed forces had acted to cut their losses before his personal discrediting and snowballing public hostility could be transferred from his government to the military as an institution.[39] Despite his pledge to "deepen the Revolution," the new president, General Roberto M. Levingston (b. 1920), was just a placeholder, one whose viability was rapidly eroded as Lanusse's influence continued on the rise. The appointment as economics minister of Aldo Ferrer, a left-of-center nationalist with a reputation for being a structuralist-developmentalist (hence with minimal concern for fiscal policies relative to the pursuit of growth), enraged major business interests, which had grave reservations about his scheme for deepening vertical integration, particularly in the intermediate goods sector, while stimulating internal demand through wage increases and public works programs.[40] Suggestions by Levingston—who was beset by external sector economic difficulties related to his strategy of marginalizing foreign creditors and investors in an attempt to build a state-domestic capital alliance—that he might want to stay on for four or five years did not sit well with major military movers and shakers or, for that matter, with civilian leaders. In November a joint declaration of Perón and radical leader Ricardo Balbín entitled "The Hour of the People" roiled the political waters by demanding a return to democracy. This declaration was not at all adequately offset by Levingston's issuance of a "Buy Argentine" decree designed to appeal to nationalist sentiments and rally support from industrialists and businessmen.

In these circumstances Levingston's twenty-one-week government ended when the second Cordobazo of March 12–15, 1971, with the chilling spectacle of almost three days of rioting strikers in control of Argentina's interior industrial center, brought Lanusse to the presidency on March 24; he also retained his post as army commander. By this time "Lanusse and the more lucid sectors of the military recognized it was illusory to think that the authoritarian system could be maintained without far reaching changes."[41] Hence the political chess game of 1971–1973 would pit a wily political strategist in Lanusse against an all-time true international grandmaster in Perón. After surviving an attempted coup in October 1971, Lanusse developed a strategy for engineering an impasse in which he might be drafted to enter the electoral lists and thus stay on in power. Shortly after publication of his Political Parties Law, Perón made a surprise return to Argentina in mid-November 1972, receiving a tumultuous welcome from a half million supporters waiting at the airport and leaving a month later—after having got his ducks in a row for the succession. Lanusse failed to mobilize sufficient military support to call off the elections at a point when at least four out of five Argentines wanted the military out of power. Moreover, Perón undermined him by making public a secret visit from a Lanusse representative in a way that forced the president to foreswear any intention to be a candidate.

Lanusse, who had legalized the PJ in January 1972, counted on a legal provision requiring candidates to be in the country on election day to thwart Perón, who he was sure would not hazard returning again against the government's express wishes. Lanusse and many other supposedly astute politicians mistakenly breathed a sigh of relief when the little-known Héctor Campora, the party's second vice president, received the Peronist nomination. Taking on the imposing name of the Justicialist Liberating Front (FREJULI) the Peronists added Frondizi's Independent Left Movement (MID) as an ally and nominated Solano Lima of the Popular Conservatives (PCP) as Campora's running mate. In the March 11 balloting, the freest since Perón's original election in 1946, carried along on the slogan "Campora to Office, Perón to Power," the FREJULI candidate received 5.9 million votes, 49.6 percent of the total, to a little over 2.5 million—21.3 percent—for the UCRP's perennial hopeful Ricardo Balbín. Francisco Manrique, a conservative of a paternalistic bent, and Oscar Alende trailed with just under 15 percent and almost half that, respectively. The turnout of over 11.9 million out of a registered electorate of 14.3 million—some 85 percent— was by far a new record. This electoral tidal wave gave FREJULI 45 of 69 seats in the senate to go with 142 of 243 in the lower house and all of the governorships that were up for election.

The second stage of Perón's comeback was ignited, as following Perón's arrival in the country on June 20, Campora and the vice president obediently resigned in early July, creating necessity for a new presidential election on September 23. Perón duly triumphed with an overwhelming 62 percent of the vote to just over 24 percent for eternal bridesmaid Balbín. At 7.4 million votes, Perón's backing was easily an Argentine record. A persistent Manrique received almost 13 percent, a small drop from March.[42] Some 84 percent of Argentine workers voted for their champion, who enjoyed the support of three-fifths of the lower middle class, but only half that proportion of the more prosperous upper middle class. Perón, complete master of the urban regions, supplemented his sparser support in less developed interior areas through the adhesion of local leaders, with their control of local political structures. In addition, some conservatives who had come to fear revolution more than Peronism voted for the aging strongman in hopes that he might be able to tame the Montenero terrorists.

Back in power after eighteen years in the political wilderness, the Peronist movement was deeply divided on a left-right cleavage overlaying a generational one. Hence, to avoid favoring one side or the other, Perón chose his third wife, María Estella Martínez de Perón (b. 1931; she used the name Isabel), a former cabaret entertainer with whom he had hooked up on his way into exile, to be vice president. Little did he dream that in just over a year this politically inexperienced young woman would be in over her head as the country's president under even more difficult conditions.

On October 12, 1973, at the age of seventy-eight, Perón returned to the presidency for what would be a short and troubled stay. Peronism was deeply divided between a new generation of youths who had grown up while Perón was in exile and looked at him as a man of the left, many accustomed to the armed struggle as Montoneros, and his old associates from before 1955, who knew his early quasi-fascistic roots and who had shifted to the right as they aged. For most of Perón's short tenure José Ben Gelbard served as economy minister, with the misfortune of having to deal with deteriorating international economic conditions.

Eight and a half months after Perón's return to power, when he was the indispensable element in holding the party together, Perón finally did what the military had long been counting on: He died. Isabelita, as the widow Perón was popularly known, was poorly prepared to deal with the heavy burdens of governing a country in crisis. She was in way beyond her depth and heavily under the influence of José López Rega, a longtime right-wing associate of the late president, who soon became her lover as well as her astrologer and minister of social welfare. Argentina's first woman president ran through economic ministers at a rate that ensured there would be no coherent economic policy.

Worse, if that were possible, under the sway of this Argentine Rasputin, Isabelita gave a free hand to right-wing paramilitary groups, particularly the Argentine Anticommunist Alliance (AAA), which López Rega had founded, to kidnap and kill leftist guerrillas. She also authorized the nationalization of oil exploration contracts held by Exxon and Shell, telecommunications franchises of Siemens and IT&T, and foreign banks, moves designed to appease all the country's different varieties of nationalists. (At this time Brazil was moving through decompression of its authoritarian regime in the direction of political opening and eventual full transition to democracy.)

López Rega's influence peaked in May 1975, when he was able to place a friendly general as army commander and make university professor Italo Argentino Luder defense minister. After the first-ever general strike against a Peronist government in June 1975, the overwhelmed chief executive lost what small degree of control she had over the situation, a condition which was worsened in July by the military's depriving her of López Rega's company and advice by forcing him to flee the country to escape trial on charges embracing almost everything from corruption to sedition. In mid-October she took a five-week leave of absence, during which senate president Luder filled in (having relinquished his cabinet post in order to return to the congress). The military's confidence that by letting Isabel Perón make a bigger mess of things, their eventual intervention would be warmly welcomed by the public was not misplaced. Between April 1975 and March 1976, inflation easily topped 700 percent, with the rate for March compounding into 17,000 percent a year.[43] By early 1976 the president's credibility was already gone, and almost everyone saw the coup coming, not difficult since a wide range of political, economic, and social groups were pleading with the military to take over. In not-very-secret meetings with top officers these pillars of civil society were being told that they had better be sure that a military coup was what they really wanted, because when the military did take over again, they would stay as long as they deemed necessary to get the job of restructuring and purifying the country done, using whatever measures might be necessary, no matter how extreme. Indeed, it was with a sense of relief that the Argentine public witnessed the military oust Isabelita, by now a diminutive of scorn, not affection, as she was informed on March 24, 1976, that her tenure in office had been terminated by the armed forces. Five days later General Jorge Rafael Videla (b. 1925) was sworn in as the president of a military junta implementing the "process of national reorganization." Few Argentines, most of whom heaved a sigh of relief, had any inkling that the door was opening on the darkest days in their country's life. For the new regime unleashed a campaign of terror against all groups it considered subversive. This campaign would lead to unimaginable horrors as the "dirty war" escalated beyond any control, generating at least 20,000 "disappearances."[44]

Initially Videla chose to give economic liberalism a full chance to work under José Martínez de la Hoz, who set out to reinsert Argentina into the global economy through imposition of the criteria of efficiency and comparative advantage. Protectionist import barriers were lowered, subsidies were drastically reduced, the public sector was severely cut back, and social expenditures were sharply curtailed. All this rationalization of industrial policy was accompanied by a brutal compression of real wages.

In keeping with the ideas of their University of Chicago mentors, holding that hyperinflation was essentially a result of excess demand, the economic team followed an orthodox stabilization program with a mid-1977 fiscal reform and a May–November 1978 effort to "deindex" the economy while reducing costs and imposing greater market discipline. (At this juncture the Augusto Pinochet dictatorship installed in Chile in late 1973 appeared to most observers to be having notable success with similar policies.) Macroeconomic indicators at first supported the government's contention that these policies were essential for economic recovery. Between 1976 and 1978 exports exploded from $3.9 billion to $6.4 billion, and imports expanded modestly from $3.0 billion to $3.9 billion. The near tripling of Argentina's trade surplus to $2.6 billion and the even greater growth of foreign exchange reserves to $6 billion (from the 1976 low of $1.8 billion) were accompanied by GDP growth of 6 percent in 1977 and almost 7 percent in 1979, compared to zero growth in 1976 and a negative 4 percent in 1978. Although a sharp jump in imports in 1979 reduced the trade surplus to $1.1 billion on record exports of $7.8 billion, foreign exchange reserves still peaked at $10.4 billion. Since GDP growth was a robust 6.8 percent and inflation dropped slightly (to a still preoccupying 180 percent), the "new political economy" impressed more than only its architects. With recirculation of petrodollars making low interest loans readily available, scant attention was paid to the huge jump in foreign debt—from $9.74 billion in 1976 to over $21 billion by 1980; after all, it just showed how credit-worthy the country was. But this transitory picture of popular satisfaction with a temporarily booming economy would fade even faster than did national euphoria over winning the 1978 soccer World Cup—milked for all it was worth (bought with bribes in money, land, and cars given to the Peruvian team for letting the host country score at will to get into the finals on goal differential). Indeed, the early 1980s would see the Argentine military regime's bright dreams turn into the darkest of nightmares.

Into Democratic Daylight Under Renovated Peronism

Although the 1980s dawned grim and unpromising for Argentina, by 1983 the sun had broken through the clouds, and by 1997 a much more broadly based regime would have surpassed the duration of the middle-class democracy the country had enjoyed from 1916 to 1930. A crucial difference was that this time no global economic crash loomed on the horizon to undercut a democracy both significantly more mature and with substantially broader and deeper roots. Hence it would be able to survive, although with pain and suffering, the stormy weather that would accompany the turn into the twenty-first century. A deeply ingrained pattern of military tutelage of the nation's political life was broken—since from 1930 to 1983 senior army officers occupied the presidency for all but fourteen years, with no civilian serving out his constitutional term. (At this point Brazil was well embarked upon a gradual, orderly, scripted return of the government to civilian hands that would be completed in 1984, whereas Mexico was a case study in arrogance of power in the hands of a hegemonic political party now a half century in power and, as with Argentina's military masters, seeing no reason to change. Events would soon provide both the Mexican mandarins and the Argentine militarists with sudden reality checks, with the latter compelled against their wishes to mend their ways.)

The distinctive feature of Argentina's escape from continued authoritarian military rule was a fundamental error in judgment on the part of the last in a series of military heads of government, which led by mid-1982 to a monumental mistake in the form of a military adventure directed against Britain. In all probability the transition to democracy would have occurred, but very likely not until the latter part of the decade and with much more suffering and bloodshed in a continuation of the "dirty war" that remains far and away the greatest trauma of Argentina's life as a nation.[45] As the Videla government moved into to its final stage, the rosy economic panorama of 1979 became shrouded in clouds of doubt as 1980 imports exploded to $10.5 billion, causing a $2.5-billion trade deficit with a resulting sharp drop in foreign exchange reserves to $7.6 billion. At a meager 1.2 percent, economic growth lagged behind population increase, creating widespread dissatisfaction with a reduction of inflation that still left it at 101 percent for the year. Many banks, including the largest private one, were insolvent and had to be liquidated; the result was increasing pressure on the budget. Foreign debt totaled $35.6 billion at year's end, a preoccupying burden. Deteriorating economic conditions continued to plague the government of General Roberto Viola (b. 1925), who took over on the basis of seniority from Videla on March 29, 1981, when the president reached the army's retirement age. Although an April 1980 bank panic had been overcome, by early 1981 grave concerns about the country's economic future had led to a massive wave of capital flight. As had become customary, many of the preceding government's fiscal policies were reversed. Hence, although the trade deficit was eliminated through increasing exports and reducing imports, foreign exchange reserves were halved as GDP shrank by a staggering 6.1 percent, with industry bearing the brunt of the contraction at a very troubling negative 15.2 percent, and inflation remained stable. The dreaded monster of stagflation was a highly evident fact. With the economy in shambles and violent terrorism largely subdued at the cost of nearly 30,000 killed, agitation for elections rose.

There was little surprise when General Leopoldo Fortunato Galtieri (b. 1926), an excellent horseman with an antiquated cavalry orientation, replaced the ailing Viola as president in November 1981, as Viola had proven to be little more than a male military equivalent of the ill-fated Isabelita Perón. The installation of Roberto Alemán as economic czar signaled a return to monetarist orthodoxy complete with currency devaluations, a two-tiered exchange rate, and heavier use of interest rates as an instrument of fiscal policy. Retaining command of the army in his own hands, Galtieri, an Argentine General George S. Patton Jr. (down to the britches, riding boots, and twin pistols) with something of a Douglas MacArthur complex, initiated an attack upon the Falkland—to Argentina the Malvinas—Islands in April 1982. The military hoped to rally patriotic sentiment while distracting attention from social and economic woes that had sparked a mass antigovernment labor rally in Buenos Aires. In this aim they failed abjectly, as, after sustaining a humiliating defeat, they surrendered to the British on June 14. (Galtieri's battle plan was about as brilliant as that of politically ambitious George Armstrong Custer 106 years earlier for a glorious victory over the Sioux and Cheyenne at Little Big Horn.)

At least Galtieri escaped with his life, but he was immediately replaced as army commander-in-chief by General Cristiano Nicolaides, and two and a half weeks later, General Reynaldo Bignone assumed the presidency as a temporary space filler with the task of negotiating the armed forces' withdrawal from power on the least demoralizing conditions possible.[46] With the economy in a shambles, as GDP shrank by another 5.1 percent in 1982, inflation rose to 165 percent, and foreign exchange reserves dropped to $3.2 billion, Domingo Cavallo, a young critic of the policies followed since 1976, became president of the Central Bank, hoping to do something about the ravages financial speculation had been causing. (In the early 1990s he would be the architect of Argentina's most successful economic plan, ironically, under a Peronist president.) In his short tenure as Argentina's central banker, he pushed through a drastic financial reform, liquidating two-fifths of the private sector's debt in only six months. Clearly, in 1983 Argentina had a very deep hole to climb out of politically. Since 1930 this once-thriving democracy had had twenty-four presidents, sixteen of them generals, and had experienced twenty-six successful coups plus at least an equal number of serious conspiratorial attempts at seizing power by force. Only two elected presidents—Generals Justo and Perón—had served out full terms during this span of over half a century. Economically the pit was equally deep, with per capita GDP having shrunk by 15 percent during the last three years of military rule; a huge explosion of foreign debt, up by nearly $40 billion during the seven years of military rule; and inflation running at 400 percent a year—all of which had resulted in a massive wave of capital flight.[47]

The crucial October 3, 1983, elections brought the Radical Party back to power behind Raúl Ricardo Alfonsín Foulkes (b. 1927). This military academy graduate, former congressman, and unsuccessful aspirant for his party's nomination for the 1973 presidential election received 7.66 million votes, 52 percent of the national total, carrying the more developed provinces, including the Federal Capital District (where he garnered 1.28 million votes), Buenos Aires (which gave him 2.85 million votes), Córdoba, and Mendoza. The Peronists, under their legal name of the Justicialist Party (PJ), ran a faltering and lackluster campaign behind a stodgy candidate, Italo Luder, an international law professor who had briefly occupied the presidency during Isabel Perón's 1975 forced leave of absence. They polled just over 40 percent—some 5.94 million votes—of which 2.34 million came from Buenos Aires and 550,000 from the Federal Capital District.[48] Yet the Peronists won control of a dozen of the country's nineteen provinces along with an advantage of twenty-one to eighteen in the senate, where seven independents held the balance of power as a result of selection by provincial legislatures, where the Peronists were still strong, and the overrepresentation of small provinces (as in Brazil and Mexico and, for that matter, the United States). In the lower house the UCR came away with a slim majority with 129 of 254 seats compared to 111 for the Peronists. This was the first time since the movement's founding in the mid-1940s that the Peronists had lost a major national election in which they were allowed to participate. Argentines between eighteen and twenty-seven were voting for a president for the first time and those between

twenty-eight and thirty-six for just the second time. The PJ's poor electoral performance undercut party head Lorenzo Miguel's prestige, and a struggle for party control
ensued between the renewal and orthodox factions. At this nadir of leadership, labor
leader Saul Ubaldini attempted to make the CGT the chief pole of opposition to the
Alfonsín government, launching a campaign of strikes and demonstrations that had
little lasting effect, but were almost inevitable given labor's regained sense of empowerment following its ineffectiveness under the post-1976 military regime.

Alfonsín was the favored heir of the UCR's grand old man, Ricardo Balbín, who
had finally passed away in late 1981. Insisting that democracy had to take priority
over economic recovery, Alfonsín forced more than half the country's generals and
admirals into retirement and slashed the armed forces' budget. To balance pressures
from the military and human rights advocates, he started legal action against both the
members of the first three post-1976 juntas and seven left-wing terrorist leaders from
the dirty-war period. Although strikes were frequent, he needed to be more concerned about the sensitivities of the military, apparent when the presidential commission looking into the dirty war issued its report in July 1984. His greatest handicaps
were the nearly insolvent economic situation he inherited from the military regime
and the highly unrealistic public expectations that a return to democratic civilian rule
would in and of itself resolve socioeconomic problems that were the result of bad
policies and poor administration by evil and incompetent men—when in reality they
had deep structural roots.[49]

Reinstalling orthodox liberal Roberto Alemán (who had served under both Frondizi and Galtieri) as economics minister, Alfonsín's government ultimately proved unsuccessful in its efforts to launch the country along the road to sustained economic
growth. The hole was just too deep as Alfonsín had inherited a country in the fourth
year of a deep recession, with a fiscal deficit of 15 percent of GDP and an external
debt nearing $50 billion, requiring 70 percent of the country's export earnings for its
servicing—with foreign exchange reserves down to a worse-than-crisis level of $102
million. Unlike in Brazil and even fiscally troubled Mexico, massive loans had not
been contracted to acquire capital goods or improve productivity. Instead, huge
amounts had been spent on importing luxury items or had left the country through
capital flight. Alfonsín refused to give priority to paying off debts run up by the "illegitimate" military regime, and by 1985 the struggle to restore any substantial degree
of order to the economy had failed. Modest GDP expansion of 2.8 percent for 1983
and 2.6 percent in 1984 turned into shrinkage of 4.7 percent during 1985 before recovering in 1986 to 5.4 percent, then sagging to 1.4 percent for 1987. Foreign trade
stagnated, with 1985 the best year, as a trade surplus was generated on exports of $8.4
billion and imports were held to $3.9 billion. This healthy surplus was halved the fol-
lowing year as exports shrank and imports grew, a negative trend that continued
through 1987, when foreign sales of $6.2 billion and purchasing abroad reaching $5.6
billion cut the surplus to under $600 million.

Harvard-educated Juan Sourroulle had replaced Bernardo Grinspun as economics
minister in February 1985, when Argentina failed to comply with the terms of its
September 1984 agreement with the IMF. Sourroulle launched the Austral Plan four
months later. Based upon a heterodox shock involving deindexing prices, a new currency anchored on fixed parity with the dollar, and temporary wage and price controls, this plan's aim was to eliminate the "inertial" effects of past inflation. Government

deficits were cut by reducing spending and increasing taxes, and the economy was to be opened by lowering tariffs and attracting foreign investment.[50] Although the year's inflation was 383 percent, that for the six months the plan was in effect dropped to 20 percent and down to 3 percent a month by year's end—raising visions of possible long-term success. In a move beneficial to the government budget, Alfonsín curbed the autonomy of the Fabricaciones Militares, the heart of the sprawling military-run industrial complex that had come to produce many civilian products as well as military hardware. The Peronist-controlled senate stymied a law instituting government monitoring of union elections.

This early success for the plan allowed the reunited Radical Party (UCR) to triumph over the Peronists by a 43-percent to 35-percent margin in the November 1985 congressional elections. (This victory probably influenced José Sarney's decision to use his analogous economic plan as the horse to ride to victory in Brazil the next year.) Then, in April 1986, administered prices and a "crawling peg" system of frequent minidevaluations of the currency (rather than often traumatic occasional large adjustments) were phased in. As the budget deficit rose and the trade balance declined, inflation by the third quarter climbed back to 8 percent a month, totaling 87 percent for the year. On the positive side, an expansion in industry by 26 percent between October 1985 and September 1986 lifted GDP by 11 percent. Further midcourse corrections in the plan were made in February 1987, allowing a new agreement to be reached with the IMF. However, as had become a pernicious habit in Argentina, dramatic short-term gains from a new economic plan were mistaken for fundamental corrections, so were not followed up by needed, but politically unpopular, reforms. A December 1986 law set a deadline for filing human rights violation cases, and the June 1987 "Due Obedience Law" relieved military officers of responsibility if they had been following orders. The regular services made no trouble, but Alfonsín never managed to establish effective control over the intelligence organizations.[51] (After serving their purpose of mollifying currently serving and recently retired officers still in a position to make trouble, these laws benefiting human rights violators were subsequently annulled along with the 1990 pardon of the chief dirty-war generals, and 500 ex-officers were charged.)

Congressional and governorship elections took place in September 1987 in an economic climate marked by growth that had slowed to a crawl, inflation that had risen to an annual rate of 180 percent, and foreign debt that had burgeoned to a staggering $57 billion—some 80 percent of GDP—up over $7 billion in a single year after holding steady during 1984–1986. These dismal economic factors impinged heavily upon the electoral outcome. In a stunning reversal from two years earlier the Peronists elected nineteen of twenty-two governors along with a 41- to 37-percent edge in the congressional races. This outcome coincided with a change in control of the PJ as the orthodox wing, which had been holding on by its fingertips, gave way to the renewal faction, now led by Antonio Cafiero, who combined the party presidency with his newly won governorship of Buenos Aires. By mid-1988 inflation was out of control at over 25 percent a month, leading to the Spring Plan in August, nonviable in the preelectoral atmosphere—since any economic plan requires governmental credibility to succeed. With the presidential campaign in full swing, inflation exploded to 80 percent in March 1989 (on its way to 200 percent in July) while the austral sank like a stone from seventeen to the dollar to over two hundred between

February and June. Hence it was no surprise when the May 14, 1989, presidential elections saw Peronist Carlos Saul Menem (b. 1930) garner 47 percent of the vote to only 37 percent for the UCR's Eduardo Angeloz. Peronists came away with half the chamber seats, compared to a third for the radicals. In clear recognition of the need to move forward, Alfonsín agreed to leave office six months early.[52] (This election just preceded an analogous one in Brazil, putting an end to the unprecedentedly harmonious relationship between presidents Alfonsín and Sarney.)

Peronism, back in power owing to the failure of the Radical Party administration to manage the economy adequately, was highly rejuvenated by Menem, a demagogic maverick from the interior who had forced the issue of Peronism's first primary as a way to even the playing field with the entrenched party bosses who would have dominated a convention. Then, in July 1988, he upset party insider Cafiero, Buenos Aires governor, with 53 percent of the 1.7 million ballots cast by the party faithful. Now the exuberant Menem was out to prove himself a worthy successor to the charismatic *caudillo* who had inspired him in his youth. His inauguration marked a series of democratic milestones: It was the first time in sixty-one years that one freely elected president had handed over power to another; the first time since 1951 that there had been two constitutional presidential elections in a row; and only the second time that an election had changed the governing party.

Menem's parents had arrived in Argentina in 1912 from Syria, with the future president born nearly two decades later, after the family had prospered in the wine business. A recent law school graduate when Perón was overthrown in 1955, he was elected governor of La Rioja in 1973, being arrested three years later in the wake of Perón's demise, and spending five years in prison under the military regime. With democratization he had returned to the La Rioja governorship in 1985 and had established a good working relationship with President Alfonsín. Quite consciously, he had decided that showmanship was a key element of electoral success in the new Argentina and had developed a flamboyant style, often viewed as over the top by foreign observers, but going over very well with the Argentine populace. Much attention was given to very public attacks by his equally vain wife, who was upset by being dumped soon after becoming Argentina's first lady, and by financial scandals involving her family, but these things did Menem little political harm.

Breaking with the practice of issuing mere stabilization plans, Menem intended to restructure as well as revitalize the economy. By the end of 1989 the congress had given him the necessary tools in the form of the Law for the Reform of the State and the Law Regarding Economic Emergency. Utilizing these special powers, Menem began a sweeping program of privatization of government-owned and mixed-capital enterprises, including utilities; suspension and elimination of direct and indirect subsidies to the private sector; and a badly needed reorganization of the financial sector. In the face of hyperinflation he stayed the course instead of abandoning his program, realizing that, in light of the grim economic and fiscal inheritance from the Alfonsín government, it had not had anywhere near enough time to show positive results. Indeed, when he had come to office, inflation was raging out of control at 200 percent monthly. Privatization, downsizing of the bureaucracy, elimination of red tape through deregulation, and improvement of tax collection were pushed as Menem's sweeping free-market reforms constituted a sharp break with the "nationalist, statist, and populist import-substitution model that had prevailed in one form or another, for most of the preceding half-century."[53] As this half century had included Perón's governments, Menem demonstrated determination not to be a prisoner of the past. Much as had become prevalent in Brazil, Menem had frequent recourse to executive decrees, legally binding until repealed by the congress or declared unconstitutional by the courts. Indeed, by the end of 1993, he had issued 308 such measures—ten times as many as in Argentina's prior life as a nation. (This constructive record was compiled by Menem at the time Brazil was struggling through the Fernando Collor fiasco and coping under the caretaker government of Itamar Franco. Since Mexico was in the throes of the controversially elected Carlos Salinas administration and Alberto Fujimori was still largely an unknown quantity while Chile was still early in its return to democracy and Venezuela in sharp decline, Menem was the unrivaled star in the Latin American political firmament.)

On the labor side, as with the Labour Party's Tony Blair in Britain, this Peronist did not favor the country's workers, neither strengthening the unions nor giving labor the type of influence they desired in the party and the government. His reforms, although taming inflation and renewing economic growth, also led to a quantum increase in unemployment. In pursuit of the goals of state solvency and market efficiency, Menem pursued his trademark program of privatization of state enterprises, chiefly in the fields of energy and communications, netting $24 billion by 1994 by selling these businesses off outright or converting them into joint ventures. Unfortunately for the longer run, most of this financial windfall was used to cover the federal government's budget deficits rather than being invested in increasing production or used to pay down the country's mounting foreign debt. The human costs involved the jobs of one-third of the nearly 250,000 individuals employed in public enterprises. Moreover, direct government employment was reduced from just over 2 million to 1.8 million by the laying off of 217,000 public employees, evenly divided between the federal payroll and those of the provinces and municipalities. Subsidies to the private sector were slashed from $7.9 billion in 1989 to $4.4 billion for 1992. With central government tax collections raised from $13.7 billion to $24.4 billion by 1992, small fiscal surpluses in the early 1990s replaced deficits that had averaged over 12 percent of GDP at the transition from military rule and 5 percent under Alfonsín.

Argentina had not yet found a developmental model to replace that of primary product exports combined with import-substitution industrialization that had perished with the 1970s. Essentially Menem was following a neoliberal market-oriented approach in keeping with the precepts of the "Washington Consensus," the fashionable economic formula for the period following the traumatic debt crisis. He and his successors would have to cope with an ingrained propensity of Argentines to be extremely impatient with economic programs, demanding immediate short-run results rather than understanding the need for long-term investments. A further complicating factor was a pervasive tendency to look at the situation as one in which one sector's gains inevitably came at the expense of other sectors, hence attentive to perceived threats to a delicate equilibrium of social forces. With Peronism traditionally having one leg firmly planted in the unions, but the other resting with the urban poor, policies benefiting its increasingly important rural constituencies were often not well received, and those aimed at the middle class were viewed with suspicion.

In late 1990 a group of eight self-styled renovationist congressmen split with the PJ over Menem's decision to pardon ex-presidents Videla and Viola as well as ranking officers of their governments who had been convicted of human rights violations. At the same time, with some elements of the military restive over punishments for human rights violations during the dirty war and the closing down of a military career as a road to political advancement—as it had been when they had chosen to become officers—some sort of coup attempt was overdue in a country where even the Alfonsín government had had to deal with multiple conspiracies.[54] Indeed, as early as April 15, 1987, under Alfonsín's rather relaxed rule there had been a junior officer uprising behind Lieutenant Colonel Aldo Rico protesting alleged offenses to the armed forces as an institution in the form of "unjust" trials for human rights violations. The mutineers seized control of the infantry school at the Campo de Mayo almost bordering on the presidential palace. Riding a wave of massive support from political parties and civic organizations, Alfonsín dramatically went to the school by helicopter to demand the mutineers' surrender. Only the leader was arrested, while the 150 others received only light wrist slaps.

This lack of forceful response apparently set a bad precedent, as Rico escaped in January 1988 and barricaded himself and his supporters at the Monte Caseros base. At the same time, retired air force officers seized the Buenos Aires airport. When the protest fizzled out in a few days, 282 were arrested, but only 20 brought to trial. Such kid glove treatment resulted in December in mutinous behavior by 400 at the infantry school—from which the armed forces got a pay raise, a bonus, and a new army chief of staff. Then, under the Menem government, on November 23, 1989, a leftist attack on the La Tablada regiment was designed to forestall a supposed coup attempt by the romanticized Carapintadas, camouflage face-painted elite troops, although this may have been a provocation by military intelligence. On December 3, 1990, some 500 officers associated with paratrooper leader Colonel Mohamed Ali Seindelin rose up, this time only a block from the presidential palace, being put down by forces loyal to the government after thirteen deaths and hundreds of injuries. Menem gained public approval for his vigorous response to this challenge and the subsequent life prison term given to the coup leader. The government effectively portrayed these rebels, who strove to picture themselves as fed-up patriots, as ambitious and self-serving militarists.

Relief from high inflation rates and lack of economic growth came after the April 1991 installation of the able and innovative Domingo Cavallo as economy minister. With Menem's firm backing he implemented an economic plan bearing his name, which dollarized the Argentine economy by making local currency and the US dollar equal and alternative with full convertibility. Made possible by an $8-billion trade surplus in the recession year of 1990, this bold move brought inflation down sharply from an annual rate of over 1,800 percent in 1990 to only 4 percent in 1994, viewed by a thankful public as a near miracle, while GDP growth averaged 8 percent a year for the first four years of the plan—the highest for any four-year period in the twentieth century. Yet, while productivity in the manufacturing sector rose one-third between 1991 and 1994, real wages dropped by 13 percent. Moreover, many of the workers left unemployed by the closing of inefficient firms that had shown a profit only with tariff protection, if not subsidies, did not find jobs with new higher-tech enterprises. With very serious implications for the future, the extreme exchange rate inflexibility established by the Convertibility Law of 1991 led to overvaluation of the peso, seriously compromising the ability of Argentine exports to remain competitive in international markets. Now unable to use monetary policy or the exchange rate as macroeconomic instruments, Argentine governments were forced to overrely on fiscal adjustments. Events would prove that getting out of dollarization was much more difficult, especially in political terms, than entering had been. For, long terrorized by the specter of hyperinflation, the Argentine middle class valued price stability over policies that would keep the economy in better balance over time. Hence, convertibility became politically untouchable and would be maintained for almost a decade—well into a period in which fiscal flexibility and autonomy in monetary policy would have stood the country in better stead.

Menem's economic policies paid spectacular short- and medium-range political dividends that carried him to a tenure in office second only to that of Perón himself. September 1991 midterm elections were a tremendous Peronist victory that could be interpreted only as a mandate for Menem. Eduardo Duhalde, his former vice president, was elected governor of Buenos Aires Province, leaving the opposition with victories only in the Federal Capital District (the city of Buenos Aires), Córdoba, and one interior province. Menem and Alfonsín signed a 1993 pact for elimination of the ban on presidential reelection as part of a broader reform of the constitution, jointly gaining 211 out of 305 seats in the resulting constituent assembly, which duly approved the change.[55] A coalition of leftist splinter parties, under the imposing name of the Grand Front (Frente Grande), received only 4 percent of the vote in the October 1993 congressional elections. In the congress this grouping gained the adhesion of Radical Party (UCR) elements alienated by what they considered Alfonsín's unprincipled deal with Menem. Disgruntled UCR voters helped quadruple the front's performance in the April 1994 constituent assembly elections to 12.7 percent, even carrying the federal capital. At the same time the Peronists still garnered 37.7 percent of the national vote (a modest dip from 42.3 percent in the previous year's balloting), and the UCR dropped sharply to not quite 20 percent from over 30 percent in the constituent assembly elections.

Dissident Peronist senator José Octávio Bordón, leader of the 1990 defection from the PJ, folded his recently formed Open Politics for Social Integrity movement, with its acronym PAIS ("fatherland"), into a coalition with the Grand Front and splinter opposition parties called FREPASO, the Fatherland Solidarity Front. This group's hopes to exploit scandals and illicit dealings by family members in the upcoming presidential election proved to be wishful thinking. Although encountering significant support in Buenos Aires city, which it carried in the late 1993 balloting, the new political grouping failed to make headway against the established parties in the rest of the country. For to a greater extent than in Brazil,

> the transition to democracy in 1983 did not involve the creation of competitive and open politics in many provinces. Indeed, at the provincial level, continuity was more frequent than change and members of the families that had controlled provincial politics for much of the 20th century were returned to power in many provinces. . . . Provincial elites play a preeminent role in national politics in Argentina: they sustain national government by providing congressional support and electoral votes, but at the same time are sustained by national governments through the transfer of federal resources and their non-involvement in provincial affairs.[56]

Eerily reminiscent of Brazil's "politics of the governors" in the late nineteenth and early twentieth centuries, this fundamental feature of Argentine political life is strikingly exemplified in San Luis, where the Rodríguez Saá clan, affiliated since the 1970s with Peronism, continued a hegemony dating back to the Roca era in the late 1880s. Current party boss Adolfo Rodríguez Saá (namesake of the family patriarch who dominated the province in the years leading up to World War I) began his career in the provincial legislature during Perón's 1973 return to the presidency, becoming governor with the restoration of democracy in 1983. Reelected in 1987, 1991, 1995, and 1999, he then moved to the national scene as a federal deputy in 2003. Two years later he became a senator, assuming a seat held since 1985 by his brother, who had replaced him as governor in 2003 and would be reelected in 2007. Moreover, Adolfo's record nineteen-year tenure as governor had ended in 2001 through his selection by congress as the country's president. Despite the fiasco of his very brief stint as the country's chief executive, by 2003 he received 87.4 percent of the vote for a seat in congress while his brother polled 90.1 percent for governor. In fact, by 2007 the Rodríguez Saá machine withstood efforts to undercut it by President Néstor Kirchner, again garnering over 80 percent of the vote.[57]

This persistence and tenacity of old-style machine politics is possible because control of the state allows provincial leaders to develop clientelistic networks dependent upon subsidies, job programs, or handouts from the provincial government. Politics remains highly personalized, so political loyalties are also based on direct personal ties as much as upon personalities, thus maintaining the elite's electoral base. Very rationally,

> governors seek to maintain the political game in their provinces closed and insulated from national politics in order to strengthen control of their geographical domain. . . . This is possible because governors have a great deal of political, and to a lesser extent, financial autonomy; they also tend to control the provincial branch of their party if it is a national party and the design of electoral lists; hence they also control the national legislators that belong to their party. And they usually have loyal voters. This means that governors can deliver important numbers of votes in presidential elections.[58]

In the May 1995 presidential balloting, the first for reelection of an incumbent since the Perón election in 1951, Menem, riding a wave of public approval for having tamed hyperinflation, received 49.5 percent of the vote, along with 137 of 257 chamber seats, in swamping FREPASO's Bordón, recipient of a respectable 29.6 percent, and the UCR standard-bearer, lost in the dust at 17 percent. This was the first time that a radical nominee finished worse than runner-up in a fair presidential election. On the congressional side the Peronists rebounded to 43 percent compared to the UCR's 21.8 percent and FREPASO's 21.2 percent. Yet signs that things might not go as well during Menem's second term were already evident on the economic front, as fears that the peso/dollar parity could not be maintained combined with fallout from the Mexican crisis (the Tequilla effect) had led in early 1995 to a loss of nearly 19 percent in bank deposits, an alarming $8.5 billion. For given their long tradition of intense pressure for favors and protection from the government, Argentine economic agents were inclined to seek the quick profits of currency speculation—even if this speculation had very negative effects on the national economy. (At this juncture

Brazil appeared to have found the highly elusive economic promised land as Fernando Henrique Cardoso's Real Plan had carried him to the presidency in late 1994. In Mexico the governing party renewed its control of the government by electing Ernest Zedillo to the presidency by a comfortable margin in mid-1994, but he inherited a grim economic situation leading to a sharp contraction of the economy during his first year in office.)

By the 1995 elections the positive features of the recent reform of the 1853 Constitution were in effect. The right to reelection was balanced with a reduction of presidential terms to four years, as was the case in Brazil when the constitutional obstacle to Cardoso's reelection was removed. Popular election of senators for six-year terms replaced the outdated practice of selection by provincial legislatures for nine-year terms. To avoid the possibility of minority presidents, a plague of the Andean countries, a runoff provision was included if the front-runner did not receive 40 percent of the vote or win by 10 percent over his nearest rival. Menem reshaped the party as well as its relationship to the labor movement. In his first term he "bypassed the party in filling government posts and in picking candidates for elected offices, gave party leaders little input into government policy, and increased the isolation of the national party leadership from party members and from provincial party organizations."[59] Menem continued by capturing the national party leadership he had been ignoring, taking advantage of their weak ties to the membership, unions, and provincial party leaders. In a blow to his political near hegemony, in June 1997 in the first-ever election of a Federal Capital District (Buenos Aires) mayor, Radical Party (UCR) senator Fernando de la Rúa (b. 1937) garnered 40 percent of the vote to 27 percent for the FREPASO candidate and not quite 18 percent for the Peronist hopeful, the appointed incumbent. For by this time lavish patronage spending and revenue sharing with the provinces needed to be cut back in the face of mounting budget deficits—triggering Cavallo's resignation and subsequent airing of dirty linen. Indeed, Argentina had entered a recession just as Menem had won his second term in 1995, and net capital inflows no longer easily covered current accounts deficits, thus allowing for accumulation of foreign exchange reserves—a warning of possible troubles ahead. For a foreign debt that had been a high $45 billion at the end of the military regime and had doubled by 1994 hit $129 billion in 1997—on its way to $148 billion by 1999.

The June 1997 electoral reality check was confirmed shortly thereafter as the two opposition parties allied before the partial congressional elections and obtained 61 seats on nearly 46 percent of the vote to 75 on 36 percent of the ballots for Menem's PJ—down from 43 percent of the vote in 1995. This outcome dropped the Peronists to 119 seats from the 131 they had held and raised the opposition alliance to 106 seats. Winning by a margin of over three to one in the capital and comfortably in Buenos Aires province, the opposition alliance poised for a strong run at the presidency in 1999. But first Argentina would slide into a deeper recession in 1998, with the perplexing result that just as more and more economists turned against convertibility, the Argentine public became increasingly in favor of keeping the dollar/peso peg perceived by them as their only protection in a highly volatile economic situation. Desiring a third term at any price, Menem opted to go where the votes were and maintain convertibility—which assured people that they could at any time change their holdings and accounts on a par basis into good, rock-solid US greenbacks. In making this fateful decision, the president set the stage for allowing his political ambitions to undo his very positive economic accomplishments. Menem's single-minded mission for reelection unleashed a spending race between the federal government and leading Peronist governors determined to thwart his unconstitutional gambit—with fiscal prudence thrown to the winds. Other victims of the no-holds-barred struggle were badly needed tax reform, liberalization of labor markets, and revamping of the revenue-sharing system between the central government and the provinces. In the spending orgy Argentina's already troublesome debt burden burgeoned.

Duhalde (b. 1939), Menem's chief rival within Peronist ranks, had blocked the president's efforts to move toward a constitutionally highly questionable third term, so he received no help from a frustrated Menem when running against the radicals' de la Rúa, who had edged out Graciela Fernández to become the FREPASO-UCR alliance nominee. Thus, Argentina went to the polls on October 24, 1999, with a clear choice to make. Since over three-quarters of the record 24 million registered voters participated, they assumed in the process a share of responsibility for the winner's subsequent performance. The UCR, eager to return to power after eleven years of Menem and Peronism, won handily with 48.5 percent of the vote for de la Rúa to 38.1 percent for Peronism's Duhalde (as ex-economics czar Cavallo and his "Action for the People" trailed with a 10 percent share).[60] In the congressional voting for half of the lower house, the UCR-FREPASO alliance came away with 63 deputies to reach 127 chamber seats compared to the Peronists' 50 deputies-elect (giving them only 101 including holdovers), and 17 for minor parties (which had 12 carried over). Hence the results were a continuation of a trend that saw Peronism under Menem peaking in 1995–1996—exactly when the Cavallo Plan ran out of steam. Indeed, Menem's legacy included a foreign debt that in gross terms had exploded to $170 billion and an unmanageable fiscal deficit. The new president's problems would start almost immediately after he took office and overwhelm him barely halfway into his term, as Argentina sank into malaise morphing into a grave crisis. (By this point, riding on economic stability, Cardoso had won reelection in late-1998 and Zedillo was guiding Mexico to the first mass-participation, free, and competitive election in its history.)

Crisis, Recovery,
and the Kirchners, 2000 to 2010

The new century started disastrously for Argentina. Indeed, de la Rúa soon had ample reason to rue his apparent good fortune in having won the 1999 presidential election, as the April 2000 congressional revision of the employment law—removing safeguards and benefits the workers had enjoyed since Perón's time—led to strikes and disturbances. This social unrest was aggravated in October when the vice president, drawn from the ranks of FREPASO, resigned in protest over the president's refusal to break with radical politicians accused of having bribed senators to make the labor law more flexible. The result was a situation the president publicly recognized as "a veritable catastrophe." Unfortunately, he was only one of the country's political leaders who had invested a risky amount of his political capital in the panacea of convertibility. Moreover, the ready availability of dollars had addicted consumers to foreign goods. Should events shake their blind faith in the dollar as an absolute guarantee of stability, the result could be not just trauma, but full-blown panic.

The Argentine economic crisis that had begun as a mild recession in 1998 deepened by 2002 into the worst crisis in the country's history (comparable only to that of 1930, which combined the impact of the world depression with the overthrow of the Yrigoyen government), one that was tearing the social fabric apart and producing political chaos. The nation's per capita GDP, highest of major countries in the region at roughly $11,000 in terms of purchasing-price parity, declined precipitously, as GDP dropped to near its 1993 level and unemployment soared well above 20 percent. Admitting defeat in dealing with the situation, the apparently highly qualified government defaulted on the country's massive foreign debt of about $155 billion before it devastated savings and investment by making a hollow mockery out of currency convertibility as local money lost three-quarters of its value relative to the dollar. As one informed observer portrayed the political impact of what was generally considered "collapse" of the Argentine economy:

> The toll on politics has been no less dramatic: between October 2000 and August 2002, there were five cabinet crises, two presidential resignations, one Senate crisis, and five ministers of the economy. The streets in downtown Buenos Aires are now full of abandoned retail stores and angry protesters. ¡Que se vayan todos! (Kick everyone out!) reads the omni-present graffiti. [61]

Argentines wondered how it could be that a mere decade since their country had apparently saved itself from hyperinflation and despair by pegging its currency to the dollar, and despite tens and tens of billions of dollars in loans from the IMF—accompanied by fulsome praise of the country's economic management from the international financial community—they had wound up in an unimaginable disaster. The public was understandably perplexed because for the first time in many of their lifetimes Argentina had seemingly got its politics and economy in order during Menem's decade-long administration. Some of the most extensive market reforms in the world had been initiated, civilian control over the military had been consolidated, and stronger instruments of governmental accountability had been instituted. The historically bitterly hostile major parties had even negotiated an unprecedented pact to reform the constitution in 1994, and the stable democracy previewed in the halcyon days of 1916–1930 appeared to have arrived. Indeed, in early 2000 a Harvard political scientist heralded "The 'Normalization' of Argentine Politics."[62]

The era of twenty-four presidents in twenty-eight years (1930–1958) that had followed the collapse of the early-twentieth-century democratic experience were almost universally held to be part of the country's past—alongside the repressive military rule preceding 1983's reestablishment of democracy. Moreover, important macroeconomic indicators were positive in 2001, including a trade surplus of $7.5 billion (compared to a deficit of $3.1 billion in 1998) that cut the current accounts deficit from $11.9 billion to under $4.6 billion. What most Argentines had overlooked was that by the end of 2000 a foreign debt nearing $150 billion equaled 51.4 percent of GDP, and the $25.5 billion required for debt service used up 71.3 percent of export earnings. As Argentina started down the slippery slope to insolvency, the IMF increased its support, supplying a loan of $13.7 billion at the end of 2000 and arranging $26 billion in financing from other sources—asking in return for pension reform and curbs on fiscal transfers to the provincial governments—paralleling steps recently taken in Brazil. The IMF's largesse was further tied to the Argentine government's maintaining a stringent monetary policy and further tightening fiscal policies.

Bringing Cavallo back once more as economics minister, the de la Rúa administration pursued deficit reduction, considered by the IMF crucial for macroeconomic stability. Cuts of $1.6 billion (about 3 percent of the federal budget) were announced in early July, on the eve of a major government bond offering, and with the presidency undergoing angioplasty. Instead of reassuring investors, shaken by Cavallo's proposal to replace the dollar as currency peg by a mixed basket of stable currencies, this further austerity move was interpreted as a sign that the crisis was deepening. Hence bonds could be sold only at 14 percent interest, 50 percent higher than the preceding month. After the IMF came up with an additional $8 billion in August, near year's end the government announced additional drastic budget cuts totaling $9.2 billion, nearly 18 percent of approved expenditures.[63]

Not surprisingly the electorate was upset, cutting the progovernment vote nearly in half from late 1999 as congressional elections in mid-October (for 130 of 251 chamber seats and 72 seats in the senate) gave the Peronists 65 lower-house seats and 40 in the upper house to 35 and 25 for the governing UCR and its allies—resulting in a strong plurality in the chamber and a majority in the upper house, with FREPASO and a small party each having seventeen seats, mostly carryovers. Spoiled and blank ballots reached historic highs, especially in Buenos Aires, which contained two-fifths of the country's electorate. The election did not change the fact that to maintain its highly overvalued currency, Argentina required large dollar reserves, as anyone at any time was entitled to exchange each peso for a dollar. Only the huge IMF loans made a continuation of this policy possible—at the cost of increasing foreign debt to an unpayable level—at least in political terms, if technically possible in strictly economic ones. Public and private foreign debt reached $146 billion in 2001, with reserves halved (from $35 billion to only $18 billion). The extremely high ratio of debt to export earnings came at a time when the GDP shrank by an additional 11 percent. At the end of the year Argentina defaulted on debt service, seeking to force creditors to settle for as little as twenty-five cents on the dollar—something the creditors stubbornly resisted (later insisting that the economically recovering country, having escaped disaster, could afford a far less deep discount on renegotiated debt). Massive bank runs resulted in a breakdown of convertibility only partially contained by Cavallo's imposition of strict limits on withdrawals and currency movements, leading the IMF to withhold a scheduled $1.26-billion disbursement.

With the middle class badly hurt and the informal (off-the-books) economy starved almost out of existence, rampant unrest featuring widespread looting and twenty-seven deaths forced de la Rúa to resign on December 20, an action leading to the temporary elevation to the presidency of the senate's Adolfo Rodríguez Saá, a Peronist, as word that Argentina's rich had spirited $20 billion out of the country led to renewed rioting. Following Rodríguez Saá's resignation after only ten days in office, the presidency passed to chamber presiding officer Eduardo Camaño. As soon as the New Year's holiday was over, the nation found itself in the paradoxical situation of the man who had lost the election only two years earlier being invited to assume the presidency. Duhalde soon found that he had made a bad deal in return for not much more than a footnote in history, as he was unable to mobilize congressional or public support for his emergency measures. Yet this grave political crisis, like Collor's removal from office in Brazil a decade earlier, was handled constitutionally with the congress playing the central role and the military remaining a highly interested, but sideline observer. Three days later currency parity was ended—and the value of the peso dropped precipitously by over 70 percent. Unemployment soon exceeded 25 percent, and half of all Argentines found themselves below the poverty line— compared to 22 percent in 1994.

The supreme court contributed to the growing sense of panic by throwing a monkey wrench into the executive's plans by declaring that the freezing (*corralito*, "penning up") of bank accounts was unconstitutional and trying to overturn the government's enactment of a six-month ban on legal challenges to limits on bank withdrawals. In late April Cavallo, his aura of invincibility shredded, resigned in the face of IMF intransigence and lack of support for plans to exchange frozen accounts for government bonds. Roberto Lavagne became Argentina's sixth economic minister in a year (a dramatic contrast with Pedro Malan's eight-year stint in Brazil). Buffeted by political ill winds from all directions, Duhalde called presidential elections for late March 2003—following the precedent of Alfonsín in 1988 by cutting six months off his already truncated term. In November, fed up with IMF insistence on policy changes before providing further help, the government failed to make a payment due to that international body, holding that the IMF had failed to support Argentina's efforts to renegotiate $55 billion owed to private foreign investors. At the same time, the year's inflation was held to 40 percent, an outcome confounding critics and observers who had predicted runaway hyperinflation. Indeed, the country's economic recovery was already under way. The problem was that nobody believed it as dismayed pessimism had morphed into desperate depression.[64]

Presidential succession split Duhalde's Peronists three ways. Ex-president Menem led the April 27, 2003, balloting with 24.3 percent, followed closely by Néstor Carlos Kirchner (b. 1950), who had just finished twelve years as governor of a Patagonian province. Former economics minister Roberto López Murphy finished in the money with 16.4 percent, to 14.1 percent for both anticorruption crusader Eliza Carrió and the third Peronist, Rodríguez Saá—who had briefly held down the presidency in December 2001. With public opinion polls showing 60 percent support for Kirchner—Peronism's new face—Menem avoided an embarrassing defeat by conceding the runoff, allowing Kirchner to take office in late May 2003. On the positive side, the voting turnout had been nearly 80 percent, and blank and spoiled ballots had dropped 25 percent—a clear indication that individuals alienated from the political process in 2001 had opted to play a constructive role in avoiding further political decay.

After six consecutive years of decline, the battered Argentine economy grew by 8.7 percent in 2003. Of course this instant growth further increased the popularity of the new president as he exploited the fact that Peronism was a "loose and heterogeneous confederation of provincial party bosses" to reestablish presidential leadership to where it had been in Menem's salad days.[65] Indeed, with a term running well into

2007 and reelection allowed, Kirchner was aware that, should Lula fail to gain reelection in Brazil in 2006, he could well emerge as the dean of Latin American presidents. Meanwhile, this resourceful and ambitious leader burnished his nationalist reputation and began to reverse Menem's sweeping nationalizations. But Argentina's recovery faced a setback in March 2004 in the form of a severe energy shortage. Although drought was a contributing factor, the main culprit was lack of investment in production and distribution following the utility privatizations of the Menem era—despite contractual obligations by the purchasers to invest. Owners of the large utility companies blamed their inaction on a court-imposed freeze on rates and the sharp devaluation of the peso, combining with inflation to yield low rates and leading to revenues falling behind costs. Overwhelmingly the public accused the utility companies (many foreign-owned) of inflating costs and hiding revenue in order to cover the profits they withdrew and remitted.

Bolstered by over 8 percent economic growth again in 2004, Kirchner's government took a firm stand on sharply reducing foreign debt through a program of exchanging existing bonds for new ones with a deep reduction in face value. This bold move paid off with a March 2005 agreement on $103 billion in bonds held by private investors at a very deep percentage discount. Foreign exchange reserves were up to nearly $20 billion as a current-accounts surplus was achieved. By playing hardball with creditors and refusing adamantly to let debt renegotiation take priority over social needs, Kirchner sought to stem Brazil's bid to be recognized as the region's spokesman. Indeed, his increasingly protectionist trade policies took the blush off hitherto close relations with Brazil.[66] Kirchner's lack of a congressional majority, since rival Peronists had done well in 2003, was remedied by the partial congressional elections of late October. His wife, fifty-three-year-old Cristina Fernández de Kirchner, gave up her senate seat from her hometown province to run in the crucial Buenos Aires constituency, decisively winning by 46 percent to 20 percent. In the process this future president defeated the wife of ex-president Duhalde and helped bring in sixty-nine congress members on her well-tailored coattails compared to only eleven for Duhalde's bloc (as the UCR won nineteen seats), thus giving the president a very strong plurality in the chamber to go along with his majority in the upper house, where his candidates won seventeen of the twenty-four seats being contested (to only four for Duhalde's Peronist faction and three for the UCR).

Viewed as a certain winner in a 2007 reelection bid, the astute Kirchner decided to run his wife instead, setting up the prospect of alternating in the presidency for a number of terms. On October 28, 2007, Cristina Kirchner rolled up 45 percent of the presidential vote, essentially double that of her nearest competitor, Eliza Carrió of the left-of-center Civic Coalition (CC) with 23 percent, and leaving former economics minister Roberto Lavagne, backed by the once powerful UCR, far behind.[67] Her electoral sweep included more than three-quarters of the country's twenty-three governors, 160 of 257 seats in the lower house of the national congress, and 47 of 74 senate seats. Moreover, dissident Peronists came away with 10 seats in the former and 5 in the latter. The opposition was in shambles, with the Civic Coalition reduced to 31 seats in the chamber, just ahead of the once-dominant UCR with 30. The trifurcated opposition was virtually impotent, with the rival Civic Coalition and the UCR also facing competition from the center-right Republican Proposal (PRO). This new factor on the political scene emerged dramatically with the mid-June runoff victory

for Buenos Aires city executive by wealthy businessman Maurício Macri (b. 1959). A
political outsider best known for his successful presidency of the famed Boca Junior
soccer club (analogous to Arsenal, Real Madrid, or Inter Milan), Macri received 61
percent of the vote in the country's second largest reservoir of electoral clout. Running for congress in 2003 with the slogan "a passion for getting things done," he had
stunningly proven to be a new kind of urban political leader, something of a New
York mayor Michael Bloomberg with greater personal charisma. He was essentially
"a media figure who managed to establish close links with public opinion at the time
and to blur and then cross the classic left-right divide, without drawing strength from
institutional party sources."[68]

How vast and swift were the changes in the politics of Argentina's metropolis was
clear from the fact that as recently as 1999 the traditional parties had received 63.5
percent of the vote there, falling in 2001 to only 36.5 percent and down to a mere 3.3
percent in 2003 before recovering to 27.5 percent in 2005. These figures contrasted
with 85, 57.6, 50.5, and 66.1 percent for the same years in surrounding Buenos Aires
province. It could be said that the party system was "unfreezing" there and in the
country's second city, Córdoba (73.4, 78.8, 57.6, 52.1, and 56.3 percent for the traditional parties between 1995 and 2005), while in Buenos Aires city it had "collapsed."[69]
In 2007 three-quarters of the voters in the metropolis supported newly created political organizations that, like Macri's PRO, relied upon media rather than party structure.
Hence it was not surprising that voters there, free of preexisting party ties, were more
heavily influenced by the course of the campaign. Elsewhere, however, Peronists had
managed to recover from the 2001–2002 crisis, going so far as to change laws to facilitate reelection and enhance their ability to elect legislative majorities by concentrating votes in fewer parties. With such a growing gap between the changing politics of
the country's largest urban concentration and the survival of traditional ways in the interior, the key question was which would prevail down the road.

Señora Kirchner's 2007 victory came as no surprise because her husband had left
an exceedingly positive legacy, having brought the country back from perceived disaster to 9 percent per year GDP growth led by a substantial expansion of exports
benefiting from soaring global commodity prices. On his watch unemployment had
dropped from 20 to 9 percent as poverty had been cut almost in half from a dismal 50
percent to 27 percent. Moreover, he had reversed the decade-long Menem string of
wage-depressing policies, causing real wages to rise by 70 percent, and he had extended social security benefits to a million workers in the informal (off-the-books)
sector of the economy. In the political realm, he had gained annulment of the laws
limiting prosecutions from the dirty-war period of the military regime. In addition,
the "other" Kirchner capitalized on the organizational strength of the PJ throughout
the country—running up 70 percent landslides in several interior provinces reminiscent of Lula's performance a year earlier in the less developed states of Brazil. The
other side of the political coin was the near collapse of the Peronists' historical rival,
the UCR. Néstor Kirchner had convinced five of that party's governors and more
than a third of its 476 mayors to come over to his side, constituting the "K Radicals."
Indeed, one of them was Cristina Kirchner's vice presidential running mate.

Señora Kirchner, whose political views were to the left of her husband's, soon
found that governing the country was not completely a bed of roses. Early in her
presidency she became involved in a lengthy impasse with agricultural producers,

who resorted to demonstrations and stoppages to make her backtrack on changes in tariff and tax rates, ending with her own vice president's breaking a congressional stalemate by voting against her. Two years of bad harvests were followed by a disastrous one in which the wheat crop was the smallest since 1902, and beef production dropped so low as to raise the unthinkable prospect of needing to import meat (as Brazil continued to make heavy inroads in Argentina's traditional markets). Still, populist and nationalist gestures kept her overall approval ratings quite high even with the 2008 economic downturn leaving GDP down 2.6 percent since she took office. Hence, fearing further economic declines, the government moved the midterm elections up to midyear. Yet despite the central bank's spending US$100 million a day to support the peso as election day neared, it sank to its lowest value in over seven years relative to the dollar.

Argentine voters returned to the polls on June 28, 2009, to elect one-third of the senate (for a six-year term) along with just over half of the lower house (to serve for four years). With an electorate of over 27.8 million and the Kirchners proclaiming governability (meaning consolidation of their hold on the government) to be the central issue, the balloting stacked up essentially as a referendum on "La Presidenta's" leadership of the country. It turned out, however, to constitute a sobering reality check for the administration and a major shot in the arm for the opposition. The CC, led by the Social and Civic Action (ASC) slate and including the UCR and Socialist Party (PS) as well as a variety of small independent groups, received 28.9 percent of the national vote to go along with 17.7 percent for the PRO (increases of 9.1 and 12.3 percent). The Kirchners' Victory Front limped home with 30.8 percent, a bare plurality and over 12 percent below its 2007 performance. Néstor Kirchner resigned the Peronist Party's presidency after the list he headed in Buenos Aires city came in third (as a new leftist "Projecto Sur" movement took second place behind the PRO), and the party was also repudiated by voters in his home state. In terms of seats, the two major opposition parities came away with 78 and 32 seats in the Chamber of Deputies, equal to the Kirchner supporters' 110 (but representing a gain of 37 against a loss of 19). In the aftermath, Santa Fé senator Carlos Reutemann (governor in 1991–1995 and 1999–2003), who broke with the Kirchners in 2007, emerged as a potential threat to their hegemony in 2011. A national hero as a leading Formula One racer, he would be a formidable presidential candidate, especially if allied with PRO leaders Macri and Francisco Narváez and their strong base in the Buenos Aires region. Hence in a fundamental sense Argentine democracy was the winner, since a reinvigorated opposition increases competition and restores the possibility of alternation in power.

For all their strength and ambition, the Kirchners are democrats, if only because at bottom this is a democratic country of democratically minded people. Levitsky and Murillo make a convincing case for "Why Argentina Is Not Venezuela," citing a "broad societal commitment to civil liberties and an extensive infrastructure of civil society organizations committed to their defense." They also point out that Argentine federalism plays a role, governors and provincial political bosses being powerful political actors, particularly through their ability to heavily influence the legislative nomination process.[70]

Despite this setback, the Kirchners and other Argentine Peronists had no reason to feel envious of their counterparts elsewhere in the region, for Brazil's Lula was nearing the end of his tenure in office with no guarantee of being able to elect his successor; in

Mexico Felipe Calderón's most optimistic hope in his midterm elections was to maintain his congressional pluralities, an aspiration in which he was almost immediately disappointed, emerging with legislative support inferior to that of the Kirchners and constitutionally banned from seeking another term; Colombia's Uribe was legally barred from succeeding himself and, in the absence of a viable candidate, was forced to seek a constitutional change enabling him to run once again; Garcia in Peru was in a much better position than he had been in back in 1988, but that was of little consolation as he coped with a host of problems; and Michelle Bachelet in Chile was rapidly approaching the end of her single four-year term. Even Hugo Chávez in Venezuela, securely entrenched in power, could wish he had the degree of well-organized support from almost all sectors of society mobilized by the Kirchners.

Notes

1. Solid histories include Luis Alberto Romero, *A History of Argentina in the Twentieth Century* (University Station: Pennsylvania University Press, 2002), and David Rock, *Argentina, 1516–1982: From the Spanish Colonization to the Falklands War* (Berkeley and Los Angeles: University of California Press, 1985), with economic factors in Laura Randall, *An Economic History of Argentina in the Twentieth Century* (New York: Columbia University Press, 1978), and Carlos Díaz Alejandro, *Essays on the Economic History of Argentina* (New Haven, CT: Yale University Press, 1970).

2. Robert Potash, *The Army and Politics in Argentina,* Vol. 1, *1928–1945: Yrigoyen to Perón* (Palo Alto, CA: Stanford University Press, 1969). The 1931–1935 period is covered in detail on pp. 57–90.

3. The 1936–1939 period is treated in ibid., pp. 91–140. Of interest is Mark Falcoff and Ronald H. Dolkart, eds., *Prologue to Perón: Argentina in Depression and War, 1930–1943* (Berkeley and Los Angeles: University of California Press, 1975).

4. Ibid., p. 183. The 1937–1943 period is examined in pp. 141–199. Valuable insights into the ensuing years are contained in Frederick C. Turner and José Enrique Miguens, eds., *Juan Perón and the Reshaping of Argentina* (Pittsburgh, PA: University of Pittsburgh Press, 1983).

5. Biographical studies include Joseph Page, *Perón: A Biography* (New York: Random House, 1983); Robert J. Alexander, *Juan Domingo Perón: A History* (Boulder, CO: Westview Press, 1979); and Robert D. Crassweller, *Perón and the Enigmas of Argentina* (New York: Norton, 1987).

6. Events from the coup to the consolidation of Perón's presidential bid (in October 1945) are discussed in Potash, *Army,* Vol. 1, pp. 200–282.

7. Perón's cultivation of army support is detailed in ibid., pp. 249–252. Quite useful on the ensuing years is Donald C. Hodges, *Argentina 1943–1987: The National Revolution and Resistance,* expanded ed. (Albuquerque: University of New Mexico Press, 1988). Economic policies in their political context are discussed in Paul H. Lewis, *The Crisis of Argentine Capitalism* (Chapel Hill: University of North Carolina Press, 1990), and William C. Smith, *Authoritarianism and the Crisis of the Argentine Political System* (Stanford, CA: Stanford University Press, 1989).

8. Invaluable from late 1945 on is Robert Potash, *The Army and Politics in Argentina,* Vol. 2, *1945–1962: Perón to Frondizi* (Palo Alto, CA: Stanford University Press, 1980).

9. On Evita Perón consult Alicia Ortiz, *Eva Perón* (New York: St. Martins Press, 1993), and Nicolas Frazer and Marysa Navarro, *Eva Perón* (New York: W.W. Norton, 1985).

10. The maneuvering is covered in Potash, *Army,* Vol. 1, pp. 269–282.

11. This pivotal "bonding" event is discussed in Douglas Madsen and Peter G. Snow, *The Charismatic Bond: Political Behavior in Time of Crisis* (Cambridge, MA: Harvard University Press, 1991), pp. 46–51.

12. Potash, *Army*, Vol. 2, p. 44, discusses the election and the socioeconomic situation on pp. 6–8.

13. José Luis de Imaz, *Los que Mandan (Those Who Rule)* (Albany: State University of New York Press, 1970), provides much information on the social composition of the Argentine army.

14. The early chapters of Smith, *Authoritarianism,* and Lewis, *Crisis of Argentine Capitalism,* treat the economic situation. Potash, *Army*, Vol. 2, pp. 92ff., provides detail on the 1949 crisis.

15. James W. McGuire, *Peronism Without Perón: Unions, Parties, and Democracy in Argentina* (Stanford, CA: Stanford University Press, 1997), pp. 59–66, discusses Perón's negativism toward parties, an attitude shared by Vargas during his first fifteen-year stay in office.

16. In all probability Perón was aware of Evita's grave medical condition, and hence wished to reward her with the vice presidency because she would not be around for a possible run to succeed him five years later. He could not let the military leaders in on her impending death and so had to absorb the serious political costs of first offending senior officers, then backing down.

17. The election is covered in Potash, *Army*, Vol. 2, pp. 135ff.

18. See the discussion of the Evita Perón Foundation in McGuire, *Peronism*, pp. 64–73. Lewis, *Crisis of Argentine Capitalism,* p. 202, estimates that as much as $700 million was diverted to overseas accounts (which stood Perón in good stead after his ouster in 1955).

19. Potash, *Army*, Vol. 2, pp. 171ff., covers the Perón-church split. A more pro-Peronist perspective is in McGuire, *Peronism*, pp. 66–75.

20. Potash, *Army*, Vol. 2, p. 197, treats the Lonardi-Aramburu relationship.

21. The thinking of key figures of the military regime is discussed in ibid., pp. 227–249. The labor-Peronist viewpoint is articulated in McGuire, *Peronism*, pp. 68–83. See also Juan E. Corradi, *The Fitful Republic: Economy, Society, and Politics in Argentina* (Boulder, CO: Westview Press, 1985).

22. The Aramburu government's repressive activities represented the harder-line faction of the military with roots back in the 1951 anti-Perón conspiracy, a point at which Lonardi was one of the most senior generals, and Aramburu was eighteen years younger. This difference was almost generational as the former began his career under the presidency of General Roca in the early years of the twentieth century, whereas the latter finished his schooling and was commissioned during the period of radical domination in the early 1920s. Lonardi was in his mid forties at the time of the 1930 Revolution, but Aramburu was just emerging from his mid twenties, so the former was a decade senior to Perón, and the latter was eight years the strongman's junior. In a hierarchical institution like the Argentine army, such seniority and age-cohort differences did matter.

23. Potash, *Army*, Vol. 2, pp. 255ff., covers the mid-1957 constituent assembly elections.

24. Ibid., pp. 263–279, covers the presidential elections and their aftermath.

25. See ibid., pp. 308–337, for a meticulously reconstructed account of events from mid-1959 to August 1961. Useful sources on the Argentine political economy, at this juncture, are Gary W. Wynia, *Argentina in the Postwar Era: Politics and Economic Policy Making in a Divided Society* (Albuquerque: University of New Mexico Press, 1978), and Carlos H. Waisman, *Reversal of Development in Argentina: Postwar Counterrevolutionary Policies and Their Structural Consequences* (Princeton, NJ: Princeton University Press, 1987).

26. As elections were for half the chamber, it was possible to let the Peronists win without their coming close to a majority in the lower house. The built-in time bomb was that a repeat performance three years later would put them in control. Hence, as these elections approached, Frondizi could not both fulfill his commitment to the Peronists and keep the military satisfied.

27. Potash, *Army*, Vol. 2, pp. 338ff., discusses the repercussions of this incident and Frondizi's consequent ouster. See also McGuire, *Peronism*, pp. 84–90.

28. Robert Potash, *The Army and Politics in Argentina*, Vol. 3, *1962–1973: From Frondizi's Fall to the Peronist Restoration* (Stanford, CA: Stanford University Press, 1996), picks up the story at this point in pp. 4–92. See also McGuire, *Peronism*, pp. 90–92, 111–153.

29. On the abortive coup see Potash, *Army*, Vol. 3, pp. 93–101.

30. The elections of 1963 are dealt with in ibid., pp. 116–117.

31. On the Illia administration's handling of relations with the military, consult ibid, pp. 118–193.

32. Consult Smith, *Authoritarianism*, pp. 37–47. Also useful, reflecting a close understanding of the cultural context is Lewis, *Crisis of Argentine Capitalism*. On p. 256, Lewis comments on widespread tax evasion, smuggling, bribery of government officials, black marketeering, and capital flight as negative features in the late 1950s and the 1960s crying out for reform.

33. On the situation see McGuire, *Peronism*, pp. 151–159. The pithy comment is from Lewis, *The Crisis of Argentine Capitalism*, p. 273.

34. Smith, *Authoritarianism*, p. 51; pp. 48–118 discuss the Onganía regime up to mid-1968.

35. Ibid., pp. 67–68.

36. Potash, *Army*, Vol. 3, pp. 228–241, treats the deterioration of the Onganía-Lanusse relationship.

37. The Cordobazo is discussed from different perspectives in ibid., pp. 246–255; Smith, *Authoritarianism*, pp. 127–133; and McGuire, *Peronism*, pp. 157–159, with the Monteneros analyzed in Richard Gillespie, *Soldiers of Perón: Argentina's Monteneros* (Oxford, UK: Clarendon Press, 1982), pp. 89–95.

38. The decline of the Onganía regime is reconstructed in Potash, *Army*, Vol. 3, pp. 255–292, and discussed by Smith in *Authoritarianism*, pp. 120–168.

39. Potash, *Army*, Vol. 3, pp. 293–308, analyzes Onganía's ouster, and pp. 309–357 cover his successor's short term. Also see McGuire, *Peronism*, pp. 150–156, and Lewis, *Crisis of Argentine Capitalism*, pp. 375ff.

40. On his views see Aldo Ferrer, *The Argentine Economy*, trans. by Marjory M. Urquidi (Berkeley and Los Angeles: University of California Press, 1967).

41. Smith, *Authoritarianism*, p. 188. Lanusse is discussed in Potash, *Army*, Vol. 3, pp. 357–393.

42. Perón's dramatic return to power is recounted in McGuire, *Peronism*, pp. 163ff., as well as in Smith, *Authoritarianism*, pp. 209–221. The military's misperceptions and ensuing miscalculations are masterfully dealt with in Potash, *Army*, Vol. 3, pp. 394–496, and Perón's final stay in power is covered in Guido de Tella, *Argentina Under Perón, 1973–1976: The Nation's Experience with a Labour-Based Government* (New York: St. Martins Press, 1983).

43. Detail is available in de Tella, *Argentina Under Perón*, with Isabelita's short and unhappy presidency covered in McGuire, *Peronism*, pp. 165–170, and Smith, *Authoritarianism*, pp. 231–242.

44. Consult Paul H. Lewis, *Guerrillas and Generals: The "Dirty War" in Argentina* (Westport, CT: Praeger, 2002), and María José Moyano, *Argentina's Lost Patrol: Armed Struggle, 1969–1979* (New Haven, CT: Yale University Press, 1995), as well as Jacobo Timmerman's moving personal account in *Prisoner Without a Name, Cell Without a Number* (New York: Random House, 1981). The Videla government is analyzed in Smith, *Authoritarianism*, pp. 231–242.

45. Useful is Monica Peralta Ramos and Carlos H. Waisman, eds., *From Military Rule to Liberal Democracy in Argentina* (Boulder, CO: Westview Press, 1987).

46. On the political repercussions of the Malvinas war see McGuire, *Peronism*, pp. 176–180.

47. Ibid., p. 185, as well as Smith, *Authoritarianism*, pp. 241–266.

48. On the Alfonsín government see ibid., pp. 267ff., and McGuire, *Peronism*, pp. 183–207.

49. Edward C. Epstein, ed., *The New Argentine Democracy: The Search for a Successful Formula* (Westport, CT: Praeger, 1992), is useful for the first half of this period.

50. The change of economic gurus is discussed in Smith, *Authoritarianism*, p. 287.

51. A near-lame-duck civilian president besieged with problems managing to gain control of a renegade intelligence community accustomed to going its own way was a nearly impossible task. On civil-military relations see J. Patrice McSherry, *Incomplete Transition: Military Power and Democracy in Argentina* (New York: St. Martin's Press, 1997), and David Pion-Berlin,

Through Corridors of Power: Institutions and Civil-Military Relations in Argentina (University Station: Pennsylvania State University Press, 1997).

52. This election reopened the question if some Peronist strategists truly wished to win in 1983 when they put up a weak candidate, or whether they realized that popular expectations far outran possibilities for their fulfillment in the midst of economic malaise. Menem was not on the radar screen as a viable contender in 1983. He required the events of the next five years to emerge as the antiestablishment Peronist standard-bearer and to take office under more favorable circumstances.

53. On Menem see McGuire, *Peronism,* pp. 216–226. Interesting ideas are found in Javier Corrales, *Presidents Without Parties: The Politics of Economic Reform in Argentina and Venezuela in the 1990s* (University Station: Pennsylvania State University Press, 2002). Paul H. Lewis, *Authoritarian Regimes in Latin America: Dictators, Despots, and Tyrants* (Lanham, MD: Rowman & Littlefield Publishers, 2006), pp. 234–239, perceptively analyzes Menem.

54. The military conspiracies are covered in McSherry, *Incomplete Transition,* and Pion-Berlin, *Through Corridors of Power.*

55. A competent discussion of Argentine democratization is the chapter by Carlos H. Waisman in Larry Diamond, Jonathan Hartlyn, Juan J. Linz, and Seymour Martin Lipset, eds., *Democracy in Developing Countries: Latin America* (Boulder, CO: Lynne Rienner, 1999), pp. 71–129.

56. Jacqueline Behrend, "Argentina and the 'Closed Game' of Provincial Politics," presented at the Latin American Studies Association's congress, Rio de Janeiro, June 11–14, 2009 (available at the LASA Web site), pp. 2, 4.

57. Ibid, pp. 11–17.

58. Ibid, p. 6.

59. McGuire, *Peronism,* p. 241. The formation of FREPASO and the 1995 elections are covered in pp. 249–251.

60. This election was unique in that the loser would come to the presidency midway through the winner's constitutional term—in effect splitting the presidential tenure.

61. See Javier Corrales, "The Politics of Argentina's Meltdown," *World Policy Journal,* 19:3 (Fall 2000), pp. 29–36.

62. Steven Levitsky, "The 'Normalization' of Argentine Politics," *Journal of Democracy,* 11:2 (April 2000), pp. 56–69.

63. Very useful is Hector E. Shamis, "Argentina: Crisis and Democratic Consolidation," *Journal of Democracy,* 13:2 (April 2002), pp. 81–94.

64. Steven Levitsky and María Victoria Murillo, "Argentina Weathers the Storm," *Journal of Democracy,* 14:4 (October 2003), pp. 152–166.

65. Ibid., p. 164.

66. See Chrystiane Silva and Carlos Rydlewski, "Diplomacia do Faz-de-Conta," *Veja* (September 15, 2004), pp. 112–114.

67. Steven Levitsky and María Victoria Murillo, "Argentina: From Kirchner to Kirchner," *Journal of Democracy,* 19:2 (April 2008), pp. 16–30, reprinted in Larry Diamond, Marc F. Plattner, and Diego Abente Brun, eds., *Latin America's Struggle for Democracy* (Baltimore: Johns Hopkins University Press, 2008), pp. 109–123.

68. Tomás Bril Mascarenhas, "Party System Collapse After a Multidimensional Crisis: Empirical Evidence and Theoretical Insights from post-2001 Argentine Subnational Politics," presented at the Latin American Studies Association's congress, Rio de Janeiro, June 11–14, 2009 (available on the LASA Web site).

69. Ibid., p. 6.

70. Levitsky and Murillo, "Argentina from Kirchner to Kirchner."

9

Colombia, Peru, Venezuela, and Chile Since 1930

Latin America is still only a decade into the new century. As was true in analogous situations in 1880, 1910, 1940, 1965, and 1990, important, perhaps eventually defining, trends are in midstream. Decisions will soon be made that may go a long way toward deciding the course and outcome of the rest of this exciting and potentially momentous period. (It may turn out with hindsight that recent years have been essentially an extension of the 1980–1999 period, with a new one still to take shape in the near future.) From a political development perspective, it is clear that Brazil is a consolidated, increasingly institutionalized mass-participation democracy, at least in the electoral arena. Argentina has recovered the substantial ground lost between 1930 and 1983, and its democracy now functions on a much larger scale than when 839,000 votes were enough to return Yrigoyen to office in 1928. Whatever lies ahead for Mexico, its democratic transition launched in 2000 with the opposition victory in the presidential election appears to be complete, with final consolidation awaiting beyond the 2012 test at the ballot box.

What of the other four countries? Certainly each has come a long way on the road of political development since 1930, but three of them still have a good distance to travel. The exception, Chile, in many ways is at the head of the class—including the three much larger countries just discussed. But back in the 1930s Chile enjoyed a much clearer and larger lead. From the perspective of the 1930s, Colombia was Chile's chief challenger for leadership in political development; now Colombia rates high marks for effort, maintaining democratic processes in the face of the great strains imposed by determined, generation-long insurgency compounded by endemic and deeply entrenched drug trafficking. Peru and Venezuela entered the post-1930 era some distance behind Chile and Colombia in terms of viable political structures and processes. Eighty years later they have made up some ground but are both still unconsolidated, imperfect, and possibly imperiled democracies. From an analytical angle, they are not as readily subject to explicit comparison as Brazil, Mexico, and Argentina. Nevertheless, the challenges, failures, shortcomings, and accomplishments along the zigzag road toward political development merit close attention from the viewpoint of intrinsic comparability if not systematic comparison. Hence similarities and differences as they have developed since 1930 need to be highlighted as they are serially examined.

Colombia: Promising Start, Rampant Violence, Democracy Under Fire

The quarter century after 1930 would be a very turbulent one. Beginning with a return to civilized, if intense, competition between the two historical parties, Colombia would move through roughneck competition with virtually no holds barred until the rivalry became cutthroat—involving tens of thousands of throats cut along with hundreds of thousands of victims of other very personal means of slaughtering one's political enemies. Relative peace would be restored through military dictatorship before the parties would agree to bury the hatchet, or rather the machete, in order to launch a unique experience in cogovernment.[1] As the power of the state increased, so did the benefits of its control both as a patronage vehicle and for economic success, as the "increasing 'state-orientation' of the economy and the social order led to a point where it became impossible to conceive of any large-scale enterprise in any sector of activity without the protection and goodwill of the state."[2]

Colombia's 1930 elections were heavily impacted by the onset of the world depression. Not having run a candidate in 1926, the Liberal Party (PL) took advantage of divisions in conservative ranks to come back with a "national concentration coalition" engineered by Enrique Olaya Herrera (b 1881), who made skillful use of his good relations with US bankers to win support of those conservative businessmen most concerned with continuing a flow of foreign investment. The mainstream conservatives were split over the administration's draconian antisubversive laws, which were passed in the wake of 1928 labor unrest. Divisions in the liberals ranks were chiefly between a reformist wing led by future president Alfonso López Pumarejo (b. 1886) and a center-right faction headed by Bogotá newspaper publisher Eduardo Santos, another future president; at this juncture this faction supported Olaya. Even after being elected Olaya felt he needed to cooperate with the Conservative Party (PC) in the interests of his priority goal of reactivating the economy. Hence he included conservatives in his cabinet as a means of gaining bipartisan support for his legislation. Olaya's main ally in this political venture was influential Antioquía Conservative Party leader Carlos Restrepo, who was willing to collaborate with moderate liberals in the interests of the stability prerequisite for foreign financing and investment. These moderate conservatives were primarily concerned with maintaining the status quo, which was, after all, chiefly of their making.

Olaya never did figure out how to get reforms started without precipitating a break between moderate and reformist liberals or how to satisfy the partisan appetites of liberals in the countryside while governing in partnership with conservatives. For Colombia's political culture viewed political domination as the supreme objective of both the parties because domination ensured a monopoly of patronage and the spoils of the political war, whereas failure to control the government meant at best the short and dirty end of the stick.[3] In 1931, the moderate, even behind-the-times Law 83 recognized the right to form unions (subject to a slew of conditions), and economic policies combined protectionism with a rather timid taste of state intervention. But by 1934 exports were back to their predepression value, and industry was growing at the same modest rate as before 1929. Partisan confrontations in rural areas and growing class cleavages in the cities were toned down by a 1933 Peruvian invasion of Leticia, a small southward protrusion extending to the Amazon, resulting in a minor war that led to an increased sense of national unity.

In 1934 López gained election as president but did not initially have control of the congress. Unlike his predecessor, he believed in party government, not bipartisan coalition. Gaining a congressional majority in 1935, he managed to enact important parts of his Revolucíon en Marcha, a very rough functional equivalent of Roosevelt's New Deal, although a relatively pale shadow of Lázaro Cárdenas's program in Mexico. Overhaul of the regressive tax system to include levies on income and wealth, expansion of education, an import-substitution program of industrialization bolstered by protective tariffs, and a beginning of agrarian reform were among López's major accomplishments, along with a 1936 election law reform that ended literacy and property requirements for voting. However, even these laws were too much for much of the moderate wing of what was, after all, an elite-led Liberal Party. Critics thought it differed too little from the preaching of "wild radical" dissident Jorge Eliécer Gaitán Ayala (b. 1898) and his Revolutionary Left National Union (UNIR, Spanish for "unite"). Those who had any inkling that López wanted to bring Gaitán and his followers back into the Liberal Party (PL) fold and use them to move it leftward were irate toward the president.[4]

In 1937 López lost control of both the congress and his party, being, in part, a victim of the single four-year term, which prematurely clipped his political wings. Liberal rural bosses were unhappy with his emphasis on urban labor and concerned about his lack of cooperation with their efforts to regain ground at the local level lost during the long era of conservative domination, a venture that required both patronage and use of government agencies to disadvantage, if not harass, political enemies. For if conservatives were considered rivals in the cities, in the countryside politics was a bare-knuckle game, so, making no bones about it, the liberals and the conservatives were enemies, an enmity often backed up by blood feuds going back at least as far as the turn-of-the-century Thousand Days War. This dissatisfaction within liberal ranks led to a shift away from reformist López toward the moderate wing, in which Eduardo Santos (b. 1888) was the rising star. In late 1937 Santos defeated Dário Echandia, López's choice, for the nomination.

The conservatives, still divided since their 1930 split, decided not to run a candidate against Santos, backing him as a great improvement over the "radical" López. So in 1938 Santos became president by a walkover. His four years in office were marked by a reorientation of policies toward capitalist industrial and agricultural development. His most significant reform was removing education from the control of the Catholic Church, and he reached agreement with the Vatican requiring that henceforth bishops and higher prelates be Colombian citizens.

López staged a comeback in 1942 because the moderates lacked any eligible candidate of his national stature, and Gaitán's radical wing was only in the process of reintegration into the PL. Defeating a dissident moderate liberal backed by Santos, who received an impressive 41 percent of the vote in an election lacking a Conservative Party (PC) contender, López pledged to complete the unfinished work of his "Revolution on the March." Unfortunately, wartime economic conditions were not conducive to costly social programs. The moderate factions of the liberals and conservatives voted together to control the congress and thwart López. Aided greatly by Santos's *El Tiempo,* the country's most influential newspaper, López's intraparty rivals and interparty foes capitalized on a series of improprieties by members of the president's family, although none by the president himself, to keep him on the defensive and wear him down. After the embarrassment of being held prisoner by army officers in the southern city of Pasto, López decreed a state of siege, using the exceptional powers the decree gave him to greatly accelerate the organization of labor unions. This strengthening of a labor power base sparked intensified personal attacks from ex-president Santos and his followers.[5]

López, who had already experienced in 1937 the uncomfortable feeling of impending lame-duck impotence, resigned in 1945 in order to avoid the same trauma. The uneventful remaining year of his term was served by young Alberto Lleras Camargo, who considerably later would be enshrined in the pantheon of outstanding Colombian presidents alongside López, although not for anything he did in this caretaker stint, during which he avoided being politically sandwiched between Santos and Gaitán by forming a national union government with the moderate conservatives of Mariano Ospina Pérez. By 1946, the Liberal Party (PL) was so deeply split that, like US Republicans in 1912, they fielded two candidates on election day. Gabriel Turbay was a moderate with long mainstream service to the party. Jorge Eliécer Gaitán Ayala, a highly unique figure in the annals of Latin America, not just Colombia, was a charismatic spellbinder as well as an outsider, more for his dark color than for lower-class origins per se, as Benjamin Disraeli had originally been to the British political establishment in the mid nineteenth century. Turbay was running for an office he had had his eye set on since youth, while Gaitán, a spoiler at this point, was running to take the party away from him and move it sharply to the left. The last-minute candidacy of Mariano Ospina Pérez (b. 1891), scion of a highly respected traditional conservative family, ended sixteen years during which that party had not put up a presidential candidate. Ospina received only 566,000 votes (42 percent) to Turbay's 437,000 votes, and in finishing third Gaitán obtained 364,000 votes, so he clearly cost Turbay a probable victory.[6]

For his first two years, Ospina maintained the national union coalition from the Lleras Camargo interregnum, not feasible over the long haul once the radical and bellicose Gaitán took over the PL leadership in 1947, and strikes and civil unrest in urban areas supplemented the usual rural violence accompanying a shift of power from one party to its enemies (as the antagonism went well beyond the bounds of rivalry). By that time Ospina was losing strength within the PC to one of the most destructive leaders to master the art of turning a political drama into a tragedy: Laureano Eleutério Gómez Castro (b. 1889), leader of the reactionary faction of the conservatives, who favored restructuring the state and the society along corporatist lines. For him, this restructuring required reestablishing Conservative Party hegemony as it had been at the beginning of the century no matter if this necessitated approximating genocide. Like inquisitioners of the sixteenth and seventeenth centuries, he was doing God's will, an end justifying any means—in this case not only tens of thousands of needless deaths, but the destruction of Colombian democracy.[7]

Gaitán's faction won 55 percent of liberal votes in the 1947 congressional elections, in which the liberal total of 806,000 votes significantly exceeded the conservatives' 654,000 votes. So the Liberal Party decided by late 1947 that they would march into the late 1950 elections united behind Gaitán. Given the decided demographic edge they held over Conservative Party voters, this decision made Gaitán's election a near certainty, and he was determined not to stop short of a Cárdenas-type revolutionary administration as López had, but even to go beyond it. The radical transformation of Colombia he had in mind would leave the Conservative Party with no political future as surely as Perón's regime was in the process of doing in Argentina. The task of stopping this political "anti-Christ," as Gómez viewed Gaitán, could not be left to the ballot box; a bullet would be much surer. On April 9, 1948, in the heart of Bogotá, the deed was done. This dastardly murder was carried out at the time and very near the place that the hemisphere's top diplomats were gathered to convert the outdated Pan-American Union into and Organization of American States (OAS) which would function as a peacekeeping body under the aegis of the then spanking new United Nations. One of the many politically active radical students drawn to this event was Cuban law students' spokesman Fidel Castro, a stripling of twenty-one.

In the short run Gaitán's murder triggered the Bogotazo (rampant rioting in the capital), in which at least 2,000 perished and much of downtown Bogotá was destroyed. In the medium run it opened the way for Gómez to become president. It also unleashed La Violencia ("the violence"), the closest approximation to genocide Latin America had experienced, ravishing the country through 1953 and leaving nearly 300,000 bodies in its wake.[8] A virtual lame duck, and with liberals and conservatives rapidly approaching a state of civil war in the countryside, Ospina banned all public meetings in March 1949 and then removed liberal governors from office, putting an end to even a pretense of national union. In November Gómez haughtily refused to consider any type of accord with the liberals (to him "damned heretic Protestants"). The liberals proposed impeachment of Ospina Pérez, who reacted by declaring a state of siege entailing the closing of legislative bodies and the suspension of civil liberties. With elections moved up a year to November 27, 1949, Gómez was chosen president by a vote of 1.14 million to 14 as the Liberal Party boycotted what they considered fraudulent elections. Gómez had long wanted to be president in the worst possible way. Now he was! (Latin American experience strongly indicates that election boycotts prove to be ineffectual and sometimes self-defeating gestures.)

Gómez was a reactionary's reactionary, classifiable as an ultraright, near-fascist, fanatical Catholic. Often expressing a desire to return Colombia to the days of Ferdinand and Isabella, he officially called for a "Hispanic Counterrevolution." An end to the separation of church and state was an early priority goal, and fiscal austerity and attraction of foreign capital were cornerstones of his rather primitive economic policy, centering on dismantling almost everything done under liberal presidents. Still, favorable exports and increasing foreign investment provided a reasonable degree of prosperity. But with deaths from politically motivated violence passing 200,000 and no end in sight, Gómez went too far when he tried to push through a constitution involving a concentration of powers that would make the president a near autocrat, reduce the congress to a rubber stamp, and centralize authority in Bogotá. He had been on leave from the presidency since November 1951 to see to health problems. Attempting to reassume office in June 1953, he was blocked by a coalition of all political factions except Laureanista conservatives, and Colombia's first successful military coup in over a century installed General Gustavo Rojas Pinilla (b. 1900) in power.[9] (Gómez's arrogant overreaching for power would be duplicated by both demagogic Brazilian president Jânio Quadros in 1961 and Chilean dictator Augusto Pinochet in 1988.)

Starting with broad support, this general, whose political ties were to the conservatives, alienated supporters. Although he was an ardent supporter of Dominican dictator Rafael Trujillo, he attempted to entrench himself in power garbed as a Peronist. Originally Rojas staffed his government with Ospinista conservatives, but early on he offered an amnesty to insurgents on both sides. Embodying a more populist stance, his late 1953 and 1954 tax reforms angered coffee growers and industrialists, who were hardest hit. Heavy public works expenditures led to balance-of-payments problems accompanied by inflation and capital flight. The final straw was setting up a National Secretariat of Social Assistance (SENDAS) along the lines of the Evita Perón Foundation and putting his daughter in charge of it. When she was booed at the Bogotá bull ring, Rojas Pinilla turned his security goon squads loose on the offending spectators. Hence, as the period ended, liberals and conservatives were beginning to consult on a plan for Rojas Pinilla's removal. The dictator's efforts to fuse urban workers and the peasantry together in a political base to counter the elite's traditional domination of Colombia's politics posed a threat to both conservatives and liberals, and his reduction of the death toll of La Violencia by half through repression did not win him the allegiance of the middle class—because the violence still caused at least 15,000 deaths a year.

For Colombia 1956 saw delicate negotiations under way between the historically antagonistic liberals and conservatives on the establishment of an alliance as a long-term institutionalized power-sharing arrangement, rather than just an ad hoc alliance to overthrow the military dictatorship of Rojas Pinilla—who besides being undemocratic was a threat to the traditional hegemony of those two elite-led parties. The period would end with the parties well advanced along a road of an incrementally staged return to full political competition without reliance on institutionalized power sharing. The road followed required effective political leadership from a variety of individuals, rather than one or two exceptionally skilled guides. In the broad comparative picture the Colombian National Front (Frente Nacional) stands out as the clearest and most dramatic example of the political learning process in the totality of Latin American experience. Moreover, this exercise in political innovation contrasts positively in its originality and viability with the far more common practice of adopting or adapting US–western European devices and stratagems. It called for sixteen years of alternating the presidency between the two parties while evenly dividing legislative seats at all levels. In departments where one party held the governorship, the other would have the mayoralty of its capital, these roles being switched every four years. To ensure coresponsibility for important laws, a two-thirds congressional majority was required. This regime involved a two-party liberal-conservative monopoly over running candidates for elective office. The agreement in principle was sealed at Benidorm, Spain, in July 1956, with the final details agreed upon at Sitges, Spain, in August 1957, shortly after Rojas Pinilla's ouster.

Negotiation of this historic accord while Rojas Pinilla was still ensconced in power was a major feat of diplomacy requiring cooperation of leaders who, until a few years earlier, had been responsible for violent partisan conflict. Only memories of the carnage of La Violencia enabled them to persist, viewing the National Front as the only sure guarantee against a return to an unthinkable bloodbath. (Similarly, traumatic memories of the civil war would, in the second half of the 1970s, enable all parties in post-Franco Spain to cooperate in democratization.) The National Front agreement in hand, the parties cooperated with legalist military sectors and others alienated by Rojas Pinilla's personal aggrandizement to force the dictator out of office in May 1957. With the National Front incorporated into the constitution through a plebiscite in December, early 1958 saw congressional elections giving the followers of ex-president Laureano Gómez, an edge over those of ex-president Mariano Ospina Pérez. Although each party would get half the congressional seats, the liberals held a decided vote edge over the conservatives at 2.13 million to 1.56 million, as for the first time women exercised the right to vote. Alberto Lleras Camargo (b. 1906)—austere and intellectual—had held things together as provisional president during the 1943–1945 period, after which he spent a decade as Secretary General of the Organization of American States in Washington. Now, the chief architect of the National Front was not allowed to rest on his laurels; in the absence of a viable conservative candidate to be the initial helmsman of the new system, Lleras was drafted to confront the daunting task of making this experiment work in a country of some 15 million inhabitants still more rural than urban, more agricultural than industrial, and all accustomed to an environment of political violence and repression.[10]

In the 1960 congressional balloting the Liberal Party edge over its Conservative Party partners fell to 1.48 million to 1.06 million: Knowing in advance that half the seats would go to each party severely dampened partisan enthusiasm. While adopting vigorous measures to reduce banditry and violence, the Lleras Camargo administration also instituted a series of programs to improve the living conditions of the masses, including increased expenditures on education, expansion of water and sewage systems, and construction of public housing. As Lleras made "cogovernment" work, engineering a substantial economic recovery accompanied by social peace, turnout for the 1962 congressional voting rose, the liberals garnering 1.7 million votes versus 1.3 million votes for the conservatives. The Revolutionary Liberal Movement (MRL) of Alfonso López Michelsen, son of ex-president Alfonso López Pumarejo, rose from 20 to 31 percent of the liberal vote, largely on the basis of López Michelsen's criticism of the National Front, making this progressive movement a serious contender for rivaling the Liberal Party. With ex-president Ospina Pérez stronger within the Conservative Party than Gómez, the unproven Guillermo León Valencia (b. 1908) became the coalition candidate and hence the new president, as only half the 5.4 million registered voters bothered to cast their ballots in May 1962. The official nominee of the National Front was legitimized by 1.64 million voters, while 626,000 unhappy liberals voted for López Michelsen.[11]

Vacillating and unpredictable, León Valencia undercut much of the economic planning done by his predecessor, as he struggled to govern a country whose population had risen to over 17 million, 53 percent urban. Indeed, the momentum built up under Lleras Camargo was lost, and the country marked time waiting for the end of León Valencia's "do-next-to-nothing" government. Deteriorating economic conditions, including rising inflation, provided an environment propitious for increasing social unrest. During León Valencia's essentially ineffective government, leftist insurgents founded the National Liberation Army (ELN) in 1962 and the communist Armed Forces of the Colombian Revolution (FARC) in 1964. These negative factors contributed to a paltry 37 percent turnout in the 1964 congressional elections, with the liberals garnering 1.14 million votes to 802,000 for the conservatives; Rojas Pinilla's vaguely Peronist National Popular Alliance (ANAPO) received 310,000 protest votes. By the second half of 1965, León Valencia was reduced to declaring a state of siege to permit harsher actions to maintain social order. Ending as one of Colombia's least-well-regarded chief executives, he caused public faith in the government to sag.

In 1966, when Lleras Camargo's fifty-eight-year-old businessman cousin, Carlos Lleras Restrepo, boy wonder finance minister back in 1938, was the National Front's nominee, only 2.94 million voters turned out for the March congressional balloting (with the Liberal Party enjoying a slight advantage). In May, 2.64 million of a registered 6.61 million voters—a mere two-fifths—participated in ratifying the two parties' presidential choice, with 1.9 million of these approving Lleras Restrepo to be the front's new pilot.[12] As this forceful and energetic liberal reinvigorated the economy and modernized the state, making good use of a competent cabinet and building on the foundations laid down by Lleras Camargo, López Michelsen brought his dissident MRL back into the mother party. To end this political equivalent of a rigid body cast featuring parity and alternation, it was agreed that the equal division of legislative seats and cabinet positions would cease in 1978, to be followed by an "equitable" division of offices, proportional to the votes received. The beginning of electoral participation by new parties was moved up to 1970 from 1974, and the two-thirds majority requirement for significant legislation was eliminated.

In March 1968, midterm congressional balloting, with participation at 2.5 million (just 37 percent of the electorate) the Conservative Party rallied to 1.16 million votes to 989,000 for the official Liberal Party (plus a substantial showing for the MLR). In the aftermath, Lleras Restrepo lifted the state of siege imposed by his predecessor in May 1965. The Liberal Party insisted that forty-seven-year-old moderate Misael Pastrana Borrero be the Conservative Party's nominee as the National Front's candidate in 1970 rather than Belisario Betancur Cuartas, who probably had more support within his party. Despite low inflation and diversification of exports, this insistence on a successor who would carry on Lleras Restrepo's constructive policies almost put the National Front experiment in peril.

Still, in April 1970, Pastrana narrowly edged Rojas Pinilla, who got on the ballot via the technical argument that ANAPO was a conservative faction, not a third party. The margin of 1.63 million votes to 1.56 million votes (with dissident conservatives polling 908,000 votes) showed that the National Front was running out of steam, either from voter fatigue or from a public perception that it was no longer needed. Indeed, most conservatives voted for one of the splinter candidates or even for Rojas Pinilla. On the congressional side, the Liberal Party received 1.47 million votes, while ANAPO forged ahead of the pro–National Front conservatives by 1.41 million votes to 1.08 million.[13]

As Pastrana, governing a country whose population had reached 22 million, cut back on Lleras Restrepo's reforms, new groups joined the political fray as well as the insurgent battlefield, the most significant being the National Liberation Army (ELN) and the 19th of April Movement (M-19), a radical offshoot of ANAPO, much as the Monteneros in Argentina were a radicalized wing of Peronism. The thorny issue of agrarian reform, which when initiated by Lleras Restrepo had met with heavy opposition in the congress, was brought up again with emphasis now upon productivity, not redistribution. Pastrana selected the construction sector as the engine of growth for the economy because of the employment it created, which increased purchasing power and spurred demand for domestically produced consumer goods. Since Álvaro Gómez Hurtado—never-say-die Laureano's son and political heir—was the official Conservative Party candidate for president in 1974, when alternation was scheduled to end, sixty-one-year-old López Michelsen became the Liberal Party nominee (a behind-the-scenes victory for Júlio César Turbay Ayala, who was planning a future presidential bid) over grizzled veteran Lleras Restrepo. With the election truly competitive, turnout rose sharply to over 5.2 million as López Michelsen trounced Gómez Hurtado 2.93 million votes to 1.64 million, with María Eugenia Rojas de Moreno, Rojas Pinilla's very un-Evita-like daughter, trailing badly at only 500,000 votes in this contest among offspring of former presidents.[14] The post–National Front period began in the midst of rising inflation and unemployment, which led the government to implement unpopular austerity measures. During López Michelsen's turbulent term, in which economic limitations forced him to set aside his initial social reformism (embodied in his heralded "To Close the Gap" and "Integrated Rural Development" programs), the drug problem sprouted and the military became increasingly restive. Belatedly, López Michelsen realized that drug trafficking was having seriously deleterious effects on society and politics, although, perversely, it was stimulating the economy.

Congressional balloting in April 1976 gave the Liberal Party an advantage of 1.7 million votes to 1.3 million over the Conservatives as only 3.3 million Colombians participated. With labor violence stemming from rapidly rising prices triggering states of siege from 1977 on, the Conservative Party, longing to get back in power, nominated Betancur as their standard-bearer for the 1978 elections. February 1978 congressional elections saw the Liberal Party widen its margin, with 2.3 million votes to 1.65 million for their now ex-coalition partners—as only 34 percent of the electorate took part.

This vote gave the Liberals 62 senate seats and 111 in the chamber to 49 and 88, respectively, for the Conservatives, as they finally regained voters from the moribund ANAPO. After two decades of the National Front, it appeared that the time had arrived to take the training wheels off the political bicycle and try full-scale competition with all the risks it might entail. (Venezuela had been on this road for some time, and Peru was embarking upon it, with Brazil taking its first tentative steps in this direction—but Argentina was not, and Chile was steaming along on the opposite track.) This bold decision proved to be the tonic needed to revive voter interest, as the decline in electoral turnout began to turn around.

Lleras Restrepo was forced to give up a comeback try by the greater liberal support for his archrival, Júlio César Turbay, who, despite being a poor campaigner requiring help from the still revered Lleras Camargo, in June 1978 maintained the Liberal Party's hold on the presidency by only a 150,000 vote margin—at 2.5 million to 2.36 million—as just 5.1 million out of an electorate swollen to 12.6 million cast their ballots.[15] Still, Colombia had its sixth duly elected chief executive in a row, and for a second time a photo-finish election had been taken in stride. Having established democracy in the late 1950s and 1960s, when most other Latin American countries were under authoritarian rule, Colombia was well beyond a transition to democracy.

It would, however, have undreamed-of problems, which reared their extremely ugly heads just around the corner: intractable insurgency and the emergence of a drug industry that together threatened to become the base of a parallel government.

Although Colombia's political development would not take major strides forward during the 1980s and 1990s, the country did manage to stave off the very serious threat to viable representative processes posed by the enormous wealth and power amassed by the ruthless entrepreneurs of the drug trade. To do so without seriously violating democratic norms was no mean accomplishment; neither was its success at all a foregone conclusion. Indeed, the performances of several Colombian presidents during this period compared favorably with those of both their predecessors, who had allowed the country get into this predicament, and their contemporaries in other Latin American countries, especially their Andean neighbors. Moreover, political leadership at least passed into the hands of a new generation of vigorous and quite modern individuals within the country's distinctive framework of a resilient two-party system.[16]

After 1978, Colombia, a country reaching a population of 25 million, had as its president a sixty-two-year-old middle-class descendant of Lebanese immigrants. Near the midpoint of Turbay's term, which featured a move back toward statist development and a freer hand for the military, the M-19 insurgents held fourteen foreign ambassadors hostage for sixty-one days, causing a profound embarrassment to the government. Moreover, the drug trade expanded by leaps and bounds with the authorities appearing clueless and ineffective. The resulting sense of malaise impacted the country's political life, as turnout in 1980 state and municipal elections was a mere 30 percent (4.2 million out of an eligible 13.8 million), reflecting apathy as well as fear. Within this low participation the liberals held onto a 2.3-million-vote to 1.6 million edge in local balloting. Still a power within the Liberal Party, Lleras Camargo favored late-1960s Bogotá mayor Virgilio Barca Vargas in 1982, while ex-president Alfonso López Michelsen sought a comeback. This liberal split, reminiscent of 1946, allowed the conservatives behind Belisario Betancur (b. 1923) to sneak back in. The liberals had defeated the conservatives in the March congressional balloting by a 3.1-million to 2.2-million margin, but in May Betancur's 3.2 million votes overcame López Michelsen's 2.8 million, with newcomer Luis Carlos Galán Sarmiento siphoning off 730,000 votes, as turnout rose to just above 50 percent.[17]

Betancur, a populist inclined to bypass the party and appeal directly to the middle classes, inherited a bleak economic landscape marred by recession, fiscal deficits, rising foreign debt, troublesome inflation, and high unemployment. These problems prevented him from launching new programs or redistributing income—particularly as government revenues were strained by existing patronage arrangements. Attempting to regulate the financial sectors and drifting away from the United States, Betancur encountered opposition from the military, which distrusted his efforts to negotiate an end to the FARC, ELN, and M-16 insurgencies. Following the latter's dramatic attack on the Palace of Justice in November 1985 and a devastating volcano eruption, and with the narcotics traffickers mounting a near parallel government in Medellín and Cali, Betancur became a virtual lame duck subject to a high degree of control by the military. Meanwhile, the March 1984 midterm elections saw both parties splintered, with the opposition liberals enjoying a 53-percent to 42-percent advantage over the conservatives. Well intentioned as it was, Betancur's 1984 "National Dialogue" (of all-embracing peace talks) failed to advance the cause of domestic peace.

In 1986 Álvaro Gómez Hurtado tried yet again for the conservatives, as Virgilio Barca, now sixty-five, won the liberal nod over Galán and cruised to a lopsided victory of 4.2 to 2.6 million votes (58 percent to 36 percent of the valid ballots cast). In the congressional elections preceding the presidential balloting, the liberals had won handily, with 49 percent for the official slate plus 7 percent for Galán's "New Liberals."[18] As yet another step toward full competition, coalition government ended after almost thirty years, as the conservatives refused what was in their view an insulting offer of three ministries. Efforts to shift to a government-loyal opposition model failed in the face of deep divisions within each of the parties—the Liberal Party being vividly depicted by critics as a "stewpot of scorpions." Governing a country of 30 million inhabitants, 70 percent urban, Barca, who had an engineering PhD from MIT, sat by ineffectively as initially favorable economic conditions deteriorated after midterm. Ex-president Pastrana's son Andrés, candidate for mayor of Bogotá, was kidnapped in early 1988, as was Gómez Hurtado in May, while crime rates soared almost beyond global comparison. The situation was grim as homicides passed an annual rate of 10,000 in 1980 and doubled by 1988 on their way to 30,000 by 1992. (In late 1995, Gómez Hurtado's name would be added to the shameful casualty list of victims of lawlessness.) Peasant populations in guerrilla-controlled areas embraced the growing of coca, and the FARC instituted a tax on the production and transportation of drugs in "its" territory. In some ways the bloodshed was equal to that of the 1948–1953 La Violencia period. Not only were there various competing violent guerrilla movements in combat with the military, but the drug lords had developed private armies with even better equipment and arms than the armed forces or the insurgents. As the campaign of military repression failed to produce results and the judicial system broke down—through a combination of bribery and intimidation—right-wing paramilitary death squads (some financed by legitimate businessmen, but others by drug cartels) emerged to play a larger role. Barca's version of a peace plan left the guerrillas better off than before—in possession of "neutral zones" free from even patrol activities by the army. Meanwhile, in an effort to force the government to cancel oil exploration contracts with foreign firms, the ELN carried out over 100 attacks on the nation's largest oil pipeline between January 1988 and the middle of the next year.

Insurgency and drug trafficking became intertwined in a symbiotic relationship. Using marijuana profits for capital, by the early 1980s Colombians became central in the global cocaine business. Already in 1979 Colombia had edged past Mexico, exporting 41 tons of cocaine and nearly 16,000 tons of marijuana. A $3-billion business by that time, the drug business grew during the 1980s until the unofficial key personality of the country was drug lord Pablo Escobar Gaviria. A crusading justice minister was murdered as early as 1984, while the governor of Antioquía and the police chief of Medellín were among the summer 1989 murder harvest. As John Martz has pointed out, many, if not most, of the insurgents were no longer ruled by ideology or a burning desire for political reform, but their "primary motive [is] material; they [are] flourishing with the benefits gained by robberies, kidnappings, bribery, and under-the-table deals with members of Colombia's economic elite."[19]

Liberal divisions allowed thirty-four-year-old Andrés Pastrana Arango to win the Bogotá mayoralty election, a win that launched once more a new generation of an old presidential family on the road to the country's top office. Then in August 1989 leading liberal presidential contender Galán was murdered (shades of Gaitán forty-one years earlier), with blame falling on the drug traffickers. On the positive side, the M-19 converted itself into a legal party (as Venezuelan guerrillas had done earlier, and Salvadoran insurgents would soon do). Barca had by this time decreed a state of siege.

In one month the military arrested over 10,000 persons while confiscating properties and prized possessions of drug traffickers, but not capturing any of the really big fish. In the wake of Galán's tragic demise, his campaign manager, César Gaviria Trujillo (b. 1947), handily defeated even younger Ernesto Samper Pizano (b. 1951), the favorite of the party's left wing, for the liberals' 1990 presidential nomination (an event paralleling developments in Mexico a few years later). The May balloting was held in a climate of terror provoked by violence unleashed by the nation's drug barons. In addition to Galán, two other presidential candidates had been slain during the campaign and more than 300 people killed by a rash of bombings. In the four months immediately preceding the election hired guns of the Medellín cartel alone gunned down 149 policemen in retaliation for the government's continued rejection of offers to pay the country's foreign debt in return for amnesty.[20] Still, the March congressional elections gave the Liberal Party a 117-to-72-seat margin in the lower house accompanied by a 72-to-41 advantage (including holdovers) in the senate as conservative electoral support fell to 33 percent. Conservative division was deep, with future president Andrés Pastrana's New Democratic Force (FDN) faction electing 9 new senators to 5 for Gómez Hurtado's split-off.

Amid a turnout of just over 40 percent of the 18 million registered voters, Gaviria won easily with 48 percent of the vote, double the percentage received by three-time loser Gómez Hurtado, running on a dissident National Salvation Movement (MSN) slate after having been denied the conservative nomination. The Social Conservative Party (PSC) candidate was left far behind with an embarrassing 12.4 percent, which effectively ended his future political hopes. (The actual figures were 2.9 million to 1.4 million, with a movement of former guerillas slightly more than matching the PSC's showing.) The future of the traditional conservatives appeared bleak after this crushing defeat, since in both 1978 and 1982 they had garnered 47 percent of the national vote. On the same ballot, 87 percent of the voters approved holding a constituent assembly to reshape the country's basic charter.

At age forty-three the country's youngest chief executive, Gaviria, who formed a coalition cabinet to enhance national unity and resolve, had a good economic performance featuring shrinking the government through privatization and decentralization. Gaviria turned from the stick to the carrot, following a policy of "talking to people who were talking to the drug lords," but apparent victory with Escobar's negotiated "surrender" in June 1991 appeared ridiculously hollow in light of Escobar's July 1992 "escape" and proof that he had freely run his drug business from his private luxury prison mansion (which he had been allowed to have built for himself). Failure to recapture him demoralized the government temporarily. However, with the late 1993 death of Escobar, who had benefited from a near–Robin Hood image among the underprivileged masses of the Medellín region, Gaviria's stock soared. During his presidency an innovative new constitution was written, followed by liberal victories in the October 1991 midterm balloting that gave the party 87 of 161 chamber seats and 56 of 102 in the upper house, along with March 1992 state and local elections in which the liberals won 18 of 27 governorships and elected the mayors of 18 of the country's 23 largest cities. In March 1994 Samper won the liberal primary as the party scored heavily in congressional elections, but in May he was pushed hard to edge out Andrés Pastrana by 20,000 votes (2.586 million to 2.566 million, or 45.1 percent to 44.8 percent) on a turnout of only 6 million out of 17 million registered voters, a margin rising to 133,000—on 50.6 percent to 48.5 percent—in the June runoff.[21]

Hardly was Samper settled in office when his campaign manager was arrested on charges of having accepted large contributions from Cali drug lords, an arrest resulting in investigations that would hamstring the ambitious young president. Samper's campaign-financing scandal led directly to US destabilization efforts and his having to stave off impeachment by wheeling and dealing with senators—many of whom had drug-money skeletons in their own closets. Meanwhile the FARC was making important gains (it would peak in 1999–2000 at 17,000 active troops), and Colombia had moved from a center of processing and transshipment of drugs to the global leader in coca cultivation and cocaine production. Homicides had risen to an insufferable 62 per 100,000. This multifaceted crisis set the stage for a conservative resurgence in 1998. When the dust settled in late June from the heated campaign, Pastrana was the winner in the runoff by 49 percent to 46 percent, becoming the first man in Colombia ever to surpass the 6-million-vote mark as turnout rallied to 60 percent. But this victory came only after a neck-and-neck first round, in which Pastrana trailed the liberal candidate 34.6 percent to 34.3 percent as half the 2.8 million votes received then by dissident liberal Noemi Sanen, a former foreign minister, went to Pastrana rather than to his liberal foe. Since the liberals retained sizable majorities in both houses of the congress, Pastrana would be doomed to a frustrating and essentially unproductive presidency.

Unfortunately Pastrana (like Betancur and Barca) met with failure in attempts to bring about a negotiated solution to the decades of armed insurgency, the leitmotif of his administration. Pastrana's Plan Colombia left the armed insurgent groups in complete control of a very large portion of rural Colombia, 42,000 square miles. Very substantial amounts of military and economic aid from the United States not only failed to bring a solution to the violence problem any nearer but also made few appreciable inroads into the drug industry, which was flourishing at century's end.[22]

Moreover, management of the economy had severely deteriorated—with GDP shrinkage for 1999 of 4.2 percent before recovery of the lost ground in 2000 and 2001 and a rise of 1.9 percent in 2002. Hence the troubled country entered the new century mired in Pastrana's futile efforts to negotiate peace with the entrenched insurgents, a policy abandoned in February 2002 as Pastrana admitted failure. A month later the liberals won 54 of 161 seats in the chamber and 29 of 102 in the senate, to the Conservative Party's 21 and 13 seats. Those expecting that this resurgence would once again give the liberals control of the government in what had become a routine alternation in office were in for a major surprise. Indeed, the demise of the traditional parties that had recently occurred in Venezuela was just around the corner—although it would be engineered by a centrist statesman (rather than a radical leftist demagogue).

In late May, Álvaro Uribe Véliz (b. 1952), a dissident liberal running as an independent, received 53 percent of the presidential vote to only 31.7 percent for the Liberal Party's Horacio Serpa.[23] A former governor of Antioquía (whose capital is Medellín), Uribe was inaugurated in August and left little doubt that he would take a much harder line toward forces threatening the country's governability. In June 2003

Uribe announced a long-term "Policy for Defense and Democratic Security" and began talks toward demobilization of the right-wing paramilitaries, institutionalized in the form of the United Self-Defense Forces of Colombia (AUC) and often as busy working with the drug traffickers as with combating the guerrillas. When no results were reached through talks with the major guerrilla groups, at the beginning of 2004 the government launched a major offensive in the vast region stretching from just south of the capital to the Ecuadoran border. This shift in policy was partially spurred by sharply falling oil production—which customarily produced a third of government revenues—and the consequent need to attract new investment by demonstrating that the government was in control of the situation. For the 2001 decision to reduce the mandatory share of state enterprise Ecopetrol in joint ventures from 50 to 30 percent and the subsequent institution of a sliding scale of royalties proved inadequate (in the face of the risks to lives and property posed by the rebels) to spur an upturn in investment by foreign oil companies. Sound economic policies under Uribe allowed GDP to grow by 3.9 percent in 2003, rising the next three years to robust annual rates of 4.8, 5.2, and 6.8 percent—the highest in twenty-eight years.

Moreover, Plan Colombia (with an original price tag of $7.5 billion, $3.5 billion of which was sought from the United States) was beginning to show results in terms of strengthening the Colombian army.[24] Despite sharp increases in US assistance, which had risen from $67 million in 1996 to $1 billion by 2001, accompanied by growth of military advisers and civilian security consultants, during the months after July 2004 only limited progress was made in the direction of disarming the 15,000-man antirebel paramilitaries, authors of mass killings and protection of drug trafficking. Indeed, in many ways these paramilitary groups, which enjoyed powerful military and political backing, even within the congress, constituted a greater obstacle to political normality than did the entrenched rebel groups they used as their justification for existence. Like the rebel groups, they had enjoyed a sizable safe haven ceded to them by the government on the highly flawed reasoning that safety from attacks and interference would increase their willingness to disarm.[25]

On the political front, local and departmental elections in October 2004 brought leftist Luis Garzón, a 2002 presidential contender and head of the newly formed leftist Alternative Independent Democratic Pole (PDA), in as mayor of Bogotá. At the end of November the constitution was amended to allow Uribe to run for a second term in 2006, and a year later the supreme court upheld the amendment's legality, with a very positive public perception. By this time intensified efforts to demobilize the paramilitaries had made progress. This program was complicated by the fact that, along with drug traffickers, many of the paramilitaries had come to constitute the backbone of a rising middle class in rural areas and small towns and therefore exercised a significant degree of local political influence. (Others had embraced crime as a way of life and would have no interest in laying down their arms.)

A neat and quiet individual, Uribe turned out to be a giant among Colombian chief executives. The country's voters, the great majority of whom could not remember life before the guerrilla insurgency, and most of whose memories did not extend back beyond the rise of the *narcotrafficantes,* were satisfied that, unlike either of the traditional parties when they had been in power, Uribe was making headway on both fronts. Projecting an image of moderation and determination, he made his central planks "security for all" and "democratic security," pledging to achieve peace without resorting to a police state. Moreover, although still high, homicide and kidnapping rates were down sharply since his first election in 2002. The March 12, 2006, congressional balloting reflected a strong comeback for the right as Uribe's "Colombia First" coalition—led by Radical Change (CR), Colombia Democrática (CD), the Social National Unity Party (PSUN), and the remnants of the discredited Conservative Party—came away with 61 of the 102 Senate seats to go along with 90 in the 166-member lower house, and the opposition Liberal Party retained only 18 chamber seats. Indeed, its new rival on the left, the PDA, made a better showing, winning 35 seats. Despite efforts of the guerrillas to intimidate voters in the countryside, 40 percent of the 26.7 million eligible voters cast their ballots in this dress rehearsal for the presidential elections.

With turnout in the May 28 presidential election exceeding 12 million, Uribe swamped his rivals with a landslide 62 percent to 22 for Carlos Gaviria Díaz of the PDA, and only 12 percent for liberal Horacio Serpa (making him a three-time loser). Despite larger public subsidies to each of his two chief challengers than received by his own campaign, Uribe's vote was 2 million higher than in 2002, as he stressed governing rather than campaigning and refused to take part in television debates or even to give press interviews. Indeed, he went out of his way to make it clear that his reelection was grounded on his proven performance rather than on any of the presumed electoral advantages of incumbency. For its part, the FARC abandoned a policy of voter intimidation in favor of seeking votes for Uribe's opponents. The president's triumph in thirty-one of the country's thirty-three departments resulted in part from progress in disarming the right-wing paramilitaries—of whom 35,000 had turned in their weapons—and in denying reelection to a number of their champions in the outgoing congress. As an unforeseen side effect of this progress in strengthening public safety and internal security, a series of embarrassing political scandals at the state level came to light.[26]

With some trepidation Uribe accepted Venezuelan president Hugo Chávez's offer to broker the release of prisoners held by the FARC. But in late November 2007, following Chávez's unacceptable direct communications with top Colombian military figures, Uribe withdrew this acceptance and denounced his neighbor for having turned it into an opportunity to legitimize the Colombian guerrillas and seek to undermine Colombia's government. Chávez responded by saying that no relations with Colombia were possible until Uribe was removed from power. Relations became even more strained afterward, as a result of clashes between FARC and the army across the Ecuadorean border river. On March 1, 2008, Colombian air-to-ground missiles destroyed a guerrilla safe haven, killing a major FARC leader and capturing a desktop computer containing incriminating records of Venezuelan financial and arms support. Within four months a well-planned raid rescued Colombian ex-presidential candidate Ingrid Betancourt from her six-year ordeal as a FARC captive. Meanwhile, FARC's founder, widely known by his nom de guerre of Manuel Marulanda, had died of natural causes and the movement had suffered additional leadership and cadre losses.

Nearing the end of his second term, Uribe had accomplished the major feat of "pulling his country back from the brink of a general unraveling" and extending legitimate state presence to almost all of Colombia's 1,099 municipalities. By 2007 the armed forces had been built up nearly 70 percent from their 1999 low to a decently trained and equipped 260,000-man level—with its professional cadre increased from only 20,000 to 78,000. Over the same time span the FARC had seen its strength dwindle 40 percent to 10,000.[27] Hence it is not surprising that in late August 2009 congress approved a national referendum to legalize a third consecutive term, which, since his popularity remains above 80 percent, he would be very likely to win in May 2010.

Peru: The Army Versus APRA, Belated Dawn of Democracy

The depression-influenced overthrow of Augusto Leguía in 1930, given his modernizing and populist, if not deeply reformist, orientation, like Yrigoyen's ouster in Argentina, allowed the return to power of backward-looking advocates of the old order. It was in opposition to this retrograde tendency that Haya de la Torre would build the Popular Revolutionary Alliance of the Americas (APRA) into a mass movement. But the military would not permit the Apristas to come to power, even outlawing the party from 1934 to 1945. In that year conservative Manuel Prado—in power since 1939—allowed them limited legality, soon erased by a military coup leading the decade-long semidictatorial regime of General Manuel Odría.[28] Thus the initial period (1930–1955) for Peru would start out much worse than in neighboring Colombia (and Chile, but not Venezuela). Indeed, by 1930 Leguía's policies had earned him the animosity of important groups: Agro-exporters were alienated by his economic policies, traditional landowners resented his expansion of political organization into "their" fiefdoms, and the provinces in general looked askance at his turning a cold shoulder to their wants while he lavished public works upon Lima. Economic decline, reflected in unemployment and popular dissatisfaction, left the autocratic chief executive vulnerable in much the same basic way as his counterparts in Brazil, Argentina, and Colombia when the full weight of the depression was felt. Hence the man who was arguably the outstanding political leader Peru had yet seen (to a limited degree a cross of Argentina's Roca and Yrigoyen) fell in August 1930 before a coup headed by Colonel Luis Sánchez Cerro (b. 1890).

Initial consensus dissipated rapidly as it became clear that the new administration, like that of General Uriburu in Argentina, was heading back toward the pre-1919 days, perhaps even toward conditions that had prevailed before Leguía had first come to power in 1908. Challenged by rival governments controlled by middle-class elements in regional centers, Sánchez Cerro agreed to new elections in October 1931. This military figure combined his anti-Leguía role, Indian appearance, lower-class background, and personal appeal to build an ad hoc movement of an updated *caudillo* nature. He was opposed by a programmatically based mass movement that would mobilize plurality support down through the 1980s: APRA. Founded in Mexico in 1924 by Victor Raúl Haya de la Torre (b. 1895), its unchallenged leader well into his, and the party's, old age, APRA preached a complex populist ideology with a near-religious fervor, operating out of a network of "Houses of the People." Mixing Andean indigenist and Marxist ideas, Aprismo (as the movement and the ideology were called) advocated an anti-imperialist and antioligarchic alliance of the middle class, the workers, and the peasants. APRA's 1931 program featured a state-led mixed economy complete with central planning, government development banks, and the nationalization of strategic economic sectors, with foreign investment on terms set by the state. Tariff protection, progressive direct taxation of export sectors, agrarian reform, and universal adult suffrage for a corporatist-structured government were other key proposals. In short, from the viewpoint of the conservative groups that had overthrown Leguía, APRA was much more threatening than what they had already found clearly unacceptable.[29]

A hierarchical structure with Haya even more its maximum chief than was Calles in Mexico, APRA expected to come to power through the 1931 election. As the electorate now embraced 25 percent of all adult males compared to only 15 percent in 1919 (and only 15 percent of them registered as white), APRA's confidence seemed justified. But when the vote tabulating was finished, the official results gave Sánchez Cerro 51 percent to Haya's 35 percent. The "outdated, reactionary, personalist" had managed to combine victory in the landlord-controlled interior provinces with support from the Lima *lumpen* proletariat to thwart political progress. In Aprista eyes, and not unreasonably given both the past history of Peruvian elections and the situation in other Latin American countries at the time, the elections had been fraud-ridden and hence invalid. Had not this been the outcome in Brazil a short year before? Violence and near civil war followed the outlawing of APRA. Having witnessed many of their comrades massacred by the army, Aprista rebels near the northern city of Trujillo killed imprisoned army officers before laying down their arms. Rather than being forgotten over time, a sense of outrage would be kept alive in the mythology and lore of the Peruvian military and was used as a justification for barring from political activity the "cowardly murderers," a category embracing all Apristas, even if they had not been born at the time. This military veto of Aprista participation in government would have a paralyzing and distorting effect upon Peruvian national life until the mid-1980s. Still, on occasion APRA would find some sympathy in the form of junior officer support for their revolts—like the sympathy the UCR had encountered in Argentina in the 1890s.

In April 1933 Apristas retaliated for the slaughter of their supporters after the Trujillo incident by assassinating Sánchez Cerro, thereby giving General Oscar Benevides a chance to come back to power; he was selected by the constituent assembly to serve out Sánchez Cerro's term. When Apristas rebelled again in 1934, the party was outlawed, being subjected to severe repression until 1945. Benevides came into office when the depression had shrunk government revenues to only $19 million and his predecessor had defaulted on Peru's foreign debt. In 1933 petroleum provided three-fifths of the government's meager income. As other sectors of the economy stabilized, revenues rose $50 million, reducing dependence on petroleum to one-fourth. Establishing a social security system for industrial workers and building low-cost housing in Lima as well as highways everywhere, Benevides rode out the depression, along the way canceling the 1936 electoral outcome and extending his term, even adopting some of the reforms proposed by the Apristas, if only to appease and coopt part of their potential electoral base. Taking over in 1939, as the official candidate in a controlled election, civilian aristocrat Manuel Prado Ugarteche (b. 1889) allowed unions to organize, doubled the number of government jobs for the middle class, and reduced the cost of basic foodstuffs in the cities. A much more able politician than his military predecessor, Prado relaxed persecution of the Apristas without endangering internal order. In so doing he made skillful use of both a successful border war with

Ecuador in 1941 and favorable wartime economic conditions. The political situation, already improved under Prado, looked even better after World War II. Peru took part in the region's general swing toward democracy in the immediate postwar period.

In 1945 a broad center-left coalition carried a distinguished jurist from the Arequipan middle class into office. José Bustamante y Rivera (b. 1894) received two-thirds of the vote—a significant part of it from Apristas integrated into his National Democratic Front (FDN). At 28 percent of the adult male population, voting was up modestly from the last competitive balloting in 1931. Continuing the trend of the Benevides and Prado governments, Bustamante's policies favored industrialization, the urban middle class, and some lower-income groups. Exporters were hit hard by tax increases, whereas tariff and credit policies benefited industry. Housing and school construction programs were continued. Still the coalition fell apart as APRA sought to dominate the administration from its dominant position in the congress. As APRA bested the communists within the labor movement and sought advantages for rural workers and tenants opposed by landlords, the political situation wavered between polarization and impasse. In July 1947 conservative opponents used an obscure legal provision to close the congress, allowing the president to rule by decree. As proved to be the case in Venezuela the next year, Peru's democratic "false dawn" proved dishearteningly short.

Following an attempted coup by APRA on October 27, 1948, the military seized power behind General Manuel Odría (b. 1897), who would hold office to 1956, following an election in 1950 legitimizing his occupation of the presidency. Odría's chief backers were the agro-exporters, anxious to be back on top where they were certain God intended them to be. Odría's personalistic authoritarian regime attracted foreign investment and stimulated industrialization, much of it by multinationals. US direct investment grew rapidly, heavily concentrated during the 1950s in mining before subsequently diversifying into manufacturing and banking. Large increases in exports followed on the heels of these investments, and the US strategic stockpiling of minerals in the early 1950s stimulated Peruvian exports of lead and zinc as well as copper and iron ore. New irrigation projects on the coast led to rapid increases in the production and export of sugar and cotton, but existing oil fields neared exhaustion.[30] Antiunion, but proworker, the paternalistic authoritarian provided substantial material benefits to the most organized components of the masses. Creating a labor ministry, he extended social security coverage and lavished special attention upon the housing field. Straddling the old and the new in a simpler version of what Vargas had done in Brazil, he built a network of political support among conservative landowners through rather traditional political brokerage and massive irrigation projects for the sugar and cotton producers and at the same time cultivated a new personal power base among the teeming population of the squatter settlements ringing Lima (the *callampas,* or mushroom slums). With an eye both on Perón's Argentina and the Peronist-type governments in Bolivia and Chile after 1952, he used his wife's charitable activities to cultivate slum dwellers' community organizations. Odría calculatingly harked back to Leguía as architect of the good old days, launching a tripling of construction expenditures during the Korean War export boom. But that war ended, and by 1955 he faced increasing political opposition, beginning with the agro-exporters, who felt he had abandoned them, his original backers, for the populist road. Again, as at the end of the preceding period with earlier strongman Leguía, the provinces resented the concentration of public works and expenditures in the capital region. By late 1955 Odría was encountering formidable political opposition for the first time. The next year he would give in to it and hold elections—the first in which women could vote. (Odría looks better in retrospect than at the time because most subsequent Peruvian chief executives have performed worse than he did in providing eight years of stability with moderate economic growth. Moreover, although no Perón, he was more politically astute than near contemporaries Rojas Pinilla and Pérez Jiménez, and arguably at least the peer of Chile's Ibáñez.)

As Peru entered the last half of the 1950s, experimentation with changing political alignments and alternative development strategies continued as industrialization gave rise to new elite sectors and middle classes not linked to APRA, massive migration to urban marginal areas, and spotty, but significant, social mobilization in the countryside. This experimentation was reflected in alternation of military and civilian rule as the 1956–1968 period would see two constitutionally elected governments separated by a year-long interim military junta. Then 1968 would witness the beginning of a transformation-oriented military regime, which would be eased out in the mid-1970s by more traditional officers, who at the end of this period were ready to hand over power to the same civilian leader the armed forces had ousted in 1968.

Behind this zigzag course beginning in 1956 lay the unresolved problems of the preceding period, especially the still-intransigent military opposition to APRA. Spurred by the economic decline that followed the Korean War boom, in late 1955 and early 1956 agro-exporters, industrialists, dissident military factions, unions, and a variety of new middle-class political organizations joined forces to oppose any plans President Odría might harbor to rig the election. In the face of spreading unrest the country's strongman relaxed censorship but refused to legalize APRA, and he threw his support to Hernando de Lavalle, a Lima businessman being put forward as a national unity candidate. Hence, in the mid-June 1956 balloting, former president Manuel Prado, a member of the urban financial elite, emerged victorious in a three-way race in which women voted for the first time, bringing participation up to around one-third of the adult population. Prado's 45 percent plurality included very substantial support from backers of the still illegal APRA. A dramatic harbinger of the future was the strong 37 percent showing of Fernando Belaúnde Terry (b. 1912), a young US-educated architect from a prominent Arequipa family who had achieved national notice as dean of the architecture school at the capital's prestigious San Marcos University. Entering the contest very late against strong opposition by the incumbent government, he emerged as the closest approximation of a popular democratic leader Peru had yet produced. To a considerable extent he bottled some old Aprista wine in new containers, but he added a distinctive younger-generation flavor.

Despite lack of party organization, Belaúnde carried the city of Lima and most of the urban centers of the south. His support, upon which he would build for future presidential bids, came largely from newer and younger middle-class and professional elements that had emerged with the post–World War II surge of industrialization; from the population of southern cities, where APRA had never sunk deep roots; and from older middle-class sectors alienated by APRA's growing conservatism. On the strength of support from APRA, to which he had held out the tantalizing prospect of legalization, Prado swept the north, and he narrowly defeated Belaúnde along the central coast. Lavalle, burdened by the Odría administration's unpopularity, finished a poor third with only 18 percent, mostly coming from the more backward areas of the sierra still dominated by conservative landlords. As no reapportionment had taken place for over three decades, the rural areas of the sierra were heavily overrepresented at the expense of the burgeoning cities of the coast. Hence the Pradist Democratic Movement (MDP) won 75 of 180 lower-house seats and a majority of 30 out of 53 seats in the senate, with Apristas running as independents gaining 40 and 12, respectively, while Odría-Lavalle backers moped over their mere 25 and 2. Not having fielded candidates in half the country, Belaúnde's supporters had only a token representation in the new congress. Looking ahead, Belaúnde established a new party, Popular Action (AP), spending the next six years overseeing its construction, and in the process successfully carrying his message to all parts of the country. As put by a contemporary student:

> Belaúnde does not seek to erect a "palace of ideas" as Victor Raúl [Haya de la Torre] did in the 1930s—a philosophy providing answers to all problems of public and private life. What he offers is not a doctrine but a style, or rather a style plus an eclectic principle. Some of APRA's old themes reappear, but they have been re-interpreted and brought up to date. . . . Belaúnde, however, presents a lyrical vision of Peru's destiny ranging from the socialism of the Incas to modern concepts of planning.[31]

If the future might be Belaúnde's, the present belonged to Prado. His support came from businessmen producing for the internal market, politically moderate agro-exporters, and groups in the provinces with whom he had established clientelistic ties in his earlier term as president. Although he would face stiff opposition throughout his six-year term, Prado enjoyed a much stronger political base than had José Luis Bustamante y Rivera in the country's most recent democratic experience. The military was favorably inclined because of the successful war with Ecuador in Prado's previous term, and the Apristas followed a policy of *convivencia* ("coexistence") and were consulted on significant issues and given a leading role on labor issues, while disassociating themselves from the government's most unpopular measures.[32]

Although Prado's initial policies favored industry and other sectors producing for the internal market and his late-term policies, particularly when Pedro Beltrán was prime minister in 1959–1961, benefited agro-exporters, the Apristas acted with restraint and provided him with a high degree of labor peace. For they believed that those essentially coastal interests would eventually turn against the large landowners of the sierra as inefficient and anachronistic drags upon expansion of the internal market. With their core constituencies of the pre–World War II middle class and the comfortably entrenched union leadership now among the well-situated sectors of Peruvian society, Aprista strategists viewed Prado's backers as an incipient bourgeoisie with whom they could form a populist alliance. The Apristas also looked forward to legalization as a reward for their cooperation with the administration. Ensnared in the past, they underestimated both the depth of military antagonism and the growing appeal of Belaúnde's mix of populism and nationalism. Like the Prado administration, the Apristas were all but blind to a new factor about to explode into the political equation: rural unrest in the south. Trotskyite agronomist Hugo Blanco built a locally strong militant peasant movement in the La Convención Valley in 1958, and this movement would be the acorn from which revolutionary movements would grow. Peasant communities invaded wool-producing estates in the higher reaches of the central sierra, including those of the US-owned Cerro de Pasco Corporation. Prado did not dislodge invading *comuneros* or break strikes by *colonos,* so many landowners sold plots to their tenants or even abandoned their estates. The church, changing under the influence of Vatican II, began to sell off its lands to peasants. Anticipating that the passing of agrarian reform legislation was only a matter of time, other landowners began to decapitalize their properties, transferring assets into urban investments.

In 1962 Peru faced the prospect of a fully competitive election, as for the first time in thirty-one years, APRA founder and historical chief Victor Raúl Haya de la Torre was allowed to run for the presidency. He faced formidable competition from both Belaúnde and ex-president Odría. The June 10 balloting gave Haya 33 percent of the vote to Belaúnde's 32.1 percent and 28.4 percent for Odría—who combined conservative rural support with clients from the Lima shantytowns built up under his presidency. Minor candidates divided the slim remaining slice of the electorate. While the new congress was nearing agreement on an Odría-Haya deal, the military seized power on June 18 and promptly canceled the election results on the grounds of alleged fraud—an act that received Belaúnde's support. The military junta announced that it would hold "clean" elections within a year, and to the surprise of many observers—including a large proportion of US Kennedy administration officials—it fulfilled its promise.[33] During its year in power the junta established the National Planning Institute (INP), staffing it with young civilian technocrats. In preparation for the new elections the congress was reapportioned in line with the 1961 census, membership of both houses was reduced, and a new system of proportional representation was installed.

Even with these changes, the June 1963 balloting was almost a carbon copy of that a year earlier, but the small difference was crucial. The Christian Democrats (PDC), who had received just under 3 percent of the 1962 vote, allied with Belaúnde and Popular Action, helping him near 39 percent of the vote compared to APRA's slight rise to 34 percent and Odría's dip to 26 percent. This outcome prevented a need for the decision to be made by the congress and placed Belaúnde, whom most of the military had expected to win the year before, squarely in the president's chair. However, governing would not be easy, since the AP-PDC alliance fell far short of a majority in either house of congress, having 19 of 44 senate seats, but only 52 of 140 seats in the lower house. The backbone of the opposition was APRA, with 58 seats in the lower house and 18 in the upper house, generally supported by the National Odrista Union (UNO), with its 24 and 7 seats.[34] This minority situation posed two special problems because the Peruvian system contained elements of parliamentary government in that the cabinet was presided over by a prime minister requiring congressional approval and subject to a vote of censure—a requirement used to force Belaúnde to change 178 ministers during his five years in office. Moreover, there were no midterm elections with the president, senators, and deputies elected at the same time for coterminous six-year terms. Hence Belaúnde was to have no opportunity to improve his inadequate legislative base. Indeed, for his first four years as president the APRA-Odría coalition held a three-fifths majority in each house. By the time this obstructionist bloc broke up, Belaúnde's Christian Democratic allies had disintegrated, with Lima mayor Luis Bedoya Reyes splitting off and founding the Popular

Christian Party (PPC)—a blow because the formation of this party negated the value of Belaúnde's having the PDC head's daughter as his very personal and inseparable private secretary.

High hopes on the part of the Peruvian public for reforms and development by this president, fitting the profile ostensibly desired by Washington under the Alliance for Progress launched with great fanfare in February 1961, were doomed to disappointment. APRA, viewing Belaúnde as a "thief" of much of its program and as an opportunist for currying military support, played an obstructionist role to the hilt. (Indeed, its attitude bore a striking similarity to the UCRP's position a short time before in Argentina, where it preferred to see the military take over to cooperating with Frondizi and his UCRI branch of the radicals, and had some elements in common with the situation that would come to a head in Brazil by March 1964.) Equally destructive were the actions of the United States, which cut off all aid to Peru and used its very considerable, often decisive, weight in international bodies such as the IMF, the World Bank (IBRD), and the Inter-American Development Bank to relegate Belaúnde's government to pariah status. As a result, Peru under Belaúnde received less foreign aid per capita than any other major Latin American country, so—unless he was willing to abandon all of his reforms and developmental projects—Belaúnde was forced to finance a growing deficit with increased amounts of short-term borrowing, drawing down foreign reserves, and printing money. (This policy was eerily reminiscent of the extremely shortsighted US policy toward the Kubitschek government in Brazil in 1959–1960.) Peru's foreign debt consequently rose from a modest $237 million to $695 million during Belaúnde's tenure, and the public sector became more prominent in the economy. At the same time, domestic capital drifted out of the agro-export sector into real estate, finance, commerce, and local industrial ventures.

A dispute had been simmering for some years over US-owned International Petroleum Company (IPC), which held a concession originally issued to a British firm, then later transferred to American interests. IPC insisted that it had also acquired the original tax breaks, which under Peruvian law became void if the concession changed hands. Peru claimed that IPC was extremely far behind with its tax obligations, and the Belaúnde administration broke the impasse by taking over the company. Under the 1962 Hickenlooper Amendment (originally aimed at Castro's Cuba) the US government was required to cut off all aid to a country expropriating American property and investments without prompt repayment. Peru's answer was that the overdue taxes significantly exceeded the value of IPC, so in forgiving these debts Peru had paid for IPC. The Hickenlooper Amendment, unlike other similar congressional fiats designed to tie the hands of the US executive branch, allowed no "wiggle room" for the administration to use its discretion, much less make an exception. Hence Belaúnde was forced to finance his government's development projects through borrowing in European capital markets at high and rising interest rates. His back against the wall, in August 1968 Belaúnde reached a controversial agreement by which IPC relinquished its concession to the government's petroleum company in exchange for being granted a larger role in the profitable areas of refining and marketing. To the leftists this deal smelled like a sellout, whereas the military used charges of a secret page missing from the version of the agreement made public to justify ousting Belaúnde from office. (The ballyhooed IPC issue proved to be largely a smokescreen manipulated by the military, which was determined not to let Haya de la Torre be elected as Belaúnde's successor. By the time international courts ruled emphatically in Peru's favor in the IPC case, Belaúnde's government was history; essentially his six-year term had been cut to five.) Although Belaúnde certainly made mistakes, the deck was stacked against him much more than it had been against Frondizi in Argentina, much less Goulart in Brazil, and as the future would demonstrate, Peru was considerably less governable than more politically developed Argentina and Brazil. Hence the harsh judgment of Belaúnde's "failures and blunders" rendered by Collier and Collier is somewhat overdrawn, although their fundamental conclusion that his mistakes affected only the timing of the coup is valid. Collier and Collier also state that the armed forces' self-definition of its role gave them a determination to take the reins of government into their own hands since

> the military increasingly believed that the democratic regime was incapable of taking needed initiatives in areas such as these [agrarian reform and labor-capital relations], and began planning the implementation of such [basic] reforms through the militarization of the state . . . promoting fundamental economic and social reform as an indispensable prerequisite for national security, for preempting what they perceived as the growing radicalization of Peruvian society.[35]

In the last quarter of 1967 APRA began to cooperate with the right wing of AP, and in early 1968 it was helping the government cope with Peru's growing economic difficulties. Bringing together the financial, industrial, and agro-export elite and encompassing private-sector leaders with strong ties to foreign capital, this coalition of forces marginalized the traditional landowners of the highlands—thus earning their animosity.[36] This new coalition offered a chance for the Belaúnde government to salvage something out of its term in office. Armed with a sixty-day grant of special emergency powers from the congress, a new cabinet moved swiftly and with resolve to reactivate and stabilize the economy. Unfortunately, it was too late for Belaúnde to redeem promises of a comprehensive agrarian reform. A tidal wave of violent land seizures had taken place following Belaúnde's election in mid-1963, but late in the year he had been forced by the APRA-Odrista congressional majority to repress the guerrilla movements in the southern and central highlands and had become preoccupied with future outbreaks. This rural unrest led some military thinkers gradually to believe that agrarian reform was badly needed to head off insurgencies, if not to coopt peasant support as Acción Democrática had done in Venezuela in 1945–1948 and again after 1958. But the military would not entrust this agrarian reform to an Aprista government. (Vice president Edgardo Seone had won the AP nomination over Belaúnde's adamant misgivings but in reality had almost no chance of being elected.)

APRA's belated cooperation with Belaúnde was motivated by its hopes not only to participate freely in the scheduled 1969 elections, but to win and be allowed to take office. In June 1968 it nominated its aging founder, Haya de la Torre, and because Belaúnde was constitutionally barred from running for a second term, and because the AP had no other national figure—as would be the case with the Christian Democrats in Chile in 1970—his election appeared to be a strong possibility. The military was not ready to relent in its veto of APRA in general and bête noire Haya in particular. Because a coup close to the 1969 elections would have been too obviously meant to block Haya and would thus have incurred the risk of strong domestic reaction and international condemnation, the step had to be taken soon and appear to be directed against Belaúnde—before he could do anything to bolster his popular support. Hence, on October 3, 1968, a coup led by armed forces commander-in-chief General Juan Velasco Alvarado (b. 1910) brought an abrupt end to the suspense about the upcoming elections: There would be none. The resulting "Revolutionary Government of the Armed Forces," a junta composed of the senior serving officer of each branch, selected Velasco Alvarado as president and then each officer assumed the post of his service's minister. The most important regional commanders were allotted normally civilian ministries, with key colonels lodged in a newly created cabinet secretariat, where they sought to function as the regime's brain trust.[37]

Largely unnoticed, the thinking of younger elements of the military had been undergoing critical changes since the days of the 1962–1963 junta (a de facto government following a coup). These officers, of generally lower-middle-class provincial backgrounds, had reassessed the military's essentially conservative position in Peru's political life. The Center for Higher Military Studies (CAEM) and the intelligence schools had evolved a doctrine linking national security to development. This thinking had evolved into support for agrarian reform, nationalist energy policies, and an emphasis on systematic planning. In time, the progressive officers realized that the opportunity for progress in these directions under Belaúnde had been lost, and since working with APRA was unthinkable, the armed forces would have to take the essential measures themselves—as they perceived had happened in Brazil (under Castelo Branco and Costa e Silva) and Argentina (under Onganía). Hence they strongly supported Velasco's government, giving it a broad base of military support.

Consensus within the military began to crack as more conservative officers shied away from confrontation with the United States over the IPC dispute—which these same officers had used to the hilt to discredit Belaúnde—and questioned stressing the social aim of redistribution over that of production in the field of agrarian reform. During the first part of 1969 Velasco forged a coalition of military radicals and centrist developmentalists to isolate his critics. His position consolidated, and enjoying substantial popular support through the nationalization of IPC, Velasco embarked on an ambitious agenda of structural reforms. The redistribution of over 8 million hectares (roughly 20 million acres) of land undercut both the agro-exporting elites and the Aprista rural unions. Most major foreign firms were expropriated, and basic industry was reserved for a substantially expanded state sector. Local capitalists were provided attractive fiscal incentives to invest in the "reformed private sector," where profit sharing and worker participation in management were instituted. As the coming to power of Allende in Chile in 1970 monopolized international attention, foreign pressures were all but absent in Peru.

The alliance between the radicals and the developmentalists within the military rested upon a tripod made up of Velasco's exceptional leadership (matched only in the annals of the Peruvian armed forces by that of Odría in the 1948–1956 era); economic prosperity; and agreement on structural reforms. The salad days of the regime peaked in 1972 with the creation of SINAMOS, the National System of Social Mobilization, an agency well suited to play a major role in a corporatist restructuring of society. In practice, there was considerable popular resistance to such top-down de-politicization, even when packaged as "popular participation." In a context of successful borrowing in the eurodollar market, which trebled Peru's foreign debt over Velasco's tenure, and certainly compared very favorably with the ultimate failure of Onganía and his successors in Argentina, the Peruvian experiment seemed to many observers to be working reasonably well.[38]

Matters began to become unraveled after a nearly fatal illness in February 1973 left Velasco not only debilitated, but also increasingly impulsive and impatient, a state reflected in his rejecting criticism and relying increasingly upon the more radical officers and favoring them in promotions and assignments. Velasco's problems mounted when the oil shock and ensuing world recession led to a precipitous economic deterioration as prices for oil imports shot up, export earnings dropped, and foreign credit dried up. Moreover, a natural disaster devastated the fish-meal industry; fish meal was Peru's second largest export. Labor and agrarian reforms and active participation of new sectors led to increased conflict over relative shares of economic benefits and input in policy implementation. In addition, the overthrow of Allende in neighboring Chile in September 1973 removed the lightning rod of a South American government to the left of Peru's as a focus of Cold War policies of the United States and its allies. Active participation in the nonaligned movement and purchase of a large number of tanks from the Soviet Union took on a more controversial meaning. (The purchase made no military sense in mountainous Peru, and because it was a credit operation, it incurred future international liabilities that complicated later foreign debt negotiations. It seems to have been part of Velasco's efforts to become a significant actor within the global nonaligned movement (harking back to Egypt's Gamal Abdel Nasser, India's Jawaharlal Nehru, and Yugoslavia's Marshal Tito) by making Lima the site of its next summit.)

The alliance between radicals and developmentalists was coming apart. In May 1974 the leading conservative voice in the cabinet was forced out, and soon thereafter Velasco made public "Plan Inca," said that it had been his master blueprint since the beginning, and expropriated all newspapers not yet in government hands. (From a comparative perspective, the situation in Peru was beginning to bear an eerie resemblance to that in Argentina in the final months of Onganía's government.) In March 1975 Velasco suffered a stroke that accelerated his physical and mental decline. (He would die in 1977.) In this situation ambitious General Javier Tantalean Vanini became a catalyst of division. His marital ties to a prominent Aprista family and corruption in the ministry he had long headed worried moderates, some of whom were more attuned to what was going on under Geisel in Brazil than to the mess in Argentina or the dictatorial regime in Chile. Extraction of the armed forces from government before they became hopelessly divided and factionalized became an important goal, one requiring an exit strategy that would prevent a demoralizing retreat. So at the end of August 1975 Velasco was eased out, not in favor of Tantalean Vanini, but of war minister General Francisco Morales Bermúdez (b. 1921), who would direct the course of affairs first as prime minister, then as president. As the radical nationalists in the military were elbowed out, Belaúnde and other leading Popular Action personalities who had exited following the 1968 coup were permitted to return to the country, and the new government courted both them and APRA as counterweights to the popular forces orphaned by its abrupt shift away from progressive social policies. By February

1977 the military government, by now fully purged of Velasquista activists, announced plans for constituent assembly elections and, in August, decreed that these would be held in June 1978. Preferring the election of a new government to the military regime's buying more time with the election of a constituent assembly (a ploy that would delay choice of a new government), Belaúnde had the AP abstain from voting. Their absence made an opening, a temporary one as it proved, for Luis Bedoya Reyes of the PPC and his version of the Chilean military government's policies to move center stage.

In this fluid political situation, Haya de la Torre and APRA attempted to seize the political initiative, whereas the left was highly fragmented. When the votes for the new national legislative body were in, APRA had won a plurality of 35.4 percent, about its historical share, and the diverse elements of the left totaled 36 percent, the PPC coming in second at 24 percent. Presiding over the constituent assembly, Haya shaped a constitution strengthening presidentialism and setting the minimum for election to the presidency at 36 percent of the vote for the 1980 balloting (up enough from the old one-third so that it would have averted the 1962 election from having ended up in the hands of the congress); the requirement subsequently rose to 40 percent. So as this period, which began in 1956 with a transition to civilian rule, came to its end, Peru was again poised to trade military government for civilian government through the ballot box.

Peru had a rocky, uneven, and essentially unconsolidated transition back to civilian rule and competitive political life. Yet despite the thorny problems posed by ingrained terrorism and an ineradicable drug industry, it did move far beyond the generation-long impasse occasioned by the military's deep-seated antipathy for APRA and that party's prolonged retention of major, if not necessarily majority, popular support.[39] By the end of the period Peru's voters had soured on all of the existing parties, and several new political movements arose—including that of a populist figure who would enjoy massive support for most of the 1990s. Peru entered the 1980s with the Apristas divided and still mourning historical party leader Haya de la Torre, who had just passed away. As APRA's presidential candidate and his more conservative running mate sniped at each other, ex-president Belaúnde Terry successfully campaigned as a democratic populist, garnering 45.5 percent of the votes in the May 1980 elections, compared to 27.4 percent for Aprista Armando Villanueva, 9.6 percent for Lima's ex-mayor Luis Bedoya (PPC), and 13.8 percent for the several left-wing hopefuls. Villanueva gracefully stepped aside, eliminating the need for a runoff, and Belaúnde negotiated an alliance with his old Christian Democratic junior partners from the 1960s to obtain a majority in the congress.

One extremely challenging problem Belaúnde faced coming into office in July 1980 that he had not had to face in his previous presidency was the persistent violence unleashed by the Shining Path (Sendero Luminoso) insurgents.[40] Advocates of a peasant-based republic through violent revolution on the principles of Mao Tse-tung at his most radical, they were responsible for nearly 2,000 deaths in 1983 and some 3,600 in 1984, along with untold acts of barbarism and destruction of property approaching $1 billion. (Eventually, the guerrilla-sparked violence would be responsible for the loss of 70,000 lives.) This group's sensational terrorist activities cast a pall over Belaúnde's attempts to spur economic development and alleviate social problems. With Belaúnde unable to live up to unrealistic expectations based on a rosy retrospective view of his earlier administration, a new-look APRA came to power in 1985 behind young, handsome, and smooth-talking Alan García Pérez (b. 1949). Not only did this emulator of Spain's Felipe González and Julio Iglesias draw just over 53 percent of the vote, but he also carried his party to majorities in both houses of the congress. The left made a significant comeback, with 24.7 percent of the vote for Lima mayor Alfonso Barrantes, as the incumbent governing party, Popular Action, fell into near irrelevance with only 7.3 percent. On the positive side, this was the first time in forty years that one duly elected president was succeeded by another. Yet soon the country was near chaos, as the immature president demonstrated a high-handed and autocratic style and an economic policy that wavered from one pole to another. After promising to reverse the statist policies of the preceding governments, he abruptly turned around again. Drug traffickers and extreme-left terrorists were running amok compared to the Belaúnde years, when the Shining Path insurgency had got under way in the early 1980s, followed by the Tupac Amaro Revolutionary Movement in mid-1984. Hence, by the end of the 1980s, the electorate was desperate for change, with García's approval rating having plummeted from 95 percent to a dismal 15 percent. Inflation of 1,722 percent in 1988 exploded to 2800 percent in 1989 as GDP fell by 9 percent, then by 12 percent. It was no surprise that an independent candidate won the late 1989 Lima mayoralty election.

Prior to the 1990 elections, foreign exchange reserves were squandered, a fitting end to García's mishandling of the debt crisis. His failing performance was testimony to how APRA's inability to come to power in the 1930s, combined with Haya de la Torre's dominance of the party until he was a very old man, had stunted the development of new leadership. García's shortcomings were magnified by the fact that as a party, the "new" APRA had a complete lack of governmental experience—although this lack had been against their will and should be laid at the military's doorstep. Long anticipation as to what Apristas might do in office helped explain the unreasonably high expectations when they finally did come to power a half century or so late—more than two decades after their knocking on the door in the 1962 elections. Perversely, this lack of experience in governing also contributed to their lamentably poor performance in the nation's government in the mid-1980s.

Against this background of disenchantment as well as persistent terrorist activity, a new providential man decided to catalyze a break with the past and rebuild the nation's political institutions. Unfortunately, Alberto Keinya Fujimori (b. 1938) was not de Gaulle, and Peru was not post-1958 France. For the better part of a decade Fujimori would, however, be a serviceable Peruvian version of Argentina's Menem in a country that had known no outstanding political leadership since the end of the Leguía era in 1930. (Haya de la Torre might have been such a person had the military allowed him to come to power, but he also could well have been another in a series of political leaders talking the political talk much better than walking the walk.) The 1990 race saw the old parties pushed aside by personalist campaigns of conservative author Mário Vargas Llosa (27.6 percent in the April balloting) and Japanese-Peruvian agronomist Fujimori (24.6 percent), as APRA's standard-bearer won only 19 percent; two leftist hopefuls shared 11 percent. In the resulting runoff, Fujimori, head of the National Agrarian University, came from behind to win going away (56.5 percent to 34 percent) by promising an almost painless way out of the economic chaos—whereas his overconfident rival stressed the sacrifices and stern tests ahead for the nation. Peru's situation was grave, with GDP having fallen 30 percent in three years, out-of-control inflation at 7,600 percent a year, and service on $23 billion in foreign debt two years in arrears. Adding to public dismay was the fact that political violence had claimed close to 3,000 lives in the twelve months preceding the election.[41]

Seeking to mobilize popular support by dramatic action and to focus dissatisfaction against his opponents, in April 1992 Fujimori abruptly suspended the constitution, an action that led to a cutoff of US aid. Bolstered by the capture of Abemael Guzmán Reynoso, supreme leader of the Shining Path insurgents, Fujimori held elections for a constituent assembly in November, and eleven months later he gained approval of a new constitution by a narrow 52 percent to 48 percent margin in a national referendum. With thousands of rebels turning in their arms, Fujimori rode high on a tidal wave of popular support as inflation dropped to 15 percent and GDP grew by 13 percent in 1994, while incidences of politically related violence fell by 80 percent. This dramatic recovery, along with a brief reopening of the border war with Ecuador, paved the way for Fujimori's reelection in April 1995 with 64 percent of the vote—an unprecedented second consecutive term paralleling Menem's Argentine feat, and preceding that of Cardoso in 1998 in Brazil. Fujimori's centralized, executive-dominated government and free-market orientation led to massive privatization—reaching $3.5 billion by mid-1995—linked to commitments by purchasers to sizable new investments. In the year he took office inflation had soared to over 7,600 percent, falling to 139 percent in 1992, 27 percent in 1993, and 15 percent for 1994. So in October 1995 an agreement with creditors reopened access to international capital markets.

With 67 of 120 seats in the congress and none of the traditional parties reaching the 5 percent threshold for representation, Fujimori, intimately tied to the intelligence services, was able to reduce somewhat his hitherto heavy dependence on the military, which he had redeployed away from the country's borders to concentrate on internal security. Still his style became increasingly authoritarian, and the shady past and highly questionable dealings of his head of the National Intelligence Service (SIN) attracted adverse attention. The revamped political system remained highly personalist and poorly institutionalized. In mid-December 1996 the Tupac Amaro Revolutionary Movement (named after the last Inca leader to have rebelled against the Spanish) proved that insurgency was alive, dramatically grabbing the spotlight from the Shining Path by seizing over six hundred hostages at the residence of the Japanese ambassador and holding onto the most prominent politicians and diplomats until being killed by assault teams in February 1997. By that time signs of "Fuji fatigue" were evident. Insurgency, no longer acute, remained and was on the upswing, having over the years cost at least $14 billion in direct economic losses. Scandals abounded involving Fujimori's controversial gray eminence intelligence chief Vladimiro Montesinos. In 1999 Alejandro Toledo Manrique (b. 1946), an Indian from the interior who began as a shoeshine boy but later earned a Stanford University PhD in economics, led the opposition to Fujimori's bid for a third term that was highly dubious from a legal standpoint. Fujimori and fraud triumphed in the short run, as he purged the supreme court when it ruled against him, but by the end of 2000 he would head in disgrace to exile in Japan. Sadly, better days were not necessarily ahead. (Menem was destabilizing Argentine politics by trying for a third term, but the damage he did was minor compared to Fujimori's undermining of Peru's fragile electoral democracy.)

Running for a coalition called Peru Posible ("Possible Peru"), Indian-ancestry Alejandro Toledo encountered blatant electoral fraud in the April 2000 presidential balloting, which credited incumbent third-term seeker Alberto Fujimori with 49.8 percent of the votes to Toledo's 40.3 percent. Convinced that the end-of-May runoff was being rigged, Toledo dropped out at the last minute, permitting Fujimori to claim 57 percent of the vote and be reinaugurated in late July. Three weeks later the lid blew off a scandal involving intelligence chief and presidential crony Vladimiro Montesinos's illegal sale of weapons to Colombia's FARC guerrillas. The surfacing of a videotape showing Montesinos personally making a large cash payoff to a congressman quickly followed this grave misdeed, a revelation that in turn led to a nearly unanimous congressional vote to disband the National Intelligence Service. (In mid-2001 Montesinos was arrested in Venezuela and a year later convicted of abuse of authority and sentenced to nine years in prison, with five more years added on another charge in March 2003 and additional indictments pending.) When proof of a secret $48-million account emerged in October, and with the opposition taking control of the congress, the jig was finally up. Fujimori was voted out of power in mid-November as having a "moral incapacity" to exercise the office, and he rushed unceremoniously into exile in Japan.

As both vice presidents resigned, a caretaker government under congressional head Valentín Paniagua held elections in April 2001 in which Toledo defeated ex-president García by 36.5 percent to 25.8 percent, with Lourdes Flores of National Unity (UN) coming in a strong third. In the early June runoff, García picked up the lion's share of Flores's votes, receiving 47.8 percent of the vote, but still fell short of Toledo's 52.2 percent. Once again this was a warning not to count a supposedly discredited Latin American ex-president out, particularly if—like García—he had the chutzpah to say that he had made every mistake possible in his first term, so that now the nation deserved the benefit of the lessons he had learned from this dismal performance.) Toledo's party came away with 41 of 120 congressional seats to APRA's 27 and 15 for the UN. The parties of the Fujimori regime collapsed from 52 to a lonely 4 congressmen. This outcome offered a skilled politician (in the mold of Brazil's Lula) good prospects for putting together a working majority in the unicameral congress, which Toledo did.

The Toledo government, in its own way, affords another lesson in the difficulties of governing in the aftermath of a political crisis brought on by a protracted undemocratic regime. As in Argentina in 1983, when Alfonsín had to clean up the mess left by an inept military government (and dealt effectively with restoring the economy but was unable to do as much in the political arena), Toledo met with considerable success in the economic sphere. Indeed, real annual GDP growth averaged close to 5 percent, very possibly the highest in the region. Inflation was under control, and export earnings, fueled by increased mining production, more than doubled to $17 billion in 2005. But the benefits of this sustained growth failed to reach the poorer half of the population—not by coincidence largely Indian. They had expected much from Toledo, who as the country's first president of indigenous descent in seventy years had featured this heritage and his humble origins in his campaign. Yet, with internationally respected Pedro Pablo Kuczynski as finance minister, in office Toledo showed more of his professional economist side, favoring macroeconomic indicators over continuing high unemployment and stagnant real wages. As recognized by a leading student of the country, he did make significant advances in the political realm, since

> democratization advanced under Toledo. To give closure to the violence of
> the 1980s and 1990s, the government appointed the Commission for
> Truth and Reconciliation in 2001. In 2003, the commission produced a
> rigorous, although controversial, report. The media, most of which had
> been mouthpieces for the Fujimori regime during its final years, became
> unshackled. Although judicial, police, and military reforms advanced halt-
> ingly, decentralization was achieved; elections for regional governments
> were held in November 2002 and regional governments were duly in-
> stalled. A new law on political parties sought to reduce their prodigious
> number, requiring parties to win 4 percent of the vote in order to obtain
> any congressional seats.[42]

Also on the plus side, earnest efforts were made to prosecute ex-government of-ficials responsible for Fujimori-era corruption and human rights violations. Spymas-ter Montesinos was the prize culprit brought to justice, but the total reached nearly 1,500. This record of achievements raises the key question of why near the end of his term Toledo's approval ratings fell into the dreaded single-digit range. In addition to the unfulfilled aspirations of the indigenous masses, unrealistically high as these may have been, there was the backlash from his anticorruption campaign. Elite ele-ments that had benefited from the Fujimori-Montesinos era were desperate to put an end to this cleansing threat before it reached them. Hoping to bring about Toledo's downfall, they brought to bear all the weapons at their disposal to discredit him, using their control of the media to devastating effect. Toledo helped by follow-ing a luxury-filled lifestyle that could be spun as an affront to the masses of poor Pe-ruvians. As McClintock perceptively points out, controlled media had portrayed Fujimori as "an austere workaholic, inaugurating one public-works project after an-other in remote villages."[43] Fairly or not, Toledo was being measured against this in-flated standard as well as "assumptions of what was appropriate for people of indigenous descent."

Hence the stage was set for someone who could convince voters of a serious commitment to social justice and personal integrity. Although he was legally ineligi-ble to run for office and faced multiple indictments, in November Fujimori dramati-cally flew from his safe haven in Japan to Chile, where protracted extradition proceedings could keep his name on Peruvian front pages. He was hoping that public opinion would pressure the courts to allow his candidacy. With this added fuel, presi-dential succession came to dominate the political scene. Early on the front-runners were 2001 near-winner Lourdes Flores from the conservative National Unity (UN) coalition and former military officer Ollanta Humala, a fiery ultranationalist sup-ported by Venezuelan strongman Hugo Chávez, for the far-leftist Union for Peru (UPP). Advocating both nationalization of the country's natural resources and repudiation of the trade pact with the United States, Humala stoked hostility to Chile—reaching back to proclaim General Andrés Cáceres as his hero. On April 9 former president García of APRA, still viewed by many as brilliant and charismatic, improved slightly, but crucially, on his performance the last time around and came in second to Humala. His subsequent alliance with Flores sealed Humala's defeat, as García (with 24.3 percent) and Flores (at 23.8 percent) jointly had outpolled the early campaign favorite by a sizable 48.1 percent to 30.6 percent margin. Hence not even appeals to the voters of the fourth- and fifth-place finishers could save Humala from a 52.6 to 47.4 percent loss on June 4.

Clearly Humala had been hurt by revelations that his claim of coming from poverty and indigenous roots was an audacious invention. He had been raised in Lima and educated in expensive private schools. As an army officer in the early 1990s he had been involved in the brutal repression of rural dissident groups, and his 2000 uprising against the Fujimori government had in reality served as a smokescreen for Montesinos's escape from the country. Peruvian voters had chosen to give their 1985–1990 failure a second chance, hoping that, as he had promised during the campaign, he had learned well from the mistakes of his youth. In fact, as his term moved forward, this claim increasingly seemed to be the case, despite his lacking a legislative majority. For the congressional balloting, which took place along with the first round of the presidential election, left the opposition UPP with 45 seats compared to 36 for APRA, the country's one strong and permanent party, with 17 seats for Flores's UN, and 13 going to the Fujimori Alliance for the Future (AF) led by his daughter Keiko.[44]

In April 2009 Fujimori, the man who had led the country through the 1990s into the disaster-ridden next decade, was convicted of a wide variety of human rights crimes committed when he was president and was sentenced to twenty-five years' imprisonment. Meanwhile, the once mercurial and still at times impetuous García had put aside many of his highly innovative campaign proposals in favor of sound management of the country's economy and an effort to restore confidence in government. Abandoning his earlier nationalist stance, García embraced the recently negotiated trade agreement with the United States and continued the infrastructure developments under way. Despite 9 percent GDP growth during his first year in office, his approval ratings plummeted as the public thought he had done a poor job of dealing with earthquake relief and that his social programs were devoid of real substance. Although García retained support in APRA's strongholds on the northern coast, the southern part of the country felt neglected and became openly hostile, and he had very difficult relations with many governors.

García's main problem, however, was dealing with newly mobilized indigenous groups in the interior. In June 2008 he changed laws protecting Indian territories to conform with the free trade agreement, leading to vigorous protests that forced him to repeal two of the laws. These protests, chiefly involving petroleum drilling, resurged in April 2009, causing García to proclaim a state of emergency in early May and subsequently to send in the army to forcefully disperse demonstrators blocking a major highway junction. Two cabinet members resigned in the aftermath of this bloody incident, and congress repealed the most objectionable laws. Still, García had until April 2011 to convince Peruvian voters that he merited a second term.

Venezuela: Dictatorship,
Democracy, New-Style *Caudillo*

Venezuela was the only country in which the 1930s opened with no significant change. Juan Vicente Gómez and his Táchira cronies were still as firmly entrenched in power as they had been for over two decades. Hence nothing changed until after his death from natural causes at the end of 1935. Even then he cast a long shadow, as General Eléazer López Contreras (b. 1883), his defense minister, presided over a controlled transition—confirmed as president by the congress—until 1941. At first tolerant of change, he tightened up under criticism from his peers and concern by foreign investors—before relaxing restrictions again after a general strike. In that initial liberalizing phase, Rómulo Betancourt (b. 1908) and fellow young Marxist associates formed the Venezuelan Revolutionary Organization (ORVE), which then joined with other progressive parties that had sprung up. The congress, a carryover from the Gómez era, reacted harshly to all this unwonted, and to them unwanted, leftist activity, which also involved a flurry of union organization.[45] The July 1936 Constitution was a major disappointment to liberals and radicals because it did not contain major reforms and they were hoping for something at least along the lines of the 1917 Mexican revolutionary constitution. In October the umbrella National Democratic Party (PDN) was denied legalization. A hastily enacted labor law, to be the carrot in a carrot-and-stick approach by the government toward the working class, fell short of both the 1931 Brazilian law and the 1924 Chilean law. Then in 1940 López Contreras, now cozying up to the conservatives, withdrew legal recognition from a third of the existing unions. Shortly thereafter he turned the presidency over to his defense minister, General Isaias Medina Angarita (b. 1897)—ratified by an election in which under 5 percent of the population voted.

In the favorable political climate of the World War II period, party activity finally flourished, led by Democratic Action (AD), successor to the ill-fated PDN; the Independent Electoral Organizing Committee (COPEI); and the Democratic Republican Union (URD). Medina agreed with Betancourt and AD on a mutually acceptable presidential candidate for 1945; then this individual's health problems undercut this effort at unity and AD joined young officers in an October 1945 coup. Thus began the *trienio,* three years of boisterous, dramatic, and—in the short run—unsuccessful radical political reform. The initial junta contained four representatives of AD and two from the army, with Betancourt soon presiding over a "Revolutionary Governing Council." This impatient young man quickly changed the 1946 petroleum law to provide for an unprecedented 50-50 split of revenues between the oil companies and the government. Moreover, foreign companies in Venezuela were required to invest in nonextractive productive activities, and a new constitution with a social welfare orientation was promulgated. Elections at all levels were made direct, with all over eighteen entitled to vote.

This government was abruptly ended by a military coup in late 1948, but out of this learning period would result the successful implantation of democracy a decade later. In this process Betancourt, who had spent his second exile in 1939–1941 observing Chile's democratic practices, gained experience that would prove invaluable as he guided the country's destinies from 1958 to 1963. For under his youthful leadership AD polled nearly 1.1 million votes (71 percent) in the 1946 constituent assembly elections, attaining 137 of 160 seats, and, with support from 70 percent of the electorate, won control of the congress and placed respected novelist Rómulo Gallegos (b. 1884) in the presidency in December 1947—as the electorate exploded to over 35 percent of the population (women voted for the first time).[46] With a high degree of fusion between party and state, Betancourt remained the country's chief political operator, and another future president from the generation of 1928, Raúl Leoni, served as the extremely active labor minister. Land reform and organization of the peasants received priority attention, enrollment in primary education nearly quadrupled, and government oil revenues doubled. Yet this damn-the-torpedoes-full-speed-ahead strategy, by going too far, too fast, on too many fronts, catalyzed a classic backlash mobilization, one aggravated by the US Cold War desire for stable anticommunist regimes—particularly one in a major supplier of oil located in close proximity to the Panama Canal. Other parties were alienated by the "arrogant, monopolistic" stance of AD, which denied them an opportunity to build a popular base, and the military listened to US interests.[47] (This heavy pressure for conservative governments had been brought to bear in Chile and Brazil a year earlier.)

Opposition coalesced around López Contreras; then conspirators who found that ex-president too right-wing gravitated to Medina Angarita. Awareness of this plotting pushed AD into a more antimilitary mood, leading to consideration of arming organized workers and setting up a peasant militia like the one in early 1930s Mexico. The sense of impending crisis spurred AD to further speed up the already hectic pace of organizing both the urban and the rural masses. In October 1948 a radical agrarian reform law was enacted. The AD government's relations with COPEI, a Christian Democratic Party, and the Catholic Church deteriorated from uneasy to openly hostile. Hence COPEI founder Rafael Caldera Rodríguez (b. 1916), a leading spokesman for the "generation of 1935" (activist university students at the end of the Gómez era), and rising leader Luis Herrera Campíns (b. 1925)—both future presidents—shed no tears when on November 24, 1948, many of the same officers who had helped the AD come to power in 1945 staged a coup to oust it. While conservative economic interests and the international oil companies were jubilant over this turn of events, Venezuela's communists were far from unhappy because the AD had been squeezing them out of their dominant role in the urban labor movement.

Developments in the political sphere quickly disappointed the parties that had opposed the Gallegos government. Colonel Carlos Delgado Chalbaud (b. 1909), minister of defense during the *trienio,* originally headed the military junta, which set out to dismantle the state-labor alliance and demobilize AD's organized popular base. The party was banned, as was its labor arm, the Confederation of Venezuelan Workers (CTV), and AD leaders went to jail or exile, or they hid. In November 1950, before he could try to become constitutional president as his contemporary Odría had just done in Peru, Delgado Chalbaud was murdered by security agents linked to one of his junta mates, the extremely ambitious Colonel Marcos Pérez Jiménez (b. 1914). PJ, as he came to be known, controlled the government from his post as minister of defense until seizing the presidency at the beginning of December 1952. He went beyond his ill-fated predecessor in reversing the economic and social policies of the AD *trienio,* particularly in rural areas.[48] Close to Dominican Republican dictator Rafael Trujillo and attuned to developments in Peru as well as Argentina, Pérez Jiménez established an Independent Electoral Front (FEI) to carry him through an election in

which COPEI and the Republican Democratic Union (URD) could safely be allowed to participate as legitimizers, with the stronger AD banned and suppressed.
This scenario was knocked into a cocked hat when voters cast their ballots overwhelmingly for the URD's Jovito Villalba. Alleging widespread power failures, the
dictator interrupted the vote counting; a week later he was announced as the winner.
Since the URD was understandably reluctant to accept perhaps the greatest electoral
fraud ever perpetrated in a region accustomed to the manipulation of election returns, it, too, was outlawed. By the beginning of 1953 the country was free of any organized opposition activity.

Once again Venezuela was under the heel of a Tachirense (a native of the Andean
province of Táchira) *caudillo* dictator—one at least as ruthless as his professed role
model Gómez had been, but nowhere as able. Still, conditions were favorable for
Pérez Jiménez as industry grew rapidly for a tremendous expansion of oil production
as the dictator abandoned the AD program of husbanding this precious nonrenewable resource. An inept hybrid of Trujillo and Perón and a counterpart of Rojas
Pinilla next door in Colombia, Pérez Jiménez, in power for nearly a decade, and far
more effective at repression than construction, increasingly faced demands for a return to democracy from a coalition of the civilian parties that had briefly flourished
before the 1948 military coup. Taking the name Patriotic Junta and clearly encouraged, if not inspired, by the National Front's contemporary success in Colombia, they
spooked Pérez Jiménez in December 1957 into abruptly substituting a plebiscite for
the scheduled legitimizing elections that he had attempted in 1952 (and that had
worked so well for Odría in Peru in 1950). This ploy backfired, with a national general strike, backed by the church and business organizations on January 21, igniting a
crisis in which the army refused to repress the protest after casualties had risen to 300
dead and 1,000 injured. Pérez Jiménez fled into exile as a military junta took over.[49]

For Venezuela, even more than for its neighbor, Colombia (and in sharp contrast
to other Latin American countries), 1956–1979 would be marked by forward movement and the establishment of a viable democratic system. Indeed, by the end of the
period the erstwhile intransigently revolutionary left would abandon violence and
reincorporate into normal electoral-political competition. In a dramatic demonstration that statesmanlike and pragmatic need not be antithetical qualities and might
even go hand in hand, the democratic parties agreed upon a formula reconciling
power sharing with responsiveness to the electorate's wishes. The parties that had
overthrown the dictator agreed in midyear on a "minimum program of government,"
followed up by the October 1958 Pact of Punto Fijo, signed by all presidential candidates and establishing a weaker and more flexible analogue to Colombia's National
Front. The leaders of the democratic parties, particularly Betancourt and Caldera, had
learned well from the 1945–1948 fiasco. They, along with Jovito Villalba of the Republican Democratic Union (URD), agreed on the importance of coalitions instead
of the leading party's going it alone; the need for procedural, if not substantive, consensus; the avoidance of divisive extremes in party programs and concentration on
common ground; the encouragement of controlled and channeled growth of participation; and the exclusion of the revolutionary left, including the Venezuelan Communist Party (PCV), as unsatisfiable maximalists, even though they had been allies in
the struggle against the dictatorship. (In essence these thoughtful leaders were Hunt-

ingtonians even before Samuel Huntington had formulated his axioms concerning reform and "reform-mongers.")[50]

The first two governments, after an excellent brief caretaker regime under Admiral Wolfgang Larrazabal Ugeto, strove to build legitimacy and make democracy the only game in town. Betancourt and the AD easily won the late 1958 elections with 49 percent of the vote and formed a broad coalition government with runner-up URD (31 percent) and COPEI, which found to its dismay that it lacked the electoral appeal it thought it had earned, garnering only 15 percent of the electoral harvest. Concerned with alleviating the fears of the groups that AD had alienated in 1945–1948, Betancourt named only three AD stalwarts to his fifteen-member cabinet along with representatives of COPEI and the URD as well as sympathetic independents (in recognition of the fact that the party spectrum included no entity from the right). The president negotiated an agreement on high protective tariffs in exchange for acceptance by the business sector, represented by the Venezuelan Federation of Chambers and Associations of Commerce and Production (FEDECAMARAS), of a major role for the state sector in a mixed economy. When Fidel Castro as well as Trujillo tried to do Betancourt in, the armed forces decided that he must not be the communistic madman reactionaries had made him out to be. Moreover, AD's repudiation of Marxism, which led to a raucous defection in April 1960 by the great majority of its Youth Federation, who were convinced of the need for radical mobilization in support of a socialist revolution and soon became the Leftist Revolutionary Movement (MIR), was clearly genuine. For his part, Betancourt skillfully used rising oil revenues to keep the military well paid and supplied with the latest equipment. It was essential for him to do this because the MIR, followed by the PCV, had initiated terrorist activities in the capital in late 1960, extending guerrilla movements into the countryside the following year and forming the Armed Forces of National Liberation (FALN) in 1962. Betancourt and the AD, which had lost its lower-house majority with the 1960 defection of the radical wing and the subsequent abandonment of the coalition by the URD (which was moving left while the AD was moving toward the center), suffered an even more serious defection at the beginning of 1962 by a left-wing faction that the mainstream party had criticized for its aggressive ideological self-righteousness. In mid-1963, a critical election year, the government ordered the arrest of all known communists and pro-Castro extremists, subsequently stripping MIR and PCV legislators of congressional immunity and imprisoning them. Meanwhile the AD and allied parties established large numbers of new unions affiliated with them and won control of the Confederation of Venezuelan Workers (CTV) away from the PCV and other extreme left groupings. Even more important, the Betancourt government rapidly implemented an extensive agrarian reform program coupled with aggressive organization of a rural labor movement.

The AD retained power through the December 1963 election of Betancourt's right-hand man, organizational secretary Raúl Leoni (b. 1906). However, with two new, largely urban, parties intensifying competition, AD's vote dropped by a third to 32.8 percent, although ally COPEI increased its vote to 20.2 percent of the total, passing the URD, which plummeted to 18 percent. Riding on a wave of urban dissatisfaction, conservative intellectual Arturo Uslar Prieti's National Democratic Front (FND) took the larger slice of the 26 percent going to the new parties, with the lesser share going to the Popular Democratic Front (FDP) of leftist elements that had defected from the MIR when that entity opted for armed struggle. Leoni's centrist administration would be troubled not only by the continued rise of virulent insurgency by Castroite extremists, but also by internal party division, since he lacked Betancourt's enormous prestige as well as his exceptional political acumen. Relying on the coalition partners essential for a congressional majority, Leoni welcomed back the URD and gave business interests a role in policymaking (as had already happened with the PRI in Mexico). Opposed to abandonment of a reformist stance, progressive Luis Prieto faced off against moderate Gonzalo Barrios in a September 1967 party primary. Although very possibly having majority support among AD militants, Prieto was not the candidate Betancourt and Leoni thought needed to hold the coalition together.

Concerned that Betancourt would seek to return to the presidency in 1973, when he would again be eligible, Prieto broke away and founded the Peoples' Electoral Movement (MEP) to run as a dissident (à la Teddy Roosevelt and his Bull Moose Party in the US presidential election of 1912). This split, like those in Colombia in 1930 and 1946 did for the Liberal and Conservative Parties, allowed COPEI and Caldera to come to office in December 1968 with the narrowest of margins—28.9 percent to 28.2 percent, only 31,000 votes—from an electorate that had expanded to 4.13 million from 3.36 million just five years earlier and 2.91 million in 1958, a growth of 42 percent in a decade. The MEP polled a respectable 19.3 percent, the URD continued to fall out of favor with only 12 percent, and both the FDP and the FDN demonstrated a failure to put down roots (coming away with only 7 and 4 percent, respectively). Despite the first loss in a national election in its history, the AD still held 66 lower-house seats and 19 in the senate to 59 and 16 for COPEI.[51]

Caldera demonstrated why he had been in Betancourt's shadow. His victory resulted from AD's division, not from any dramatic increase in support for him or his party. Early on he legalized MIR and PCV and issued an amnesty that attracted most participants in the armed struggle away from guerrilla tactics that had failed to produce results and back into "normal" political competition.

With a limited base of support in the congress, Caldera and the AD entered into an "institutional pact" providing that for the next three administrations the party winning the presidency would name the presiding officer of the senate and the losers would get the presidency of the lower house and coparticipation in executive positions. Only after a major impasse did the parties agree in 1970 to an informal coalition in the congress. This was facilitated by COPEI's moving toward the center when in office—as AD had done when it was the governing party—making these parties overlapping multiclass parties (as the Labour and Conservative Parties overlapped in Britain, and as Christian Democrats and Social Democrats were beginning to do in Germany.)

The election of December 1973 reflected a continuation of the trend toward a two-party system as AD and Copei combined for over 85 percent of the vote.[52] A reunited AD won the presidency for a younger leader, Carlos Andrés Pérez (b. 1922), who received 48.8 percent of the vote to the COPEI candidate's 36.7 percent, as Betancourt wisely decided that a renovation of party leadership was more important than any personal ambitions on his part. (This statesman-scholar was well aware of the irreparable harm Yrigoyen's ambitions in 1928 had done to the radicals in Argentina.) As 1974 brought the global energy crisis and its big boom in oil revenues—with the entire petroleum industry by now in Venezuelan government hands—he could be a distribution-oriented populist. The political benefits Pérez reaped led the last of the guerrillas to give up their armed struggle and enter electoral politics. Still, Pérez had to concern himself more with economic policy than had his three predecessors. With growth down and inflation rising, he stepped up social welfare and investment expenditures, after 1976 giving these policies the label of "growth before redistribution." With Venezuela's rising oil revenues acting as a cushion against the increased costs of imports resulting from international inflation, Pérez did not have to worry about a depletion of foreign exchange revenues, so he could concentrate on maintaining consumer purchasing power—which inevitably led to subsidized prices. As found by Echeverría in Mexico, whose situation bore the greatest similarities to Venezuela's condition, foreign borrowing appeared to be the least painful option. (Venezuela's happy situation in this regard contrasted strikingly with that in Peru at the same time.)

With AD lacking a candidate of the incumbent's stature, COPEI behind Herrera Campíns won back the presidency in December 1978, the margin being 46.6 percent to 43.3 percent on a record vote of 2.48 million to 2.31 million with the electorate swollen to 6.2 million—an increase of over 31 percent in ten years. On the congressional side, 38.7 percent of the vote resulted in 86 deputies and 21 senators for each of the major parties, leaving only 21 seats in the lower house for all other parties combined. Hence, when in most of the area democratic transitions were only getting under way or were not yet moving forward, Venezuela's appeared to be fully consolidated. But its political development would bog down during the 1980s and 1990s, dramatically so when compared to the great forward movement of the preceding two decades. Yet disastrous backsliding was avoided and foundations for future progress were preserved. Leadership, one of Venezuela's strong suits in the first thirty-five years of the post–World War II era, let the country down. Concurrently, there was a failure to continue learning from the past. Political elites that had absorbed lessons from the adversities of 1948–1958 and astutely applied them during four presidencies became overconfident and, in a basic sense, complacent. When the performance of the next pair of administrations (1979–1988) proved lackluster, both leading parties' response, avidly seized upon by the electorate, was to go back and choose former distinguished chief executives to come back and reassume power under greatly changed circumstances. The results were acutely disappointing, but the processes of competitive civilian electoral democracy survived.[53]

As the 1980s dawned, Venezuela was still in a highly favorable political situation compared to the tensions and turbulence prevailing in much of the region. The protracted insurgency had died down to sporadic flare-ups, but by 1982 economic conditions were seriously deteriorating as oil revenues, counted on for 90 percent of foreign exchange earnings and the bulk of government revenues, plunged in the final years of COPEI stewardship. With the state responsible for 65 percent of GDP and with more than 1.2 million persons on its payroll, there was great reluctance to make deep cuts in federal expenditures, which neared $23 billion in 1982. As it entered an election year, the Herrera Campíns government faced a pressing foreign debt burden of at least $36 billion, half of it short-term; a growing trade deficit; shrinking foreign exchange reserves; surging inflation; a badly deteriorating exchange rate; and out-of-control deficit spending. In late February 1983 the bolivar was devaluated by 40 percent, and a highly artificial exchange rate structure was imposed, followed by a temporary debt moratorium. Dissatisfaction with the government's management of the economy soared to 87 percent. Under these circumstances the AD pulled itself together to regain power at the end of 1983 behind Jaime Lusinchi (b. 1924), a veteran congressional leader. Despite the prestige and proven track record of COPEI standard-bearer Caldera, Lusinchi won by a landslide, with a margin of 3.8 million votes—a record 56.8 percent of the valid vote cast—to 2.3 million for the veteran ex-president. The 3.3 million to 1.9 million margin of AD over COPEI in simultaneous congressional balloting, with less that 1.4 million for the plethora of smaller parties, gave the AD the highest proportion it had received in a national legislative election in Venezuela's multiparty system at 49.9 percent. This translated into a 29-to-13 advantage over COPEI in the senate and 112 to 61 in the 200-member Chamber of Deputies.

The 1983 election marked the peak of two-party dominance, as Lusinchi and COPEI's Eduardo Fernandez combined for 90 percent of the presidential vote, and their parties received 79 percent of the valid legislative votes. It also marked a low point for the left, as Euro-Communist intellectual Teodoro Petkoff of the Movement Toward Socialism (MAS), in alliance with the MIR, received a dispiriting 270,000 presidential votes to go along with 5.7 percent of those for the congress, while older Marxist warhorse José Vicente Rangel did even worse with a disheartening 220,000 votes. The MIR's 1.6 percent sliver of the congressional vote matched the dismal 1.7 percent for the Venezuelan Communist Party (PCV). The registered electorate had grown from 1978's 6.2 million (with 5.5 million actually voting) to well over 7.5 million, of whom 6.6 million cast valid ballots.[54] Such a high degree of participation in an electorate dominated by first- and second-time voters was exceptional by any comparative standards. (In 1958 the electorate had been 2.9 million, passing 4.1 million a decade later, and exceeding 4.7 million by 1973.)

To outside observers at this point Venezuela appeared to be in by far the best political health of any of these seven countries, but below the surface dangerous erosions were about to turn into sinkholes. Although political deterioration set in during Lusinchi's disappointingly lackluster administration, in the face of public disenchantment AD retained power at the end of 1988 by running ex-president Carlos Andrés Pérez, associated in the public eye with the prosperity of the oil-boom-fed mid-1970s, although the AD lost the control of congress it had achieved in 1983. Disillusion set in early, as Pérez encountered a difficult economic situation that kept him from fulfilling expectations for a return to populist policies. Nonetheless, he survived rather poorly planned and organized military coup attempts in February and November 1992, with their leader, Lieutenant Colonel Hugo Chávez Frías (b. 1954), being imprisoned after the second and more serious try. (Yet it bears remembering that an even worse-planned adventure of this type had lifted Fidel Castro out of the political sideshow in Cuba in 1953, and Chávez would not have to wait long to attain Venezuela's presidency.) In Chávez's view Pérez had improperly used military force to repress popular demonstrations against price rises resulting from IMF insistence on an end to food and fuel subsidies. Economic problems mounted, escalating seriously with a January 1993 bank crisis that cost the country $10 billion over the next year and a half, wiped out its foreign exchange reserves, helped spur inflation to an annual rate of 100 percent, and contributed mightily to a rise in unemployment to 18 percent. This time, with no international oil crisis to bail him out and evidence of corruption bursting out, the president's support eroded until the supreme court and the senate forced him to resign or be impeached in May 1993, with the election campaign already well under way.

Not deterred by the fiasco resulting from having reached back into the past to elect a previous occupant of the presidential palace, the Venezuelan electorate decided to compound the error. In a December 1993 presidential race featuring an overcrowded field, Rafael Caldera (president 1969–1973) was elected as an "antiparty" candidate (as had been the case with Fujimori in Peru), running against his own child, COPEI, as well as a plethora of other candidates. With a great deal of quantity, but little quality, from which to choose, only three-fifths of registered voters cast ballots. Obviously the younger generation of Venezuelans did not share the enthusiasm of their parents for the parties and system that had brought democracy after the cruel 1948–1958 authoritarian night. For this experience had not been part of their lives, while being left out of the benefits was. Long preeminent, after the December 1993 elections AD dropped to only 27 percent of the seats in the lower house and 32 percent of the senate seats. As the candidate of a catchall coalition of splinter parties calling itself Convergencia ("Convergence"), with only 17 percent of the vote, the aging Caldera was a minority president in all senses of the word, badly needing AD support in the congress.[55] More seriously, the party system that had performed so well since the mid-1940s was clearly on its last legs. (The fact that Caldera was elected with a minimal plurality by a coalition of splinter and ad hoc parties running against not only AD but even his old party COPEI was a strong indication of voter disillusionment with the parties that had dominated the political scene since 1958. These parties, like the Chilean Radical Party by the 1950s as well as APRA and AP in Peru by 1990, had failed to adjust to an electorate swollen by the entrance of both young "first timers" and the urban underclass.)

By the mid-1990s Venezuela's population was up 400 percent from the 1936 immediate-post-Gómez era, and Caracas had grown sevenfold. The once dominant Andean region had dropped from nearly 20 percent of the country's population to half that. So structural changes appear to have been needed for a system that had relied upon two major disciplined parties' keeping the congress weak in relation to the executive. But this was not the type of government Caldera was inclined or able to offer. Yet, after starting very badly, once Caldera learned how much times and Venezuela had changed, he paid more attention to the views of planning minister Teodoro Petkoff, once a leader of the armed insurgency.

Having been amnestied by Caldera and calling himself an heir to Bolívar as well as a fervent admirer of Peru's Fujimori, ex-coup maker Chávez ran successfully for the presidency at the end of 1998 as the candidate of the "Patriotic Pole," which included his personalistic Fifth Republic Movement (MVR), attacking the "rancid oligarchs" with devastating effect. This man of the people (son of a small-town schoolteacher) took office in February 1999. Independent Henrique Sallas Romer, running on the Venezuelan Project (PRVZL) ticket, had eventually received the backing of both COPEI's and AD's electorally unexciting nominees but still lost to Chávez's 56.4 percent of the vote (settling for 39.5 percent). Yet Chávez came away with only a minority in the congress, where the traditional pillars AD and COPEI won fifty-five and twenty-seven seats in the chamber, with nineteen and six in the Senate (on 22 percent and 11 percent of the vote), whereas Sallas's PRVZL came in with twenty-four seats in the lower house and two in the Senate on 12 percent of the vote. This outcome left the opposition bulwarks well ahead of the Chávez coalition's seventy chamber and eighteen senate seats (mainly for the MVR and its 21 percent of the vote, but also including allies Movement Toward Socialism at 9 percent and Causa Radical with 3 percent). Clearly at this juncture a major shift in voter loyalties away from historically dominant parties was taking place, one roughly analogous to the severe erosion of support the Radical Civic Union was undergoing at that time in Argentina (or that experienced by the Chilean Radical Party in the 1950s).[56]

Chávez seized the opportunity to mobilize, organize, and incorporate new elements into the political arena. Unwilling to be hampered by this congress, Chávez gained 81.5 percent approval—of the 39 percent who bothered to vote—in a late April referendum on his proposal for a constituent assembly, then two months later won 117 of 128 seats for the body that wrote his kind of a strong executive constitution. Courtesy of an ingenious system of gerrymandering districts and manipulating delegate lists, this overwhelming 93 percent majority was achieved with only 53 percent of the votes cast. The resulting ultrapresidential charter, ratified in mid-December 1999, also bestowed upon its architect the right to an extended term beginning in 2000. This second term would prove controversial and troubled but would also mark a watershed in Venezuelan politics as well as have a broader regional impact. Under the new constitution, Chávez handpicked a twenty-one-member "minicongress" at the beginning of February 2000, subsequently postponing elections for a single-chamber national legislature from late May to the end of July.[57] At that time a low turnout yielded a 57 percent endorsement of Chávez, an outspoken admirer of Bolívar, Castro, Fujimori, and Panama's late Omar Torrijos. His MVR won 80 of 165 congressional seats on 44.4 percent of the vote, as its ally, MAS, came away with 21 posts. Once nearly hegemonic, AD led the opposition with 30 seats on 26.1 percent of the vote, with its traditional rival, COPEI, settling for a mere 8 congressmen and an anemic 5.1 percent electoral support. Only 6.6 million of 11.7 million registered voters bothered to vote—as a large proportion of Chávez's foes did not support the opposition candidate. Local elections in December evoked a small turnout of only 23 percent of eligible voters—reflecting an extremely high degree of alienation from traditional political processes.

On the economic front a new hydrocarbons law enacted in 2001 raised royalties from 16.7 percent to 30 percent while limiting foreign participation in new oil projects to 49 percent. This law gave Chávez both increased government revenues and nationalist support in a rapidly polarizing political environment. His efforts to extend "enabling powers" allowing him to rule by decree in several policy areas, ranging from property into the field of education, aroused opposition escalating into national protests culminating in a two-day civil stoppage in December. As depicted by a pair of close students of Venezuela, "By 2002, the country was gripped by the worst polarization that Latin America had seen since the heyday of the Sandinistas in 1980s Nicaragua."[58] A protracted oil workers' strike starting at the end of 2001 and continuing into 2002 led to widespread violence once the Confederation of Venezuelan Workers (CTV) and the Federation of Chambers and Associations of Commerce and Production (FEDECAMARAS) threw their support behind it. After at least seventeen individuals were killed near the presidential palace on April 11, dissident army units arrested Chávez and installed a junta under FEDECAMARAS president Pedro Carmona—who acted in a high-handed and, in the eyes of many, arrogant manner that included immediately closing the congress and dismissing all elected governors. As with Perón's arrest in Argentina in 1945, a pro-Chávez uprising by the presidential guard restored Chávez to power within two days, as much because of as despite clear signs of US backing for the provisional regime. A general strike from November 2002 to February 2003 was ended only after international mediation resulted in a shaky agreement for a recall election some time the next year. As Chávez loyalists replaced striking workers, the revenues of PDVSA (the cumbersome acronym for what had been known as Petrovén) declined by over 12 percent in the third quarter of 2003 as oil exports fell by 27 percent (a decrease that would result in a massive 17.6 percent shrinkage of GDP for 2003). When the recall was finally held on August 15, 2004, Chávez emerged relegitimized as his supporters prevailed by a margin of 59 percent to 41 percent with a 70 percent turnout of an electorate reaching 14 million. Now his favorite catchwords of integration, solidarity, and complementarity could be supplemented with "Bolivarian Socialism" and a philosophy of as much representative democracy as necessary, but as much participatory democracy as possible. Increased power and extended tenure in office would be tenaciously pursued at every opportunity. To this end, Chávez folded the organizations backing him into a United Socialist Party of Venezuela (PSUV).

Buoyed by soaring petroleum prices, which rising 47 percent in 2004 spurred a GDP growth of 17 percent, making up the previous year's drop, the very determined Chávez prepared for a bid to remain in power beyond the late 2006 elections. Having packed the supreme court with an additional twelve justices and won every plebiscite held, Chávez was riding high. October 2004 regional elections, which a demoralized and disorganized opposition had largely ignored, left the government with control of all but two states and 90 percent of municipalities, strengthening Chávez's hand, particularly as nine new governors were ex-military allies. Bolstered by lavish social expenditures, the increasingly autocratic populist's approval ratings consistently ran above 70 percent. Congressional balloting in late 2005 reflected Chávez's continued support, as all significant opposition parties boycotted the balloting. Meanwhile, the self-assured *caudillo* raised eyebrows abroad by his anti-US rhetoric and gestures and the purchase in the first part of 2005 of $7 billion in armaments, including 100,000 Russian AK-47 rifles. Moreover, he used subsidized oil exports to create dependency on Venezuela in some of the small Caribbean islands as well as to support leftist movements in South American countries. As Fidel Castro's health deteriorated, Chávez skillfully positioned himself as the focus of anti-US sentiment in the region. In December 2007 Chávez put his plan for indefinite tenure as president, concentration of powers, and more socialist means of property ownership to a national referendum. To his dismay, voters rejected his proposals by a close vote of 51 to 49 percent. Then, in November 2008 regional balloting, the opposition emerged victorious in five states as well as the capital district. Although Chávez backers came out on top in seventeen states, those won by his opponents contained nearly half the country's population, with oil-rich Zulia the major prize.

Getting the supreme court to rule that a constitutional change was not the same as an amendment and extending the provisions to all elected offices, not just the presidency, a highly persistent Chávez managed to resubmit the end-of-term-limits proposal to a national referendum on February 15, 2009. With just over 70 percent of an electorate nearing 16.7 million casting their ballots, and following a very heated campaign, he carried the day by a margin of 6.3 million votes to 5.2 million (54.8 percent to 45.2 percent). Emboldened by this victory, by March 2009 Chávez had taken aggressive measures to strip his opponents of the most important powers of their offices and had forced the leading figure, Zulia's Manuel Rosales—who had had the temerity to run against him for the presidency—into exile with a barrage of charges and indictments. Juan Vicente Gómez ruled Venezuela for twenty-seven years, a record Chávez could break only in 2025. (After all, Castro had not only eclipsed Porfirio Díaz's Western Hemisphere longevity record of thirty-five years by 1994, but by 2000 had gone on to break Francisco Franco's all-Hispanic record.)

Chile: Redemocratization, Disaster, Return to Enhanced Democracy

The period from 1930 through 1955 would see a good deal of political change in Chile, much more than in Colombia, Peru, or Venezuela. Strangely, the period began with Colonel Carlos Ibáñez del Campo's losing his hold on dictatorial power, and it closed with retired General Ibáñez halfway through a term as a freely elected president governing Chile as a semi-Peronist. In between, the country had a brief experience with revolving-door presidents, an encore performance by Arturo Alessandri, a popular-front government, and a Cold War–era president elected with communist votes but shifting to the right. Meanwhile, copper would assume the importance previously held by nitrates.[59] Subsequently thriving in the 1960s, Chilean democracy would fail to survive its most severe crisis in the 1970s but would find its way back by the end of the next decade and go on to new heights.

When Colonel Carlos Ibáñez del Campo, having seized power in 1927, formed a new congress in 1930, the seats were allocated among the political parties according to previous negotiations, with Ibáñez's infant new organization getting a junior partner's share.[60] The 1931 elections produced a victory for Juan Esteban Montero Rodríguez, the military strongman's minister of interior, supported by the Conservative, Liberal, Democratic, and Radical Parties. Unable to develop an effective program, as these parties supported different policies and had diverse ideas about Chile's political future, Montero drifted to the right until overthrown in June 1932. After extreme instability, a self-declared "socialist republic" headed by Colonel Marmaduke Grove Vallejo (b. 1879) lasted only twelve days in September 1932 before being replaced by the moderate Carlos Dávila Espinoza, who shifted back toward Ibáñez-like policies during his brief passage through the presidency. Two additional provisional presidents later, Arturo Alessandri, the democratic president through much of the 1920s, was back in office courtesy of an October 30, 1932, election in which he received 54.7 percent of the vote to 17.7 percent for Grove, running from exile. Candidate of the democrats and the radicals, Alessandri was supported by many liberals tired of the political turmoil and, in retrospect, reacting positively to his earlier presidency. (As demonstrated time and time again throughout the region, nothing makes a president look good more than less successful successors.) As with Yrigoyen's encore performance in Argentina after 1928, and as it would be with Alfonso López in Colombia a decade later, those who expected a renewed wave of reform measures were quickly disappointed as liberals and even conservatives played major roles in policymaking. Conservative Gustavo Ross as treasury minister followed orthodox recovery-from-depression policies designed to get business on its feet. In a development that would have its major impact substantially later, the Chilean Socialist Party (PSCh) was founded in 1933. For the upper and middle classes the uneventful Alessandri administration was more comforting than the Justo administration was to their counterparts in Argentina.[61]

The 1938 elections found politically conscious Chileans concerned about the sad turn of events in Spain, where the Civil War had shifted in favor of Franco's fascistic Nationalists. The Comintern's policy of popular fronts of democratic and antifascist forces made the Chilean Communist Party (PCCh) available for alliances, so right-wing radical Pedro Aguirre Cerda (b. 1878) had both socialist and communist backing, along with that of the fading democrats, and he also received considerable support from admirers of Ibáñez and elements of the right unhappy with the liberal-conservative coalition's candidate. These two parties of the right came away from the polls with 48 percent of the seats in the lower house compared to 40 percent for the popular-front parties, led by the radicals at 20 percent and the socialists with 13 percent. In this politically uncomfortable situation, centrist Aguirre Cerda found himself reassuring the right because of his unwillingness to rely on the left.

In fact, this was the dilemma of the Radical Party, with a wing leaning in each direction. By the premature end of Aguirre Cerda's government in 1941, immobilism was its hallmark—although there had been some industrialization, expansion of the state's role, and respect for workers' rights.

On February 1, 1942, Juan Antonio Ríos Morales (b. 1888), another right-leaning radical, was elected president over ever-available Ibáñez, the candidate of the right—in part owing to ex-president Alessandri's pushing the liberals into the Ríos camp. With a cabinet extending over into liberal and business ranks, and under the slogan "To govern is to produce," Ríos promoted social stability. Suspected of profascist sympathies, he reluctantly joined the Allies at the beginning of 1943. One by-product of his administration was the ouster of Marmaduke Grove as head of the Socialist Party (for being too open to alliances) and his replacement by young Salvador Allende Gossens (b. 1908), who would be a key protagonist in the political drama and tragedy after this period's end. Allende produced no miracles as the party's presidential candidate in 1946, receiving a very anemic 2.5 percent of the vote. The Socialist Party had become discredited for collaborating with a government that had produced no significant reforms and whose economic policies had allowed the deterioration of working-class income relative to other social sectors that were supporting opposition parties. Meanwhile both President Ríos's possible accomplishments and potential failures were cut off when ill health forced him out of office near the end of January 1946.

On September 4 Gabriel González Videla (b. 1898), from the left wing of the Radical Party, was elected president in an extremely close election over a near-reactionary candidate. The margin of González Videla's victory was provided by the Communist Party, which received three seats in his cabinet—which also included as finance minister future president Jorge Alessandri Rodríguez—son of "Don Arturo." Under heavy US pressure in 1948 González Videla enacted a "Law for the Defense of

Democracy," which proscribed the PCCh, replacing it in his coalition with liberals who had opposed his election. This was one of the most dramatic impingements of the Cold War upon politics in any Latin American country, even going beyond the ouster of AD in Venezuela. Foreign observers, but not individuals closely following Chilean politics, were surprised when Ibáñez, who had been serving as a senator, won the September 4, 1952, election as candidate of an array of newly formed electoral vehicles (ad hoc political organizations brought into being only for one-time electoral purposes) and older splinter parties. In a general rejection of the traditional parties a near majority of the electorate (46.8 percent) decided to gamble on Ibáñez's recent rebirth as a Peronist—in the first balloting that included women. The candidate of the right received less than 28 percent, and that of the left, Socialist senator Salvador Allende, trailed badly with a mere 5.5 percent. (Eighteen years and three tries later, Allende would come out on top, although with only 36 percent of the vote—a victory that had fatal consequences for the country, resulting in a military takeover within three years.) Electoral reform and legalization of the Communist Party led the list of Ibáñez's political accomplishments, although there was little positive on the economic side of the ledger. As the period ended, Ibáñez was pondering the implications for him and his government of Perón's recent fall from power.[62]

Although initial omens appeared highly favorable, for Chile the quarter century beginning in 1956 would provide a very trying roller-coaster ride. Indeed, in many ways it would be the most critical watershed in Chile's history, its negative legacy becoming fully evident only in the ensuing period. Starting out with the election of a respectable conservative, Chile would then see a reformist government under Latin America's outstanding Christian Democrat, followed by the peaceful election of a Marxist—who would be violently overthrown only halfway into his constitutional term. This traumatic event led to a military dictatorship, bringing with it a level of repression never dreamed of by essentially democratic Chileans. The period began favorably as, deprived of his outside mentor, Perón (ousted from power in Argentina in September 1955), President Ibáñez decided to maintain the ship of state on an even keel by not having a candidate of his own for the 1958 succession. The January 1, 1956, general strike to protest the recommendations of the US-sponsored Klein-Saks economic study mission was met with a state of siege and arrest of its chief architect, Marxist union leader Clotario Blest. In the aftermath of this fiasco the labor movement remained quiescent owing to a combination of internal recriminations and the specter of repression. Ibáñez's economic and financial officials followed orthodox policies and attempted to balance the budget. Inflation dropped in 1956 and 1957, but a surge in 1958 resulted in large part from labor's protest of wage restraints; the government was sensitive to that part of the dissatisfaction coming from white-collar workers traditionally linked to the radicals. As would often be the case in Chile, as well as in many other countries, policy consistency was sacrificed to political conveniences, viewed around election time as necessities. This breach rekindled the debate between monetarists and structuralists, with the government moving back toward orthodox stability measures it believed had kept the 1959 inflation from rising above the disquieting 38 percent that it did reach.

Following repeal in 1958 of the controversial Law for the Defense of Democracy, Ibáñez legalized the Communist Party. As reflected by the 1957 congressional elections, the antiparty sentiment that had elevated him to office in 1952 was on the wane, but the right still benefited from quirks in the antiquated electoral law. As would be the case subsequently in Peru, reforms in 1958 greatly reduced the possibilities of voting fraud in the rural areas that had provided the conservatives with a captive electorate. By so doing, it afforded an incentive for the parties of the center and the left to seek support from the peasantry. This move toward modernizing politics also led to the incoming president's abandonment of a policy of filling key bureaucratic posts with civilian technicians and a return to staffing the executive branch with party politicians. The 1958 presidential balloting was in every sense a critical election, one that had in its second- and third-place finishers the future victors of 1964 and 1970. In a very tight race, Chile's constitutional reputation stood up to the test posed, as Jorge Alessandri Rodríguez (b. 1896), candidate of the right-wing parties, edged out the standard-bearer of the left, socialist Salvador Allende, by less than 35,000 votes. Significantly for the future, the young Christian Democratic Party (PDC) behind Eduardo Frei Montalva (b. 1911) elbowed past the radicals for third place. Alessandri's winning margin was 31.6 percent of the vote to 28.9 percent for Allende, with Frei garnering an attention-getting 20.7 percent of voter preferences while the radicals' near demise was sealed by their getting only 15.6 percent. The very small 41,000 votes for a "spoiler" candidate, a defrocked Catholic priest rumored to have been sponsored by the US Central Intelligence Agency (CIA), was larger than the difference between Alessandri and Allende. (There is little doubt that the Eisenhower administration would have mounted some form of covert operation to block Allende from taking office at this juncture—probably focused on thwarting his requisite congressional selection.)[63] One thing was glaringly clear from the election: the Radical Party had come to the end of its long run as a political force by 1958.

Jorge Alessandri, a respected businessman with experience in both houses of congress as well as the cabinet, and son of the renowned two-time ex-president Arturo Alessandri Palma, hero of the 1920s and 1930s (when his nemesis had been Ibáñez), steered Chile along to the major challenge of the 1964 elections. To do this, he attenuated, with tension, but not serious crises, the impact of the Cuban Revolution. His election as the candidate of the liberals and the conservatives arose out of changes that had come to maturity during the Ibáñez years. The traditional rural clientelistic "managed" vote (submissive to their patron's wishes) elites had depended on in the past had been undermined, so Alessandri pointed the way to a new, essentially urban coalition of the right involving professionals, small businessmen, and, with the decline of the radicals, white-collar workers. Labor during the Alessandri government shifted from its antipolitics, general strike orientation, which had proven a failure, to reentering the arena of electoral and parliamentary politics through close alignment with parties. Opposition gains in the 1961 congressional balloting led the president to ease up on restrictive wage policies at the cost of a rise in inflation. Slippage by the right in the 1963 municipal elections caused large industrial entrepreneurs to cool toward Alessandri, who in any case was not eligible for reelection. Hence both conservatives and liberals had to closely examine their options for the looming presidential succession.

In 1964 Salvador Allende, a respected socialist senator who had received less than 6 percent of the 1952 vote as a symbolic candidate and had been edged out by Alessandri in 1958, again carried the banner of the left under the Revolutionary Popular Action Front (FRAP) label, while the right lacked a candidate with significant electoral appeal, throwing its support to the Christian Democrats' Eduardo Frei in a move to prevent a possible Allende victory. This polarized situation in an electorate that had exploded from 1.16 million in 1958 to 2.92 million led to a campaign in which funding flowed in from the United States and Western European countries on the one side and from the Soviet Union, both directly and through Cuba, on the other. The result was a landslide victory for pragmatic Christian Democratic reformer Eduardo Frei with just over 56 percent, a rare majority in a country whose multiparty politics had for over a generation led to plurality presidents' needing to have their victory ratified by the congress. Yet with a view to the future, Frei's not-so-easy "easy" win was misleading, since the conservatives and the liberals had backed his election as a lesser of two evils and had no intention of supporting his programs. Allende's nearly 39 percent, although far behind Frei's vote, represented a substantial gain for the left over 1958, so the runner-up was able to keep FRAP together and on the "Peaceful Road to Socialism" as he looked ahead to 1970, when the popular centrist could not run to succeed himself. The left's strategy was to team with the right to prevent Frei from being sufficiently successful to pose the threat of a Christian Democratic victory in 1970. Hence archenemies, although looking forward to politically, if not literally, destroying each other down the road, often worked in tandem in congress to hamstring Frei's reform programs. Calling for "Revolution in Liberty" and "Chileanization" of the US-owned copper mines, Frei demonstrated awareness that a growing proportion of the population wanted more than just improved access to education and health care.

The Christian Democrats had had their roots in the Conservative Party's youth wing before migrating into the Falange in the latter 1930s. Constituting themselves as a party only in 1957, they emerged in 1958 as a serious contender as dramatically as Belaúnde and Popular Action had arrived on the Peruvian political scene in 1956. As formulated by Frei, the party's ideals were a creation of a reformist, communitarian third way between the poles of Marxism on the one hand and liberal capitalism on the other. Rejecting class conflict, the Christian Democrats wished to establish social justice by way of a humanitarian society shaped along the lines of Christian families. PDC ideologues saw the peasantry, the urban unemployed, and women as natural constituencies. In practice the party found its support within the middle class and the petty bourgeoisie and became a party more of the center than of the center-left. With only minority support in the congress, despite garnering an unprecedented 42 percent of the vote in the 1965 congressional elections, as the rightist parties ran their own chamber and senate slates and adopted an oppositional stance in repudiation of his slogan of "Revolution in Liberty," Frei found himself in the classic uncomfortable position of the centrist reformer fighting a two-front war against the left and the right while being pulled in both directions by elements within his own multiclass, catch-all party. In his first two years Frei moved cautiously and thus alienated the progressive wing of his party without appeasing the right opposition, which viewed any reforms with distaste as catalysts of revolutionary appetites. In 1967 internal dissension came to the fore with factions seeking to improve their clout through the congressional elections. With the reformist wing headed toward alliance with Allende's forces, in 1968 the administration shifted toward the right.

If any other Chilean administration is taken as a standard, Frei's accomplishments were far from inconsequential. Despite opposition from the right, he managed to enact an agrarian reform program providing for the expropriation of properties in excess of a certain size, but with exceptions for those being efficiently managed and highly productive. By the end of his term 3.4 million hectares, over 8 million acres of land, had been distributed to 35,000 families, and 115,000 rural workers had been extended the benefits of unionization. In the mining field, Frei succeeded in getting congressional approval for "Chileanization," or majority ownership of the mines by Chileans. Still, with labor remaining free of government control and linked to opposition parties, labor relations were confrontational when not conflictual. Frei's understandable policy of breaking, resisting, and circumventing the labor arm of his political enemies had the effect of further radicalizing the unions. Thus, in the view of a leading contemporary observer, while aiming at depolarizing the situation, Frei's actions "aggravated polarization and worsened the deadlock"[64] As a highly qualified scholar saw the situation, "In Chile, political structures that had facilitated popular participation, in a way which would not have been possible during the early stages of industrialization in Europe, proved too much of a threat to elites, and seemed too brittle to facilitate any compromise between elites and populist demands."[65]

Despite having coped reasonably well with the dilemmas inherent in this sticky situation, Frei, trapped in the single-term limitation that had waylaid Kubitschek in Brazil a decade earlier, was forced to sit by and see the progressive wing of his party join Allende's alliance in 1969, which, along with the left wing of the crumbling Radical Party, made Allende's new, broader Popular Unity (UP) coalition more formidable than the FRAP had been. For its part, the PDC went into the campaign saddled with a candidate not only less reformist than Frei, but lacking his popularity and charisma. As in 1958, the balloting was extremely close, with Allende receiving 36.3 percent of the vote over the nominee of the National Party (a merger of the liberals and the conservatives) standard-bearer, ex-president Jorge Alessandri, with 34.9 percent. Hence the election went, as had all recent ones except the one in 1964, into the hands of congress, where the Christian Democrats followed the democratic tradition of ratifying the first-place finisher—but only in return for a promise from Allende not to change the rules of the electoral game before the next presidential succession. US efforts to convince the national legislators not to vote for Allende failed, as did efforts designed to promote a military coup, with the assassination of strict constitutionalist General René Schneider the critical element.[66] Thus, just as twelve years earlier Alessandri had narrowly edged Allende, the latter now nosed him out. Just and fair as this result may have been, its outcome proved to be tragic, as half a term of Allende, gentleman that he was, would lead to fifteen years of repressive dictatorship. For nations, as for individuals, the path to hell may be paved with good intentions, especially if these bring out very bad intentions on the part of enemies. This was certainly the case, as Allende found himself caught between the opposition and the more radical elements of his own coalition. Although this was not in itself an impossible situation, bearing some similarities to Frondizi's earlier problems in Argentina, there was one critical difference: the determination of the United States to be rid of a second Marxist regime in the hemisphere, recently demonstrated in the Dominican intervention of 1965.

Allende's Popular Unity coalition enjoyed the support of just over one-third of the congress and faced the unremitting hostility of the United States and its allies. Under these handicaps his valiant pursuit of the "peaceful road to socialism" proved unattainable. This unfortunate outcome resulted even though Allende benefited from constitutional reforms in 1969–1970 that had strengthened the executive vis-à-vis the congress. As was in the cards, labor did very well under Allende's government, for which they would pay later, with the United Confederation of Workers (CUT) legally recognized, public employee unions legalized, and a two-thirds rise in the minimum wage in 1971, nearly twice as high as the previous year's increase in the cost of living. In an adoption of a structuralist approach, few restraints were initially placed on wages, which generally were negotiated well in excess of government guidelines—a practice the PDC adopted as payback for the many things the FRAP had done to make life miserable for the Frei government. The Christian Democrats felt, quite justifiably, that the Frei government had been subjected to opportunistically partisan hamstringing by the FRAP, which had frequently operated in conjunction with the extreme right to block or eviscerate the administration's legislative proposals. Because the left had obstructed the Frei government, some degree of parliamentary payback by the PDC was both rational and understandable.[67] The agrarian reform program was revised to greatly reduce the area of exceptions, and in a move with eventual near fatal results, the copper mines were fully nationalized. Copper needs to be smelted, and the smelting refining facilities were not located in Chile; the countries where they were located proved reluctant to buy minerals they felt had been improperly taken from their nationals. Until the ore is sold, mining creates major expenditures and there is no offsetting income—a lesson the Allende government learned the hardest possible way. At the same time, renewal of violent tactics in the countryside pursued by UP's militant maximalist revolutionary wing during Frei's administration brought strong reaction from the right, while the armed forces became increasingly divided.

While socialist measures went too far for the opposition, they were only a timid beginning in the eyes of the left wing of Popular Unity. Thus, Allende was increasingly hampered by deep divisions in his government and even deeper ones within its power base. The Leftist Revolutionary Movement (MIR) had never embraced the Via Pacífica, or peaceful road, to socialism. Dedicated to violence, having pronounced Maoist sympathies, the MIR was joined by the Movement for Unitary Popular Action (MAPU) and its followers in the labor movement in taking actions to bring about the establishment of socialism ahead of and beyond the government through land seizures and factory occupations. Extremely vociferous, these sectarian groups of the extreme left made no secret of their belief not only that existing structures and practices needed to be swept aside, but also that counterrevolutionaries and other reactionaries could expect to be sacrificed on the altar of revolution. In an unruly process of uprooting and replacing, rather than reforming and transforming, formal institutional channels of policymaking and political compromise broke down or were bypassed.[68] The behavior of the radical left wing was out of line with Allende's sincere, if idealistic, belief that in Chile, if nowhere else, because of its unique characteristics and traditions, it would be possible to install socialism through democratic institutions. He was both a dedicated socialist and a convinced democrat. He felt that it was possible to unite all classes, or at least important segments of all, against monopolists, the landed oligarchy, and foreign capitalist sectors. As with the contemporary Velasco Alvarado regime in Peru, there would be three forms of economic enterprises differentiated by ownership: private; social; and mixed, with the second eventually predominating as the first was reduced in scope, often bypassing into if not through the mixed model. This scenario presumed permanent tenure of the left in power, which Allende believed could be accomplished by electoral processes. Those to his left within UP felt that establishment of a socialist system had to be done quickly, as their confidence in maintaining power through parliamentary processes ranged from limited to nonexistent.

Popular Unity, particularly its Socialist Party component, performed well in the 1971 municipal elections, feeding a euphoric sense of invincibility on the part of the coalition's more exalted elements. The critical test of the Via Pacífica would be the 1973 midterm elections for congress. But growing economic problems cast doubt on how the public would judge the government at that point, when short-term economic factors might blind them to appreciating what fruits UP's actions would eventually bring. With inflation on the rise by mid-1972, this prospect of electoral defeat became preoccupying. The stakes of polarization were raised with the formation of a National Association of the Private Sector (FRENAP) to coordinate opposition by business, finance, and industrial groups on the one hand and the dramatic and disruptive October 1972 truckers' strike on the other. Along with other moves by the right, including middle-class housewives' parading in the streets banging on their empty pots to protest shortages and high prices, the scenario was eerily reminiscent of that in Brazil in the early 1960s leading up to Goulart's ouster at the end of the first quarter of 1964. Indeed, Brazilians were among the array of outsiders advising the anti-Allende forces.

The gains Allende had counted upon as a result of the March 1973 congressional elections did not materialize, with the UP gaining a scant eight seats on 34.6 percent of the vote—no significant progress over 1970. Hence the government would have to continue without adequate legislative support. The Christian Democrats had, in line with Chilean tradition, voted in 1970 for the congressional selection of Allende as the most-voted candidate. In return they had negotiated an agreement with him that his government would not make any fundamental changes in the rules of the electoral game, an understanding that, if honored, would give the PDC a favorable prospect for returning to power in 1976, when Allende would not be eligible to stand for reelection, but Frei could run again. Frei and his associates strongly suspected that, under heavy pressure from the rebellious MIR and MAPU, which insisted on complete socialization at any cost, Allende would go along with a proposal to replace the existing congress with a Soviet-style parliament. Having hoped to avoid this dilemma by obtaining a legislative majority in the 1973 elections, Allende was thrown into a quandary by UP's failure to get a popular mandate. The left's significant gains in congressional balloting since 1961—from 22 percent to nearly 35 percent—had come chiefly at the expense of the radicals, who had declined precipitously from over 21 percent to under 4 percent. The Christian Democrats' share of the vote had risen from 16 percent to almost 29 percent over the same span (while the right had declined from 38 percent to 21 percent), so there was little room for the left to keep growing unless there was an extremely sharp and "un-Chilean" shift from 1970 to 1973.

US-backed "destabilization" activities had been under way for some time, as many American Republicans had not taken kindly to the failure of efforts to convince the Chilean congress in 1970 to choose, as was then their legal right, Alessandri as president. (The law had subsequently been changed to provide for a runoff election instead of a congressional decision.) Earlier many of these activities were aimed at further undermining an already poor economic situation, but newer covert operations were in the field of psychological warfare, concentrating on fears among the military that they and their families were on hit lists to be eliminated after an impending complete seizure of power by UP. After the congressional elections, the crisis deepened rapidly, with the chamber, where the Christian Democrats were now ready to vote with the right, calling openly, on August 22, for military intervention.[69]

September 11, 1973, saw General Augusto Pinochet Ugarte (b. 1915) come to power over the blood-drenched bodies of Allende and many of his supporters. Indeed, by December 1,500 of them had been killed, joining the president, who committed suicide rather than surrender when fighting for Chile's equivalent of the White House became hopeless. (In this gesture he followed the precedent set by José Manuel Balmaceda nine decades earlier when he was defeated in the armed struggle with the congress and the military.) Chile entered a reign of terror exceeding even the worst days of the Argentine military regime. Acutely aware of the strength of UP's organizations and the dedication of its cadres, as well as the fact that they were not thoroughly discredited in the eyes of the public (as had been the case in Brazil and soon would be in Argentina), the new holders of power set out to obliterate them.[70]

A traditional type of army officer, Pinochet had entered the military academy in 1932 at age sixteen, graduating four years later. Attending Chile's War Academy (Chile's equivalent of the US Army Staff and Command School at Fort Leavenworth) from 1949 to 1952, by then a major, he remained there as an instructor while also attending law school. Following a successful, but not spectacular, career as a senior officer during which he avoided political involvement, he was selected to command the capital-area garrison at the onset of Allende's government, rising to command of the army in late August. This strategic position made the reluctant conspirator the vital swingman for any coup (equivalent to Castelo Branco and Costa e Silva in Brazil in 1964). Once dug in as head of the armed forces junta, this throwback to the officers turned out by the Prussian military mission in the late 1880s overcompensated for his earlier hesitancy to become involved in the plotting, exceeding any of Brazil's or even Argentina's military presidents in centralizing power and exercising it with zest—outdoing his ideological opposite, Peru's Velasco Alvarado, at his peak. Pinochet presided over a junta composed of the chiefs of the four armed services, as in Chile these included national militarized police established in the nineteenth century as a counterweight to the army. In a trajectory reminiscent of Spain's Franco in the late 1930s, Pinochet soon became Supreme Chief of the Nation and, by year's end, President of the Republic before adding the title of Chief Executive in mid-1974.

The Pinochet-led junta was extremely repressive in its opening period, torturing and killing individuals associated with the Allende regime or active in left-wing movements, with an energy and gusto not seen in Argentina until the dirty war and never found in Brazil or Peru. Thousands of such "subversives" disappeared, with human rights violations reaching 35,000. Despite the extreme polarization preceding the coup, most Chileans still wavered somewhere in the middle. As aptly put by a leading scholar, they were neither Marxists nor Pinochetists, but rather "dubious spectators caught in a system they had not chosen."[71] Under the force of circumstances, they became conformists. With no parties allowed and sectoral organizations severely restricted, the military services became avenues for a rough form of interest articulation and the junta a vehicle for a limited degree of aggregation. The most liberal, or at least the most modernization-oriented, of the services was the air force, making General Gustavo Leigh an often independent, if not dissident, voice until he was purged in July 1975. The Pinochet regime did meet with considerable, even notable, success in rebuilding the country's shattered economy, a feat that eluded many military and civilian governments across the region. Initially following the path of gradualism, the government shifted to shock treatment in 1975 under the baton of Sérgio de Castro, their answer to Roberto Campos and Delfim Netto in Brazil. The country was opened up to competition by relying on private enterprise and market forces; hence price controls were eliminated, tariffs were reduced, nationalization of mines was retained, but land was returned to its former owners. From 1977 to 1981 Chile's economy expanded at an annual rate of 6 to 8 percent. Continuity of what came to be called "Chicago Boys'" economic policy—for the university at which the leading lights had done their doctoral work—continued until de Castro's departure from the government in 1982.

Although restoring Chile's economic viability and fiscal solvency, Pinochet proved a much more ruthlessly dictatorial figure than Chile had ever seen. Indeed, his highly authoritarian and repressive regime, which had in mid-1977 implanted a plan for institutionalizing its permanence in power to the end of the century, was fully entrenched as the decade ended—sufficiently to last for another eight years. Indeed, the 1980s opened with the Pinochet regime firmly entrenched in power and beginning to gain international acceptance, as Franco had managed to do in Spain by the late 1940s. As late as 1988, after fifteen years in power, General Augusto Pinochet still presided over a united army, enjoyed a solid core of civilian support, and had a constitutional blueprint for remaining in power another decade—despite the demise of military regimes in all of Chile's neighbors and the rest of the region. Yet in a very short time he was out of power and Chile had resumed its democratic heritage.[72] In 1980 Pinochet imposed an authoritarian new constitution, ratified through a procedurally questionable plebiscite by an announced, but widely doubted, two-thirds majority. It enshrined the duty of the armed forces to ensure the survival of the state, legalized control of the media to prevent injury to the state and the people, and outlawed both strikes and labor courts as ways of settling union-management disputes. Most significantly, the constitution provided for a plebiscite in 1988 through which the junta's candidate could receive an additional eight years as president.[73] In installing this mechanism for continuing in power, Pinochet and his advisers counted on three factors favoring legitimization of his rule: satisfaction with the country's economic situation; fear of a return to the turmoil of the early 1970s; and division of the opposition. All three of these considerations, as well as the international environment, would undergo significant change by the time the referendum came around. First, the sustained economic growth, ranging from 6 to 8 percent annually from 1977 through 1981, ended abruptly in 1982 as low copper prices pulled the rug out from under loyalty-gaining social programs, modest as they were. In this context, neoliberal elements organized the Independent Democratic Union (UDI) while traditional right-wingers attempted to revive the National Party (PN).[74]

Hence, by the mid-1980s, heartened by the return to civilian democracy in neighboring countries previously friendly to the Pinochet regime, Chile's political parties increasingly advocated elections and a return to competitive political processes. The strongest of these parties, the PDC, riding on the memory of ex-president Eduardo Frei, called openly for a no vote in the upcoming referendum. Since it was free of any involvement with the Allende government—Frei having defeated the socialist leader in 1964 and backed his ouster in 1973—and enjoyed a close relationship with the Catholic Church, the PDC could not be attacked by the military regime as subversive or soft on communism. When a broad coalition of opposition parties, including the socialists as well as the PDC, issued a joint program on the eve of the balloting and the church carried out a massive voter registration campaign, the handwriting was on the wall for Pinochet and his supporters. So on October 5, 1988, Chile's electorate upset Pinochet's carefully laid plans with a 54.7 percent no vote (to 34 percent favoring Pinochet's guaranteed continuance in power), as close public and international scrutiny of the balloting and vote counting stymied efforts to manipulate the electoral outcome. Concertacíon's innovative campaign strategy centered on establishing direct lines to the voting public, bypassing existing intermediary organizations in favor of door-to-door campaigning. Appealing to all Chileans to come together in support of democracy, Concertacíon avoided harping upon the misdeeds of the incumbent regime, much less calling for retribution. Instead, the allied democratic parties stressed their leaders' comprehension of the people's problems and sharing of their concerns.[75]

The question remaining was whether the regime could muster a civilian candidate capable of defeating the prodemocracy forces. Surprising the government with its unity, the opposition formed the Concertacíon dos Partidos por la Democracia behind the PDC's Patricio Aylwin Alcozar (b. 1918) running against the regime's Hernan Buchi, the incumbent finance minister. To guarantee the military regime's acceptance of subsequent electoral outcomes, the opposition agreed to retain the 1980 constitution subject to removal of some of its most democracy-inhibiting provisions. After laborious negotiations, the modifications were approved in a May 1989 referendum. The initial presidential term was set at four years, with the next term returning to the traditional six years, and the number of elected senators was raised to dilute the influence of the nine Pinochet-appointed senators while maintaining their existence. Still the great autonomy of the armed forces, their budget guarantees, and the exaggerated role of the National Security Council remained, along with other "authoritarian enclaves."

On December 14, 1989, Chile had its first competitive and free elections since 1970. with 55.2 percent of the valid vote, 3.5 million out of 6.8 million, going to Aylwin as he defeated the pro-Pinochet candidate by a margin of nearly 1.3 million votes and his PDC received the lion's share of the coalition's support (26.6 percent of the total turnout compared to 29.4 percent for Buchi's coalition). Taking office on March 11, 1990, for a four-year term, Aylwin faced the task of establishing democracy with the dictator still on the political scene and vetoing any punishment of regime members for atrocities committed from 1973 on. Although enjoying control of the chamber, where 51.5 percent of the vote (26 percent for the PDC) gave them sixty-nine seats, the Concertacíon lacked a majority in the senate despite winning twenty-two of its thirty-eight elected seats (thirteen for the PDC). On the opposition side, out of a total of forty-eight the UDI had eleven seats in the chamber, and National Renewal, essentially a successor to the PN, held twenty-nine seats, second to the PDC's thirty-eight.[76] As Pinochet was legally entrenched as both a life-term senator and army commander-in-chief, he enjoyed considerable bargaining power—a sharp contrast with the Argentine and Peruvian situations, and quite distinct from that in Brazil. Yet in some ways the residual threat posed by his presence helped maintain the unity of the democratic forces beyond the point at which it otherwise might well have unraveled. For as time passed Pinochet became a sick old man preoccupied with avoiding trial and punishment abroad for his crimes against humanity. Still the government had to content itself with investigation and publicity about human rights violations, rather than prosecution and punishment. Fortunately, most of the public accepted this as all that was feasible under the constraining circumstances.

The very thoughtful and carefully progressive government proved adept in managing the economy, so in 1993 Eduardo Frei Ruiz-Tagle, in his early fifties and son of PDC founder and 1964–1970 president Eduardo Frei Montalva, received 55.5 percent of the total votes for a victory of 3.7 million votes to 1.9 million votes over the right's candidate, Arturo Alesandri Besa—another bearer of a distinguished political lineage, who garnered 33.6 percent of the vote. Hence the second Eduardo Frei embarked upon a six-year term as consolidator of Chile's democratic transition, pushing forward along the rails laid down by his predecessor—on balance the most successful of immediate postauthoritarian chief executives (Argentina's Alfonsín, Brazil's Sarney, and Peru's Belaúnde Terry).[77] On a different level, Frei's election repeated the 1958 success of Jorge Alessandri, another presidential son, which in turn had multiple precedents in Chile's nineteenth century. Frei clearly performed better than had the younger Alfonso López in Colombia—indeed, well enough that in 2009 Concertacíon would once again choose him to be its presidential candidate, giving him the unique chance to become the region's first son of a president to become a two-time president.

In the lower house of the congress, seventy seats gave Concertacíon solid control, as the PDC held thirty-seven, and each of its major allies, the socialists and the Party for Democracy (PPD), had fifteen. The RN had twenty-nine and the UDI had fifteen. Aylwin had concentrated with some success on reducing poverty, so Frei could pay increasing attention to education and infrastructure. In 1995 GDP grew by 8.4 percent, with inflation an annual 8.2 percent and the unemployment rate down to 4.5 percent. Savings and investments equaled 31.7 percent of GDP, so democratic Chile enjoyed respect for able management of the economy, which had been the military regime's claim to respectability. More important, the popular support that prosperity engendered allowed the government to emerge victorious in its one major confrontation with right-wing forces. Convicting retired General Manuel Contreras, former head of Pinochet's feared secret police, in June 1995 for the brazen 1976 murder in Washington, D.C., of Orlando Letelier, the government was faced with a four-month standoff with military elements protecting him. In the end he was imprisoned with the courtesy of military, rather than civilian, guards. Then in 1997 Pinochet and the other service heads were finally retired, and judges appointed by the ex-dictator began to reach retirement age. At the end of the year, stand-alone congressional elections gave the president's party 23 percent of the vote (compared to 27.2 percent in 1993) as its allied parties fared relatively well, maintaining the government's chamber majority at 69 of 120 seats on 50.5 percent of the vote, with a turnout of 86 percent.[78] Positioning itself for the presidential succession, the PDC garnered 39 seats in the lower house (on 19 percent of the vote) to 16 for the PPD and 11 for the socialists. On the opposition side the RN came away with 23 and the UDI with 17.

A presidential election at the end of 1999 carried Chile forward into the second decade of its reestablishment of democracy. In a context of rising unemployment Social Democrat Ricardo Lagos Escobar (b. 1938) of the PPD ran against a very respectable conservative, Joaquín Lavín Infante, mayor of the wealthy Santiago suburb of Los Condes, defeating him in a tight mid-January 2000 runoff by a margin of 51.3 percent to 48.7 percent—after a squeaker of 48 percent to 47.5 percent on December 12, as 90 percent of registered voters cast their ballots.[79] (The minuscule 0.5 percent margin on the first ballot was attributed by many observers to Lavín's very effective use of television.) Taking a page from Concertacíon, he concentrated upon direct contact with the voters, communicating empathy for their problems. Indeed, party symbols were absent from his campaign, and he stressed diagnoses of the country's problems rather than putting forth policy proposals.[80] The closeness of the election, combined with the decline in the Concertacíon's share of the vote, in part reflecting some Christian Democrats' reluctance to cast their ballots for a socialist, raised expectations of greater electoral competition in the near future. Nevertheless, a former Pinochet government official had narrowly lost to an Allende protégé, who, to gain election, pledged to continue Frei's free-market economic policies. This showing was a testimony to the pragmatism of once quite ideological Chilean politics. With an economics doctorate from Duke University, Lagos had been education minister in Aylwin's government and public works minister under Frei, thus being highly qualified for the presidency.

Indeed, he carried Chile into the twenty-first century in the best political shape of any country in the Western Hemisphere, not just of Latin America (since the United States was going from a near impeachment of a Democratic president to a highly controversial election eventually won by the Republican contender after very contentious court proceedings). The 2000 municipal elections demonstrated the Concertacíon's continued dominance as it elected 169 mayors and 1,039 municipal councilmen. The PDC remained its senior partner with 85 mayors and 424 local legislators. The conservative opposition's Alliance for Chile won 165 city halls, chiefly in smaller communities, accompanied by only 684 local legislators, led by RN with control of 72 city halls and 292 municipal lawmakers. The left was all but shut out, electing a single mayor and only 23 councilmen.[81] As the increasingly sophisticated electorate went to the polls for the third time in just two years in November 2001, the governing alliance received 62 of 120 chamber seats on the strength of 48 percent of the vote. Again the Christian Democratic Party (PDC) was the alliance's strongest leg with twenty-four seats to twenty-one for the Party for Democracy (PPD) and eleven for the Chilean Socialist Party (PSCh). The opposition Alliance for Chile earned fifty-seven seats on 44 percent of the vote. With half the senate's thirty-eight elected seats at stake, that body ended up almost evenly divided as the Concertacíon edged the Alliance twenty to sixteen.[82]

By early 2005 maneuvering for the next round of presidential balloting at year's end was under way. With the economy continuing its strong performance and the country enjoying social peace, especially compared to its Andean neighbors, the center-left coalition remained in a strong position to continue in office, as Michelle

Bachelet Jeria (b. 1951), the preferred candidate of the incumbent chief executive, won the Concertacíon's nomination over experienced cabinet minister Soledad Alvear, seeking to regain the spot for the Christian Democrats (a globally rare contest between two women for a governing political entity's presidential nomination). In mid-December Bachelet opened a lead in the first round of the presidential sweepstakes. Then on January 15, 2006, this avowed agnostic and proudly independent single mother improved from 45.9 percent of the vote in the first round to 53.5 percent. In so doing she defeated multimillionaire businessman Sebastián Piñera, who had edged out Joaquín Lavín 25.4 percent to 23 percent to get into the runoff. This 500,000 vote margin for the Concertacíon standard-bearer was an improvement over incumbent Ricardo Lagos's narrow victory five years before.

This spunky daughter of an air force general who had paid with his life for his loyalty to Allende stressed competence and experience in her campaign while staying away from demagogic promises or pledges of drastic sea changes. A medical doctor who lived in the United States both as a preteen and thirty-three years later as a student at the Inter-American Defense College, the new president had studied in East Germany after her 1975 exile from Chile. For as a socialist student leader, she had undergone imprisonment and torture in the wake of Allende's ouster. Following the end of the Pinochet regime, she had acted as an adviser to the health ministry and had graduated from the Chilean War College. When Lagos became president, she served first as health minister, then made her unique mark in the sensitive and strategic position of a female defense minister before winning the triple crown of Socialist Party nomination, being selected over a Christian Democratic rival as the coalition's candidate, and election to the presidency. Dr. Bachelet's triumph reflected voters' choice to continue the string of enlightened centrist governments Chile had had since its 1989 return to democracy. To combat perception by the electorate that there was only a process of rotating the top jobs among leading figures of the same parties (fatal to AD and COPEI in Venezuela), Bachelet "successfully portrayed herself as the candidate of renewal and change, promising to forge a more inclusive and open 'government of citizens.'"[83] She enjoyed a strong position in the congress with 65 of 120 seats in the chamber and 20 of 38 in the upper house. Her cabinet, composed equally of men and women, contained a plurality of Christian Democrats, including Alejandro Foxley, Aylwin's finance minister, as foreign minister, as well as the outgoing president's son. By this time it was apparent that the armed forces had adapted to their new role as public servants in defense of the country from their earlier pretension to be "guardians of the nation."

With only a four-year term (reduced from six by a 2005 constitutional amendment that also forbade reelection) Bachelet did not have time to waste. Indeed, she started off with a well-publicized effort to implement all thirty-six of her specific campaign promises, chiefly with regard to societal problems, within the first 100 days. She was somewhat taken aback by determined student protests and was diverted from her goals by the necessity of dealing with destructive floods. Nearing the end of her term, she was largely holding the fort. Because the free-market policies followed by her predecessors resulted in sustained high growth and substantial job creation, she did not appear inclined to make fundamental changes in what had worked well. As Valenzuela points out, "By reaching out to opposition leaders, Chilean governments since 1990 have made it clear that their country's 'democracy of accords' includes more than just the parties of the Concertacíon."[84] Indeed, Chilean governments have reassured the business community that they will continue skillful management of the economy, respect for the Central Bank's independence in fiscal policy, and export promotion. As for the "Presidenta," her successor will be chosen on December 11, 2009 in a free and highly competitive election.

This time around former president Eduardo Frei won the Concertacíon nomination, thus returning the PDC to senior partner status after two social democratic presidents. Early favorite ex-chief executive Ricardo Lagos dropped out of contention owing to problems encountered by his trademark Transantiago transportation system, while Soledad Alvear stepped aside after the PDC's relatively poor showing in the October 2008 municipal balloting. Beginning to tire of a coalition in power for nearly two decades, Chilean voters gave its parties only 28.7 percent of the vote, with the PDC electing 136 mayors on 1.83 million votes (18 percent of the total) and the PSCh—the president's party—winning in 72 contests (on the strength of 594,000 votes, just 9.3 percent). The opposition Alianza did better, with the Independent Democratic Union (UDI) receiving 1.28 million votes, 20 percent of the national total good for 129 mayors, and the National Renewal (RN), with the support of 841,000 voters (13.2 percent), winning 121 city halls. Complicating the picture was the fact that the Party for Democracy (PPD), a charter member of the governing coalition that in recent elections had lost ground to the socialists, went its own way as the backbone of "Concertacíon Progressista," taking 443,000 votes (7 percent) with it as a third force (and with its allies electing 102 mayors). Hence the end-of-2009 presidential race was three ways, with many observers predicting a win by the united opposition's Piñera.

Chile's democratic regime is both broadly participant and highly competitive. Yet although Chile's quality of democracy at the end of the first decade of the twenty-first century ranked the highest in Latin America, Brazil and Argentina could boast of having been democracies for five and six years longer, respectively, with Colombian and Venezuelan democracy going back even further, indeed, more than a half century, if in some respects lagging. For the former is marred by endemic insurgency and the latter by a sharp decline in the quality of its formerly enviable democratic credentials—flaws carried over from Colombia's tradition of political violence and Venezuela's propensity toward caudillism. Not fully consolidated, democracy in Mexico has made the most progress in recent years, while Peru had taken the greatest strides in extending meaningful political participation to an indigenous near-majority previously excluded, marginalized, and manipulated. Hence each country can rightly take pride in some signal accomplishment on the long road to political development, but rather than resting on its laurels needs to take stock of the myriad problems remaining and resolve to push ahead with determination and a degree of understanding exceeding that of previous generations.

Lessons from the past and elements for a forward-looking strategy for Latin America's continued and sustainable political development are pulled together and presented in the remaining pair of brief chapters—where matters that have already been described and discussed are refocused and analyzed.

Notes

1. Sound histories include David Bushnell, *The Making of Modern Colombia: A Nation in Spite of Itself* (Berkeley: University of California Press, 1993), and Frank Stafford and Marco Palacios, *Colombia: Fragmented Land, Divided Society* (New York: Oxford University Press, 2002).

2. Paul Oquist, *Violence, Conflict, and Politics in Colombia* (New York: Academic Press, 1980), p. 152.

3. Ibid., p. 14.

4. See Richard E. Sharpless, *Gaitán of Colombia: A Political Biography* (Pittsburgh, PA: University of Pittsburgh Press, 1978); Herbert Braun, *The Assassination of Gaitán: Public Life and Urban Violence in Colombia* (Madison: University of Wisconsin Press, 1985); and W. John Green, *Gaitanismo, Left Liberalism, and Popular Mobilization in Colombia* (Gainesville: University Press of Florida, 2003).

5. This period is covered in Harvey Kline, *Colombia: Democracy Under Assault*, rev. ed. (Boulder, CO: Westview Press, 1994).

6. For politics up through Gómez consult John D. Martz, *The Politics of Clientelism: Democracy and the State in Colombia* (New Brunswick, NJ: Transaction, 1997), pp. 53–62.

7. See James F. Henderson, *Colombia: The Laureano Gómez Years, 1889–1965* (Gainesville: University Press of Florida, 2001).

8. On La Violencia consult Orlando Fals Borda, *Subversion and Social Change in Colombia*, trans. by Jacqueline Skiles (New York: Columbia University Press, 1969), and Mary Roldon, *Blood and Fire: La Violencia in Antioquía, Colombia, 1946–1953* (Durham, NC: Duke University Press, 2002).

9. The Rojas Pinilla period is captured in Vernon Lee Fluharty, *Dance of the Millions* (Pittsburgh, PA: University of Pittsburgh Press, 1957), and John D. Martz, *Colombia: A Contemporary Political Survey* (Chapel Hill: University of North Carolina Press, 1962), pp. 63–74.

10. Consult Jonathan Hartlyn, *The Politics of Coalition Rule in Colombia* (New York: Cambridge University Press, 1988). On Lleras Camargo see Martz, *Politics,* pp. 75–97.

11. On the León Valencia government, see ibid., pp. 99–118.

12. Ibid., pp. 119–142, treats the Lleras Restrepo administration.

13. Ibid., pp. 143–159, deals with events during Pastrana's presidency.

14. The government of the younger López is discussed in ibid., pp. 161–183.

15. Ibid., pp. 185–206, covers the Turbay period. Also useful is Richard Maullin, *Soldiers, Guerrillas, and Politics in Colombia* (Lexington, MA: Lexington Books, 1973).

16. For this period see Kline, *Colombia,* and Hartlyn, *Politics.*

17. Betancur's term is covered in Martz, *Politics,* pp. 209–241.

18. The Barca administration is treated in ibid., pp. 243–264. There is a good overall analysis of the state of Colombian democracy by Jonathan Hartlyn and John Dugas, "Colombia," in Larry Diamond, Jonathan Hartlyn, Juan J. Linz, and Seymour Martin Lipset, eds., *Democracy in Developing Countries: Latin America* (Boulder, CO: Lynne Rienner, 1999), pp. 249–397.

19. Martz, *Politics,* p. 135, as well as Harvey Kline, *State Building and Conflict Resolution in Colombia, 1986–1994* (Tuscaloosa: University of Alabama Press, 1999), and Charles Berquist, Ricardo Peñaranda, and Gonzálo Sánchez G., eds., *Violence in Colombia 1990–2000: Waging War and Negotiating Peace* (Wilmington, DE: Scholarly Resources Books, 2001).

20. Gaviria is treated in Martz, *Politics,* pp. 265–289. Also see Russell Crandall, *Driven by Drugs: U.S. Policy Toward Colombia* (Boulder, CO: Lynne Rienner, 2002).

21. Hartlyn and Dugas, "Colombia," as well as Martz, *Politics,* pp. 297–304.

22. The younger Pastrana did not have as much to live up to as had López Michelsen, because his father was not in the same league as the first Alfonso López.

23. Consult Eduardo Posada-Carbo, "Colombia's Resilient Democracy," *Current History,* No. 670 (February 2004), pp. 68–73.

24. Consult Arlene B. Tickner, "Colombia and the United States: From Counternarcotics to Counterterror," *Current History,* No. 661 (February 2003), pp. 77–85.

25. Peter De Shazo, Tanya Primiani, and Phillip McLean, *Back from the Brink: Evaluation of Progress in Colombia 1999–2007* (Washington, DC: Center for Strategic and International Studies, November 2007).

26. Eduardo Posada-Carbo, "Colombia Hews to the Path of Change," *Journal of Democracy,* 17:4 (October 2006), pp. 80–94. Reprinted in Larry Diamond, Marc F. Plattner, and Diego Abente Brun, eds., *Latin America's Struggle for Democracy* (Baltimore: Johns Hopkins University Press, 2008), pp. 169–183.

27. De Shazo, Primiani, and McLean, *Back from the Brink,* p. 16.

28. A sound history is Peter F. Klarén, *Peru: Society and Nationhood in the Andes* (New York: Oxford University Press, 2000).

29. The literature on APRA includes Grant Hilliker, *The Politics of Reform in Peru: The Aprista and Other Mass Parties of Latin America* (Baltimore: Johns Hopkins University Press, 1971), and Peter F. Klarén, *Modernization, Dislocation, and Aprismo* (Austin: University of Texas Press, 1973). There is also a perceptive discussion in Charles D. Ameringer, *The Socialist Impulse: Latin America in the Twentieth Century* (Gainesville, FL: University Press of Florida, 2009), pp. 91–119.

30. Odría's eight years are treated in Klarén, *Peru,* and Hilliker, *Politics of Reform.*

31. François Bouricaud, *Power and Society in Contemporary Peru* (New York: Praeger, 1970), pp. 230–231. Also useful on the period is James L, Payne, *Labor and Politics in Peru* (New Haven, CT: Yale University Press, 1965).

32. The APRA alliance with Prado is analyzed in Ruth Berins Collier and David Collier, *Shaping the Political Arena: Critical Junctures, the Labor Movement, and Regime Dynamics in Latin America* (Princeton, NJ: Princeton University Press, 1991), pp. 696–701.

33. The military seizure of power is studied in Arnold Payne, *The Peruvian Coup d'Etat of 1962: The Overthrow of Manuel Prado* (Washington, DC: Institute for the Comparative Study of Political Systems, 1968).

34. The extremely pragmatic, if not opportunistic, alliance of APRA with Odría is examined in Collier and Collier, *Shaping the Political Arena,* pp. 701–704.

35. Ibid., p. 718. The most conceptualized and sophisticated study of Peru at this juncture is Alfred Stepan, *The State and Society: Peru in Comparative Perspective* (Princeton, NJ: Princeton University Press, 1978). Another relevant work is Howard Handelman, *Struggle in the Andes: Peasant Political Mobilization in Peru* (Austin: University of Texas Press, 1975).

36. APRA's relations with Belaúnde are covered in Collier and Collier, *Shaping the Political Arena,* pp. 704–710.

37. Consult Stepan, *State,* as well as Abraham F. Lowenthal, ed., *The Peruvian Experiment: Continuity and Change Under Military Rule* (Princeton, NJ: Princeton University Press, 1975).

38. A sound work on the military regime is Cynthia McClintock and Abraham F. Lowenthal, *The Peruvian Experiment Reconsidered* (Princeton, NJ: Princeton University Press, 1983). See also Cynthia McClintock, *Peasant Cooperatives and Political Change in Peru* (Princeton, NJ: Princeton University Press, 1981), and David Collier, *Squatters and Oligarchs: Authoritarian Rule and Policy Change in Peru* (Baltimore: Johns Hopkins University Press, 1976).

39. There is a competent treatment of Peru's troubled situation by Cynthia McClintock, "Peru," in Larry Diamond, Jonathan Hartlyn, Juan J. Linz, and Seymour Martin Lipset, eds., *Democracy in Developing Countries: Latin America* (Boulder, CO: Lynne Rienner, 1999), pp. 309–365. Also useful is Catherine M. Conaghan and James M. Malloy, *Unsettling Statecraft: Democracy and Neoliberalism in the Central Andes* (Pittsburgh, PA: University of Pittsburgh Press, 1994).

40. The rich literature on the Peruvian insurgencies includes Steve J. Stern, ed., *Shining and Other Paths: War and Society in Peru, 1980–1995* (Durham, NC: Duke University Press, 1998);

David Scott Palmer, ed., *The Shining Path of Peru* (New York: St. Martins Press, 1992); and Cynthia McClintock, ed., *Revolutionary Movements in Latin America: El Salvador's FMLN and Peru's Shining Path* (Washington, DC: United States Institute of Peace Press, 1998).

41. Fujimori's election is discussed by McClintock, "Peru." Paul H. Lewis, *Authoritarian Regimes in Latin America: Dictators, Despots, and Tyrants* (Lanham, MD: Rowman & Littlefield, 2006), pp. 239–242, shows insight into Peru at this point.

42. See Cynthia McClintock, "An Unlikely Comeback in Peru," *Journal of Democracy*, 17:4 (October 2006), pp. 95–110, reprinted in Larry Diamond, Marc F. Plattner, and Diego Abente Brun, eds., *Latin America's Struggle for Democracy* (Baltimore: Johns Hopkins University Press, 2008), pp. 154–168.

43. Ibid., p. 157.

44. Ibid., pp. 160–164.

45. See Daniel C. Hellinger, *Venezuela: Tarnished Democracy* (Boulder, CO: Westview Press, 1991), and David E. Blank, *Politics in Venezuela* (Boston: Little, Brown, 1973).

46. Robert J. Alexander, *Rómulo Betancourt and the Transformation of Venezuela* (New Brunswick, NJ: Transaction Books, 1982), covers the *trienio*.

47. John D. Martz, *Acción Democrática: Evolution of a Modern Political Party in Venezuela* (Princeton, NJ: Princeton University Press, 1966), is the standard work on the AD.

48. Phillip B. Taylor, Jr., *The Venezuelan Golpe de Estado de 1958: The Fall of Marcos Pérez Jiménez* (Washington, DC: Institute for the Comparative Study of Political Systems, 1968).

49. Ibid.

50. See Alexander, *Rómulo Betancourt*.

51. Worth consulting are David E. Blank, *Venezuela: Politics in a Petroleum Republic* (New York: Praeger, 1984), and Enrique Baloyra and John D. Martz, *Political Attitudes in Venezuela: Societal Cleavages and Public Opinion* (Austin: University of Texas Press, 1979).

52. See John D. Martz and Enrique Baloyra, *Electoral Mobilization and Public Opinion: The Venezuelan Campaign of 1973* (Chapel Hill: University of North Carolina Press, 1976).

53. Consult Howard R. Penniman, ed., *Venezuela at the Polls: The National Elections of 1978* (Washington, DC: American Enterprise Institute for Public Policy Research, 1980).

54. See the author's series, especially No. 4, *Venezuelan Election Project: Results and Future Prospects* (Washington, DC: Center for Strategic and International Studies, January 1984).

55. Useful through the 1980s is Daniel C. Hellinger, *Venezuela*. His coverage is extended in Steve Ellner and Daniel Hellinger, eds., *Venezuelan Politics in the Chávez Era: Class, Polarization, and Conflict* (Boulder, CO: Lynne Rienner, 2004). For a perceptive analysis of the decline of Venezuela's democracy see the chapter "Venezuela," by Daniel H. Levine and Brian F. Crisp, in Larry Diamond, Jonathan Hartlyn, Juan J. Linz, and Seymour Martin Lipset, eds., *Democracy in Developing Countries: Latin America* (Boulder, CO: Lynne Rienner, 1999), pp. 367–426. See also the vivid portrayal of Chávez in Bart Jones, *Hugo: The Hugo Chávez Story from Mud Hut to Perpetual Revolution* (Hanover, NH: Steerforth Press, 2007), as well as Steven Ellner and Miguel Tinker Salas, eds., *Hugo Chávez and the Decline of "Exceptional Democracy"* (Lanham, MD: Rowman & Littlefield, 2007).

56. See José E. Molina V. and Carmen Pérez B., "Radical Change at the Ballot Box: Venezuela's 2000 Elections," *Latin American Politics and Society*, 46:1 (Spring 2004), pp. 103–134. Interesting ideas are expressed in Javier Corrales, *Presidents Without Parties: The Politics of Economic Reform in Argentina and Venezuela in the 1990s* (University Station: Pennsylvania State University Press, 2002).

57. Consult Jennifer McCoy and David Meyers, *The Unraveling of Representative Democracy in Venezuela* (Baltimore, MD: Johns Hopkins University Press, 2004), and Jennifer McCoy, "One Act in an Unfinished Drama," *Journal of Democracy*, 16:1 (January 2005), pp. 109–123.

58. See Javier Corrales and Michael Penfold-Becerra, "Venezuela: Crowding Out the Opposition," *Journal of Democracy*, 18:2 (April 2007), pp. 99–113, reprinted in Larry Diamond,

Marc F. Plattner, and Diego Abente Brun, eds., *Latin America's Struggle for Democracy* (Baltimore: Johns Hopkins University Press, 2008), pp. 184–198.

59. Informative histories include Brian Loveman, *Chile: The Legacy of Hispanic Capitalism*, 3rd ed. (New York: Oxford University Press, 2001), and Simon Collier and William F. Slater, *A History of Chile, 1808–1994* (Cambridge, UK: Cambridge University Press, 1993).

60. Consult Donald W. Bray, *Chilean Politics During the Second Ibáñez Government*, microfilm/microform (Palo Alto, CA: Stanford University, 1961).

61. A solid political analysis is Federico G. Gil, *The Political System of Chile* (Boston: Houghton Mifflin, 1966)

62. See Arturo Valenzuela, *The Breakdown of Democratic Regimes: Chile* (Baltimore: Johns Hopkins University Press, 1978).

63. Quite useful on this period is Federico G. Gil, Ricardo Lagos E.[Chile's recent president], and Henry A. Landsberger, *Chile at the Turning Point: Lessons of the Socialist Years, 1970–1973*, trans. by John S. Gitlitz (Philadelphia: Institute for the Study of Human Issues, 1979).

64. Valenzuela, *Breakdown*, pp. 37–38.

65. Robert Pinkney, *Democracy in the Third World* (Boulder, CO: Lynne Rienner, 1994), p. 47.

66. See Peter Kornbluh, ed., *The Pinochet File: A Declassified Dossier on Atrocity and Accountability* (New York: New Press, 2003).

67. As Huntington points out, the far left often fears that successful reform programs will reduce the prospects of revolution and so cooperates with its mortal enemies to undermine reformers. See Samuel P. Huntington, *Political Order in Changing Societies* (New Haven, CT: Yale University Press, 1968), Chapter 5.

68. Of interest is former US ambassador Nathaniel Davis, *The Last Two Years of Salvador Allende* (Ithaca, NY: Cornell University Press, 1985).

69. See Paul E. Sigmund, *The Overthrow of Allende and the Politics of Chile, 1964–1976* (Pittsburgh, PA: University of Pittsburgh Press, 1977), and John Dinges, *The Condor Years: How Pinochet and His Allies Brought Terrorism to Three Continents* (New York: New Press, 2003).

70. Essential are Genaro Arriagada, *Pinochet: The Politics of Power*, (Boston: Unwin Hyman, 1988); Mary H. Spooner, *Soldiers in a Narrow Land* (Berkeley and Los Angeles: University of California Press, 1994); J. Samuel Valenzuela and Arturo Valenzuela, eds., *Military Rule in Chile: Dictatorship and Repression* (Baltimore: Johns Hopkins University Press, 1986); Pamela Constable and Arturo Valenzuela, *A Nation of Enemies: Chile Under Pinochet* (New York: W. W. Norton, 1991); and Marcelo Pollack, *The New Right in Chile, 1973–97* (New York: St. Martins Press, 1999).

71. Valenzuela, *Breakdown*, p. 163.

72. Essential are Valenzuela and Valenzuela, *Military Rule;* Constable and Valenzuela, *A Nation;* and Spooner, *Soldiers.*

73. Arturo Valenzuela, "Chile," in Larry Diamond, Jonathan Hartlyn, Juan J. Linz, and Seymour Martin Lipset, eds., *Democracy in Developing Countries: Latin America* (Boulder, CO: Lynne Rienner, 1999), pp. 191–247, provides a coherent analysis of the reestablishment of democratic political life in Chile.

74. See Marcelo Pollack, *The New Right in Chile, 1973–97* (New York: St. Martins Press, 1999), pp. 73–81, as well as Paul E. Sigmund, ed., *Chile 1973–1998: The Coup and Its Consequences* (Princeton, NJ: Princeton University Program in Latin American Studies, 1999).

75. Taylor C. Boas, "Varieties of Electioneering: Success Contagion and Presidential Campaigns in Latin America," presented at the Latin American Studies Association's congress, Rio de Janeiro, June 11–14, 2009). Available on the LASA Web site, pp. 14–16.

76. Pollack, *New Right*, pp. 83ff.

77. On the elections see Pollock, *New Right,* pp. 164–193, 184–195, with the nature of RN discussed in pp. 115–116 and the congressional lineup in pp. 149ff.

78. Ibid., pp. 164, 174–180.

79. Boas, "Varieties of Electioneering," pp. 16–18.

80. Pollack, *New Right,* pp. 153, 180–184.

81. See Paul W. Posner, "Local Democracy and the Transformation of Popular Participation in Chile," *Latin American Politics and Society,* 46:3 (Fall 2004), pp. 55–58, and John M. Carey and Peter M. Scavelis, "Insurance for Good Losers and the Survival of Chile's Concertación," *Latin American Politics and Society,* 47:2 (Summer 2005), pp. 1–22.

82. Peter Scavelis, "Electoral System Coalitional Disintegration and the Future of Chile's Concertación," *Latin American Research Review,* 40:1 (2005), pp. 56–82.

83. Arturo Valenzuela and Lucia Dammert, "Problems of Success in Chile," *Journal of Democracy,* 17:4 (October 2006), pp. 65–79, reprinted in Larry Diamond, Marc F. Plattner, and Diego Abente Brun, eds., *Latin America's Struggle for Democracy* (Baltimore: Johns Hopkins University Press, 2008), pp. 139–153.

84. Ibid., p. 144.

PART 3

◇ ◇ ◇

Comparative Perspectives and Outlook

10

Comparative Perspectives on Latin America's Political Development

Latin America's political experience has been marked on the dark side by corruption, egoism, injustice, inertia, inequality, violence, exclusion, and shortsightedness. But these negative factors have often been balanced by courage, determination, persistence, resilience, imagination, responsiveness, and occasionally innovation. Although the picture is still very mixed today, these positive elements are becoming more widespread and pervasive, gradually displacing their dysfunctional opposites from center stage and pushing them toward the wings—albeit not entirely eliminating them from the drama of national life, much less from its setting. Although politically motivated violence persists, it has been eliminated in some countries, brought under control in others, and contained in a few more. At the same time, consolidation of democratic political processes based on broad popular participation, linked to increasingly effective governmental structures, and rooted in a congruently modernizing political culture is well advanced in the Latin American countries that contain the overwhelming bulk of the region's population. This current state stands in sharp, even stark, contrast to the situation as recently as the late 1970s and carrying over into the 1980s, when authoritarian military regimes were still entrenched in such leading countries as Brazil, Argentina, and Chile.

This progress is all the more notable because, as has been shown in the preceding chapters, many Latin American countries have undergone divisive experiences that left long-lasting traumatic aftermaths impeding rational political development. Unfortunately, some of these conflicts persisted for a full generation or, in a few cases, even beyond. Although a good number of these conflicts have been overcome in recent years and the negative impact of others has been attenuated, several persist in some countries, retarding progress toward viable competitive political processes. But in contrast to cases in the past where animosities prevented civil cooperation even well beyond the generation in which they were rooted, more recent experience is marked with examples of pragmatic outcomes. Because democratic politics necessarily often involves difficult compromises and uneasy alliances between yesterday's—and possibly tomorrow's—rivals, if not opponents or even enemies, this pragmatism is salutary.[1]

A major measure of democratic stability is the handing over of power from one freely elected chief executive to another. An even more significant landmark, and a much rarer one, is the replacement of a democratically elected president by another one of a different political persuasion. Both these highly favorable occurrences have been markedly more frequent since the 1990s than ever before in the region's experience. Indeed, they have become commonplace and expected. Such alternation or even rotation of parties in power is still extremely rare in most parts of the world.

Latin America's experience dramatically underscores the fact that there is no quick and easy path to political development. Its political development has followed a very tortuous and painful zigzag course, with one generation often prone to repeat the mistakes of the preceding ones. In large part this recalcitrance is rooted in the major authoritarian corporatist components of Latin America's political culture. As captured by Wiarda:

> Most Latin American countries have the formal institutions of democracy—elections, legislatures, political parties, and so on—but are not very democratic underneath. They are *electoral democracies* but not liberal democracies. They have the *institutions* of democracy (relatively easy to change) but not its underlying *practices* or *political culture*.[2]

But the region also demonstrates that over a span of generations political culture can change sufficiently to support and even nourish democratic processes despite a country's extremely authoritarian starting point and subsequent highly antidemocratic experiences.

Overall, change in political culture is most strongly correlated with the scale and timing of postindependence immigration but can eventually occur without a significant influx of new and different people. Only in the case of Mexico is proximity to the United States a factor modifying political culture; otherwise, it is the result of far more broadly based and profound processes than the US example or "Yankee" influence. Traditional attitudes appear to change more slowly in those countries and regions where the Catholic religion retains a strong hold. Thus, in Chile and urban Brazil, political culture has modernized in part because of the rapid spread of Protestantism, particularly of a Pentacostal and Evangelical nature.

Latin America has become one of the more politically developed regions of the world. In good part this was to be expected, given the substantial length of experience as "independent" nations of most of its components—ranging from over a century and three-quarters to almost two centuries. Much of this distinct improvement in the region's political status is the result of hard work and lessons learned—although often belatedly. Several first- and second-try democracies, including Peru and Venezuela, show signs of stress and strain; there are solid reasons to doubt that most of this progress is merely another "false dawn" like the ones in Argentina in the 1912–1930 period and in Brazil between 1946 and 1964. In this respect, it must be asked to what degree the establishment of democracy in Latin America required countries to become essentially urbanized. For it is strikingly evident that the region's consolidating democracies at the beginning of the twenty-first century are overwhelmingly urban in contrast to the situation prevailing when the wave of democratic regimes collapsed in the late 1950s and early 1960s. Latin American societies have undergone vast changes in the past generation, changes that have transformed the societal foundations of political life. A decided majority of Latin America's population is urban; soon urbanites will become the overwhelming population bulk. Hence the patrimonialism of the past, albeit still a drag upon political development, is definitely on the wane.

Comparative Conceptualization

A key question is under what circumstances surges in political development have taken place in Latin America—and why they have eventually run out of momentum. Looking back, one finds that such leaps forward have resulted from an accumulation of fundamental socioeconomic changes that have rendered the existing political regime obsolete and created a gap between those privileged by the political status quo, but no longer creating the nation's wealth, and those individuals and groups that, having been elevated by the ongoing socioeconomic transformations, seek a commensurate voice in political affairs. When political participation was much more restricted, leadership was the fundamental catalyst of whether this developmental spurt would be accomplished sooner or later. Very often the key to prompt fulfillment was realization by individuals already on the political stage, but blocked in their quest for the nation's highest office, that the support of these emergent elements was key to their own aspirations, and that measures had to be taken to empower them. Usually coming from the "modernizing" wing of a dominant political party, as in turn-of-the-century Argentina, once in power these leaders adopted policies that shifted public resources into the hands of the new elites to enhance their productivity. In most cases these newly dominant elements would eventually use their political influence for profitability instead of productivity. If their heyday was prolonged, they would become the old oligarchs in a repeat of the dialectic that had opened their way to power. In other cases the elite they replaced has found new allies—often in the military—to dislodge them from power and provide for a temporary comeback, as in Argentina between 1930 and 1943. All in all, Latin American experience strongly confirms the view that it is the social conditions resulting from economic development, not the latter's level in and of itself, that influence electoral outcomes—with leadership playing a major role in determining how long the apparently inevitable time lag will be.[3]

Samuel Huntington's widely influential ideas on the relationship between societal changes and political development, as formulated in his 1968 classic, *Political Order in Changing Societies,* have proven essentially sound in the light of Latin American experience.[4] For example, in Brazil social mobilization—changes in the social order that undercut existing political culture—in the early twentieth century outpaced political institutionalization (which strengthens political structures and processes by giving them complexity, coherence, autonomy, and adaptability). By the late 1920s this imbalance left the country in a clearly praetorian position of inadequate interest-mediating organizations and channels relative to increased pressures for participation. The outcome was regime change through the 1930 Revolution, leading to a system in which Vargas's leadership made the new mix of structures and processes sufficient for a time in terms of adaptability, complexity, and coherence, basic components of political institutionalization, albeit lacking in the dimension of autonomy. As the

economic development and social change unleashed by Vargas's policies spurred further social mobilization, particularly during World War II and his final term in the
early 1950s, the political system was again praetorian (hence prone to instability)
rather than civic by 1964, the result being the establishment of an authoritarian military regime.

Cumulative economic development and modernization under Brazilian governments pursuing growth gave rise to further social mobilization (through the impact
of industrialization, urbanization, increased education, and the spread of mass media).
Because political institutionalization lagged badly, the military itself adopted a decision to expand adaptability, autonomy, and coherence to go along with the increased
complexity through reestablishing competitive political processes capable of channeling vastly expanded demands for participation. Thus, despite the continuing social
mobilization in the 1980s, Brazil's political system became and has remained civic—
indeed increasingly so. By the 1990s Brazil came to possess a political infrastructure
of mediating structures and participatory processes adequate to the advanced level of
mobilization that had been reached in its urban industrial society, although in need of
further strengthening.

In Mexico the developmental thrust of the Díaz era led to a surging tide of social
mobilization while political institutionalization stood still. Hence an extremely praetorian situation of institutionalization failing to keep up with social mobilization at
the beginning of the twentieth century resulted in a revolution that failed to institutionalize itself politically and thus brought on a protracted period of instability
whose destructive effects retarded social mobilization. This state of affairs ended in
the late 1920s and the 1930s through the establishment of a hegemonic party that
provided a great deal of complexity and sufficient coherence along with a modicum
of adaptability for several decades before facing the challenges posed by further social
mobilization by means of a growing degree of autonomy in the 1990s. Thus Mexico
avoided the praetorianism that plagued most of the region in the 1960s and 1970s
and subsequently became an increasingly civic political system before it became
democratic, supporting the proposition that political development must move ahead
in advance of democratization (as economic growth usually precedes redistribution).
Argentina, although for decades ahead of the game in terms of its absolute level of
political institutionalization, slipped by 1930 into a praetorian situation through the
sustained surge of social mobilization unleashed by sustained early-twentieth-
century economic growth and societal modernization. Rescued by semidemocratic
and mobilizational (in the basic sense of arousing groups to pursue participation)
Peronism in the mid to late 1940s, it slipped back into praetorianism when faltering
institutionalization stalled relative to accentuated social mobilization by the mid-
1950s. As authoritarian military regimes failed to foster significant political institutionalization, Argentina remained mired in praetorian conditions until the early
1980s, when, much as in Brazil, reestablishment of competitive political life brought
with it a flourishing of political institutionalization that caught up with social
mobilization—which in the Argentine case slowed sharply as a result of having already reached a very high level.

Huntington's global/universal scheme also helps clarify the course of Colombia's
political life. In Colombia political institutionalization closed the gap with relatively
slow social mobilization during the 1930s, only to see a marginally civic system de-

railed in the late 1940s by charismatic populist Gaitán's assassination and the consequent precipitous decline in adaptability and coherence. The resulting descent into a blood-drenched praetorian period of direct political fighting was ended in 1958 by the reestablishment of a balance between social mobilization and political institutionalization by means of the innovative National Front system of power sharing. Despite the emergence of grave insurgency and drug-trafficking problems, the resurrected civic system has survived despite continuing social mobilization, with elections serving as much-needed escape valves for societal tensions.

Peru, Venezuela, and Chile have all followed political development paths congruent with basic elements of Huntington's empirical theorizing. In particular they bear out his conceptualization of the relationship between reform and revolution, including the former's role in the achievement of "containment" rather than revolution as the outcome of praetorian situations. In Venezuela the loyalty-gaining reforms of post-1958 AD administrations (building on agrarian reform initiatives of their earlier brief stay in power) led to mobilization of the rural masses within a civic political system rather than against it. Hence, even though alienated urban groups attempted to launch armed revolution, they were never able to forge an alliance with significant elements of the rural population. Thus Venezuela remained a civic system for nearly a generation despite continuing social mobilization. Only in the last half of the 1990s did its political institutionalization lose adaptability and decline in coherence. Even then the country did not move into the praetorian realm, continuing to decide who would hold power through the ballot box even in a highly polarized atmosphere. Indeed, Chávez became president through electoral processes and emerged victorious in a series of frequent tests at the polls, and continues to enjoy widespread mass support.

In the case of Chile, reform proved to be more a catalyst of revolution than an alternative to it, for reasons compatible with Huntington's appraisal of this equation, yet even the establishment of a Marxist government came through constitutional processes. In Chile social mobilization was matched by political institutionalization until the economic crisis of the late 1920s—which accelerated the erosion of established political beliefs and values to the point of their breakdown. Still a full-blown praetorian situation was avoided as the Ibáñez regime proved to be transitory, and the country was back on the civic path within five years, staying there for another four decades. The systematically reformist Frei government in the last half of the 1960s attempted a strategy, which was working in Venezuela, of undercutting revolutionary tendencies through loyalty-gaining reforms. Under the different circumstances of Chile—where the miners were the most important segment of the labor movement, there were well-established parties to the left of the Christian Democrats, and a praetorian regime had not recently been ousted as in Venezuela in 1958. Hence, these reforms had at least as much of a catalytic effect (whetting appetites for more) as an ameliorative one. The civic political order survived in the 1970 elections through the elevation of the radical left to power, but as the Allende government's policies accelerated social mobilization that undermined fragile and in some ways brittle institutionalization, upsetting the attenuated civic balance, the country slid rapidly into praetorianism. Instead of having a revolutionary outcome, this crisis resulted in a counterrevolutionary military coup. Subsequently the Pinochet regime failed to keep its restrictive version of political institutionalization ahead of the substantial social mobilization resulting from the societal effects of sustained economic development through which the military hoped to gain legitimacy. In the late 1980s, the return to competitive politics resurrected the institutional pillars of the previous civic system, strengthening them through the broad-based inclusionary Concertacíon and reestablishing a decidedly civic balance.

Peru provides a test of the limits of Huntington's conceptualization of the course of political development. Because his propositions are probabilistic and never intended to be determinist, this lack of a perfect fit need not be perplexing or disconcerting—two adjectives that unfortunately too frequently do apply to Peru's troubled political life. To a significantly greater degree than in Colombia, the crux of the problem is that Peruvian nation building is still incomplete owing to both geographic and ethnic factors. In important respects Lima is the effective capital of just the country's heartland, not of the outlying areas. Moreover, by excluding the most broad-based political movement from a central and continuous role in the country's political institutionalization, the army's generation-long veto of the Apristas—extending from the early 1930s into the mid-1980s—prevented the system from being truly civic. Hence it was susceptible to military intervention. Recent decades have been marked by substantial social mobilization, accompanied only sporadically by significant political institutionalization. To a substantial degree the Fujimori 1990s witnessed the country move the balance between these factors from praetorian into precariously civic.

Huntington's original analytic scheme was concerned with political development in terms of stability and viability, not with whether political development leads to democracy. But Latin America's experience also underscores the essential validity of views propounded at the end of the 1960s by Dankwart A. Rustow concerning the fact that democratization is a lengthy and generally discontinuous process. He saw its genesis in a "preparatory phase" during which "well-entrenched social forces" engage in a prolonged and inconclusive struggle over fundamental class, ethnic, and religious conflicts.[5] This struggle is likely to be the result of the emergence of a new elite "that arouses a depressed and previously leaderless social group into concerted action," and the forces and issues involved can vary widely from case to case and even over the course of the transition in a single country. Since polarization and intensity are hallmarks of the struggle, progress toward democracy is far from ensured, much less inevitable. Moreover, the minimum period for bringing about democracy is likely to be at least a generation, of which a major proportion is taken up by the preparatory phase. The shift to the "decision phase" comes when these exhausting and often violent struggles end in stalemate. Then angry and frustrated elites may decide that their interests could be better served by a basic compromise on procedures than by continuing the conflict. These elites calculate that it is feasible to employ their bargaining skills to get the better of their rivals within some crucial aspect of democratic processes that has been mutually accepted; for all parties this "genesis" of democracy tends to be a second-best outcome, if not a Hobson's choice or lesser evil. Once agreed to by the contending elites, this generally distasteful, or at least reluctant, option for democracy gains acceptance first from professional politicians and then from the politically active citizens, in what Rustow calls the "habituation phase." Still, early failure to resolve some urgent political question may well lead to erosion of this acceptance and even to the demise of democracy.

Although compromise can usually be found on economic issues and social policy, religious, national, and racial divisions prove more intractable. Rustow sagely points out that each of the major tasks along the slow road toward democracy has its own logic and natural protagonists. Hence democratization is apt to be a stop-and-go process that requires, at times, societal changes to catch up with those in the political realm, or even the emergence of political leaders whose socialization, and thus political culture, differs from that of the preceding phase. What Rustow did not take into account when writing in 1970 was the possibility of a military seizure of power that would derail democracies, an adverse development that would become a tidal wave in much of the world, but that fortunately in a wide array of Latin American countries only interrupted the habituation phase, necessitating a renewed decision in favor of democracy.

At a basic level, Latin America's experience fits Rustow's conceptualization reasonably well. In Brazil a very restricted elite-dominated formal democracy existed from 1894 through 1930 on the foundation of the earlier constitutional monarchy. It foundered on the question of full incorporation of the middle class. Following the paternalistically authoritarian Vargas era—a response to sharp political polarization that had led to armed conflict—a reborn electoral democracy survived from 1946 into 1964. Its failure to resolve issues concerning greater participation of the working class triggered two decades of authoritarian military rule. A much more broadly based democratic regime emerged in 1985 and became both institutionalized and stabilized in a renewed process of habituation. Hence successful democratization was eventually accomplished on the fourth try within a century of a republican framework of government. For Mexico the road to democratization has also been highly discontinuous, but much more violent. The battle for power that lasted from 1910 to the late 1920s led to the formation of a hegemonic governing party rather than real political competition. With significant democratic features implanted under Cárdenas (president 1934–1940), its long string of electoral successes pushed the final decision phase into the late 1990s, with habituation still at an early stage. This path stands in marked contrast with that of Argentina, where in 1912–1914 the basic decision was undertaken to go beyond the constrained elite democracy of the preceding four decades. Sadly, the military's seizure of power in 1930 renewed a prolonged struggle that ended with a decision to reinstall full democracy in 1983. Colombia saw its habituation to democratic processes interrupted in the late 1940s by Gómez's violent crusade against the liberals, but within a decade most conservatives had opted for a return to democratic processes within the conciliating framework of the National Front. Despite elements wedded to violence, habituation to democracy has progressed for the great majority of Colombians.

Peru poses a phenomenon Rustow didn't foresee: the decision of the armed forces to veto a major political movement for over a half-century. Although a decision phase that included the military opened in the late 1970s, habituation proved difficult, in large part owing to an absence of national unity (Rustow's only precondition for democracy) rooted in the limited political incorporation of the sizable indigenous population. For Venezuela, the preparatory phase lasted until 1958, the ensuing decision phase being relatively short, as habituation began within a decade. Much earlier than any other country in the region, Chile made the decision to adopt some significant democratic procedures back in the 1830s, and habituation ran nearly its full course in another generation. A century later the Pinochet dictatorship constituted a temporary, albeit traumatic, aberration.

Latin America's recent experience has been, on balance, decidedly positive with respect to formal democracy, with its emphasis upon free elections, universal suffrage, and a reasonable degree of administrative accountability to elected authorities as well as freedom of expression and association. The region has also made outstanding progress in broadening participation along with substantial, if still quite uneven, headway in eliminating systematic differences in participation across class and ethnic lines. With respect to gender, the gap in the more developed of Latin American countries is comparable to that in English-speaking North America and in western Europe—with the rate of improvement in Latin America probably higher than in these regions of industrialized democracies. But "deepening" of democracy in terms of reducing social and economic inequalities presents a less rosy picture. A significant school of thought, led by Evelyne Huber, holds that "the structure of the state and state-society relations are critically important to the chances of democracy." The state needs enough strength and autonomy to avoid being an instrument for advancing the interests of dominant groups. Instead it should be responsive to pressures from civil society. This responsiveness, these scholars argue, is often lacking as mobilization of the subordinate classes declined with the disappearance of obvious threats to the democratic system, and the political parties generally failed to forcefully and effectively articulate the demands of these social strata. High voter turnout by the masses, although a good thing, often does not result in the translation of the voters' interests into government policies:

> The political space left empty by weak popular organizations and the failure of political parties to establish organizational ties to subordinate classes has been filled by clientelistic networks. These networks link lower class individuals and informal social groups to individual politicians; they serve at best as transmitters of temporary particularistic favors, not as channels to mobilize citizens into influencing policy formation.[6]

Huber et al. appropriately single out countries with weak political parties, including Brazil and Peru, as failing to provide effective citizen input into policy making. Clearly the current situation in these countries supports such a contention. There is also considerable validity to these authors' concerns about presidents coming to power through loose electoral coalitions and often viewing legislatures and courts as obstacles to their exercise of power, rather than being elevated to office by a strong party whose legislative support they require. This negative attitude by such chief executives undermines the national legislature and the judiciary as levers for affecting policy and renders generally ineffective the voters' pressure on the party they voted for to provide the programs it promised. Yet, as has been shown, in many countries the legislative branch is a meaningful part of the policymaking process, and political parties are as effective as in a number of Europe's older democracies. Indeed, in Brazil, Mexico, Argentina, Colombia, Peru, and Chile the present chief executives do need to treat their national legislatures as "legitimate partners in Government."[7] Moving to the question of just how the past affects the present, I would argue that all cases bear out the contention of Scott Mainwaring and Arturo Valenzuela, two leading figures in the contemporary study of Latin American politics, that an approach stressing "path dependency," helps bridge the gap between structural dependency, with its emphasis upon the past as determining the future, and its antithesis of "replacement," which holds that the present essentially negates or at least neutralizes the past. In this balanced view, structural, institutional, and cultural constraints impose broad limits or shape the general nature of outcomes that are then determined by contingent choices that impact upon political, economic, and social trajectories.[8] (I would add that the legacies of the past not only linger but sometimes even resurge.)

Challenges and Differentiating Factors

With respect to Latin America of the early twenty-first century, as social scientists we must concentrate on what explains the great differences in degree of ability to obtain and maintain democratic processes among the region's countries. As individuals deeply concerned about Latin America's future, we must ask whether there is anything about the recent decades of sustained headway toward democratic political development that justifies optimism that this time the pendulum might not swing back as was the case in the early 1960s as well as in the late 1940s. The chief factor linking societal transformations to political change appears to be the great expansion of political participation, which engenders and spreads a sense of political efficacy, a feeling of some small share of responsibility for the results obtained by popularly elected governments and a stake in their survival. Although during the post–World War II populist era in many countries governments were chosen by electorates greatly expanded over any previous democratic interlude, voters were still a distinct minority of the population.

The vast expansion of the electorate in recent decades in the great majority of Latin American countries is of the greatest significance with respect to democratic political development. The challenge of broadened participation has been both critical and difficult in all countries that have eventually succeeded in developing into stable democracies. In this realm, compared to earlier global experience, Latin America has done very well in greatly increasing the number and proportion of voters without seriously destabilizing the fundamental institutions of its political systems. Brazil and Mexico provide dramatic cases. Brazil's registered electorate of over 135 million now includes two-thirds of its population, a more than elevenfold increase of the only 11.5 million eligible voters in 1950—when Vargas was swept back into power. Mexicans with a voice in choosing their governmental officeholders have increased exponentially since 1952, the last balloting before women could vote, and now exceed 78 million.

Numbers and proportions do not tell the whole story. Racial and ethnic factors also play a significant role in the integration of societal sectors into national political life. For first the middle-class and then the urban-working-class incorporation into politics was most easily, hence in most cases first, accomplished in those few countries, like Argentina, where no significant racial or ethnic factor was involved. In Argentina, and to a more limited extent in Chile, those knocking on the door for admittance into the political arena were essentially European, as were the elites who were being asked to accommodate to the newcomers' inclusion in what had hitherto been a quite restricted club. This adjustment was eased by the fact that the broadened membership would as a practical matter remain stratified on the basis of social status because the elites possessed formidable political assets beyond their mere individual votes.

In Brazil, the broadening of political access to include recent immigrants moved ahead much faster and farther than it did with respect to Afro-Brazilians, color proving to be a far greater deterrent than just socioeconomic factors. Hence the factory workers who benefited under Vargas in the 1930s and 1940s were overwhelmingly white, as, for that matter, were the workers appealed to by Goulart in the early 1960s or even the cadres of the contemporary Workers' Party (which, as one of its recently disaffected founders laments, remains much more a party of unions than of workers).[9] In Mexico the relative continued political marginalization of the rural proletariat is far from unrelated to its high proportion of Indians, and the meaningful participation of many rural sectors is facilitated by their identification as essentially *mestizo*. Elements feeling left out have found a home in the Party of the Democratic Revolution (PRD), as well as in the much smaller Workers' Party (PT). In Argentina all significant elements of society have been incorporated into national life through Peronism. In Colombia such groupings long ago channeled their frustrations and alienation into insurgency, and in Venezuela they have become the backbone of Chávez's support. The Andean countries have begun to incorporate their indigenous populations into national political life—generally with at least short-term destabilizing effects, as demonstrated by recent developments in Peru. As a practical political matter in the majority of countries, the growing numbers of individuals with minority racial/ethic heritages residing in urban centers are significantly less excluded from the political process than those living in distant rural areas, and there is a continuing flow of these rural migrants toward the cities.

Optimism about Latin America's political future is rooted in the happy combination of increasingly urban and modern societies, vastly broadened political participation, a more favorable international environment, and a growing capacity to learn from past experience. This situation is fairly general throughout this far-flung and diverse region, but its core is the South American continent, particularly giant Brazil and its Southern Cone neighbors of Argentina and Chile. Yet less than four decades ago these same countries constituted the backbone of authoritarian militarism in the hemisphere. Hence it appears that the foundations for a democratic order are cumulative, perhaps even sedimentary. At least this is a proposition meriting examination in the context of the years ahead. If Latin American countries on the whole have made impressive progress with regard to the challenges of participation and incorporation, has this progress been matched in the area of distribution and social justice? Although the answer is a qualified no, the historical sequence in older democratic parts of the world have generally involved a significant time lag, for it is largely through effective political participation that underdog groups gain a more equitable share of socioeconomic goods and benefits. Hence the most relevant question is whether there is strong evidence of this scenario's at least beginning to occur in Latin America. Because it is precisely the region's economic engine and largest society, in Brazil, that has one of the world's most extremely skewed income distributions, significant movement has a heavy impact upon the regional equation. This move toward reducing inequality has begun to occur through social welfare programs that are the hallmark of Lula's present administration, but they could well be blunted by the recession that took hold in 2009. Although Mexico could—and should—do more than it has to equalize income distribution, Latin America's number-two country (Mexico) is not such an extreme case and has more of a foundation upon which to build.

Analogous to the incorporation of new groups, certain socioeconomic problems profoundly impacting on politics must be dealt with along the course of political development. Painful as it may be to bite the bullet on some of the problems that are never easy and that universally involve confrontation if not open conflict, once successfully disposed of, these challenges are removed from the agenda of tests still to be encountered and met. For countries that have avoided the thorny issues or bought time with palliative measures, agrarian reform is the most pressing. In the long run its emergence into the active political arena is not only necessary, but also salutary, even if temporarily destabilizing. Agrarian reform in its broadest sense of alterations in land tenure patterns sufficient to provide land and employment to a sizable portion of the marginalized rural masses is often the most difficult, intractable, and violence-generating of the distributive-participatory tasks faced on the road to the construction of a socially just and inclusive polity. Because the interests adversely affected are most often well entrenched in the country's existing power structure—much as slaveholders were in the past—decisive action is often postponed until tensions in some areas, most commonly land seizures or organized invasions by squatters, have escalated into widespread violence. Understandable as such procrastination may be, its continuation in the face of clear symptoms of growing unrest is politically short-sighted. At present Brazil faces the greatest need to move farther and faster in this field. Mexico took decisive action beginning in 1934 but needs to create a new generation of beneficiaries. Colombia, Venezuela, and Peru at least partially dealt with agrarian reform in the 1960s, and Chile in the 1970s.

Where the Region Stands:
Is Democracy the Only Game in Town?

As Latin America reaches the end of the first decade of the new millennium, many of the democratic gains from the 1980s and 1990s have been consolidated. Brazil has been free from military tutelage for a quarter of a century, and Mexico has escaped from the constraints of the long PRI power monopoly and become a highly competitive electoral democracy. These positive trends have opened the opportunity for further democratic political development but do not guarantee that it will occur. Argentines have successfully come out of one of their most troubled political crossings, and Colombia has developed a capability for coexisting with intractable insurgency and drug trafficking, containing, but not eliminating, these threats to stable democracy. Peru appears to be stabilizing, and Venezuela has opted for what Chávez has given the less fortunate in the past dozen years. Chile is basking in two decades of quality democracy. In a global situation dominated by the US-led "war on terrorism," with its focus on the Middle East and Asia, the centrality of the Brazilian third of the region to other Latin American countries continues to grow. Continued progress in Brazil would not guarantee forward movement for the South American continent, of which it constitutes half, much less for the northern third of Latin America, where Mexico is the dominant component. But backsliding or decay there would hamstring advances and negate even significant gains in countries of lesser weight, as well as have a heavy negative impact on the whole array of regional performance averages—economic, social, and political.

Political development in Latin America has taken enormous strides over the past century and has leaped forward since the early 1980s. Headway had been made toward stable representative political systems with a high degree of institutionalization and a broad base of participation, often against adverse headwinds. In progressing toward the consolidation of democratic processes the most important threshold to be crossed is the recognition by all significant power contenders that democracy has become the "only game in town," with elections—not military coups or revolutions—deciding who will control the machinery of government. Such a near-universal commitment to the ballot box as the fundamental arbiter of who will hold government office is difficult to attain. Once reached and consolidated, this kind of electoral democracy generally remains viable unless the resulting governments fail woefully in their responsibility to manage the economy with some degree of competence. The realization that the electoral process has become definitive—rendering other, sometimes deeply rooted, ways of gaining power obsolete—is arrived at only through a protracted process and is both painful and only reluctantly accepted by elements on both the right and the left. These polarized and intransigent actors cling tenaciously to their favored practice of winning through force rather than persuasion. At last, democratic electoral politics have become the only game in town in the vast majority of the region's countries, whereas it was only in the mid-1980s that competitive elections were rarely held, and if they did take place, their results were often brushed aside by authoritarian military regimes. This highly favorable development, in almost all cases following on the heels of authoritarian military regimes, has come about through a variety of paths. Munck and Leff stress that modes of democratic transition shape the ensuing regime and course of politics by affecting "the pattern of elite competition, institutional rules crafted during the period of transition, and disposition of key actors to accept or reject the new rules of the game."[10] These authors' scheme of transition modes is based on the identity of the actors impelling change and the strategies they employ. The identity of the actors ranges from the incumbent elite through a combination of incumbent and counterelites, to the latter alone. The strategies they use run from accommodation through its combination with confrontation, to essentially confrontational. In the resulting matrix, reform from below, transaction, extrication, and rupture are possible modes of transition (as, in theory at least, are conservative reform, social revolution, and revolution from above).

Chile, where the impetus came from the opposition following an accommodationist strategy, illustrates reform from below, resulting in fairly balanced elite competition. Argentina, with moderate elements of both the regime and the opposition as agents of change using a strategy involving more confrontation than accommodation, with the opponents of military rule playing the major role, illustrates reform through rupture. The lack of opposition to democratization led to an early breakup of the antiauthoritarian alliance, as both the radicals and the Peronists strove to become hegemonic, unlike the Christian Democrats and the socialists who remained allied in Chile. In Munck and Leff's analytical scheme, Brazil, with a similar mix of actors, who used much more accommodation than confrontation, exemplifies reform through transaction, which resulted in a very complex transition process in which a plethora of political parties competed, with lines blurred between exregime and former opposition elements—and the eventual alignments are still being worked out. As Colombia and Venezuela had their transitions from authoritarian military regimes in the late 1950s, they do not easily fit a conceptualization based essentially on 1980s developments. Both seem to come fairly close to reform from below, followed by competition between two parties operating within a framework of cooperation roughly analogous to Chile's Concertacíon. This conceptualization is not fully appropriate for Mexico, which did not have an authoritarian military regime, but it can be said that the impetus for change came chiefly from the opposition, abetted by reformist elements within the governing party. However, this transition was a process of infusing formally democratic institutions already in place with meaningful and vital competitive content. For its part, Peru falls between reform through transaction and the extrication mode, being somewhat more confrontational in the strategy of opposition elements, yet still essentially accommodationist, and with regime moderates having been the most significant actors. Overall, the region's essentially democratic conditions can and should, in both the empirical and normative senses of that word, be maintained if the social and economic benefits of political participation, through effective leverage on distribution, are extended to the previously excluded sectors of society.

Violence and militarism were long endemic in the region and have proven persistent. But although violence is still far from absent in Latin American politics, it has greatly decreased over time.[11] As has clearly been shown in preceding chapters, the early decades of national existence were marked by violence and conflict, with force usually deciding who would hold power. However, the longest and bloodiest periods of resort to force came one, two, or even three generations after independence. Starting with the Thousand Days' War in Colombia at the end of the nineteenth century, massive and protracted civil strife moved to Mexico in the second and third decades of the twentieth century before exploding in Colombia in 1948 and continuing in a chronic rather than acute stage down to the present.

In the late 1990s violence increased in the region's two largest countries as armed struggles over land in the vast interior of Brazil accelerated, and the Zapatista rebels in southern Mexico have continued to demand attention. Often lost from sight was the calming influence of the refusal of the Cardoso and Zedillo administrations to overreact and use of their countries' federalism to decentralize the issue. Mexico deserves especially high credit for its progress in overcoming a heritage of intense conflict, beginning with its conquest and extending through a bloody independence struggle, war against a foreign-imposed monarch in the 1860s, and two decades of revolution and civil war after 1910. In the opening years of the twenty-first century large-scale organized insurgencies have become relatively rare throughout the region. Moreover, compared to the circumstances in southeast Europe, as well as Africa and Asia, organized armed violence is isolated and sporadic. Indeed, for Latin America crime-related urban violence has become a much more serious problem, one generally calling for attention to social problems, not military repression.

The dramatic shift from the "normality" of military rule as late as the 1970s and early 1980s to its complete disappearance in little more than a decade does not guarantee that this historical and deep-seated phenomenon has been effectively banished, never to rear its ugly head again. Military intervention in politics has always been a function of inclination and opportunity, conditioned by tradition. The at least adequate performance of civilian governments in the 1990s and 2000s has greatly diminished opportunities, and relatively long periods of civilian governments weaken a "savior of the nation" tradition important in legitimizing coups. Much less can be said with certainty concerning inclinations, for armed forces are hierarchical institutions in which there is a substantial time lag between initial socialization and arrival at a level giving an officer some weight in decision making. Still, permanent and adequately institutionalized civilian supremacy over the military appears to have been established in a number of Latin American countries. Mexico in the 1930s and early 1940s shows that the less individuals select a military career with political ambitions in mind, the lower the collective inclination to seek opportunity or pretext to intervene. Yet Mexico's success in taming militarism was greatly facilitated by the fact that the professionalized officer corps was decimated, if not destroyed, in the 1911–1928 fighting. Moreover, the elimination of intraparty competition through the establishment of the hegemonic PRI all but eliminated the opportunity factor. Indeed, Mexico's uniqueness for a long generation was a hegemonic party dominated for six years at a time by an extremely powerful president who then ceded leadership to a successor essentially of his choice. In this manner order and stability prevailed under civilian rule from the 1930s through the 1990s.[12] As this time span included at least two protracted periods of military interventions and authoritarian regimes in most of the rest of Latin America, Mexico's order and stability were no mean accomplishment.

It remains to be seen whether changes in recruitment and socialization are sufficient to engender and maintain a sea change in such a deeply rooted tradition as military intromission in political affairs. Yet Brazil, Argentina, and Chile have taken giant strides in this direction. In the first the armed forces have adjusted to a near abandonment of their once-treasured "moderating power," and in the second, the military as an institution still bears deep scars from its dismal performance as the nation's self-appointed savior in 1976–1983. In the special case of Chile, statesmanlike behavior on the part of the democratic politicians carried the country through the potentially dangerous period when ex-authoritarian strongman Pinochet still nominally held command of the army. Despite the continuing insurgency problem, since 1957 Colombia has avoided political interference by its military, and Peru also has substantially domesticated the armed forces, which governed the country as recently as 1977. Venezuela remains a case apart as Chávez continues to use the army as a major pillar of his regime.[13]

In sum, Latin America has become one of the politically most stable regions in the world, with South America measuring up very favorably against Europe in terms of democracy. It must go on in the years ahead to consolidate these gains and improve equity and social welfare. Strong foundations have been built and sturdy walls erected, but the temple of democracy still needs to be finished and furnished. That is the challenge for the coming decades as well as the present generation.

Notes

1. Recent scholarship on the region as a whole includes a number of books providing insight and provoking thought. Among them are Peter H. Smith, *Democracy in Latin America: Political Change in Comparative Perspective* (New York: Oxford University Press, 2005); Manuel

Antonio Garreton, Peter Cleaves, Marcelo Cavarozzi, Jonathan Hartlyn, and Gary Gereffi, *Latin America in the Twenty-first Century: Toward a New Sociopolitical Matrix* (Boulder, CO: Lynne Rienner, 2002); Mark Falcoff, *A Culture of Its Own: Taking Latin America Seriously* (New Brunswick, NJ: Transaction Books, 1998); Forrest D. Colburn, *Latin America at the End of Politics* (Princeton, NJ: Princeton University Press, 2002); José Nun, *Democracy: Government of the People or Government of the Politicians?* (Lanham, MD: Rowman & Littlefield, 2003); Manuel Antonio Garreton M. and Edward Newman, eds., *(Re)Constructing Democracy in Latin America* (New York: United Nations University Press, 2001); and Ronaldo Munck, *Contemporary Latin America,* rev. ed. (New York: Palgrave/Macmillan, 2008).

2. Howard J. Wiarda, *Dilemmas of Democracy in Latin America: Crises and Opportunity* (Lanham, MD: Rowman & Littlefield, 2005), p. 230.

3. An often contradictory literature has finally shaken down to a generalized agreement that rather than a relationship between high levels of economic development or rates of economic growth and democratization, economic factors impact upon the political realm largely through their societal effects. Stimulating works enriching this debate include Patrice Franko, *The Puzzle of Latin American Economic Development,* 2nd ed. (Lanham, MD: Rowman & Littlefield, 2003), and Charles H. Wood and Bryan R. Roberts, eds., *Rethinking Development in Latin America* (University Station: Pennsylvania University Press, 2005), as well as Evelyne Huber, ed., *Models of Capitalism: Lessons for Latin America* (University Station: Pennsylvania University Press, 2002).

4. Samuel P. Huntington, *Political Order in Changing Societies* (New Haven, CT: Yale University Press, 1968).

5. Dankwart A. Rustow, "Transitions to Democracy: Toward a Dynamic Model," *Comparative Politics,* 2:2 (April 1970), pp. 337–363, reprinted in Lisa Anderson, ed., *Transitions to Democracy* (New York: Columbia University Press, 1999), pp. 14–41.

6. Evelyne Huber, Dietrich Rueschemeyer, and John D. Stephens, "The Paradoxes of Contemporary Democracy: Formal, Participatory, and Social Dimensions" in Lisa Anderson, ed., *Transitions to Democracy* (New York: Columbia University Press, 1999), p. 181.

7. Ibid.

8. Scott Mainwaring and Arturo Valenzuela, eds., *Politics, Society, and Democracy: Latin America* (Boulder, CO: Westview Press, 1998), p. 105.

9. Cristovam Buarque speaking at the Bildner Center for Hemispheric Affairs of the City University of New York Graduate Center, November 2005.

10. Gerardo L. Munck and Carol Skolnik Leff, "Modes of Transition to Democratization: South America and Eastern Europe in Comparative Perspective" in Lisa Anderson, ed., *Transitions to Democracy* (New York: Columbia University Press, 1999), pp. 193–194.

11. Consult Miguel Angel Centeno, *Blood and Debt: War and the Nation-State in Latin America* (University Station: Pennsylvania State University Press, 2002), and David R. Mares, *Violent Peace: Militarized Interstate Bargaining in Latin America* (New York: Columbia University Press, 2001).

12. Roderick A. Camp, *Mexico's Military on the Democratic Stage* (Northport, CT: Praeger, 2005).

13. See J. Samuel Fitch, *The Armed Forces and Democracy in Latin America* (Baltimore: Johns Hopkins University Press, 1998); Kirk S. Bowman, *Militarization, Democracy, and Development: The Perils of Praetorianism in Latin America* (University Station: Pennsylvania University Press, 2002); Brian Loveman, *Por la Patria : Politics and the Armed Forces in Latin America* (Wilmington, DE: Scholarly Resources Books, 1999); and Craig L. Arceneaux, *Bounded Missions: Military Regimes and Democratization in the Southern Cone and Brazil* (University Station: Pennsylvania University Press, 2001).

11

A Look into the Future

Political development is a long-term and almost never straight-line process. It was only in the mid-1960s that Latin America was entering a period when authoritarian military regimes were all but universal, a situation that prevailed for nearly two decades. Only forty years farther back, Latin American governments were, almost without exception, the result of elite-dominated successions resulting from fraudulent elections if not naked seizures of power. The few exceptions were destined to succumb to the political fallout of the world economic crisis unleashed in 1929–1930. Indeed, at that time, when World War I had given way to the optimistic 1920s in the developed world epitomized by western Europe and the United States, Brazil was caught up in a series of military uprisings that would culminate in its 1930 Revolution. Mexico was still immersed in the long bloody civil war that its 1910 Revolution had substituted for a repressive dictatorship. Colombia was a one-party oligarchical regime resulting from the fratricidal slaughter of its Thousand Days' War at the turn of the century. Although Argentina was enjoying a heady dose of democracy, this house of cards would come tumbling down with the dawn of a new decade in 1930. Chile was on the brink of trading constitutional civilian rule for a military dictatorship, and Venezuela had long been under an autocrat who had an equally long tenure still before him.

As has already been shown, change in the region since 1930 has been more profound and substantial than it was in Europe during any equivalent time span. Yet, to document how much more politically developed and broadly participant Latin America is today compared to fifty or ninety years ago is, in and of itself, only part of the story. What is truly important is an understanding of why and how this progress came about as well as an appreciation of the challenges and obstacles to its continuation. Beyond the changes in political structures and processes already examined, the past most pervasively influences the present through the political socialization that all persons undergo, particularly in their early years. Everyone is subject to particularly intense impact from traumatic events such as wars or protracted economic crises. Fortunately in this respect most of Latin America's countries are to one degree or another distancing themselves from past national traumas. Only those persons who are into their eighties have even fading childhood memories of the Great Depression of the 1930s, and World War II is still a vivid memory for only the segment of the population in their seventies. With democratization dating back to the late 1970s or early 1980s in most of the region, traumatic memories of the military regimes of the 1960s and 1970s are essentially the province of individuals in their sixties, or at least their late fifties. Some of the older of the middle-aged individuals holding a high proportion of the region's political offices had their prime socializing experiences during the populist 1950s, but even more were socialized during the 1960s or even the 1970s.

During the years ahead, this fading of the fairly recent past (in terms of processes, personalities, and events) will be accentuated, with the tens of millions of individuals born after 1980 already politically active and those born after 1990 entering the political arena in significant numbers, first as voters and activists, then as candidates for local offices. Electoral democracy is fast being taken for granted by an increasing proportion of the population, remaining a novelty perhaps only in Mexico.

Leadership:
Essential Element or Desirable Catalyst?

One of the most serious lacks in contemporary Latin America is leadership. A critical factor in mobilizing developmental advances in any part of the world, leadership has been in serious decline globally for most of the past generation. In the world as a whole the high point with respect to political leadership was the middle of the twentieth century. The vast majority of the great leaders of that generation had been born in the latter part of the nineteenth century, most of them in the 1890s. Latin America was not left out of this global phenomenon, with Cárdenas in Mexico, Vargas in Brazil, and Perón in Argentina—Perón, the youngest of these three nation shapers, being born in 1895. But just as the rest of the world, including the United States, has since failed to produce individuals comparable to this generation, so has Latin America. Indeed, in Latin America the contemporary era has seen little quality political leadership in Argentina, a country that from the late nineteenth through much of the twentieth century gave rise to Roca, Yrigoyen, and the Peróns, with even Menem a standout on a number of criteria. Brazil, favored with Vargas, Kubitschek, and Cardoso during the post–World War I era, presently sees Lula avoiding serious missteps, much as Sarney did, more than having filled the shoes of his distinguished predecessors. Colombians, unable to point to an outstanding leader since Rafael Reyes early in the twentieth century, are forced to reassess past presidents such as Alfonso López less unfavorably, as, prior to Uribe, more recent ones have overwhelmingly been lackluster at best. In Mexico, to find a figure worthy of admiration the public must hark back to Cárdenas—now seventy years out of office and with his namesake grandson already a fairly senior figure on the political scene—and jump back all the way to Juárez in the third quarter of the nineteenth century. In Peru, Leguía from the pre-1930 era is the last first-rate leader, and Chávez's controversial role in Venezuela follows a series of, at best, marginally adequate presidential performances in a country that just a generation ago produced a Betancourt.

It is highly sobering to reflect that the contemporary ho–hum crop of chief executives has resulted from broad-based and often highly competitive electoral politics. This fact leads to the uncomfortable question of whether these leadership doldrums arose despite democracy or in some significant ways because of it. Hence it becomes imperative to scrutinize critically the present processes of political recruitment in these countries. Why have federal systems with governorships as executive training grounds not provided more qualified candidates? How important are political party systems in advancing or blocking the rise of able executives? Given the need to mobilize massive electoral support, has it become more important to be a skilled campaigner than to possess the attributes of political leadership that would make for a more effective president once in office? With the elevated cost of campaigns, has wealth or the ability to raise enormous sums of money come to overshadow executive abilities and political acumen? Clues to these questions can be found in the recent past, but the wave of presidential elections in 2010–2012 must be critically examined from this perspective.

Latin America has a very deep and widespread tradition, far more pronounced than in any other part of the world, of seemingly discredited leaders making surprising—often stunning—political comebacks. These returns to power during the nineteenth century can be explained largely in terms of their frequently involving forceful usurpation of power, the indirect election process in many of these countries, the very small populations in a large proportion of them, and, particularly, limited urbanization. However, this second-time-around trend continued unabated around the bend into the twentieth century with Roca, Yrigoyen, and Perón in Argentina; Brazil's Rodrigues Alves and Vargas; six examples in Peru (including the 2010 incumbent); three cases in Venezuela (all since 1945); and two in Chile (with another very possible by 2010). The adoption of immediate reelection during the past decade and a half in Brazil, Argentina, Colombia, Venezuela, and Peru was in large part a response to this phenomenon.

Which leaders catalyzed the most profound transformations in their countries? The roster in order of enduring political development includes Brazil's Vargas (president 1930–1945 and 1951–1954), Cárdenas in Mexico (president 1934–1940), Perón of Argentina (president 1945–1955 and 1973–1974), Betancourt in Venezuela (president 1946–1947 and 1958–1963), and Lleras Camargo of Colombia (president 1945–1946 and 1958–1962). When it comes to depth instead of stars, Brazil, aside from Vargas, has enjoyed quality political leadership only from 1956 through 1960 with Kubitschek, a Vargas heir, and with Cardoso (president 1995–2002). Surviving mediocre leadership much of the time, Brazil was launched into political decay by Bernardes and Washington Luis in the 1920s as well as through the manifold shortcomings of Quadros and Goulart in 1961 to early 1964. From the downfall of the Díaz regime in 1911, Mexico's political leadership, with the lonely exception of Cárdenas, rarely rose above merely competent. Argentina's process of political recruitment functioned best at the beginning of the twentieth century, with Roca, Saénz Peña, and Yrigoyen all effective before the fifteen-year interregnum of mediocrity preceding Perón, whose institutional legacy provided both Menem for a decade and the Kirchners. By way of contrast, Colombia's leadership rarely rose above adequacy and more often fell below a passing mark than above it. Other than Betancourt, in pre-Chávez Venezuela only Caldera in his first term was more than an average chief executive, while in Peru, Fujimori, the best of a poor lot of performers, ended poorly with Belaúnde nearer his level than down with the rest. Chile has had its ups and downs, with the first Alessandri closest to a star, followed a third of a century later by the elder Frei. It has, however, had a series of quite competent chief executives since the reestablishment of democracy in 1990. This is a notable accomplishment in light of its small population (one-eleventh that of Brazil and only a seventh of Mexico's).

The proof of the pudding with regard to leadership lies in the extent and duration of legacy, broadly defined. Perón and Peronism in Argentina rank first in this respect, as almost three and a half decades after the great man's death Peronists remain the country's leading political force. Vargas, although the parties he founded did not survive the military regime, influenced a very wide range of today's political leaders and forces in Brazil. More important, he initiated fundamental social and economic changes in Brazil that are the foundation of recent progress there. As a coherent effort at comprehensive implementation of the Mexican Revolution, delayed by civil war and warlordism, Cárdenas's epoch in Mexico stands out and remains a point of reference for contemporary politicians. On the down side, without the deeply embedded *caudillo* tradition in Venezuela, embodied in the twentieth century by Gómez, who channeled it toward militarism, there would be no Hugo Chávez today.

Aside from the merits of individual leaders, there has been progress in the broader picture of who holds and exercises power. A century ago entrenched economic elites dominated Latin American politics, often almost unchallenged; seventy-five years ago the impact of the world economic crisis was the determinant factor; then forty-five years ago the military became arbiter of national destiny throughout the region. At least now, in all but a few cases of relatively small countries, the decision as to who will govern is in the hands of the people, and complex social orders have led to increasingly pluralistic politics. Indeed, the past two decades have been a sometimes-difficult learning process in how to exercise this newly won power wisely as well as more effectively. In this regard there is greater independence, and concentration on the country's current situation is more common than in the past. Now more than before, neighbors may have governments of the determined right, or of the hopeful left, or of the uncertain center, but they are at least governments chosen by the people in response to their own perceived needs and recent experience. Although bad choices have been made and more are likely in the future, electoral democracy still constitutes a major step forward along the boulder-strewn road to political development.

It is readily apparent that leadership has been and continues to be a vital variable, although a frustratingly idiosyncratic one, conditioned by contextual factors and cultural values. As it has been often in the past and is now generally around the rest of the world, it is in short supply in Latin America. Brazil seems to be in reasonably good shape for having had political recruitment interrupted by two decades of military rule. Lula's good qualities, added to those of his predecessor, not only raise the bar at least back to where it was in the late 1950s but almost guarantee that whoever replaces him will have to possess strong presidential credentials. Mexico provides cause for concern because Fox turned out to have been a much better campaigner than a chief executive and because, no matter what his performance, Calderón cannot be reelected. On the positive side, Mexico's system is now truly competitive, and offering even longer-term hope, Mexico's congress, long a rubber stamp, finally seems to be emerging as a leadership proving ground, and Mexico is now operating like a true federal system—approaching in this respect Argentina, if not Brazil. Therefore its governors can now gain valuable political as well as administrative experience.

By contrast, Argentina's recent track record raises warning signs. Both de la Rúa and Duhalde, effective campaigners as well as experienced administrators at the state and metropolitan levels, failed abysmally as presidents. Clearly more effective than either of them, Kirchner did not rise to the level reached by Menem during his first eight years in office, and Señora Kirchner did not get off to a strong start. However, having a truly federal system, Argentina has governorships as well as cabinet positions and congressional leadership posts as training grounds and structures for political recruitment. Colombia's profound problems eluded solution under a series of unremarkable presidents, in part at least because of the confining constraints of a single four-year term, which prematurely shifted political attention to the succession question. With the late 2004 constitutional amendment Uribe escaped this fate. Over time governorships and mayoral offices may come to play roles more similar to those in Brazil and Argentina. Peru and Venezuela afford cause for serious concern. Toledo was barely adequate on his best days, which were alarmingly few. Positive for much of his extended presidency, Fujimori's final legacy still casts a pall over the Peruvian political scene. Political recruitment remains excessively unstructured in Peru, but even more so in Venezuela. Chávez rose from being a military plotter with no normal political or governmental experience and is concerned with his personal continuation in office à la Castro to the exclusion of grooming any successor. But anti-Chávez groups are characterized by their absence of any dynamic leadership, and his intention appears to be to rival Guzmán Blanco and even Gómez in terms of tenure. By contrast, Chile has put together a string of competent chief executives since its return to democracy, and its sophisticated party system appears capable of meeting future requirements.

Over the longer term, the quality of political leadership in Latin America could well improve for two reasons. First, the restoration of democratic processes, including filling offices through competitive elections, dates back in most countries to the early and mid-1980s. This amount of time allows for the emergence and maturation of a new generation of leaders not decimated or stunted by the authoritarian experiences of the 1960s and 1970s. Second, although women still have the decidedly short end of the officeholding stick, this gender disparity is slowly narrowing. Having more women as mayors, governors, national legislators, and department heads broadens and deepens the pool of potential candidates and has already increased the possibilities for them to become chief executive. Cristina Kirchner and Michelle Bachelet (the latter elected solely on her own merits) have already made it, with a woman, Dilma Rousseff, also Lula's choice as his successor.

If competence is increasingly likely among Latin American leaders (except perhaps those few emerging without administrative experience, like Lula), "visionary" leadership is less likely to achieve power—if managing to emerge to contender status. "Transforming" leaders have been rare, except for the happy coincidence of Vargas, Perón, and Cárdenas at the same time, because in the past the vision of a large proportion of them has been tempered by the heavy responsibilities of office.[1] "Radical" leaders are apt to be elevated to power only in countries where—as in Venezuela in the 1990s—a large proportion of the politically participant population (often newly enfranchised) feel that they have been denied a fair share of governmental benefits.

Convergence, or Each Its Own Way?

As elsewhere in the world, Latin American countries do influence each other by actions upon, or even within, the country being influenced. There is, however, very little evidence that developments in one Latin American country significantly affect events in another, either by individual example or by demonstration effect. The major exception seems to have involved South America in the early 1950s. In this instance the Peronist experience in Argentina briefly extended its influence into a majority of the continent's nations. Although a portion of this influence was a result of conscious efforts on the part of the Argentine regime, a substantial proportion resulted from governments or opposition forces in other countries perceiving the Peronist model as suitable for, or at least adaptable to, their circumstances as well as reacting against US neglect.

The Peróns were unquestionably charismatic leaders as well as skillful political operators, and Peronism is a political phenomenon with aspects of style, program, and political philosophy appropriate for other sections of the continent. Evita's mid-1952 death not only forced Perón to focus on domestic matters but caused him to shift toward the defensive and underscored potential weaknesses of his model, which never did show brightly in the strictly economic field. By late August 1954, Vargas was dead and the interim Brazilian government was friendly to the United States and hostile to Perón for his past ties to Vargas. Hence the interest in emulation of Peronism turned into a fleeting infatuation instead of a lasting attraction. With Perón's removal from office in September 1955 the affinities of political strategies that had briefly prevailed quickly dissipated and disappeared.

With rare exceptions of "intimate" or "penetrated" neighbors, Latin American publics have paid very little attention to what was happening in other countries of the region. Until recently this indifference was perhaps reasonable, as such developments had no significant impact upon their lives or even the course of national affairs. Now greater attention is becoming not only rational but also highly desirable, particularly in situations of economic interchange. Argentina, not only Uruguay and Paraguay, are heavily affected by Brazilian economic performance through that country's great specific weight within the Southern Cone Common Market (Mercosur). Politically concerned Chileans are increasingly aware that close ties to Mercosur are an important option, so some knowledge of what is going on in Brazil should supplement Chilean preoccupation with neighboring Argentina and Peru. Since Spanish and Portuguese are more similar on the printed page than in their spoken forms, the spread of print media across national borders has facilitated "knowing thy neighbor" even if he lives down the block. However, the most significant influence in informing some Latin Americans about other countries is television. Pictures not only speak as eloquently as thousands of words but also do not require familiarity with the language of their subjects.

It remains an open question whether this pervasive lack of influence of one country's experiences on another's—or others'—may be changed by the effects of continued economic integration, as clearly has been the case in Europe. For a long period such economic cooperation was limited to relatively minor subregional groupings such as Central America, the New Caribbean, or the West Coast South American countries of the ineffective Andean Pact. Beginning near the end of the authoritarian period, and picking up momentum through the late 1980s and the 1990s, the solid edifice of a dynamic free trade area began to take shape, with previously hostile rivals Brazil and Argentina at its core. Under their leadership and encompassing other newly industrialized countries of South America, the Southern Cone Common Market came into existence, subsequently adding Chile and Peru, with Venezuela's adhesion held up by Brazil's reluctant senate for more than two years.[2]

Although there is no "typical" Latin American country, the range of variation in the political sphere has been reduced compared to any time in the past. The prior peak of convergence was in the late 1960s and early 1970s, when authoritarian military governments in Brazil, Argentina, Peru, and Chile prevailed alongside a semiauthoritarian civilian regime in Mexico. Indeed, a case might well be made that the similarities of those repressive regimes helped erase some of the preceding country-to-country differences, and that the ensuing processes of transition to democracy reinforced similarities. There is now some real sense of discussing central tendencies in terms of a basic Latin American mode—which fits the greatest number of countries—instead of an essentially meaningless mean (homogenizing average) or misleading median (the midpoint along a continuum of differences). Brazil differs from any synthetic model largely in terms of scale, even more than degree, and certainly more than kind. Mexico has finally emerged from not-so-splendid isolation as a hegemonic single-party regime to having a competitive multiparty system. Colombia no longer has the rigid, elite-dominated vertical two-party system it had for generations. Argentina is becoming more Latin American. Long accustomed to viewing their country as a displaced corner of Europe, Argentines increasingly realize that, like it or not, their future is tied up with that of their neighbors, Brazil being reluctantly admired for its heft and Chile for its accomplishments.

A compelling lesson from Latin America's experience is that successful democratization requires a significant degree of political development. Much of this may take pace during "false dawns," early and ultimately impermanent efforts at establishing democracy. As Huntington has pointed out on a global basis, the first two waves of democratization were followed by demoralizing reverse waves. That beginning in 1922 swept away democracy in thirteen of the seventeen countries that had embraced it between 1910 and 1931, and the second, starting in the early 1960s, reduced democratic regimes from a peak of fifty-two to only thirty. Twenty-three of the twenty-nine countries democratizing between 1974 and 1990 (the third wave) had prior democratic experience.[3] These "cyclical, second try, and interrupted" democracies included Brazil, Argentina, Colombia, Peru, Venezuela, and Chile. Most important, all instances of democratization in Latin America have been protracted processes involving disheartening setbacks followed—often after the passage of considerable time—by resolute efforts to regain lost ground before shifting to making new headway.

For Brazil, drawing meaningful lessons from its own past experience and applying them in the political arena has been both slow and partial but shows signs of accelerating. Moreover, given Brazil's many facets of uniqueness—its size and population, its Portuguese and monarchical heritage, and its nearly equal mix of European- and African-origin peoples (the latter exceeding in number that component throughout the rest of the region)—the experience of other countries has been considered essentially irrelevant. Many of the same considerations apply in Mexico's case. Here the Cárdenas period in the 1930s and, in more limited ways, the Zedillo administration

(1995–2000) with its conscious effort to adapt to changed conditions offer rays of hope, but the jury must remain out until the country gets past Fox into the next administration. Largely in light of their particular bilateral relationship with the United States, Mexicans essentially feel that the rest of Latin America holds no lessons for them. So overall, more than half the region's inhabitants are insular in their view of the possible sources of relevant lessons from anywhere.

Argentina appears to have at last developed a capacity for learning from previous setbacks and failures on the road to political development, but although both Colombia and Venezuela have demonstrated a good deal of progress in this respect in the past, their record since the 1990s reflects at least partial amnesia. Moreover, neither views the other as significantly similar. In the former, the National Front was an outstanding example of recrafting institutions and procedures to prevent a recurrence of past problems, whereas in the latter after 1958 Acción Democrática systematically applied lessons from 1945–1948 failures. Chile has been a quite good learner, but Peru is near the opposite pole, generally failing to see lessons from its own history, much less the experience of other countries.

Whither Latin America?

As the late Roger Hilsman reminds us, the future crouches in the present, while the present is itself still emerging from the past.[4] How this process has occurred and is occurring affords no certainty for understanding what lies ahead, but it does provide significant clues. In a changing world straight-line projections are extremely hazardous, but not to try to peer through the dusk of uncertainty and the fog of impermanence at least down to the next corner and reflect on what may lie around it would be to shirk a scholar's responsibility to put knowledge and understanding to work on behalf of more reasonably informed public policy. As shown above, all political participants, leaders and followers alike, are very much products of the political socialization they underwent as much as a half-century earlier. Combining this salient fact with the persistence of many practices and the inertia of structures and procedures confirms the lesson of Latin America's history that substantial change for the region as a whole is very likely to be slow and gradual.

Estimating where Latin America may be in 2015 requires peering down the road rather than looking around the corner. As of 2010 the dawn of the next decade is only as far ahead as 2005 is behind. For many countries this short period encompasses only the completion of the present administration and a single presidential succession. In Brazil, Colombia, and Chile this change in administration comes in 2010, in Argentina and Peru the following year, and for Mexico in mid-2012. If, as seems highly possible, even probable (although far from certain), the region can reach the end of the next decade without recourse to coups and a resurgence of militarism, its historical cycle of political booms and busts may well have been broken. With most transitions to democracy dating back at least to the first half of the 1980s, democracy would by 2020 have endured for thirty-five to forty years.

Does this roseate scenario mean that the future of democracy in Latin America is guaranteed? Clearly not, for a serious and prolonged economic downturn could destabilize what are generally still immature democracies. But in terms of political development many of these countries are strapping and healthy adolescents, and some are vigorous young adults. This condition contrasts very favorably with the infirm and infant statuses that characterized the democratically inclined polities leveled to the ground by the bulldozers of Cold War militarism during 1962–1973.

To venture beyond 2015 becomes an exercise in futurology, a quite different and much more speculative matter, because contingencies, both internal and international, multiply and uncertainties proliferate. Any such predictions must perforce rest upon the accuracy of those already made for the shorter run, so it is upon these that the final considerations in this book are focused. As the twenty-first century moves forward, the fundamental question hanging over Latin America is whether the dramatic trend toward democratization since 1980 can be consolidated—both by being extended to the laggards and by being deepened in the mainline countries. Having begun at the end of the 1970s, this predominance of positive political development has already far outlasted typical swings of the pendulum in Latin American political life, which have generally lasted twenty-five to thirty years. If there are no international crises, which in the past have impinged upon, often shortening, previous democratic surges—like the world depression at the beginning of the 1930s or the Cold War beginning in the late 1940s—this time the answer is largely in the hands of the region's own inhabitants: elites, masses, and the often amorphous sectors in between.

Will the countries of Latin America find their political bearings in the years ahead and manage to combine democracy with social progress and economic development?[5] This is the 590-million person question over which the first years of the new millennium cast some gray clouds of gloom, but not necessarily of doom. The hope of dedicated radicals of the left that there was a quick, if violent, road to the promised land is all but dead, lingering on only as a treasured illusion of the past. The belief of the right that neoliberal policies anchored in privatization and relative price stability would usher in an era of prosperity as well as stability also proved illusory as the downside of globalization has made itself felt. As so often in the past, world developments—this time the war on terrorism—have pushed the region to the familiar ground of low priority for the United States and the other industrial powers. To change this lack of sustained international interest, Latin American nations will first have to deal more effectively with their own sociopolitical problems and then—having demonstrated their competence—act on the international scene with much greater unity of purpose.

Each country of Latin America faces a salient priority problem. For most of the countries, the immediate challenge is to recognize what this problem is and to find the necessary resolve to at least begin its amelioration—even if a lasting solution may be a long-term task. For some countries the problems are more pressing and more intractable than for others. Standing in the way of their solution is not only lack of resources, both material and human, serious as this is in many cases, but also failure to create widespread awareness of the need for action. Denial, so prevalent in individual human behavior, too often proves to be a collective phenomenon—especially when recognition of a critical shortcoming brings with it difficult and unpleasant choices. Protracted denial and the inaction it entails only aggravate the problem and increase the costs of dealing with it. Indeed, delay may do so beyond the capability of the political system to cope effectively.

In terms of political maladies, Colombia, Peru, and Venezuela remain the most critical cases—each in its own way. Although, as has been shown, it is hazardous to speak of a "learning process" in terms of a body politic, educationally advanced Argentina appeared for a long time and in important aspects to be a slow learner, with many Argentines accustomed to a European-type lifestyle and clinging hard to hope for a miracle cure rather than fully accepting the need for bitter medicine and possibly painful surgery. Fortunately, at the beginning of 2003, that country showed some awareness of the life-threatening nature of its infirmities and elected a government pledged to pursue painful treatment if necessary to restore the country to the robust health it enjoyed before 1930 and largely recaptured under Perón. With this sense of urgency somewhat dissipated, Argentina needs to remember that, lacking the natural resources essential for heavy industry, its highly educated population is its greatest asset in a high-tech and increasingly service-oriented world. Its political structures and processes are adequate to the country's needs as long as its political culture continues to evolve away from that engendered in the yesterdays of agro-exporting elites. Fortunately, in Argentina no significant sector of its society is failing to participate meaningfully in its political life. Moreover, Argentina's well-structured party system is a significant asset in this quest for sustained political development.[6]

In sharp contrast, Brazil has laboriously achieved a relatively high degree of political development without benefit of effectively integrative political parties. In light of its great size—over four times that of Mexico, three times that of Argentina, and seven and a half times that of Colombia—and great diversity, the creation of truly national parties with coherent programmatic content continues to be an intimidating task. Yet this task remains the most important structural one, as substantial progress in this direction is required for full consolidation of recent political gains. In the policy arena Brazil must continue with agrarian reform, the massive problem on which the Cardoso administration made a significant beginning, and for which the Lula government aroused expectations by pledging to give it a higher priority. In terms of long-range enlightened self-interest, agrarian reform should be given a much higher priority by the next administration. However, if we take into account the short-range political imperatives, one or two steps up the ladder may be all that can realistically be expected. For the peculiarities of Brazil's electoral system militate against responsiveness to the agrarian reform constituency and reward not offending powerful advocates of the status quo.

Hence, in the political realm, Brazil urgently needs to enact and put into effect reforms long discussed but not acted upon. At the heart of the problem is Brazil's highly defective electoral system, nominally a form of proportional representation, but one that in effect has candidates most directly in competition with members of their own party and spreading their campaign efforts across an excessively wide constituency—the entire state. Here Brazil needs to innovate as creatively as the German Federal Republic did after World War II, not continue debating whether to copy the system the Germans crafted for their specific problems and needs. Again, as in many other Latin American cases, the need is to adapt, not adopt. The present system has the most damaging effects in the major states, beginning with the absurdity of having seventy members of the lower house, as well as the entire state legislature, elected at large from a state with a population greater than that of California—precisely the tragicomic situation that exists in São Paulo.

From the 1930s on Mexico created an inclusive hegemonic single party, the political equivalent of a full body cast, to escape the chronic civil strife unleashed by its 1910 Revolution. Its daunting challenge from the 1990s forward has been, and continues to be, how to fully dismantle the hegemonic semicorporatist PRI structure without losing the valuable benefits of stability that it brought for over a generation. There are no party or electoral system problems as in Brazil. Rather, the priority need is continuing change in Mexico's political culture, particularly as it bears upon the behavior of interest groups still caught midstream in transition from attitudes shaped in a corporatist system to ways of thinking congruent with increasing pluralism. As is always the case, thinking has to change before behavior can. In the policy arena, Mexico has three urgent needs. The first is to improve levels of living for the rural and small-town masses. A situation in which a very large proportion of the populace believes that its hopes for a better life lie in the breadwinners' leaving home and finding work among the vast US underclass of illegal unskilled workers is politically unhealthy. The underlying imperative is to create better employment opportunities and more adequate social programs within Mexico. In light of the low rate of population increase, this goal is not unattainable in a context of sustained economic growth. Relations with the United States are not just important to Mexico; they are absolutely paramount. The relationship is so asymmetrical as to render the term *lopsided* a gross understatement. As has often been noted, when the United States sneezes a number of Latin American countries catch cold, but only Mexico comes down with pneumonia. Ironically, it is this extreme degree of dependence that gives Mexico some degree of leverage in its dealings with its behemoth of a neighbor. For the threat of an unstoppable torrent of illegal immigration unleashed by socioeconomic deterioration in Mexico is, along with the heavy financial stake of US banks and investors, the prime factor in giving Mexico a meaningful priority in US foreign policy.

At the present the bilateral relationship, summed up as "too close for comfort," is essentially going nowhere. President Calderón needs to obtain from the Obama administration cooperation on the immigration issue that was not forthcoming from the Bush administration—at a time when the war on terrorism holds center stage in the US foreign policy realm. The second pressing policy need, if Mexico is to consolidate its newly established democracy, is to curb the cancerous growth of drug trafficking and its pervasive corruption of the law enforcement and judicial systems. The huge amounts of money mobilized by the Mexican producers of marijuana and the transshippers of South American cocaine have enabled them to corrupt even the highest levels of Mexico's antidrug forces. The rooting out of police corruption needs to become an even higher priority, transformed into a crusade requiring courage as well as determination.

Colombia's salient challenge is very different from those of Argentina, Brazil, or Mexico. The pervasively corrupting influence of the entrenched illegal-drugs industry has undermined its formal electoral democracy, which was characterized by well-rooted and highly competitive national parties. Hence the priority need is to accomplish what administration after administration has failed to do: reestablish control over areas long dominated by well-armed and experienced insurgent movements. Failing such control, efforts to curb the drug trade are doomed to failure, further undermining public faith in government. This is a long-term task that has been inhibited by Colombia's democratic political system, in which presidents until

2006 had a single four-year term. In effect this stipulation means that noticeable progress had to be made in at most three years before attention turned to the selection of the next governmental gladiator. With a second term, Uribe has made significant headway, but curbing the drug trade and the insurgencies remains an extremely severe challenge for the 2010–2014 chief executive, be it him or someone else. Hence a very substantial proportion of the Colombian population views another four years of Uribe as preferable to the alternatives. Admittedly, drug and insurgency problems separately present a formidable political challenge; when combined, their containment may well strain a political system's capabilities to their limit, and a solution might be unattainable. Drug production and export vastly enhance the resources available for corruption. Beleaguered revolutionaries turn to providing protection to the drug traffickers in return for the financing of arms purchases. The relationship is symbiotic as well as pernicious, as the more serious the drug problem, the more the government must divert resources to combating it, reducing the ability to concentrate on anti-insurgency measures.

Peru's most pressing challenge is to successfully complete the incorporation of its indigenous population into the political process. It must also devise and implement a program to eliminate the roots of violent insurrection, rather than just "manage" and contain the threat provided by the Sendero Luminoso and Tupac Amaro revolutionary movements. Moreover, the resources available to any Peruvian president are very limited in comparison to the resources available in the four larger and much richer countries. Unfortunately, the current administration is barely keeping its head above water and no better alternative is on the horizon. For Venezuela the high-priority problem has been moving on to new leadership after having spent most of the 1990s under presidents whose political prime had been during the 1960s and 1970s. The result of failure to renovate leadership cadres by the established parties was the explosion to power of Chávez, who in important ways has aggravated the problem through his adoption of an updated version of paternalistic caudillism rather than modernization of governmental structures and political processes. By any comparative standards Chile is in the fortunate position of needing only to maintain the momentum built up over the last two decades.

Latin America and the World

What is happening politically in Latin America today is still not viewed in most of the world as of any great concern. Gradually, however, Brazil is stirring up greater curiosity, even serious interest, in larger portions of the world than was the case even in the 1994–2002 period. Few of the globe's less-developed countries could identify with the accomplishments of a government headed by one of the world's leading social scientists. For many of these countries, Brazil's recent experience under an authentic representative of its disadvantaged masses is far more relevant and, for a few at least, hope-inspiring. Indeed, this once strident socialist's acceptance of free-market capitalism and the need for development over redistribution, resulting in an option to pursue social justice through distribution of the fruits of growth stemming from sustained investment, may well be the West's most attractive billboard and convincing showcase in gaining the hearts and minds of Africa—nearly a quarter of the world's nations. The more people of that continent can see life improving for the 98 million Afro-Brazilians, the greater their interest in Brazil's formula for democracy and development might become (although the level of awareness concerning Latin America in Africa is still dismayingly low).

Argentina's dramatic decline in the opening years of the twentieth century and its overshadowing by huge northern neighbor Brazil, as well as Mexico's ensnarement in an unavoidable junior partnership with the United States, has served to enhance European interest in Brazil, all the more so as it manifests its independence from the United States on global trade issues and demonstrates an increasing ability to be a leader of like-minded countries outside Latin America. (This European interest is reflected in substantial support for Brazil's bid for selection as a permanent member of an enlarged UN Security Council.) Chile may be handling its affairs with competence bordering upon distinction, but it remains a small country geographically remote to most of the region as well as to Europe, whereas Brazil's heterogeneity as well as its great size and central location make it a much more broadly relevant example. As the exports of its well-over-$2-trillion economy have expanded and show continued growth, its deepening as well as extending network of trade relations both enhances ties and underscores mutuality of interests as it enhances them.

The current international situation presents opportunities as well as challenges to Latin America. It is not a distinct culture or civilization in Huntington's sense (as are the Islamic and Asiatic religion areas). Indeed, South America is very clearly an offshoot of western Europe. Mexico still fits this categorization but is slowly sliding toward becoming a variant of the predominant English-speaking portion of North America, particularly the United States. Overwhelmingly Christian and speaking the tongues of the Iberian Peninsula, the region also has its economic ties essentially with Europe and the United States. Indeed, this Latin American affinity to the North Atlantic community of nations may turn out to be Western Christian civilization's saving grace in the more pessimistic of Huntington's scenarios. Combined with the increased incorporation of the eastern European countries as the West's buffer against the Muslim world, Latin America's continuing population growth helps offset the global demographic shift away from the still-dominant western civilization/culture.[7] In a world in which the Islamic countries enjoy a much higher rate of demographic expansion than the Christian West (with half the world being neither), Latin America's relative weight within the West is on the rise. Including Latin America, the West is a solid four-continent bloc (including Australia and New Zealand "down under"), with Islam confined to a third of vast Asia and less than half of Africa. Within the Western Hemisphere, Latin America's population already outweighs that of the United States and Canada by a margin gradually approaching two to one, as Brazil and Mexico together essentially match the United States.

Increasingly it seems that differences between the North American portion of sprawling Latin America and its larger southern continent component are no longer diminishing but instead may be growing. If former cultural outsider Brazil has become significantly more Latin American, Mexico seems to be becoming less so as a result of increasingly intimate interaction with the United States.

As a part of this unequal, but far from one-way, process, the southwestern region of the United States—from second-most-populous Texas across to a California close to rivaling Colombia or Argentina in its number of inhabitants—is increasingly

Mexicanized. This process is only in a secondary sense a process of Latin American-ization or being Hispanicized in a broader sense, but it does have such an effect when combined with the large and diverse Latino population in New York and the heavy concentration of Cubans and Haitians in southern Florida (soon to overtake New York as the country's third most populous state). At the same time, however, Mexico, by losing its uniqueness with the end of PRI hegemony and the narrow presidential succession process this entailed, has become more like the rest of the region politically. Because it greatly outweighs all of Central America and the Caribbean, Mexico exerts a very heavy influence in this respect of similarity versus difference involving the North American and South American portions of Latin America.

In sum, electoral democracy is well rooted in Latin America, and participation has become very broad, although its quality in a number of countries still leaves much to be desired. The social dimension of democracy remains a matter for concern, especially with regard to income inequality. Progress in this and other facets of justice is the region's greatest challenge. In this regard Chile leads the way, but will the larger countries follow? In any case, Latin America has come to be an important part of the global scene and a very significant component of the community of democratic nations. Moreover, its best days still lie ahead, as many of its countries are just achieving maturity and are on the brink of fulfilling their potential. Its successes in the realms of democracy and socioeconomic progress make Latin America worthy of examination and possible emulation by nations less well advanced along the road to political development. Past failures and setbacks also provide lessons about overcoming obstacles to the development of viable political systems responsive to the will of citizens.

Notes

1. These types are discussed in Arnold M. Ludwig, *King of the Mountain: The Nature of Political Leadership* (Lexington: University Press of Kentucky, 2002), pp. 31–41.

2. Consult Francisco Domínguez and Marcos Guedes de Oliveira, eds., *Mercosur: Between Integration and Democracy* (Pieterlen, Switzerland: Peter Lang AG, 2004), as well as Laura Gómez-Mera, "Explaining MERCOSUR's Survival: Strategic Sources of Argentine-Brazilian Convergence," *Journal of Latin American Studies*, 37:1 (February 2005), pp. 109ff. A wide range of thoughtful and informed viewpoints on South American integration was put forth at a conference held in Brasília in July 2009 by the Fundacão Alexandre Gusmão, the think tank of the Brazilian foreign ministry. Many of these viewpoints are available at www.funag.gov.br. Illustrative of the foundation's wide range of interests is an annual competition, the Prémio América do Sul, for the best monograph on *Peru; Evolução Recente e Futuro* was the 2009 winner with a not insignificant first prize of R30,000 (along with R15,000 and R10,000 for second and third place). The foundation is headed by Ambassador José Jeronimo Moscardo de Souza, a former culture minister as well as one-time Brazilian ambassador to UNESCO.

3. See Samuel P. Huntington, *The Third Wave: Democratization in the Late Twentieth Century* (Norman: University of Oklahoma Press, 1991), pp. 41–44.

4. Roger Hilsman, *The Crouching Future: International Politics and U.S. Foreign Policy, a Forecast* (Garden City, NY: Doubleday, 1975).

5. Jorge A. Castañeda and Marco A. Palacios, eds., *Leftovers: Tales of the Latin American Left* (New York: Routledge, 2008), provides insight and stimulation concerning a range of views on this critical issue.

6. Smith considers Argentina one of the more institutionalized party systems with long-lived parties and high voter identity (low electoral volatility). See Peter H. Smith, *Democracy in Latin America: Political Change in a Comparative Perspective* (New York: Oxford University Press, 2005), pp. 176–182. By sharp contrast, Brazil has very low institutionalization of its party system combined with being next to the bottom (trailed only by Peru) in terms of electoral volatility and popular affinity for its political parties.

7. Samuel P. Huntington, *The Clash of Civilizations and the Remaking of World Order* (New York: Simon & Schuster, 1996).

Glossary

abertura	Political "opening," an early stage in a transition from an authoritarian regime to democracy.
acuerdos	"Accords" or "agreements," usually in the nature of backroom deals among political brokers.
Apristas	Followers of the APRA party in Peru.
ayuntamientos	Urban governing councils introduced to parts of Spanish America on the eve of independence.
bandido	"Bandit," a term applied to both criminals and political opponents.
braceros	Mexican harvest workers in the United States in the 1940s into the 1960s.
callampas	Urban slums of Lima, Peru, so named for their tendency to spring up like "mushrooms."
campesinos	Rural laborers and subsistence farmers, often imprecisely rendered into English as the narrower category of peasants.
cartorial	Used in Brazil in reference to the nature of a political system in which appointments to governmental office were exchanged for electoral support and public employment used to satisfy the clientelistic needs of the elite.
caudillos	Spanish-American personalist political leaders first arising in the aftermath of the wars for independence. They utilized private armies to control a region of the country and then to seize control of the capital city.
Científicos, Los	The positivist technocratic elite of the Díaz regime in Mexico.
clientelism, clientelist, clientelistic	The terms for political processes rooted in patron–client relationships of asymmetrical exchanges of political support for material and personal benefits featuring, but not limited to, patronage positions and other jobs.
colonos	Peruvian rural workers.
comuneros	Populations of essentially indigenous communities that in the late colonial period sometimes rose up in opposition to the so-called Bourbon reforms and demanded a voice in political decisions. In twentieth-century Peru it meant rural dwellers living in communities rather than on the landed estates.
concertación	Literally "working in concert"; denotes a type of formal political alliance with a defined purpose (rather than only transitory convenience).

continuismo	The pronounced tendency up through World War II of Latin American chief executives to remain in power beyond and despite constitutional limitations.
convergencia	"Convergence," often used for an alliance sharing some central aim.
convivencia	"Coexistence," the term for political collaboration between strange bedfellows; particularly applied to the alliance of conservatives and Apristas in Peru during the late 1950s and early 1960s.
coronel (pl. *coroneis*)	The name given to political bosses in the interior of Brazil, especially in the northeastern region; derived from their holding commissioned ranks in the National Guard during the monarchy.
coronelismo	The type of patron-client political processes shaped by the *coroneis*.
Cortes	The Spanish national legislature.
criollos	Europeans born in the New World; in English, Creoles.
derrubadas	Political efforts by the Brazilian government of Floriano Peixoto in 1890–1891 to oust provincial governors who had sided with his predecessor.
descamisados	Literally "shirtless ones," the term for the Buenos Aires lower-class followers of the Peróns.
dispositivo militar	The structure of military support arranged by Brazilian presidents to ensure their survival in office.
distensão	"Decompression"; a stage of dismantling the most authoritarian features of the Brazilian military regime followed by the government of Ernesto Geisel in the mid-1970s.
ejido	A collective holding of agricultural lands by Mexican Indian communities.
estancias	The name in southern South America, especially Argentina, for large agricultural landholdings.
estanciero	The owner of an *estancia*.
fazenda	The Portuguese equivalent of a *hacienda* or *estancia*, that is, a large rural landholding.
fazendeiro	The owner of a *fazenda*; collectively *fazendeiros* were the dominant elite of large landowners in the colonial and early independence periods of Brazil.
fueros	Special legal rights, including having their own courts, enjoyed by the military and the church in colonial and early independent New Spain.
gaucho	"Cowboy," a resident of the Brazilian state of Rio Grande do Sul or with an accent in Spanish for cowboys, especially in the La Plata region.

gobernación	"Government," often the name for the ministry in charge of governmental affairs and internal security.
gorila	Colloquial term for hard-line right-wing advocates of continued military rule, especially in Argentina.
hacendados	Large landholders (owners of *haciendas*) in most of Spanish America.
haciendas	The name in most of Spanish America for large rural landholdings.
Iberian	Collective, geographically based term for Spain and Portugal together.
interventor	A trusted political leader imposed by Getúlio Vargas in Brazil after the 1930 Revolution to replace elected governors.
junta	A multimember de facto governing body resulting from the overthrow of a duly constituted government, generally composed of military figures.
linha dura	"Hard-line," that is, militantly intransigent; usually applied to the faction of a military establishment advocating control of the government by the armed forces.
llanero	A cowboy of the Venezuelan *llanos,* or plains.
logias	"Lodges," a name used for politically active, often conspiratorial, military cliques, especially in Argentina.
Maximato	Transitional political regime established in Mexico by Calles (as Jefe Máximo) bridging the end of the civil war until a representative electoral regime was put in place by Cárdenas.
mestizo	An individual of mixed European and Indian ancestry.
Mineiros	The inhabitants of the key Brazilian state of Minas Gerais.
pampean	Referring to inhabitants of the fertile pampas (grassland plains) covering much of northern Argentina.
patrimonial, patromonialist, patromonialism	Analytical terms pertaining to a political system or processes characterized by unequal patron–client types of obligations rooted in ascribed, inherent, and often inherited status difference.
Paulistas	The residents of São Paulo.
pelucones	The conservative "bigwigs" in Chilean politics of the 1820s and 1830s.
peninsulares	Individuals born in Spain who migrated to the New World in the colonial period.
pipolos	The liberal "newcomers" or "pipsqueaks" in Chilean politics of the 1820s and 1830s.
poder moderador	"Moderating power," meaning the authority of the Brazilian emperor to function as the fourth branch of government, particularly as the manipulating balance wheel of the parliamentary system.

Porfiriato	The thirty-five-year rule of Porfirio Díaz in Mexico beginning in the mid-1870s.
Porteños	The residents of Buenos Aires.
praetorian	A predisposition of a political system toward instability, militarism, or authoritarianism as a result of insufficient political institutionalization for the country's degree of social mobilization.
puta	"Whore"; used pejoratively in political life for enemies.
reerguimento	Brazil's financial "resurrection" under President Rodrigues Alves in 1903–1905.
rurales	The brutal rural police of the Díaz regime in Mexico.
salvações	"Salvations," political efforts by the Brazilian government of Marshal Hermes da Fonseca on the eve of World War I to oust entrenched conservative political machines in the interior by means of intervention on the side of their opponents by local military commanders.
sexénio	Mexico's single six-year presidential term.
tenentes	"Lieutenants"; a name for reform-minded activist young officers in Brazil during the 1920s and 1930s.
tenentismo	The political movement catalyzed and led by the *tenentes*.
unicato	The political system installed in Argentina by Roca's centralizing powers in the capital and concentrating them in the hands of the president.
unitários	Advocates of a unitary government in Argentina in the first half of the nineteenth century.
vereadores	Municipal councilmen in Brazil.
viceroy	A very high royal governor of a vast portion of the New World literally functioning in the stead of the king (*rey* or *rei*).

Index